Taxes For Dummies® 2004 Edition

by Eric Tyson, MBA, and David J. Silverman

D0800194

Eric & David's Time-Tested Strategies for Tax-Wise Living

$ **Use tax laws to reduce your taxes.** If you educate yourself about the tax laws and incentives, you can dramatically and permanently reduce the taxes that you pay over the course of your lifetime. Now more than ever, with the recent major tax law changes, it pays to understand tax reduction strategies.

$ **Use retirement accounts as a simple but powerful way to reduce your income taxes.** The new tax laws dramatically increase the amount you can contribute to these accounts. Lower income earners also will be able to get free government matching money from contributions (see Chapter 21).

$ **Take control of your taxes.** Find out enough about the tax laws by reading the relevant sections of this book so that you can prepare your own return or intelligently hire a good tax preparer. Don't forget to review your return when someone else prepares it.

$ **Try preparing your own return.** If your situation hasn't changed since last year, you're probably wasting your hard-earned dollars paying a tax preparer to plug your new numbers into this year's return. Unless your finances are complicated or the tax laws have dramatically changed in an area that affects you, try preparing your own return. If you get stuck or want another opinion, you can always go to a preparer at that point.

$ **Get, and stay, organized.** Try keeping your tax and financial documents organized year-round. This practice saves many hours not only when you prepare your tax return but also when you make important financial decisions.

$ **Remember that the IRS is not always right.** Whether providing advice over the phone or challenging taxpayers' returns, the IRS makes mistakes, so don't panic if you get a call from Uncle Sam. If you haven't knowingly cheated or defrauded the IRS, you have little to fear from audit notices or other IRS letters. Calmly organize your supporting documents to prove your case.

$ **Learn from your return.** After you've gone to all the time and trouble of preparing your tax return, don't let that effort go to waste. Use the information to identify areas for better financial management in the coming year. Especially helpful is Part V of this book. It helps you plan ahead to take advantage of the recently passed tax law changes.

$ **The more you consume, the more you pay in taxes.** As you earn and spend your income, you not only must pay income tax on your earnings, but you also incur sales and other taxes on your purchases. Moreover, many of the best tax breaks available for people at all income levels are accessible only if you're able to save money to invest.

$ **Invest tax-wisely.** Don't overlook tax implications when investing your money. Remember, it isn't what you make, it's what you get to keep that matters.

$ **Don't buy real estate *only* for tax purposes.** Owning your own home and other real estate can be an investment that helps reduce your taxes. But don't purchase real estate just because of the tax benefits — these benefits already are reflected in the price that you pay for a property.

$ **Know when estate planning matters.** The recent tax law changes significantly increase amounts that you can pass onto your heirs and reduce the estate tax rate. Read up on this issue (see Chapter 26) so that you know when and what you need to do to arrange your financial affairs.

$ **Keep taxes in perspective.** There's more to life than working and making money. If you do such a good job reducing your taxes that you gain great wealth, don't forget to enjoy it and share it with others.

For Dummies: Bestselling Book Series for Beginners

Taxes For Dummies® 2004 Edition

by Eric Tyson, MBA, and David J. Silverman, EA

Quick Reference Card

Highlights of Recent Tax Law Changes

We've highlighted the biggest changes in the lists below to entice you to read the relevant chapters of this book so that you get your piece of the tax reduction. Please pay special attention to Chapter 27 and to Part V, which help you begin taking action now and in the months and years ahead to legally cut your tax bills.

- **$ Lower income tax rates.** The lowest individual income tax bracket is now only 10 percent, and the rates of higher tax brackets also are reduced.

- **$ Greater retirement account contribution limits and incentives.** Significantly higher amounts can be contributed to retirement savings plans. IRAs and SEP-IRAs enjoy the greatest percentage increases in contribution amounts. Those 50 years of age and older can contribute more than younger workers. The government also will begin matching contributions for modest income earners. And, in future tax years, more retirement plan options will allow for tax-free withdrawal of investment earnings. See Chapter 21 for the details.

- **$ Lower tax rates on long-term capital gains and stock dividends.** Appreciation on investments held more than one year and sold and on corporate stock dividends will now be taxed at a maximum 15 percent rate. See Chapter 23 for the whole scoop.

- **$ More tax benefits for children.** In addition to increasing the child tax credit, recent tax law changes expanded the refundability of the child tax credit for lower-income families. And the adoption tax credit has been made permanent with double its maximum value — as does the exclusion of company-paid adoption aid from taxable income. Many parents who work and pay for dependent-care expenses also will enjoy increased tax credits. Refer to Chapter 25.

- **$ Education tax assistance.** Many parents can begin taking advantage of up to a $3,000 tax deduction toward college costs. Some taxpayers also will be able to claim more tax deductions on student loan interest. Section 529 college savings plans will begin allowing tax-free withdrawals when funds are used to pay for qualified higher education expenses. See Chapter 25.

- **$ Estate tax reduction.** The size estate that may be passed free of federal estate taxes will mushroom to $3.5 million by the year 2009, and the highest estate tax rate on large estates gradually will decline. In 2010, the estate tax actually disappears but then is reinstated in 2011! Turn to Chapter 26 for the details.

- **$ Marriage penalty relief.** The 15 percent tax bracket is widened for married couples filing jointly, and the standard deduction for married couples filing jointly is now twice the amount allowed a single taxpayer. Other provisions lessen but don't eliminate the marriage penalty.

Last-Minute Tax Tips

- **$ Double-check your return for mistakes that can cost you money, time, and audits.**

  Put your name and Social Security number on every page, check the arithmetic, attach W-2s and any 1099s where federal tax was withheld, and sign and date the return. Verify that you've transferred over from last year's return items that you need for this year's return.

- **$ Scavenge for overlooked deductions, especially if you're self-employed.**

  Determine whether you can save money by electing the filing status of married filing separately or head of household.

- **$ Make sure the data is correct on the forms that you receive from financial institutions and your employer(s).**

- **$ File extension(s) (Forms 4868, 2688), if necessary, to allow yourself enough time to fill in the forms correctly and ensure that you take all the deductions to which you're legally entitled.**

  Don't make the mistake of waiting until you have the money to pay before filing. The penalty for doing so can be as much as 25 percent of the tax that you still owe. Ouch!

- **$ Keep copies of everything that you file with the IRS and your state and obtain a mailing receipt if you file at the last minute and a lot of money (or a big issue) is at stake.**

For Dummies: Bestselling Book Series for Beginners

Praise for Taxes For Dummies

"The book does a terrific job of explaining the tax code. The tax advice...is on target and has depth. Smart chapters — not just thumbnail sketches — for filling out forms."

> — Gannett News Service

"Among tax advice books is far and away the best. *Taxes For Dummies* is fun to read and teaches about the tax system itself. The book also provides excellent advice about dealing with mistakes — created by you or the Internal Revenue Service. And it talks about fitting taxes into your daily financial planning. In other words, it's a book you can use after April 15, as well as before."

> — Kathy M. Kristof, *Los Angeles Times*

"The best of these books for tax novices. Substitutes simple English for tax-code complexities."

> — *Worth* magazine

"User-friendly income-tax preparation and sound financial advice you can use throughout the year."

> — *The Seattle Times*

"This book is the most accessible and creative. It's also the best organized of the lot, presenting information in the order you need it to complete your tax forms."

> — *USA Today*

"*Taxes For Dummies* will make tax preparation less traumatic...It is a book that answers — in plain English, and sometimes with humor — many puzzling questions that arise on the most commonly used tax forms."

> — Stanley Angrist, *The Wall Street Journal*

"This is a lot of book for the money, filled with good examples...and level-headed advice. It follows the line-by-line format but also has year-round reference value for taxpayers who plan ahead...A human heart beats in this highly intelligent tax tome."

> — Michael Pellecchia, syndicated columnist

"$$$$ — Highest rated among the annual tax guides . . . superb writing and friendly organization."

> — *Publishers Weekly*

More Bestselling For Dummies Titles by Eric Tyson

Investing For Dummies®

The complete guide to building wealth in stocks, real estate, mutual funds, and small business. With updated coverage on everything from Internet brokerages to information sources, this friendly guide shows you how to assess your situation, gauge risks and returns, and make sound investments.

Personal Finance For Dummies®

Discover the best ways to establish and achieve your financial goals, reduce your spending and taxes, and make wise personal finance decisions. *Wall Street Journal* bestseller with over 1 million copies sold in all editions and winner of the Benjamin Franklin best business book award.

Home Buying For Dummies®

America's #1 real estate book includes coverage of online resources in addition to sound financial advice from Eric Tyson and frontline real estate insights from industry veteran Ray Brown. Also available from America's best-selling real estate team of Tyson and Brown — *House Selling For Dummies* and *Mortgages For Dummies*.

Small Business For Dummies®

Take control of your future and make the leap from employee to entrepreneur with this enterprising guide. From drafting a business plan to managing costs, you'll profit from expert advice and real-world examples that cover every aspect of building your own business.

Taxes

FOR

DUMMIES®

2004 EDITION

**by Eric Tyson, MBA,
and David J. Silverman, EA**

WILEY

Wiley Publishing, Inc.

Taxes For Dummies®, 2004 Edition

Published by
Wiley Publishing, Inc.
111 River Street
Hoboken, NJ 07030-5774
www.wiley.com

About the Authors

Eric Tyson, MBA, is a financial counselor, best-selling author, syndicated columnist, writer, and lecturer. He works with and teaches people from myriad income levels and backgrounds, so he knows the financial and tax questions and concerns of real folks just like you.

After toiling away for too many years as a management consultant to behemoth financial-service firms, Eric decided to take his knowledge of the industry and commit himself to making personal financial management accessible to all of us. Despite being handicapped by a joint B.S. in Economics and Biology from Yale and an MBA from Stanford, Eric remains a master at "keeping it simple."

An accomplished freelance personal-finance writer, Eric is the author of other *For Dummies* national bestsellers on Personal Finance, Mutual Funds, Investing, and Home Buying. His work has been critically acclaimed in hundreds of publications and programs including *Newsweek*, *The Los Angeles Times*, *Chicago Tribune*, *Kiplinger's Personal Finance Magazine*, *The Wall Street Journal*, and NBC's *Today Show*, ABC, CNBC, PBS's *Nightly Business Report*, CNN, FOX-TV, CBS national radio, Bloomberg Business Radio, and Business Radio Network.

David J. Silverman, EA, is an enrolled agent, which means that he can represent clients before the Internal Revenue Service. He has served on the Advisory Group to the Commissioner of Internal Revenue. David has a Certificate in Taxation from New York University and has been in private practice in Manhattan for over 25 years.

He regularly testifies on tax issues before both the Senate Finance Committee and the House of Representatives Committee on Ways and Means. As the result of his suggestions regarding penalty reform that he made while testifying before these committees, legislation was enacted that reduced the amount of penalties that may be assessed in a number of key areas.

David is the author of *Battling the IRS,* which has received critical acclaim in *The New York Times*, *Money*, *The Wall Street Journal*, and numerous other publications. David has been a contributing editor and wrote a monthly column for *Smart Money* magazine and writes a monthly tax column for *Golf Digest*. David is frequently interviewed on national TV and radio as an expert on tax issues. He can be reached at his Web site, www.silvermanstaxadvice.com.

Dedication

My deepest and sincerest thanks to my family, friends, clients, and students for their enthusiastic support and encouragement. My wife, Judy, as always, gets special mention for inspiring my love of books and writing.

—Eric Tyson

To my wife, Betsy, who provided the inspiration; my late father, Louis, whose writing skills I hope I inherited; and my daughters, Joanna and Lisa, who assisted with the essential research and editing.

—David J. Silverman

Authors' Acknowledgments

Our sincere thanks to Mark A. Luscombe and Leslie Bonacum of CCH Incorporated for their expert assistance in helping with researching key areas. Their contribution was invaluable in helping us bring clarity to an overly complex, confusing, and often contradictory tax system. Special thanks to the people at CCH Incorporated who provided the technical review: Glenn Borst and Jim Solheim. Every chapter in this book was improved by their knowledge, insights, and experience.

We'd also like to thank all the good people at Wiley Publishing, Inc. Special recognition goes to Kathy Cox, Tim Gallan, Neil Johnson, and Kristin DeMint.

Publisher's Acknowledgments

We're proud of this book; please send us your comments through our Dummies online registration form located at www.dummies.com/register/.

Some of the people who helped bring this book to market include the following:

Acquisitions, Editorial, and Media Development

Senior Project Editor: Tim Gallan

Acquisitions Editor: Kathy Cox

Copy Editors: Neil Johnson, Kristin DeMint

Technical Editor: CCH Incorporated: Glenn Borst, JD; Jim Solheim, JD, LLM

Editorial Manager: Christine Meloy Beck

Editorial Assistants: Melissa S. Bennett, Elizabeth Rea

Cover Photo: © Getty Images

Cartoons: Rich Tennant, www.the5thwave.com

Production

Project Coordinator: Kristie Rees

Layout and Graphics: Amanda Carter, Joyce Haughey, Kristin McMullan, Jacque Schneider, Julie Trippetti, Erin Zeltner

Proofreaders: Laura Albert, Andy Hollandbeck, Betty Kish, Dwight Ramsey, Rob Springer

Indexer: Sherry Massey

Special Help: Michelle Dzurny, Laura K. Miller, Chad R. Sievers

---

Publishing and Editorial for Consumer Dummies

Diane Graves Steele, Vice President and Publisher, Consumer Dummies

Joyce Pepple, Acquisitions Director, Consumer Dummies

Kristin A. Cocks, Product Development Director, Consumer Dummies

Michael Spring, Vice President and Publisher, Travel

Brice Gosnell, Associate Publisher, Travel

Kelly Regan, Editorial Director, Travel

Publishing for Technology Dummies

Andy Cummings, Vice President and Publisher, Dummies Technology/General User

Composition Services

Gerry Fahey, Vice President of Production Services

Debbie Stailey, Director of Composition Services

Contents at a Glance

Table of Contents

Introduction

● ●

Welcome to *Taxes For Dummies,* 2004 Edition — the up-to-date revision of our annual best-selling book by your humble authors — Eric Tyson and David J. Silverman. These pages answer both your tax-preparation and tax-planning questions in plain English and with a touch of humor.

Our book can help you make sense of the newest tax laws. We also promise to help relieve your pain and misery (at least the tax-related portion), legally reduce your income tax bill, and get you through your tax return with a minimum of discomfort.

We also help you keep your mind on your taxes while you plan your finances for the upcoming year. As you probably know, Congress and political candidates engage in what seem like never-ending discussions about ways to tinker with our nation's tax laws. Where appropriate throughout the book, we highlight how any resulting changes may affect important decisions you'll need to make in the years ahead.

In addition to helping you understand how to deal with federal income taxes, we explain how to handle and reduce some of those pesky and not-so-insignificant taxes slapped on by states and other tax-collecting bodies.

We also show you how to steer clear of breaking tax laws. The fact that Congress keeps changing the tax laws makes it easy for many honest and well-intentioned people to unknowingly break those laws. We explain how to clear the necessary hurdles to keep the taxing authorities from sending threatening notices and bills. But, if you do get a nasty letter from the tax police, we explain how to deal with that frightful situation in a calm, level-headed manner so that you get the IRS off your case.

What's New in This Edition

While you were out basking in the sun, enjoying a barbecue, or being annoyed by some relatives during the most recent Memorial Day weekend, the U.S. Congress and our president were putting the finishing touches on yet another major tax bill — the Jobs and Growth Tax Relief Reconciliation Act of 2003. Among other changes, this bill reduces the federal income tax rates, significantly reduces the tax rate on stock dividends and long-term capital gains, and dramatically increases small business write-offs for equipment purchases. Please see Chapter 27 for an overview of the major tax law changes that kick in during the past year.

Throughout this book, we highlight new tax provisions with this icon. Although searching for and reading passages marked with this icon quickly tells you what's new, don't overlook the many tax-reducing strategies and recommendations throughout the rest of the book.

Why Buy This Tax Book?

At their worst, some annual tax-preparation books are as dreadful as the IRS instruction booklets themselves — bulky, bureaucratic, and jargon-filled. In particular cases, preparation books simply reproduce dozens of pages of IRS instructions! At their best, these books tell you information you won't find in the IRS instructions — but the golden nuggets of tax information often are buried in massive piles of granite. _Taxes For Dummies_ lays out those golden nuggets in nice, clean, display cases so that you won't miss a single one. There's still plenty of granite, but we promise not to use it to bury you — or key insights!

Between the two of us, we have more than five decades of experience providing personal financial and tax advice to real people just like you. We understand your tax and financial concerns and know how to help solve your quandaries!

Most people's tax concerns fall into three categories: filling out their forms properly, legally minimizing their taxes, and avoiding any penalties. _Taxes For Dummies_ addresses these concerns and helps take some of the pain and agony out of dealing with taxes. Here are the various practical ways that you can use this book to complete your forms, legally reduce your taxes, and avoid penalties:

- **As a reference:** For example, maybe you know a fair amount about your taxes, but you don't know where and how to report the dividends you received from some of your investments. Simply use the Table of Contents or Index to find the right spot in the book with the answers to your questions. On the other hand, if you lack investments — in part, because you pay so much in taxes — this book also explains legal strategies for slashing your taxes and boosting your savings. Use this book before _and after_ April 15.

- **As a trusted advisor:** Maybe you're self-employed, and you know that you need to be salting money away so that you can someday cut back on those long workdays. Turn to Chapter 21 and find out about the different types of retirement accounts, which one may be right for you, how it can slash your taxes, and even where to set it up.

- **As a textbook:** If you have the time, desire, and discipline, by all means go for it and read the whole shebang. And please be sure to drop us a note and let us know of your achievement!

Your Tax Road Map

If you've already peeked at the Table of Contents, you know this book is divided into parts. Here's a brief description of what you can find in each of the six major parts.

Part I: Getting Ready to File

This part helps you understand how and why taxes work the way they do in the United States of America. You can explore how to fit taxes into your personal financial life. Here, you can also master time-tested and tax advisor–approved ways of getting organized and ready to file your tax returns. We also help you figure out what taxes you have to pay and what other tedious tax forms you're required to complete at other times of the year.

Part II: Tackling the Various Forms 1040

In this part, we walk you through the process of completing the multiple versions of Form 1040 and confronting the typical challenges that taxpayers face. We promise not to reprint pages from the incomprehensible IRS manuals, and we try to make the process of filling out your Form 1040 as painless as possible.

Part III: Filling Out Schedules and Other Forms

Schedules A, B, and C. No, this isn't an elementary school class! In this part, we show you, line by line, how to complete the common Form 1040 schedules — such as the ones for itemized deductions, interest and dividend income, profit and loss from a business, capital gains and losses, and so on. You'll also be happy to know that we give you a brief primer on other useful forms, such as the ones that self-employed and retired people must complete to make estimated tax payments throughout the year.

Part IV: Audits and Errors: Dealing with the IRS

No matter how hard you try to ward off nasty letters from the IRS, sooner or later you may receive that dreaded thin envelope from the friendly tax folks with a message challenging your return. The operative word here is *challenge*. As long as you think of this situation as an opportunity to play show and tell, you'll do fine.

So you'll be tickled to know that *Taxes For Dummies* goes beyond dealing with the annual ritual of filing your tax return by offering tips, counsel, and a shoulder to cry on. You find out how to sweep the IRS off your doorstep swiftly, deftly, and without breaking a sweat. And you can keep those pesky IRS agents out of your bank account while you keep yourself (and your loved ones) out of jail.

Part V: Year-Round Tax Planning

Because taxes are a year-round obligation and an important piece of your personal finance puzzle, this part provides tons of practical planning advice that you can use in May, and July, and October, and the rest of the year. We show you how to accomplish common financial goals, such as purchasing a home or squirreling away enough loot so you don't have to work into your 80s and 90s — all in a tax-wise manner.

You may be tempted to skip this section after you make it past April 15, but don't make that mistake. Part V can pay off in tens of thousands of dollars someday, saving you headaches and heartaches when you file returns each and every year.

Part VI: The Part of Tens

These top-ten lists often cover big-picture issues, such as the ten most important changes that are new for this year, which cry out for top billing in their very own section. You may also enjoy plowing through these short (but highly useful) chapters in record time.

Appendix

Appendixes usually include horrible little technical details that are best avoided by normal readers. In this book, however, you can find the most-used tax forms and schedules, which you can tear out, cut out, photocopy (yes, the IRS lets you use photocopies of most forms to do your tax return), and use for filing.

Icons Used in This Book

This target marks recommendations for making the most of your taxes and money (for example, paying off your non-tax-deductible credit-card debt with your lottery winnings).

The info by this friendly sign will be of great interest if you want to discover ways to reduce your taxes — and all the suggestions are strictly legit.

This is a friendly reminder of stuff we discuss elsewhere in the book or of points we really want you to remember.

This alert denotes common, costly mistakes people make with their taxes.

Don't become shark bait. This icon alerts you to scoundrels, bad advice, and scams that prey on the unsuspecting taxpayer.

This nerdy guy appears beside discussions that aren't critical if you just want to know the basic concepts and get answers to your tax questions. However, reading these gems can deepen and enhance your tax knowledge. And you never know when you'll be invited to go to a town meeting and talk tax reform with a bunch of politicians!

Just to keep you off balance, Congress continues to enact new tax laws, and the IRS keeps tinkering with the tax code. This icon alerts you to the changes that you need to know about.

Some tax problems are too complex to be handled in any one book. If you're one of the unlucky ones who's in a tax situation that can spell big trouble if you get it wrong, consult a tax advisor to be on the safe side. We tell you how to select one in Chapter 2.

Part I
Getting Ready to File

The 5th Wave   By Rich Tennant

"Death and taxes _are_ for certain, Mr. Dooley; however, they're not mutually exclusive."

In this part . . .

Do you feel disorganized? Do you not know where to turn for tax help? Are you in a bad mood about all the forms you must complete and the taxes you have to pay? We can't eliminate all those forms and taxes, but we can help you to think about your taxes in the context of your overall financial situation and what our great politicians do with all the money you send them. But maybe you already know that! Although it's not as much fun as complaining about government waste, you'll also find out how to get organized — and stay organized — throughout the year. And we explain how to find competent tax help, should you be at your wits' end.

Chapter 1

The U.S. Tax System and Rates

. . . .

In This Chapter

▶ Making sense of our tax system

▶ Thinking intelligently about taxes year-round

▶ Understanding the importance of marginal taxes

▶ Comprehending state taxes and the Alternative Minimum Tax

. . . .

*M*ost everyone — including your humble authors — finds taxes to be a pain. First, everyone faces the chore of gathering various complicated-looking documents to complete the annual ritual of filling out IRS **Form 1040.** If your past financial year wasn't exactly like the preceding one, you may need to become acquainted with some forms that are new to you. Perhaps you need to figure out how to submit a quarterly tax payment when you no longer work for a company and now receive self-employment income from independent contract work. Maybe you sold some investments (such as stocks, mutual funds, or real estate) at a profit (or loss), and you must calculate how much tax you owe (or loss you can write off).

Whenever money passes through your hands, it seems that you pay some kind of tax. Consider the following:

✔ When you work and get paid, you pay all sorts of taxes: federal, state, and local taxes (on top of having to deal with the migraines your bosses and difficult customers give you).

✔ After paying taxes on your earnings and then spending money on things you need and want (and paying more taxes in the process), you may have some money left over for investing. Guess what? Your reward for being a saver is that you also pay tax on some of the earnings on your savings.

Even if your financial life is stagnant, tax law changes during the past year may require you to complete some new forms and calculations. You can expect many of these situations in the years ahead thanks to the mammoth proportions of *The Economic and Tax Relief Reconciliation Act of 2001, The Job Creation and Worker Assistance Act of 2002,* and *The Jobs and Growth Tax Relief Reconciliation Act of 2003.* And, if you're like most people, you're currently missing out on some legal tax reduction tactics.

Unfortunately, too many people think of taxes only in spring, when it comes time to file that dreadful annual return. Throughout this book, you can find all sorts of tips, suggestions, and warnings that help you discover the important role that your taxes play in your entire personal financial situation year-round. In fact, we devote a major part of the book (Part V) to showing you how to accomplish important financial goals while legally reducing your taxes.

Understanding Our Tax System

You'll pay more in taxes than you need to if you don't understand the tax system. Who wants to pay more when you already feel like you're paying plenty and you work hard for what money you do earn?

When you try to read and make sense of the tax laws, you quickly realize that you're more likely to win the lottery than figure out some parts of the tax code! That's one of the reasons that tax attorneys and accountants are paid so much — to compensate them for the intense and prolonged agony of deciphering the tax code, day after day after day!

But here's a little secret that'll make you feel much better: You don't need to read the dreadful tax laws. Most tax advisors don't read them themselves. Instead, they rely upon summaries prepared by organizations and people who have more of a knack for explaining things clearly and concisely than the IRS does. CCH, Incorporated — the organization responsible for technically reviewing this fine book — has compiled a *Federal Tax Reporter* publication that details all federal tax laws. This publication now has in excess of 55,000 pages!

We hope that you include this book as a comprehensible resource you can count on.

Taxes For Dummies, 2004 Edition, helps you discover how the tax system works and how to legally make the system work for *you.* You'll quite possibly be bothered by some of the things this book shows you that don't seem fair. But getting angry enough to make the veins in your neck bulge definitely won't help your financial situation or your blood pressure. (We don't want to see your medical deductions increase!) Even if you don't agree with the entire tax system, you still have to play by the rules.

A brief history of U.S. income taxes

Federal income taxes haven't always been a certainty. In the early twentieth century, people lived without being bothered by the federal income tax — or by televisions, microwaves, computers, voice mail, and all those other complications. Beginning in 1913, Congress set up a system of graduated tax rates, starting with a rate of only 1 percent and going up to 7 percent.

This tax system was enacted through the 16th Amendment to the Constitution, which was suggested by President Teddy Roosevelt (a Republican), and pushed through by his successor, President William H. Taft (another Republican), and ultimately ratified by two-thirds of the states. (Sorry, Mr. Forbes, Mr. Bush, and Mr. Limbaugh — not all Republicans have been anti-tax-and-spend!) Note that we, your good authors, are Independents, which means that we happily take swipes at Republicans, Democrats, and other political pundits throughout our book.

In fairness, we must tell you that the 1913 federal income tax was not the first U.S. income tax. President Abraham Lincoln (Republican) signed a Civil War income tax in 1861, which was abandoned a decade later.

Prior to 1913, the vast majority of tax dollars collected by the federal government came from taxes levied on goods, such as liquor, tobacco, and imports. Today, personal income taxes, including Social Security taxes, account for about 85 percent of federal government revenue.

In 1913, the forms, instructions, and clarifications for the entire federal tax system would have filled just one small, three-ring binder! (And we're not even sure that three-ring binders existed back then.) Those were, indeed, the good old days. Since then, thanks to endless revisions, enhancements, and simplifications, the federal tax laws — along with the IRS and court clarifications of those laws — can (and should) fill several dump trucks. Since World War II, the size of the federal tax code has swelled by more than 400 percent! And, according to the Tax Foundation — a nonprofit, nonpartisan policy research organization — complying with the tax laws costs everyone in the U.S. more than $200 billion annually.

You can reduce your taxes

The tax system, like other public policies, is built around incentives to encourage *desirable* behavior and activity. Home ownership, for example, is considered good because it encourages people to take more responsibility for maintaining properties and neighborhoods. Therefore, the government offers all sorts of tax benefits *(allowable deductions)* to encourage people to own homes (see Chapter 24). But if you don't understand these tax benefits, you probably don't know how to take full advantage of them, either.

Even when you're an honest, earnest, well-intentioned, and law-abiding citizen, odds are that you don't completely understand the tax system. This ignorance wreaks havoc with your personal finances, because you end up paying more in taxes than you need to.

Adding insult to injury, you may step on a tax land mine. Like millions of taxpayers before you, you can unwittingly be in noncompliance with one or more of the ever-changing tax laws at the federal, state, and local levels. Your tax ignorance can cause mistakes that may be costly if the IRS and your state government catch your errors. With the proliferation of computerized data tracking, discovering errors has never been easier for the tax cops at the IRS. And when they uncover your boo-boos, you have to pay the tax you originally owed *and* interest *and,* possibly, penalties. Ouch!

So don't feel dumb when it comes to understanding the tax system. You're not the problem — the complexity of the income tax system is. Making sense of the tax jungle is more daunting than hacking your way out of a triple-canopy rain forest with a dinner knife. That's why, throughout this book, we help you understand the tax system, and we promise not to make you read the actual tax laws.

You should be able to keep much more of your money by applying the tax-reducing strategies we present in this book.

- ✔ You may be able to tax shelter your employment earnings into various retirement accounts such as 401(k) and SEP-IRA plans. This strategy slashes your current income taxes, enables your money to grow tax-free, and helps you work toward the goal of retirement.

- ✔ The less you buy, the less sales tax you pay. You can buy a less expensive, more fuel-efficient car, for example.

- ✔ When you invest, you can invest in a way that fits your tax situation. This strategy can make you happier and wealthier come tax time. For example, you can choose tax-friendly investments (such as tax-free bonds) that reduce your tax bill and increase your after-tax investment returns.

Beyond April 15: What you don't know can cost you

Every spring, more than 100 million tax returns (and several million extension requests) are filed with the IRS. The byproduct of this effort is guaranteed employment for the nation's more than 1 million accountants and auditors, and 2 million bookkeeping and accounting clerks (not to mention more than a few tax-book authors and their editors). Accounting firms rake in more than $30 billion annually, helping bewildered and desperately confused taxpayers figure out all those tax laws. So that you can feel okay about this situation, keep in mind that at least some of the money you pay in income taxes actually winds up in the government coffers for some useful purposes.

Given all the hours that you work each year just to pay your taxes and the time you spend actually completing the dreaded return, on April 16, you may feel like tossing the whole tax topic into a drawer or closet until next year. Such avoidance, however, is a costly mistake.

During the tax year, you can take steps to ensure that you're not only in compliance with the ever-changing tax laws, but also that you're minimizing your tax burden. If your income — like that of nearly everyone we know — is limited, you need to understand the tax code to make it work for you and help you accomplish your financial goals. The following case studies demonstrate the importance of keeping in mind the tax implications of your financial decisions throughout the year.

The costs of procrastination

Consider the case of Sheila and Peter, the proud owners of a successful and rapidly growing small business. They became so busy running the business and taking care of their children that they hardly had time to call a tax advisor. In fact, not only did they fail to file for an extension by April 15, but they also didn't pay any federal or state income taxes.

By August, Peter and Sheila finally had time to focus on the prior year's income taxes, but by then they had gotten themselves into some problems and incurred these costs:

- **A penalty for failure to file,** which is 5 percent per month of the amount due, up to a maximum of 25 percent (for five months).

- **Interest on the amount due,** which at that time was running about 9 percent per year. (*Note:* This rate is adjusted over time based on current interest rate levels.)

- **A larger tax bill** (also caused by lack of planning), which turned out to be far more expensive than the first two expenses. Because they had incorporated their business, Peter and Sheila were on the payroll for salary during the year. Despite the high level of profitability of their business, they had set their pay at too low a level.

  A low salary wouldn't seem to be a problem for the owner and only employee of a company. The worst that you'd think could happen to Peter and Sheila is that they might have to eat more peanut butter and jelly sandwiches during the year. But because they received small salaries, the contributions they could make to tax-deductible retirement accounts were based on a percentage of only their small salaries.

  The rest of the business profits, however, had to be taken by Sheila and Peter as taxable income, because they had their company set up as an *S Corporation.* (We explain the different types of corporations and their tax consequences in Chapter 22.) This gaffe caused Sheila and Peter to pay thousands in additional taxes, which they could've legally — and easily — avoided.

- **Loss of future investment earnings,** which means that over time Sheila and Peter actually lose *more* than the additional taxes. Not only did Peter and Sheila miss out on an opportunity to reduce their taxes by making larger deductible contributions to their tax-sheltered retirement accounts, but they also lost the chance for the money to compound (tax-deferred) over time.

The consequences of poor advice

Getting bad advice, especially from someone with a vested interest in your decisions, is another leading cause of tax mistakes. Consider the case of George, who wanted advice about investing and other financial matters. When he received a solicitation from a financial advisor at a well-known firm, he was game to give it a whirl. The polished, well-dressed advisor, who was actually a *broker* (someone who earns commissions from the financial products that he or she peddles), prepared a voluminous report complete with scads of retirement projections for George.

Part of the advice in this report was for George to purchase some cash-value life insurance and various investments from the broker. The broker pitched the insurance as a great way to save, invest, and reduce George's tax burden.

Through his employer, George could invest in a retirement account on a tax-deductible basis. However, the broker conveniently overlooked this avenue — after all, the broker couldn't earn fat commissions by telling people like George to fund their employers' retirement accounts. As a result, George paid thousands of dollars more in taxes than he needed to.

Funding the life insurance policy was a terrible decision for George, in large part because doing so offered no upfront tax breaks. When you contribute money to tax-deductible retirement accounts, such as 401(k) plans, you get to keep and invest money you normally would've owed in federal and state income taxes. (See Chapter 21 to find out more about retirement accounts and check out Chapter 23 for the other reasons why life insurance generally shouldn't be used as an investment.)

Understanding Your Income Tax Rates

Many people remember only whether they received tax refunds or owed money on their tax returns. But you *should* care how much you pay in taxes, and you should understand the *total* and the *marginal* taxes that you pay, so you can make financial decisions that lessen your tax load.

Although some people feel happy or fortunate when they get refunds, you shouldn't feel so good. All a refund really indicates is that you overpaid your taxes during the prior year. When you file your income tax return, all you do is balance your tax checkbook, so to speak, against the federal and state governments' versions of your tax checkbook. You settle up with tax authorities regarding the amount of taxes you paid during the past year versus the total tax that you actually are required to pay, based on your income and deductions.

Last year, the IRS issued about $180 billion in individual income tax refunds. If you figure that even at a 4 percent interest rate from shorter-term bonds, taxpayers threw away about $7 billion in interest on money that they could've invested.

Total taxes

The only way to determine the total amount of income taxes you pay is to get out your federal and state tax returns. On each of those returns is a line that shows the *total tax* (line 60 on Form 1040 returns). Add the totals from your federal and state tax returns, and you probably have one of the largest expenses of your financial life (unless you have an expensive home or a huge gambling habit).

You need to note that your taxable income is different from the amount of money you earned during the tax year from employment and investments. *Taxable income* is defined as the amount of income on which you actually pay taxes. You don't pay taxes on your total income for the following two reasons. First, not all income is taxable. For example, you pay federal income tax on the interest that you earn on a bank savings account but not on the interest from municipal bonds (which are essentially loans that you, as a bond buyer, make to state and local governments).

A second reason that you don't pay taxes on all your income is that you get to subtract deductions from your income. Some deductions are available just for being a living, breathing human being. For tax year 2003, single people receive an automatic $4,750 *standard deduction,* and married couples filing jointly get $9,500. (People older than 65 and those who are blind get slightly higher deductions.) Other expenses, such as mortgage interest and property taxes, are deductible to the extent that your total itemized deductions exceed the standard deductions.

A personal budget or spending plan that doesn't address, contain, and reduce your taxes may be doomed to failure. Taxes are such a major portion of most people's expenditures that throughout this book we highlight strategies for reducing your taxable income and income taxes right now and in the future. Doing so is vital to your ability to save and invest money to accomplish important financial and personal goals.

Your marginal income tax rate

"What's marginal about my taxes?" we hear you asking. "They're huge! They aren't marginal at all!" _Marginal_ is a word that people often use when they mean small or barely acceptable. Sort of like getting a C– on a school report card (or "just" an A– if you're from an overachieving family).

But when we're talking about taxes, _marginal_ has a different meaning. The government charges you different income tax rates for different parts of your annual income. So your _marginal tax rate_ is the rate that you pay on the last dollars you earn. You generally pay less tax on your _first,_ or lowest, dollars of earnings and more tax on your _last,_ or highest, dollars of earnings. This system is known as a graduated income tax. Graduated tax brackets are recorded in Greece as far back as 2400 B.C.

Are your income tax rates fair? You be the judge

With the possible exceptions of abortion and gun control, the issue of whether the tax system is fair inspires some of the more emotionally charged dialogue (and preachy monologues from radio talk show commentators). By _fair,_ we mean how much total tax you're asked to pay and how that total compares with what your neighbors, your co-workers, and people in various states pay.

Like most Americans, you probably think you pay too much in taxes. It may not be much comfort to you, but the average total taxes that citizens in the United States pay are low when compared with what citizens of other industrialized countries in Europe and Asia pay. However, low and moderate income earners in the U.S. pay higher income taxes than their overseas friends, and high-income earners generally pay less.

A tremendous debate rages, and much gnashing of teeth is heard, about how much high-income earners and the wealthy (relative to other taxpayers) should pay in taxes. On the far right of the political spectrum, politicians and commentators argue that burdening the people who work hard and generate jobs (that is, the high-income earners) with oppressive taxes is unfair and economically harmful. At the other end of the spectrum, you hear diehard liberals pleading that the well heeled don't pay their fair share and need to face higher taxes to help pay for deserving programs for the poor and disadvantaged.

As with many disagreements, the people at the polar extremes think they're right (intellectually, not politically speaking) and that the other side is wrong. The politically liberal have a tendency to idealize how well government solves problems, and they therefore advocate more taxes for more programs. On the other hand, the politically conservative have a tendency to idealize how well the private sector meets the needs of society at large in the absence of government oversight and programs.

Although we can agree that easy access to tax revenue encourages some wasteful government spending and pork-laden programs, we also know that taxes must come from somewhere. The questions are how much and from whom? Equity, fairness, and stimulation of economic growth are concerns in the design of a tax system. You rarely hear blustery commentators or news programs thoughtfully discuss these issues.

Our advice is to keep an open mind, listen to all sides, and remember the big picture. Back in the 1950s (an economic boom time), for example, the highest federal income tax rate was a whopping 90 percent, more than double its current level. And whereas during most of the past century the highest income earners paid a marginal rate that was double to triple the rate paid by moderate income earners of the time, that gap was greatly reduced during the 1980s. However, the highest income earners continue to pay the lion's share of taxes. In fact, the top 1 percent of all income earners pay about 30 percent of all income taxes. The top 20 percent pay more than three-quarters of the total individual income taxes collected.

The fact that *not all income is treated equally* under the current tax system isn't evident to most people. When you work for an employer and have a reasonably constant salary during the course of a year, a stable amount of federal and state taxes is deducted from each of your paychecks. Therefore, you may have the false impression that all your earned income is being taxed equally.

Table 1-1 gives the federal tax rates for singles and for married people filing jointly.

Table 1-1	2003 Federal Income Tax Brackets and Rates	
Singles Taxable Income	*Married-Filing-Jointly Taxable Income*	*Federal Tax Rate*
Less than $7,000	Less than $14,000	10%
$7,000 to $28,400	$14,000 to $56,800	15%
$28,400 to $68,800	$56,800 to $114,650	25%
$68,800 to $143,500	$114,650 to $174,700	28%
$143,500 to $311,950	$174,700 to $311,950	33%
More than $311,950	More than $311,950	35%

Remember that your marginal tax rate is the rate of tax that you pay on your *last,* or so-called highest, dollars of income. So, according to Table 1-1, if you're single and your taxable income during 2003 totals $34,000, for example, you pay federal income tax at the rate of 10 percent on the first $7,000 of taxable income. You then pay 15 percent on the amount from $7,000 to $28,400 and 25 percent on income from $28,400 up to $34,000. In other words, you effectively pay a marginal federal tax rate of 25 percent on your last dollars of income — those dollars in excess of $28,400.

After you understand the powerful concept of marginal tax rates, you can begin to see the value of the many financial strategies that affect the amount of taxes you pay. Because you pay taxes on your employment income and on the earnings from your investments other than retirement accounts, many of your personal financial decisions need to be made with your marginal tax rate in mind. For example, when you have the opportunity to work over-time or moonlight and earn some extra money, how much of that extra compensation you get to keep depends on your marginal tax rate. Your marginal tax rate enables you to quickly calculate the additional taxes you'd pay on the additional income.

Conversely, you can delight in quantifying the amount of taxes that you save by reducing your taxable income, either by decreasing your income — for example, with pretax contri-butions to retirement accounts — or by increasing your deductions.

Actually, even more can be made of your marginal taxes. In the next section, we detail the painful realities of income taxes levied by most states that add to your federal income burden. If you're a higher income earner, pay close attention to the section later in this chapter where we discuss the *Alternative Minimum Tax.* And as we discuss elsewhere in this book, some tax breaks are reduced when your income exceeds a particular level — here are some examples:

✔ Itemized deductions, which we discuss in Chapter 9 and record on Schedule A, are reduced for tax year 2003 when your *adjusted gross income* (AGI — total income before subtracting deductions) exceeds $139,500 ($69,750 for married persons filing separately).

✔ Personal exemptions are a freebie — they're a write-off of $3,050 in tax year 2003 just because you're a living, breathing, human being. However, personal exemptions are whittled away for single-income earners with AGIs of more than $139,500, married per-sons filing separately with AGIs of more than $104,625, and married people filing jointly with AGIs of more than $209,250.

✔ If you own rental real estate, you may normally take up to a $25,000 annual loss when your expenses exceed your rental income. Your ability to deduct this loss begins to be limited when your AGI exceeds $100,000.

✔ Your eligibility to fully contribute to *Roth Individual Retirement Accounts* (see Chapter 21) depends on your AGI being less than or equal to $95,000 if you're a single taxpayer or $150,000 if you're married. Beyond these amounts, allowable contributions are phased out.

Your marginal tax rate — the rate of tax you pay on your last dollars of income — should be higher than your *average tax rate* — the rate you pay, on average, on all your earnings. The reason your marginal tax rate is more important for you to know is that it tells you the value of legally reducing your taxable income. So, for example, if you're in the federal 28 percent tax bracket, for every $1,000 that you can reduce your taxable income, you shave $280 off of your federal income tax bill.

State income taxes

Note that your *total marginal rate* includes your federal and state tax rates. As you may already be painfully aware, you don't pay only federal income taxes. You also get hit with state income taxes — that is, unless you live in Alaska, Florida, Nevada, South Dakota, Texas, Washington, or Wyoming. Those states have no state income taxes. As is true with federal income taxes, state income taxes have been around since the early 1900s.

You can look up your state tax rate by getting out your most recent year's state income tax preparation booklet. Alternatively, we've been crazy — but kind — enough to prepare a helpful little (okay, not so little) table that can give you a rough idea of your state tax rates (see Table 1-2).

Table 1-2		State Marginal Tax Rates			
State	**Filing Status***	**Taxable Income**			
		$25,000+	**$50,000+**	**$100,000+**	**$250,000+**
Alabama	All	5%	5%	5%	5%
Alaska	(No personal income tax)				
Arizona	Singles	3.74%	4.72%	4.72%	5.04%
	Marrieds	3.2%	3.74%	4.72%	5.04%
Arkansas	All	7%	7%	7%	7%
California	Singles	6%	9.3%	9.3%	9.3%
	Marrieds	2%	6%	9.3%	9.3%
Colorado	All	4.63%	4.63%	4.63%	4.63%
Connecticut	All	4.5%	4.5%	4.5%	4.5%
Delaware	All	5.55%	5.55%	5.95%	5.95%
District of Columbia	All	7.5%	9.3%	9.3%	9.3%
Florida	(No personal income tax)				
Georgia	All	6%	6%	6%	6%
Hawaii	Singles	7.60%	8.25%	8.25%	8.25%
	Marrieds	6.80%	7.60%	8.25%	8.25%

State	Filing Status*	Taxable Income			
		$25,000+	$50,000+	$100,000+	$250,000+
Idaho	All	7.8%	7.8%	7.8%	7.8%
Illinois	All	3%	3%	3%	3%
Indiana	All	3.4%	3.4%	3.4%	3.4%
Iowa	All	6.8%	7.92%	8.98%	8.98%
Kansas	Singles	6.25%	6.45%	6.45%	6.45%
	Marrieds	3.5%	6.25%	6.45%	6.45%
Kentucky	All	6%	6%	6%	6%
Louisiana	All	4%	6%	6%	6%
Maine	Singles	8.5%	8.5%	8.5%	8.5%
	Marrieds	7.0%	8.5%	8.5%	8.5%
Maryland	All	4.8%	4.8%	4.8%	4.8%
Massachusetts	All	5.3%	5.3%	5.3%	5.3%
Michigan	All	4.2%	4.2%	4.2%	4.2%
Minnesota	Singles	7.05%	7.05%	7.85%	7.85%
	Marrieds	5.35%	7.05%	7.05%	7.85%
Mississippi	All	5%	5%	5%	5%
Missouri	All	6%	6%	6%	6%
Montana	All	8%	10%	11%	11%
Nebraska	Singles	5.01%	6.68%	6.68%	6.68%
	Marrieds	3.49%	6.68%	6.68%	6.68%
Nevada	(No broad-based income tax)				
New Hampshire	All	5% only on dividend and interest income on stocks and bonds			
New Jersey	Singles	1.75%	5.525%	6.37%	6.37%
	Marrieds	1.75%	1.75%	5.525%	6.37%
New Mexico	Singles	6%	7.9%	8.2%	8.2%
	Marrieds	6%	7.1%	8.2%	8.2%
New York	Singles	6.85%	6.85%	6.85%	6.85%
	Marrieds	5.25%	6.85%	6.85%	6.85%
North Carolina	All	7%	7%	7.75%	8.25%
North Dakota	Singles	2.10%	3.92%	4.34%	5.04%
	Marrieds	2.10%	2.10%	3.92%	5.04%
Ohio	All	4.46%	5.20%	6.9%	7.5%
Oklahoma	All	6.65%	6.65%	6.65%	6.65%

(continued)

Table 1-2 *(continued)*

State	Filing Status*	Taxable Income			
		$25,000+	**$50,000+**	**$100,000+**	**$250,000+**
Oregon	All	9%	9%	9%	9%
Pennsylvania	All	2.8%	2.8%	2.8%	2.8%
Rhode Island	All	Flat rate of 25.5% of federal income tax liability			
South Carolina	All	7%	7%	7%	7%
South Dakota	(No personal income tax)				
Tennessee	All	6% only on interest and dividends from stocks and bonds			
Texas	(No personal income tax)				
Utah	All	7%	7%	7%	7%
Vermont	All	Flat rate of 24% of federal income tax liability			
Virginia	All	5.75%	5.75%	5.75%	5.75%
Washington	(No personal income tax)				
West Virginia	All	4.5%	6%	6.5%	6.5%
Wisconsin	All	6.5%	6.5%	6.5%	6.75%
Wyoming	(No personal income tax)				

* Filing status "married" refers only to married couples who file jointly.

The second tax system: Alternative Minimum Tax

You may find this hard to believe, but there's actually a *second* federal income tax system (yes, we groan with you as we struggle to understand even the first complicated tax system). This second system may raise your income taxes higher than they'd otherwise be. We'll explain.

Through the years, as the government has grown hungrier for revenue, taxpayers who slash their taxes by claiming many deductions have come under greater scrutiny. So the government created a second tax system — the *Alternative Minimum Tax (AMT)* — to ensure that higher income earners with relatively high amounts of itemized deductions pay at least a minimum amount of taxes on their incomes.

If you have a bunch of deductions from state income taxes, real estate taxes, certain types of mortgage interest, or passive investments (such as limited partnerships or rental real estate), you may fall prey to the AMT. The AMT is a classic case of the increasing complexity of our tax code. As incentives were placed in the tax code, people took advantage of them. Then the government said, "Whoa, Nelly! We can't have people taking *that* many write-offs." Thus was born the AMT.

At the federal level lurk two AMT tax brackets: 26 percent for AMT income up to $175,000, and 28 percent for everything that's more than that amount, except for capital gains. The AMT restricts you from claiming certain deductions and requires you to increase your taxable income. So you must figure the tax you owe under the AMT system *and* under the other system and then pay whichever amount is *higher* (ouch!). Unfortunately, the only way to know for certain whether you're ensnared by this second tax system is by completing — you guessed it — another tax form (see Chapter 8).

Chapter 2

Tax Return Preparation Options and Tools

In This Chapter
▶ Preparing your own tax return
▶ Getting IRS assistance
▶ Understanding the pros and cons of tax-preparation software and Internet sites
▶ Hiring help: Preparers, EAs, CPAs, and tax attorneys

*B*y the time you actually get around to filing your annual income tax return, it's usually too late to take advantage of many tax-reduction strategies for that tax year. And what can be more aggravating than, late in the evening on April 14 when you're already stressed out and unhappily working on your return, finding a golden nugget of tax advice that works great — if only you'd known about it last December!

Be sure to review Part V, which covers the important tax-planning issues that you need to take advantage of in future years. In the event that you've waited until the last minute to complete your return this year, be sure to read Part V thoroughly after you file your return.

If you're now faced with the daunting task of preparing your return, you're probably trying to decide how to do it with a minimum of pain and taxes owed. You have several options for completing your return. The best choice for you depends on how complex your tax situation is, how much you know about taxes, and how much you enjoy a challenge.

Doing Your Own Return

You already do many things for yourself. Maybe you cook for yourself, do home repairs, or even change the oil in your car. You may do these chores because you enjoy them, because you save money by doing them yourself, or because you want to develop a particular skill.

Sometimes, however, you hire others to help you do the job. Occasionally, you may buy a meal out or hire someone to make a home improvement. And so it can be with your annual income tax return — you may want to hire help, but you may end up, like most people, preparing your own return.

Doing your own income tax return is an especially good option if your financial situation doesn't change much from year to year. You can use last year's return as a guide, filling in the new numbers, doing the required mathematical operations on the new return, making a copy of your completed return (you always need to keep a copy of your tax return for your files), and putting it in the mail.

You may need to do some reading to keep up with the small number of changes in the tax system and laws that affect your situation (this book can help). Given the constant changes to various parts of the tax laws, you simply can't assume that the tax laws that apply to your situation are the same from one year to the next just because your situation is the same.

Another benefit of preparing your own return includes the better financial decisions that you make in the future by using the tax knowledge you gain from learning about the tax system. Most tax preparers are so busy preparing returns that you probably won't get much of their time to discuss tax laws and how they may apply to your future financial decisions. Even if you can schedule an audience with the preparer, you may end up sitting in his or her office thinking about how much more your bill will reflect when he or she adds the cost of the personal tutorial you're sitting through.

Last, but not least, doing your own return should be your lowest-cost tax-return-preparation option. Of course, we're assuming that you don't make costly mistakes and oversights and that the leisure time you forego when preparing your return isn't too valuable!

You bought this book, and that was a smart move. You're confident enough to tackle the tax forms yourself, but you're savvy enough to know you need expert guidance through the thicket of annual tax law changes. Give our advice a try before throwing in the towel and paying hundreds of dollars in tax-preparation fees. And if you stay alert while preparing your return, reading the list of deductions that don't apply to you may motivate you to make changes in your personal and financial habits so that you *can* take some of those deductions next year.

Using IRS Publications

In addition to the instructions that come with the annual tax forms that the good old Internal Revenue Service mails to you every year, the IRS also produces hundreds of publications that explain how to complete the myriad tax forms taxpayers must tackle. These booklets are available in printed form or through the IRS's Web site (www.irs.gov; see the section "Internal Revenue Service" later in this chapter for more on what the site has to offer). Additionally, the IRS provides answers to common questions through its automated phone system and through live representatives. If you have a simple, straightforward tax return, completing it on your own using only the IRS instructions may be fine. This approach is as cheap as you can get, costing only your time, patience, photocopying expenses, and postage to mail the completed tax return.

Unfortunately (for you), IRS publications and employees don't generally offer the kind, helpful advice that we provide in this book. For example, here's something you don't see in an IRS publication:

> STOP! One of the most commonly overlooked deductions is . . . You still have time to . . . and whack off hundreds — maybe thousands — of dollars from your tax bill! HURRY!

Another danger in relying on the IRS for assistance is that it has been known to give wrong information and answers. When you call the IRS with a question, be sure to take notes about your phone conversation, thus protecting yourself in the event of an audit. Date your notes and include the name of the IRS employee with whom you spoke, what you asked, and the employee's responses. File your notes in a folder with a copy of your completed return.

In addition to the standard instructions that come with your tax return, the IRS offers some pamphlets that you can request by phone:

- ✔ Publication 17: *Your Federal Income Tax* is designed for individual tax-return preparation.
- ✔ Publication 334: *Tax Guide for Small Business (For Individuals Who Use Schedule C or C-EZ)* is for (you guessed it) small-business tax-return preparation.

These guides provide more detail than the basic IRS publications. Call 800-TAX-FORM (800-829-3676 for those who hate searching for letters on phone keypads) to request these free guides. (Actually, nothing is free. You've already paid for IRS guides with your tax dollars!)

The IRS also offers more in-depth booklets focusing on specific tax issues. However, if your tax situation is so complex that this book (and Publications 17 and 334) can't address it, you need to think long and hard about getting help from a tax advisor or from one of the other sources recommended in the "Hiring Help" section later in this chapter.

IRS publications present plenty of rules and facts, but they don't make it easy for you to find the information and advice you really need. The best way to use IRS publications is to *confirm facts* that you already think you know or to check the little details. Don't expect IRS publications and representatives to show you how to cut your tax bill.

Perusing Tax-Preparation and Advice Guides

Privately published tax-preparation and advice books are invaluable when they highlight tax-reduction strategies and possible pitfalls — in clear, simple English. We hope you agree with the reader and reviewer comments in the front of this guide that say *Taxes For Dummies* is top of the line in this category. Such books help you complete your return accurately and save you as much money as possible. The amount of money invested in a book or two is significantly smaller than the annual cost of a tax expert. And books like this one come with commonly needed tax forms, saving you time and hassle.

Taxes For Dummies covers the important tax-preparation and planning issues that affect the vast majority of taxpayers. A minority of taxpayers may run into some nitpicky tax issues caused by unusual events in their lives or extraordinary changes in their incomes or assets. This book may not be enough for those folks. In such cases, you need to consider hiring a tax advisor, which we explain how to do later in this chapter (see the section, "Hiring Help").

Buying Software

If you don't want to slog through dozens of pages of tedious IRS instructions or pay a tax preparer hundreds of dollars to complete your annual return, you may be interested in computer software that can help you finish off your IRS **Form 1040** and supplemental schedules. If you have access to a computer and printer, tax-preparation software can be a helpful tool.

Tax-preparation software also gives you the advantage of automatically recalculating all the appropriate numbers on your return if one number changes — no more painting out math errors with a little white brush or recalculating a whole page of figures because your dog was sleeping on some of the receipts. (Just don't let your cat walk on your keyboard or another family member use the computer before saving and printing out your return!)

The best tax-preparation software is easy to install and use on your computer, provides help when you get stuck, and highlights deductions you may overlook. If you get a headache trying to figure out how to do something with the software, the best packages have accessible and helpful technical support people you can call in your time of need. Remember, though, that these people are software techies, not tax techies. Don't expect to get an explanation of whether you can deduct your last trip to Hawaii as a business expense.

Before plunking down your hard-earned cash for some tax-preparation software, know that it has potential drawbacks. Here are the big ones:

- **Garbage in, garbage out.** A tax return prepared by a software program is only as good as the quality of the data you enter into it. Of course, this drawback exists no matter who actually fills out the forms; some human tax preparers don't probe and clarify to make sure that you've provided all the right stuff, either. Tax software programs also may contain glitches that can lead to incorrect calculating or reporting of some aspect of your tax return.

- **Where's the beef?** Some tax software packages give little in the way of background help, advice, and warnings. This lack of assistance can lull you into a false sense of security about the completeness and accuracy of the return you prepare.

- **Think, computer, think!** Computers are good at helping you access and process information. They don't exercise judgment or think for you (although someday they may do more, if the artificial intelligence gurus realize their dreams). Meanwhile, remember that your computer is great at crunching numbers but has a far lower IQ than you have!

TaxCut and *TurboTax* are the leading programs, and they do a reasonable job of helping you through the federal tax forms. One way to break a tie between good software options is considering price — you may be able to get a better deal on one software package (*TurboTax* carries a higher suggested retail price). Procrastinating also offers some benefits, because the longer you wait to buy the software, the cheaper it generally gets — especially when you buy it after filing for an extension. You also want to make sure to check whether the tax software you buy can import the data from the checkbook software you've been using to track your tax-deductible expenses throughout the year.

No matter which program you buy, don't waste your money on *electronic filing,* which the programs promote, unless you're chomping at the bit to receive a large refund (electronic filing gets a refund to you a few weeks earlier than normal filing). Filing your tax return online enriches the software companies and saves the IRS on data entry (they should pay us to file electronically) but doesn't save you any hassles; you still must mail in your W-2 and yet another IRS form **(Form 8453-OL)**.

Accessing Internet Tax Resources

In addition to using your computer to prepare your income tax return, you can do an increasing number of other tax activities via the Internet. The better online tax resources are geared more to tax practitioners and tax-savvy taxpayers. But in your battle to legally minimize your taxes, you may want all the help you can get! Use the Internet for what it's best at doing — possibly saving you time tracking down factual information or other stuff.

On the Internet, many Web sites provide information and discussions about tax issues. Take advice and counsel from other Net users at your peril. We don't recommend that you depend on the accuracy of the answers to tax questions that you ask in online forums. The problem: You can't be sure of the background, expertise, or identity, in many cases, of the person with whom you're trading messages. However, if you want to liven up your life — and taxes make you mad — a number of political forums enable you to converse and butt heads with others. You can complain about recent tax hikes or explain why you think that the wealthy still don't pay enough taxes!

The following sections describe some of the better sites out there.

Internal Revenue Service

When you think of the *Internal Revenue Service* — the U.S. Treasury Department Office charged with overseeing the collection of federal income taxes — you probably think of the following adjectives: bureaucratic, humorless, and stodgy. Difficult as it is to believe, the IRS Web site (www.irs.gov) offers fun graphics and some mildly amusing writing. For example, one headline article on the IRS's homepage was "Teenager Tanya Taylor Tries to Tackle Taxation Training Interactively." The article was about a then high school junior Tanya Taylor of Tyler, Texas, taking home her first paycheck. "Many of my friends thought they got to keep *all* of their pay," Tanya chuckled, adding, "Boy, were they shocked to see all of the deductions! Fortunately, my boss gave me a heads-up of what to expect." The article goes on to explain how Tanya's employer had Tanya visit the IRS Web site so she could find out about the taxes that are deducted from her paycheck and where that money goes.

The IRS site also has links to state tax organizations, convenient access to IRS forms (including those from prior tax years), and instructions. To be able to read and print the forms, you need a software program like Adobe Acrobat Reader, which you can download for free from many Internet sites, including the IRS site or the Adobe Web site at www.adobe.com. To download forms from the IRS site, start browsing at www.irs.gov/formspubs/index.html.

You can complete your tax forms online at the IRS site using Adobe Acrobat Reader. The IRS site even features a place for you to submit comments on proposed tax regulations, with a promise that the "comments are fully considered." Is this the IRS we know and love?

Directories

A number of sites on the Web claim to be *directories*. Be forewarned that some sites marketing themselves as providing collections of all the best tax stuff on the Internet may not be nearly as objective as they lead you to believe. Some sites may simply provide links to other sites that pay them a referral fee.

Dennis Schmidt's Tax and Accounting Sites Directory (www.taxsites.com) is organized into various categories, such as state taxes, tax forms, software, and law. This site is a comprehensive collection of tax Web sites. There are no frills, graphics, reviews, or even commentary. Schmidt is a professor of accounting at the University of Northern Iowa.

Research

For true tax junkies, the U.S. Tax Code On-Line (www.fourmilab.ch/ustax/ustax.html) is a search engine that enables you to check out the complete text of the Internal Revenue Code. Hyperlinks embedded in the text provide cross-references between sections at the click of a mouse. (We know we promised not to subject you to the tax code, but if you're interested, it's all laid out for you.)

CCH Incorporated's site (www.cch.com) is geared toward tax and legal professionals who need to keep up with and research the tax laws. Access to most of the site's resources is granted by subscription only.

Tax preparation sites

A number of Web sites enable you to prepare federal and state tax forms and then file them electronically. For example, at H&R Block's site (www.hrblock.com), you enter your data on interview forms that are provided, and the necessary calculations are performed. Although using the Web site to perform your calculations is free of charge, H&R Block charges you $29.95 if you want to print your filled-out IRS forms (requires using Adobe Acrobat Reader software) or file them electronically through the site. Preparing and filing state forms (most, but not all, state forms are available on the site) costs extra.

A lower-cost alternative worth your consideration can be found at CCH Incorporated's Complete Tax Web site (www.completetax.com), where you enter data on interview forms and calculate your tax. For only $24.95, you can print your completed return and electronically file your tax return with the IRS and any state that accepts electronic returns.

 Unless you're using a speedy modem connection on your computer (such as a cable modem or DSL connection), preparing tax forms online can be painfully slow compared to having a software program on your hard drive. Remember that if you're simply after the tax forms, we provide many of them in the back of this book, and plenty of the sites mentioned in this section offer such documents for free.

Hiring Help

Because they lack the time, interest, energy, or skill to do it themselves, some people hire a contractor to handle a home-remodeling project. And most people who hire a contractor do so because they think that they can afford to hire a contractor. (Although sometimes this last part isn't true, and they wind up with more debt than they can afford!)

For some of the same reasons, some people choose to hire a tax preparer and advisor.

By identifying tax-reduction strategies that you may overlook, competent tax practitioners can save you money — sometimes more than enough to pay their fees. They may also reduce the likelihood of an audit, which can be triggered by blunders that you may make. Like some building contractors, however, some tax preparers take longer, charging you more and not delivering the high-quality work you expect.

Deciding whether you really need a preparer

Odds are quite good that you can successfully prepare your own return. Most people's returns don't vary that much from year to year, so you have a head start and can hit the ground running if you get out last year's return — which, of course, you copied and filed!

Preparing your own return may not work as well whenever your situation has changed in some way — if you bought or sold a house, started your own business, or retired, for example. In such an event, start by focusing on the sections of this book in Parts II and III that deal with those preparation issues. If you want more planning background, check out the relevant chapters in Part V.

Don't give up and hire a preparer just because you can't bear to open your tax-preparation booklet and get your background data organized. Even if you hire a tax preparer, you still need to get your stuff organized before a consultation.

As hard and as painful as it is, confront preparing your return as far in advance of April 15 as you can so that if you feel uncomfortable with your level of knowledge, you have enough time to seek help. The more organizing you can do before hiring a preparer, the less having your return prepared should cost you. Avoid waiting until the 11th hour to hire an advisor — you won't do as thorough a job of selecting a competent person, and you'll probably pay more for the rush job. If you get stuck preparing the return, you can get a second opinion from other preparation resources we discuss in this chapter.

If you decide to seek out the services of a tax preparer/advisor, know that tax practitioners come with various backgrounds, training, and credentials. One type of professional isn't necessarily better than another. Think of them as different types of specialists who are appropriate for different circumstances. The four main types of tax practitioners are preparers, enrolled agents, certified public accountants, and tax attorneys.

Preparers

Among all the tax practitioners, *preparers* generally have the least amount of training, and more of them work part-time. H&R Block is the largest and most well-known tax-preparation firm in the country. In addition, other national firms and plenty of mom-and-pop shops are in the tax-preparation business.

The appeal of preparers is that they're relatively inexpensive — they can do basic returns for $100 or so. The drawback is that you may hire a preparer who doesn't know much more than you do! As with financial planners, no national regulations apply to tax-return preparers, and no licensing is required. In most states, almost anybody can hang out a tax-preparation shingle and start preparing. Most preparers, however, complete some sort of training program before working with clients.

Preparers make the most sense for folks who don't have complicated financial lives, who are budget-minded, and who dislike doing their own taxes. If you aren't good about hanging onto receipts or don't want to keep your own files with background details about your taxes, you definitely need to shop around for a tax preparer who's going to be around for a few years. You may need all that paperwork stuff someday for an audit, and some tax preparers keep and organize their clients' documentation rather than return everything each year. (Can you blame them for keeping your records after they go through the tedious task of sorting them all out of the shopping bags?) Going with a firm that's open year-round may also be safer, in case tax questions or problems arise (some small shops are open only during tax season).

Enrolled agents (EAs)

A person must pass IRS scrutiny to be called an *enrolled agent (EA)*. This license enables the agent to represent you before the IRS in the event of an audit.

The training to become an EA generally is longer and more sophisticated than that of a typical preparer. Continuing education also is required; EAs must complete at least 24 hours of continuing education each year to maintain their licenses.

Enrolled agents' prices tend to fall between those of a preparer and a certified public accountant (CPAs are discussed in the next section). Tax returns with a few of the more common schedules (such as Schedule A for deductions and Schedule B for interest and dividends) shouldn't cost more than a couple hundred dollars to prepare. If you live in an area with a relatively high cost of living, expect to pay more.

The main difference between enrolled agents and CPAs and attorneys is that EAs work exclusively in the field of taxation, which makes them more likely to stay attuned to the latest tax developments. Not all CPAs and attorneys do. In addition to preparing your return (including simple to complex forms), good EAs can help with tax planning, represent you at audits, and keep the IRS off your back. You can find names and telephone numbers of EAs in your area by contacting the National Association of Enrolled Agents (800-424-4339; www.naea.org).

Certified public accountants (CPAs)

Certified public accountants (CPAs) go through significant training and examination to receive the CPA credential. Maintaining this designation, a CPA must complete at least 40 hours worth of continuing education classes every year.

CPA fees vary tremendously. Most charge around $100 per hour, but CPAs at large accounting firms and in high-cost-of-living areas tend to charge somewhat more. Some CPAs charge $300-plus per hour.

Competent CPAs are of greatest value to people completing some of the more unusual and less user-friendly schedules, such as K-1 for partnerships. CPAs also are helpful for people who had a major or first-time tax event during the year, such as the child-care tax-credit determination. (Good EAs and other preparers can handle these issues as well.)

Whenever your return is uncomplicated and your financial situation is stable, hiring a high-priced CPA year after year to fill in the blanks on your tax returns is a waste of money. A CPA once bragged to Eric (your humble coauthor of this book) that he was effectively making more than $500 per hour from some of his clients' returns that required only 20 minutes of an assistant's time to complete.

Who's best qualified — EA, CPA, or preparer?

Who is best qualified to prepare your return? That really depends on the individual you want to hire. The CPA credential is just that, a credential. Some people who have the credential will try to persuade you not to hire someone without it, but don't always believe this advice.

Some tax-preparation books perpetuate the myth that only a CPA can do your taxes. In one such book, in a chapter about choosing a tax preparer, entitled "How to Prepare for Your Accountant," the authors say, "Choosing an accountant isn't something that should be done casually. There are more than 300,000 certified public accountants." These authors then recommend that you ask a potential preparer, "Are you a certified public accountant?" (As you may have guessed, the firm behind the book is a large CPA company.)

What about all the non-CPAs, such as enrolled agents, who do a terrific job helping prepare their clients' returns and tax plans throughout the year?

If you can afford to and want to pay hundreds of dollars per hour, hiring a large CPA firm can make sense. But for the vast majority of taxpayers, spending that kind of money is unnecessary and wasteful. Many enrolled agents and other tax preparers are out there doing outstanding work for less.

Paying for the additional cost of a CPA on an ongoing basis makes sense if you can afford it and if your financial situation is reasonably complex or dynamic. If you're self-employed and/or file many other schedules, hiring a CPA may be worth it. But you needn't do so year after year. If your situation grows more complex one year and then stabilizes, consider getting help for the perplexing year and then using other preparation resources discussed in this chapter or a lower-cost preparer or enrolled agent in the future.

If you desire more information about CPAs in your area, we suggest that you contact the local organization of CPAs in your state. To locate your state's group, call toll-free directory assistance at 800-555-1212 and ask for the number for your state's "Society" or "Association" of CPAs. You can also visit the American Institute of Certified Public Accountants listing of state CPA associations at www.aicpa.org/states/info/index.htm. If you're considering hiring a CPA, be sure to ask how much of his or her time is spent preparing individual income tax returns and returns like yours.

Tax attorneys

Unless you're a super-high-income earner with a complex financial life, hiring a *tax attorney* to prepare your annual return is prohibitively expensive. In fact, many tax attorneys don't prepare returns as a normal practice. Because of their level of specialization and training, tax attorneys tend to have high hourly billing rates — $200 to $300-plus per hour isn't unusual.

Tax attorneys sometimes become involved in court cases dealing with tax problems, disagreements, or other complicated matters, such as the purchase or sale of a business. Other good tax advisors also can help with these issues.

The more training and specialization a tax practitioner has (and the more affluent the clients), the higher the hourly fee. Select the one that best meets your needs. Fees and competence at all levels of the profession vary significantly. If you aren't sure of the quality of work performed and the soundness of the advice, get a second opinion.

Finding Tax Preparers and Advisors

The best tax advisors don't usually cold-call you at home, trying to get your business. The challenge for you is to locate a tax advisor who does terrific work, charges reasonable fees, and thus is too busy to bother calling to solicit you! Here are some resources to find those publicity-shy, competent, and affordable tax advisors:

- ✔ **Friends:** Some of your friends probably use tax advisors and can steer you to a decent one or two for an interview.

- ✔ **Co-workers:** Ask people in your field which tax advisors they use. This strategy can be especially useful if you're self-employed.

- ✔ **Other advisors:** Financial and legal advisors also can be helpful referral sources, but don't assume that they know more about the competence of a tax person than you do. Beware of a common problem: Financial or legal advisors may simply refer you to tax preparers who send them clients.

- ✔ **Associations:** Enrolled agents (EAs) and certified public accountants (CPAs) maintain professional associations that can refer you to members in your local area. See the relevant sections earlier in this chapter.

Never decide to hire a tax preparer or advisor solely on the basis of someone else's recommendation. To ensure that you're hiring someone who is competent and with whom you will work well, please take the time to interview at least two or three prospective candidates. In Chapter 31, we list key questions that you need to ask prospective tax advisors before hiring them. Because you've gone to the trouble and expense of tracking down this book, please make use of it — you've got many more chapters to check out. The more you know before you seek a tax advisor's services, the better able you'll be to make an informed decision and reduce your expenditures on tax preparers.

Chapter 3

Getting and Staying Organized

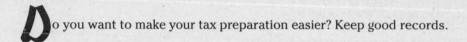

In This Chapter

▶ Understanding the benefits of keeping good records

▶ Organizing, organizing, and organizing some more

▶ Deciding how long to keep records

▶ Knowing what to do when records aren't available

▶ Using the Cohan Rule

o you want to make your tax preparation easier? Keep good records.

Do you want to make sure you claim every deduction you're entitled to? Keep good records.

Do you want to survive an IRS audit and not pay additional tax, interest, or penalties? Keep good records.

Do you want to save money by not paying tax preparers $50 to $200 an hour to organize your stuff? Keep good records.

 If you're like most people, you probably aren't a good bookkeeper. But without good records, you may be in trouble, especially if you're ever audited. Furthermore, some tax preparers and accountants love to see you walk into their offices with shoeboxes full of receipts. Knowing that they can charge you a hefty hourly fee and then turn around and pay someone else $20 an hour to organize your receipts brightens their day.

You may realize when you sit down to complete your tax return that you're going to have to rummage through a box of paper scraps containing not only your important tax records, but also cool things like your homework assignments from seventh grade and your 1996 holiday shopping list.

Or this may be the year that you know you can itemize deductions on Schedule A and save those big bucks — if only you could remember where you stashed your medical bills and the receipts from your favorite charity.

 A recent General Accounting Office report revealed that more than one million taxpayers overpaid the IRS a staggering half a billion dollars by using the standard deduction rather than itemizing their deductions on Schedule A. We tell you how to avoid this disaster in Chapter 9. What is disturbing about this report is that half of these taxpayers used tax preparers to do their returns.

Finally, perhaps you can easily imagine yourself the night before an IRS audit wondering how you're going to support your claim for all those business entertainment costs. Do you know what happens when you're audited and you can't document your claims? First, you get socked with additional tax and interest. Then come the penalties — and the IRS has a lengthy list of them.

But enough horror stories! You know that you must take some steps now to avoid the misery associated with not keeping good records. It may be too late for you this time around, but it's never too late to establish good habits for next time. In this chapter, you discover a few tried and proven ways of keeping track of everything you need to survive — not only this tax-preparation season, but also in future tax situations.

To deal effectively with the IRS, you need documentation, because the tax laws place the burden of proof primarily on the taxpayer. Do you think this policy means that you're guilty until proven innocent? Unfortunately, the answer is *yes*. But don't let that depress you. Remember that documentation is required only if you're audited. Even if you're not being audited, you still need to organize your records now. If you *are* audited and lack the tax records that you need to support your case, don't throw in the towel. This chapter shows you how to overcome such a problem — just in case you failed Recordkeeping 101.

As a result of the IRS horror stories broadcasted on TV, Congress shifted the burden of proof for when taxpayers and the IRS end up in court. But don't get too excited over this provision. The fine print is murder. You still have to present credible evidence and be cooperative (Boy Scouts to the head of the line), and the provision applies only to tax audits that began after July 22, 1998. Shifting the burden of proof doesn't mean that you can sit back and say, "Prove it." Remember, too, that few cases go to court. The Taxpayer Bill of Rights in Chapter 19 explains the fine print.

Keeping Good Records

Tax records pose a problem for many people because the IRS doesn't require any particular form of recordkeeping. In fact, the IRS recommends, in general terms, that you keep records only to file a "complete and accurate" return. Need a bit more detail? Read on.

Ensuring a complete and accurate tax return

"Hey, my return *is* complete and accurate," you say. "All the numbers are within the lines and neatly written without any math errors." In case you don't feel like flipping through countless pages of government instructions on what constitutes a "complete and accurate" return, we thought you'd like to check out several common problem areas at a glance and the types of records normally required.

- **Charitable contributions:** No longer is a canceled check alone sufficient to support this deduction. When you make a donation of $250 or more, you need a written receipt from the charity indicating the amount of money you gave or a description of the property you donated. Technically, you must have those receipts by the time you file your return. (See Chapter 9 for more information.)

- **Dependent care expenses:** If you plan to claim someone as a dependent, you need to be able to prove (if you're audited) that you provided more than 50 percent of that person's total support. This proof applies especially to college students and children of divorced parents. The length of time that you provide the support doesn't mean anything — it's the total cost that matters. So be ready to show how much you paid for your dependent's lodging, food, clothes, healthcare, transportation, and any other essential support stuff. (See Chapter 4 for the rules for claiming dependents.)

- **Car expenses:** If, for the business use of your car, you choose to deduct the actual expenses rather than the standard mileage rate (which is 36 cents per mile for tax year 2003), you need to be able to show the cost of the car and when you started using it for business. You also must record your business miles, your total miles, and your expenses, such as insurance, gas, and maintenance. You need a combination of a log and written receipts, of course!

✔ **Home expenses:** Besides the records of your purchase price and purchase expenses, save all the receipts and records of improvements and additions that affect the value of your residence. House sales are discussed in Chapter 12.

✔ **Business expenses:** The IRS is especially watchful in this area, so be sure to keep detailed proof of any expenses that you claim. This proof can consist of many items, such as receipts of income, expense account statements, and so on. Remember that the IRS doesn't always accept canceled checks as the only method of substantiation, so make sure that you hang on to the bill or receipt for every expense you incur (see Chapter 11 if you're self-employed, and "Lines 20–26: Job Expenses and Most Other Miscellaneous Deductions" in Chapter 9 if you're an employee).

Setting up a recordkeeping system

The tax year is a long time for keeping track of records that you'll need (and where you put them) when the filing season arrives. So here are some easy things you can do to make your tax-preparation burden a little lighter:

✔ **Invest in an accordion file.** You can buy one with slots already labeled by month, by category, or by letters of the alphabet, or you can make your own filing system with the extra labels — all this can be yours for less than $10.

✔ If $10 is too much, you can purchase a dozen or so of those manila file folders for about $5 (or less). Decide on the organizational method that best fits your needs, and get into the habit of saving all bills, receipts, and records that you think you can use someday for your tax purposes and for things that affect your overall financial planning. This basic advice is good for any taxpayer, whether you file a simple tax return on **Form 1040EZ** or a complicated **Form 1040** with several supplemental schedules. Remember that this plan is only minimal, but nevertheless is much better than the shoebox approach to recordkeeping.

✔ If your financial life is uncomplicated, then each new year you can set up one file folder that has the year on it (so in January 2004 you establish your 2004 file). During the year, as you receive documentation that you think you'll use in preparing your return, stash it in the folder. In January 2005, when you receive your dreaded Form 1040 booklet, toss it in the file, too. Come springtime 2005, when you finally force yourself to sit down and work on your return, you have everything you need in one bulging file.

✔ If you're a 1040 user and a real perfectionist, you can arrange your records in a file according to the schedules and forms on which you'll report them. For example, you can set up folders such as these:

- **Schedule A:** Deductible items (such as mortgage interest, property taxes, charitable contributions, and job-related expenses)

- **Schedule B:** Interest and dividend income stuff

- **Schedule D:** Documents related to buying, selling, and improving your home, and the sale and purchase of investments such as stocks and bonds

You 1040 filers have so many options that you truly need to take the time to learn about your return — we can help you there — so that you can anticipate your future tax needs.

Tracking tax information on your computer

A number of financial software packages enable you to keep track of your spending for tax purposes. Just don't expect to reap the benefits without a fair amount of upfront and continuing work. You need to learn how to use the software, and you need to enter a great deal of data for it to be useful to you come tax time.

Watch out for state differences

Although the IRS requires that you keep your records for only three years, your state may have a longer statute of limitations with regard to state income tax audits. Some of your tax-related records may also be important to keep for other reasons. For example, suppose that you throw out your receipts after three years. Then the fellow who built your garage four years ago sues you, asserting that you didn't fully pay the bill. You may be out of luck in court if you don't have the canceled check showing that you paid.

The moral is: Hang on to records that may be important (such as home improvement receipts) for longer than three years — especially if a dispute is possible. Check with a legal advisor whenever you have a concern, because statutes of limitations vary from state to state.

If you're interested in software, consider personal finance packages such as Quicken (from Intuit) or Microsoft Money. With these packages, you can keep track of your stock portfolio, pay your bills, and balance your checking account, and best of all, get help with tabulating your tax information. Just remember that the package tabulates only what you enter. So if you use the software to write your monthly checks but neglect to enter data for things you pay for with cash, for example, you won't have the whole picture.

Deciding when to stash and when to trash

One of the most frequently asked questions is how long a taxpayer needs to keep tax records. The answer is easy — a minimum of three years. That's because the statute of limitations for tax audits and assessments is three years. If the IRS doesn't adjust or audit your 2000 tax return by April 16, 2004 (the three years starts running on April 15, 2001), it missed its chance. Because April 15, 2001, fell on a Sunday, the due date for filing your 2000 return was extended to Monday, April 16, 2001. Therefore, on April 17, 2004, you can start disposing of your 2000 records, if you want, and then you can celebrate because you've gone another year without an audit! (If you filed after April 15 because you obtained an extension of time to file, you must wait until three years after the extension due date rather than the April 15 tax date. The same is true when you file late — the three-year period doesn't start until you actually file your return.)

However, we must add one point to the general three-year rule: Save all records for the assets that you continue to own. These records can include purchase slips for stocks and bonds, automobiles, the purchase of your home (along with its improvements), and expensive personal property, such as jewelry, video cameras, or computers. Keep these records in a safe-deposit box in case you suffer a (deductible casualty) loss, such as a fire. You don't want these records going up in smoke! Some taxpayers take the practical step of videotaping their home and its contents, but if you do, make sure that you keep that record outside your home. You can save money on safe-deposit box fees by leaving your video with relatives who may enjoy watching it because they don't see you often enough. (Of course, your relatives may also suffer a fire or an earthquake.)

In situations where the IRS suspects that income was not reported, IRS agents can go back as far as six years. And if possible tax fraud is involved, forget all time restraints!

Reconstructing Missing Tax Records

The inscription above the entrance to the national office of the Internal Revenue Service reads:

Taxes are what we pay for civilized society.

But any taxpayer who has ever had a tax return examined would probably enjoy a little less civilization.

Our experience shows that the number-one reason why taxpayers must cough up additional tax when they're audited is lousy recordkeeping. They don't get themselves into this situation by fabricating deductions, but rather because most taxpayers aren't very good bookkeepers and they fail to produce the records that properly substantiate the deductions they have a right to claim.

When taxpayers misplace tax records or simply don't save the ones that they need to be able to claim the deductions they're allowed under the law, all is not lost. Other ways exist for gathering the evidence that establishes what was actually spent — but obtaining the necessary evidence may prove time-consuming. And yet, when you consider the other option — paying additional tax, interest, and penalties on disallowed deductions from an audit where you couldn't prove what you spent — your time and energy will be amply rewarded. The following sections describe some ways to reconstruct lost or forgotten records. (You may also want to look at Chapters 16 and 17, which tell you how to fight back against an IRS audit when it comes to tax records.)

Property received by inheritance or gift

The starting point for determining whether you made or lost money on a sale of a property is the property's tax basis. (Remember, to the IRS, *property* can be more than just real estate; it also includes stocks, bonds, cars, boats, and computers.) *Tax basis* is an IRS term for cost. Your basis usually is what you paid for something.

However, the rule for determining the tax basis for property you inherited or received as a gift is different. Because you don't know the cost of the inheritance or gift, the tax basis for determining the taxable gain or loss of property you inherited is the *fair market value* of the property on the date of the titleholder's death. For property received as a gift, the tax basis is the donor's cost. But in some instances, the tax basis can also be the fair market value on the date you received the gift. For example, if your father left you 100 shares of General Motors that were worth $10,000 when he died, the $10,000 is your cost for tax purposes. If he gave you the shares before he died, and the shares cost him $5,000, then $5,000 is your tax basis. (See Chapter 12 for more about determining tax basis so you can figure out whether you have a taxable profit or deductible loss.)

A rather simple rule exists — at least in theory. IRS instructions state that a taxpayer who sells a property received as an inheritance must use the value stated in the decedent's **Form 706, Estate Tax Return** as the cost for determining a profit or loss. For a gift, the recipient usually has to use the value on the date the donor acquired the item. If you're required to use the gift's value on the date of the gift, use the value in the donor's **Form 709, Gift Tax Return.** The only problem is that these tax returns may no longer be available or may no longer exist when you need them, especially when someone sells an asset that he or she inherited many years earlier.

When you inherit something, don't automatically assume that its fair market value as reported on the estate tax return is correct, especially where real estate and art are concerned. The IRS constantly challenges the value placed on an item for estate tax purposes, and so can you. Now for something about date-of-death values that rightfully falls under the heading of, "The devil you know is better than devil you don't." The 2001 tax bill that drastically changed the estate tax modified the rule that enabled heirs to use the date-of-death value as their cost. Thankfully this change doesn't take place until 2010. When it does, some inherited assets will be valued for capital gain purposes at the date-of-death value and other assets at the decedent's original cost. So while the death tax will be a thing of the past when 2010 rolls around, some heirs will end up paying the capital gains tax that the dearly departed never did. Isn't this one problem you wish you had?

Establishing the value of real estate (farm or residence) received by inheritance, when original tax records aren't available, isn't as formidable a task as it may first appear. You can use one of four methods to compute your tax basis: newspaper ads, local real estate board and broker records, the assessed value of the property, and the *Consumer Price Index (CPI)*. (You know the CPI: It tells you that what cost $10 last month costs $50 this month. Seriously, it probably costs $10.02, and the CPI is an official government measure that tells how much prices increase over time.)

Researching newspaper ads

If the property value you're trying to determine is for property acquired by gift, the deed tells you when the donor acquired the property. If the property was inherited, the date-of-death value is what you must determine. With this plan in hand, you're ready to proceed.

Start at your local library or your local newspaper office to find a copy of the newspaper printed on the date for which you're trying to establish the value. The classified ads in the real estate section should reveal the price of similar property offered at the time. Back issues often are kept on microfilm, so you can look backward or forward for six or so months in case you can't find any values for a particular date.

If a piece of real estate exactly like yours wasn't offered for sale at that time, you may have to find an ad for one as close as possible in description to yours and simply estimate the price. For example, suppose that you're trying to figure out how much Uncle Jesse's farm was worth when he left it to you in 1980. You now want to sell the 100-acre farm and farmhouse and you're searching for its value in 1980. You check out some 1980 ads from *The Daily Bugle* and find

- ✔ An ad showing a house and 50 acres for $75,000
- ✔ An ad showing a house and 60 acres for $85,000

Because the farm with ten more acres was selling for $10,000 more, assume that an acre was worth around $1,000. The IRS will find your assumption reasonable. Therefore, Uncle Jesse's farm has 40 more acres than the one selling for $85,000, so you can figure that the value of the farm in 1980 was $125,000 ($85,000 + $40,000).

The IRS won't simply accept the statement that you looked up this information. Remember, all IRS agents act as if they come from Missouri (the "Show Me" state — in case you were absent from school the day your fifth grade teacher lectured on state mottoes). If you go to all the trouble to visit the library, make sure you come away with a photocopy of the paper's real estate section. The IRS requires documentation, especially when you use an alternative method to establish what something is worth.

Consulting local real estate board and broker records

If your trip to the library or local newspaper office comes up short, try the local real estate board or a real estate broker (one may owe you a favor or want to hustle for your business). Individual brokers or local real estate boards usually keep historical data on property sold in their respective areas. Again, you may have to estimate selling prices if you don't find a property exactly like yours.

Obtaining assessed values

The *assessed-value method* may uncover the most accurate estimate of a property's value. Because property taxes are collected on the basis of assessed values, try to obtain the assessed value of the property on the date you're interested in. With that information and the percentage of the fair market value that the tax assessor used in determining assessed values, divide the percentage into the assessed value to come up with the market value.

You can obtain assessed values for property (and the percentage of the fair market value of property assessed in its vicinity) from the government office that receives or collects property taxes, which usually is found in the courthouse of the county where the property is located. Don't forget to get a copy of this information. For example, if the assessed value was $2,700 and the percentage of the fair market value at which the property was assessed was 30 percent, the fair market value was $9,000 ($2,700 ÷ 30 percent).

Using the Consumer Price Index

Unlike baseball, when you're assessing the value of real estate, you're not out on three strikes. When all else fails, use the Consumer Price Index (CPI) method. Because you already know the amount for which you sold the property, another trip or call to the library enables you to determine the increase in the Consumer Price Index between the acquisition date and the sale date. For example, say you sold a tract of land for $300,000. If the CPI went up three times since you inherited it, your tax basis is $100,000.

Determining the property's acquisition date depends on how you acquired the property. If you inherited it, the acquisition date is the date of the previous owner's death. If the property was a gift, the acquisition date is the date the property originally was purchased by the person who gave you the gift.

If your local library doesn't have CPI data, you can obtain it by writing to the U.S. Department of Labor, 200 Constitution Avenue NW, Washington, DC 20210. This information also is available on the Internet at the Consumer Price Index home page (www.bls.gov/cpi/home.htm). Click on "Tables Created by BLS" *(Bureau of Labor Statistics)*.

Securities received by inheritance or gift

Establishing the price of a stock or a bond on a particular date is much easier than coming up with the value of other property, especially if the stock or bond is traded on a major securities exchange.

When you inherit a stock or bond, your tax basis usually is the value of the stock or bond on the deceased's date of death. Sometimes an estate — to save taxes — uses a valuation date that is six months after the date of death. If you receive the security as a gift, you often have the added task of establishing the date when the donor acquired the security, because you normally must use the value on that date (including any commission expense). Not to confuse you, but sometimes you must use the value on the date you received the gift. We explain all this in Chapter 12. You can write to the transfer agent to find out when the stock was acquired. The *transfer agent* is the company that keeps track of the shares of stock that a company issues. Your stockbroker can tell you how to locate the transfer agent, or you can consult the *Value Line Investment Survey* at your local library.

After you determine the acquisition date, either the back issue of a newspaper or a securities pricing service can provide the value of the security you're looking for on any particular day. A back issue of a newspaper won't reveal whether any stock dividends or splits (affecting the share price) occurred since the acquisition date. A good pricing service can provide that information.

One service that we recommend for determining the value of stocks and bonds (plus any stock splits or stock dividends) is Prudential-American Securities, Inc., 921 E. Green St., Pasadena, CA 91106; phone 626-795-5831; Web site www.securities-pricing.com. This company charges $3 to determine the value of a stock or bond on a given day, with a minimum fee of $10.

Also, consider checking with the investment firm where the securities were (or are still) held. The firm may be able to research this information — maybe even for free.

Improvements to a residence

How many homeowners save any of the records regarding improvements that they make, even when those expenditures are substantial? Not nearly enough. Why? Because improvements to a home quite often are made during a 30- to 40-year span, and saving records for that many years is a lot to ask of anyone. For example, landscaping expenditures — one tree or bush at a time — can really add up.

The point of counting every tree and bush and other improvement to home sweet home is to raise the *basis,* or total investment, that you have in your residence so that you can reduce your taxable profit when you sell. (See Chapter 12 for details.)

Although the 1997 law eliminated the fiendish recordkeeping requirements for sales of $500,000 or less for couples filing jointly and $250,000 for singles, for sales above these amounts you still need records to prove, for example, that you didn't make more than these threshold amounts ($500,000/$250,000). And if you buy a house today, say for $350,000, you don't know what the sales price will be in 10, 20, 30, or more years when you finally sell it. Here's hoping it's $1 million. So tax records are still important.

Before you estimate how much you spent on residential improvements, you first have to determine what improvements you spent the money on. This step is necessary because if you can't document the amount spent, you at least can establish that an improvement was made. Your family photo album (which may contain before and after pictures) is probably the best source for obtaining such information.

Obtaining a Certificate of Occupancy

If you can't get a receipt from the contractor who made improvements to your home, hike down to the county clerk's office to obtain a copy of the Certificate of Occupancy (the house's birth certificate, so to speak), which shows what your house consisted of when it was built. Records at the county clerk's office also reveal any changes in the house's assessed value as the result of improvements you made, along with any building permits issued. Any of these documents can clearly establish whether improvements were made (assuming, of course, that you *did* obtain the proper permits for these improvements).

Getting an estimate

When original invoices, duplicate invoices, or canceled checks aren't available, obtain an estimate of what the improvement would cost now, and then subtract the increase according to the Consumer Price Index (as explained in "Using the Consumer Price Index" earlier in this chapter). This procedure can help establish a reasonable estimate of what the improvement originally cost.

Casualty losses

A casualty loss is probably the most difficult deduction to establish. Few people consistently save receipts on the purchase of personal items, such as jewelry, clothing, furniture, and so on. If the casualty loss occurred because of a fire or hurricane, any receipts that you may have had were probably destroyed along with your property. Although a police, fire, or insurance company report establishes that a casualty loss was sustained, how do you establish the cost of what was stolen or destroyed? The answer: with a little bit of luck and hard work.

For example, the value of an expensive necklace that was stolen was once established by using a photograph that showed the taxpayer wearing the necklace. The taxpayer then obtained an appraisal from a jeweler of the cost of a similar necklace. Because jewelry is a popular gift, receipts sometimes don't exist.

Although you can prove to the IRS that you have enough money to afford the lost or stolen item, the IRS also needs proof that you had the item in your possession. For example, suppose that your $10,000 Rolex watch is stolen (we feel for you). To make the IRS folks happy, you must prove two things:

- That you can afford the Rolex, which your total income from your tax return can prove.

- That you had the Rolex, which can be established by a statement from a friend, a relative, or an acquaintance asserting that you actually owned the item. If the Rolex was a gift, a statement from the giver also helps.

Effective August 5, 1997, an appraisal used to obtain a disaster loan from the Federal Emergency Management Agency (FEMA) can be used as evidence for tax purposes to claim a casualty loss.

Business records

If business records have been lost or destroyed, you can often obtain duplicate bills from major vendors. You shouldn't have a great deal of trouble getting copies of the original telephone, utility, rent, credit card, oil company, and other bills. Reconstructing a typical month of automobile use can help you make a reasonable determination of the business use of your automobile. If that month's use approximates an average month's business use of an auto, the IRS usually accepts such reconstructed records as adequate substantiation.

Using duplicate bank statements

If all your business income was deposited in a checking or savings account, you can reconstruct that income from duplicate bank statements. Although banks usually don't charge for copies of bank statements, they do charge for copies of canceled checks. These charges can be quite expensive — about $4 to $5 per check — so do some legwork before ordering copies of all your checks. For example, obtain a copy of your lease and a statement from your landlord saying that all rent was paid on time before you request duplicate copies of rent checks.

Ordering copies of past returns

By ordering copies of past returns with **Form 4506, Request for Copy or Transcript of Tax Form,** you can have a point of reference for determining whether you have accounted for typical business expenses. Past returns reveal not only gross profit percentages or margins of profit, but also the amounts of recurring expenses.

Requesting Copies of Lost Tax Returns

Last year's tax return is the starting point for filling out this year's tax return. It serves as a guide to make sure you don't forget anything. But what if you can't locate your 2002 return? Or suppose you need a return from a previous year but can't find it?

You can request a copy of your previous returns and all attachments (including Form W-2) by using Form 4506. Send the completed Form 4506 to the Internal Revenue Service Center where you filed the return. You must pay a $39 charge when you file the form, but there is no charge for asking for a copy of Form W-2 or a Tax Return Transcript showing all the lines from your original return. Most banks accept this type of document in lieu of your tax return when you're applying for a loan. It can take up to 60 days to receive a copy of a tax return. Transcripts, however, don't take as long, even though you order them on Form 4506 as well. Transcripts are available for the current year and the three previous years.

Returns filed six or more years ago may or may not be available for making copies, but tax account information generally still is available for those years.

If you need a record of the changes the IRS made to your original return showing any penalties, interest, and payments made subsequent to filing your return or showing if an amended return was filed, you need a *Record of Tax Account Information.* This printout must be ordered by phone.

Ordering a Tax Return Transcript or a Record of Tax Account Information by phone is quick. Simply call 800-829-1040, and you will be prompted through a series of automated questions. When asked if you have a question about your personal tax records, press 2. There will be more automated questions, and you will likely be put on hold before you speak with a live person who will process your request. The Tax Return Transcript of Record of Tax Account Information should arrive by mail in about 7 to 10 days.

Understanding the Cohan Rule

Before we end this discussion about undocumented claims, we must tell you about the case of George M. Cohan and the resulting *Cohan Rule.* It's the story of one person's victory over the IRS, and it may inspire you to defend your own rights as a taxpayer. Even if some of the rights that taxpayers earned because of his victory have been eroded over the years, Cohan's battle for the right to estimate deductions still has repercussions today.

In 1921 and 1922, George M. Cohan deducted $55,000 in business-related travel and entertainment expenses. The IRS refused to allow him any part of these entertainment and travel deductions on the grounds that it was impossible to tell how much Mr. Cohan spent because he didn't have any receipts to support the deductions he claimed.

Mr. Cohan appealed to the Second Circuit Court of Appeals, and the court established the *rule of approximation.* The court instructed the IRS to "make as close an approximation as it can, bearing heavily, if it chooses, upon the taxpayer whose inexactitude is of his own making." (Isn't "inexactitude" a lovely way of saying "no records"?)

For more than 30 years, the *Cohan Rule* enabled taxpayers to deduct travel and entertainment expenses without having to substantiate what they spent. Taxpayers had only to establish that it was reasonable for them to have incurred travel and entertainment expenses in the amount they claimed they spent.

Congress changed the law regarding travel, use of a car, and entertainment expenses in the early 1960s. Since that change, taxpayers no longer can deduct travel or entertainment expenses without adequate substantiation.

The *Cohan Rule* still applies, however, to other expenses whose records are not available. Under the *Cohan Rule,* the Tax Court routinely allows deductions based on estimates for the following deductions:

- Petty cash and office expenses
- Delivery and freight charges
- Tips and business gifts
- Cleaning and maintenance expenses
- Small tools and supplies
- Taxi fares
- Casualty losses (fire, flood, and theft losses)

For some expenses, obtaining receipts for what you spend is impractical, if not downright impossible. Petty cash and tips are just two examples of such expenses.

The *Cohan Rule* doesn't mean that you can stop keeping receipts and simply use estimates. You must have a valid reason for relying on the *Cohan Rule,* such as impracticability or lost or destroyed records. In fact, taxpayers have had penalties assessed against them for not attempting to obtain duplicate records that were lost when they moved, and for periodically destroying all business records immediately upon the filing of their tax returns. One court held that the unexplained loss of corporate records carries a strong presumption that the records would have prejudiced the taxpayer's position.

In case you're scratching the back of your head and wondering if any of this will work, the question you have to ask yourself is, if you were sitting on a jury and saw this evidence, would you believe it? If the answer to this question is *yes,* guess what? You're going to prevail.

Chapter 4

No Form Fits All (Or, What Kind of Taxpayer Are You?)

● ●

In This Chapter

▶ Understanding the differences between the tax forms

▶ Deciding on a filing status

▶ Walking through joint return issues

▶ Understanding the Innocent Spouse Rule

▶ Calculating personal and dependent exemptions

▶ Getting Social Security numbers for dependents

▶ Filing returns for dependents

▶ Answering the where, when, why, and how filing questions

● ●

ou have to make some key decisions before grabbing those good ol' tax forms and marking them up. Even though you're anxious to begin, read the relevant portions of this chapter first. We explain some important issues you must resolve each tax year before you knuckle down to complete your return.

What Rendition of 1040 Shall We Play?

If you could get across town by taking one bus rather than having to transfer and take two, you'd do it, right? That is, unless you enjoy riding city buses, sightseeing, or wasting time and money by transferring.

Like your transportation options, you have a few choices of tax forms — three, to be exact. In order, from mind-challenging (read *simplest* in IRS jargon) to mind-numbing (read *complex*), they are **Form 1040EZ, Form 1040A,** and **Form 1040.**

The simpler forms are easier to finish because they have fewer lines to complete and far fewer instructions to read. Having to read additional IRS instructions is like having to diagram sentence structures from a Faulkner novel.

The simpler forms save you time and maybe a headache or two, but — and this is an important *but* — the simpler forms offer you far fewer opportunities and options to take deductions to which you may be entitled. Thus, in a rush to save yourself a little work and time, you can cost yourself hundreds, maybe thousands, in additional tax dollars.

Can I itemize? Should I itemize? And what the heck are itemized deductions?

Deductions are just that: You subtract them from your income before you calculate the tax you owe. (Deductions are good things!) To make things more complicated, the IRS gives you two methods for determining the total of your deductions: itemized and standardized deductions. The good news is that you get to pick the method that leads to the best solution for you — whichever way offers greater deductions. If you can itemize, you should, because it saves you tax dollars. The bad news is that if you choose to itemize your deductions, you must use **Form 1040.**

The first method — taking the standard deduction — requires no thinking or calculations. If you have a relatively uncomplicated financial life, taking the standard deduction is generally the better option. Symptoms of a simple tax life are: not earning a high income, renting your house or apartment, and lacking unusually large expenses, such as medical bills or losses from theft or catastrophe. Single folks qualify for a $4,750 standard

deduction, and married couples filing jointly get a $9,500 standard deduction in tax year 2003. If you're age 65 or older, or blind, your standard deduction is increased by $1,150 if single, and by $950 if married.

Some deductions — moving expenses, the penalty for early withdrawal from savings, and so on — are available even if you don't itemize your deductions. The bad news: You have to file Form 1040 to claim them. The good news: We tell you how to do this in Chapter 7.

The other method of determining the total of your allowable deductions is itemizing them on your tax return. This method is definitely more of a hassle, but if you can tally up more than the standard deduction amounts, itemizing saves you money. Use Schedule A of IRS Form 1040 to total your itemized deductions.

See Chapter 9 for more about using Schedule A to itemize deductions.

Form 1040EZ

Here's the lowdown on this *EZ-est* of tax forms. (They actually test-marketed this form before they started using it — very much like Procter & Gamble does before they try something new, like purple-colored Crest. Unfortunately, the IRS has a bit of an advantage over Procter & Gamble — if you don't like the forms, you can't switch to Brand X.)

The easiest form to fill out and file is the 1040EZ. All you need to do is insert your name, address, occupation, Social Security number, wages, unemployment compensation, and taxable interest. Your refund can be deposited directly into your bank account. To find out whether you should use this form, see "Who Can File a 1040EZ?" in Chapter 5. Form 1040EZ is a breeze. You don't have to make any computations if you don't want to. Just plug in the numbers and skip the math, if you'd like. If you owe, the IRS bills you. And if you're due a refund, the IRS sends you a check. How EZ! (Just don't forget to attach your W-2s.)

Form 1040A

For those of you who are several rungs up the economic ladder, congratulations! You have just graduated from Form 1040EZ. Your reward is Form 1040A. But there's something you need to know: The best way to be certain that you should use Form 1040A is to review Form 1040 before reaching for Form 1040A. Check to make sure there isn't any deduction or tax credit you can use on Form 1040. To find out whether you qualify for Form 1040A, see "Who Can File a 1040A?" in Chapter 5.

Form 1040 (the long form)

Because Forms 1040A and 1040EZ are easier to complete than Form 1040, you should use one of them unless Form 1040 allows you to pay less tax. But if you don't qualify for filing Form 1040A or 1040EZ, you must use Form 1040.

This is the form that everybody loves to hate. *The Wall Street Journal* believes that the form was invented by tax professionals — the newspaper's editors even refer to our tax laws as the "Accountants and Lawyers Full Employment Act." We think that complicated tax laws should be called the "IRS Guaranteed Lifetime Employment Act."

If you itemize your deductions, claim a host of tax credits, own rental property, are self-employed, or sell a stock or bond, you're stuck — welcome to the world of the 1040.

If you have the option of using or not using the 1040, a quick review of Schedule A (see Chapter 9) helps you find out whether it's worth your while to itemize.

If you're depressed because you have to use the simpler forms for your 2003 return and you want to be able to deduct more and have more favorable adjustments to your income in the future, all is not lost. At a minimum, you can make things better for 2004 by planning ahead. (Be sure to read Part V, "Year-Round Tax Planning.") You may be able to do some last-minute maneuvering before you file your 2003 return. We direct you to these maneuvers as we walk you through the line-by-line completion of your return.

Choosing a Filing Status

When filing your return, you must choose the appropriate filing status from the five filing statuses available for 1040A and 1040 users. (Users of Form 1040EZ must file as *single* or as *married filing jointly,* with no dependents.) You select a status by checking the appropriate box directly below your name on page 1 of Form 1040, where it says "Filing Status":

- ✔ Single
- ✔ Married filing jointly
- ✔ Married filing separately
- ✔ Head of household
- ✔ Qualifying widow(er) with dependent child

Each filing status has its own tax rates. As a general rule, you pay the lowest tax by filing jointly or as a qualifying widow(er), and then come head of household and single. Those who are married filing separately pay tax at the highest rate. However, like every rule, a few circumstances exist in which married filing separately saves couples money, as explained later in this section. In addition, you can select a different filing status every year. For example, because you filed jointly last tax year doesn't mean you automatically have to file that way for this tax year.

Single

Most people who aren't married file as *single.* The IRS doesn't recognize couples living together, regardless of sexual orientation, as being married for filing purposes.

However, if you were widowed, divorced, or legally separated by the end of the tax year (December 31, 2003) and provided support to dependents, such as children or an elderly parent, you may be able to save yourself some tax dollars by filing as *head of household* or as a *qualifying widow(er)*. You can find out more in the upcoming section, "Head of household."

Married filing jointly

If you're married, you probably share many things with your spouse. One of the more treasured tasks you get to share is the preparation of your annual tax return. In fact, this may be the one time during the year that you jointly examine and combine your financial information. Let the fireworks begin!

 Filing jointly usually offers the greatest tax savings when one spouse has no income or significantly less income than the other. The reason? Some of the income of the spouse with the larger income will be brought down to lower tax brackets by filing jointly. When both spouses have substantially the same amount of income, their total federal tax will be about the same whether they file jointly or separately. For more on this phenomenon, see the sidebar "The marriage penalty" later in this chapter.

For your 2003 return, you're considered married if you got married by or were still married as of the end of the tax year — December 31, 2003. In some rare instances, married folks can save money by filing their taxes as *married filing separately*. This somewhat oddball status can be useful for couples who have large differences between their two incomes and can claim more itemizable deductions by filing separately. See the section "Married filing separately," later in this chapter, to determine whether you can save money by filing separately.

 If you file a joint return for 2003, you may not, after the due date for filing, amend that return to change to a married filing separately filing status. You're "jointly" stuck!

You can file jointly if you meet any of the following criteria:

- ✔ You were married as of December 31, 2003, even if you didn't live with your spouse at the end of the year.
- ✔ Your spouse died in 2003, and you didn't remarry in 2003.
- ✔ If your spouse died during the year, you're considered married for the entire year, providing you didn't remarry. You report all your income for the year and your spouse's income up to the date of his or her death.
- ✔ Your spouse died in 2004 before you filed a 2003 return.

You and your spouse may file jointly even if only one of you had income or if you didn't live together all year. However, you both must sign the return, and you're both responsible for seeing that all taxes are paid. That means if your spouse doesn't pay the tax due, you may have to.

 The *Innocent Spouse Rule* (explained later in this chapter) can, in some instances, relieve a spouse who was unaware of his or her spouse's shenanigans from sharing joint responsibility for what is owed.

A couple legally separated under a divorce decree may not file jointly. On the other hand, if one spouse lived away from the home during the entire last six months of the tax year (July 1, 2003, through December 31, 2003), the remaining spouse, if taking care of dependents, may be able to file under the more favorable head of household status (see "Head of household," later in this chapter).

 Although this suggestion is decidedly unromantic, if you're considering a late-in-the-year wedding, especially in December, you may want to consider the tax impact of tying the knot so soon. A considerable number of couples pay higher total taxes when they're married versus when they were single.

Spouses who are nonresident aliens or dual-status aliens

If one spouse is a nonresident alien and does not pay U.S. income taxes on all his or her income, regardless of the country (or countries) in which it is earned, then the couple may not take the married filing jointly tax status.

The same is true when your spouse is a dual-status alien — that is, if during the year, your spouse is a nonresident as well as a resident. You may file jointly if:

✔ You were married as of December 31, 2003, even if you did not live with your spouse at the end of 2003.

✔ If your spouse is a nonresident alien, or if either of you are dual-status aliens, you can make a special election to file jointly. IRS Publication 519 *(U.S. Tax Guide For Aliens)* explains how to make this election.

Some couples have been known to postpone their weddings until January and use the tax savings to pay for the cost of their honeymoons! Others choose not to marry, and they cohabitate instead. Although we don't want to criticize or condone such decisions, it is unfortunate that such a high tax cost of getting married exists for a sizable minority of couples (see "The marriage penalty" sidebar, later in this chapter).

Married filing separately

The vast majority of married couples would pay more taxes if they chose to file separate returns. The IRS won't stand in the way of your doing this. However, by filing separately, you may be able to avoid the marriage penalty and save on your combined tax bill. To determine whether filing separately is to your benefit, you should figure your tax both ways (married filing jointly and married filing separately).

Besides saving money, another reason you may choose to file separately is to avoid being responsible for your spouse's share of the joint tax bill whenever you suspect some kind of monkey business (for example, your spouse is underreporting taxable income or inflating deductions).

Even though married filing separately on your federal return might work out to be the same as filing jointly, don't overlook the possibility that by filing that way you might save state taxes.

If you file separately, be aware that the following restrictions may apply:

✔ You can't take the standard deduction if your spouse itemizes deductions. Both spouses must itemize their deductions, or both must claim the standard deduction.

✔ You can't claim the credit for child and dependent care expenses in most cases. The amount of income you can exclude under an employer dependent care assistance program is limited to $2,500 instead of the $5,000 by filing jointly.

✔ You can't claim a credit for qualified adoption expenses.

✔ You can't take the earned income credit.

✔ You can't exclude from your taxable income the interest you earned from series EE U.S. Savings Bonds issued after 1989, even if you paid higher education expenses in 2003.

✔ You can't take the credit for being elderly or disabled unless you lived apart from your spouse for all of 2003.

✔ You may have to pay more tax on the Social Security benefits you received in 2003.

✔ You usually report only your own income, exemptions, deductions, and credits. Different rules apply to people who live in community property states (see the sidebar "Filing separately in community property states," later in this chapter).

- You can't deduct interest paid on your student loan.

- You may have a lower Child Tax Credit than you would have if you filed jointly. The Child Tax Credit is a $1,000 tax credit for every child under the age of 17 (see Chapter 5).

- If you own and actively manage real estate, you can't claim the passive loss exception (see the particulars in "The $25,000 special allowance" section in Chapter 13).

- You can't claim the Hope Scholarship and Lifetime Learning credits.

- You can't claim the $3,000 IRA deduction for a nonworking spouse. And you may not be able to deduct all or part of your $3,000 IRA contribution if your spouse is covered by a retirement plan.

- You can't transfer funds from a traditional IRA to a Roth IRA.

- Your capital loss limit is $1,500 instead of $3,000.

- You can't claim the new $3,000 tuition and fees deduction for higher education expenses.

- Income levels at which personal exemptions and itemized deductions start being reduced are half the amount for joint filers.

Instead of filing separately, you may be able to file as a head of household if you had a child living with you and you lived apart from your spouse during the last six months of 2003. See the "Head of household" section later in this chapter for more information.

Emotional estrangement doesn't qualify as living apart for head of household status. In a recent Tax Court case, a couple became estranged but continued to reside in the same dwelling. The court rejected the idea that *emotional estrangement* equated to actual separation. *Living apart* requires geographical separation and living in separate residences.

Marriage is a tax issue that can be confounding. Most of the time, you pay lower taxes if you're married, but because of certain vagaries of the tax law and the way our society is shifting toward more two-income families, you can end up paying more tax than two unmarried persons with the same income would. The new 2003 law brought partial relief from the marriage penalty by increasing the standard deduction to $9,500 from $7,950, increasing the amount of income taxed at 10 percent to $14,000 from $12,000 and increasing the amount of income taxed at 15 percent to $42,800 from $35,450. According to the IRS, these changes will bring marriage penalty relief to 34 million couples by an average of $589. Complete elimination of the marriage penalty is dependent upon which political party controls the White House and the two chambers of Congress. To see whether you need to escape the marriage penalty, you have to prepare three returns — two separate and one joint. We know it's a time sink, so you may want to spend $50 and spring for a computerized tax program that does the number crunching for you. (See Chapter 2 for our software recommendations.)

Married couples most likely to save tax dollars filing separately are those who meet both of the following criteria:

- Couples who have two incomes
- Couples who have hefty deductions for medical expenses, miscellaneous itemized deductions, or casualty losses

If you fall under this umbrella, by all means complete the three tax returns to determine which filing status works best for you.

Here's an example to show how those deductions come into play. To figure out your medical deduction, take your medical expenses and subtract 7.5 percent of your adjusted gross income (AGI). For example, if your AGI is $100,000 and you have medical expenses of $10,000, you perform the following calculation: Multiply $100,000 by 7.5 percent ($7,500); then subtract this amount from your $10,000 of medical bills. This leaves you with a $2,500 medical deduction. For miscellaneous deductions, you subtract 2 percent of your income instead of 7.5 percent. And for personal casualty losses, subtract 10 percent of your income.

As Table 4-1 shows, these deductions may be a lot more valuable if you file separately. Say your spouse had an $11,000 casualty loss. If your income is $80,000 and your spouse's is $70,000, none of that $11,000 casualty loss is deductible. The math: $11,000 minus $15,000 ($150,000 × 0.10) equals -0-, which means that you're not entitled to a casualty deduction. But by filing separately, your spouse gets to deduct $4,000, because 10 percent of your spouse's income amounts to only $7,000. For the purpose of this illustration, the $100 non-deductible portion of casualty loss and the rate reduction credit isn't being considered.

Table 4-1	Filing Jointly versus Separately: A Sample Couple		
	Jointly	*Husband*	*Wife*
Gross income	$150,000	$80,000	$70,000
Casualty loss	$11,000	$0	$11,000
Less 10% of income	($15,000)	($0)	($7,000)
Deductible casualty loss	$0	$0	$4,000
Medical expenses	$7,250	$500	$6,750
Less 7.5% of income	($11,250)	($6,000)	($5,250)
Deductible medical	$0	$0	$1,500
Miscellaneous deductions	$3,200	$1,500	$1,700
Less 2% of income	($3,000)	($1,600)	($1,400)
Deductible miscellaneous	$200	$0	$300
Taxes	$5,000	$3,000	$2,000
Mortgage interest	$9,500	$9,500	$0
*3% itemized deduction phase out	($315)	($308)	($7)
Total itemized deductions	$14,385	$12,192	$7,793
Personal exemptions	$6,100	$3,050	$3,050
Taxable income	$129,515	$64,758	$59,157
Tax	$26,445	$13,222	$11,654

When your income exceeds $139,500 filing jointly, or $69,750 filing separately, your total itemized deductions (not including medical and casualty deductions) gets reduced by 3 percent of the difference between your income and the $139,500 threshold ($150,000 – $139,500 = $10,500 × .03 = $315).

Amounts may vary slightly depending on whether you use the tax tables or the rate schedules.

The potential for savings doesn't stop there. Say your combined income is $209,250 or more, congratulations! But as a reward for your financial success, a portion of your personal exemptions starts getting whittled away. (Personal exemptions are those $3,050 deductions you get for yourself and each of your dependents.) When one spouse's income is less than half that amount, you may be better off filing separately and piling the personal exemptions onto that person's return, if that spouse is otherwise entitled to the dependency exemption.

It's worth doing the numbers. For example, in Table 4-1, the sample couple saves a total of $1,569 by filing separately. Their combined separate tax bill comes to only $24,876 instead of $26,445.

Filing separately in community property states

Community property states are Arizona, California, Idaho, Louisiana, Nevada, New Mexico, Texas, Washington, and Wisconsin. If you and your spouse live in one of these states, you have to follow your state's law in determining what is community income and what is separate income, if you want to file separately.

In a community property state, each spouse, as a general rule, must report one-half of the joint income. However, this step isn't necessary if:

✔ You and your spouse lived apart for the entire year

✔ You and your spouse filed separately

To qualify, at least one of you must have salary, wages, or business income — none of which was transferred between you and your spouse. Child support is not considered a transfer. You can also disregard the community property rules and file a separate return without having to report any portion of the community property income where your spouse fails to inform you of the income and acted as if the income was exclusively his or hers. Nor does the IRS require you to include an item of community property income on your separate return where you didn't know of the income, had no reason to know of it, or where it would be unfair to make you pay tax on income. This is an area where you should either read IRS Publication 555 *(Federal Tax Information on Community Property)* or consult a tax advisor.

If you think you could have saved money in a previous year by filing separately, sorry. There's nothing you can do about it now. After you file a joint return, you can't turn back the clock and change it to separate returns. On the other hand, if you and your spouse filed separately, you can (within three years from the due date of your return or two years from the date the tax was paid) file an amended return and switch to filing jointly. You may want to do this if, when audited, some of the deductions you and your spouse claimed were disallowed, or if you get an insurance recovery greater than you expected, reducing the amount of the casualty loss. If you're making estimated tax payments during the year, it doesn't matter whether you make joint or separate payments. You can still file your actual return however you wish and divide the estimated tax payments in accordance with the rule for joint refunds in Chapter 19.

Head of household

You may file as head of household if you maintain a home under one of the following conditions:

✔ You paid more than half the cost of keeping up a home (see Table 4-2 to compute that figure) that was the main home during 2003 for a parent whom you can claim as a dependent. Your parent did not have to live with you in your home.

✔ You paid more than half the cost of keeping up a home in which you lived and in which one of the following also lived for more than half of the year (temporary absences, such as for school, vacation, or medical care, count as time lived in your home):

- Your *unmarried* child, adopted child, grandchild, or stepchild. This child does not have to be your dependent. But you still enter the child's name in the space provided on line 4 of Form 1040A or Form 1040.

- Your *married* child, adopted child, grandchild, or stepchild. This child must be your dependent. But if the married child's other parent claims him or her as a dependent under the IRS rules for children of divorced or separated parents, this child doesn't have to be your dependent. Enter this child's name on line 4 of Form 1040A or Form 1040.

- Your *foster* child, who must be your dependent and must have lived with you the entire year.

- Any of the following relatives that you can claim as a dependent: parents, grandparents, siblings, step relatives, in-laws, and, if related by blood, your uncle, aunt, nephew, or niece.

- You're related by blood to an uncle or aunt if he or she is the brother or sister of your father or mother. You're related by blood to a nephew or niece if he or she is the child of your brother or sister. If you are just living with someone, that won't cut it.

- A child kidnapped by someone other than a relative (see IRS Publication 501, *Exemptions, Standard Deduction and Filing Information*). Bizarre but true: Such a child is considered to still be a member of a household for the head of household status even though he or she is missing.

✔ You *cannot* file as head of household if your child, parent, or relative described in the preceding list is your dependent under a multiple support agreement. We get into this distinction later when we discuss personal exemptions.

✔ You are married but you did not live with your spouse. Even if you were not divorced or legally separated in 2003, you may be able to file as head of household if you fulfill all these requirements:

- You've lived apart from your spouse for the last six months of 2003, and you're filing a separate return.

- You paid more than half the cost of keeping up your home in 2003, and your home was the main residence of your child, adopted child, stepchild, or foster child for more than half of the year. Temporary absences, such as for school, vacation, or medical care, are counted as time lived in your home.

- You must claim this child as your dependent (or the other parent claims the child under the rules of children of divorced or separated parents). If this child is not your dependent, be sure to enter the child's name on line 4 of Form 1040A or Form 1040.

✔ If all the preceding factors apply, you may also be able to take the credit for child and dependent care expenses, the earned income credit, and the $1,000-per-child tax credit (for child tax credit purposes, the child has to be your dependent). You can take the standard deduction even if your spouse itemizes deductions. More details are in Chapters 5 and 6.

In the case of a birth or death of a dependent, you must have provided more than half the cost of keeping up a home that was that person's home for more than half the year, or if he or she wasn't alive that long, then they must have been a member of your household during the period of the tax year that he or she *was* alive.

Table 4-2	How to Compute the Cost of Maintaining a Home	
	Amount You Paid	*Total Cost*
Property taxes	$	$
Mortgage interest expense	$	$
Rent	$	$
Utility charges	$	$
Upkeep and repairs	$	$
Property insurance	$	$
Food consumed on the premises	$	$
Other household expenses	$	$
Totals	$(a)	$(b)
Subtract Total (a) from Total (b) and enter here		($)

Note: If you paid more than half of the total cost you qualify for head of household status.

The marriage penalty

Some couples' first year of marriage brings surprises. Others find that the song remains the same. But of all the many things that newlyweds discover about being married, one of the most annoying is the *marriage penalty,* a tax-law inequity that forces millions of married couples to pay more tax than they would if they were single and living together.

Briefly, the penalty occurs for this reason: When two people get married, the second person's income is effectively added on top of the first person's income, which can push the couple into higher tax brackets. Not only that, but the couple may also lose some itemized deductions and personal exemptions with a higher combined income.

You should know, however, that not all couples pay higher taxes. In fact, in most cases couples find that their joint tax bill is less. Another situation occurs with couples in which one spouse doesn't earn any income or has a low income. Those couples sometimes receive a marriage bonus.

Yet, according to *The Wall Street Journal,* a study by the Congressional Budget Office determined that 21 million couples paid an average of $1,400 more in taxes per couple than they would've paid on the same income had they remained single.

The tax law changes enacted in 1993 made the marriage penalty even worse because the tax rates were raised for higher-income earners. And many of the tax benefits enacted in 1997 are phased out for higher-income couples.

Couples more likely to be hit with the marriage penalty are two-income-earning households, especially spouses who have similar individual incomes and/or are higher-income earners. Why? Because U.S. tax brackets are graduated, which simply means that you pay a higher tax rate at higher-income levels (see the discussion in Chapter 1).

Can you do anything about it? In a small number of cases, married couples can cut their tax bills simply by filing separately.

Some people opt for another approach — not marrying, or getting a divorce. By living together as unmarrieds, you and your significant other each pay taxes at the individual rate. We're not advising this course, but it's simply what we hear and see. You also need to know that you can't divorce in December just to save on your taxes and then remarry the next year. Taxpayers who've tried this scam in the past have been slapped with penalties in addition to the extra taxes they would've owed if they'd stayed away from divorce court.

If you decide not to stay married for the long haul just to save on income taxes, be warned that unmarried couples aren't eligible for any of the significant survivor's Social Security benefits if one partner passes away or splits. A person who doesn't work is particularly vulnerable; if he's married and his spouse passes away or divorces him, the nonworking spouse qualifies for Social Security benefits based on the working partner's income history and Social Security taxes paid. If you aren't married and you don't work, you aren't entitled to Social Security benefits if your partner leaves you.

The cost of keeping up a home doesn't include clothing, education, medical expenses, vacations, life insurance, or transportation. These are personal support items that are taken into account to determine if you are entitled to claim a $3,050 personal exemption deduction for the support of a dependent. See the section "Figuring Personal and Dependent Exemptions," later in this chapter, for more on when and how to claim these deductions.

Qualifying widow(er) with dependent child

If you meet all five of the following tests, you can use the tax table for married filing jointly.

- ✔ Your spouse died in 2001 or 2002, and you did not remarry in 2003.
- ✔ You have a child, stepchild, adopted child, or foster child whom you can claim as a dependent.
- ✔ This child lived in your home for all of 2003. Temporary absences, such as for vacation or school, count as time lived in your home.

> ✔ You paid more than half the cost of keeping up your home for this child.
>
> ✔ You could have filed a joint return with your spouse the year he or she died, even if you didn't actually do so. (But you can't claim an exemption for your deceased spouse.)

If your spouse died in 2003, you may not file as a qualifying widow(er) with a dependent child. But see whether you qualify for filing jointly and refer to the "Filing a Return for a Deceased Taxpayer" section near the end of this chapter.

And if you can't file as a qualifying widow(er) with a dependent child, see whether you can qualify as a head of household. If you don't meet the rules for a qualifying widow(er) with a dependent child, married filing a joint return, or head of household, you must file as a single.

For example, suppose that a mother with children died in 2001, and the husband has not remarried. In 2002 and 2003, he kept up a home for himself and his dependent children. For 2001, he was entitled to file a joint return for himself and his deceased wife. For 2002 and 2003, he may file as a qualifying widow(er) with dependent children. After 2003, he may file as head of household, if he qualifies. If he doesn't qualify, he files as single.

Protecting Yourself with the Innocent Spouse Rule

Many taxpayers not experiencing marital bliss, or those in the throes of divorce proceedings, continue to file jointly if doing so cuts their current tax bill. This decision may be shortsighted because of the ramifications of one spouse not paying his or her share of the tax bill. Here's why.

When you file jointly, you're separately and jointly liable for any unpaid tax. Forget the legalese for a second. What it means is that if your spouse is a deadbeat and doesn't pay any tax owed, you may end up paying more than your fair share of the tax, or maybe all of it.

Under certain circumstances — if you didn't know about any omission of income or inflated deductions, for example — the *innocent spouse rule* may protect you, as we discuss later in this section. Don't look for speedy action on a request for innocent spouse relief. It takes the IRS about a year to process a request. Of the cases that meet one of the three criteria for relief, the IRS has been approving or partially approving about 45 percent of them.

Consider the real-life example of a couple who filed a joint tax return. The following year, they divorced. A year later, the IRS sent a notice stating that the husband failed to report $45,000 of income on the couple's joint return. A bundle of tax was now owed. Guess who got stuck for it? Need a hint? Let's just say she didn't need the extra expense. Under the new rules, this innocent spouse can get off the hook for the tax on the $45,000.

Filing separately, however, isn't entirely a one-way street. Certain tax breaks, such as deductions for losses on real estate that you actively manage, can't be claimed on a separate return if you and your spouse live together. Nor can you take an IRA deduction for a non-working spouse if you file separately. When filing separately, you can't take the earned income credit or claim a deduction for dependent care unless you and your spouse lived apart for the last six months of the tax year. In addition, you can't claim the Hope Scholarship or Lifetime Learning credits if you file separately.

Another drawback to filing separately is that you can't use one spouse's losses to offset the other's capital gains. For example, if you have a $6,000 capital gain and your spouse has a $9,000 capital loss, on a joint return you can net the two and claim a $3,000 loss. On separate returns, you're required to report your $6,000 gain, while your spouse can deduct only $1,500 of his or her $9,000 loss. Also keep in mind that by filing separately, half or maybe more of any Social Security payments automatically becomes taxable. When you file jointly or as a single person, the tax bill on your Social Security is almost always smaller.

To determine each spouse's share of a joint refund, see "You Haven't Received Your Refund" in Chapter 18. This knowledge can really help if things get sticky (maybe even nasty) in a divorce.

Getting innocent spouse relief: Determining if you are eligible under the new rules

If you filed a joint return and didn't know — and had no reason to know — that your spouse was playing fast and loose with the deductions on your return or wasn't reporting all his or her income, you aren't responsible for any additional interest or penalties when the IRS discovers these discrepancies. This rule is known as *traditional relief.* A second type of innocent spouse relief is called *separate liability,* and a third is called *equitable relief.* We explain all three in this section.

Although you're responsible for any unpaid tax on the original return, the "didn't know or had no reason to know" rule can get you off the hook for the unpaid tax if you didn't know that the money intended to pay the tax was used for other purposes. The law also allows the IRS to grant innocent spouse relief if it would be inequitable to hold a taxpayer liable for part or all of the correct but unpaid tax. Don't count on the IRS's benevolence in cases like these, however. Here's how *traditional relief* works:

- At the time the return was filed, you didn't know and had no reason to know that the tax wouldn't be paid.
- The unpaid tax is attributable to your spouse.
- It would be unfair after considering all the facts and circumstances to hold you liable for the tax.

Even if you don't meet all the criteria in the preceding list for getting off the hook for the unpaid tax, you may still qualify for relief if, "after taking into account all the facts and circumstances," holding you liable for what the IRS is demanding would be inequitable. This is known as *equitable relief.*

Here is what the IRS looks at when reviewing this type of request:

- Your marital status — separated or divorced helps.
- If you would suffer an undue economic hardship. *Undue hardship* means a significant hardship. It has to be more than an inconvenience. It means you would incur a substantial personal or financial loss. Need an example? You wouldn't be able to pay your rent or medical bills if you got stuck for the tax.
- If you were abused by your spouse.
- If an agreement obligates your spouse to pay the tax.

The following will weigh against you:

- Marital status — you're not divorced or separated.
- You had some knowledge that the tax wasn't going to be paid.
- You benefited (beyond normal support) by not paying the tax.
- You agreed that you'd pay all or part of the tax.
- Determining whether a reasonable person in similar circumstances would have known of the understatement of tax. This test gives people the most grief.

Under what circumstances can the IRS say you aren't responsible for all or part of any unpaid tax? Your spouse runs off in the middle of the night with all your dough and jewelry. While this is extreme behavior, here is what the new law is intended to address. Suppose that the IRS discovers an additional $20,000 of income, $5,000 of which the IRS proves you had knowledge of. You and your spouse are responsible for the tax on the $5,000 that you knew about. Your spouse is solely responsible for the tax on the remaining $15,000.

Here is a real-life Tax Court case: A husband withdrew part of his retirement account and put it into the couple's joint checking account. He used $100,000 of it to pay off the mortgage on their home. He assured his wife that their accountant said that the money could be withdrawn tax-free from his retirement account to pay off their mortgage. The couple later divorced, and the IRS went after the wife for the unpaid taxes on the money that was withdrawn from the retirement account. The Tax Court denied the wife's request for innocent spouse relief because she had knowledge of the withdrawal being deposited into their joint checking account. That she didn't have knowledge of the correct treatment of it on her joint tax return didn't matter, so she ended up being deceived twice. Once by her former husband and once by believing that the innocent spouse rule would protect her.

If the IRS is hounding you for back taxes and you think the innocent spouse rule might apply, give it a whirl. You have nothing to lose; no downside exists. Applying for innocent spouse relief can only improve your chances of getting off the hook.

Electing separate tax liability

Innocent spouse relief is available even if the IRS claims you "should have known" that your spouse was using creative accounting in filing your joint return. You can elect to limit your liability for any additional tax owed to what you would owe if you filed a separate return.

Here's how the separate tax liability election works: Jack and Jill, who are now separated, filed jointly. They reported $150,000 of salary income. Jack earned $60,000, and Jill earned $90,000. The IRS audited their return and discovered that Jack failed to report $15,000 of interest he earned on assets held in his name only. The IRS assesses a $4,500 tax deficiency. Jill knew about a bank account in Jack's name that generated $5,000 of interest. Jill can only be held liable for one-third of the deficiency, or $1,500 ($4,500 × ⅓ [$5,000 ÷ $15,000]), if Jack doesn't pay the entire tax assessment. That's because Jill knew about one-third of the unreported interest income. Had she not known about the bank account, Jill wouldn't be liable for any portion of the $4,500 in extra tax.

To elect separate liability, you have to be divorced, legally separated, or not living with your ex for 12 months prior to making the election. In addition, you must have had no knowledge about the concealed income or phony deductions. This "actual knowledge" is a lower standard than the "knew or should have known" standard required for regular innocent spouse relief. "Knew or should have known" can be inferred; "actual knowledge" can't be inferred based on indications that the electing spouse had reason to know. Sounds like a distinction without a difference, doesn't it? The IRS can claim you should have known. The IRS can't claim that you had knowledge if you didn't. Even if you can't meet the rules for separate liability (for example, if you aren't divorced, separated, or living apart), the IRS has the authority to grant separate liability relief if it feels not doing so would be inequitable. This authority also extends to situations where the tax shown on the return is correct, but you can't pay because of your ex-spouse's shenanigans. It's worth remembering, however, that the folks at the IRS aren't overly charitable.

Additional innocent spouse rules

Transferring assets between spouses so that one spouse ends up owing all the tax but has no assets that the IRS can seize won't work.

Whether you elect innocent spouse relief under the traditional or the separate liability method, the election must be made on IRS **Form 8857, Request for Innocent Spouse Relief (And Separation of Liability and Equitable Relief).**

You must elect innocent spouse relief within two years from the day the IRS begins to enforce collection. A demand or notice addressed to either or both spouses isn't considered "collection activities." Neither is a notice that offsets a refund in a different year to pay what is owed or is a notice of lien. A garnishment or notice of intent to levy is and so is a lawsuit by the IRS against you. For example, if the IRS sends you a notice of intent to levy, you have two years from that date to file Form 8857. If all you receive is a notice demanding payment, no time limits are placed on when you can no longer request innocent spouse relief.

Relief is available under this provision for all taxes, no matter how old. You can apply for relief even if you were denied innocent spouse relief under the old law.

No collection activity may be undertaken while your application for relief is pending. And if relief is denied, you can appeal to the U.S. Tax Court. You have 90 days after the notice of denial to make your appeal.

Now for the bad news: The IRS must notify your ex and give him or her the opportunity to object to what you're doing.

When a married couple separates, the IRS should be informed of each spouse's new address so that all notices received by one spouse are received by the other. You can take care of this by filing **Form 8822, Change of Address.**

The Taxpayer Bill of Rights enacted in 1996 enables you to ask what the IRS is doing to get your ex-spouse to pay and how much he or she has paid. Because of possible hostility toward an ex-spouse, the IRS won't reveal the spouse's home or business address.

For more on this subject, take a peek at IRS Publication 971 *(Innocent Spouse Relief)*.

Figuring Personal and Dependent Exemptions

You 1040A and 1040 filers have another hurdle to jump: Lines 6a–6d of these forms ask you to figure your total number of exemptions. (You 1040EZ filers have line 5 to contend with, but it's a breeze. We explain it in Chapter 5, in the section "How to Fill Out a 1040EZ.")

Each exemption that you're entitled to claim reduces your taxable income by $3,050, so exemptions are a *good* thing, right? There are two kinds of exemptions: personal exemptions and dependent exemptions. They're discussed in the following two sections.

Personal exemptions

You can take one personal exemption for yourself and one for your spouse. Here are the details.

- ✔ **Your own:** You may take one exemption for yourself unless someone else can claim you as a dependent. For example, if your parents can claim you as a dependent but they choose not to, you still can't claim an exemption for yourself. This situation usually applies to teenagers with part-time jobs. If that is the case, check the Yes box on line 5 of Form 1040EZ; don't check box 6a on Form 1040 or 1040A.

- ✔ **Your spouse:** If filing jointly, you can take one exemption for your spouse, provided that your spouse can't be claimed on someone else's return.

If you file a separate return, you can claim your spouse as a dependent only if your spouse is not filing a return, had no income, and can't be claimed as a dependent on another person's return.

If, by the end of the year, you obtain a final decree of divorce or separate maintenance, you can't take an exemption for your former spouse even if you provided all of his or her support.

If your spouse died and you didn't remarry, you can claim an exemption for your spouse only if you file jointly. For example, Mr. Jones died on August 1. Because the Joneses were married as of the date of Mr. Jones's death, Mrs. Jones can file a joint return and claim an exemption for her husband. Mrs. Jones reports all of her income for 2003 and all of Mr. Jones's income up to August 1.

On a separate return, you can take an exemption for your deceased spouse only if this person had no income and couldn't be claimed as someone else's dependent.

Dependent exemptions

You can claim an exemption for a dependent if you provide more than half of his or her support and this person passes the five dependency tests. (Don't forget that if you claim someone, that person can't claim a personal exemption on his or her own tax return.)

Personal and dependency exemption phaseout

Depending on your filing status, each $3,050 exemption to which you are entitled is whittled away in $61 increments ($122 for married filing separately) as your income rises above these limits:

Married filing separately	$104,625
Single	$139,500
Head of household	$174,400
Married filing jointly or qualifying widow(er)	$209,250

Here's how it works: For every $2,500 or part of $2,500 of income above these amounts, you have to reduce every $3,050 exemption by 2 percent. For example, if your income is $148,500 and you're single, your personal exemption is reduced to $2,806.

Here's the math:

Your exemption		$3,050
Your income		$148,500
Phaseout amount		$139,500
Difference		$9,000
$9,000 ÷ $2,500	(3.6 rounded up to 4)	4
4 × 0.02		8%
$3,050 × 0.08		$244
Exemption allowed ($3,050 − $244)		$2,806

We suggest that you pick up the wonderful (and free) IRS Publication 17 *(Your Federal Income Tax)* and use the official worksheet. Call 800-TAX-FORM (800-829-3676) to order the publication. (You can also find the worksheet in the 1040 instruction booklet.)

Okay, you may open your booklets and begin the tests now. Any person who meets all five of the following tests qualifies as your dependent:

Test 1: Member of your household or relative

Your dependent must live with you the entire year as a member of your household. But a person related to you by blood or marriage does not have to live with you for the entire year as a member of your household to meet this test. (A cousin meets this test only if he or she lived with you as a member of your household for the entire year.)

If you file a joint return, you don't need to show that a dependent is related to both you and your spouse. The dependent only needs to be related to one of you.

Temporary absences are ignored. If a person is placed in a nursing home for constant medical care, the absence is also considered temporary.

Here are some more details you may need to consider:

- ✔ **Death or birth:** A person who died during the year but was a member of your household until death meets the *member of your household test.* The same is true for a child who was born during the year and was a member of your household for the rest of the year. A child who was born and died in the same year qualifies, but a stillborn child doesn't. The child must have been born alive — even if for just a moment — to qualify as an exemption.

- ✔ **Violation of local law:** A person doesn't meet the member of your household test if your relationship violates local law.

- ✔ **Adoption:** Before the adoption is legal, a child is considered to be your child if he or she was placed with you for adoption by an authorized adoption agency (and the child must have been a member of your household). Otherwise, the child must be a member of your household for the entire tax year to satisfy this test.

- ✔ **Foster care:** A foster child or adult must live with you as a member of your household for the entire year to qualify as your dependent. However, if a government agency makes payments to you as a foster parent, you may not list the child as your dependent.

Test 2: Married person

If your dependent is married and files a joint return, you can't take this person as an exemption. However, if the person and the person's spouse file a joint return to get a refund of all tax withheld, you may be able to claim this person if the other four tests are met.

Test 3: Citizen or resident

The dependent must be one of the following:

- ✔ A U.S. citizen or U.S. resident alien
- ✔ A resident of Canada or Mexico
- ✔ Your adopted child who is not a U.S. citizen but who lived with you all year in a foreign country

A child who isn't a U.S. citizen or resident and lives abroad (in a country other than Canada or Mexico) can't be claimed as a dependent.

Test 4: Income

The dependent's gross income must be less than $3,050. Gross income does not include nontaxable income, such as welfare benefits or nontaxable Social Security benefits. Income earned by a permanently and totally disabled person for services performed at a sheltered workshop school is generally not included for purposes of the income test.

Children of divorced or separated parents and persons supported by two or more taxpayers

The parent who had custody of the child for most of the year is the one entitled to claim the child as a dependent — provided that both parents together paid more than half of the child's support.

A noncustodial parent can claim the child if any of the following apply:

↳ The custodial parent gives up the right to claim the child as a dependent by signing **Form 8332, Release of Claim to Exemption for Child of Divorced or Separated Parents.** The form allows for the release of an exemption for a single year, a number of years, or all future years. The noncustodial parent must attach this form to the return.

↳ A decree or separation agreement signed after 1984 provides that the noncustodial parent is unconditionally entitled to the exemption and the custodial parent is not. You must list the child's name, Social Security number, and the number of months the child lived in your home. You also must attach a copy of the cover page of the decree or agreement with the custodial parent's Social Security number written next to his or her name, along with the page that unconditionally states that you can claim the child as a dependent. Don't forget to attach a copy of the signature page of the decree or agreement.

↳ A decree or separation agreement signed before 1985 provides that the noncustodial parent is entitled to the exemption, and that this parent provided $600 or more toward the child's support.

↳ In the extreme right column on line 6 of your 1040 where you list your total exemptions, you must list the number of dependents who didn't live with you separately from the number who did.

As a note of caution, if you fail to pay child support in the year it is due, but pay it in a later year, it is not considered paid for the support of your child in either year.

Even if you can't claim a child because your ex-spouse is claiming the child, you still can claim the child's medical expenses, and you're entitled to the Child and Dependent Care Credit if you're the custodial parent. When the child reaches his or her majority, the custodial parent rules no longer apply. The parent who provides more than 50 percent of the child's support is entitled to the exemption.

Note: The special rules for divorced or separated parents don't apply to parents who never married each other. In such situations, you either have to provide more than half the support of the child or enter into a multiple support agreement (**Form 2120**).

Of course, there are exceptions. Your child can have a gross income of $3,050 or more under one of the following conditions:

↳ He or she was under the age of 19 at the end of 2003.
↳ He or she was under the age of 24 at the end of 2003 and was also a student.

Your child is considered a student if he or she is enrolled as a full-time student at a school during any five months of 2003. A school includes technical, trade, and mechanical schools. It does not include on-the-job training courses or correspondence schools.

Test 5: Support

You must have provided more than half the dependent's total support in 2003. If you file a joint return, support can come from either spouse. If you remarried, the support provided by your new spouse is treated as support coming from you. For exceptions to the support test, see the sidebar "Children of divorced or separated parents and persons supported by two or more taxpayers." (You can't miss it with a title like that!)

Support includes food, a place to live, clothing, medical and dental care, and education. It also includes items such as a car and furniture, but only if they're for the dependent's own use or benefit. In figuring total support, use the actual cost of these items, but figure the cost of a place to live at its fair rental value. Include money the person used for his or her own support, even if this money wasn't taxable. Examples are gifts, savings, Social Security and welfare benefits, and other public assistance payments. This support is treated as *not* coming from you.

Total support doesn't include items such as income tax and Social Security taxes, life insurance premiums, or funeral expenses. A person's own funds aren't considered support unless they're actually spent for support. For example, your mother received $2,400 in Social Security and $400 in interest. She paid $2,000 for rent and $400 for recreation. Even though her income was $2,800, she spent only $2,400 for her own support. If you spent more than $2,400 for her support, you can claim her as a dependent because you provided more than half her support.

Even if you did not pay more than half of a dependent's support, you may still be able to claim this person as a dependent if all five of the following apply:

- ✔ You and one or more eligible persons paid more than half of the dependent's support. An eligible person is someone who could have claimed the dependent but didn't pay more than half of the dependent's support.

- ✔ You paid more than 10 percent of the dependent's support.

- ✔ No individual paid more than half of the dependent's support.

- ✔ Dependency tests 1 through 4 are met.

- ✔ Each eligible person who paid more than 10 percent of support completes **Form 2120, Multiple Support Declaration,** and you attach this form to your return. The form states that only you will claim the person as a dependent for 2003.

Securing Social Security Numbers for Dependents

You must list a Social Security number on line 6c column (2), Form 1040 and 1040A, for every dependent. If your dependent was born and died in 2003 and didn't have a Social Security number, write Died in column (2). No Social Security number, no deduction, and no right to claim head of household status. To obtain a Social Security number, contact the Social Security Administration at 800-772-1213 or on the Web at www.ssa.gov. Click on "Your Social Security Number" in the upper left corner. You can either download the one-page application for a Social Security card, **Form SS-5,** or have one mailed to you. Based on your zip code, you'll be directed to the nearest Social Security office. Take your driver's license, your child's original birth certificate (no duplicates), and another form of ID for your child, such as a birth announcement or a doctor's bill, together with the SS-5. It takes about two weeks to get a number.

If you're in the process of adopting a child who is a U.S. citizen or resident and cannot get a Social Security number until the adoption is final, you can apply for an *adoption taxpayer number* that can be used instead of a Social Security number. To get one, file **Form W-7A, Application for Taxpayer Identification Number for Pending U.S. Adoptions.**

Filing for children and other dependents

If you as the parent can claim a child (or someone else) as a dependent on your return, the dependent must file a return under any of the following circumstances:

✔ The dependent had unearned income (interest, dividends, capital gains, and so on), and the total of that income plus earned income exceeds $750.

✔ The dependent had no unearned income but had earned income that exceeds $4,750.

✔ The dependent had gross income that exceeds the larger of (a) $750 or (b) the earned income up to $4,500 plus $250.

For example, suppose that your teenager has interest income of $200 and salary from a summer job of $450. This dependent doesn't need to file because the total income was less than $750. If your teenager had no unearned income but earned $2,000 from a summer job, he or she wouldn't have to file either because the earned income was under $4,750.

But here's an important point: The dependent must file to *get back* the tax that was withheld from his or her paychecks. This situation can be avoided, however, if a dependent who starts to work claims an exemption from having tax withheld by filing Form W-4 with the employer. That way, he or she won't have to file a return to get back the tax that was withheld. When he or she reaches $4,750 in income, withholding will have to start, and a new W-4 must be filed with the employer. In 2004, the $4,750 threshold increases to $4,850.

You may encounter another wrinkle in the IRS rules for this exemption from withholding to apply — the teenager's investment income (interest) can't exceed $250. If it does, she can't claim an exemption from withholding if her total income exceeds $750. There's no such thing as being too young when introducing your kid to our convoluted tax laws.

A child under the age of 14 with more than $1,500 in investment income is subject to the *Kiddie Tax*. This income is considered earned by the child's parents at the parents' tax rate (see "Line 41: Tax" in Chapter 8 for more details on this wonderful tax law nuance).

Filing a Return for a Deceased Taxpayer

When someone dies, a separate taxpaying entity is created — the decedent's estate. If the estate has more than $600 in income or has a beneficiary who is a nonresident alien, it must file **Form 1041, U.S. Income Tax Return for Estates and Trusts.** This filing is in addition to the decedent's final tax return.

Suppose the decedent died before April 15. The executor must file a tax return for that individual for the prior year and for the current year. For example, if someone died on April 1, 2004, a return must be filed for 2003, and a final return for 2004 must be filed by April 15, 2005, reporting all of the deceased's income and deductions for the period January 1, 2004, through April 1, 2004.

Even though the decedent's income has to be prorated for the year and reported on the final return up to the date of death, and on the decedent's estate's return (Form 1041) for income received after the death, the decedent's personal exemption ($3,050) doesn't have to be prorated. Neither does the standard deduction.

If the surviving spouse didn't remarry in the same year as the death, a joint return can be filed. The surviving spouse reports all his or her income and deductions for the entire year and the deceased's up to the date of death. If you remarry in the same year that your spouse dies, you can file jointly with your new spouse, but not with your deceased spouse.

Medical expenses paid within one year of the decedent's death can be deducted on the decedent's final return or by the estate.

If the deceased owned E or EE Savings Bonds and chose not to report the interest during his or her lifetime, the tax on the interest has to be paid by the survivor, unless an election is made to report the interest on the decedent's final return. This might make sense if the deceased died early in the year and had little income and large deductions.

Either the surviving spouse or the executor can sign the deceased's final personal income tax return. Write DECEASED, the decedent's name, and the date of death at the top of page 1 of the 1040.

Must I File?

Yes, you must file a tax return when your income exceeds the amounts for your age and filing status, as shown in Table 4-3.

Table 4-3	When You Must File		
Marital Status	*Filing Status*	*Age**	*Filing Required When Gross Income Exceeds*
Single, divorced, legally separated	Single	Under 65	$7,800
		65 or older	$8,950
	Head of household	Under 65	$10,050
		65 or older	$11,200
Married with a child and living apart from spouse during last 6 months of 2003	Head of household	65 or older	$11,200
Married and living with spouse at end of 2003 (or on date of spouse's death)	Married (joint return)		$15,600
		65 or older (one spouse)	$16,550
		65 or older (both spouses)	$17,500
Married (separate return)		Any age	$3,050
Married and not living with spouse at end of 2003 (or on date of spouse's death)	Married (joint or separate return)	Any age	$3,050
Widowed before 2003 and not remarried in 2003	Single	Under 65	$7,800
		65 or older	$8,950
	Head of household	Under 65	$10,050
		65 or older	$11,200
Qualifying widow(er) with dependent child		Under 65	$12,550
		65 or older	$13,500

* If you turn 65 on January 1, 2004, you are considered to be age 65 at the end of 2003.

When to file

If you don't file by April 15, 2004, you'll have to pay penalties and interest. If you live or work outside the United States, you have an automatic extension of time to file until June 15, 2004.

If you know that you can't file by April 15, you can get an automatic four-month extension of time to file — until August 16, 2004 (August 15 falls on a Sunday so you have until Monday, August 16) — by filing **Form 4868, Application for Automatic Extension of Time to File U.S. Individual Income Tax Return.** Keep in mind that this form must be filed by April 15, 2004. If you use a credit card to pay the balance owed for 2003, you don't have to separately file Form 4868; it's done automatically for you. We explain how to pay by credit card in the first section of Chapter 5 — line 12. Extensions of time to file can also be obtained by calling 888-796-1074 or by using your personal computer and a tax software program. The choices are endless, so don't blow the April 15 filing date.

Form 4868 doesn't, however, extend the time to pay. You'll be charged interest and a late payment penalty of 0.5 percent a month if you don't pay at least 90 percent of your tax by April 15, 2004. (*Note:* You'll be charged interest on outstanding tax owed.) If you still can't file by August 16, 2004, you can obtain an additional two-month extension of time to file until October 15, 2004, by filing **Form 2688, Application for Additional Extension of Time to File U.S. Individual Income Tax Return.** This form must be filed by August 16. Most tax software programs allow for the electronic filing of Form 4868, or it can be filed the old-fashioned way, by mail. You can't get an extension beyond October 15. Filing Form 2688 is done strictly by snail mail.

If you don't file

You *can* end up crushing rocks. But it's more likely that you'll be assessed penalties that make crushing rocks seem like a stroll in the park. Annually, the IRS prosecutes only 5,000 individuals (you can't call them taxpayers) for tax evasion. Some 80 percent are members of organized crime or drug dealers, and the balance is made up of high-profile individuals and others. You don't want to be one of the others. Even though the government currently is interested in high-profile CEOs from companies like Enron and Tyco, you never know who they may decide to take an interest in. The IRS moves in mysterious ways.

If you don't file, based on the information reported to the IRS by your employers, the IRS either prepares a substitute return and assesses a late filing penalty of 25 percent, a late payment penalty of 0.5 percent a month to a maximum of 25 percent plus interest (and possibly a 75 percent fraud penalty), or issues a summons for you to appear with your tax records so that the IRS can use those records to prepare a more accurate return. Interest and penalties are charged whichever way the IRS decides to proceed.

Tax software and antipiracy

The two leading programs, H&R Block's *TaxCut* and *TurboTax* by Intuit are just about identical according to *The Wall Street Journal*'s personal technology expert Walter S. Mossberg. Intuit's "insulting approach" turned Mossberg off in his January 2003 evaluation of the two programs. The reason? In an effort to curb piracy, users must contact Intuit to activate the software, which limits the use of TurboTax to a single PC. Also be aware when installing TurboTax that you will also be installing a hidden antipiracy program that will always be running in the background to monitor the program whenever it is being used.

Where to file

The IRS Web site lists all the addresses to which you can send your forms. Just look for the "Where To File" link in the "Resources" section.

How to file

Okay, so this whole book is supposed to be about this subject. But what we mean here is that you have several ways to get the forms — and the check, if necessary — to IRS Central: You can file the old-fashioned way through the U.S. Postal Service, or you can file electronically, or by phone.

Electronic filing

We should define this one: Your return is filed either over a telephone line or one of those faster cable connections either by you or a company that offers this service. All you need is a computer and a modem.

Electronic filing is free. Through a link on the IRS Web page (www.irs.gov), a group of software companies are offering free online tax filing. Why are they doing this? To ensure that the IRS won't jump into the online tax filing market with a competitive product. If free electronic filing sounds too good to be true, you are probably right. It has been our experience that when someone offers something for nothing, usually a gimmick is involved. Some companies may have something up their sleeves and try to solicit you for their financial services or products. One catch, we noticed — although the federal return is free, a fee is charged for your state return. So be on the lookout for the fine print.

Each participating software company has set its own eligibility requirements for free filing. Generally, those requirements are based on age, Adjusted Gross Income (AGI), eligibility to file Form 1040EZ, eligibility to claim the Earned Income Credit, state residency, and active duty military status (if applicable). Each company has a description of the criteria for using its free service.

The advantage of electronic filing is that you get your hands on your hard-earned refund in 10 days, which is about three weeks faster than by mail. Also, you can have your refund deposited directly into your bank account. Your state return gets filed along with your federal return at the same time. One transmission does it all.

Some tax preparation firms will not only prepare and electronically file your return, they'll also loan you money based on the projected amount of the refund. These clever loans are called *refund anticipation loans*.

Our principal objection to paying someone to electronically file your return is that it's too pricey. Here's why: According to the IRS, the average refund is $1,980. Some tax preparation firms can arrange for an on-the-spot loan for the amount of your refund. According to the Consumer Federation of America and the National Consumer Law Center, the typical loan for the average refund of $1,980 bears a 222.5 percent annual percentage rate. This is the result of the loan being repaid within 10 days when the refund is deposited into a special account set up by the lender. A class action suit was once settled against H&R Block involving deceptive business practices concerning their refund loans. This tax filing season, you will probably notice a number of car dealerships offering tax preparation services. They are hoping that by offering this service together with refund anticipation loans, they can seduce more people into driving off the lot with one of their latest models. How's that for one-stop shopping?

Filing by phone

Single or married taxpayers who qualify to use Form 1040EZ can file their returns by means of a touch-tone telephone. However, if the IRS didn't mail you a *1040EZ TeleFile* booklet tax package, you can't file by phone. If the IRS does mail you a *1040EZ TeleFile* booklet, but you lose it, you can't file by phone. Finally, if you're married, have unemployment compensation to report as income, or need to claim deductions for being over 65 or blind, you can't file by phone. The *TeleFile* worksheet in your 1040EZ package guides you through the process. Depending on where you live, you can also file your state return at the same time.

Only the IRS would include more rules when trying to make things easier!

A Final Bit of Advice

Here's an old saying from a wise man — the father of one of us. He said, "Son, there are two kinds of payments in the world you should avoid: too early and too late." That kind of advice also applies to filing your taxes. Filing taxes late leads to IRS interest and penalties; paying your taxes too early, or withholding too much, is simply an interest-free loan to the federal government. Thanks for the advice, Dad.

Tax strategies for the unemployed

The unpleasant truth in any economic downturn is that more and more people find themselves between jobs. Although this revelation is hardly a startling one, here is a point that we'd like to make: Dramatic changes in your financial situation call for dramatic changes in your tax strategies. Here are some tax strategies to help the unemployed regroup and move on with the least amount of tax pain.

✔ **Unemployment Insurance:** Unfortunately unemployment insurance is taxable. On average, about a third of what you earn belongs to the government. Only the balance is yours. So unless you provide in advance for the taxes you expect to owe on this governmental benefit, you can expect a nasty surprise next April 15. The ins-and-outs of unemployment insurance are covered in the discussion about line 19 in Chapter 6. We even cover what to do if you're forced to repay some of those weekly checks because of the law that requires you actively be looking for work while you're unemployed . . . but you weren't.

✔ **Severance pay:** Severance pay generally is taxable, unless it is a payment for a physical injury or illness. Payment for emotional distress as a result of a settlement involving age, sex, or racial discrimination is taxable. Sorry! Not only that, but the IRS demands that you report the entire amount of the settlement on your tax return, and not the net amount after the cut your lawyer takes. The IRS insists that the legal fee can be claimed only as a miscellaneous itemized deduction, which subjects many taxpayers to the Alternative Minimum Tax. See Chapter 9.

✔ **Job Hunting and Networking:** Job-hunting expenses are deductible as a miscellaneous itemized deduction (see Chapter 9). The type of expenses that are allowed are printing and mailing resumes, telephone, travel, professional counseling, and similar expenses. The hitch: You can't make a career switch and deduct these expenses. You have to be looking for work in the same field or type of position to be able to claim this deduction.

Even though most experts advise that networking is the best way to land a job, expenses incurred while networking generally are not deductible. The IRS believes that establishing relationships isn't related to your job description sufficiently enough to warrant a deduction. Like every IRS rule, there always seem to be exceptions. For example, evenings of networking sponsored by and for graduate-school alumni probably will pass muster. What the IRS requires in order for you to be able to nail down a networking deduction is for you to say, "Please hire me." See Chapter 9.

(continued)

(continued)

✔ **Moving Expenses:** If you must relocate to find employment, which isn't all that unusual, and your new employer doesn't reimburse you, a substantial part of your moving expenses can be deducted. You don't have to itemize your deductions to be entitled to this deduction. You can claim the standard deduction as well as a moving expense deduction. See Chapter 15.

✔ **Withdrawals from an IRA, pension, or 401(k):** Forgive us if we state the obvious. Being strapped for cash when you're between jobs is a situation in which many people find themselves. Before you dip into a retirement as a source of funds to tie you over, you must be mindful that taking a distribution is taxable, and if you are younger than 59½, the withdrawal is subject to a 10 percent penalty. Some notable exceptions to the penalty include you're tapping into an IRA to pay for health insurance premiums when you're unemployed and you're either receiving unemployment insurance for at least 12 consecutive weeks or paying medical expenses that exceed 7.5 percent of your income or for qualified higher-education expenses. The penalty also doesn't apply to withdrawals that are received over your lifetime in the form of an annuity. This last exception applies to all retirement plans. See Chapter 9, lines 15 and 16.

✔ **Starting a business:** Chapter 9 has it all when you're considering what you can and can't deduct and what to look out for. If your new business loses money, you may very well have a Net Operating Loss, which entitles you to carry the loss back to a prior year and obtain a refund. Whether it's consulting or a retail store, you face a host of rules with which you must comply, including the rules concerning a home office deduction.

✔ **Sale of a home:** The first $500,000 ($250,000 if single) of profit on the sale of a home that was your principal residence for at least two of the past five years is exempt from tax. If you fail to meet the two-year requirement because you lost your job, you're nevertheless entitled to a portion of the exemption, so flip over to Chapter 12 for the low-down on how to pull this off.

✔ **Education credits and deductions:** The Lifetime Learning Credit entitles you to a direct credit against your tax of 20 percent on up to tuition and related expenses. There is a limit to what you can earn and still be eligible to claim the credit, so Chapter 8 is a must read (line 47). What expenses qualify? Brushing up classes that make you more marketable even if it involves a career change, for one. Eligible expenses include undergraduate- or graduate-level and professional-degree courses, and any course that you take at an eligible institution to acquire new or improve your old job skills.

If you don't qualify for the Lifetime Learning Credit, don't overlook the Tuition and Fees Deduction (Chapter 7, line 26). The rules are less stringent than the Learning Credit or the Hope Scholarship Credit, but income limits still are in effect. You can claim a deduction of up to $3,000, if you qualify, and you don't have to itemize your deductions.

When it comes to employment-related education expenses, you don't get only two strikes and you're out. You still have one more swing at a deduction. If you can't pull off the Education Credit or the Tuition and Fees Deduction, deducting your education expenses as a miscellaneous itemized deduction is a possibility. (See Chapter 9.)

✔ **Health Insurance Credit:** This credit allows workers dislocated as the result of foreign competition and uninsured retirees who are receiving pension benefits from the federal governments Pension Benefit Guarantee Corporations (PBGC) to claim a refundable credit equal to 65 percent of their health insurance expenses. Individuals can elect to forego the credit and, instead, have the government pick up the tab directly for 65 percent of their health insurance premiums. See Chapter 8, line 67, box c.

✔ **Trade Adjustments Assistance (TAA) Allowances:** If you were laid off because of foreign competition you may very well be eligible for a cash allowance, the health insurance credit, and retraining. So be sure to contact the U.S. Department of Labor.

Part II
Tackling the Various Forms 1040

The 5th Wave   By Rich Tennant

"I got excellent advice on my tax return from a very knowledgeable guy. All the while he cleaned my windshield and checked the air pressure in my tires."

In this part . . .

Rituals make the world go 'round. And what ritual is quite so enjoyable as completing one's tax return? Visiting your local department of motor vehicles to renew your driver's license? Waiting in line at the post office to buy some stamps? Cleaning up an overflowing toilet? Figuring out who to call when you lock your car keys in the trunk?

It all starts with Form 1040 in its three guises: 1040EZ, 1040-A, and plain old 1040. After you get the form right, you have the challenge of finding the tax documentation needed to plug answers into those small lines. And just when you're ready to start (after pulling out your hair), you find yourself wading knee-deep through those dreadful IRS instructions.

Thanks to the *For Dummies* translation of jargon into plain English, here is what you need to know to get an A+ on tax return preparation. And we show you some tricks along the way to make it easier on yourself next time around. (By the way, did you know you can purchase stamps through the mail and eliminate those trips to the post office?)

Chapter 5

Easy Filing: 1040EZ and 1040A

• •

In This Chapter

▶ Living the really EZ life: Using the 1040EZ

▶ Living the semi-easy life: Using the 1040A

▶ Letting the IRS do the math for you

• •

*1*t's best to begin a challenging part of the book with something EZ. Trust us, things get much more complicated in a hurry. However, if you can file a simplified tax form, you'll be able to bypass much of what's in the rest of Part II of this book. For now, though, take a look at the easier forms (1040EZ and 1040A). They're easier because you don't have as many lines to fill out, as many schedules to complete and attach, or as many receipts and records to dig out.

The most difficult decision to make is whether to choose the 1040EZ or the 1040A (the infamous *Short Form*). From then on, it's downhill. In fact, the forms are so simple that the IRS computes the tax for you.

Who Can File a 1040EZ?

With the 1040EZ (see Figure 5-1), all you have to do is fill in the numbers — a snap with this short form. The IRS likes this form because an optical scanner can process it. You'll like this form, too, because you don't have to do the math. The nice folks at the IRS do it for you (see the sidebar "Let the IRS figure your tax," later in this chapter). You may use the 1040EZ if you meet all of the following criteria:

✔ You are single or are married filing jointly and don't claim any dependents.

✔ You (and your spouse, if married filing jointly) are younger than age 65 and are not blind, which otherwise entitles you to increase your standard deduction.

✔ You have income only from wages, salaries, tips, taxable scholarships or fellowship grants, unemployment compensation, dividends from the Alaska Permanent Fund, and qualified state tuition program earnings — and not more than $1,500 of taxable interest income.

✔ Your taxable income (line 6) is less than $50,000. That's taxable income after deducting $7,800 if single or $15,600 if married.

✔ You aren't receiving any advance *earned income credit (EIC)* payments. You can find out whether you received any advance EIC payments by referring to box 9 of your W-2. (See "Box 9" in Chapter 6 for more on advance EICs.)

✔ You aren't itemizing deductions (on Schedule A) or claiming any adjustments to income (for example, an IRA or student loan interest deduction) or tax credits (such as child-care expenses).

Form **1040EZ**	Department of the Treasury—Internal Revenue Service **Income Tax Return for Single and Joint Filers With No Dependents** (99) **2003**		OMB No. 1545-0675

Label
(See page 12.)
Use the IRS label.
Otherwise, please print or type.

L A B E L   H E R E

Your first name and initial	Last name	Your social security number
If a joint return, spouse's first name and initial	Last name	Spouse's social security number
Home address (number and street). If you have a P.O. box, see page 12.	Apt. no.	
City, town or post office, state, and ZIP code. If you have a foreign address, see page 12.		

▲ **Important!** ▲
You **must** enter your SSN(s) above.

Presidential Election Campaign (page 12) ▶

Note. Checking "Yes" will not change your tax or reduce your refund.
Do you, or your spouse if a joint return, want $3 to go to this fund? . . . . . . ▶

     You   Spouse
☐ Yes ☐ No ☐ Yes ☐ No

Income

Attach Form(s) W-2 here.
Enclose, but do not attach, any payment.

Note. You **must** check Yes or No.

1 Wages, salaries, and tips. This should be shown in box 1 of your Form(s) W-2.
   Attach your Form(s) W-2.   1

2 Taxable interest. If the total is over $1,500, you cannot use Form 1040EZ.   2

3 Unemployment compensation and Alaska Permanent Fund dividends
   (see page 14).   3

4 Add lines 1, 2, and 3. This is your **adjusted gross income.**   4

5 Can your parents (or someone else) claim you on their return?
   Yes. Enter amount from   **No.** If **single,** enter $7,800.
   ☐ worksheet on back.   ☐   If **married filing jointly,** enter $15,600.
                 See back for explanation.   5

6 Subtract line 5 from line 4. If line 5 is larger than line 4, enter -0-.
   This is your **taxable income.** ▶ 6

Payments and tax

7 Federal income tax withheld from box 2 of your Form(s) W-2.   7

8 **Earned income credit (EIC).**   8

9 Add lines 7 and 8. These are your **total payments.** ▶ 9

10 **Tax.** Use the amount on **line 6 above** to find your tax in the tax table on pages
    24–28 of the booklet. Then, enter the tax from the table on this line.   10

Refund
Have it directly deposited! See page 19 and fill in 11b, 11c, and 11d.

11a If line 9 is larger than line 10, subtract line 10 from line 9. This is your **refund.** ▶ 11a
▶ b Routing number ☐☐☐☐☐☐☐☐☐   ▶ c Type: ☐ Checking ☐ Savings
▶ d Account number ☐☐☐☐☐☐☐☐☐☐☐☐☐☐☐☐☐

Amount you owe

12 If line 10 is larger than line 9, subtract line 9 from line 10. This is
    the **amount you owe.** For details on how to pay, see page 20. ▶ 12

Third party designee

Do you want to allow another person to discuss this return with the IRS (see page 20)? ☐ **Yes.** Complete the following. ☐ **No**
Designee's name ▶   Phone no. ▶ ( )   Personal identification number (PIN) ▶ ☐☐☐☐☐

Sign here
Joint return? See page 11.
Keep a copy for your records.

Under penalties of perjury, I declare that I have examined this return, and to the best of my knowledge and belief, it is true, correct, and accurately lists all amounts and sources of income I received during the tax year. Declaration of preparer (other than the taxpayer) is based on all information of which the preparer has any knowledge.

Your signature	Date	Your occupation	Daytime phone number ( )
Spouse's signature. If a joint return, **both** must sign.	Date	Spouse's occupation	

Paid preparer's use only

Preparer's signature ▶	Date	Check if self-employed ☐	Preparer's SSN or PTIN
Firm's name (or yours if self-employed), address, and ZIP code ▶		EIN	
		Phone no. ( )	

For Disclosure, Privacy Act, and Paperwork Reduction Act Notice, see page 23.   Cat. No. 11329W   Form **1040EZ** (2003)

Figure 5-1:
Form 1040EZ
page 1.

If you can't file Form 1040EZ, all is not lost. You may be able to use another simplified form: 1040A (see "Who Can File a 1040A?" later in this chapter).

Filling Out a 1040EZ

The IRS has provided nice little boxes where you can put your numbers (but please leave off the dollar signs). What a considerate organization!

Rounding off dollars

No pennies please, even though the form has a column for cents. You're allowed to round to the nearest dollar. Drop amounts under 50 cents and increase amounts from 50 to 99 cents to the next dollar. If you have one W-2 for $5,000.55 and another for $18,500.73, enter $23,501 ($5,000.55 + $18,500.73 = $23,501.28) not $23,502 ($5,001 + $18,501).

Line 1: Total wages, salaries, and tips

Enter your wages (from box 1 of your W-2 form). If your employer hasn't provided you with this form by January 31, 2004, go squawk at your payroll and benefits department. If you're interested in what all those boxes on your W-2 mean, see Chapter 6, line 7.

Line 2: Taxable interest income of $1,500 or less

Enter your interest income on line 2. You can locate this amount in boxes 1 and 3 of your 1099-INTs, which your bank and other investment companies should provide. If this amount is more than $1,500, you can't use the 1040EZ. Sorry!

If you're in a higher tax bracket, you may be able to gain a higher return with your savings by choosing tax-free investments. This applies to you when you're in the 25 percent federal income tax bracket that begins at $28,400 in taxable income — line 6 on the 1040EZ — as a single filer, or $56,800 as a married couple filing jointly. See Chapter 23 to find out how to keep more of your investment income.

Line 3: Unemployment compensation and Alaska Permanent Fund dividends

Once upon a time, unemployment compensation wasn't taxable. But that was before "tax reform." To report your unemployment compensation received during the tax year, enter on line 3 the amount from box 1 of **Form 1099-G** that your state sends you.

Although you can elect to have tax withheld at the rate of 10 percent on your unemployment, so you won't be caught short next April 15, this offer is one that most people are likely to refuse. **Form W-4 V, Voluntary Withholding Request** is used to request this election. Check box 5 of the form and submit it to the unemployment office where you file for benefits.

To get the lowdown on Alaska Permanent Fund dividends, skip ahead to line 13 in the 1040A section of this chapter. Please don't be annoyed when we ask you to do this. It's because we don't want to bore you by constantly having to repeat the same instructions all over the place.

Line 4: Adjusted gross income

Add the amounts of lines 1, 2, and 3 together and enter the total here. The figure on Line 4 is your *adjusted gross income (AGI)*.

Line 5: Deductions and exemptions

From your AGI, you have to subtract your standard deduction and personal exemption. The amount you can deduct is indicated to the left of the boxes, but you first have to take the IRS *yes-or-no test*. Read the question on line 5: "Can your parents (or someone else) claim you on their return?" Mark your answer. (Aren't you glad this isn't an essay test?)

If you checked "yes," you have to use the worksheet on the back of the form to figure your standard deduction. That's because you're not entitled to deduct either the $7,800 or $15,600 on line 5. There is also an additional restriction if your parents are entitled to claim you as a dependent; you aren't entitled to a personal exemption for yourself. As an example, pretend that you're preparing the return of a teenage dependent who earned $3,300 last summer. Because we know that at first glance this worksheet (on page 2 of the form) looks intimidating, we help you wade through it.

Line A.	Enter the amount of her wages		$3,300
	Additional amount allowed by law		$ 250
		A.	$3,550
Line B.	Minimum standard deduction	B.	$ 750
Line C.	The larger of A or B	C.	$3,550
Line D.	Maximum standard deduction if single	D.	$4,750
Line E.	The smaller of C or D	E.	$3,550
Line F.	Exemption amount (because you claim her, enter 0)	F.	0
Line G.	Add lines E and F and enter that amount on line 5 on Form 1040EZ	G.	$3,550

If you checked "no" on line 5 (1040EZ), because no one else can claim you on his or her return, your life is just that much simpler now. Enter in the boxes the amount for single ($7,800) or married ($15,600), whichever applies. You should feel good about this number that you're deducting from your taxable income. The IRS is effectively saying that this amount of income is tax-free to you.

Line 6: Taxable income

Subtract the amount that you entered on line 5 from line 4, and enter the remainder here. Line 6 is your taxable income. If line 5 is larger than line 4, enter 0.

Line 7: Federal income tax withheld

Enter your federal tax withheld (shown in box 2 of your W-2) here. Your federal income tax withheld is the amount of tax that you already paid during the tax year. Your employer withholds this money from your paycheck and sends it to the IRS. Don't overlook any withholding from box 4 of Forms 1099-INT or 1099-G, the forms where interest income and unemployment compensation are reported.

Line 8: Earned income credit

Single filers whose adjusted gross income (from line 4) is less than $11,230 may be eligible for the earned income credit (see "Line 63: Earned income credit" in Chapter 8 for more details about this credit). The credit can be as high as $382 for a single filer with no kids and is subtracted from your tax. For joint filers with no kids, the income limit is $12,230. The credit can be as high as $4,140 for a joint filer with two kids. If you don't owe tax, the credit is refunded to you. Remember, if you have kids and want to claim the credit, you *can't* use Form 1040EZ! You don't have to compute the credit. Just look up the credit for your income in your instruction booklet and enter that amount here.

A number of studies show that almost a third of the people who claim this credit have no right to do so. So here's what happens to people who get caught. In addition to all the penalties the IRS can impose, anyone who fraudulently claims this credit is ineligible to claim it for ten years. For taxpayers who are merely careless or intentionally disregard the rules, the penalty is two years.

Line 9: Total payments

Add the amounts on lines 7 and 8, and put the sum here.

Line 10: Tax

To figure your total federal income tax for the year, look up the amount on line 6 in the tax tables (available at www.irs.gov) for your income bracket and filing status. For example, if you're single and your taxable income (on line 6) is $32,100, find the row for $32,100 to $32,150 and read across to the "Single" column. In this example, your tax is $4,841.

When you've found the appropriate row and column for your taxable income and filing status — and while you have your finger in the right place — enter the amount here on line 10.

Line 11a: Refund time!

The last computation that you have to make is quite simple. Look at lines 9 and 10. If the amount on line 9 is larger than line 10, you're going to get a refund. Just subtract line 10 from line 9 and enter the amount on line 11a. The amount on 11a is your refund!

You can have your refund deposited directly into your bank account, which should speed up your refund by more than three weeks. However, a number of people we know are reluctant to take the IRS up on this offer. Their reason: "The IRS knows too much about me already."

If we haven't scared you away, the sample check in Figure 5-2 shows you how to get the information that the IRS needs to wire the money to your account from your check. Your routing number referred to on line 11b is the nine-digit number at the bottom left in Figure 5-2. On line 11c, check the type of account and then enter your account number. That's the number to the right of the routing number in Figure 5-2.

PAUL MAPLE
LILIAN MAPLE
123 Main Street
Anyplace, NY 10000

1234

15-0000/0000

20

PAY TO THE
ORDER OF _____ $ [   ]

SAMPLE

_____ DOLLARS

ANYPLACE BANK
Anyplace, NY 10000

Routing
Number
(line 11b)

Account
Number
(line 11d)

For

I: 250000005I :200000"¨86" 1234

Figure 5-2:
A sample
check.

Line 12: Amount you owe

Yes, you guessed it. When the amount on line 10 is larger than that on line 9, you still owe because not enough tax was withheld from your paycheck or paid by you during the year. Subtract line 9 from line 10 and enter the amount on line 12. Fess up and pay up.

Plastic anyone? Whether you file your return electronically, by mail, or by IRS *TeleFile,* you'll be able to charge the balance due with a toll-free call. Official Payments Corporation (888-2-PAY-TAX, that's 888-272-9829) expects to accept most major credit cards. Currently, MasterCard, American Express, Visa, and Discover cards are on board, and partial payments are allowed. You can pay the balance on your 2003 return, make estimated tax payments (Form 1040ES), and make a payment when you request an extension of time to file. Another authorized payment company that accepts plastic is Phone Charge Link2GovCorporation (888-658-5465).

The four reasons why paying with plastic isn't especially attractive are

- Credit-card companies typically charge a 21 percent rate of interest.

- Resolving billing disputes can prove to be a nightmare. Once a payment is made, it cannot be canceled. A stop payment can be placed on a check.

- Credit-card companies may potentially release confidential information when they sell the mailing list of their customers, which most of them do.

- Credit-card holders pay a "convenience fee" of about 2.49 percent on top of their interest charges, because the IRS doesn't pay the fee that credit-card companies normally collect from merchants. You'll be advised of the "convenience fee" right upfront. If it's too high, hang up.

We can think of better ways to earn frequent-flyer miles.

The new and friendlier IRS has become quite ingenious! It constantly is coming up with more convenient (convenient for whom?) payment methods such as:

- Checkless payments. The IRS has your bank deduct your payment directly from your account. Balance due, estimated tax (Form 1040ES), and extension of time to file payments (Form 4868) can be made this way. To sign up for this marvelous option, dial 800-555-4477.

- Electronic and TeleFile filers will be prompted to a payment option that allows for the direct payment from your account by your bank. You can file early and direct your bank to send what you owe on April 15, 2004. That's the last day this delayed payment option is available.

✔ What's your pleasure? If you use *TurboTax* (other software may also include this feature), you can choose how you want to pay — by check, direct transfer from your account, or by credit card.

Finishing up

Don't forget to attach your W-2s to your return. Staples are just great! (And staples are preferable to tape and paper clips. You don't want your W-2s going one way at IRS Central and your tax return going another.) If you owe money, make sure that you write your Social Security number in the lower-left corner of the front of your check, along with the notation `2003 FORM 1040EZ INCOME TAX` — just in case the folks at the IRS think you're trying to make a payment on your new boat but sent them the check by mistake.

Make out your check to the United States Treasury. Checks are no longer made out to the IRS. Sign your return and mail it to the IRS Service Center for your area. Normally, an addressed envelope is provided with your tax form. If you don't have the address, see the addresses provided in the back of this book.

The IRS offers two other ways to file your return — electronically and by phone — so flip back to Chapter 4, "How to file" if you find this intriguing.

Who Can File a 1040A?

You have the gracious permission of the IRS to use the 1040A if you meet all of the following conditions:

✔ You have income only from wages, salaries, tips, taxable scholarships, fellowship grants, pensions or annuities, taxable Social Security benefits, withdrawals from your individual retirement account (IRA), unemployment compensation, interest, and dividends.

✔ Your taxable income (line 27, page 2) is less than $50,000. That's not your total income. It's your income after all allowable deductions.

✔ You aren't itemizing deductions.

When you meet all the criteria for filing Form 1040A, be sure to check the section "Who Can File a 1040EZ?" earlier in this chapter to determine whether you can file the even easier Form 1040EZ.

You can also use Form 1040A (see Figure 5-3) and claim the earned income credit, the deduction for contributions to an IRA, nondeductible contributions to an IRA, educator expenses, tuition and fees deduction, the credit for child and dependent care expenses, the credit for the elderly or the disabled, child tax credits, education credits, an adoption credit, or the student loan interest deduction. You may use the 1040A even if you made estimated tax payments for 2003, or if you can take the exclusion of interest from series EE U.S. Savings Bonds issued after 1989.

You can't use 1040A if you received a capital gain distribution on Form 1099-DIV that includes entries in boxes 2b, 2c, 2d, or 2e. Why? Drop down to line 10 to find out.

Completing Form 1040A

We hope you've already figured out your filing status and exemptions. If you need help, see Chapter 4. You can round off to the nearest dollar so you don't have to fiddle with pennies. See the sidebar "Rounding off dollars," earlier in this chapter.

Line 6: Exemptions

Make sure you provide Social Security numbers for the youngsters (see Chapters 4 and 25 to find out how to obtain Social Security numbers for your children). Every dependent needs a Social Security number — even someone born on December 31. The IRS will disallow all exemptions without a Social Security number and will kick you out of head of household status and penalize you $50 for every missing number. You can claim an exemption for yourself, your spouse, your kids, and other dependents on line 6. Enter the information for items a through d. Each exemption entitles you to a $3,050 tax deduction.

Lines 6a and 6b: Exemptions for you and your spouse

This line is where you claim an exemption for you and your spouse. Living together doesn't count.

If someone else can claim you as a dependent, you can't check the box on 6a and claim an exemption for yourself. Not being able to claim yourself as an exemption also impacts the amount of the standard deduction to which you're entitled on line 24. Just keep this bit of news in the back of your mind — we explain it all when you get to that line.

Line 6c: Dependents

This line is as easy as pie. List each dependent's name, Social Security number, and relationship to you, and indicate whether your child qualifies for the Child Tax Credit (column 4). The following tax tip explains what this credit is about.

Subject to the income limitations, each kid younger than 17 on December 31 can cut your tax bill by $1,000. So check the box if this applies to you, and don't forget to claim this Child Tax Credit on line 33. The credit may be refundable if it exceeds your tax. If you have three or more kids, you're given the option of computing the refundable portion in one of two ways. You choose the method that produces the largest refund. All others get a shot at just one of these methods, which, by the way, is the simpler method. The refundable portion is claimed on line 42. **Form 8812, the Additional Child Tax Credit** is where the refundable portion of the credit is computed. The one-method way of computing (where you don't have more than two kids) requires that only lines 1–6 be filled out. The two-method way (three or more kids) requires that you fill out all 13 lines of the form. We explain it later in this chapter under "Line 33."

Tally all the exemptions you claimed on lines 6a through 6c.

If you're eligible for the Child Tax Credit and want to take immediate advantage of this tax savings, you can do so by submitting a new **Form W-4, Withholding Allowance Certificate,** to your employer. For example, if you're entitled to a $3,000 child credit (three kids) and get paid monthly, your monthly take-home pay will increase by $250. We explain how to complete Form W-4 in Chapter 15.

Don't confuse the Child Tax Credit with the credit for child and dependent care expenses. See "Line 45" in Chapter 8 for the rules on claiming the Dependent Care Credit. Be aware that if you received the $400-per-child advance payment of the Child Tax Credit last summer as a result of the credit being increased from $600 to $1,000, you'll find computing the credit somewhat more complex this year. Life just doesn't get any easier!

Form **1040A**	Department of the Treasury—Internal Revenue Service **U.S. Individual Income Tax Return** (99) **2003**	IRS Use Only—Do not write or staple in this space.

Label (See page 19.) / **Use the IRS label.** Otherwise, please print or type.

Your first name and initial — Last name — Your social security number

If a joint return, spouse's first name and initial — Last name — Spouse's social security number

Home address (number and street). If you have a P.O. box, see page 20. — Apt. no.

City, town or post office, state, and ZIP code. If you have a foreign address, see page 20.

▲ **Important!** ▲ You **must** enter your SSN(s) above.

Presidential Election Campaign (See page 20.) — Note. Checking "Yes" will not change your tax or reduce your refund. Do you, or your spouse if filing a joint return, want $3 to go to this fund? ▶ You □Yes □No Spouse □Yes □No

Filing status Check only one box.
1 □ Single
2 □ Married filing jointly (even if only one had income)
3 □ Married filing separately. Enter spouse's SSN above and full name here.
4 □ Head of household (with qualifying person). (See page 20.) If the qualifying person is a child but not your dependent, enter this child's name here. ▶
5 □ Qualifying widow(er) with dependent child (See page 21.)

Exemptions
6a □ **Yourself.** If your parent (or someone else) can claim you as a dependent on his or her tax return, **do not** check box 6a.
b □ **Spouse**
c **Dependents:**

(1) First name Last name	(2) Dependent's social security number	(3) Dependent's relationship to you	(4) ✓ if qualifying child for child tax credit (see page 23)
			□
			□
			□
			□
			□

If more than six dependents, see page 21.

No. of boxes checked on 6a and 6b ___
No. of children on 6c who: lived with you ___ did not live with you due to divorce or separation (see page 23) ___
Dependents on 6c not entered above ___
Add numbers on lines above ___

d Total number of exemptions claimed.

Income
Attach Form(s) W-2 here. Also attach Form(s) 1099-R if tax was withheld. If you did not get a W-2, see page 24. Enclose, but do not attach, any payment.

7 Wages, salaries, tips, etc. Attach Form(s) W-2. — 7
8a **Taxable** interest. Attach Schedule 1 if required. — 8a
b **Tax-exempt** interest. **Do not** include on line 8a. — 8b
9a Ordinary dividends. Attach Schedule 1 if required. — 9a
b Qualified dividends (see page 25). — 9b
10a Capital gain distributions (see page 25). — 10a
b Post-May 5 capital gain distributions (see page 25). — 10b
11a IRA distributions. — 11a / 11b Taxable amount (see page 25). — 11b
12a Pensions and annuities. — 12a / 12b Taxable amount (see page 26). — 12b
13 Unemployment compensation and Alaska Permanent Fund dividends. — 13
14a Social security benefits. — 14a / 14b Taxable amount (see page 28). — 14b
15 Add lines 7 through 14b (far right column). This is your **total income.** ▶ 15

Adjusted gross income
16 Educator expenses (see page 28). — 16
17 IRA deduction (see page 28). — 17
18 Student loan interest deduction (see page 31). — 18
19 Tuition and fees deduction (see page 31). — 19
20 Add lines 16 through 19. These are your **total adjustments.** — 20
21 Subtract line 20 from line 15. This is your **adjusted gross income.** ▶ 21

For Disclosure, Privacy Act, and Paperwork Reduction Act Notice, see page 57. — Cat. No. 11327A — Form **1040A** (2003)

Figure 5-3: Form 1040A page 1.

Line 7: Wages, salaries, and tips

Enter your wages from box 1 of your W-2s, which your employer(s) should provide, on this line. If you're interested in what all those other boxes on your W-2 mean, see Chapter 6, line 7.

Line 8a: Taxable interest income

Enter your interest income on line 8a (you can find this amount on your 1099-INT: box 1 from banks and S&Ls, and box 3 from U.S. Savings Bonds). If you're rolling in interest dough (at least more than $1,500), you have to fill out and attach **Schedule 1 (Interest and Dividend Income).** Just think of it as homework that you must hand in — unless you want the IRS to keep you after school. To complete Schedule 1, just put down the name of the payer and the amount in the amount column. If you need help with any part of it, call us (only kidding!). Actually, cruise ahead to Chapter 10, which walks you through completion of the nearly identical Schedule B, the schedule that taxpayers use to tally interest and dividend income for the cumbersome 1040. For example, if you need help determining what kind of interest income is taxable, the section "Line 1: Taxable interest" in Chapter 10 should help.

When you're in a higher tax bracket (the 25 percent federal income tax bracket beginning at $28,400 in taxable income as a single filer — line 27 on the 1040A — or $56,800 as married filing jointly), you may be able to make a higher return with your savings by choosing tax-free investments. See Chapter 23 to see how to keep more of your investment income.

Line 8b: Tax-exempt interest

If you received any tax-exempt interest (such as from a municipal bond or a tax-free money market fund), enter this amount on line 8b. This amount doesn't increase your taxable income unless you're receiving Social Security. If you collect Social Security benefits, tax-exempt interest is used to figure out how much of your Social Security is subject to tax. That's why this tax trap is here. Line 8b is not a harmless little line to some folks. At lines 14a and b, we explain how this nasty bit of business plays out.

Line 9a: Ordinary dividends

Once upon a time, dividends came in one flavor that was taxed at the same rate as other income. Now dividends come in two categories. The first is your total dividends, which are called ordinary dividends. That's the amount in box 1a on **Form 1099-DIV, Dividends and Distributions,** which you enter on line 9a. The other category is called qualified dividends. *Qualified dividends* are taxed at reduced rates of 15 percent or 5 percent. Normally the tax rate on qualified dividends is 15 percent, but for taxpayers whose taxable incomes (line 27) place them in the 10 percent or 15 percent tax brackets, the rate drops to 5 percent. You enter qualified dividends, which are reported to you in box 1b of Form 1099-DIV, on line 9b. Lines 9a and 9b tell the IRS which dividends are taxed at lower rates and which are not.

The portion of your total dividends (line 9a) minus your qualified dividends (line 9b) ends up being taxed at the rate for the bracket in which your taxable income (line 27) places you. Now that couldn't be simpler, could it?

Knowing whether a dividend qualifies for the reduced rate requires you to understand when a dividend isn't a dividend. This necessity is the result of financial institutions carelessly labeling distributions as dividends when they really aren't. Banks loosely call what they pay out for deposits in money-market, bond, and other funds dividends. These *dividends* clearly are interest payments and under the new law must be reported as such and do not qualify for the lower tax rate.

Only dividends that are paid to shareholders of U.S. corporations, foreign corporations traded on a U.S. stock exchange, or foreign corporations that are either incorporated in a U.S. possession or from a country that has full tax treaty benefits with the U.S are eligible for the reduced rate. So brokerage firms, mutual funds, banks, and corporations need to clean up their dividend labeling acts, or a whole bunch of people will end up unnecessarily paying more tax than they have to or perhaps considerably less than they have to.

You need to pay closer attention than ever before to the 2003 Form 1099-DIV, Dividends and Distributions that you receive.

Dividends that you receive by virtue of your mutual fund receiving qualified dividends *are* eligible for the lower tax rate. Similarly, you must meet other requirements, such as owning the stock or the fund for 60 days, to qualify for the lower rate. We explain all these issues in greater detail in Chapter 10.

The reduced dividend rate doesn't apply to dividends paid by

- ✔ Credit unions
- ✔ Insurance companies
- ✔ Bond or money-market funds
- ✔ Savings banks and savings and loans
- ✔ Banks on certificates of deposits
- ✔ Farmers' cooperatives
- ✔ Real-Estate Investment Trusts (REITs)
- ✔ Borrowers of securities who make payments in lieu of dividends

Enter the amount from box 1a of your 1099-DIV on line 9a. If this amount is more than $1,500, you have homework to do on Schedule 1 (see Chapter 10 if you get stuck).

Line 9b: Qualified dividends

Enter the amount of the qualified dividends from box 1b of Form 1099-DIV, Dividends and Distributions on this line. Flip back to line 9a for a quick refresher on qualified and total dividends and how each category is taxed and check out Chapter 10 for more details.

Qualified dividends are taxed along with capital gains at 15 percent. If your taxable income (line 27) is below $28,400 when your filing status is single or married filing separately, $56,800 when married filing jointly, or $38,050 when filing as a head of household, your dividend ends up being taxed at only 5 percent. You'll probably find this hard to believe, but starting in 2008 the 5 percent rate is reduced to zero for these taxpayers.

Unless you use the tax computation worksheet that we provide at line 41 in Chapter 8 or the qualified dividend and capital gain worksheet in the Form 1040A Instruction Booklet, you *will* overpay your tax. Paying what you have to is bad enough, but if you ignore our advice and end up paying more, don't expect a thank you from the IRS. However, if all you have is $10 of qualified dividends, for example, and you don't have a tax software program that automatically does the computations for you, we'll be understanding if you decide that it's hardly worth the hassle to go through the computations to have your $10 in qualified dividends taxed at 5 percent or 15 percent rather than 25 percent.

Line 10a: Capital gain distributions

Guess what? Just like dividends, capital gain distributions from mutual funds now come in two varieties — distributions received before May 6, 2003, and distributions received on or after that date. This date is of extreme importance, because the new law, whose official moniker is the Jobs Growth Tax Relief Act of 2003, reduces the maximum tax rate on capital gain distributions from 20 percent to 15 percent. But — and there's always a *but* in the tax world — only gains received on or after May 6, 2003, are eligible for the new rate. An even lower rate — 5 percent — applies to gains after this date for anyone whose taxable income (line 27) is less than $28,400 if single or married filing separately, $56,800 if married filing jointly, or $38,050 if filing as a head of household.

What we're about to tell you should rightfully be highlighted with an "Old/New Law" icon. Why? Because capital gain distributions received before May 6, 2003, are taxed at the old 20 percent maximum tax rate. Be mindful that this 20 percent rate gets reduced to 10 percent or perhaps even 8 percent when your taxable income (line 27) is below the amounts that we listed in the previous paragraph for your filing status.

Normally capital gain distributions are entered on Schedule D (see Chapter 12), which normally means that you can't use Form 1040A. However, the exception to that rule applies when the only capital gains that you have are from mutual funds. In that case, you don't have to report them on Schedule D and thus automatically get kicked out of filing 1040A and into the long Form 1040. If this exception applies to you, enter your capital gain distribution(s) that were reported on Form 1099-DIV, Dividends and Distributions on line 10a. Another rule — yes, we know, rules, rules, and more rules — enables you to use Form 1040A only when the entries on any 1099-DIV that you receive are limited to boxes 1a, 1b, 2a, or 2b. If you have any amounts in boxes 2c through 2f or in boxes 5 or 6, you automatically are bumped up to the major leagues and must use Form 1040 and its Schedule D. In Chapter 10, we explain what those harmless (Ha!) little boxes are there for. Here's a quick explanation: The amount in box 2f informs you whether, for some reason, any part of the distribution must be taxed at the 28 percent rate rather than the normally lower capital gain rates. Box 2c informs you whether a gain received before May 6, 2003, depending on your bracket, is taxed at the lower 8 percent tax rate. Because boxes 2d and 2e apply only in rare circumstances, rather than explain them twice, we'll wait until Chapter 10 to fill you in. Chapter 12 gives you the scoop on the heady concept of how capital gains are taxed and the right amount to enter in line 10.

Here is how you enter the amounts from boxes 2a and 2b of Form 1099-DIV: Enter amounts from box 2a on line 10a. If you have an entry in box 2b, enter that amount on line 10b.

Line 10b: Post-May 5 capital gain distributions

Enter amounts from box 2b Form 1099-DIV here. Couldn't be simpler, right? This line lets the IRS know that this particular capital gain is taxed at the new rate. The difference between boxes 2a and 2b gets taxed at the old (20 percent) capital gain rate.

Before we leave lines 10a and 10b, remember that you must be keenly aware that if you want the reduced capital gain rates to apply, you must use the capital gain worksheet in your instruction booklet when you get to line 28. That's the line where you compute your tax. We supply you with a worksheet in Chapter 8, line 41, so you can make this tax-saving computation.

Lines 11a and 11b: Total IRA distributions

The custodian of your IRA, bank, or investment company should send you a **Form 1099-R, Distributions from Pensions, Annuities, Retirement or Profit-Sharing Plans, IRAs, Insurance**

Contracts, etc., by January 31 for the prior tax year if you withdrew money from your IRA. The amount in box 1 of this form is entered on line 11a, and the amount in box 2a is entered on line 11b. Because this is an IRA, the amounts in boxes 1 and 2a are usually the same.

But if you made nondeductible contributions to your IRA, not all the money you withdraw is taxable. To compute what's taxable in such instances, you're going to have to fill out **Form 8606, Nondeductible IRAs** (see "Lines 15a and b: Total IRA distributions" in Chapter 6 for the lowdown on IRA distributions). If you elected to have tax withheld on your IRA payments, don't forget to enter the tax withheld (from box 4 of your 1099) on line 39, together with the tax withheld from your paychecks as reported on your Form W-2.

Coverdell ESAs

A Coverdell Education Savings Account is similar to a nondeductible IRA. Based on your income, you're allowed to contribute, but not deduct, up to $2,000 per beneficiary until they reach age 18. The age limit can be ignored for someone with special needs. The beneficiary doesn't have to be your dependent. The earnings on the account are tax-free and so is money withdrawn from the account if it is used to pay either elementary, secondary, or higher education expenses. We explain how this little tax shelter works in Chapter 25. IRS Publication 970 *(Tax Benefits for Education)* also explains Coverdell IRAs, but like many IRS instructions, you may need a couple of college degrees to understand it.

Distributions from Coverdells are reported in box 1 on **Form 1099-Q, Payments from Qualified Education Programs.** The 1099-Q is issued to the beneficiary. If the beneficiary's education expenses exceed the withdrawal, none of the earnings from the account included in the withdrawal are subject to tax. If that isn't the case, the beneficiary must use the worksheet provided in Publication 970 to determine how much (if any) of the withdrawal is taxable. The taxable portion is reported on line 21 of Form 1040, which means Form 1040A no longer is an option. The taxable portion also is subject to a 10 percent penalty that's reported on **Form 5329.** Guess what the name of the form is, **"Additional Taxes."** There is also a 6 percent additional tax when more than $2,000 per year is contributed or if contributions are made after the kid hits 18.

In any year that you use Coverdell distributions to pay education expenses, you can't claim the Hope or Lifetime Learning credits (line 31) or the tuition and fees deduction (line 19).

You can use the funds in a Coverdell to make payments to a Qualified Tuition Program (more commonly referred to as Section 529 Plan), and you can now contribute to a Coverdell IRA and a 529 Plan in the same year. We highlight these plans briefly at line 31 and in detail in Chapter 25.

Now that dividends and capital gains are taxed at rates as low as 5 percent for a child who's 14 or older, parents may want to reconsider these special methods when saving for college. The potential tax-free benefits of these savings accounts with their numerous restrictions may be outweighed by the extremely low tax rate a child might pay when the assets are held in his or her name.

Lines 12a and 12b: Total pensions and annuities

If you received income from a pension or an annuity during 2003, the payer will provide you with a 1099-R showing the amount you received in box 1 and the taxable amount in box 2a. (See "Lines 16a and b: Total pensions and annuities" in Chapter 6 to find out whether the pension plan computed the correct amount.) Enter the amount from box 1 on line 12a and the amount from box 2a on line 12b. If income tax was withheld, enter the amount from box 4 on line 39, along with the tax withheld from your salary as indicated on your W-2. To understand what all those boxes on your 1099-R mean, flip to "Lines 16a and b" in Chapter 6.

Line 13: Unemployment compensation and Alaska Permanent Fund dividends

Because most people will have to deal only with unemployment compensation, let's start there. Once upon a time unemployment benefits weren't taxable; now they are. Enter on line 13 the amount from box 1 of **Form 1099-G, Certain Government and Qualified State Tuition Program Payments,** which your state will send you (see "Line 19: Unemployment compensation" in Chapter 6 to find out more about this issue).

Alaska not only doesn't have an income tax, but every year residents also receive a distribution (dividend) from the state's permanent trust fund. The money comes from the state's oil revenues. In 2003, the distribution was $1,108. Not a bad reason to go north. Normally dividends and distributions are reported on Form 1099-DIV. Distributions from the Alaska Permanent Fund aren't. The state sends a notice of payment.

For folks in Alaska, if you're filing Form 1040EZ, enter your distribution from the Permanent Fund on line 3. For 1040 filers, it goes on line 21. In case you're asking who makes up these rules, aliens from outer space wouldn't be a wild guess.

Lines 14a and 14b: Social Security benefits

Yes, you have to pay tax on your Social Security benefits whenever your income is more than the income levels indicated on the worksheets in "Lines 20a and 20b: Social Security benefits" in Chapter 6.

Basically, if you're single and your gross income — lines 7, 8a, 8b, 9, 10, 11b, 12b, and 13, plus one half of your Social Security, minus your educator expense (line 16) and IRA (line 17) deductions — exceeds $25,000 ($32,000, if married), then up to 50 percent of your Social Security can be taxed. If you excluded income on U. S. Savings Bonds **(Form 8815, Exclusion of Interest from Series EE and I U.S. Savings Bonds Issued After 1989)** or for adoption benefits **(Form 8839, Qualified Adoption Expenses),** you must add these amounts to the total. See "Lines 20a and b," Chapter 6, for the items that go into this computation. And it gets worse. If you're single and the preceding computation exceeds $34,000 ($44,000 if married), as much as 85 percent of your Social Security can be added to your taxable income.

Enter on line 14a the amount from box 5 of **Form SSA-1099** (which reports the amount of Social Security you received). Also, don't forget to add the amount from your spouse's SSA-1099. These forms should be sent by the Social Security Administration by January 31, 2004. (If you've moved or haven't received mail for some other reason, you may need to contact the Social Security Administration at 800-772-1213 to find out where your Form SSA-1099 is.) To determine the taxable amount of your Social Security, you have to complete the Social Security worksheet provided in Chapter 6. Enter the taxable portion of your Social Security on line 14b. For most 1040A filers, none or very little of their Social Security should be subject to tax.

To make paying your taxes easier, Congress passed a law that enables you to have tax withheld on your Social Security at rates of 7 percent, 10 percent, 15 percent, or 25 percent, so that you won't owe a bundle next April 15. Send **Form W-4V, Voluntary Withholding Request** to the Social Security folks when you want tax withheld.

Line 15: Total income

Here you put the total of lines 7 through 14b. All those numbers to add!

Line 16: Educator expenses

Teachers who incur unreimbursed, out-of-pocket expenses for supplies that they bring to the classroom for the benefit of their students are entitled to deduct up to $250 for books, supplies, computer software and equipment, and supplemental material used in the classroom. Unless Congress extends this deduction, 2003 will be the last year it can be claimed. It had a short life of only two years, 2002 and 2003. We explain the fine print about who an eligible educator is, how to claim the deduction, and how the 900-hour school year rule applies in Chapter 7, line 23. Prior to this change in the law, teachers had to itemize their deductions to be able to deduct their out-of-pocket expenses. Don't forget that expenses in excess of the $250 that qualify for this deduction still can be claimed as an itemized deduction (see Chapter 9).

Line 17: Your (and your spouse's) IRA deduction

You're entitled to deduct up to $3,000 for contributions to IRAs. Do it if you can! However, if you're covered by a retirement plan at work, this deduction may be reduced or eliminated. See Chapters 7 and 21 for more than you can imagine about this issue. You have to make this computation based on the IRS rules and enter the amount on this line.

Tax-deductible and nondeductible IRAs, along with Roth IRAs, now are somewhat more flexible savings vehicles, with more people eligible to contribute to them. See Chapter 21 for details.

Let the IRS figure your tax

Instead of struggling with all the math, subtracting this from that, and looking up the tax for your tax bracket, the IRS will figure the tax for you. For 1040EZ and 1040A filers who don't want the hassle of doing the math, letting the IRS compute your tax after you enter your basic information on the forms is headache-free. If you're entitled to a refund, the IRS will send you a check. If you owe money, the IRS will bill you. And if you're entitled to the earned income credit or credit for the elderly or disabled, you don't have to spend hours filling out the forms.

Be careful, though: Even the IRS makes mistakes (no kidding!). If you're entitled to one of the credits, check the IRS computation (the credits will be itemized on it) when you receive your bill or refund check.

Here's how 1040EZ filers do it: On lines 1 through 8, fill in the lines that apply to you. If your income is less than $11,230, you could be entitled to the earned income credit. So print EIC on line 8, in the blank space to the right of the text, "Earned income credit (EIC)." By doing this, you alert the IRS that you're entitled to the earned income credit.

Attach your W-2s. Sign your return and send it to the IRS Service Center for your area. Ignore all the "subtract this line from that and enter it here" on Form 1040EZ. The IRS does all that fun stuff.

For 1040A filers, fill in any of lines 1 through 26 that apply. If you're entitled to a credit for child and dependent care expenses, you must complete Schedule 2 (the child and dependent care form) and attach it to your return. Enter the amount of credit on line 29.

If you're entitled to claim a credit for the elderly or the disabled, attach Schedule 3, and, on lines 1 through 9 of Schedule 3, check the box for your filing status (single, married, and so on). On Form 1040A, line 30, in the space to the right of the words "Schedule 3," print CFE. You won't have to tackle this nightmarish form. The IRS will prepare it for you.

If you're entitled to the earned income credit, the IRS will fill in the credit for you. Print EIC in the blank space on line 41. Fill in page 1 of Schedule EIC and attach it to your 1040A.

Fill in lines, 31, 32, 33, 34, and 37 if they apply.

Sign your return. Attach your W-2s and make sure that your Schedule 2 or 3 is attached if you're claiming any child-care or elderly and disabled credits. If you're claiming a child or adoption credit, attach those schedules. Mail your return to the IRS Service Center for your area.

Here's a warning, however: Although this method sounds EZ, it may lead to a false sense of security because you may overlook something like an important deduction that can work to your tax advantage. Also, the IRS is not infallible and may make an error.

The rules on line 17 also apply to your spouse's IRA. And even if your spouse isn't employed, you can also deduct $3,000 for him or her for a total deduction of $6,000 (again, see Chapter 7). You have to do the math and enter the amount here.

Not only has the IRA contribution limit been increased to $3,000 (that's $6,000 per couple), people who are age 50 or older can put away an extra $500 or $1,000 if both spouses are older than 50. In the years ahead, the contribution limits rise even more. For the details, please see Chapters 7 and 21.

Line 18: Student loan interest deduction

You can deduct up to $2,500 of interest that you paid on a loan used to pay for higher education (what comes after high school) and certain vocational school expenses. Ask the vocational school whether it qualifies for this deduction if you have to borrow to pay the tab. The interest you paid is reported on **Form 1098-E, Student Loan Interest Statement.**

A host of rules must be met before this deduction can be nailed down, the main one being that if you're single, the deduction quickly gets whittled away once your income hits $50,000 and disappears altogether at $65,000. For joint filers, it starts to shrink at $100,000 of income, with the deduction getting wiped out at $130,000. In Chapter 7, we explain who's entitled to the deduction, for how many years it can be claimed, and what loans and education expenses qualify. You can deduct interest for the full term of the loan rather than merely for 60 months, which was the case prior to 2002.

The beauty of the student loan interest deduction is that you don't have to itemize your deductions to claim it. You can claim the standard deduction (see "Line 24: Standard deduction") and this deduction. This interest deduction should be of great benefit to recent graduates.

Line 19: Tuition and fees deduction

A higher-education deduction of up to $3,000 is available, even if you don't itemize your deductions. The deduction can be claimed for you, your spouse, and your dependents. You can't claim this deduction for any person for whom you're claiming a Hope Scholarship or Lifetime Learning Credit (See Chapter 8, Line 47, Education credits). You don't have to be a full-time student to claim this deduction, and your income can't exceed $65,000 if single or $130,000 if filing a joint return. Unlike many other deductions and tax credits that have a phase-out range that entitles you to a partial deduction or credit, if your income exceeds the basic limits by even $1, you can kiss the higher-education deduction goodbye. Ouch! People who are married but filing separately are not eligible for this deduction. Flip ahead to Chapter 7, Line 26, "Tuition and fees deduction," for tips on planning for how to compute the deduction.

Sport, hobby, or noncredit courses don't qualify for the deduction, unless the course is either required as part of a degree program or taken to improve job skills.

Line 20: Total adjustments

Add lines 16 through 19. What could be easier?

Line 21: Adjusted gross income

Now you get to subtract the total of the deductions that you claimed on lines 16 through 19 and entered on line 20 from your total income (line 15). Do the subtraction and enter that amount here.

Don't forget that you may be entitled to an earned income credit if your adjusted gross income is less than $29,666 and one child lived with you. The cutoff is $33,692 if two children lived with you, and $11,230 if you don't have kids. These amounts are for single taxpayers. For married taxpayers, the amounts are $30,666, $34,692, and $12,230, respectively. See "Line 63: Earned income credit" in Chapter 8 for more details. Your tax is figured on page 2 of the form, so turn the page over.

Line 22: Successful transcription of adjusted gross income to back of Form 1040A

You enter your adjusted gross income on line 22 (which you already totaled on line 21). Be careful; don't transpose numbers!

Lines 23a and 23b: Standard deduction questions

Check the appropriate box(es). If you or your spouse is 65 or older or blind, you're entitled to an increased standard deduction. To figure the increased amount, refer to Table 9-1 (in Chapter 9), the standard deduction chart for people 65 or older or blind. Enter that amount on line 24.

If you're married filing separately and your spouse itemizes deductions, check box 23b and enter 0 on line 24. You aren't entitled to any standard deduction because both you and your spouse must use the same method. Unless you want to claim a zero standard deduction because your spouse is itemizing his or her deductions, you must abandon using Form 1040A to be able to itemize your deductions on the regular 1040.

Line 24: Standard deduction

So many choices! Find your filing status and enter the number here.

- Single: $4,750
- Head of household: $7,000
- Married filing jointly or qualifying widow(er): $9,500
- Married filing separately: $4,750

If you checked the first box on line 23a because you are older than 65, you're entitled to increase your standard deduction by $950 if married, and by $1,150 if single. If you checked box 23b, enter 0 on this line. For someone who is single, blind, and older than 65, the standard deduction is increased by $2,300 for a total of $7,050. If you and your spouse both are older than 65, your standard deduction of $9,500 increases by $1,900 for a total of $11,400. If all the boxes on line 23a are checked (older than 65 and blind), the increase in the standard deduction is $3,800, for a total of $13,300.

If your parent or someone else can claim you as a dependent, use Table 9-2 (in Chapter 9), the standard deduction worksheet for dependents, to compute your standard deduction. Enter that amount (instead of the standard deduction to which all others are entitled).

If you think that you can get a higher deduction by itemizing your deductions on Schedule A, you can't file with Form 1040A. The standard deduction versus itemized deduction option is available only when filing Form 1040.

Line 25: IRS subtraction quiz

Go ahead and subtract the amount you have on line 24 from your adjusted gross income on line 22. Put the result of this mathematical computation here. If you ended up with a number on line 24 that was larger than the one on line 22 (and you started to wonder how you can subtract a larger number from a smaller number), you have to start over from the beginning. No! Just kidding! If line 24 is larger than line 22, you place 0 on line 25.

Line 26: Total number of exemptions times $3,050

Multiply the number of exemptions you claimed on line 6d by $3,050 and enter the total here.

Line 27: Taxable income

Now subtract the amount on line 26 from line 25, and carefully place that number here. Well done! You've arrived at your taxable income.

Line 28: Find your tax

Using the tax tables (available at www.irs.gov) to find your tax means that you don't have to make a mathematical computation to figure your tax. For example, if you're single and your taxable income is $43,610, look up the bracket between $43,600 and $43,650 and read across to the single column. The appropriate tax is $7,716.

Unless you use the tax computation worksheet that we provide at line 41 in Chapter 8 or the qualified dividend and capital gain worksheet in the Form 1040A Instruction Booklet and you have entries on line 9b or lines 10a or b you probably will overpay your tax.

Line 29: Credit for child and dependent care expenses

Use Schedule 2 to figure this amount. See "Line 45: Credit for child and dependent care expenses" in Chapter 8 for more details.

Line 30: Credit for the elderly or the disabled

Use Schedule 3 to compute this credit. See "Line 46: Credit for the elderly or the disabled" in Chapter 8 for further explanation.

Line 31: Education credits

"The more you learn, the more you earn." The government likes it when you further your education because it can collect more tax.

Here is the lowdown on the *Hope Scholarship Credit* and the *Lifetime Learning Credit*. Remember that credits reduce your tax, dollar for dollar. Both credits are claimed on **Form 8863, Education Credits (Hope and Lifetime Learning Credits),** although you can't take both credits (for the same student) in the same year. The next two sections explain how the two credits work.

The Hope Scholarship Credit

This credit amounts to $1,500 per student per year for the first two years of college. The credit is equal to 100 percent of the first $1,000 of tuition expenses (but not room, board, or books) and 50 percent of the next $1,000 of tuition paid. The credit can be claimed for you, your spouse, and your dependents. But if you earn too much, you won't be eligible to claim the credit. For married taxpayers, the credit starts to phase out at $83,000 of income and is completely lost at $103,000. And if you're married, you have to file jointly to be entitled to the credit. For single taxpayers, the phaseout starts at $41,000 and is wiped out when their incomes reach $51,000. If students haven't completed their first two academic years as of the beginning of 2003, you still can claim the credit as long as you don't claim it for more than two years.

The credit isn't available for anyone convicted of possession or distribution of a controlled substance. And students must carry at least one half of the normal course load.

The Lifetime Learning Credit

This credit entitles you to a 20 percent credit on up to $10,000 of tuition expenses (but not room, board, or books) paid. This $2,000 credit (up from $1,000 last year) is per family and not per student, like the Hope Credit. The same income limits and stipulations about who can claim the credits that apply to the Hope Credit also apply to this credit. Unlike the Hope Credit, however, the student doesn't have to carry at least one half of the normal course load.

If for some reason you forgot to claim either credit in 2000, 2001, or 2002, you still can do so. But times are a-wasting. See Chapter 19 on how to amend a return.

The IRS can check to see whether you're entitled to either credit, because educational institutions now are required to issue **Form 1098-T, Tuition Payments Statement,** listing a student's name, Social Security number, whether the student was enrolled for at least half the full-time workload, whether the courses lead to a graduate level degree, and the amount of tuition paid.

You cannot claim any credit for tuition that was paid and then refunded. For example, if your child dropped a class after the beginning of a semester and tuition was refunded, turn to the section on line 47 in Chapter 8 to see how to handle this situation.

Here is how the two credits work in conjunction. For any individual student, you can claim only one of the credits. For example, say your daughter completed her second year of college in June of 2003 and started her third year of college in September. You can claim the Hope Credit for her 2003 second-year expenses, or the Learning Credit for all her 2003 expenses — but not both. For 2004 you no longer are entitled to claim the Hope Credit for her, but you can claim the Lifetime Learning Credit. In figuring eligible expenses, only the expenses paid in 2003 for the academic period beginning in 2003 and before April 1, 2004 count. You lose any benefit from the credit for 2003 if you pay tuition for a period after April 1, 2004.

You can't claim the Hope or the Lifetime Learning credit for a student and the tuition and fees deduction (line 19) during the same year. It's either one or the other.

The rules regarding which person among family members is eligible to claim these education credits have changed dramatically. These new rules apply to divorced parents where one parent claims the child as a dependent and the other parent foots the tuition bill or where, because of the income phase-out limits, a parent can't claim the credit. As a result, a way now exists for the student to claim the credit and shelter any income he or she might have. We explain these sophisticated tax-planning techniques at line 47 in Chapter 8.

Sport, hobby, or noncredit courses don't qualify for the credit, unless the course either is required as part of a degree program or is taken to improve job skills.

A host of education provisions are available. A tuition and fees deduction (line 19), easier-to-deduct student loan interest (line 18), and a number of enhancements to Education IRAs (recently dubbed *Coverdell Education Savings Accounts*) are a few of the education goodies contained in the new law (see Chapter 25, line 11).

Qualified tuition programs

Under a qualified tuition program, a parent, grandparent, or other donor purchases tuition credits or certificates for a child (the beneficiary) to pay for college. The amount contributed to the program is not tax deductible. Unlike the Coverdell program, your contributions (and the earnings on those contributions) to this kind of tuition program are not limited. Commonly referred to as Section 529 Plans, none of the earnings are taxable as long as what was saved is used for college expenses. Payments made by the plan are reported on **Form 1099-Q, Qualified Tuition Program Payments** (under Section 529). If any of the earnings have to be reported because money was paid out that wasn't used for college expenses, it gets reported on line 21 of Form 1040. So make sure the dough was used for what it was intended. See Chapter 25 for more about these programs.

Line 32: Retirement Contributions Credit

This credit is designed to encourage joint filers with incomes below $50,000 ($37,500 for heads of households and $25,000 for single filers) to save for retirement. You can claim a credit against your tax that's equal to a percentage/equivalent of up to the first $2,000 that you contribute to either a Roth, a Traditional IRA, a 401(k), or as elective deferrals to their employers' retirement plans. Now for the fine print! If money was taken out of one of these accounts between January 1, 2001, and the date that you file your 2003 return, including any extension of time to file, you must reduce the maximum $2,000 amount by the amount you withdrew. Whoo! For example, say you withdrew $1,500 from your IRA in 2001. Even though you contribute to your IRA the $3,000 maximum allowed in 2003, the maximum amount on which you can compute the credit is $500 ($2,000 – $1,500).

Depending on the amount of your income, the credit can be either 50 percent, 20 percent, or 10 percent of the first $2,000 you saved. Say you are single, earned less than $15,000, and put $1,500 into an IRA, your credit is $750 ($1,500 × 50 percent). Where did these percentages and income levels come from? **Form 8880, Credit for Qualified Retirement Savings Contributions.** This form is laid out as a worksheet. Don't be intimidated; it's only adding and subtracting.

Three other rules apply. You must be at least 18 by December 31, 2003, not someone else's dependent, and not a student enrolled full-time at a school during any five months of 2003. That means graduates of the class of June 2003 won't be eligible to claim the credit until 2004. Oh, by the way, the credit evaporates at midnight on December 31, 2006. A school includes technical, trade, and mechanical schools, but it does not include on-the-job training courses or correspondence schools.

Line 33: Child Tax Credit

Every child younger than 17 on December 31 who you can claim as a dependent can cut your tax bill by $1,000, if your income is less than $75,000 ($110,000 for joint returns, $55,000 for married persons filing separately). To claim the credit, your dependent must be either your son, daughter, adopted child, stepchild, foster child, grandchild, great-grandchild, or even your great-great-grandchild. The child also must be a U.S. citizen or resident.

The credit increases from $600 to $1,000 for 2003, and based on your 2002 tax return, the $400 difference, assuming you were entitled the maximum $600 in 2002, should already have been mailed to you last summer. Consequently, the $1,000 credit to which you're entitled to for 2003 must be reduced by the $400 you received last summer. Here's something that will pleasantly surprise you. If you received an advanced payment but can't claim the credit in 2003 because your income is too high, you don't have to pay back the advance. Even though the advanced payment was based on your 2002 return, rebate checks were not sent for children who wouldn't be younger than the age 17 cutoff as of December 31, 2003.

Divorced couples who take turns claiming the dependency exemption for a child every other year may end up facing a problem they never expected, because the parent who claimed the child in 2002 will have received the rebate check. As a result, parents who claim the dependency exemption for 2003 may *want* to claim the full $1,000 credit — because they didn't receive the rebate checks — but they won't be able to because $400 of the credit already has been disbursed to the other parent.

A child placed with you by an authorized placement agency for adoption is considered an adopted child, even if the adoption isn't final. A foster child has to live with you for the entire year. A child who was born and then died in that year qualifies.

Although part of your Child Tax Credit starts getting whittled away when your income exceeds $110,000 and you're filing jointly ($55,000 filing separately and $75,000 if you are single), Form 1040A filers can ignore these limits, because they can't use Form 1040A when their taxable incomes exceed $50,000. It would be extremely unusual if a married taxpayer's total income on a 1040A exceeded $110,000, for example, and the couple's taxable income was under $50,000. They would have to have about 16 kids to accomplish such a feat!

To compute the Child Tax Credit, the IRS directs you to a worksheet in your instruction booklet. We lay out a plain English version below. You can use this worksheet if your income doesn't exceed the $110,000, $55,000, and $75,000 limits just mentioned, or if you aren't claiming a credit for three or more kids and the Adoption Credit. If the rule just recited prevents you from using this worksheet, you must use the worksheet in Publication 972: *(Child Tax Credit)*.

Line 1: Based on the number of kids qualifying for the credit, enter the credit to which you are entitled (one kid $1,000, two kids $2,000, and so on). $_____

Line 2: Enter the amount of your advanced child tax credit. $_____

Line 3: Subtract line 2 from line 1. If line 2 is larger than line 1, you can't take this credit nor do you have to pay back the amount on line 2. $_____

Line 4: Enter your tax from line 28. $_____

Line 5: Enter the amounts from:

Credit for child and dependent care expenses — line 29 $_____

Credit for elderly — line 30 $_____

Education credit — line 31 $_____

Retirement savings contributions credit — line 32 $_____

Total the above amounts, if any $_____

Line 6: If the total of the amounts listed in line 5 is equal to or larger than line 4, you cannot claim a child tax credit because there is no tax to reduce. If line 4 is larger than line 5, subtract line 5 from line 4. $_____

Line 7: Is the amount on line 3 more than line 6? If yes, enter the amount from line 6. This is your Child Tax Credit, because the credit can't exceed the tax, but see the tip below because you may be entitled to the Additional Tax Credit. If line 3 is more than line 6, enter the amount from line 3. Carry this to line 33 of your 1040A. $_____

This credit comes in two varieties:

- ✔ **The Child Tax Credit:** Most people who are eligible to claim this credit will find it easy to compute by following the preceding line-by-line instructions.

- ✔ **The Additional Child Tax Credit:** This one comes into play when the regular Child Tax Credit exceeds your tax. People with three or more kids get to compute the refundable credit two ways and then choose the method that produces the largest refund. If you have fewer than three kids, you can use only one method, which — if nothing else — makes your tax return less complicated. You compute whether you are entitled to the additional credit on **Form 8812, Additional Child Tax Credit.** Enter the amount from line 13 of Form 8812 on line 42.

Line 34: Adoption credit (Form 8839)

Both the adoption credit and the exemption from income for employer-reimbursed adoption expenses increased by $160 to $10,160. The income phaseout range where the credit begins to disappear before your eyes is between $152,390 and $192,390.

In 2003, if you adopt a child with special needs, you can claim the credit even if you didn't incur adoption expenses (see Chapter 25).

If your employer pays or reimburses you for the adoption expenses, you don't get to claim the credit, but you don't have to pay tax on the first $10,160 that you receive. Both the credit and exemption are computed on **Form 8839, Qualified Adoption Expenses.** The amount of the credit you're entitled to per line 18 of the form is entered on line 34. If your employer reimbursed your adoption expenses, or paid them directly, the amount reimbursed that escapes tax is computed on page 2 of Form 8839. See "Line 50" in Chapter 8 to determine what expenses qualify, what adoptions qualify, when the credit starts to evaporate as your income gets too high, and when the credit is due to expire.

Line 35: Total credits

Compute your total credits, add the amounts from lines 29 through 34, and enter them here.

Line 36: Another IRS subtraction problem

Gee whiz, it never ends, does it? Now subtract your total credits (line 35) from the amount on line 28. Enter that remainder here. However, if your total credits are more than the amount on line 28, you get the easy way out and can enter 0.

Line 37: Advance earned income payments

This amount is in box 9 of your W-2s, which your employer provides for you.

This is a smart move. By filing **Form W-5, EIC Advance Payment Certificate,** with your employer, you don't have to wait until you file your return to claim this credit. Depending on the amount of your wages, up to $1,528 (the 2003 maximum amount — it increases every year) can be added to your paycheck throughout the year. This advance payment is only available when you have at least one qualifying child — see line 6 in Chapter 8.

Line 38: Total tax

Add lines 36 and 37 to arrive at your total tax.

Line 39: Total federal income tax withheld

Get this amount from box 2 of your W-2s or box 2 of your W-2G. And don't forget to add in any tax withheld and listed in box 4 of Forms 1099-INT, 1099-R, and 1099-DIV. These forms report the amount of federal income tax you already paid during the tax year — you want to make sure that you get credit for the total tax withheld from your income. Otherwise, you'll double-pay!

Line 40: 2003 estimated tax payments and amount applied from 2002 return

If you made quarterly tax payments, enter the amount here. You can be penalized for not paying at least 90 percent of your tax by means of withholding and quarterly tax payments. The IRS doesn't like to wait until April 15 to collect most of the tax you owe. For more on estimated tax penalties, see Chapter 19.

If you have income such as interest, dividends, pension, and IRA withdrawals, and the tax you owe for 2003 after what was withheld will be at least $1,000, you should have been making quarterly estimated payments on **Form 1040ES, Estimated Tax for Individuals.** If you don't meet one of the exceptions to this rule, you'll be penalized (see "Line 73" in Chapter 8). See also Chapter 15 to determine whether you have to make estimated tax payments for 2004.

Line 41: Earned income credit

You may be entitled to an earned income credit if your AGI (line 22) is less than $34,692 and two children lived with you, or $30,666 if one child lived with you (less than $12,230 if no child lived with you). These AGI limits are for joint filers. For single or head of household filers, the AGI limits are $11,230 with no kids, $29,666 with one child, and $33,692 with two kids. See "Line 63: Earned income credit" in Chapter 8 for more details. If you qualify for the credit and have a qualifying child, you must fill out **Schedule EIC** (earned income credit) and attach it to your return.

The credit can be as high $4,204 for someone with two kids. The exact amount of the credit is based on your income, filing status (married or single) and whether you have one, two, or no children. If the credit exceeds your tax, the difference is refundable. Not bad!

Anyone who fraudulently claims the earned income credit is declared ineligible to claim it for ten years. For people who are reckless or intentionally disregard the rules, the penalty is two years. The IRS initiated a program this year where 25,000 filers must precertify that their children lived with them for more than 6 months to be eligible for the credit. The IRS actually wanted to contact twice as many filers, but Congress wouldn't let them.

Line 42: Additional Child Tax Credit

This is the refundable portion of the Child Tax Credit that we explain in "Line 33: Child Tax Credit." To get part of the credit refunded, you have to file **Form 8812, Additional Child Tax Credit.** Flip back to line 33 for a quick refresher.

Line 43: Total payments

Now you get to add. Find the sum of lines 39, 40, 41, and 42.

Line 44: We smell refund!

Subtract your total tax (line 38) from your total payments (line 43) — if line 38 is smaller than line 43. Here's your refund! Don't spend it all in one place.

Although refunds are fun, large ones are a sign that you made the IRS an interest-free loan. More was withheld from your salary than should have been. You can lower the amount of tax withheld by filing Form W-4 with your employer's payroll department. See "Form W-4" in Chapter 15 for a quick guide through this form.

Lines 45a and 46: What to do with your refund

If you have a refund but think you're going to owe tax in 2004 and can't trust yourself to hang on to the cash, you may want to apply some or all of the refund toward next year's tax (do this on line 46).

Applying the refund toward next year's tax is an excellent option for people who must make quarterly estimated payments, because doing so can significantly reduce the amount of those payments, and perhaps even eliminate the first of those payments, which is due on April 15, 2004. This way your money works for you. For example, say you must make an estimated payment of $1,500 for 2004 on April 15, and you've overpaid your 2003 taxes by $1,000 (which shows up as a refund on your 2003 return). If you apply the entire $1,000 overpayment toward the $1,500 estimated tax that is due, you have to pay only $500 instead of paying the full $1,500 and having to wait for your $1,000 refund. Once you make this choice, you can't change your mind and ask for it back. It can, however, be claimed as an additional payment on your 2004 return.

Lines 45b–d: Direct deposit of your refund

You can speed up the receipt of your refund by almost three weeks and minimize the chances of its loss or theft by requesting that it be deposited directly to your account. *Note:* Consider whether you want to share this type of confidential and personal information — your bank account numbers. See the instructions under "Filling out a 1040EZ," earlier in this chapter. If you want your refund extra pronto (up to almost three weeks sooner), jot down the routing number from one of your checks on line 45b. (That's the nine-digit number shown in Figure 5-2.) On line 45c, check the type of account. Your account number is the number to the right of your routing number as shown in Figure 5-2; enter your account number on line 45d.

Line 47: Amount you owe

Those are three of the most dreaded words in the English language. If the amount on line 38 is greater than that on line 43, subtract line 43 from line 38. Put your Social Security number on the check and write 2003 FORM 1040A on the line at the bottom left of your check. Make out the check to the United States Treasury.

If you want to charge what you owe on a credit card, go back to line 12 in the section on filling out a 1040EZ for the ins and outs on how to do this. (Before you whip out your plastic, though, read our cautions at the end of "Line 12: Payment due" in the "Filling Out a 1040EZ" section, earlier in this chapter.) You can also have the IRS withdraw the balance you owe directly from your account. How's that for a friendlier IRS!

Line 48: Estimated tax penalty

If you owe $1,000 or more in tax, and the sum of the estimated tax payments you made in 2003 plus your withholding doesn't equal 90 percent of your tax, you'll be assessed a penalty. You can escape this penalty in a number of ways. Turn to "Line 73" in Chapter 8 to see if there's hope for you. **Form 2210, Underpayment of Estimated Tax,** is used to both compute or to escape the penalty. Chapter 19 has valid excuses that should work.

Final Instructions

Put your John or Jane Hancock(s) on your form. (That means sign it, okay? Don't get funny and write in *John Hancock;* the IRS doesn't have our sense of humor.) Attach your W-2s and any 1099s where tax was withheld, as well as your check or money order (if required) to the form and mail it to the IRS Service Center for your area. Check out the IRS Web site for the correct address if you're missing the preaddressed envelope that comes with your Form 1040A instruction booklet.

The IRS offers another way for you to file your return — electronically — so flip back to "How to file" in Chapter 4, if you find this method intriguing.

Chapter 6

Form 1040: Income Stuff

Surely you remember the old war slogan "Divide and conquer!" (We think Alexander the Great or some other real famous warrior said it.) Well, that's our strategy here. We break down each section and each line of Form 1040 and pound each one into submission.

Note: You're going to be jumping into a deeper section of the pool here. If you're unsure about which Form 1040 to use (EZ, A, or the "long" version), you need to take one step back to Chapter 5. Likewise, if you're unsure of your filing status (single, married filing separately, married filing jointly, head of household), take two steps back to Chapter 4.

Now for Chapter 6, which deals with the guts of the return, the income section (see Figure 6-1). Each heading has the specific line references of Form 1040 listed first. After you go through a segment, plug the correct number onto the same line of your 1040 and move on.

Income	7	Wages, salaries, tips, etc. Attach Form(s) W-2		7	
	8a	**Taxable** interest. Attach Schedule B if required		8a	
Attach Forms W-2 and W-2G here. Also attach Form(s) 1099-R if tax was withheld.	b	**Tax-exempt** interest. **Do not** include on line 8a	8b		
	9a	Ordinary dividends. Attach Schedule B if required		9a	
	b	Qualified dividends (see page 23)	9b		
	10	Taxable refunds, credits, or offsets of state and local income taxes (see page 23)		10	
	11	Alimony received		11	
	12	Business income or (loss). Attach Schedule C or C-EZ		12	
	13a	Capital gain or (loss). Attach Schedule D if required. If not required, check here ▶ ☐		13a	
	b	If box on 13a is checked, enter post-May 5 capital gain distributions	13b		
If you did not get a W-2, see page 22.	14	Other gains or (losses). Attach Form 4797		14	
	15a	IRA distributions	15a	b Taxable amount (see page 25)	15b	
	16a	Pensions and annuities	16a	b Taxable amount (see page 25)	16b	
Enclose, but do not attach, any payment. Also, please use Form 1040-V.	17	Rental real estate, royalties, partnerships, S corporations, trusts, etc. Attach Schedule E		17	
	18	Farm income or (loss). Attach Schedule F		18	
	19	Unemployment compensation		19	
	20a	Social security benefits	20a	b Taxable amount (see page 27)	20b	
	21	Other income. List type and amount (see page 27)		21	
	22	Add the amounts in the far right column for lines 7 through 21. This is your **total income** ▶		22	

Figure 6-1: The Income section of Form 1040 lists how much you made in 2003.

Lines 6a–6d: Exemptions

We don't like to repeat ourselves, so go back to our explanation in Chapter 5 on Form 1040EZ to find out how to complete lines 6a through 6d.

Lines 7–22: Income

Income is, in brief, money or something else of value that you receive regardless of whether you work for it.

Most people know that wages earned from toiling away at jobs are *income.* But income also includes alimony, certain interest, dividends, and profits on your investments, and even your lottery winnings or prizes won on *Wheel of Fortune.*

All people who work for an employer will receive the famous **Form W-2, Wage and Tax Statement,** which your employer issues at tax-year's end. That form helps you find out what you earned during the year and what was taken away from you.

In this chapter, you discover the meaning of all those various boxes on your W-2 (your regular income stuff). We show you how to use this and other information to complete all those other line numbers in the big section of Form 1040 called "Income," lines 7 through 22. These lines are the guts of your return. So we not only make sure you get it right, we also point out the tax savings techniques you need to employ.

We must warn you that you may become dejected to see your other nonemployment income (which you report in the lines ahead) as taxable income. We'll make sure that we highlight foolproof ways to keep this tragedy from happening again next year.

You can round off to the nearest dollar, so you don't have to fiddle with pennies. (See the sidebar, "Rounding off dollars," in Chapter 5.) It only takes a minute or two; we promise.

Line 7: Wages, salaries, tips

To fill in the blank on line 7, scrounge around for your W-2 (see Figure 6-2). You should receive your W-2 from your employer by January 31, 2004. It's a three-part form. Why three parts? Copy B gets mailed with the federal return; Copy C is filed with your neat and organized tax records; and the state copy is affixed to your state return. Your employer sent Copy A to the folks at the Social Security Administration. If you look at the lower-left corner of your W-2s, you see what to do with each copy.

If you're self-employed and you don't receive a W-2, you get to skip this line, but you're going to end up doing tons more work completing Schedule C so you can fill in line 12 of the 1040. For farmers, it's Schedule F. Retirees can skip 'em both — one of the many perks of retirement!

If your W-2 is wrong, contact your employer to have it corrected as soon as possible. Otherwise, you'll pay too much or too little tax — and you wouldn't want to do that. If you didn't receive your W-2, call your employer. If that doesn't work, file **Form 4852, Employees' Substitute Wage and Tax Statement,** which is a substitute for missing W-2s (and missing 1099-Rs). The magnanimous IRS allows you to estimate your salary and the amount of tax withheld on this form. You then attach Form 4852 to your tax return. You can get that form or any other form by calling the IRS toll-free (800-829-3676) or downloading it from the IRS Web site at www.irs.gov.

What those W-2 boxes mean

Each of the numbered boxes on your W-2 contains either welcome information (like your gross income, which momentarily makes you feel rich) or the type of information that surely will have you shaking your head in disbelief (like the total amount of different types of taxes that you paid throughout the year, which effectively makes you feel poor again). If you notice in the discussion ahead that we're skipping over some of those silly little boxes, rest assured that we explain them when we need to in the chapters ahead.

a Control number		22222	Void ☐	For Official Use Only ▶ OMB No. 1545-0008		

b Employer identification number		1 Wages, tips, other compensation $	2 Federal income tax withheld $
c Employer's name, address, and ZIP code		3 Social security wages $	4 Social security tax withheld $
		5 Medicare wages and tips $	6 Medicare tax withheld $
		7 Social security tips $	8 Allocated tips $
d Employee's social security number		9 Advance EIC payment $	10 Dependent care benefits $
e Employee's first name and initial	Last name	11 Nonqualified plans $	12a See instructions for box 12 $
		13 Statutory employee ☐ Retirement plan ☐ Third-party sick pay ☐	12b $
		14 Other	12c $
			12d $
f Employee's address and ZIP code			

15 State	Employer's state ID number	16 State wages, tips, etc. $	17 State income tax $	18 Local wages, tips, etc. $	19 Local income tax $	20 Locality name
		$	$	$	$	

Form **W-2** Wage and Tax Statement (99) **2003**

Copy A **For Social Security Administration**—Send this entire page with Form W-3 to the Social Security Administration; photocopies are **not** acceptable.

Cat. No. 10134D

Department of the Treasury—Internal Revenue Service
For Privacy Act and Paperwork Reduction Act Notice, see separate instructions.

Do Not Cut, Fold, or Staple Forms on This Page — Do Not Cut, Fold, or Staple Forms on This Page

Figure 6-2: Form W-2 shows how much dough you earned and how much you paid in various taxes to the government.

Box 1: Wages, tips, and other compensation

Your taxable wages, tips, other compensation, and taxable fringe benefits are listed here. This is a biggie. Everything but the kitchen sink was thrown into box 1. Common examples are your salary, your tips, and the taxable portion of any fringe benefits like the personal-use part of your company car. Other stuff that your employer tossed into box 1 includes back pay, bonuses, commissions, severance or dismissal pay, and vacation pay. That whopping $7 per day that you were paid for jury duty isn't reported on your W-2. It gets reported on line 21 of your 1040.

Because box 1 is a catchall, the figure in it may be larger than your actual cash salary. Get it over with — fill in the amount on line 7. If you have one or more W-2s, add 'em up and put in the total.

Box 8: Allocated tips

If you worked in a restaurant and didn't report all your tip income to your employer, box 8 includes the difference between your share of at least 8 percent of the restaurant's income and what you reported. This amount doesn't mean that you're entitled to this money. Your employer figures what 8 percent of the restaurant's income amounts to. This is the minimum amount of tip income the employees have to pay tax on. Your employer then computes your share, which doesn't let you off the hook. The IRS can always audit the restaurant's books and determine, for example, that the tip rate was in fact 15 percent. Ouch! This income is not reported in box 1. Therefore, you must add it to the amount on Form 1040 (line 7). You must also enter this amount on **Form 4137, Social Security and Medicare Tax on Unreported Tip Income.** You get an earful about this form in the section "Line 56: Social Security and Medicare tax on unreported tip income," in Chapter 8.

Box 9: Advance EIC (Earned Income Credit) payment

If you're filing jointly and your income is less than $34,693 with two or more qualifying dependents, less than $30,666 with one dependent, or less than $12,230 and no dependents, you may be entitled to the earned income credit (see the stuff under "Line 63: Earned income credit" in Chapter 8 for more information). Here are the income limits that apply to single or head of household filers to determine their EIC eligibility: no qualifying kids, $11,230; one child, $29,666; and two kids, $33,692. If you have at least one child and your salary is less than $29,666 (2003 amount for single or head of household filers) or $30,666 for joint filers, you can file **Form W-5, EIC Advance Payment Certificate** with your employer, and instead of waiting until you file your return to have this credit refunded, you can have up to $1,528 added to your paycheck throughout the year.

You can obtain this form from your employer or by calling the IRS at 800-829-3676.

The purpose of the EIC is to refund a portion of the Social Security and Medicare tax to low-income workers if their income is below the appropriate income threshold discussed in the preceding paragraph.

Box 10: Dependent-care benefits

If your employer has a day-care plan or provides day-care services, this box includes the reimbursement from your employer for day-care costs or the value of the day-care services that your employer provides. The amount in box 10 above $5,000 is taxable and is also included in box 1. Don't report it again!

To determine whether any portion of the amount below $5,000 is taxable, you have to complete Part III of **Form 2441, Child and Dependent Care Expenses.** If any part of that amount is taxable, include it with the amount that you enter on line 7 of Form 1040. Next to that total write DCB (which stands for dependent care benefits). The reason that you're being directed to Form 2441 is that the portion of the tax-free child-care benefits that you received reduces the amount of your child-care and dependent-care expenses that are eligible for the child-care credit. If you forfeited any of your dependent-care or flexible-spending account because you didn't incur the expense, cruise over to Chapter 15 where we explain how to handle this situation when preparing Form 2441.

Box 12: See Instructions for Box 12

This cryptic message is meant to direct you to the instructions on the reverse side of your W-2 to find out what the symbols in this box mean. This box includes your 401(k) contributions, the premium on group life insurance of more than $50,000 (that amount also is included in box 1), nontaxable sick pay, employer contributions to your medical savings account, and uncollected Social Security and Medicare taxes on tips that you reported to your employer (and that your employer wasn't able to collect from you — the letter "A" will be next to the amount). Uncollected Social Security tax is added to your final tax bill and is reported on Form 1040 (line 60) along with other taxes that you owe. Next to it, write UT, which stands for *uncollected tax on tips.* A list of codes, A through V, on the back of your W-2 explains what each code stands for in box 12. Some of the items entered in boxes 12a through 12d also are entered in box 1 (Wages); others aren't. Make sure that you don't enter on line 7 of your 1040 something that was already included box 1. You don't want to pay more tax than you have to, do you? A silly question, but we thought we'd ask it anyhow.

Box 13: Statutory employee

Full-time life insurance salespeople, agents, commission drivers, traveling salespeople, and certain home-workers can file as self-employed rather than as employees. This status enables them to deduct their business expenses on **Form 1040, Schedule C (Profit or Loss From Business)** or on **Schedule C-EZ.**

Don't report the amount of your W-2's box 1 on line 7 of your Form 1040 if you want to deduct your business expenses *and* "Statutory Employee" in box 13 is checked. Report your wages and expenses on Schedule C or Schedule C-EZ. By doing it this way, you will be able to deduct all your travel, entertainment, auto, and other business-related expenses instead of having to claim them as itemized deductions. (See Chapter 11 for loads of Schedule C stuff.) Line 1 of Schedules C and C-EZ has a box to check if you are claiming business expenses as a statutory employee. Business expenses taken as itemized deductions are reduced by 2 percent of your *adjusted gross income (AGI)* and then shaved a second time if your income is too high. It also keeps these expenses out of the clutches of the dreaded *Alternative Minimum Tax (AMT),* which we explain in Chapter 8. So reporting business expenses on Schedule C clearly is to your advantage. Additionally, deducting these expenses on Schedule C lowers your AGI, which means that you pay less tax. You can do this stuff only if the statutory employee box is checked.

Line 8a: Taxable interest income

If your interest income (from boxes 1 and 3 of all your **Form 1099-INTs**) is $1,500 or less, enter the amount on this line. If this amount is more than $1,500, you must complete Schedule B. No biggie! Schedule B is easy to complete. For more information, you have permission to cruise to Chapter 10 to dive further into that schedule. When you get the total, come back and fill it in. With the exception of municipal bonds, all the interest that you earn is taxable. If you need examples, the IRS publications have pages of them. But don't report the interest that you earn on your IRA or retirement account; that interest is taxed only when you withdraw the funds.

If you keep lots of your money in bank accounts, you may be missing out on free opportunities to earn higher interest rates. Chapter 23 discusses money market funds, a higher yielding alternative to bank accounts.

Different definitions of what you earned

Many of the boxes on your W-2 include wage information that you don't need to include on your Form 1040. Think of them as FYI boxes. They simply show you the different ways that the IRS computes income for assessing different taxes.

For example, box 3, "Social Security wages," reports the amount of your wages for the tax year that is subject to Social Security taxation (not the benefits that the Social Security Administration is paying you!). Your Social Security wages may differ from your wages as reported in box 1 because some types of income are exempt from income tax but are not exempt from Social Security tax. For example, if you put $3,000 in a 401(k) retirement plan in 2003, box 3 is going to be $3,000 higher than box 1.

Box 5, "Medicare wages and tips," reports the amount of your wages that is subject to Medicare tax. For most people, their wages that are subject to Medicare equal their total wages that are reported in box 1. Although the amount of your wages that is subject to Social Security tax is 6.2 percent up to $87,000, there is no maximum on wages subject to the 1.45 percent Medicare tax.

Box 7, "Social Security tips," is the amount of tips that you received and reported to your employer. This amount is included in box 1, so don't count it again!

Box 11, "Nonqualified plans," pertains to retirement plans in which you can't defer the tax. Distributions to an employee from a nonqualified or a nongovernmental Section 457 (Deferred Compensation Plan) are reported in box 11 and in box 1. Distributions from governmental Section 457 plans are reported on Form 1099-R. Be thankful that this applies to only a few people.

Box 12, "See instructions for box 12," is for entering 401(k) contributions (code D), adoption benefits (T), Archer medical savings accounts (R), and excludable moving expenses (P). Taxable fringe benefits, such as your personal use of a company car and reimbursed employee business expenses, are included in box 1 of your W-2 and not here.

The first $5,250 of employer-paid educational expenses is tax-free. Although benefits above that amount are taxable, see Chapter 9, lines 20–26, to determine whether you can claim a deduction for any portion of the taxable amount. The exclusion now applies to graduate-level courses. Aren't you glad you went back to school so that you can understand all this stuff? Up to $190 per month of employer-provided parking and $100 per month for the total of commuter transit passes and commuter van pools are considered tax-free fringe benefits (these are the 2003 amounts). If, however, you opt for the cash, they're taxable.

Also, if you're in a higher tax bracket, you may be able to earn a higher return with your savings by choosing tax-free investments instead of keeping money in bank accounts. (You're in the 25 percent federal income tax bracket beginning at $28,400 in taxable income — line 40 on the 1040 — as a single filer, or $56,800 as a married couple filing jointly.) See Chapter 23 to learn how to keep more of your investment income.

Line 8b: Tax-exempt interest

Because municipal bond interest is not taxable, you're not going to receive a 1099. Your year-end statement from your stockbroker includes this information. The IRS wants you to fill in the interest that you received on tax-exempt bonds. Plug it in. Just so you know: Although this interest isn't taxable, the number is used to compute how much of your Social Security benefits may be subject to tax.

Surprisingly, some people who invest money in tax-exempt bonds actually shouldn't. These people often are not in a high enough income tax bracket to benefit. If your taxable income isn't at least $28,400 if you're filing as a single (or $56,800 if married filing jointly), you shouldn't be so heavily into tax-exempt bonds. You'd be better off moving at least some of your money into taxable bonds or stocks (where gains can be taxed at rates as low as 5 percent, 10 percent, or 15 percent). See Chapter 23 for more information about investments that are subject to more favorable tax rates.

Line 9a: Ordinary dividends income

Dividends are income that you receive from stocks and mutual funds that you own. They're reported on **Form 1099-DIV, Dividends and Distributions.** Most people receive dividends that are either classified as ordinary, qualified (which are subject to reduced tax rates), capital gain distributions (which also are taxed at reduced tax rates), and nontaxable. Be careful, though: You don't have to own a $100,000 nest egg to fill in this line; you may own one or two mutual funds and need to put some information here.

Once upon a time ordinary dividends came in one flavor, taxed at the same rate as other income. Now ordinary dividends come in two categories. The first category is the total of the amounts reported in box 1a on all the Forms 1099-DIV that you receive. That total is entered on line 9a. The other category is called *qualified dividends*. They're the kind of dividends that qualify (or make the grade) for the reduced 15 percent or 5 percent tax rates. Normally the maximum tax rate on qualified dividends is 15 percent, but the rate drops to 5 percent for taxpayers whose taxable incomes (line 40) place them in the 10 percent or 15 percent tax brackets. The total of your qualified dividends, which are reported to you in box 1b, Forms 1099-DIV, is entered on line 9b. Lines 9a and b tell the IRS which of your dividends are taxed at lower rates and which are not.

The portion of your total dividends (line 9a) less your qualified dividends (line 9b) ends up getting taxed at the rate for whatever bracket in which your taxable income (line 40) places you. Now that couldn't be simpler, could it?

You need to understand when a dividend is and isn't a dividend to find out whether yours qualifies for the reduced rate. Sound confusing? Well you can blame financial institutions that carelessly label distributions as dividends when they really are not. Banks loosely refer to distributions paid investors and depositors for money-market funds, bond funds, and other investment accounts as dividends, when they clearly are interest payments and, under the new law, must be reported as such on your return.

Only dividends paid to shareholders of U.S. corporations, foreign corporations traded on a U.S. stock exchange, or foreign corporations that either are incorporated in a U.S. possession or are from a country that has full tax treaty benefits with the U.S are eligible for the reduced rate. So brokerage firms, mutual funds, banks, and corporations must clean up their dividend labeling acts, or many of their customers will end up paying more tax than required or perhaps considerably less than they have to. We figure that not many people will complain when these financial institutions get it wrong and their customers end up paying less tax.

In Chapter 10, we give you the lowdown on which types of dividends qualify for the reduced rates and on all the rules that must be met so that you pay less tax on qualified dividends.

This year you must pay closer attention than ever before to the 2003 Forms 1099-DIV that you receive.

When your dividend income is less than $1,500, enter the amount from boxes 1a and b on lines 9a and b. If you have more than $1,500 in dividend income, you must fill out Schedule B. Again, we send you to Chapter 10 to find out how to complete Schedule B.

Line 9b: Qualified dividends

Enter the total of the qualified dividends from boxes 1b of all your Forms 1099-DIV on this line. Flip back to line 9a for a quick refresher on qualified and total dividends and how each category is taxed. We also go into reporting dividend income in greater detail in Chapter 10.

Qualified dividends are taxed at the same 15 percent rate as capital gains. However, your qualified dividend income is taxed at 5 percent when your taxable income (line 27) falls below $28,400 and your filing status is single or married filing separately, $56,800 when married and filing jointly, or $38,050 when filing as a head of household. You probably find this hard to believe, but starting in 2008, the 5 percent rate drops to zero for people with incomes below these levels.

Unless you use the tax computation worksheet that we provide at line 41 in Chapter 8 or the qualified dividend and capital gain worksheet in the Form 1040A Instruction Booklet, *you will overpay your tax.* Paying what you have to is bad enough, but if you ignore our advice and end up paying more, don't expect any thank-yous from the IRS. On the other hand, if you have only $10 of qualified dividends, and you don't have a tax software program that automatically calculates your tax, we'll understand when you decide that making the computations necessary for your $10 to be taxed at the lower 5 percent or 15 percent rates is hardly worth the hassle.

Capital gain dividends reported on Form 1099-DIV are entered on line 13 of Schedule D. If your capital gain distributions are your only capital gains or losses for the year, you may be able to skip filling out Schedule D. See the sections "Line 13a: Capital gain (or loss)" and "Line 13b: Post-May 5 capital gain distributions" later in this chapter to find out more about capital gain dividends.

Line 10: Taxable refunds, credits, or offsets of state and local income taxes

As a general rule, state and local income tax refunds are taxable because you deducted your state tax payments on last year's federal income tax return as an itemized deduction.

State and local tax refunds that you receive are reported on **Form 1099-G,** a form that your state department of revenue sends to you. If you chose to apply part or all of your 2002 state tax overpayment to your 2003 estimated state or local tax payments that you have to make (instead of having it refunded), the overpayment still is considered a refund even though a check wasn't sent to you. Box 2 of Form 1099-G has the amount of your refund.

But, like just about every tax rule, there is an exception. For example, your refund isn't taxable if you claimed the standard deduction in a prior year instead of itemizing your deductions.

Even though you may itemize your deductions, only the part of your refund that represents the amount of your itemized deductions in excess of the standard deduction is taxable. That means you have to do some number crunching to make this computation. The following worksheet (see Table 6-1) gives you the answer. Suppose that your 2002 state refund was $800, you filed jointly, and your itemized deductions were $8,150.

Table 6-1	State and Local Income Tax Refund Worksheet		
		Example	*Your Computation*
1.	Enter the income tax refund from Form(s) 1099-G (or similar statement).	1. $800	1.
2.	Enter your total allowable itemized deductions from your 2002 Schedule A (line 28).	2. $8,150	2.
3.	Enter on line 3 the amount shown below for the filing status claimed on your 2002 Form 1040: Single — $4,700 Married filing jointly or Qualifying widow(er) — $7,850 Married filing separately — $3,925 Head of household — $6,900	3. $7,850	3.
4.	If you didn't complete line 37a on your 2002 Form 1040, enter -0-. Otherwise, multiply the number on your 2002 Form 1040, line 37a, by $900 ($1,150 if your 2002 filing status was single or head of household) and enter the result.	4. $0	4.
5.	Add lines 3 and 4.	5. $7,850	5.
6.	Subtract line 5 from line 2. If zero or less, enter -0-.	6. $300	6.
7.	Taxable part of your refund. Enter the smaller of line 1 or line 6 here and on Form 1040, line 10.	7. $300	7.

Line 11: Alimony received (by you)

Because the person who pays the alimony can deduct these payments from his or her taxable income (on line 32a), the spouse who receives these payments must include alimony as taxable income. You report alimony received on line 11. You'll know the figure to enter by consulting the divorce decree or separation agreement.

You need to know what alimony is before you can report it as income or deduct it as an expense. The alimony rules aren't simple — Why should they be? Why simplify divorce? — but we've tried our best to clear them up. We offer a more detailed explanation of alimony in the section, "Lines 32a and b: Alimony paid," in Chapter 7.

Here's an important tip about alimony and about separate maintenance payments and IRAs. These payments are considered income from employment that entitles you to set up and make deductible contributions to an IRA. Basically, if you receive taxable alimony, you can set up an IRA and deduct what you contribute to it — 100 percent of your alimony and employment income up to $3,000, if any, is deductible. However, your deduction may be reduced or eliminated if you're covered by a retirement plan through your work. See Chapter 21 for more on how to set up IRAs. Chapters 7 and 21 give the lowdown on both deductible IRAs and the new Roth IRA.

If you're older than 50, you can contribute an additional $500 to an IRA. The increased amounts for the catch-up contribution are explained in Chapters 7 and 27.

Line 12: Business income (or loss)

If you're self-employed, you must complete a Schedule C to report your business income and expenses. If you just receive an occasional fee and don't have any business expenses, you can report that fee on line 21 as other income. And remember, if you're a *statutory employee* (a life insurance salesperson, agent, commission driver, or traveling salesperson, for example), report the wages shown in box 1 of your W-2 form on Schedule C along with your expenses. How do you know if you're a statutory employee? Simple, box 13 of your W-2 will be checked. For a quick reminder on this statutory employee title, flip back to "What those W-2 boxes mean" at the beginning of the chapter.

As a general rule, you're better off reporting your self-employment income on Schedule C, if you're eligible to do that. Although slightly more complicated than entering your income on line 21, you can deduct business-related expenses against your income on Schedule C, and that can lower your income and the tax that you have to pay.

The amount that you enter on line 12 is the result of figuring and jumbling that you do on Schedules C or C-EZ, which is a shorter version. Check out Chapter 11 to dive into that material.

Line 13a: Capital gain (or loss)

You don't have to be Bill Gates to have a capital gain or loss. (We bet that Bill has mostly gains. How about you?) You have a capital gain when you sell stocks or bonds or investment property for a profit. When you sell an asset like your house for a profit, you have a gain that may be taxable (we cover the rules on the exclusion from tax on home sales in Chapter 12), but you have a nondeductible loss if you lose money on the sale of your house. Losses on other investments — such as stocks, bonds, and mutual funds — made outside of retirement accounts are generally deductible. Capital gains and losses get reported on Schedule D with the net result being reported here. If all you have are capital gain distributions from a mutual fund, you can skip Schedule D and enter your capital gain distribution(s) on lines 13a and b. Don't forget to check that little box to the left of the amount you entered on line 13a, if under this rule you're not required to file Schedule D. See Chapter 12 for a more in-depth explanation of capital gains and losses and of Schedule D.

Guess what? Just like dividends, capital gain distributions from mutual funds now come in two varieties: distributions received before May 6, 2003, and distributions received on or after that date. May 6, 2003, is of extreme importance, because the new law that went into effect then reduces the maximum tax rate on capital gain distributions from 20 percent to 15 percent. However, only gains received on or after May 6, 2003, are eligible for the new rate. An even lower 5 percent rate applies to gains after this date for anyone whose taxable income (line 40) is less than $28,400 if single or married filing separately, $56,800 if married filing jointly, and $38,050 if filing as head of household.

These new provisions should rightfully be tagged with an "Old/New Law" icon. Why? Because capital gain distributions received before May 6, 2003, are taxed at the old 20 percent maximum rate. Be mindful that this 20 percent rate is reduced to 10 percent or perhaps even 8 percent if your taxable income (line 40) is below the income amounts listed in the previous paragraph for your respective filing status.

Enter the amount from box 2a of Form 1099-DIV on line 13a. If you have an entry in box 2b of form 1099-DIV, enter it on line 13b.

See Chapter 8, line 41 for the various maximum tax rates for capital gains. Box 2a has the amount, and box 2f informs you whether, for some reason, any part of the distribution must be taxed at the 28 percent rate instead of the normally lower rates. Box 2c has the amount of the capital gain that may be subject to the 8 percent rate, which depends on what tax bracket you're in. Chapter 12 gives you the scoop on all these heady concepts and tells you the right amount to enter here.

Line 13b: Post-May 5 capital gain distributions

Enter the amount from box 2b of Form 1099-DIV here. Couldn't be simpler, right? This line tells the IRS that this capital gain is taxed at the new post-May 5, 2003, rate. The difference between the amounts in boxes 2a and 2b is taxed at the old capital gain rate.

Before leaving lines 13a and b, we want to remind you that you have to be vigilant about using the capital gain worksheet in your instruction booklet when you get to line 41 if you want the reduced capital gain rates to apply. Line 41 is where you compute your tax on Form 1040. We walk you through a worksheet in Chapter 8 so you can make this tax-saving computation on line 41.

Line 14: Other gains (or losses)

You guessed it, grab another form — **Form 4797, Sales of Business Property.** Fill out that form and enter the final figure on line 14. Form 4797 is used when you sell property that you've been depreciating (such as a two-family house that you've been renting out). This form is explained in Chapter 12.

Lines 15a and 15b: Total IRA distributions

One of the benefits from all those years of hard work and diligent savings is that someday, hopefully, you'll be able to enjoy and live off the fruits of your labor. Although this line number is for reporting money that you've withdrawn from an Individual Retirement Account (IRA), we must share with you some important information if you haven't yet started withdrawals and are getting to the age where you should.

You must start taking out a minimum amount from your IRA in the year that you turn 70½; however, you can delay this first distribution until April 1 of the year after you turn 70½ (see "Computing the amount you must withdraw" at the end of this section). If you choose to delay making your first distribution until the year after you turn 70½, you have to make two withdrawals in that year . . . one for the current year and one for the year you turned 70½. If you don't take out of your IRA what you are required, you'll be assessed a 50 percent penalty on the amount that you should have taken out. Suppose that you should have taken out $4,000, but you didn't. You'll have to pay a $2,000 penalty. You can request that the penalty be excused if your failure to make a minimum distribution was caused by a reasonable error or if you're taking steps to remedy the error. Illness, a computational error, or incorrect advice are three examples of a reasonable error. You compute the 50 percent penalty on Form 5329.

Note: The minimum withdrawal rule doesn't apply to Roth IRAs; you can keep money in a Roth IRA for as long as you like.

If you just discovered that you should have been taking money out of your IRA, start taking your distribution immediately. Then try to see whether you have a plausible reason to help you avoid the penalty. Math errors or illnesses are some of the valid reasons for a penalty to be excused. Next, you need a statement explaining why you didn't make the required distribution. In the statement, say that you corrected the error and are taking out what the law requires you to withdraw every year. Also, state that you don't feel that you should be penalized because it's the only time that it has happened, and you took immediate measures to correct the mistake.

Even though the IRS instructs you to explain why the penalty should be excused and what steps you have taken to correct the error and to attach that explanation to **Form 5329, Additional Taxes on Qualified Plans (Including IRAs) and Other Tax-Favored Accounts,** the IRS nevertheless requires that you pay the penalty as computed on lines 42–45 of Part VII, Form 5329. If the IRS believes that you made your case, it will refund the penalty.

Computing the amount you must withdraw from retirement accounts

When you reach age 70½, you must start withdrawing at least a minimum amount from your retirement accounts. The minimum amount you must withdraw at 70½ is computed by using the IRS life-expectancy table listed later in this sidebar. An important exception to using this life-expectancy table benefits those of you with spouses who are more than 10 years younger than you. A more advantageous life-expectancy table can be used. Using this *other* life-expectancy table means that you're not required to take out as much as with the *standard* life-expectancy table.

Here's an example of how to compute the minimum amount that must be withdrawn : If you turn 70½ in 2004, divide the value of your account on the preceding December 31 — say it was $200,000 — by the number of payout years next to your age in the life-expectancy table. In your case, it's 27.4 years. So in 2004, you must withdraw at least $7,299 ($200,000 ÷ 27.4). In 2005 you'd divide the balance in the account on December 31, 2004, by 26.5.

Minimum Distribution Life Expectancy Table

Age	Payout Years	Age	Payout Years	Age	Payout Years
70	27.4	77	21.2	84	15.5
71	26.5	78	20.3	85	14.8
72	25.6	79	19.5	86	14.1
73	24.7	80	18.7	87	13.4
74	23.8	81	17.9	88	12.7
75	22.9	82	17.1	89	12.0
76	22.0	83	16.3	90	11.4

The IRS Table goes to age 115 and older. Supplement to Publication 590, *Individual Retirement Arrangements (IRAs)* contains the entire table all the way to age 115 (it's Table III), and the life-expectancy table for someone whose spouse is more than 10 years younger (it's Table II). If you're 70, and your spouse is 45, instead of having to use 27.4 years as your life expectancy, Table II in Supplement to Publication 590 enables you to use 39.4 years.

Three lifetime-expectancy tables are found in the Supplement to Publication 590. Table III (illustrated above) is the Uniform Lifetime Table that IRA owners use when they're required to start making withdrawals. Table I (referred to as the Single Life Table) is for beneficiaries of an inherited IRA. As explained above, IRA owners whose spouses are more than 10 years younger can use Table II.

Tip: If you have more than one IRA account, you don't have to take a minimum amount out of each account. Tally the total of all your IRAs before computing the minimum amount you must withdraw. That amount can be taken from any of your IRAs. With other types of retirement accounts (non-IRAs), you have to withdraw the minimum from each account.

Beginning in 2004, your bank or broker is required to notify the IRS on **Form 5498, IRA Contribution Information** (with a copy to you) that a minimum distribution from your IRA was required. On the 2003 form, box 11 will be checked to indicate that a minimum distribution is required in 2004. They're also obliged to compute the required minimum amount whenever asked to do so.

Because it's a whole lot nicer not to part with your money in the first place, try this: On lines 42–45, write `See attached explanation of why the penalty should be excused for reasonable error`. Call it our version of "Go now and only pay when you have to." The only downside to taking this step: If the IRS doesn't waive the penalty, you'll have additional interest to pay.

Line 15a is for reporting money that you withdrew from your IRA during the tax year. If you receive a distribution from an IRA, the payer — your bank or broker — sends you Form 1099-R (see Figure 6-3).

As a general rule, distributions made from an IRA are fully taxable unless you made nondeductible contributions to the IRA, which we explain in the upcoming instructions for box 2a of the 1099-R. Here's a rundown of the important boxes that you need to read on your 1099-R to report an IRA distribution on Form 1040.

If you turn 70½ in 2003 and wait until 2004 to take a distribution, the distribution you have to take is computed on the balance in your IRA on December 31, 2002, not on December 31, 2003. The second distribution that you must take in 2004 is based on the balance in your account on December 31, 2003.

IRAs come in three varieties: deductible, nondeductible, and Roth IRAs. See Chapters 7 and 21 for more on these new investment vehicles.

Box 1: Gross distribution (Form 1099-R)

This box represents the amount of money that you withdrew from your IRA and that was reported to the IRS. Make sure that it's correct by checking to see whether the figure matches the amount withdrawn from your IRA account statement. If you made a nondeductible contribution to an IRA — that's an IRA contribution for which you didn't take a tax deduction and thus filed **Form 8606, Nondeductible IRA Contributions, Distributions and Basis** — write the number from box 1 on line 15a of your Form 1040. The taxable portion of your IRA that you computed on Form 8606 is entered on Line 15b. See Chapter 15 for information about how to fill out the form. However, if your IRA distribution is fully taxable (see the next section), don't make an entry on line 15a; write the number on line 15b instead.

Box 2a: Taxable amount

This box contains the taxable amount of your IRA distribution. However, the payer of an IRA distribution doesn't have enough information to compute whether your entire IRA distribution is taxable. Therefore, if you simply enter the amount reported in box 1 on Form 1040 (line 15b) as being fully taxable, you'll overpay your tax if you made nondeductible contributions to your IRA. If you made nondeductible contributions, you must compute the nontaxable portion of your distribution on Form 8606. And you must attach Form 8606 to your return. We show you all you need to know about this form in Chapter 15.

Box 7: Distribution code

A number code is entered in this box if one of the exceptions to the 10 percent penalty for distributions before age 59½ applies:

- Code 2 — annuity exception
- Code 3 — disability exception
- Code 4 — death exception
- Code 7 — indicated in box 7 if you're at least 59½ years old. That way the IRS knows that the 10 percent penalty for an early distribution doesn't apply. A transfer directly from one IRA account to another doesn't have to be reported to the IRS.

	☐ VOID	☐ CORRECTED			
ꟈ8ꟈ8					

Figure 6-3:
Form 1099-R
tells you
about
distributions
made from
your
retirement
accounts.

PAYER'S name, street address, city, state, and ZIP code	1 Gross distribution $	OMB No. 1545-0119 2003 Form **1099-R**	**Distributions From Pensions, Annuities, Retirement or Profit-Sharing Plans, IRAs, Insurance Contracts, etc.**
	2a Taxable amount $		
	2b Taxable amount not determined ☐	Total distribution ☐	**Copy A** **For**
PAYER'S Federal identification number	RECIPIENT'S identification number	3 Capital gain (included in box 2a) $	4 Federal income tax withheld $	**Internal Revenue Service Center** **File with Form 1096.**
RECIPIENT'S name		5 Employee contributions or insurance premiums $	6 Net unrealized appreciation in employer's securities $	For Privacy Act and Paperwork Reduction Act Notice, see the **2003 General Instructions for Forms 1099, 1098, 5498, and W-2G.**
Street address (including apt. no.)		7 Distribution code(s) IRA/SEP/SIMPLE ☐	8 Other $ %	
City, state, and ZIP code		9a Your percentage of total distribution %	9b Total employee contributions $	
Account number (optional)		10 State tax withheld $ $	11 State/Payer's state no.	12 State distribution $ $
		13 Local tax withheld $ $	14 Name of locality $	15 Local distribution $ $

Form **1099-R**   Cat. No. 14436Q   Department of the Treasury - Internal Revenue Service

Do Not Cut or Separate Forms on This Page — Do Not Cut or Separate Forms on This Page

Distributions before 59½

If you withdraw money from your IRA before you turn 59½, not only do you have to include that amount in your income, but you also owe a 10 percent penalty on the taxable amount that you withdrew (your nondeductible contributions are not subject to the 10 percent penalty). The penalty is computed on **Form 5329, Return for Additional Taxes Attributable to Qualified Retirement Plans.** Attach the form to your return and carry over the penalty to Form 1040 (line 57). The penalty doesn't apply to IRA distributions that are paid because of death or disability, paid over your life expectancy, or rolled over to another IRA.

The 10 percent penalty also doesn't apply to withdrawals from an IRA used to pay medical expenses in excess of 7.5 percent of your income. Additionally, anyone receiving unemployment for 12 consecutive weeks can withdraw money to pay health insurance premiums without paying the penalty. Self-employed people out of work for 12 weeks also can make penalty-free withdrawals to pay their health insurance premiums.

The 10 percent penalty doesn't apply to distributions paid over your lifetime or the joint lives of you and your beneficiary. You can switch out of this method after you reach 59½ and after you've used it for five years — for example, you're 56 years old and need some dough. You start taking out annual amounts based on your life expectancy. Read the IRS Supplement to Publication 590 *(Individual Retirement Arrangements)* and then follow the illustration we provide in the sidebar, "Computing the amount you must withdraw from retirement accounts" for the amount you have to withdraw every year. After receiving distributions based on your life expectancy for at least five years, you can switch out of this method. At age 61, you can withdraw the remaining balance or any part of it, if you want. You don't have to make this election for all your IRAs. You can use it with the IRA that has the largest or smallest balance.

Penalty-free (but taxable) withdrawals are allowed for the purchase of a first home and to pay college expenses. This exception to the penalty includes the first home of you and your spouse, child, or grandchild. Penalty-free withdrawals for higher education also apply to you and education expenses of your spouse, child, or grandchild. Withdrawals for graduate school also are penalty-free. No limits are placed on amounts that you withdraw for college expenses. What expenses qualify? Tuition fees, books, and room and board — as long as the student is enrolled at least on a half-time basis.

A first home doesn't mean your first ever — it simply means that you didn't own one within two years of the withdrawal. For example, you sold your home, lived in a rented apartment for three years, and then purchased a new home — this purchase qualifies for the $10,000 penalty-free withdrawal. The homebuyer's exception has a limit of $10,000, but you can stretch the withdrawals over several years. For example, if you withdraw $3,000 in December, you can withdraw $7,000 the following January. You must, however, use the funds within 120 days of withdrawal to buy, build, or rebuild a "first home." Your lifetime limit is $10,000; so once you take out $10,000, that's it.

A married couple can withdraw up to $10,000, penalty free, from their respective IRAs. For example, David and Betsy have their own IRAs; $10,000 can be taken out of each account, but $20,000 can't be taken from one account.

The rules for withdrawals from a traditional IRA and a Roth IRA are dramatically varied and different from one another. Chapter 7 has the lowdown on Roth IRAs.

Transfers pursuant to divorce

The transfer of an IRA account as a result of a divorce or maintenance decree isn't taxable to you or your former spouse. Nor is it subject to the 10 percent penalty. Here's how you deal with the reality of dividing an IRA in a divorce. If your divorce decree requires that you transfer all or part of your IRA to your former spouse, the transfer is not taxable, nor is it subject to the 10 percent early distribution penalty if you're younger than 59½.

To make sure that you don't run afoul of the 10 percent penalty, the spouse receiving the money should set up his or her own IRA account. Have the money transferred directly to that account or change the name on the account to that of the spouse. One hapless tax-payer recently learned about this preferred method the hard way. He withdrew the funds from his IRA and endorsed the check over to his ex-spouse. Although the transfer was required by his separation agreement, he ran afoul of the requirement that he didn't transfer his interest in his IRA account. The Tax Court sided with the IRS in determining that his interest in his IRA was extinguished when he withdrew the funds.

Inherited IRAs

When you inherit an IRA, you usually have the option of either withdrawing the money and paying tax on the amount withdrawn or taking the money out in drips and drabs so the IRA can continue sheltering the balance in the account from tax. We say usually, because in some instances the IRA owner predetermines whether at his or her death the account will be paid out all at once or over time. The 10 percent penalty that normally applies to withdrawals made to someone before he or she is 59½ doesn't apply to beneficiaries.

Determining how the money is taken out of the IRA and over what period of time is based on whether the account was left to a spouse (spouses have two additional choices that we explain in moment) or to someone else.

Surviving spouse

If you're the sole beneficiary of your deceased spouse's IRA, you can choose to roll that IRA over into your own IRA. It can be a new IRA account (which we suggest) or an existing one. A surviving spouse also can redesignate the account as his or her own by converting it to his or her name as the owner. The advantage to rolling over your deceased spouse's IRA into yours or redesignating the account is that if you're younger than 70½, you can delay making withdrawals until you reach that age. The money in the account continues to grow, tax-free. Another plus in electing to treat the account as your own is that you get to name who you want to inherit what's in the account at your death instead of the money going to the beneficiary the original IRA owner selected to succeed you.

If you choose not to treat the IRA as your own, how you take the money depends on whether your spouse was 70½ at the time of death. If your spouse died before the minimum distributions began at age 70½ or April 1 of the following year, you need not start withdrawing the funds until the later of December 31 of the year following your spouse's death or the year in which he or she would have turned 70½. In that year, withdrawals are based on the surviving spouse's life expectancy, which is recalculated every year in accordance with the *Expectancy Table* shown in Table I (single life) in the Supplement to Publication 590 *(Individual Retirement Arrangements)*. If the surviving spouse doesn't start making distributions over his or her life expectancy or waiting until his or her spouse would have turned 70½, then he or she has to withdraw the entire amount in the account by December 31 of the year of the fifth anniversary of his or her spouse's death.

If a surviving spouse dies before the IRA owner would have turned 70½ or before December 31 of the year following the IRA owner's death, the life expectancy of the successor beneficiary is used to determine the minimum distribution that must be made from that point on. In each succeeding year, one is subtracted from that life-expectancy number. Here's how it works. Say the surviving spouse, Florence, age 60, was waiting until her spouse would have turned 70½ before starting to make withdrawals, and she died in 2003. The IRA was left to the couple's daughter, Judy, age 35. Judy decides not to take a distribution until 2004, the year following the year of Florence's death. Based on the Single Life Expectancy (Table I) in Supplement to Publication 590, Judy's life expectancy in 2004 is 48.5 years. The beneficiary's life expectancy begins in the year the distributions start, not the year of death of the IRA owner. In 2004, Judy computes the amount that has to be withdrawn by dividing the balance in the account on December 31, 2003, by 48.5 years. In 2005, her life expectancy is one less, or 47.5 years (48.5 − 1), and so on. If Florence had begun taking distributions because 2003 was the year her spouse would have reached 70½, then Judy would be required to use Florence's life expectancy as determined in 2003, which, based on Table I, is 25.2 years. In subsequent years, Judy would subtract one from that amount to determine how much she needed to withdraw.

Here are the rules for when your spouse was withdrawing money from the IRA because he or she had reached the threshold age of 70½ when minimum distributions had to begin. Unless a surviving spouse elects to treat the IRA as his or her own, distributions must begin by December 31 of the year following the year of IRA owner's death. You have two choices for whose life expectancy can be used in determining the minimum amount that must be withdrawn. You can use either your life expectancy or that of your deceased spouse for the year he or she died and then subtract one in each subsequent year. You get to use the life expectancy that produces the best result. We'd be less than candid if we let you believe that using your deceased spouse's life expectancy is an easy concept to fathom. Unless your deceased spouse was much younger, it's hardly worth the effort. But because you paid good money for this book, we thought we'd better tell you about it.

When the IRA owner reaches 70½ and dies, each year the surviving spouse, based on his or her age, uses Table I to determine his or her life expectancy for that year. When a surviving spouse passes away, the succeeding beneficiary uses the surviving spouse's life expectancy in the year of death and then subtracts one in each successive year to determine what must be withdrawn.

Here's another option: You can roll over part of your deceased spouse's IRA and withdraw the rest of it. You have to pay tax on the part that isn't rolled over. But even though you may be younger than 59½, you're not subject to the 10 percent early withdrawal penalty that normally applies when someone withdraws money from an IRA before he or she is 59½, and you likewise won't have to pay a penalty if you choose to receive distributions as a beneficiary of the account.

Because you may be dealing with large sums of money, you may want to seek professional advice or immerse yourself in IRS Publication 590 *(Individual Retirement Arrangements)*. Also, the Roth IRA rules are somewhat different — see Chapter 7 for an explanation of them.

Marital status for calculating the minimum amount that must be withdrawn from an IRA is determined on January 1 of the year for which you're making the withdrawal, so any changes in that status caused by death or divorce are ignored. However, if you divorce during the year and change the beneficiary designation on the IRA, this rule doesn't apply.

Beneficiary other than a surviving spouse

Only surviving spouses can treat inherited IRAs as their own. Other beneficiaries must start receiving distributions from the IRAs. If the decedent was under 59½, the 10 percent early withdrawal penalty doesn't apply.

Here is where the rules get hairy. They depend on whether the owner had named a beneficiary. Not only don't large numbers of people have wills, but many folks also simply don't bother to name a beneficiary when setting up an IRA. What happens to the IRA when you don't name a beneficiary? It goes to the persons named in your will. If you don't have a will, it goes to your next of kin. If a person's estate is named as beneficiary, the beneficiaries of the estate don't qualify as IRA beneficiaries, so the IRA is considered to have no beneficiary. If a trust is named as a beneficiary, then under some conditions the beneficiaries of the trust may be considered beneficiaries of the IRA. Check with the attorney who drafted the trust on this one.

If a beneficiary is named, withdrawal amounts are determined by using the beneficiary's life expectancy in the year following the decedent's death and reducing it by 1 in each succeeding year. A minimum distribution, however, must be made in the year of the decedent's death as if he or she were alive.

If no beneficiary was named and the owner of the IRA died before minimum distributions were required (age 70½ or the following April 1), then all the money has to be taken out no later than the end of the fifth year following the owner's death. If the owner died without naming a beneficiary after minimum distributions began, withdrawals may be based on the owner's life expectancy in the year of death. Subtract 1 from that life expectancy in each subsequent year. The payments go to the owner's estate.

Although an estate can be named as a beneficiary, it isn't considered a *designated beneficiary* under the minimum distribution rules, because an estate doesn't have a life expectancy. If the account passes to someone under state law (next of kin rule), the IRA also is considered not to have a named beneficiary. However, if the terms of the IRA permit, a beneficiary can be named in a will or by some other election — a letter or note, for example.

Because the age of the eldest beneficiary is used to determine the minimum distribution at death, dividing an IRA into separate accounts makes sense if there are large differences in the ages of your beneficiaries. That way, one account can be for someone age 36 who has a 46.4-year life expectancy and the other for a 15-year-old grandchild who has a 66.8-year life expectancy. Another important change is that you no longer are required to use the life expectancy of the beneficiary you named at your required minimum distribution date. Now beneficiaries can be named after that date.

Make sure that you read the terms of your IRA agreement that you signed when you opened your account so that you understand your withdrawal options.

Withdrawal of nondeductible contributions

If you made nondeductible contributions to your IRA, use **Form 8606** to compute the taxable portion of your withdrawal. You don't have to pay tax on nondeductible contributions that you withdraw. The total of your IRA distributions is entered on line 7 of Form 8606; enter that same total on line 15a of Form 1040. The figure from line 15 of Form 8606 is carried over to line 15b of the 1040. That's the taxable portion.

Loss on an IRA

Losses on a Roth and nondeductible IRAs can be deducted. Say that you invest $2,000 in a Roth. The value drops to $1,500. You say, "The heck with it" and withdraw the $1,500. Your $500 loss is deducted as a miscellaneous itemized deduction on Line 22, Schedule A, Form 1040. To report a loss in a Roth, all your Roths have to be liquidated. This liquidation rule also applies to losses on nondeductible contributions to a traditional IRA.

Lines 16a and 16b: Total pensions and annuities

Here's where you report your retirement benefits from your pension, profit-sharing, 401(k), SEP, or Keogh plans. How these plans are taxed depends on whether you receive them in the form of an annuity (paid over your lifetime) or in a lump sum.

The amounts that you fill in on lines 16a and 16b are reported on a **Form 1099-R** that you receive from your employer or the custodian of your plan. If the amount that you receive is fully taxable, complete only line 16b and leave line 16a blank.

Pensions and annuities

If you didn't pay or contribute to your pension or annuity — or if your employer didn't withhold part of the cost from your pay while you worked — then the amount that you receive each year is fully taxable. The amount that you contributed, for which you received a deduction — such as tax-deductible contributions to a 401(k), SEP, IRA, or Keogh — isn't considered part of your cost.

If you paid part of the cost (that is, if you made nondeductible contributions or contributions that were then added to your taxable income on your W-2), you aren't taxed on the part that you contributed, because it represents a tax-free return of your investment. The rest of the amount that you receive is taxable. To compute this amount, you can use either the *Simplified Method* or the *General Rule*.

Simplified Method

You must use the *Simplified Method* for figuring the taxable amount of your pension or annuity if the starting date for your pension or annuity occurred after November 18, 1996, and the payments were from a qualified employee plan, a qualified employee annuity, or a qualified tax shelter annuity. The word *qualified* is tax jargon for a retirement plan approved by the IRS. You can't use this method if you were 75 or older at the starting date and your payments were guaranteed for more than five years at the time the payments began. Who came up with this one? In case you are wondering whether you can use the Simplified Method if your pension began on or before November 18, 1996, the answer is yes, unless, that is, you are required to use the General Rule that we explain in a moment.

Under the Simplified Method, the IRS allows you to declare as nontaxable part of the money that you receive from a certain number of payments made to you or to your beneficiary, based on your age when your pension or annuity started. The nontaxable portion is your after-tax contributions, if any, to the pension. Divide the amount of your contribution to the pension by the number of payments that the IRS allows. Use Table 6-2 to arrive at the nontaxable amount of each payment if your pension is based on one life or if it is based on two life expectancies and the pension starting date was before January 1, 1998. If your pension started before January 1, 1998, and it is based on two lives, use the age of the primary beneficiary, which usually is the employee.

Table 6-2	Simplified Method — One Life	
Combined Age at Annuity Starting Date	*Divide By*	*After 11-18-96*
55 and under	300 payments	360 payments
More than 55 and under 60	260 payments	310 payments
More than 60 and under 65	240 payments	260 payments
More than 65 and under 70	170 payments	210 payments
More than 70	120 payments	160 payments

For reasons that we can't explain, Congress won't make it simple and pick the beginning of a year as the date for making a change. If you started receiving payments after November 18, 1996, you must use the payment schedule in the right-hand column of Table 6-2.

Here's another midstream change. If your retirement began in 1998 or in later years and your pension or annuity is being paid over the life expectancies of two or more retirees — for example, the life expectancies of you and your spouse — you have to use Table 6-3. What's your life expectancy? The IRS determines everything, so send for IRS Publication 575 *(Pension and Annuity Income)*.

Table 6-3	Simplified Method — Two Lives
Combined Age at Annuity Starting Date	*Divide By*
110 and under	410 payments
More than 110 and under 120	360 payments
More than 120 and under 130	310 payments
More than 130 and under 140	260 payments
More than 140	210 payments

Suppose that you retired at age 65 and began receiving $1,000 per month under a joint and survivor annuity with your spouse (that is, an annuity that pays a benefit to you or your spouse as long as one of you still is living). Your spouse is 60, and you contributed $31,000 to the pension. Divide the $31,000 by 310 (the amount for your combined age of 125). The resulting $100 is the monthly amount that you receive tax-free. If you live to collect more than the 310 payments, you'll have to pay tax on the full amount of your pension that you receive beyond that point. Your contribution includes amounts withheld from your paycheck and any contributions made by your employer that were reported as additional income.

If you die before you receive 310 payments, your spouse continues to exclude $100 from each payment until the number of payments received, when added to yours, totals 310. If your spouse dies before the 310 payments are made, a miscellaneous itemized deduction on your spouse's final tax return is allowed for the balance of the 310 payments remaining to be paid, multiplied by $100. This deduction isn't subject to the 2 percent adjusted gross income limit. If your spouse dies with 40 payments yet to be made, a $4,000 deduction would be allowed (40 × $100).

If your annuity starting date was after July 1, 1986, but before January 1, 1987, you can take the exclusion as long as you're receiving payments. You don't need to stop at the total number of payments you determined in Table 6-2.

General Rule

You must use the *General Rule* to figure the taxability of your pension or annuity that you receive from a nonqualified (not approved by the IRS) employee plan, or a private or commercial annuity, or from a qualified (IRS-approved) plan if you were 75 or older at the starting date and your payments were guaranteed for more than five years at the time they began. You can use the *General Rule* for a qualified plan that began on or before November 18, 1996 (but after July 1, 1986), if you do qualify or do not choose to use the Simplified Method.

Under the General Rule, a part of each payment is nontaxable because it is considered a return of your cost. The remainder of each payment (including the full amount of any later cost-of-living increases) is taxable. Finding the nontaxable part is extremely complex and requires you to use actuarial tables. For a full explanation and the tables you need, get IRS Publication 939 *(General Rule for Pensions and Annuities — Nonsimplified Method)* or consult a tax advisor.

The nontaxable amount remains the same under the General Rule even if the monthly payment increases. If your annuity starting date was after July 1, 1986, and before 1987, you continue to exclude the same nontaxable amount from each annuity payment for as long as you receive your annuity. If your annuity starting date is after 1986, your total exclusion over the years cannot be more than your cost of the contract, reduced by the value of any refund feature. This means that you can't exclude more from tax than you contributed.

If you (or a survivor annuitant) die before the cost is recovered, a miscellaneous itemized deduction is allowed for the *unrecovered cost* on your (or your survivor's) final income tax return. The deduction is not subject to the 2 percent AGI limit.

Lump-sum distributions

If you were born before 1936, you can elect to have a lump-sum distribution taxed at a special optional method called 10-year averaging. To qualify for this special method, the lump sum must be your entire balance in all your employer's pension plans, and it must be paid within a single tax year. The distribution must be paid because of one of the following reasons:

- ✔ You die.
- ✔ You leave the firm.
- ✔ You are self-employed and become totally and permanently disabled.

Instead of electing the special 10-year averaging, a lump-sum distribution from your employer's pension plan can be rolled over to an IRA or to your new employer's retirement plan. If you don't need the immediate use of the money, a rollover probably is your best bet, because it allows you to continue deferring taxation of the money. (It's also best to let your employer transfer the money on your behalf.) You don't have to roll over the entire amount. The part that you don't roll over is subject to tax and possibly a 10 percent penalty if you are not 59½. Voluntary after-tax contributions that you made to the plan can now be rolled over, but we advise against doing so, because such contributions are tax-free to you when received and *aren't* subject to the 20 percent withholding tax that lump-sum distributions *are* subject to. See "Tax on early distributions," later in this chapter, for information about how to escape the penalty. A lump-sum distribution is eligible for capital gain or special averaging treatment if the participant was in the plan for at least five years. We discuss these options further in this section.

You can't roll over a hardship distribution from your employer's 401(k) plan to an IRA.

If you have your employer make a direct rollover from the retirement plan to your IRA, tax doesn't have to be withheld. If you receive the lump-sum payment directly, however, tax must be withheld. ***Remember:*** You have 60 days from the receipt of the money to roll it over. Because you'll be receiving only 80 percent if you receive the lump sum directly, you'll have to pay tax on the 20 percent withheld, unless you make up the difference with your own dough.

If you don't roll over your withdrawal within 60 days, through no fault of your own, the new law excuses the lateness. Before this change, whenever a financial institution messed up your transfer instructions (depositing the rollover in the wrong account, for example), you were stuck and ended up owing a barrel of taxes due and possibly penalties to boot. Here are some of the other excuses that will fly: being hospitalized, foul-ups by the post office, disasters, or circumstances beyond your control.

A single tax year means exactly that if you want to elect the 10-year averaging method. If, for example, you received $10,000 in 2003 and the balance in 2004, you're out of luck.

If your former employer's retirement plan includes the company's stock (say you work for GE, for example), you may want to transfer the stock to your taxable brokerage account instead of an IRA rollover account. Why? When you take the stock, you pay taxes only on the value at the time you purchased it and not the value when you left the company. For example, you bought shares through your company's retirement account that cost $10,000; the shares are now worth $100,000. You pay tax on $10,000 and not on the current value. And if you're younger than 55, the 10 percent penalty also is computed on the $10,000 value (see the section, "Tax on early distributions," later in this chapter). Only when you sell the shares are you taxed on the appreciation in value, and then you are taxed at capital gain rates that could be as low as 5 percent but no more than the new maximum 15 percent rate.

Capital gains treatment

If you reached the age of 50 before 1986, you can choose to treat a portion of the taxable part of the lump-sum distribution as a capital gain that is taxable at the 15 percent or 20 percent rates. This treatment applies to the portion that you receive for your participation in the plan before 1974. You can select this treatment only once, and you use **Form 4972, Tax on Lump-Sum Distributions,** to make this choice.

The tax on the balance of the lump-sum distribution is computed under the 10-year averaging method described in the next section. For most people, a tidy sum can be saved between the capital gain and averaging methods. Box 3 of Form 1099-R contains the capital gain amount.

Special averaging method

If you reached age 50 before 1986 (you were probably born before 1936, right?), you can elect the 10-year averaging method of the ordinary income portion of your lump-sum distribution. (This procedure also includes the capital gain portion of the distribution if you don't choose capital gain treatment for it.) To qualify, you must elect to use special averaging on all lump-sum distributions received in the tax year.

To use special averaging, you must have been a participant in the plan for at least five full tax years. You can make only one lifetime election to use this method. If you choose the special averaging method, use Form 4972 and figure your tax as if you received the distributions over ten years.

When you treat the distribution as though you received it over ten years, you must use 1986 tax rates. The instructions accompanying Form 4972 contain a 1986 tax-rate schedule. Ten-year averaging can save you a bundle.

Pension distributions on Form 1099-R

Pension distributions are reported on Form 1099-R, which is the same one used to report IRA distributions. The difference between how the information on an IRA distribution is reported to you and how the distribution from your pension is reported is as follows:

Box 3: If the distribution is a lump sum, and you were a participant in the plan before 1974, this amount qualifies for capital gain treatment.

Box 5: Your after-tax contribution that you made is entered here.

Box 6: Securities in your employer's company that you received are listed here. The appreciation in value isn't taxed until the securities are sold. Only the actual cost of the shares is taxed when they're received. See the earlier section "Lump-sum distributions."

Box 7: This box informs you if you are receiving a normal retirement payment, a distribution that's subject to the 10 percent penalty because you're under 59½, whether the distribution isn't subject to the penalty or if it's a direct rollover to an IRA, and so on. Here is a list of the codes that you will most likely encounter in Box 7:

Code 1 — Early distribution, no known exception

Code 2 — Early distribution, exception to 10 percent penalty applies

Code 3 — Disability

Code 4 — Death

Code 7 — Normal distribution

Code 8 — Excess contributions and earnings, or excess deferrals, taxable in 2003

Code 9 — PS 58 costs (premiums paid for insurance protection taxable in 2003)

Code A — May be eligible for 10-year averaging

Code G — Direct rollover to an IRA or another retirement plan

Code J — Distribution from Roth IRA and no known exception to the 10% penalty applies

Code N — Recharacterized IRA contribution made for 2003 and recharacterized in 2003 (see Chapter 7, line 24)

Code P — Distribution of excess contributions and earnings in the plan

Code R — Recharacterized IRA contribution made in 2002 and recharacterized in 2003 (see Chapter 7, line 24)

Code S — Early distribution from a SIMPLE IRA in first two years, no known exception to 10% penalty

Code T — Roth distribution and an exception to the 10% penalty applies

Box 8: If you have an entry here, seek tax advice.

Box 9: Your share of a distribution, if there are several beneficiaries.

You pay the tax on the lump sum in the year that you receive it, even though the tax on the distribution is computed as if you received it over ten years. After you pay the tax, the balance is yours, free and clear.

Form 1099-R

If you receive a total distribution from a retirement plan, you will receive a **Form 1099-R.** If the distribution qualifies as a lump-sum distribution, box 3 shows the capital gain amount, and box 2a minus box 3 shows the ordinary income amount. Code A is entered in box 7 if the lump sum qualifies for the 10-year special averaging. If you do not receive a Form 1099-R, or if you have questions about it, contact your plan administrator.

Tax on early distributions

Distributions that you receive from your employer's retirement plan before the age of 59½ are subject to a 10 percent penalty, and are taxable. But here are some of the exceptions to the 10 percent penalty on employer retirement plans:

- Death.
- Total and permanent disability.
- Distributions (after separation from service) paid over your lifetime or the joint lives of you and your beneficiary.

- Distributions made after you stopped working (retirement or termination) during or after the calendar year you reach age 55.

- Made to correct excess amounts in the plan.

- Distributions made under a Qualified Domestic Relations Order (QDRO), which is a divorce decree or order that spells out in specific detail who is to be awarded the retirement benefit. (See "Transfers pursuant to divorce" on line 15a where we discuss IRA distributions.)

- Distributions made to you (to the extent you have deductible medical expenses in excess of 7.5 percent of your adjusted gross income). You don't have to itemize your deductions for this exception to apply.

You report the penalty you have to pay on **Form 5329, Additional Taxes Attributable to Qualified Retirement Plans,** if none of the exceptions apply. Attach the form to your return and carry over the 10 percent to line 57 on Form 1040.

The penalty-free (but taxable) withdrawals allowed for first-time homebuyers and for paying college tuition don't apply to your employer's pension plan, Keoghs, SEPs, or 401(k)s — only to IRAs.

Minimum distributions

The same rule that applies to IRAs also applies to pension plans for failing to take a minimum distribution by April 1 of the year following the year you turned 70½.

The 70½ rule doesn't apply if you're still employed. You can delay making withdrawals until you retire. This rule doesn't apply to IRAs or to someone who owns 5 percent or more of a business.

Disability income

If you retire on disability, your pension usually is taxable. Sounds unfair, doesn't it? Yep! The way the IRS figures it, pensions are taxable, so how you retire shouldn't make a difference. However, nonpension payments made because of the permanent loss of use of part of the body, or because of permanent disfigurement, are exempt from tax. Sounds like a distinction without a difference.

If you're 65 or older (or if you're younger than 65 and are retired because your disability is total and permanent and you receive disability income), you may be able to claim a credit for the elderly or the disabled. You compute the credit on Schedule R (see "Line 46: Credit for the elderly or the disabled," in Chapter 8).

If you contributed to a plan that paid a disability pension, the part of the pension that you receive that is attributable to your payments isn't subject to tax. You report all your taxable disability on line 7 of your 1040 until you reach the m*inimum retirement age* — that is, the age stated in your plan when you are entitled to a regular retirement annuity — and then on line 16a or 16b. You must use the Simplified Method or the General Rule to compute the part of a disability pension that isn't taxable because of your contribution.

Veteran's Administration disability benefits are tax-free. If you're a military retiree and receive disability from other than the VA, do not include in your income the amount of those benefits that are equal to your VA benefits.

Military and government disability pensions that you receive as the result of an injury or sickness that occurred in a combat or extrahazardous area are exempt from tax. So are disability payments made to a government employee as a result of a terrorist attack outside the U.S. Since (and because of the events of) September 11, 2001, this provision covers all terrorist attacks, not only those occurring outside the U.S. and not only for government employees or the military. See Publication 3920 *(Tax Relief for Victims of Terrorist Attacks).*

Here is a quick reference list on sickness and injury benefits:

- ✔ **Workers' compensation:** Not taxable if paid under a workers' compensation policy because of a work-related injury or illness.

- ✔ **Federal Employees' Compensation Act (FECA):** Not taxable if paid because of personal injury or sickness. However, payments received as continuation of pay for up to 45 days while a claim is being decided and pay received for sick leave while a claim is being processed are taxable.

- ✔ **Compensatory damages:** Not taxable if received for injury or sickness.

- ✔ **Benefits from an accident or health insurance policy:** Not taxable if you paid the insurance premiums.

- ✔ **Disability benefits:** Not taxable if received for loss of income or earning capacity because of an injury covered by a *no-fault* automobile policy.

- ✔ **Compensation for permanent loss, or loss of use of a part or function of your body, or for permanent disfigurement:** Not taxable if paid because of the injury. The payment must be figured without regard to any period of absence from work, because payments for lost wages are taxable.

- ✔ **Reimbursements for medical care:** Not taxable, the reimbursement may reduce your medical expense deduction.

- ✔ **Life Insurance:** Death benefit paid to a beneficiary is exempt from tax.

Effective August 21, 1996, damages received for age, gender, or racial discrimination, and injury to your reputation and emotional distress not related to physical injuries or sickness are not tax-exempt. Prior to this change, courts had reached differing results on this issue.

Take a peek at the miscellaneous deductions in Chapter 9 for information about how to possibly exclude a reimbursement for medical expenses and amounts your attorney deducted off the top from your injury award from income on which you may have to pay tax. For example, because awards for age, gender, or racial discrimination are taxable, excluding your medical and legal expenses from the award will reduce the amount on which you have to pay tax.

Line 17: Rental real estate, royalties, partnerships, S Corporations, trusts

This line is an important one for all you self-starters who are landlords, business owners, authors, and taxpayers collecting royalties (like us!), and those people lucky enough to have someone set up a trust fund for them. Jump to Chapter 13 to find out more about this and good old Schedule E — the necessary form to wrestle with for this line.

Line 18: Farm income (or loss)

What comes after E? You got it. If you have farm income or losses, seek ye olde Schedule F (see Chapter 14), fill it out, and fill in the final number on line 18. It's similar to Schedule C.

Line 19: Unemployment compensation

Losing your job was bad enough. And now you receive another nasty surprise — the news that the unemployment compensation that you received is taxable. The government should have sent you a **Form 1099-G** (see Figure 6-4) to summarize these taxable benefits that you received. Unemployment compensation is fully taxable, and you enter it on line 19.

You can elect to have tax withheld at the rate of 10 percent on your unemployment, so you won't be caught short next April 15. This is one offer most people are likely to refuse.

Figure 6-4:
If you repaid some or all of the unemployment compensation benefits you received in 2003, you subtract the amount you repaid from the total amount you received and enter the difference on line 19.

ᏸᏰᏰᏰ ☐ VOID ☐ CORRECTED			
PAYER'S name, street address, city, state, ZIP code, and telephone no.	1 Unemployment compensation $	OMB No. 1545-0120 2003 Form 1099-G	**Certain Government Payments**
	2 State or local income tax refunds, credits, or offsets $		
PAYER'S Federal identification number	RECIPIENT'S identification number	3 Box 2 amount is for tax year	4 Federal income tax withheld $	Copy A For Internal Revenue Service Center File with Form 1096.
RECIPIENT'S name	5	6 Taxable grants $	For Privacy Act and Paperwork Reduction Act Notice, see the 2003 General Instructions for Forms 1099, 1098, 5498, and W-2G.
Street address (including apt. no.)	7 Agriculture payments $	8 Check if box 2 is trade or business income ▶ ☐	
City, state, and ZIP code			
Account number (optional)			

Form **1099-G** Cat. No. 14438M Department of the Treasury - Internal Revenue Service

Do Not Cut or Separate Forms on This Page — Do Not Cut or Separate Forms on This Page

Why would you have to give back some of your benefits? Because when you are collecting unemployment insurance, you have to be looking for a job. And if you aren't, the folks at the unemployment office may determine that you weren't entitled to all the benefits you received and that you owe some money back. If you gave back the benefits in the same year that you received them, no problem, just subtract what you returned from the total you received and enter that amount on line 19. You should also enter REPAID and the amount that you repaid on the dotted line next to the amount column on line 19.

But if you returned money in 2003 that you paid tax on in 2002, things aren't as easy. Suppose that in 2002 you received and paid tax on $10,000 of unemployment benefits. Then during 2003 you had to pay $2,500, as determined by the unemployment office. The $2,500 you paid back is deductible on Schedule A (see Chapter 8).

If you repaid unemployment compensation (that was less than $3,000) in 2003 that you included in gross income in an earlier year, you may deduct the amount repaid with Form 1040, Schedule A (line 27).

If the amount you repaid was more than $3,000, you can take either a deduction for the amount repaid as an itemized deduction or a credit against your tax for the amount of tax you originally paid by including this amount in your income in a prior year.

For example, suppose that in 2003 you repaid $4,000 of unemployment compensation that you received and paid tax on in 2002. Compute your 2002 tax without the $4,000 being included in your income. If your original tax was $10,000 and your tax without the $4,000 of unemployment was $8,416, you can claim the difference ($1,584) as a credit against your 2003 tax. If this credit is more than what you would save by deducting the $4,000 as an itemized deduction in 2003, enter the $1,584 on Form 1040 (line 67), and to the left of the line 67 credit, write IRC 1341. The credit to which you are entitled is considered an additional tax payment made. The term IRC 1341 comes from Section 1341 of the Internal Revenue Code of 1986. This is known as a *claim of right*.

Lines 20a and 20b: Social Security benefits

Politicians don't want to do away with Social Security; they just want to tax more of it. As a result, they have made retirement more complicated. Here's how to figure out what to plug in.

Don't forget that if you are married and file a joint return for 2003, you and your spouse must combine your incomes and your benefits when figuring whether any of your combined benefits are taxable. Even if your spouse did not receive any benefits, you must add your spouse's income to yours when figuring whether any of your benefits are taxable.

Form SSA-1099

Every person who receives Social Security benefits will receive a **Form SSA-1099,** even if the benefit is combined with another person's in a single check. If you receive benefits on more than one Social Security record, you may receive more than one Form SSA-1099. Your gross benefits are shown in box 3 of Form SSA-1099, and your repayments are shown in box 4. The amount in box 5 shows your net benefits for 2003 (box 3 – box 4). This is the amount you use to figure whether any of your benefits are taxable. If you misplaced Form SSA-1099, you can order a duplicate at the Social Security Web site (www.ssa.gov/1099/) or by phone.

How much is taxable?

The starting point for determining the taxable portion of your Social Security is your base income, which is your adjusted gross income with a few adjustments. The base income worksheet we give you shows you how to compute this amount. It's an easy computation to make, unless you or your spouse were covered by a pension and decided to make a deductible contribution to an IRA because your income was under $70,000 (for joint filers) or $50,000 (for others).

Early retirees, watch your step

People who retire early but continue working part-time to supplement their Social Security income may be in for a nasty surprise when they sit down to complete their tax returns.

If you are between the ages of 62 and 65, you lose out on $1 of Social Security benefits for every $2 you earn above $11,520 for 2003. The 2004 amount is $11,640, and the age range expands from 62 to 65 and 4 months. (Remember, this is earned income only; unearned income, such as from investments or a pension, doesn't penalize your benefits.)

This is known as the Social Security giveback, though it seems like a takeback to us. (At age 65 and 4 months, you can earn as much as you like without forfeiting any of your benefits.) Every year the full retirement age increases by two months until it reaches age 67.

Not only do you have this giveback to contend with, but more of your Social Security is subject to tax. Married couples with incomes above $44,000, and singles who make more than $34,000, will pay tax on 85 percent of their Social Security income.

The long and short of all of this is that if you're not careful, working a little extra to add to your income from Social Security income can cost you money. Suppose that you earned $2,000 above the year 2003 threshold of $11,520 and, bad luck, it pushed you from the 15 to the 25 percent tax bracket. First, you pay 7.65 percent Social Security tax on the extra $2,000 of income, which works out to $153. Next you have to pay income tax on the extra $2,000 you earned, and to make matters worse, that extra income subjected an additional $1,000 of your Social Security to tax. Then you'd have to give back $1,000 of your Social Security benefit. Your cost of making that extra two grand: $1,653!

Our advice to early retirees under the age of 65 is: Once you reach the 2004 earnings level of $11,640, take a vacation until December 31. One other point: Workers who take early retirement (age 62) and then turn 65 and 4 months in 2004, can earn up to $30,720 in the months before they reach 65 plus 4 months without forfeiting benefits. Additionally, you don't lose $1 for every $2 you earn above $30,720. It's $1 for every $3 you earn above $30,720. Think of it as a gift for reaching 65 in 2004.

Here's a suggestion. Unless you want to drive yourself crazy, stay away from making deductible contributions to an IRA if you or your spouse were covered by a pension *and* received Social Security. But in case you want to do the math in this more-complicated case, we show you how to do the calculations here.

Base Income Worksheet

Example: You're married filing jointly and have interest and dividend income of $10,000, a $20,000 pension, and you received $16,000 from Social Security.

1. Total income (1040, line 34; 1040A, line 21) before addition of taxable Social Security	$30,000
2. Social Security (box 5, SSA-1099)	$16,000
3. 50 percent of line 2	$8,000
4. Tax-exempt interest income	$0
5. Foreign earned income and housing exclusion (Form 2555, lines 43 and 48 or Form 2555-EZ, line 18)	$0
6. Qualified U.S. Savings Bond interest (Form 8815, line 14)	$0
7. Adoption benefits (Form 8839, line 30)	$0
8. Student loan interest (Form 1040, line 25 or Form 1040A, line 18)	$0
9. Tuition and fees deduction (Form 1040, line 26 or Form 1040A, line 19)	$0
10. Total of lines 3, 4, 5, 6, 7, 8, and 9	$8,000
11. Base income (add lines 1 and 10)	$38,000

Line 7 really falls under the heading, "Our tax laws are really crazy." How many people drawing Social Security benefits are involved in an adoption?

Now use one of the following worksheets to figure the taxable portion of your Social Security benefits: If line 11 is more than $44,000 (if you are married and filing jointly) or $34,000 (if unmarried), you have to use Worksheet II.

Worksheet 1

1. Base income	$38,000
2. Enter the appropriate amount below.	
Married filing jointly — $32,000	
Married filing separately and living with spouse at any time during year — $0	
All others — $25,000	$32,000
3. Subtract line 2 from line 1.	$6,000
4. 50 percent of line 3	$3,000
5. Social Security (box 5, SSA-1099)	$16,000
6. 50 percent of line 5	$8,000
7. Taxable Social Security — smaller of lines 4 and 6	$3,000

Enter the amount on line 5 ($16,000) on line 20a, Form 1040, and the amount on line 7 ($3,000) on line 20b, Form 1040. For 1040A filers, it's lines 14a ($16,000) and 14b ($3,000).

Worksheet II

Example: Assume the same facts in the example on Worksheet I, except that your AGI is $36,000, your Social Security is $16,000, and your only adjustment to your base income worksheet above is $6,000 in tax-exempt interest.

1. AGI without Social Security	$36,000
2. Tax-exempt interest	$6,000
3. 50 percent of Social Security	$8,000
4. Base income (add lines 1 through 3)	$50,000

Tier-one adjustment

5. Enter the appropriate amount below.

Married filing jointly — $32,000

Married filing separately and living with spouse at any time during year — $0

All others — $25,000	$32,000
6. Subtract line 5 from line 4.	$18,000
7. 50 percent of line 6	$9,000

8. Enter the appropriate amount below.

Married filing jointly — $6,000

Married filing separately and living with spouse at any time during year — $0

All others — $4,500	$6,000
9. The smaller of lines 3, 7, and 8	$6,000

Tier-two adjustment

10. Enter the appropriate amount below.

Married filing jointly — $44,000

Married filing separately and living with spouse at any time during year — $0

All others — $34,000	$44,000
11. Subtract line 10 from line 4.	$6,000
12. 85 percent of line 11	$5,100

Taxable portion

13. Add lines 9 ($6,000) and 12 ($5,100)	$11,100
14. 85 percent of box 5, SSA-1099 ($16,000)	$13,600
15. Taxable Social Security (smaller of lines 13 and 14)	$11,100

You would enter the amount in box 5, SSA-1099 ($16,000), on line 20a of Form 1040 and $11,100 from 15 on line 20b, Form 1040. On Form 1040A, it's $16,000 on line 14a and $11,100 on line 14b.

Repayment of benefits

In some cases, your Form SSA-1099 will show that the total benefits you repaid (box 4) are more than the gross benefits you received (box 3). If this situation occurs, your net benefits in box 5 will be a negative figure, and none of your benefits will be taxable. If you receive more than one form, a negative figure in box 5 of one form is used to offset a positive figure in box 5 of another form. If you have any questions about this negative figure, contact your local Social Security Administration office.

Lump-sum Social Security payments

If you receive a lump-sum payment of Social Security benefits in 2003 that includes benefits for prior years, you have two choices. You can consider the entire payment as the amount of Social Security received in 2003 and compute the taxable portion by using Worksheet I or II. Or you can allocate the amount that you received for a prior year as being received in that year.

It makes sense to do it the latter way, if your income was lower in a prior year. If that's the case, maybe none or perhaps less than 50 percent or 85 percent would have been taxable.

If you elect the second way of treating a lump sum that covers more than one year, you don't file an amended return for that year. Here's what you do. You compute the amount of the lump sum that would have been taxable had it been received in the prior year. You then add that amount to your income for the current year.

For example, suppose that you receive a lump-sum payment of $20,000 in 2003 that includes $10,000 of benefits for 2002. If you report the whole amount in 2003, 85 percent, or $17,000, is taxable. If you elect to treat the $10,000 for 2002 as being received for that year, you can save some dough. Why? Because, based on your 2002 income, only 50 percent of the $10,000 lump-sum income attributed to that year would have to be added to your taxable income. Because $10,000 was for 2002 and $10,000 was for 2003, only $13,500 is taxable in 2003. That's because the $10,000 attributable to 2002 only would have increased your income by $5,000, and the $10,000 attributable to 2003 increases your income by $8,500. Isn't it better to have to report only $13,500 in 2003 rather than $17,000?

If you and your spouse file a joint return and your SSA-1099s show that *your* repayments are more than your gross benefits, but *your spouse's* are not, subtract the amount in box 5 of your form from the amount in box 5 of your spouse's form to get your net benefits when figuring whether your combined benefits are taxable.

Repayment of benefits received in an earlier year

If the sum of the amount shown in box 5 of each of your SSA-1099s is a negative figure, and all or part of this negative figure is for benefits you included in gross income in an earlier year, you can take an itemized deduction on Schedule A for the amount of the negative figure — or you can claim credit for the tax that was paid on this in a prior year, because you included it in your income. We explain how to make the computation for this *claim of right* in our previous discussion of unemployment insurance on line 19.

If you're married and filing separately, you'll get caught in a special trap. Because the base exemption of $25,000 that single filers enjoy before 50 percent of their Social Security becomes taxable is not allowed for marrieds filing separately, neither are they entitled to the $32,000 single filer base exemption before 85 percent of their benefits becomes taxable. If a married couple lived apart for the entire year and filed separately, then these base exemption amounts apply. However, a recent Tax Court case held that living apart meant separate residences, not separate bedrooms. The long and short of all this is that 85 percent of married individuals' Social Security benefits end up being taxed when they file separately and didn't live apart the entire year.

Line 21: Other income

Line 21 of Form 1040 is a catchall for reporting income that doesn't fit the income categories listed on page one of Form 1040. Hey, even if you *find* some money, the IRS treats it as income! Just report all this miscellaneous income here. Don't forget to write a description of these earnings on the dotted line next to the amount.

Here are some examples of stuff that goes on line 21.

Bartering

Bartering is the trading of your services for goods or other services. You usually must declare the fair market value of goods you receive. If you participate in a barter exchange, you may get a **Form 1099-B** — and the IRS gets a copy, too. For example, suppose that you're a carpenter with a child who needs braces; you agree to make cabinets in a dentist's office in exchange for your child's braces and treatment. Although no cash changed hands, you have to pay tax on what the dentist normally would charge, because that is your income from making the cabinets. The dentist makes out better. Because the cabinets are used in his business, he is entitled to a business deduction equal to the income he has to report. Even poor Jack of Beanstalk fame had taxable income when he traded his cow for those beans.

Canceled debt

A canceled debt, or a debt paid for you by another person, is generally income to you and must be reported. For example, a discount offered by a financial institution for the prepaying of your mortgage is income from the cancellation of the debt. However, you have no income from the cancellation of a debt if the cancellation is a gift. For example, suppose you borrow $10,000 from a relative who tells you that you don't have to repay it. It's a gift! (And be sure to invite *that* relative to Thanksgiving dinner every year.) If you received a sweetheart deal on a loan, make sure that you read the rules on below-market interest rates for loans in Chapter 10.

If your debt is canceled as the result of bankruptcy or because you are insolvent, the cancellation of the debt negates your having to pay tax on the income. And you do not have to report it as income if your student loan is canceled because you agreed to certain conditions to obtain the loan — and then performed the required services. For a quick rundown on the ins and outs of canceled debts take a peek at the sidebar, "Canceled or forgiven debts that aren't taxable," at line 12 in Chapter 14.

Under the old law, only student loans from governmental or educational organizations qualified for this exclusion from income rule when professional services were rendered in exchange for the forgiveness of the loan. After August 5, 1997, loans from tax-exempt charities also qualify.

Other stuff

Here are some more examples of things to include on line 21:

- **Fees that you snare:** Maybe you're a corporate director, or a notary public, and you made some extra cash. Good job!

  If these payments are $600 or more, you will receive **Form 1099-MISC.** If you receive a fee or commission from an activity you're not regularly engaged in for business, you report it instead on line 21. Fees are considered self-employment income, which means that you may owe Social Security tax on them. You compute the Social Security tax you owe on **Schedule SE (Self-Employment Tax).** The amount of Social Security tax owed is then reported on line 55 of Form 1040, and you get a deduction for half of the tax on line 29.

- **Free tour:** The free tour you received from a travel agency or the group organizer is taxable at its fair market value. Bon voyage.

- **Gambling winnings:** Gambling winnings are taxable. But you can also deduct your gambling losses — as long as they don't exceed your winnings — as an itemized deduction on line 27 of Schedule A.

✔ **Prizes and awards:** If you get lucky and hit the lottery or win a prize in a contest, the winnings are taxable. Sorry!

However, some employee achievement awards may be nontaxable. These are noncash awards, such as a watch, golf clubs, or a TV, given in recognition for length of service or safety achievement. The tax-free limit is $400 if given from a nonqualified employer plan and $1,600 from a qualified plan. Check with your human resources department.

✔ **Jury duty:** The whopping $7 a day (more or less) that you received for jury duty goes here. If you must repay this amount to your employer because your employer continued to pay your salary while you served on the jury, you can deduct the repayment. The repayment gets deducted on line 33 of Form 1040. Write JURY PAY on the dotted line next to line 33.

✔ **Qualified tuition program payments:** These programs more commonly are known as Section 529 plans in which you prepay a student's tuition or establish an account to pay his or her higher education expenses. To the extent that any earnings are distributed that are not used to pay higher education expenses, the beneficiary, not the person who established the account, has to pay tax on those earnings. One other twist for 2003, earnings distributed from other than a state-maintained 529 Plan are taxable. So watch these dates. The earnings are reported on Form 1099-Q, box 2. Dial up Savingforcollege.com to find out how to set up a Section 529 plan. Taxable earnings on Coverdell Education Savings Accounts, if you have any, are reported on this line. See Chapter 5 for the lowdown on Coverdell ESAs.

✔ **Alaska Permanent Fund distributions (dividends):** See line 13 under 1040A filing section in Chapter 5 for the ins and outs about this kind of income.

✔ **Illegal income:** Al Capone found out about this too late.

✔ **Treasure-trove:** Say you buy a used sofa at an auction for $500 and discover a diamond ring under one of the cushions when you get it home. Guess what — you owe the tax on the value of the ring. Unfair! Just think of it as your fellow citizens wanting to share in your good fortune. Forgive us if we confronted you with a moral dilemma on what you have to do.

Frequent-flyer miles that you earn on business trips but use for personal travel are not taxable. One taxpayer stretched this rule too far. He had his travel agent bill the employer for first-class tickets. Next, he purchased coach tickets and used the frequent-flyer miles to upgrade to first class. He had the travel agent refund the difference to his personal account. The IRS held that the refunds were taxable.

Deductions

You also use line 21 to claim two types of deductions: a net-operating loss and the foreign earned income and housing exclusion.

Net operating loss (NOL)

This deduction to your income occurs when your business expenses in a prior year exceed your income for that year. Unless you elect otherwise by attaching a statement to your return that says you want to carry the loss forward, you must first carry back the loss to the two prior tax years as a deduction and then forward for the next 20 years — until the total loss is used up. Chapter 19 deals with filing amended returns and how NOLs are carried back and forward. When you carry an NOL forward from a previous year, you enter it as a negative number (for example, <$10,000> on line 21).

Losses incurred before January 1, 1998, can be carried back three years, and then carried forward for 15 years instead of 20. Despite the change, the three-year carryback will still apply to the NOL of small businesses ($5 million or less of income for the past three years) attributable to losses in a presidentially declared disaster area. Farmers are allowed a special break; losses incurred after 1997 can be carried back 5 years and forward 20 years.

As a result of the events of September 11, 2001, operating losses incurred in 2001 and 2002 can be carried back 5 years. See Chapter 19.

Foreign earned income and housing exclusion

U.S. citizens and residents working abroad are entitled to exclude up to $80,000 of their foreign salary or their self-employed income. (If you've ever considered working abroad, this exclusion may help you make up your mind.) The portion of their foreign housing costs above an annual threshold ($11,233 for 2003) can also be deducted. The exclusion isn't automatic. You have to file **Form 2555, Foreign Earned Income,** to claim the exclusion and the housing deduction, and attach it to your return. There is also a **Form 2555-EZ.**

To qualify for the exclusion, you must either be a resident of a foreign country or be physically present in a foreign country. Earnings from employment by the U.S. government don't qualify.

To qualify as a resident, you must reside in a foreign country for an uninterrupted period that includes the entire year (January 1 to December 31). So if you start working in London on March 31, 2003, you can't qualify for the exclusion under the entire-year rule, but you can possibly under the *physical presence test.* Brief trips back to the U.S. don't disqualify you from being a resident of a foreign country.

Under the physical presence test, you must be in a foreign country for 330 days during a 12-month consecutive period. If you weren't physically present or a bona fide resident for the entire year, the $80,000 exclusion has to be reduced based on the number of days you were out of the country.

To determine whether you meet the 330-day test, you may have to apply for an extension of time to file **(Form 2350, Application for Extension to File U.S. Income Tax Return).** Say you started to work in Paris on July 1, 2003 (great assignment!); you won't know until July 1, 2004, if you meet the 330-day test for the 12-month period of July 1, 2003 to July 1, 2004.

Say that you weren't in a foreign country for 330 days between July 1, 2003, and July 1, 2004. You can still claim a partial exemption for 2003 (½ of $80,000) if you meet the bona fide residence test for 2004. If you meet this test, you are considered a bona fide resident since July 1, 2003. While you are waiting to qualify as a bona fide resident for 2004, so that you can claim the foreign earned income exclusion for 2003, you can put off filing your 2003 return until January 30, 2005. Normally, a 2003 return can only be extended until October 15, 2004; Form 2350 will get you the extension to January 30, 2005.

You enter your foreign earnings from Form 2555, line 25 on Form 1040 (line 7). Then you enter the amount of those earnings that you can exclude — plus your foreign housing deduction — as a negative number on line 21 and deduct it from your income.

If your foreign earned income was $80,000 or less and you earned it as an employee (you weren't self-employed), and you're not claiming a foreign housing exclusion or a deduction for moving expenses, the friendly folks at the IRS allow you to use Form 2555-EZ; the difference is 18 lines versus 48.

Life insurance

The death benefit paid to the beneficiary of a life insurance contract is exempt from tax. However, this exception doesn't apply to advance payments made to terminally or chronically ill taxpayers.

A limited portion ($220 a day or $80,300 annually) of an advance payment on a life insurance policy won't be subject to tax if paid to a terminally or chronically ill person. Unfortunately, here is where the law gets somewhat ghoulish. A terminally ill person is someone who is certified by a doctor as having a life expectancy of less than 24 months. A person is chronically ill if he or she can't perform at least two normal daily functions, such as eating, bathing, dressing, toileting, and so on. (Only the IRS can make such a distinction.) Amounts above $220 are also excludable if they are used to pay for long-term care. That's an oxymoron if we ever heard one. The tax lingo for these advanced payments is *viatical settlements.* Aren't you glad you took Latin in high school? Viatical payments and the portions exempt from tax are reported in Section C of **Form 8853, Archer MSAs and Long-Term Care Insurance Contracts.**

To get the name of viatical brokers or companies that advance money before the death of a policyholder, contact either the National Viatical Association at 800-741-9465, or the Viatical Association of America at 800-842-9811.

Line 22: Your total income

Whew! Are you ready to do the math? Don't be stubborn or proud; grab the calculator. Add lines 7 through 21 and put the final figure on line 22. Congratulations! This amount is your total income. Because you don't want to pay tax on this amount, we tell you what deductions you're entitled to in the chapters that follow, so you can get away with paying the least amount possible.

Chapter 7

Form 1040, Part II: Adjustments to Income Stuff

Congratulations! If you're reading this chapter, you've probably made it through one of the more depressing parts of the tax return. Completing lines 7 through 22 is a bit like trying to count up the number of kindergarten students at the end of a field trip — it's hard to corral everyone, and the total keeps increasing. Despite the IRS calling this last section *Income,* most people just think of their employment earnings as income. If you've completed lines 7 through 22, you now know that the IRS definition includes a whole lot more. Ugh!

The first step in the tax-slimming process is completing the *adjustments to income* section. *Adjustments* are things that reduce the amount of income that can be taxed. It sure would be easier for you to understand if adjustments to income were simply called deductions from income. But no one ever said the IRS likes to make things simple. When you flip over your Form 1040, you'll see another section that enables you to actually deduct things.

Adjusted Gross Income

In this section (see Figure 7-1), you'll be summing your adjustments to income on lines 23 through 32a and subtracting them from your total income on line 22. The result of this subtraction is called your *adjusted gross income (AGI).* Your AGI is an important number, because it's used as the benchmark for calculating many allowable deductions — such as medical and miscellaneous itemized deductions — and the taxable amount of your Social Security income. In fact, if your AGI is too high in the eyes of the IRS, we're sorry to say that you may even lose the personal exemptions to which you thought you were entitled — the $3,050 personal exemptions that you can claim for yourself, your spouse, and your dependents.

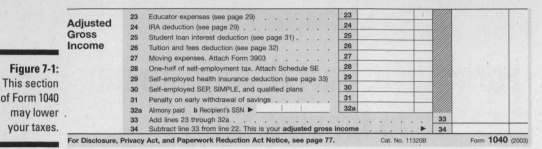

Figure 7-1:
This section
of Form 1040
may lower
your taxes.

Adjusted Gross Income	23	Educator expenses (see page 29)	**23**			
	24	IRA deduction (see page 29)	**24**			
	25	Student loan interest deduction (see page 31)	**25**			
	26	Tuition and fees deduction (see page 32)	**26**			
	27	Moving expenses. Attach Form 3903	**27**			
	28	One-half of self-employment tax. Attach Schedule SE	**28**			
	29	Self-employed health insurance deduction (see page 33)	**29**			
	30	Self-employed SEP, SIMPLE, and qualified plans	**30**			
	31	Penalty on early withdrawal of savings	**31**			
	32a	Alimony paid b Recipient's SSN ▶	**32a**			
	33	Add lines 23 through 32a			**33**	
	34	Subtract line 33 from line 22. This is your **adjusted gross income** ▶			**34**	

For Disclosure, Privacy Act, and Paperwork Reduction Act Notice, see page 77.　　Cat. No. 11320B　　Form **1040** (2003)

An important thing to keep in mind: You don't have to itemize your deductions on Schedule A to claim adjustments to income in this section. Everyone gets to make these adjustments.

Here's the line-by-line rundown of the adjustments you may be able to make. The headings refer to line numbers where you plug your data into your 1040.

Line 23: Educator expenses

Teachers who incur unreimbursed out-of-pocket expenses for supplies they bring to the classroom are now entitled to deduct up to $250. Expenses that qualify include books, supplies, computer software and equipment, and supplemental material used in the classroom. Unless Congress extends this deduction, it's valid only in 2002 and 2003. Before 2002, teachers had to itemize their deductions to deduct their out-of-pocket expenses. Expenses of more than $250 still can be claimed as an itemized deduction (see Chapter 9).

Here's a crash course on nailing down the deduction. An *educator* means a teacher, instructor, counselor, principal, or aide in a public or private elementary or secondary school who works a minimum of 900 hours during a school year. Educators who exclude U.S. Savings Bond interest from income that was used to pay college tuition (Chapter 10) or payments from a 529 plan (Chapter 5, line 11), or made withdrawals from an education savings account (Chapter 5, line 11), can claim this deduction only to the extent their out-of-pocket expenses exceed the amount that is tax-free under these education tax breaks. For example, if you excluded $750 of U.S. Savings Bond interest and have educator expenses of $500, you *cannot* claim a deduction! However, you *can* claim the $500 as a miscellaneous itemized deduction. If, on the other hand, your expenses were $1,000, you would be able to deduct $250 ($1,000 – $750). The $750 can be claimed as a miscellaneous itemized deduction.

A number of questions regarding the deduction have gone unanswered: Does work outside the classroom planning lessons, grading papers, and organizing activities count toward the 900 hours? What about extracurricular activities? Are teachers who start to work in September 2003 entitled to a deduction on their 2003 returns, based on the expectation that they will work 900 hours by the end of the current school year? Based on the spirit of the law, we believe the answer to all these questions is yes. The IRS may have a different opinion, but go for it!

Line 24: You and your spouse's IRA deduction

Individual Retirement Accounts (IRAs) were established by Congress to enable taxpayers to establish their own retirement plans. Unfortunately, IRA laws are anything but straightforward. Whether you can take *an adjustment* for a tax-deductible IRA contribution is based not only on your income level but also on whether you (and your spouse, if you're married) already are covered by some sort of retirement plan. We address those issues later in this section. Before we do, you need to determine whether you even have income that qualifies you for an IRA contribution.

In Chapter 23, we explain the various methods of how you can invest your IRA funds in mutual funds, stock, and basically the entire investment landscape. You can't, however, invest in collectibles — art, antiques, gems, stamps, coins, alcoholic beverages, or memorabilia.

For 2003 returns, you can contribute $3,000 to an IRA, and if you're 50 or older, you can contribute an additional $500. As long as your birthday falls on or before December 31, 2003, you can take advantage of this extra $500 amount, which is more commonly referred to as a catch-up contribution. In later years, you'll be able to contribute up to $5,000 and an extra $1,000 if you're 50 or older. The increased IRA limits don't kick in, however, until 2005. See Chapter 21 for details.

You don't have to wait until you turn 50 to make this catch-up contribution to your IRA. As long as you turn 50 by the end of the year, the $500 contribution can be made any time during the year. Remember, the earlier in the year that you make your IRA contribution, the sooner it starts earning income that's free of tax.

Compensation needed to qualify for an IRA

If you don't earn employment income or receive alimony and have income only from something like investments, you're *not* allowed to contribute to an IRA, period. As we explain in the next section, limits exist on how much you can contribute to an IRA if you have employment income or alimony.

You may contribute to an IRA if you have at least some of the following types of compensation:

- ✔ Salary and wages
- ✔ Commissions and tips
- ✔ Self-employed earnings from your business — reduced by your contribution to your other retirement plan (Keogh or SEP) and by the deduction allowed for one-half of the Social Security tax that you must pay as a self-employed person (see Chapter 8)
- ✔ Alimony paid to you

Congratulations! If you qualify to contribute to an IRA, you've made it past the first hurdle. But keep in mind that an age rule prohibits you from contributing to a regular IRA beginning in the year that you reach age 70½. The age rule doesn't apply to Roth IRAs.

Deductible IRA contributions

As a general rule, you can claim a deduction for the contribution that you are allowed to make to your IRA. Now for the exception to this general rule: If you or your spouse is covered by a retirement plan at work, your ability to claim a deduction may be reduced or eliminated. This restriction doesn't mean you can't make a $3,000 ($3,500 if you're 50 or older) *nondeductible* IRA or Roth IRA contribution.

What if you're not covered by an employer's plan?

If you aren't covered by a retirement plan where you work, you can make a fully deductible IRA contribution. You can skip this section on IRAs (see you later). But if your spouse is covered by a retirement plan, sorry, the next section is vital. You can't skip over it.

What if you're covered by an employer's plan?

If your filing status is single and your modified adjusted gross income is $40,000 or less ($60,000 or less for married filing jointly), you're eligible to make a fully deductible IRA contribution. Although modified adjusted gross income — it seems there's no end to terms like these — is explained in all its glory in the sidebar "How to figure partial IRA deductions," here's a shortcut that most taxpayers can use. For 1040 filers, add line 34 (your AGI), line 24 (your IRA deduction), line 25 (your student loan interest deduction), and line 26 (your tuition and fees deduction) to get your modified adjusted gross income. For 1040A filers, add line 21 (your AGI), line 17 (your IRA deduction), line 18 (student loan interest), and line 19 (your tuition and fees deduction).

If you excluded income from qualified savings bonds (Form 8815), employer-reimbursed adoption expenses (Form 8839), or foreign earned income or the related foreign housing exclusion or deduction (Form 2555), you have to add these amounts to the computation you made in the preceding paragraph.

Pause to catch your breath — here comes another big hurdle: If your income is more than the $40,000 (single) or $60,000 (married) thresholds, or if you're covered by a retirement plan but your spouse isn't, or vice versa, and your joint income is more than $150,000, your ability to deduct an IRA contribution will be reduced or eliminated completely. We explain how these income thresholds work against you in a minute. So how do you know whether you're *covered?* And what the heck is a *retirement plan?*

The simplest way to determine whether you're covered by an employer's retirement plan is to look at box 13 (the pension plan box) on your W-2 (the form that you receive early in the year from your employer that summarizes your previous year's earnings). If the retirement plan box (box 13) is marked with an *X,* you're covered by some type of retirement plan. Box 13 on your W-2 will be checked, if your employer offers you any of the following:

- Pension, profit sharing, stock bonus, or Keogh plans
- 401(k) plans
- Union retirement plans — 501(c)(18) plans for you Trivial Pursuit players!
- Qualified annuity plans
- Tax-sheltered annuities — known as 403(b) plans
- Simplified Employee Pension (SEP-IRA) plans
- Retirement plans established by a federal, state, or local government

You're considered covered, or an active participant, even if you haven't earned the full right (known as *vesting*) to the benefits under your plan. If you switch employers during the year, and one of the employers has a plan and the other doesn't, you're considered covered.

You're also considered covered by a plan when you're both salaried and self-employed, provided that you have your own Keogh, SEP, or SIMPLE Plan and you aren't covered by a plan where you're employed. You're also considered covered by a plan if you're self-employed and have a Keogh, SEP, or SIMPLE plan.

If your employer offers you a retirement plan that you can contribute to, such as a 401(k) or 403(b) and you and your employer did not add any money to your account and no forfeitures were allocated during the tax year, you're *not* considered covered during the year. Thus, you can make the maximum tax-deductible IRA contribution if your spouse also isn't covered by a pension plan. If he or she is covered by a pension plan, you can still put away the $3,000 maximum, provided your joint income is less than $150,000. More on this in a moment.

IRA planning tips

If you're currently completing your tax return for 2003, the IRA represents your last chance to make retirement contributions for 2003 (unless you had self-employment income that enables you to contribute to an SEP-IRA — see "Line 30: Self-employed SEP, SIMPLE, and qualified plans," later in this chapter). Unfortunately, you can't go back now and make contributions to your employer's plan for last year.

If you have plenty of cash around, go ahead and make the IRA contribution. You have until April 15, 2004, to be able to deduct it on your 2003 return. If you're tight on cash, foregoing the IRA contribution for the 2003 tax year may be better. Looking forward, if you can contribute through your employer's plan, odds are quite high that you may make a higher tax-deductible contribution through that plan than through an IRA. Get signed up for your employer's retirement plan and start funneling money into it now! If you have self-employment income or don't understand how the employer retirement plans work, be sure to read Chapter 21 to discover the benefits of retirement plans.

 Don't bother contributing to an IRA if you already receive Social Security benefits. Why? The paperwork is a nightmare. You need to complete the worksheets in Appendix B of Publication 590 *(Individual Retirement Arrangements)* to figure your IRA deduction and the taxable portion, if any, of your Social Security benefits. It's just too much of a hassle. If you're receiving Social Security, you're close to the age when you have to start withdrawing money from your IRA anyway. If you want to try to figure this one out, good luck. The small tax savings isn't worth paying a tax advisor to figure it out. ***Remember:*** You can't contribute to a regular IRA in the year that you turn 70 ½.

Income limitations

If you're covered by a retirement plan where you work, all is not lost. You still may be able to take the tax deduction for an IRA contribution. However, *if* what's called your *modified adjusted gross income* (explained in the "How to figure partial IRA deductions" sidebar later in this chapter) *exceeds* the following thresholds (pay attention to the filing status), you may not take the IRA deduction:

- ✔ At $50,000 and above, no deduction is allowed if you're single or a head of household. At $40,000 or less, you may take a full deduction for an IRA contribution. If your modified AGI is between $40,000 and $50,000, you're entitled to a partial deduction.

- ✔ At $70,000 and above, no deduction is allowed if you're filing jointly or as a qualifying widow or widower. At $60,000 or less, you may take a full deduction for an IRA contribution. If your income is between $60,000 and $70,000, you're entitled to a partial deduction.

- ✔ At $10,000 and above, no deduction is allowed if you're married filing separately. Below $10,000, a partial deduction is allowed. If you didn't live with your spouse for the entire year, you can ignore this rule. The single income limits apply.

- ✔ If you're married and you aren't covered by a pension but your spouse is and your joint income is below $150,000, you can take a full deduction for an IRA. If your joint income is between $150,000 and $160,000, you're entitled to a partial deduction. Above $160,000, no deduction is allowed.

If you can't take an IRA deduction or can take only a partial one, you still can make a nondeductible contribution to an IRA, as discussed later in this chapter. Although you don't get a deduction, the earnings on your contribution aren't subject to tax until you withdraw the money. The compounding of your investment earnings over many years with deferred taxation has great value.

In addition to deductible and nondeductible IRAs, the Roth IRAs, Education IRAs (formally known as Coverdell Education Savings Accounts), Archer Medical Savings Accounts (MSAs), and Medicare Plus Choice Medical Savings Accounts also offer substantial tax savings opportunities — so read on. We cover Medical Savings Accounts at line 33.

Contribution limits

The most that you can contribute in any year to your IRA is the *smaller* of the following:

- ✔ Your compensation (as we define in the previous section "Compensation needed to qualify for an IRA"), which you must include as income for the year
- ✔ $3,000

For folks aged 50 and older, it's the smaller of these two amounts plus $500.

If you're married, your spouse may also be able to contribute to an IRA. See the section "Your spouse's IRA deduction," later in this chapter.

Peter is a real person who read his IRS instruction booklet and learned that he could contribute $3,000 to an IRA. He liked investing in mutual funds, so he set up three IRA accounts with three different mutual funds and contributed $3,000 to each one, for total contributions of $9,000 for the year! IRS computers discovered this glitch when the three mutual funds each reported that Peter had made three contributions for the same tax year. Remember that $3,000 (or $3,500 if you're 50 or older) is the maximum limit that you can contribute, regardless of whether your contributions are to one or more IRAs and regardless of whether all or part of your contributions are deductible. (See the discussion of "Nondeductible IRA contributions (Form 8606)" in the next section.)

By May 31, 2004, you should receive **Form 5498, IRA Contribution Information** and **Form 5498-ESA for Coverdells** — they're similar to Form 1099. These forms show all contributions you made to your IRA for 2003.

Nondeductible IRA contributions (Form 8606)

Although your deduction for an IRA contribution may be reduced or eliminated because of the adjusted gross income modifications, you still can make nondeductible IRA contributions of up to $3,000, or 100 percent of your compensation, whichever is less, plus the $500 catch-up amount if you're 50 or older. The difference between your allowable deductible contribution, which is entered on line 24, and your total contributions made, if any, is your nondeductible contribution.

Your total deductible and nondeductible IRA contributions can't exceed $3,000 (or $3,500 if you're 50 or older).

If you can't deduct an IRA contribution, you may wonder why or how you still can contribute to an IRA. An astonishing number of taxpayers don't realize they still can contribute to an IRA even though it isn't deductible. The *growth* (from interest, dividends, and appreciation) on a nondeductible IRA contribution is sheltered from taxation the same way deductible contributions are. The value the account hopefully grows to won't be taxed until they're distributed to you years from now during retirement. The younger you are and the more years that your money can compound without taxation, the greater the value of this tax-deferred compounding.

For example, Alex is single and not yet 50. In 2003, he's covered by a retirement plan at work. His salary is $50,000, and his modified AGI is $55,000. Alex makes a $3,000 IRA contribution for that year. Because he's covered by a retirement plan and his modified AGI is more than $50,000, he can't deduct his IRA contribution.

Because Alex can't deduct the $3,000 he contributed to the IRA, he should either designate his contribution as a nondeductible contribution by completing **Form 8606, Nondeductible IRAs,** or contribute $3,000 to a Roth IRA that we discuss in the next section and in Chapter 21. However, because the growth of his IRA — deductible or otherwise — is tax-sheltered, he's still wise to contribute to an IRA, especially if he also contributes the maximum to his employer-sponsored retirement plans. See Chapter 15 for details on filling out Form 8606.

You must report nondeductible contributions to the IRS on Form 8606 even if you don't have to file a tax return for the year. If you're filing a Form 1040, you attach Form 8606 to your 1040. The penalty for not filing your Form 8606 is $50, and if your IRA contributions are more than the permissible amount, you must correct the overpayment; otherwise you may be subject to a 6 percent penalty (see Chapter 8, Line 57). The penalty is imposed annually until the excess amount is removed. You can also be penalized an additional $100 if you overstate the computation of your nondeductible contributions on Form 8606.

Say you discovered while preparing your 2003 return that you contributed too much in 2003. Three ways to avoid the penalty are

> ✔ **Considering the excess 2003 contribution part of your 2004 IRA contribution.** This way works best. For example, if you contributed $1,000 too much in 2003 and you're entitled to contribute $3,000 for 2004, then you can contribute $2,000 for 2004 and guess what? No penalty is assessed, and you're entitled to either deduct the entire $3,000 or have it count toward your nondeductible amount.
>
> ✔ **Withdrawing the excess amount by the due date (including extensions) for filing your return.** If you withdraw the excess and the earnings on the excess amount before April 15, 2004, no penalty. However, you'll owe tax on the earnings and, if you're younger than 59½, the earnings are subject to the 10 percent withdrawal penalty discussed in Chapter 6.
>
> ✔ **Withdrawing the excess contribution and paying tax on it when it's too late to use either of the other two methods, even when you didn't claim a deduction for the excess amount.** Ouch!

If after filing your return, you discover that you should have deducted your IRA contribution instead of claiming it as a nondeductible contribution (or vice versa), you can amend your return by filing Form 1040X. You also have to amend Form 8606 and attach it to Form 1040X.

The Roth and other IRAs

Deductible IRAs, nondeductible IRAs, and rollover IRAs for lump sums of your former employer's retirement plan (check out "Lump-sum distribution" in Chapter 6) are only half the story. Be aware of four other types of IRAs: Medical Savings Accounts, Education IRAs (also known as Coverdell Education Savings Accounts), Medicare Plus Choice MSAs, and Roth IRAs. See Chapter 21 for more information about the Roth IRAs and Medicare Plus Choice MSAs. Chapter 25 covers the Education IRA.

Roth contributions

The lowdown on Roth IRAs: You can contribute up to $3,000 ($3,500 if you're 50 or older) to a Roth IRA, a deductible IRA, or a nondeductible IRA in any year. You can contribute to all of them, but the total can't exceed the $3,000 or $3,500 amounts. Your spouse also can contribute either $3,000 or $3,500. Although you don't receive a deduction for your contribution, if you keep your dough in a Roth IRA for at least five years, the entire balance can be withdrawn tax-free when you retire. And like regular IRAs, you have until April 15, 2004, to contribute for 2003. Unlike regular IRAs, which prohibit contributions after you turn 70½, Roth IRAs have no age limits. A nice feature of a Roth, but not with a traditional IRA is that you can withdraw the *contributions* you made at any time without having to pay tax on it, and the withdrawal is not subject to any penalties.

A $3,000 or $3,500 contribution to a Roth IRA can be made by single taxpayers with incomes below $95,000 but can't be made by singles with incomes exceeding $110,000. Roth IRA contributions are reduced (or phased out) between incomes of $95,000 and $110,000. For joint filers, the respective phase-out limits are $150,000 and $160,000. The word income refers to *modified adjusted gross income* (explained in the "How to figure partial IRA deductions" sidebar earlier in this chapter). For example, Betsy and David, with a combined income of $175,000, file jointly. Because their income exceeds the $160,000 threshold, neither can contribute to a Roth IRA. If Betsy's and David's combined incomes had been $140,000, each could have contributed $3,000 to a Roth. If both were 50 or older, they each could have contributed $3,500 to their separate accounts.

Unlike regular IRAs, Roth IRAs have no age limits. You can contribute to a Roth even when you're 70½ or older. If you keep your money in a Roth IRA for at least five years, the following types of withdrawals are tax-free:

> ✔ Made by you after you reach 59½
>
> ✔ Made by a beneficiary (or your estate) after your death
>
> ✔ Made because you become disabled
>
> ✔ Made by you to purchase a first home (up to a $10,000 lifetime limit)

How to figure partial IRA deductions

You get a partial deduction:

✔ If your modified adjusted gross income falls between $40,000 and $50,000 when you're single, or between $60,000 and $70,000 when you're married filing jointly or a qualifying widow or widower

✔ If your modified adjusted gross income falls below $10,000 when you're married filing separately

If your modified adjusted gross income is above the phase-out limits, you are not entitled to a deduction.

Figure your partial IRA deductions by first determining your modified AGI, which is your AGI from line 34 on Form 1040 (or line 21 on Form 1040A) added to the following deductions:

✔ Your IRA deduction (Line 24)

✔ Student loan interest deduction (Line 25)

✔ Foreign earned income and housing deductions (this only applies to taxpayers who live and work abroad) per Form 2555 (see Chapter 6)

✔ The exclusion for Series EE U.S. Savings Bond interest (shown on Form 8815) explained in Chapter 10

✔ The exclusion for adoption assistance (Form 8839) — see Chapter 8

✔ Tuition and fees deduction (Line 26)

If you didn't live with your spouse at any time during the year and you file a separate return, your filing status is considered single for this purpose.

1. Depending on your filing status, enter one of the following:

   $50,000 — single or head of household

   $70,000 — joint or qualifying widow or widower

   $10,000 — married filing separately

   1._____

2. Enter your modified AGI. 2._____

3. Subtract line 2 from line 1. 3._____

4. Your IRA contribution. 4._____

(See instruction A below.)

5. See instruction B and C below. 5._____

6. Your IRA deduction. Enter the smaller of 4 or 5. 6._____

7. Your nondeductible contribution. Subtract 6 from 4. 7._____

If line 2 is larger than line 1, you aren't entitled to an IRA deduction — enter zero -0-.

A. Remember, your contribution can't exceed your compensation as we explain at the beginning of this section.

B. If line 3 is $10,000 or more, enter $3,000 (or $3,500 if you are 50 or older in 2003) on line 6 above. No further computations are required.

C. If line 3 is less than $10,000, multiply line 3 by 30 percent (0.30) or 35 percent (0.35) if you were 50 or older by the end of 2003. Round to the nearest $10. If the amount that you arrive at is less than $200, enter $200. Don't ask why. These are the rules. Simply enter the amount you arrive at or the $200 minimum on line 5.

D. Line 6 is your IRA deduction; enter this amount on Line 24 (1040) or Line 17 (1040A).

E. Your nondeductible IRA contribution is the difference between your maximum IRA contribution, which generally is $3,000, and the portion of the $3,000 you are entitled to deduct (computed on line 6 above). You must also enter this amount on line 1 of **Form 8606, Nondeductible IRAs,** where you keep track of all your nondeductible IRA contributions made through the years. For example, if only $500 of your $3,000 can be deducted, that is the amount you claim on line 24 (1040) or line 17 (1040A). The $2,500 balance is entered on Form 8606.

If you aren't covered by a pension, but your spouse is (or vice versa), enter $160,000 on line 1 and complete lines 1 through 7.

For more about the rules on first-time homebuyer expenses, see the section "Distributions before 59½" in Chapter 6.

If you withdraw money from a Roth before you are 59½, or before you have had the account for five years, see Chapter 6 to find out whether one of the exceptions to the 10 percent penalty for early distributions applies.

The five-year clock starts ticking in the tax year for which you make the first contribution. For example, say that you contribute $3,000 in 2003 for 2002. Your holding period begins on

January 1, 2002. If you also contribute $3,000 for 2003, 2004, 2005, and 2006, the earliest you can make a tax-free withdrawal is 2007. Say the account was worth $25,000 on January 1, 2007. If you're 59½, the entire $25,000 can be withdrawn tax-free; you don't have to wait five years for each of your contributions to be in the account for five years. If you inherit a Roth, you don't start a new five-year holding period; the decedent's holding period continues to count. This holding period is separate from the five-year holding period for any of your own Roth IRAs.

If you don't keep your dough in an account for at least five years, the earnings you withdraw are subject to tax. The earnings are not taxed until after you withdraw all your contributions. For example, say you put away $2,000 a year for three years and the account is now worth $7,500. If you withdraw the entire amount, only $1,500 is taxable and/or possibly subject to the 10 percent early withdrawal penalty. If you withdraw only $6,000, the entire withdrawal is tax and penalty free. It's only after you withdraw amounts that are greater than what you've contributed that you have to pay tax. That would be the $1,500 balance in the above example.

Five years means five years. Suppose that John contributed $2,000 a year for four years starting in 2000. He dies in 2004 when the account is worth $12,000. If his beneficiary withdraws the entire $12,000 in 2004, the $4,000 gain will be taxed to the beneficiary. If John's beneficiary waits until 2005, the entire $12,000 can be withdrawn tax-free. The reason? Five years from January 1, 2000, doesn't roll around until January 1, 2005.

Roth deduction phaseout

Here is how the math for the phaseout works for a single taxpayer with a modified AGI of $104,000 and a married couple with a $155,000 modified AGI:

	Single	_Married_
1. Income.	$104,000	$155,000
2. Threshold.	$95,000	$150,000
3. Subtract line 2 from line 1.	$9,000	$5,000
4. Divide line 3 by the phaseout. ($15,000 single, $10,000 married)	$9,000/$15,000	$5,000/$10,000
5. Result.	60% (0.60)	50% (0.50)
6. Maximum contribution.	$3,000	$3,000
7. Multiply line 5 by line 6.	$1,800	$1,500
8. Allowable Roth contribution. (Subtract line 7 from line 6.)	$1,200	$1,500

If the amount in line 8 is less than $200 but above zero, you can contribute $200. In addition, any result that isn't a multiple of $10 must be rounded to the next lowest $10. For example, $812 must be rounded down to $810. If you're 50 or older, enter $3,500 on line 6, because you're allowed an extra $500 catch-up amount.

Remember: The phaseout comes into play only when you're single and your income is between $95,000 and $110,000, or married with income between $150,000 and $160,000. Below $95,000 (single) or $150,000 (married), you don't have to worry about the phaseout. You are entitled to a full $3,000 or $3,500 contribution. Above $110,000 (single) or $160,000 (married), no contribution is allowed. If you're married filing separately, the phaseout starts at zero, and your $3,000 or $3,500 allowable contribution vanishes at $10,000.

IRA conversions

Before we leave the Roth arena, you need to find out something about converting a regular IRA to a Roth IRA. You can do this without incurring the 10 percent early withdrawal penalty as long as the conversion is made within 60 days of the withdrawal from the regular IRA. The best way to accomplish this feat is to have your IRA go directly from one institution to the other.

You can convert your IRA only if your income is less than $100,000 and you're not married filing separately. The amount of money that can be converted is not limited. The drawback, however, is that you must include the taxable amount in your income. For example, if you make nondeductible contributions of $10,000 to an IRA that's worth $25,000, you have to include $15,000 with your other income on your return if you convert the $25,000 to a Roth. The $15,000 you have to include with your income isn't counted toward figuring whether you meet the under-$100,000 requirement. The minimum required distribution you have to take from a retirement or IRA plan because you're past 70½ counts in determining the $100,000 threshold right now, but beginning in 2005, it won't.

When you convert a regular IRA to a Roth, you have to separately track two five-year periods; one to determine whether the money can be withdrawn free of tax, and another to determine whether the withdrawal is subject to the 10 percent penalty. That's because, unlike a regular Roth's five-year holding period, a converted Roth's five-year holding period, for the purposes of determining whether the 10 percent penalty applies, doesn't start with the year it relates to, but rather with the year the conversion takes place. Here's how this sneaky bit of business works. Say on February 25, 2004, you make a regular contribution of $3,000 to a Roth IRA for 2003 and also convert $50,000 from a traditional IRA to a Roth. The five-year period for the purposes of withdrawing tax-free whatever the total of these two sums grow to start on January 1, 2003. However, the five-year period in determining whether the $50,000 conversion is subject to the 10 percent penalty because it failed to meet the five-year rule starts on January 1, 2004. For the unsuspecting, not coordinating both five-year periods can be costly.

If a Roth contains both conversion and regular Roth contributions, the first money taken is deemed to be your regular Roth IRA contributions, and the converted amounts come next (starting with the amounts converted first).

What's wrong with a Roth?

A Roth IRA may be the worst tax idea that ever came out of Congress. Why? Because not being able to deduct a $3,000 (or $3,500 if you're 50 or older) contribution to a traditional IRA immediately costs a taxpayer in the 25 percent bracket $750. Not only does $750 earn interest for an indefinite period of time, but a taxpayer has a great deal of discretion as to how it is invested and ultimately withdrawn. With a Roth, a taxpayer gives up this savings for future savings that are unknown and impossible to calculate. Years from now, a sales or value-added tax could replace the income tax. As for future tax rates, who knows? Since 1980, the top tax rates have fluctuated between 28 percent and 70 percent. According to Rolf Auster, a professor of taxation at Florida International University in Miami, "A common misunderstanding is that somehow a Roth IRA will accumulate more after-tax funds than a deductible IRA." In the following example, Professor Auster demonstrates that is not the case. Say that a taxpayer in the 25 percent bracket has $3,000 to invest. With a nondeductible Roth, he actually has only $2,250 to invest ($3,000 less the 25 percent tax). If both

accounts earn 10 percent, after one year a deductible IRA would yield $3,300 less 25 percent tax, or $2,475. The nondeductible Roth, $3,000 less 25 percent tax which amounts to $750 because you decided to forgo the tax-deductible IRA route, or $2,250, will grow by $225 to $2,475. At the end of the day, regardless of the number of years, the after-tax balance of each account will be the same. Although a Roth will grow much faster if the full $3,000 is invested rather than just the $2,250, it takes $4,000 in before-tax earnings to invest the full $3,000. In addition, don't overlook the fact that deducting $3,000 produces a lower AGI and that income figure affects a whole range of deductions and credits that you're entitled to. If the choice is between a Roth and a nondeductible traditional IRA, then we recommend that you go for the Roth. The reason? Although contributions to both accounts aren't deductible, withdrawals coming out of a Roth are tax-free. That isn't the case with a nondeductible traditional IRA. See Chapter 21 for financial planning advice regarding what kinds of IRA are best for your situation.

Establishing a Roth for the preceding year always is a good idea when you're considering a conversion. That way you get a one-year jump on the five-year period governing tax-free withdrawals.

Say you converted $50,000 from a regular IRA to a Roth in 2003 but discovered at the end of the year that your income exceeded $100,000. Oops! You can "undo" the conversion if you transfer the money back by the due date for filing your return (including extensions) for the tax year in which you made the conversion. The conversion is treated as never having taken place. If your filing date for 2003 is April 15, 2004 — meaning that you didn't apply for an extension — you can correct your error regarding your 2003 conversion without any tax consequences if you make a trustee-to-trustee transfer back to a regular IRA by April 15, 2004. You also may want to do this if the stocks you own in the converted account took a nosedive — if, for example, the $50,000 you converted from your regular IRA to a Roth IRA during 2003 is now worth only $20,000 as you are about to file for 2003. This has happened to many people in the recent stock market decline. You're allowed to do what is known as a *recharacterization* (undoing a conversion). Otherwise you have to pay tax on $50,000 that's now worth only $20,000. You are allowed only one recharacterization a year.

Although a conversion is treated as if it never had taken place, because it was *recharacterized,* you must report it on your tax return. Enter the original conversion on line 15a Form 1040 or 11a of Form1040A. Enter zero (-0-) in either line 15b of your 1040 or 11b of your 1040A. These entries show the original conversion and a zero amount as being taxable, because you undid the conversion by means of a recharacterization. Attach a statement to your return showing the amount recharacterized, the original conversion, the earnings or loss while the money was in the Roth, and the amount back in your traditional IRA. If you make a *trustee-to-trustee transfer* when you do a recharacterization, the Roth earnings are considered being earned by the account receiving the recharacterization. A recharacterization can be made on an amended return filed within six months of your original return (including extensions). If you missed the date for recharacterizing a conversion through no fault of your own, the IRS has announced in a number of private-letter rulings that it will excuse missing the deadline.

Your spouse's IRA deduction

If your spouse is employed, the deductible amount of your spouse's IRA contribution also goes on line 24.

If your spouse is not employed outside the home, you can set up a spousal IRA and contribute up to $3,000 for him or her for a total IRA deduction of $6,000. Spouses who are 50 or older also can contribute an extra $500. You can't put $7,000 into *your* IRA alone and say that it's covering you and your spouse and both of you are older than 50. Each of you has to establish your own account. A spouse who isn't working outside the home can set up a deductible IRA even if the other spouse is covered by a pension at work, provided the couple's income doesn't exceed $150,000. If their income is between $150,000 and $160,000, a partial deduction is allowed. At $160,000, the deduction is eliminated. See the phase-out worksheet for joint filers in the earlier "Roth IRAs" section to determine whether you qualify for a partial deduction. If this phaseout works against you, don't overlook a nondeductible IRA.

The following example illustrates how to determine whether you qualify for an IRA deduction. Judy is covered by a 401(k) plan at work. Her husband, Harvey, isn't employed outside the home. The couple files jointly and has a combined income of $120,000. Harvey may make a deductible IRA contribution to an IRA, because he isn't covered by a pension plan and the couple's income is less than $150,000. Judy can't make a deductible IRA contribution because she's covered by a plan at work and, as a couple, their income is beyond the threshold ($60,000 through $70,000) for someone who is an active participant in a pension plan and is married and filing jointly. Judy is allowed to make a nondeductible IRA contribution of $3,000 ($3,500 if she is 50 or older). Judy and Harvey also are eligible to contribute to a Roth IRA.

If your spouse is employed

If your spouse is employed during the year — and each of you is younger than 70½ at the end of 2003 — you can each have IRAs and can each contribute up to the $3,000 or $3,500 limits, unless your taxable compensation (or your spouse's) is less than $3,000. Qualifying income ranges are the same as those we explain earlier in this chapter in the section "Compensation needed to qualify for an IRA." For example, Michael and Lisa file a joint return for 2003. Michael earned $28,000, and Lisa earned $1,800. Michael and Lisa can each contribute $3,000 to their respective IRAs for a total of $6,000. Even though Lisa earned less than $3,000, she is deemed to have earned Michael's $28,000 less his $3,000 IRA deduction, or $25,000, as the compensation she needs to qualify for her IRA.

If your spouse is not employed

If your nonworking spouse decides to set up his or her own IRA, the most the two of you can contribute is 100 percent of your taxable compensation up to $6,000, or $7,000 if both of you are 50 or older. You can divide your IRA contributions between your IRA and your spouse's IRA any way you choose, but you can't contribute more than $3,000 or $3,500 to either IRA. For example, if your salary is $3,500, you can contribute $3,500 — that is, $2,000 for you and $1,500 for your spouse, $1,500 for you and $2,000 for your spouse, or $1,750 for you and $1,750 for your spouse — but no more than $3,500 total. If your salary is more than $6,000, the most you can contribute to your separate accounts is $3,000.

If your spouse is younger than you, you're close to retirement age (70½), and all you can afford to contribute is $2,500, it makes sense to contribute $2,500 to your spouse's IRA. That way, the money contributed continues to grow tax-free for a longer period before it must be withdrawn.

To contribute to a spousal IRA, you need to fulfill the following requirements:

- You must be married at the end of the tax year.
- Your spouse must not have reached age 70½ by the end of the year.
- You must file a joint return.
- You or your spouse must have taxable compensation for the year. Even if you don't have taxable compensation, you're deemed to have earned your spouse's compensation less your spouse's IRA deduction.

Spouses younger than 70½

You can't make contributions to your own IRA for the year in which you reach age 70½ or in any later year. However, for any year you have compensation, you can continue to make contributions of up to $3,000 or $3,500 to your spouse's IRA until the year your spouse reaches age 70½.

Line 25: Student loan interest deduction

You can deduct up to $2,500 of interest on a loan used to pay higher education and certain vocational school expenses (ask the vocational school whether it qualifies for this deduction if you have to borrow to pay the tab).

You can claim this deduction as long as it takes to pay off the loan and as long as you're paying interest on it. Prior to 2002, the deduction was allowed for only 60 months.

For single filers, the deduction doesn't start to get eliminated until their income hits $50,000 and doesn't completely disappear until $65,000. For joint filers, the phaseout of the deduction starts at the $100,000 income level, with the deduction getting wiped out at $130,000.

The beauty of the student loan interest deduction is that you don't have to itemize your deductions to claim it. You can claim the standard deduction (see Chapter 9) and the student loan deduction. This should be of great benefit to recent graduates.

To take this deduction, you must meet the following requirements:

- ✔ You're not filing as married filing separately and no one else can claim you as a dependent.

- ✔ The loan must be incurred to pay the higher education expenses of you, your spouse, or anyone you claimed as a dependent when you took out the loan.

- ✔ The expenses must be paid within a reasonable amount of time after the loan is taken out. We wish we could tell you what's reasonable, but you know how it is: The IRS knows what's reasonable when it sees it. One way the IRS views as reasonable is when the loan proceeds are used within 60 days before the start or end of an academic semester to pay your allowable higher education expenses.

- ✔ You must be the person primarily responsible for the loan.

- ✔ The student must carry at least half the normal workload of a full-time student or be attributable to a period during which he or she met this requirement.

- ✔ The loan was taken out to pay higher education expenses for tuition, fees, room and board, books, supplies, and other necessary expenses, such as transportation.

- ✔ Loans from related family members don't qualify for the deduction.

- ✔ Revolving lines of credit don't qualify unless you agree that the line will be used only to pay for education expenses.

Students usually take out these loans because they can obtain lower interest rates, but their parents won't be able to claim the deduction, even if they make all the payments. That's because the parents didn't borrow the money. If the student is liable for the loan, the student can't claim the interest deduction when he or she can be claimed as a dependent on someone else's return.

With all of these rules, high-income taxpayers can probably do better with home equity loans (see Chapter 9).

Institutions making education loans are required to issue **Form 1098-E, Student Loan Interest Statement,** listing the interest. Your instruction booklet has a worksheet for 1040 filers to compute the phase-out amount and so do we.

Here's how the phaseout works:

	Single	*Married*
1. Income.	$53,000	$115,000
2. Threshold amount.	$50,000	$100,000
3. Subtract line 2 from line 1.	$3,000	$15,000
4. Phase-out range. ($65,000 – $50,000 for singles, $130,000 – $100,000 for joint filers)	$15,000	$30,000
5. Divide line 3 by line 4.	$3,000 ÷ $15,000	$15,000 ÷ $30,000
6. Result.	20%	50%
7. Maximum deduction.	$2,500	$2,500
8. Multiply line 7 by line 6.	$500	$1,250
9. Allowable deduction. (Subtract line 8 from line 7.)	$2,000	$1,250

You figure income for line 1 by adding the following items back to your AGI (Line 34, Form 1040 or Line 21, Form 1040A):

- ✔ Student loan interest deduction (Line 25)

- ✔ Foreign earned income and housing deductions (this applies only to taxpayers who live and work abroad) per Form 2555 (see Chapter 6)

- ✔ Tuition and fees deduction (Line 26)

- ✔ Exclusion of income for bona fide residents of American Samoa and the exclusion of income from Puerto Rico

Interest can be deducted on refinanced loans as long as the loan was refinanced with another educational institution or tax-exempt organization.

Line 26: Tuition and fees deduction

A higher-education deduction of up to $3,000 is available, even if you don't itemize your deductions. The deduction can be claimed for higher-education expenses paid on behalf of you, your spouse, and your dependents. That's $3,000 in total, not $3,000 each. You can't claim this deduction for any person for whom you're also claiming a Hope Scholarship or Lifetime Learning Credit (see Chapter 8, Line 47, Education Credits). You don't have to be a full-time student to claim this deduction, and your income can't exceed $65,000 if single, and $130,000 if filing a joint return. Unlike many other deductions and tax credits that have a phase-out range that entitles you to a partial deduction or credit, if your income exceeds those basic limits, you can kiss this higher-education deduction goodbye if your income exceeds the $65,000 or $130,000 thresholds by even $1. Ouch! People who are married but file separately are not eligible for this deduction.

Sport, hobby, and noncredit courses don't qualify for the deduction, unless the course is either required as part of a degree program or is taken to improve job skills. If you can be claimed as a dependent on someone else's return, you can't claim the deduction. This means that if your income prohibits you from claiming the deduction, your child on whose behalf the expense was incurred can't claim the deduction.

The amount of your higher-education expenses used to figure the deduction has to be reduced by:

- ✔ Distributions from qualified tuition plans

- ✔ Distributions from a Coverdell Educational IRA

- ✔ Interest on U.S. Savings Bonds used to pay higher-education expenses

You noticed that the title for line 26 is "Tuition and fees deduction." This means you can deduct only those kinds of expenses. Forget about room and board.

Just like the Hope and Lifetime Learning Credit, the timing of when higher-education expenses are paid is critical. You can't claim this deduction if you paid tuition in 2003 for a period beginning after April 1, 2004. Nor can you use these expenses to compute your 2004 deduction. People with hearts of stone made up these rules. You noticed!

Only expenses paid during the year that relates to the current academic year or the term beginning during the first three months of the following year can be deducted.

The starting point to determine whether your income exceeds the $65,000 or $130,000 levels so you can claim the deduction is your AGI (Line 34, Form 1040 or Line 21, Form 1040A). Subtract the taxable portion of your Social Security (Line 20b) from your AGI and then add the following:

- ✔ Student loan interest deduction (Line 25)

- ✔ Tuition and fees deduction (line 26)

- ✔ Foreign earned income and housing deductions (this applies only to taxpayers who live and work abroad) per Form 2555 (see Chapter 6)

In 2004 and 2005, the deduction increases to $4,000, and in those years, single taxpayers whose incomes are greater than the $65,000 limit but don't exceed $80,000, and joint filers whose incomes are more than the $130,000 threshold, but don't exceed $160,000 are entitled a $2,000 deduction.

This new higher-education deduction, which can be claimed even if you don't itemize your deductions, will enable taxpayers to deduct education expenses without having to substantiate that it is job related. Education expenses above $3,000 can be claimed as a Miscellaneous Itemized Deduction if they're employment related. See Chapter 9.

Line 27: Moving expenses (Form 3903)

If you incur moving expenses because you have to relocate, you can deduct moving expenses for which your employer doesn't reimburse you. Self-employed individuals may also deduct their moving expenses.

The place to deduct moving expenses is **Form 3903, Moving Expenses.** The deductible amount is then entered on Line 27. See Chapter 15 for more about filling out Form 3903. Don't forget to attach Form 3903 to your return.

Line 28: One-half of self-employment tax

If you're self-employed, you have to pay your own Social Security and Medicare taxes. This is one crummy drawback to being self-employed; if you worked for an employer, your employer would pay for half of your so-called self-employment tax. It's a little confusing because this tax is called a self-employment tax (not a Social Security and Medicare tax). Don't you wish the IRS would use English?

If you're self-employed and file Schedule C or Schedule C-EZ, or you're a working partner in a partnership, or if you earned income for services you provided that you reported on line 21 of Form 1040 as miscellaneous income *and* you didn't incur any expenses in earning it, you have to file **Schedule SE, Self-Employment Tax**. That's the form you use to compute the Social Security and Medicare taxes you owe. See Chapter 15 for help with completing Schedule SE.

Now for some good news (yes, there is occasionally *some* good news when it comes to taxes): Half of the self-employment tax that you must pay is deductible. Complete Schedule SE and note the following: The amount on line 5 of Schedule SE is the amount of tax you have to pay, and it's carried over to Form 1040 (line 55) and added to your income tax that's due; half of what you have to pay — the amount on line 6 of Schedule SE — is entered on Form 1040 (line 28). This amount gets deducted from your income, thereby reducing the amount of tax you have to pay.

You owe Social Security tax on the first $87,000 of your earnings at a rate of 12.4 percent and 2.9 percent Medicare tax on your entire earnings.

Line 29: Self-employed health insurance deduction

2003 was the year it finally arrived. You now can deduct 100 percent of your health insurance premiums from your income. That's up from 70 percent in 2002. Your deduction cannot exceed your net profit.

A general partner (but not a limited partner), an independent contractor, or a shareholder in an S Corporation also can claim this deduction. The deduction is allowed for premiums paid for you, your spouse, and your dependents. A portion of your long-term care premiums also qualifies for this deduction (see medical insurance premiums in Chapter 9 for the maximum deductible amount).

Because self-employed people can pay and deduct an employee's family health insurance premiums as a business expense, even if the health insurance policy covers the owner as well; and if you set up a medical reimbursement plan, you may be able to deduct your family's other medical costs as a business expense instead of claiming them as an itemized medical deduction where only the portion that exceeds 7.5 percent of your income is allowed as a deduction. A tax advisor can show you how to do this stuff. Or, for $175 a year, *Bizplan* can handle the whole thing for you (800-298-2923).

Two things make all this unattractive, however. You have to provide all employees with this coverage, and you (or the business) will incur a payroll tax expense, such as Social Security taxes, on your spouse's salary.

Line 30: Self-employed SEP, SIMPLE, and qualified plans

If you are looking for the place to deduct your Keogh contribution, this is the place. "Qualified plans" is IRS terminology for a retirement plan, such as a Keogh, that has the IRS seal of approval.

You still can open a self-employment retirement plan called a SEP in 2004 and deduct your contribution to it on your 2003 return. You have until April 15 to do this. Or, with a six-month maximum extension of time to file, you have until October 15, 2004. SEP stands for *Simplified Employee Pension,* which is basically a combination IRA/profit sharing plan. A SEP is available only for self-employed individuals and their employees, not a corporation. As a self-employed person, you can also set up a Keogh plan. Your contributions to the plan are not only deductible but also are exempt from tax until you start receiving benefits. But to make a Keogh contribution in 2004 that's deductible on your 2003 return, the plan had to be set up by December 31, 2003. (See Chapter 21 to find out about Keoghs.) If you already have a Keogh set up by the end of the tax year, see "Keogh contributions," later in this chapter.

If you have employees and want to contribute to a SEP or Keogh for yourself, you can't ignore your employees. If you go the SEP route, you have to put away money for anyone who is 21, worked for you in three of the last five years and earned at least $450. With a Keogh, you have to put away money for anyone who is 21 and worked for at least one year. This one-year requirement can be extended to two, if the employees become 100 percent *vested* (have a nonforfeitable right to what was contributed for them). With a one-year employment requirement, vesting can be stretched out for five years.

If you and your spouse are the only ones covered by the plan, you don't have to file an annual information return with the IRS until the plan's assets exceed $100,000. If you're subject to the filing requirements, file **Form 5500EZ.** If you have employees, use **Form 5500.** This form need not be filed for a SEP.

If you forgot to set up a Keogh by December 31, 2003, you can't make a deductible contribution to it for 2003. But with a SEP, you can take a deduction for 2003 as long as you set one up and contribute to it by the due date for filing your 2003 return (which can be extended to October 15, 2004). Consider a SEP-IRA for the interim and establish a Keogh by December 31, 2004, so that you can switch over to funding a Keogh for 2004.

Employers with fewer than 100 employees can establish what's known as SIMPLE plans. A cross between an IRA and a 401(k), a *SIMPLE plan* allows an employee to contribute up to $8,000 in pretax dollars with the employer matching a like amount. Unlike regular retirement plans, the nondiscrimination coverage rules don't apply. This means that the plan will qualify even if you as the owner are the only one who elects to participate. See Chapter 21 for more about SIMPLE and other small-business retirement plan options.

Regardless of whether you have a SEP, a Keogh profit-sharing, or Keogh pension, you generally can deduct up to 25 percent of your earnings to a maximum deduction of $40,000. You noticed that we said "generally." That's because when it comes to taxes, about every rule has an exception. With a defined-benefit Keogh, you can, depending on your age, get to put away substantially more than the smaller of 25 percent of your earnings or $40,000. You need to know about a few other wrinkles when deciding which type of plan is best for you, so read on. For example, with a SEP or profit-sharing Keogh, you get to choose the percentage you want to contribute every year. It can be zero or 25 percent or any percentage in between.

Another retirement plan possibility is called the *Solo (k)*, which is a cross between a 401(k) and a profit-sharing Keogh. What's unique about the Solo (k) retirement plan is that business owners without employees — consultants, independent contractors, lawyers and doctors in solo practices, and mom-and-pop shops — can put away significantly more than they can under a conventional Keogh. Here's how it works. Say the earnings of your consulting business are $40,000. Under a regular Keogh, you can contribute and deduct $8,000 (25 percent of $40,000 after deducting the $8,000). With a Solo (k), you get to contribute the $8,000 plus the maximum 401(k) limit of $12,000 for a total contribution of $20,000, as long as the combination of the two contributions doesn't exceed $40,000. There's more! If you're older than 50, you can contribute an additional $2,000 to the 401(k) portion of the plan. This extra amount isn't subject to the overall $40,000 limit. So if your income is $140,000 and you're older than 50, you can contribute $12,000 under the 401(k) arrangement plus $2,000 because you're older than 50, and another $28,000 in normal profit-sharing contributions (25 percent of $140,000 after deducting the $28,000) for a total retirement deduction of $42,000. If all you had was a regular Keogh, the most you can contribute is $28,000.

If you're both an employee and a sole proprietor, the most you can contribute to either your employer's 401(k) or the 401(k) feature of your Solo (k) is $12,000. Some taxpayers mistakenly believe they can contribute $12,000 to each 401(k). Don't be one of them. However, if your employer contributes on your behalf to a profit-sharing plan, you can also contribute to the profit-sharing feature of your plan. However, if you're an owner where you're employed, the profit-sharing plan of your separate business won't be considered a separate plan, meaning that the most you can contribute to both plans is $40,0000.

If you find this Solo (k) business intriguing, just click onto `www.401khelpcenter.com` for a list of companies that sponsor such plans. This Web site also features a calculator that instantly computes the maximum you can contribute. Just enter your age, earnings, and presto! Because the menu options at this site change so often, type in `Solo (k)` at the search button, and you'll be taken to Solo (k) menu.

Computing your SEP and Keogh deductions

We wish we could tell you that all you have to do to figure your Keogh deduction is to multiply your self-employment earnings by 25 percent. Why should the government make it that simple? You must follow two rules to arrive at the amount you are allowed to deduct.

✔ **Rule 1**. You have to reduce your earnings by deducting one-half of your self-employment tax and your Keogh contribution to get the amount that you multiply the percentage by, say it's 25 percent.

✔ **Rule 2**. The maximum amount of your earnings reduced by this adjustment that you multiply the 25 percent by can't exceed $200,000.

Although 25 percent of $200,000 is $50,000, you're limited to a maximum deduction of $40,000. Once your earnings hit $248,725, you're at the $200,000 earnings limit ($248,7255 minus your $40,000 Keogh contribution and $8,725 which is one-half your self-employment tax of $17,450 equals $200,000). The $8,725 represents the one-half $17,450 that you are allowed to deduct on line 28. As a result of having to reduce your earnings by half of your self-employment tax and your Keogh contribution, the maximum rate on earnings before these adjustments, works out to be 20 percent. The examples that follow illustrate the conversion percentages.

Example 1	
Earnings	$248,725
Less 50 percent of self-employment tax	$8,725
Balance	$240,000
Less 25 percent of $200,000 to a maximum of $40,000	$40,000
Maximum earnings base	$200,000

Example 2	
Earnings	$60,000
50 percent of self-employment tax	$4,238
Balance	$55,762
Keogh contribution (20 percent of $55,762)	$11,152
Maximum earnings base	$44,610

Twenty-five percent of $44,610 equals $11,152.

See Table 7-1, "Keogh and SEP Conversion Table," to determine your effective contribution rate based on the actual plan percentage that you choose to contribute.

Table 7-1	Keogh and SEP Conversion Table
Actual Plan Rate	*Effective Rate That You Contribute*
1%	.009901
2%	.019608
3%	.029126
4%	.038462
5%	.047619
6%	.056604

Actual Plan Rate	Effective Rate That You Contribute
7%	.065421
8%	.074074
9%	.082569
10%	.090909
11%	.099099
12%	.107143
13%	.115044
14%	.122807
15%	.130435
16%	.137931
17%	.145299
18%	.152542
19%	.159664
20%	.166667
21%	.173554
22%	.180328
23%	.186992
24%	.193548
25%	.200000

There is a kind of Keogh known as a *defined-benefit retirement plan*. With this type of pension, the annual contribution isn't determined by a percentage of your earnings or by your employees' salaries. You select an annual pension benefit that you want to receive at retirement, say $75,000. Next an insurance actuary determines — based on your age — how much you need to contribute to the pension every year to have a nest egg at retirement that's large enough to pay you $75,000 a year during retirement. If the actuary determines that you need to put away $95,000 a year to accomplish that goal, then you can ignore customary maximum annual deduction limitation of $40,000. Sounds great, but all this red tape is extremely complicated and costly to administer. You can select a retirement benefit as high as $160,000. Because the amount that you can put away every year is based on your age, you can, as a general rule, put away more money under this type of plan at about age 50. That's because at that age, you have fewer years to put money away, so a greater annual contribution to the plan must be made.

If you have a SEP or a profit-sharing plan, you can wait until you file your return in 2004 (including the extension period) to make your contribution to the plan and have it count toward 2003. Extensions of time to file until either August 15 or October 15, 2004, count toward this grace period. On the other hand, if you have a defined-benefit or a regular pension plan (other than a SEP or profit-sharing plan), your contribution must made by September 15, 2004, regardless of whether you have an extension of time to file until October 15, 2004. Dealing with the IRS rules is a virtual minefield to the unknowing.

Line 31: Penalty for early withdrawal of savings

If you withdraw funds from a savings account before maturity or redeem a certificate of deposit before it's due and you're charged a penalty, you can deduct it on your 1040 (line 31). You don't have to itemize to claim this deduction. You can deduct the entire penalty, even when it exceeds the interest income reported on the **Form 1099-INT** that you received. The penalty amount, if any, is shown in box 2 of the 1099, which the bank will send you by January 31, 2004.

Lines 32a and b: Alimony paid

The alimony you paid is deducted on line 32a; to the left of the amount, you have to enter your former spouse's Social Security number on line 32b. If you don't enter the number, you can expect to hear from the IRS because there is a $50 penalty for making this boo-boo, and your alimony deduction may be disallowed. If you paid alimony to more than one person, enter the total amount of alimony you paid on line 32a, and then list the amount and Social Security number for each recipient on a separate statement, and attach this to your return.

Before you can deduct it as an expense, you need to know what the government defines as alimony. The alimony rules aren't simple, so hang in there.

This is alimony

Payments count as alimony only if *all* the following conditions are met:

- ✔ Payments are required by the divorce decree or a separation decree.
- ✔ The payer of alimony and its recipient don't file a joint return.
- ✔ The payment is in cash (including checks or money orders).
- ✔ The spouses who are separated or divorced are not members of the same household (see the sidebar "Members of the same household," later in this chapter).
- ✔ The payments are not required after the death of the spouse who receives the alimony.
- ✔ The payment is not designated as child support.

This is not alimony

Payments do not count as alimony if *any* of the following conditions are true:

- ✔ The payment is a noncash property settlement.
- ✔ The payments are a spouse's part of community income.
- ✔ The payments are destined to keep up the payer's property.
- ✔ The payments are not required as part of the separation or divorce settlement.

Rules and exceptions to alimony

Looks simple, you say? Sorry. The rules on alimony are one of the most complex areas of the law. The reason for this absurd complexity is that each party to a divorce is trying to achieve opposite goals. The payer usually wants to deduct every payment, and the recipient wants to pay as little tax as possible. To keep everyone honest, regulations breed regulations! Here's some more information that will help you plug in the right amount on line 11 for alimony received, or line 32a for alimony paid.

Cash payments: A cash payment must be made in cash. (Makes sense, doesn't it?) Therefore, property settlements don't qualify. The transfer of a home or business is considered a property settlement.

Payments to a third party: Payments to a third party qualify as alimony if they are used in place of alimony and are requested in writing by your former spouse. These payments can be for medical expenses, housing costs, taxes, tuition, and so on.

Life insurance premiums: Life insurance premiums on your life insurance qualify as deductible alimony if the payment is required by the divorce or separation agreement and your former spouse owns the policy.

Mortgage payments: Mortgage payments are alimony if you must make mortgage payments (principal and interest) on a home jointly owned with your former spouse — and the terms of the decree or agreement call for such payments. You can deduct half of the total of these payments as alimony. Your spouse reports this same half as income. If you itemize deductions and the home is your qualified residence, you can include the other half of the interest portion in figuring your deductible interest. If the home is your ex's residence, he or she can deduct half of the mortgage interest.

Taxes and insurance: Tax and insurance payments qualify as alimony if you must make them on a home that you hold as *tenants in common* — which means that your heirs get your share when you die. (The person you own the property with doesn't get your share.) You can deduct half of the tax and insurance payments as alimony, and your spouse reports this amount as income. If you and your spouse itemize deductions, you each may deduct one-half of the real estate taxes. If the property is held as *tenants by the entirety* or as *joint tenants* (where the survivor gets it all), none of your payments for taxes and insurance qualify as alimony. If you itemize your deductions, you can deduct all of the real estate taxes.

Minimum payment period: For alimony agreements executed in 1985 and 1986, annual payments in excess of $10,000 had to continue for at least six years. For agreements made after 1986, no minimum payment period exists.

Recapture: To keep people from disguising large divorce settlements as alimony, a recapture provision was enacted for agreements executed after 1986. *Recapture* means that you have to report as income part of what you deducted during the first two years that you started paying alimony. The recapture rule applies if your average payments decline in the first three years by more than $15,000.

For example, suppose that in year one and year two, you paid and deducted $25,000 in alimony, but in year three, you paid only $5,000. You triggered the recapture rules, because your payment decreased by more than $15,000. See a tax expert. This area is one you shouldn't fool around with. However, recapture doesn't apply if your spouse dies or remarries, or if your alimony payments are geared to a fixed percentage of your income and your income decreases.

Payments after death: Alimony payments must stop at your ex-spouse's death. If you must continue to make payments after your spouse's death — because of the legalese included in the agreement — none of the payments that you made before or after death qualify as alimony that you can deduct.

Child support: A required payment that's specifically designated as child support under your divorce decree isn't deductible as alimony. Even if a payment *isn't* specially designated as child support, part of it will be considered child support, if the payment is to be reduced when your child reaches a specified age, dies, marries, leaves school, or becomes employed.

For example, suppose that you're required to pay your spouse $2,000 a month. However, when your child reaches age 21, your payment will be reduced to $1,250. Only $1,250 of your $2,000 monthly payment is considered alimony, and the remaining $750 is considered nondeductible child support.

Members of the same household

You are members of the same household even if you and your spouse separate yourselves physically in your home (or in your tropical hut, just like Gilligan and the Skipper once did after they had a fight). However, payments made within one month of departure qualify as alimony. For example, suppose that on June 1, while you're still residing in the same residence with your spouse, you make a support payment. If you move out by July 1, this payment is deductible. Any payments made prior to June 1 do not qualify. A technical exception

exists, however. If you're not legally separated under a decree of divorce or separate maintenance, a payment made under a written separation agreement, support decree can qualify as alimony even if you are members of the same household. Although this sounds like a distinction without a difference, in plain English this means that temporary payments until the separation or divorce is finalized can be deducted as alimony even if you continue to live in the same residence.

For *pre*-1985 divorce decrees, combined spouse and child support payments that are reduced when the child comes of age are treated as alimony. The IRS deemed this deal too good (of course) and thus changed the rules for agreements executed after 1984.

Payments to nonresident aliens: Alimony paid to nonresident aliens is considered U.S. source income. This means that you have to withhold 30 percent for tax and send it to the IRS, just like your employer does with the tax withheld from your salary. Find out whether the U.S. has a tax treaty with the country of your former spouse — under a number of tax treaties, alimony is exempt from withholding. See IRS Publication 901 *(U.S. Tax Treaties)* for some really interesting reading!

Normally when a property settlement is reached in a divorce, the transfer isn't taxable to either of the parties. For example, if you give shares of stock or stock options that you own to your former spouse, the transfer, depending on the type of option, may be a taxable event. However, the spouse who receives the stock or options owes the tax that his or her ex would have owed when the options are exercised or the stock is sold. This rule also applies to other assets. Chapter 12 contains the rules on stock options.

Line 33: Total adjustments

Go ahead, make your day. Add all the figures you have on lines 23 through 32a. This total represents your total adjustment — and we hope it's a big number! But alas, it may be zero. Don't despair; there are more deductions to come on the back of Form 1040.

Hey! They ran out of room — the dotted line to the left of Line 33

With all the tax law changes, the IRS was bound to run out of places on Form 1040 to list four deductions to which you may be entitled. The deductions for combination gasoline/electric vehicles, Archer MSAs (Medical Savings Accounts), expenses of performing artists, and for (the return of jury) duty pay now have a new home — the dotted line to the left of line 33. So if you want to claim any of these deductions, write in the amounts on the dotted line directly beneath line 32a and insert the types of deductions to the left of your entry, such as "Clean Fuel" when you're claiming that type of deduction. Don't forget to include this amount in the total on line 33.

Medicare Choice Medical Savings Account

The Medicare Choice Medical Savings Account is an experimental congressionally funded four-year program that is available to 390,000 senior citizens on a first-come, first-served basis. These accounts are similar in many ways to a regular Medical Savings Account. Medicare administers the program (800-633-4227, or www.medicare.gov).

Here's the lowdown on Medicare MSAs.

✔ You choose a health insurance policy with an insurance company that has a high deductible. The deductible can't exceed $6,300 (the 2000 amount).

✔ Medicare pays the premiums that are equal to what the Medicare program would have spent if you had joined another one of Medicare's Medicare + Choice health plan options.

✔ You continue paying your monthly Part B Medicare Premium ($58.70 in 2003).

✔ You set up a Medical Savings Account at a bank that is registered with the Medicare program.

At the beginning of the year, Medicare makes a deposit in your account for the entire year. We wish we could tell you the amount. The reason we can't is that the amount varies with the policy that you choose and the area where you live.

You can sign up for the plan only during November. Your Medicare MSA Plan becomes effective January 1 of the following year. You must stay with the plan for a full year.

The benefits? The earnings on your account are tax-free, and withdrawals to pay medical and dental expenses also are tax-free.

At this point you're probably thinking, who wants to be a guinea pig? Well, you'd better get used to schemes like these, because they're probably the wave of the future. Unfortunately, no financial institution has signed up with Medicare to act as trustee for these types of accounts, and no MSA insurance policies are being written in all parts of the country. Maybe by the time you buy this book, the program will be up and running.

Clean fuel–burning vehicle deduction

A deduction is allowed for using a clean fuel–burning vehicle. This is a one-time deduction of up to $2,000. Only the original purchaser can claim the deduction in the year in which such a vehicle is bought and put into use. The car doesn't have to be used in a business to claim the deduction.

Heavy clean fuel–burning trucks and buses qualify for a much higher clean fuel–burning vehicle deduction. IRS Publication 535 *(Business Expenses),* has the details on this.

Here are vehicles that up to the time of the publication of *Taxes For Dummies,* 2004 Edition, (Wiley, Inc) qualify for the deduction: the 2001, 2002, and 2003 models of the Toyota Prius; the Honda Insight for 2000, 2001, and 2002; and the Honda Civic-Hybrid for model year 2003. These vehicles qualify for this deduction, but not the electric vehicle credit (see Line 53, Chapter 8). The reason: They are not 100 percent electric.

If you purchased one of these vehicles, enter the deduction on the dotted line to the left of line 33 and write Clean Fuel next to the amount. Include the amount in your total adjustments on line 33. If you're using one of these hybrid gasoline/electric vehicles in your business, enter the deduction on Line 27, Other expenses of Schedule C (see Chapter 11).

Archer MSA (Medical Savings Account) deduction

The moniker hung on this account is for the former congressmen (Bill Archer) from Texas. You can set up a *medical savings account (MSA)* to pay your medical bills. This type of account, which is offered by insurance companies, is similar to an IRA. For information about a company that dominates this market, check out GoldenRule.com.

For single taxpayers, your MSA must have an annual deductible of at least $1,700 but not more than $2,500. For family coverage the deductible has to be at least $3,350 but not more than $5,050.

You can contribute and deduct up to $3,788 if married and $1,625 if single. A nifty feature of MSAs is that, unlike employer-provided flexible spending accounts (FSAs), an MSA isn't subject to the "use it or lose it" rule. Balances in the account can be carried forward from year to year. The earnings on the account accumulate tax-free, and withdrawals to pay medical expenses aren't subject to tax. It's much like running your own insurance company, and best of all, you get to keep the profits.

Like regular IRAs, contributions to an MSA that are made before the April 15, 2004, filing date can be deducted on your 2003 return.

You can be covered under only one high-deductible plan. (Accident, disability, dental care, vision care, long-term care, medical supplemental insurance, and per diem plans that pay a fixed daily rate if you're hospitalized aren't considered additional plans.)

Nonreimbursed medical expenses that can be withdrawn free of tax are the ones that you can deduct as a medical expense on your return if you itemized your deductions. However, the most that can be paid out of the plan for family coverage of out-of-pocket medical expenses (other than for premiums) is limited to $6,150. For single coverage, the out-of-pocket limit is $3,350. Amounts withdrawn that are more than these amounts are taxable. What you can deduct as a medical expense is spelled out in Chapter 9. However, you can't make withdrawals to pay health insurance premiums except for continuation coverage required by federal law, long-term healthcare, or while you're unemployed.

Distributions from an MSA for nonmedical expenses are subject to a 15 percent penalty, plus the tax on the distribution at the rate for your tax bracket. The penalty and income inclusion also apply if you pledge the account for a loan.

After age 65, you can withdraw funds from an MSA for any reason without paying the 15 percent penalty (but the funds still are taxable). Although not intended for this purpose, MSAs can potentially be viewed as an additional retirement account.

MSAs are part of a program that is set to expire December 31, 2003. After the expiration date, no new MSAs can be established. Taxpayers who establish an MSA by that date can continue making contributions to and paying medical expenses from their MSAs after the cutoff date. Because MSAs are established in a manner similar to IRAs, you have until April 15, 2004, to put money into one and claim a deduction for 2004.

The deduction is computed on **Form 8853, Archer MSAs and Long-Term Care Insurance Contracts.** Every year the deductible and out-of-pocket amounts are indexed and adjusted for inflation.

Expenses of performing artists

Why couldn't the IRS simply use the terms actors and musicians? Because they can't, here is what this deduction is all about: Performing artists who meet the following requirements can deduct the expenses they incur in connection with their "gigs" on the dotted line to the left of line 33 and bypass Schedule A, Itemized Deductions (see Chapter 9):

- ✔ You performed services for at least two employers and received at least $200 each from at least two of them.

- ✔ Your performing-arts expenses don't exceed 10 percent of your performing artist income.

- ✔ Your adjusted gross income (line 34) after deducting your performing artist expenses doesn't exceed $16,000.

More rules! If you're married, you must file a joint return unless you lived apart for the entire year.

When you meet all of the requirements listed above, list your performing artist expenses on **Form 2106** or **Form 2106-EZ** and enter your performing artist expenses included on line 10 of Form 2106 or line 6 of Form 2106-EZ on the dotted line 33 directly under line 32a. To the left of the entry write QPA. Include the amount you entered in the total on line 33.

When you don't meet all the requirements listed above, your performing artist expenses also are entered on either Form 2106 or 2106-EZ where the amounts from line 10, Form 2106 or line 6, Form 2106-EZ are carried over to line 20, Schedule A as a miscellaneous itemized deduction.

Jury pay returned to your employer

If you have to return jury-pay to your employer because your employer continued to pay you while you served on the jury, you can deduct that amount on the dotted line directly below line 32a. To the left of the entry write Jury Pay. Don't forget to add this amount into the total on line 33.

Line 34: Adjusted gross income

The next step is subtracting the amount in line 33 from line 22 (the total income). The result is your *adjusted gross income,* which is one of those big tax terms that you hear a good deal about. Now even you know what it means!

The IRS must think that this is a pretty important number because the good people at the Department of the Treasury have designed an easy-to-find adjusted gross income line at the bottom of the 1040 (line 34) where you enter this amount before you turn to the back of the form. Congrats! You're halfway there! This number is used to determine a host of deductions and tax credits. So, as you'll find out in later chapters, we often refer to this line.

Chapter 8

The Rest of the 1040 and Other Yucky Forms

*W*hen you turned the page of your Form 1040, you probably had that same sickening feeling that you had as a student when you turned the page on an exam — just to find more junk that you'd never finish before the bell rang! But we think that you can beat the bell this time if you take the 1040 line by line, relax, and let us help you. For some of you, the worst is over; for others, well, you've still got some nasty schedules ahead of you.

Tax Computation

You may think that because this section is entitled "Tax Computation," you're going to calculate how much tax you owe or will be refunded and be on your merry way (see Figure 8-1). Wrong! What you're going to do here is calculate your *taxable income* — that is, the income that you actually owe tax on for the year. Finding out your taxable income isn't the finish line, however, because you may have some *credits* (these are good, because they reduce your tax bill) and some other taxes (these obviously are bad) to report. Then you must settle up with the IRS and determine in the *payments section* whether you paid too much, too little, or just enough tax during the year (yeah, that part will be a little like Goldilocks, the three bears, and the porridge-tasting stuff!).

Line 35: Adjusted gross income

This line is a piece of cake. To complete line 35 at the top of the back page, turn your return back over and copy the entry you made on line 34 — both are your adjusted gross income (AGI — there's that acronym again)!

Line 36a

On line 36a, check the box if either you or your spouse were born before January 2, 1939. That makes you 65 or older in 2003 and entitles you to increase the standard deduction to which you're entitled. So you noticed that strange date, but it isn't a misprint. Most logically thinking people believe that if they were born January 1, 1939, their 65th birthdays wouldn't arrive until 2004 and thus wouldn't make them ineligible to increase the standard deduction until 2004. That isn't the IRS's way of thinking. If you were born January 1, 1939, you're considered to be 65 on December 31, 2003 and thereby are entitled to the extra standard deduction amount. Don't ask who came up with this one. We're at a loss to explain it just like you are.

Line 36a also asks you to check a box if you're blind. We realize that most people find this line somewhat of a puzzlement. After all, if someone is blind, how do they know to check the box? We hope the answer is that you bought this book so you could prepare their tax return for them.

If you check one of the boxes on line 36a and you're not itemizing your deductions, see Table 9-1 in Chapter 9 ("Over 65 or blind") to compute your increased standard deduction. If you're single or a head of household, your standard deduction is increased by $1,150, if you're age 65 or older or blind. If you're 65 or older and blind, add $2,300 to your standard deduction. For all others, that's the married folks filing jointly, the standard deduction is increased by either $950 or by a multiple of $950, such as $1,900 or $2,850. For example, if you and your spouse are 65 or older, add $1,900 to your $9,500 standard deduction. If both of you are 65 or older and one is blind, add $2,850 to the $9,500 standard deduction that married taxpayers filing jointly are allowed.

Line 36b

If you're married filing separately and your spouse itemizes deductions, then you must also itemize. If one claims the standard deduction, then both must claim it.

If you are legally married but can qualify as head of household, you are treated as if you were unmarried, and so you can claim the standard deduction even if your spouse chooses to itemize deductions. See Chapter 9, "Separate returns and limits on deductions."

Line 37: Itemized deductions (from Schedule A) or your standard deduction

This section refers to what can be a critical choice, so don't make a quick decision between the two choices the IRS offers for *deductions*. Either choice is good in the sense that the result reduces your taxable income — the income that you owe tax on. HOWEVER, and note, this is a big however: You may be cheating yourself if you automatically jump into the easier of the two choices and take the so-called *standard deduction*.

The standard deduction is tempting to take, because, without any complicated figuring, you simply take the deduction that corresponds to your filing status. For example, if you're filing as a single, you can take a standard deduction of $4,750.

If your parent or someone else can claim you as a dependent, the standard deduction to which you're entitled is limited. You're going to have to use the Table 9-2 worksheet for dependents in Chapter 9 ("Standard deduction for dependents") to figure your allowable standard deduction.

Form 1040 (2003)   Page **2**

Tax and Credits	35	Amount from line 34 (adjusted gross income)	35	
	36a	Check if: { ☐ **You** were born before January 2, 1939, ☐ Blind. } { ☐ **Spouse** was born before January 2, 1939, ☐ Blind. } **Total boxes checked** ▶ 36a		
Standard Deduction for—	b	If you are married filing separately and your spouse itemizes deductions, or you were a dual-status alien, see page 34 and check here . . . ▶ 36b ☐		
• People who checked any box on line 36a or 36b or who can be claimed as a dependent, see page 34.	37	**Itemized deductions** (from Schedule A) **or** your **standard deduction** (see left margin) . .	37	
	38	Subtract line 37 from line 35	38	
	39	If line 35 is $104,625 or less, multiply $3,050 by the total number of exemptions claimed on line 6d. If line 35 is over $104,625, see the worksheet on page 35	39	
	40	**Taxable income.** Subtract line 39 from line 38. If line 39 is more than line 38, enter -0-	40	
• All others:	41	**Tax** (see page 36). Check if any tax is from: a ☐ Form(s) 8814 b ☐ Form 4972	41	
Single or Married filing separately, $4,750	42	**Alternative minimum tax** (see page 38). Attach Form 6251	42	
	43	Add lines 41 and 42 . . . . ▶	43	
Married filing jointly or Qualifying widow(er), $9,500	44	Foreign tax credit. Attach Form 1116 if required	44	
	45	Credit for child and dependent care expenses. Attach Form 2441	45	
	46	Credit for the elderly or the disabled. Attach Schedule R . .	46	
Head of household, $7,000	47	Education credits. Attach Form 8863	47	
	48	Retirement savings contributions credit. Attach Form 8880 .	48	
	49	Child tax credit (see page 40)	49	
	50	Adoption credit. Attach Form 8839	50	
	51	Credits from: a ☐ Form 8396 b ☐ Form 8859 . .	51	
	52	Other credits. Check applicable box(es): a ☐ Form 3800 b ☐ Form 8801 c ☐ Specify _____	52	
	53	Add lines 44 through 52. These are your **total credits** . . .	53	
	54	Subtract line 53 from line 43. If line 53 is more than line 43, enter -0- . . . . . ▶	54	

Figure 8-1: The Tax Computation section of Form 1040.

The other option for taking deductions, which is itemizing them on Schedule A, takes much more work. Think of this path as the grass-roots deduction process because you must identify and tabulate numerous items so that you build enough deductions to exceed the standard one the IRS grants you.

If you're in doubt about whether itemizing saves you money or what expenses you may actually itemize, jump over to Chapter 9 right now. Take a gander at the line items on Schedule A. Even if itemizing can't save you money for this year's return, educating yourself about deductions that are available is a good idea for the future. The major expenses that you may itemize include some home ownership expenses (mortgage interest and property taxes), state income taxes, medical and dental expenses that exceed 7.5 percent of your AGI, gifts to charity, casualty and theft losses that exceed 10 percent of your AGI, job expenses, and other miscellaneous things (that exceed 2 percent of your AGI).

If your AGI (line 35) is more than $139,500 ($69,750 if married filing separately), the itemized deductions that you're entitled to enter here on line 37 have to be reduced. Sorry! Refer to Table 9-3 at the end of Chapter 9 to reduce your itemized deductions if this situation applies to you.

Line 38: Subtract line 37 from line 35

After you've either completed Schedule A for your itemized deductions or elected to take the standard deduction, enter the result on line 37, and then subtract it from line 35 and enter the result on line 38.

Line 39: Exemptions

Multiply the number of exemptions you claimed in the box on line 6d on the front side of your Form 1040 by $3,050. You already filled out line 6d by now (didn't you?), but in case you need to go back to make sure that you grabbed all the exemptions that you are allowed, turn to the section "Figuring Personal and Dependent Exemptions" in Chapter 4.

Enter the result of your multiplication on line 39. For example, if you claimed four exemptions on line 6d, enter $12,200 (4 × $3,050) on line 39. Now you understand the financial benefits of your children. A bunch of other benefits the kids provide include education credits and deductions, dependent-care and the child tax credits, so read on.

Don't forget that if your AGI (line 35) exceeds the following amounts, your deduction for personal exemptions is limited. This is how the government punishes you for earning too much. Say you're single and line 35 exceeds $139,500 — then turn to Chapter 4 to figure out how much you have to reduce your $3,050 exemption. If this rule applies, every $3,050 exemption gets reduced. The computation is a piece of cake if you follow the example we provide in Chapter 4, "Personal and dependency exemption phaseout." The income thresholds begin at:

- ✔ $104,625 for married people filing separately
- ✔ $139,500 for single filers
- ✔ $174,400 for heads of households
- ✔ $209,250 for married couples filing jointly or qualifying widow(er)

If your income on line 35 (AGI) is less than $104,625, regardless of your filing status, multiply the exemptions you claimed on line 6d by $3,050. None of the thresholds that would send you in search of your calculator apply. Be thankful for small favors.

Line 40: Taxable income

Hey, you get an easy math problem. Subtract line 39 from line 38 and enter the result on line 40. But if line 39 is more than line 38, you get to place -0- (that's a zero) on line 40. If you enter zero on line 40, you could possibly have a *net operating loss* (NOL — see "More expenses than income" in Chapter 19). Now you've arrived at another tax landmark — your taxable income, which is your AGI minus your deductions (either standard or itemized) and minus your personal exemptions. This is the amount from which you finally calculate the taxes you owe on what you earned.

Line 41: Tax

Here's where you finally calculate the total federal tax that you must pay based on your taxable income. When your taxable income is less than $100,000, you figure your tax by finding the bracket for your taxable income and filing status in the tax tables. We explained how to do this on line 28 in the Form 1040A section of Chapter 5, "Figure your tax." When your income is more than $100,000, you must use the tax rates for your filing status in the tax-rate schedules, which are also included in the back of the book.

Suppose that your taxable income is $118,800. Congratulations! You just graduated to the Tax Rate Schedules. If you're single, use Schedule X. Because your income is between $68,800 and $143,500, here's how to figure your tax:

		Tax
Taxable income	$118,800	
Less: Your starting tax bracket amount $68,800	−$68,800	$14,010
Balance	$50,000	
Tax bracket percentage for amount more than $68,800	× 28%	$14,000
Tax to be entered on line 41		$28,010

Capital gains and qualified dividends tax worksheet

Throughout this book, we've been warning you that when you get to this line, you'll end up overpaying when you have either a long-term capital gain, a capital gain distribution from a mutual fund, or qualified dividends, and you don't use the capital gain and qualified dividend tax worksheet we've provided below or the worksheet in your instruction booklet. The reason why you'll be overpaying is that last year's tax bill ushered in a number of reduced rates on capital gains and qualified dividends.

Qualified dividends

The maximum tax on qualified dividends (for a refresher on that term sprint over to line 9b in Chapter 6 and line 5 in Chapter 10) is now 15 percent. Prior to 2003, all dividends other than capital gain dividends were taxed at the rate for the tax bracket in which your total income placed you. Not only is the maximum rate now 15 percent, but for folks whose taxable incomes fall within the 10 percent or 15 percent tax brackets, the maximum tax on qualified dividends is reduced to 5 percent. In 2008, the tax rate on qualified dividends for folks in these low brackets becomes zero. Looking back, the last time that dividends weren't taxed at regular tax rates was 1936. Just like the song, "Everything Old Is New Again."

Capital gains

Unlike new maximum tax rates on qualified dividends that are retroactive to January 1, 2003, the reduced 15 percent maximum long-term capital gain rate doesn't apply to gains realized before May 6, 2003. The reason for this is that backdating the change to January 1, 2003 would be too costly, and Congress never would have approved the lower rates. Regardless of whether you agree with this decision, the result is that for 2003, we must use two sets of maximum long-term capital gain rates — one for gains realized before May 6, 2003, and the other for gains realized on or after May 6, 2003.

Under the new law, the maximum rate on the gain on the sale of collectibles didn't change; it's still 28 percent, regardless of whether the gain was realized before May 6, 2003, or on or after that date. The rate for depreciable real estate also didn't change; the rate still is 25 percent on depreciation that's recaptured. If you find this capital gains stuff somewhat confusing, you're not alone. See Chapter 12 for an updated course on the reduced capital gains rules, including what the heck *recapture of capital gain depreciation* is all about and what portion of the gain is taxed at 25 percent and what part is taxed at the lower maximum tax rates. We leave nothing out when it comes to these heady subjects.

Gains before May 6, 2003

For long-term capital gains realized before May 6, 2003, the maximum rates are 20 percent or 10 percent for individuals whose taxable incomes place them in either the 10 percent or 15 percent tax brackets. This special 10 percent rate is reduced to 8 percent whenever the asset that produced the gain was owned for more than five years. See the section "Special 8 percent rate" in Chapter 12. After May 6, 2003, this special rate for assets held longer than five years no longer applies.

Gains on or after May 6, 2003

For long-term capital gains realized on or after May 6, 2003, the maximum rate is now 15 percent. For individuals whose taxable incomes place them in either the 10 percent or 15 percent brackets, the maximum rate is 5 percent. In 2008, the 5 percent become zero for this special group. That's right! Their long-term capital gains together with their qualified dividends become tax-free.

If you compute your tax based on your taxable income using line 40 instead of using Part IV of Schedule D, you will overpay your tax, if you have a capital gain or qualified dividends. For example, suppose that you're single with a taxable income of $150,000 — which places you in the 33 percent tax bracket — and you have an $8,000 long-term capital gain that you realized on or after May 6, 2003 and $2,000 of qualified dividends. If you use the Tax Rate Schedule instead of computing your tax using Schedule D, you'll pay $3,300 on your $10,000 capital gain and qualified dividends rather than $1,500.

We offer two worksheets in Tables 8-1 and 8-2 later in this section, so you can see whether your tax computation on Schedule D is correct. Tables 8-1 and 8-2 can help you decide whether you want to skip that ugly section (Part IV) completely. Use Table 8-1 for calculating 20 percent and 15 percent gains, and use Table 8-2 for calculating gains that are taxed at the 5 percent, 8 percent, or 10 percent rates (because you're in the 10 percent or 15 percent brackets).

Just because you're eligible for the 5 percent, 8 percent, or 10 percent rates doesn't mean that your entire capital gain and qualified dividends are taxed at those rates. Only that portion of your gain and qualified dividends that normally is taxed at 10 percent or 15 percent gets taxed at 5 percent, 8 percent, or 10 percent. Confused? Don't be. Here's an example to help you unravel the mystery. You're single and your taxable income without your $10,000 capital gain is $23,400. We're assuming in this example that your capital gain occurred after May 5, 2003, and therefore, the 5 percent reduced rate applies. Five thousand dollars of your gain — which is the portion of your capital gain that increases your income to the level where you leave the 15 percent bracket ($28,400) — is taxed at 5 percent. The balance of your gain, which is $5,000, is taxed at the maximum 15 percent rate.

Tallying your capital gains and qualified dividends

Because qualified dividends now are taxed at reduced rates just like long-term capital gains, the first bit of arithmetic you need to do in computing your tax is adding your capital gains and qualified dividends. Say you have qualifying dividends of $1,000 and long-term capital gains of $12,000. Here's how you find and tally this information.

Qualifying dividends (Line 9b, Form 1040 or Form 1040A)	$1,000
Long-term capital gains (the smaller of lines 16 or 17a, Schedule D). If you didn't file Schedule D because the only capital gain that you had was from a mutual fund and you checked the box at line 13a on Form 1040, then enter the amount from 13a. 1040A filers enter the amount from line 10a.	$12,000
Total capital gains and qualifying dividends eligible for reduced rates	$13,000

If your taxable income (line 40) minus your capital gains and qualifying dividends is more than the following amounts, use Table 8-1.

  ✔ Single or married filing separately — $28,400

  ✔ Married filing jointly or qualifying widow(er) — $56,800

  ✔ Head of household — $38,050

If your taxable income (line 40) without your capital gain and qualifying dividends is equal to or less than above amounts, use Table 8-2.

Yes, we know that we're repeating this information, but it's important. So here's the worksheet (Table 8-1). For this example, you're single with a taxable income of $109,800 and a capital gain of $40,000 (the smaller of lines 16 or 17a on Schedule D), of which $30,000 is from gains realized after May 5, 2003 (line 17b, Schedule D), and $1,000 is qualifying dividends

(Line 9b, Form 1040). By following the worksheet in Table 8-1, you end up saving $4,830. Not exactly loose change, but they sure make you work for it. Who ever said saving money was easy.

Table 8-1	Capital Gains Tax Worksheet (15% or 20% Rates)		
1.	Enter the amount from line 40 of your 1040.	1.	$109,800
2.	Enter the smaller amount of your net capital gain from Schedule D, line 16 or 17a.	2.	$40,000
3.	Enter your qualifying dividends from line 9b, Form 1040.	3.	$1,000
4.	Add lines 2 and 3.	4.	$41,000
5.	If you're filing Form 4952 (that's the Investment Interest form; see "Line 13: Investment interest" in Chapter 9), enter the amount from line 4g of that form.	5.	$0
6.	Subtract line 5 from line 4. If the amount is zero or less, stop here. Use the Tax Table or Tax Rate Schedule instead.	6.	$41,000
7.	Subtract line 6 from line 1.	7.	$68,800
8.	Figure the tax on the amount on line 7. Use the Tax Table or Tax Rate Schedule (for your particular case).	8.	$14,010
9.	Enter the qualifying dividends from line 3 above.	9.	$1,000
10.	Enter the capital gains earned after May 5, 2003 (Schedule D, line 17b).	10.	$30,000
11.	Add lines 9 and 10.	11.	$31,000
12.	Calculate the tax (15%) on line 11 ($31,000 × 0.15).	12.	$ 4,650
13.	Enter the capital gains earned before May 6, 2003. Subtract line 10 from line 2 ($40,000 − $30,000).	13.	$10,000
14.	Calculate the tax (20%) on line 13 ($10,000 × 0.20).	14.	$2,000
15.	Add lines 8, 12, and 14.	15.	$20,660
16.	Figure the tax on the amount on line 1, using the Tax Table or the Tax Rate Schedule X.	16.	$25,490
17.	Enter the smaller of line 15 or line 16 here. Then enter this amount also on Form 1040 (line 41, in case you lost your place).	17.	$20,660

If you have capital gains from the sale of collectibles that are subject to the 28 percent maximum capital gain rate or recaptured depreciation that's taxed at the maximum 25 percent rate, you must use the Qualified Dividend and Capital Gain Tax Worksheet in your Form 1040 instruction booklet, or better yet, see a good tax professional. Because the new rates didn't kick in until the middle of the year, you can end up with some rather goofy results from what you may at first glance think is taxable at the 15 percent and 20 percent rates. For example, say all of these transactions took place after May 5, 2003: a long-term gain on the sale of stock of $3,000, a short-term loss on the sale of stock of $1,000, and a $1,000 long-term gain on the sale of a stamp collection for a combined total net long-term gain of $3,000. If you thought that because all of these transactions occurred after May 5, 2003, the most the $3,000 could be taxed at is 15 percent, you'd be wrong. The net $2,000 gain from the stock transactions is taxed at 15 percent, and the $1,000 gain on the stamp collection is taxed at 28 percent. Maybe the government saved money by not making the reduced capital gain rate retroactive to January 1, 2003, but they sure as heck have created an accounting headache for taxpayers.

For the 5 percent, 8 percent, or 10 percent rates to apply, your taxable income (Line 40) minus your qualified dividends and capital gains must place you in the 10 percent or 15 percent bracket and must be equal to or less than the following amounts (the amounts above which you leave the 15 percent bracket and enter the 25 percent bracket):

- Single or married filing separately — $28,400

- Married filing jointly or qualifying widow(er) — $56,800

- Head of household — $38,050

The worksheet in Table 8-2 illustrates the computations that have to be made when the 5 percent, 8 percent, or 10 percent rates apply. In this example, you're single with a taxable income of $27,900 and a capital gain (the smaller of lines 16 or 17a on Schedule D) of $8,500, of which $5,000 was from gains realized after May 5, 2003 (line 17b, Schedule D), and qualifying dividends of $1,000 (Line 9b, Form 1040). Of the gains realized before May 6, 2003, $1,000 was from the sale of an asset that you owned more than five years for which the maximum 8 percent rate applies.

Table 8-2	Capital Gains Tax Worksheet (5%, 8%, or 10% Rates)		
1.	Enter the amount from line 40 of your 1040.	1.	$27,900
2.	Enter the smaller amount of your net capital gain from Schedule D, line 16 or 17a.	2.	$8,500
3.	Enter your qualifying dividends from line 9b, Form 1040.	3.	$1,000
4.	Add lines 2 and 3.	4.	$9,500
5.	If you're filing Form 4952 (that's the Investment Interest form; see "Line 13: Investment interest" in Chapter 9), enter the amount from line 4g of that form.	5.	$0
6.	Subtract line 5 from line 4. If the amount is zero or less, stop here. Use the Tax Table or Rate Schedule instead.	6.	$9,500
7.	Subtract line 6 from line 1.	7.	$18,400
8.	Enter the smaller of line 1 or the appropriate amount below: $28,400 (single or married filing separately) $56,800 (married filing jointly or qualifying widow or widower) $38,050 (head of household)	8.	$27,900
9.	Subtract line 7 from line 8.	9.	$9,500
10.	Figure the tax on line 7, using the Tax Table.	10.	$2,414
11.	Enter the qualifying dividends from line 3.	11.	$1,000
12.	Enter capital gains earned after May 5, 2003 (Schedule D, line 17b).	12.	$5,000
13.	Add line 11 and 12.	13.	$6,000
14.	Calculate the tax (5%) on line 13 ($6,000 × 0.05).	14.	$300
15.	Enter capital gains earned before May 6, 2003 (Subtract line 12 from line 2).	15.	$3,500

16.	Enter gain on sale of assets you owned more than 5 years.	16.	$1,000
17.	Calculate tax (8%) on line 16 ($1,000 × 0.08).	17.	$80
18.	Subtract line 16 from line 15.	18.	$2,500
19.	Calculate tax (10%) on line 18 ($2,500 × 0.10).	19.	$250
20.	Add lines 10, 14, 17, and 19.	20.	$3,044
21.	Figure your tax on line 1 ($27,900) using the Tax Table.	21.	$3,839
22.	Enter the smaller of line 20 or 21. Then enter this amount on Form 1040 (line 41).	22.	$3,044

Congratulations! You saved $795 by taking this 22-step math quiz.

The worksheets in Tables 8-1 and 8-2 illustrate two examples, one where taxable income, including capital gains and qualifying dividends, places a hypothetical taxpayer in the 10 percent and 15 percent brackets and the other where taxable income after deducting capital gains and qualifying dividends still places a hypothetical taxpayer well above the 10 percent and 15 percent brackets. There could also be situations in which a portion of a taxpayer's capital gains and qualifying dividends may fall in the 10 percent and 15 percent brackets and part may not. In such situations, we advise using Tables 8-1 and 8-2 as guidelines, but make sure you use Part IV, Tax Computation Using Maximum Capital Gains Rates on page 2 of Schedule D, Capital Gains and Losses, when computing your maximum tax liability on line 41.

The Kiddie Tax: Forms 8615 and 8814

Don't jump over to the next line quite yet. If you have children younger than 14 who have investment income, you may need to complete some additional forms (see Chapter 15 for a discussion of Form 8615 and Form 8814). Form 8615 is used if your kid files his own return. Use Form 8814 if you qualify to report your kid's investment income on your return. The general rule: If your child is younger than 14, his or her investment income (interest, dividends, and so on) above $1,500 is taxed at your rate, not the child's.

Those tiny boxes on line 41: Forms 8814 and 4972

Form 8814, Parents' Election to Report Child's Interest and Dividends, is the form to use when you elect to report your kids' investment incomes on your own return instead of having the kids file their own returns. See Chapter 15 for a detailed look at your choice.

Form 4972, Tax on Lump-Sum Distributions, however, is more common. If you decide to take all of your money out of your employer's retirement plan in a lump sum, use this form to compute your tax under the 10-year averaging method if you are eligible. Using the averaging method can save you a bunch of dough. Refer to Chapter 6 ("Lines 16a and 16b: Total pensions and annuities") for a complete discussion of this issue. You had to be born before 1936 to qualify.

Line 42: Alternative Minimum Tax (Form 6251)

This line can prove to be a real bummer for some. It refers you to yet another whole tax system — the *Alternative Minimum Tax (AMT)*, which is designed to snare higher income people who reduce their taxable incomes by claiming too many (from the perspective of the IRS) deductions. You need to figure your tax under the AMT system and compare it with the regular system on Form 1040. Guess what? You pay whichever one is higher.

The AMT in brief

Here is a quick glance at how the AMT works for a couple filing jointly.

	Regular Tax	AMT
Income	$150,000	$150,000
Deductions		
Taxes	<20,000>	0
Home Equity Interest (not used to improve your home)	<5,000>	0
Mortgage Interest	<20,000>	<20,000>
Charity	<5,000>	<5,000>
Job Expenses	<15,000>	0
Exemptions (5 × $3,050)	<15,250>	0
AMT Exemption		<58,000>
Taxable Income	$69,750	$67,000
Tax	$11,064	$17,420

The unlucky taxpayer in this example had to cough up $17,420. That's $6,356 more than what his tax worked out to be under the regular method. You pay the higher of your regular tax or AMT. For simplicity, we didn't take into account all of the various deduction phaseout amounts. If your AMT is higher than your regular tax as computed in the above example, the $6,356 difference gets entered here on line 42.

You don't have to be Bill Gates to get clipped by the AMT. In 2003, a projected 1.2 million taxpayers will get hooked by the AMT. Unfortunately, things will be getting worse. Congress's Joint Tax Committee expects the number to swell to 17 million by 2010. To make matters worse, many of these newcomers will be middle-income taxpayers. The irony of the AMT is that it originally was enacted because of reports that 200 to 300 wealthy Americans paid no income tax at all. In 1969, Congress cast out a net to catch this small group and ended up hauling in 1.2 million hapless Americans.

If you have any of the types of deductions or income in the list that follows, you may be subject to the AMT. So get out your **Form 6251, Alternative Minimum Tax — Individuals,** and start calculating. The starting point is line 38 of your Form 1040 — your AGI after deducting your itemized deductions or standard deduction but before you subtract your personal exemptions to arrive at your taxable income. Enter the amount from line 38 on line 1 of Form 6251. If you claimed the standard deduction instead of itemizing your deductions, enter the amount from line 35 of Form 1040. From this amount, you have to add back the following items to arrive at your AMT income:

- Job expenses and miscellaneous itemized deductions (line 26 of Schedule A).
- Medical and dental expenses in excess of 10 percent of your income.
- Deductions for taxes (line 9 of Schedule A).
- Home equity mortgage interest not used to buy, build, or improve your home.

✔ Incentive stock options — the difference between what you paid for the stock and what it was worth when you exercised the option. (See Chapter 12 for the lowdown on handling stock options.)

✔ Depreciation in excess of the straight-line method.

✔ Tax-exempt interest from private activity bonds issued after August 7, 1986.

Although adding back the preceding items most likely will force the average taxpayer into having to compute an AMT to see whether it applies, a number of way-out items also go into figuring the AMT, such as intangible drilling expenses, circulation expenses, depletion, certain installment sales, passive activities and research, and experimental costs. Nobody can say for certain, but our best estimate is that the AMT may grab people with incomes in the $50,000 to $75,000 range.

Can you avoid the Alternative Minimum Tax? Defer those deductions and tax incentives that trigger the AMT or accelerate income, so your deductions will be within the AMT limits. Unfortunately, this maneuver requires checking your income and deductible expenses periodically throughout the year. Investing in a tax software program or a tax advisor may help ease the burden.

We wish that we could provide you with a general guide on when your AMT will exceed your regular tax, thereby causing you to have to fork over the difference. Unfortunately, we can't. But here is the IRS rule: If your taxable income, combined with your personal exemptions and the items listed earlier in this section, exceeds the following amounts, you could end up paying the AMT:

✔ Married filing jointly and qualifying widow(er) — $58,000

✔ Single or head of household — $40,250

✔ Married filing separately — $29,000

As of 1998, farmers no longer need to include certain installment sales when computing their AMTs.

Line 43: Add lines 41 and 42

Follow the instructions as indicated on the tax form.

Credits: Lines 44 to 52

Now it's time for your *credits* — and each one has a nice form for you to fill out. The credits on lines 44 to 52 may be reduced if your AMT (we just discussed it on line 42) exceeds your regular tax. Some credits can't reduce the AMT; others can, such as the Child and Dependent Care (line 45), the Elderly and Disabled (line 46), the Lifetime Learning and Hope for Education (line 4), Retirement Savings Contributions (Line 48), the Child (Line 49), and the Adoption credit (line 50). These are credits to which average taxpayers usually find they're entitled. However, there are a bunch of tax credits that we don't want you to miss.

Tax credits reduce your tax dollar for dollar. Deductions reduce only your taxable income. A $1,000 tax deduction reduces the tax for someone in the 30 percent tax bracket by only $300.

Line 44: Foreign tax credit (Form 1116)

Use **Form 1116, Foreign Tax Credit** to figure this credit. If you're not itemizing your deductions, you have to claim the foreign tax that you paid as a credit if you want to use it to reduce your tax.

Unfortunately, the computation of this credit is a killer — and even the IRS agrees. The instructions say that it should take you about 6½ hours to read the instructions, assemble the data, and fill in the form. And that's with all the instructions in English (by and large) and all the parts included! Give it a whirl. If you hate number-crunching, a computer tax software program can help (see Chapter 2). If using a computer isn't your thing, see a tax advisor. Attach Form 1116 to your return and bid it good riddance! You can either claim the foreign tax as a credit that you paid on line 44 or as an itemized deduction on Schedule A.

As a general rule, taking the credit produces a larger savings. For more on foreign taxes, refer to "Line 8: Other taxes (foreign income taxes)" in Chapter 9.

You don't have to be a multinational corporation to pay foreign taxes. With more and more people investing in international mutual funds, the foreign tax credit is being used more than ever before to reduce investors' U.S. tax bills for their share of the foreign taxes paid by the fund.

The foreign tax credit also can be used for foreign taxes paid on income earned overseas that exceeds the $80,000 exclusion and the housing allowance. (See "Work overseas" in Chapters 6 and 30 for more about this tax credit.)

You can ignore the fiendish Form 1116 if the foreign tax you paid is $300 or less ($600 for joint filers). Simply enter the foreign tax you paid on line 44 if your foreign tax is less than these amounts. This simplified method of claiming the credit is available if the only type of foreign income you had was from dividends, interest, rent, royalties, annuities, or the sale of an asset.

Line 45: Credit for child and dependent-care expenses (Form 2441)

If you hire someone to take care of your children so that you can work, you're entitled to the credit that you figure on **Form 2441.** This credit may save you several hundred dollars. To be eligible, your child must be younger than 13 or a dependent of any age who is physically or mentally handicapped. See Chapter 15 for information on Form 2441.

The maximum credit for one child jumped from $720 in 2002 to $1,050 in 2003. For two kids the credit now is $2,100, up from $1,440 in 2002. Employers who provide child care for their employees are allowed a tax credit for a percentage of their expenses.

Line 46: Credit for the elderly or the disabled (Schedule R)

You use (and attach!) Schedule R for this credit. You are entitled to claim this credit (which can amount to as much as $1,125) if you are married and both you and your spouse are 65 or older — or both of you are disabled and any age. For single taxpayers, the maximum credit is $750. See Chapter 15 for a discussion of Schedule R and the reasons most people are ineligible for this credit. If you qualify, enter this credit on line 46.

Line 47: Education credits (Form 8863)

Here is where you claim the *Hope Scholarship Credit* and the *Lifetime Learning Credit*. Remember that credits reduce your tax, dollar for dollar. You claim both credits on **Form 8863, Education Credits (Hope and Lifetime Learning Credits).** Here are snapshots of how these credits work:

- ✔ **The Hope Scholarship Credit** provides a credit of $1,500 per student per year for the first two years of college. The credit is equal to 100 percent of the first $1,000 of tuition expenses (but not room, board, or books) and 50 percent of the next $1,000 of tuition paid. The credit can be claimed for you, your spouse, and your dependents. But if you earn too much, you won't be eligible. For married taxpayers (you must file jointly), the credit starts to phase out at $83,000 of income and is completely lost at $103,000. For single taxpayers, the phaseout starts at $41,000 and is completely wiped out at $51,000.

  The credit isn't available for anyone convicted of possession or distribution of a controlled substance. A student must carry at least one-half the normal course load.

- ✔ **The Lifetime Learning Credit** is a 20 percent credit on up to $10,000 of tuition expenses (but not room, board, or books). That's up from the $1,000 credit allowed in 2002. This credit is per family, not per student, as is the case with the Hope credit. Don't confuse the word "lifetime." It means that during your lifetime, you can annually claim a credit of $2,000 now, and not a limit of $2,000 during your entire lifetime. The same income limits and family-member restrictions that apply to the Hope credit also apply to this credit. Unlike the Hope credit, a student doesn't have to carry at least one-half the normal course load. Any course to acquire or improve job skills qualifies, but not courses involving sports or hobbies.

You can claim the Hope credit for one child and the Lifetime credit for another, but you can't claim both credits for the same student.

Here is how the two credits work in conjunction. For any student, you can claim only one of the credits. For example, your daughter completed her second year of college in June of 2003 and started her third year of college in September. You can claim the Hope Credit for her 2003 second-year expenses or the Learning Credit for all her 2003 expenses — but not both. For 2004, you no longer are entitled to claim the Hope Credit for her, but you *can* claim the Lifetime Learning Credit. In figuring eligible expenses, only the expenses paid in 2003 for the academic period beginning in 2003 and ending before April 1, 2004 count. You can't claim either credit if you pay tuition in 2003 for a period beginning after April 1, 2004. Nor can you use this amount to compute your 2004 credit. People with hearts of stone made up these rules. You noticed!

If you were entitled to claim either credit in 2000, 2001, or 2002 but forgot to, you can correct that error, but time's a wasting. See Chapter 19 on how to amend your 2000 to 2002 returns.

Suppose that you or one of your kids for whom you're claiming an education credit dropped a class after the beginning of the semester. Here's what to do: If you receive a refund in 2003 or 2004 before you file your 2003 return, subtract your refund from the tuition you paid in 2003 when figuring the credit. If you receive a refund after you file your 2003 return, you have to increase your tax for 2004 by the amount of the credit that the refund gave rise to. For example, in 2003 you paid tuition expenses of $3,000 and claimed a 20 percent Lifetime Learning Credit of $600. In 2004, after you filed your 2003 return, you receive a $1,000 tuition refund. You have to increase your tax on the 2004 return by $200 ($1,000 × 20 percent). You can enter the amount on the dotted line to the left of Line 60 and write Hope or Lifetime Learning Credit next to it. Make sure that you add this amount to the total you place on Line 60.

The IRS can check to see whether you're entitled to either the Hope or Learning Credit because educational institutions now are required to issue **Form 1098-T, Tuition Payments Statement,** which lists the student's name, Social Security number, the amount of tuition paid, whether the student was enrolled for at least half the full-time workload, or whether the courses lead to a graduate-level degree.

The rules regarding which person among family members is eligible to claim the Hope or Lifetime Learning credits have been changed dramatically. This change applies to divorced parents where one parent claims the child as a dependent and the other parent foots the tuition bill, or where, because of income phase-out limits, a parent can't claim the credit. A way now exists for the student to claim the credit and shelter any income he or she may have. Say, for example, you're the custodial parent (see Chapter 4) and claim your child as a dependent, but your former spouse pays the tuition. You are considered to have made the payment and may claim an education credit. However, you can twist that stipulation in a number of ways that entitles that person who "is considered to have paid the tuition and related expenses" to claim an education credit. When the student pays the tuition and you claim the student as a dependent, you're still considered to have paid tuition. When someone else, say a grandparent, pays the tuition, the student is considered to have paid the tuition, which again entitles you to claim an education credit because tuition that's considered paid by the student is considered paid by you.

Because education credits attach to whomever claims the dependency exemption, the student or the parent, here is a nifty tax-planning technique. If you can't claim Hope or Learning Credit because your income is above the limits ($103,000 when filing jointly or $51,000 for others), maybe you need to consider not claiming the student as a dependent. Because students are considered to have paid their own tuition even though it's actually paid by their parents, they can claim the credit whenever their parents do not claim them as a dependent. Foregoing a $3,050 dependency exemption for someone in the 30 percent bracket costs the parents $915 in tax ($3,050 × 30 percent). On the other hand, the students pick up either the $1,500 Hope or up to $2,000 Learning credits.

The scenario in the previous paragraph is based on the student having income that's subject to tax. If the student doesn't have such an income, you may want to try this: Give the student an investment that has gone up in value followed by a quick sale of that investment. Doing so shifts the income and tax burden from you to the student so the student can apply either of the education credits against the tax, which makes more after-tax money available for the student to pay the tuition.

A host of other education provisions also are available, including a tuition and fees deduction for higher-education expenses (Line 26, Chapter 7), student loan interest that becomes easier to deduct (Line 25, Chapter 7), and Education IRAs (also known as Coverdell Education Savings Accounts), which have become more attractive — see Chapter 25.

You can't use the Hope or Lifetime Learning credits for a student *and* the tuition and fees deduction on Line 26, Form 1040. It's one or the other.

Line 48: Retirement savings contributions credit

The retirement savings contribution credit encourages joint filers with incomes of less than $50,000 (heads of households below $37,500 and single filers below $25,000) to save for retirement by enabling them to claim a credit against their tax for a percentage of up to the first $2,000 that they contribute to Roth or traditional IRAs, 401(k)s, or elective deferrals to their employer's retirement plan. Now for the fine print: If money were taken out of one of these accounts between January 1, 2000, and the date for filing your 2003 return, including any extension of time to file, you must reduce the maximum $2,000 amount that is subject to the credit by the amount that you withdrew. Whoo! For example, say you took $1,500 out of your IRA in 2002. Even though you contributed the $3,000 maximum allowed in 2003 to an IRA, the maximum amount that you can compute the credit on is $500 ($2,000 – $1,500).

Depending on the amount of your income, the credit can be either 50 percent, 20 percent, or 10 percent of the first $2,000 you saved. If you're single, earned less than $15,000, and put $1,500 into an IRA, your credit is $750 ($1,500 × 50 percent). Where did these percentages and income levels come from? **Form 8880, Credit for Qualified Retirement Savings Contributions.** This form is laid out in the form of a worksheet. Don't be intimidated; all that you do is add and subtract.

Three other rules apply: You have to be at least 18 by December 31, 2003, not someone else's dependent, or a student enrolled on a full-time basis during any five months of 2003. That means graduates of the class of June 2004 aren't eligible to claim the credit until 2005. The credit evaporates at midnight December 31, 2006. A school includes technical, trade, and mechanical schools. It does not, however, include on-the-job training courses or correspondence schools.

Line 49: Child tax credit

Every child younger than 17 on December 31 that you can claim as a dependent can cut your tax bill by $1,000. The credit was increased from $600 to $1,000 for 2003, and assuming you were entitled to the maximum $600 credit in 2002, the $400 difference should have been mailed to you last summer. Consequently, the $1,000 credit to which you're entitled for 2003 must be reduced by the $400 you received last summer. Here's something that may pleasantly surprise you. If you received an advanced payment, but you can't claim the credit in 2003 because your income is too high, you don't have to pay back the advance that you received on this year's credit. Even though the advanced payment was based on your 2002 return, no advanced payment checks were sent for children who wouldn't be under the age 17 cutoff as of December 31, 2003.

Divorced parents who take turns in claiming the dependency exemption for a child every other year may end-up facing a problem they never expected. That's because the parent who claimed the child in 2002 received the advanced payment check. So although in 2003, the other parent will claimed the dependency exemption, he or she won't be able to claim the full $1,000 credit because the parent who claimed the child as a dependent in 2002 received the $400 advance payment in 2003, which must be subtracted from the total credit.

The child must be a U.S. citizen or resident, and remember that this credit reduces your tax bill dollar for dollar. Part of your credit gets whittled away, however, when your income exceeds $110,000 if filing jointly, $75,000 filing as single or head of household, and $55,000 if married filing separately. The credit is reduced by $50 for every $1,000, or part thereof, that your income exceeds the above thresholds. This phaseout is on a per-child basis. For example, for joint filers with one child, the credit is completely phased out when their income reaches $120,000. If they have two children, a complete phaseout of the credit won't occur until their income reaches $140,000.

A quick formula — for every $20,000 of income above the phase-out levels, you lose the $1,000 credit for one kid. At $40,000 you would lose the credit for two kids.

To claim the credit, your dependent must be one of the following:

- Your son, daughter, adopted child, stepchild, or foster child
- Your brother, sister, stepbrother, or stepsister (or that person's child or grandchild), if you care for that individual as you would your own child
- Your grandchild, great-grandchild, or even your great-great-grandchild

This child tax credit comes in two varieties: *The Child Tax Credit* that most people find easy to compute and the *Additional Child Tax Credit* that comes into play when the regular Child Tax Credit exceeds your tax. When this occurs, part of the credit is refundable. People with three or more kids get to compute the refundable credit two ways and then choose the one that produces the largest refund. People with fewer kids get only one shot, which by the way, is the simpler method to compute. To determine the additional credit, you have to fill out **Form 8812, Additional Child Tax Credit.**

Here is how the refund works. Say, for example, that your tax is $1,800 and you're entitled to a $2,000 credit (2 kids × $1,000). By filling out Form 8812, you may discover that you're entitled to a refund of the $200 difference.

To compute the Child Tax Credit, use the worksheet in your 1040 instruction booklet. Here's a plain English version.

Line 1: Multiply the number of qualifying children by $1,000 and enter that amount on Line 1. One kid equals $1,000, two kids $2,000, and so on.

Line 2: Enter the amount of the advanced child tax credit you received last summer. Enter -0- if you didn't receive any.

Line 3: Subtract line 2 from line 1. If line 2 is larger than line 1, you can't take the credit, but you don't have to pay back the amount on line 2.

Line 4: Enter the amount from Form 1040, line 34, or Form 1040A, line 21. This is your AGI, your total income before claiming your itemized or standard deduction and personal exemptions.

Line 5: This line applies only if you are claiming a foreign income exclusion (Form 2555) because you are working abroad, because you are claiming an income exclusion from Puerto Rico, or because you are a resident of American Samoa (Form 4563). If this line doesn't apply, enter -0-.

Line 6: Add lines 4 and 5. Couldn't be simpler, right?

Line 7: Enter $110,000 if married filing jointly, $75,000 if single or head of household, or $55,000 if married filing separately.

Line 8: This is a yes or no question. Is line 6 more than line 7? If it isn't, check no and enter -0- on line 9. If line 6 is more than line 7, check yes. A yes means your Child Tax Credit starts getting whittled away because your income is too high. To figure by how much you must reduce your credit, subtract line 5 from line 4 and increase the result to the next $1,000. For example, increase $425 to $1,000 or $1,025 to $2,000, and so forth.

Line 9: If you checked no on line 6, you can skip this line. If you checked yes, multiply line 6 by 5 percent (0.05) and enter the result.

Line 10: Here's another yes or no question. If line 3 isn't more than line 9, check no and you don't have to proceed further. The reason: You went over the income limits and can't claim the child tax credit. If line 3 is more than line 9, check yes and subtract line 9 from line 3. Now for some good news: Generally the amount on line 10 ends up being the credit to which you're entitled. But because the credit can't exceed your tax, you have to pass that test by completing lines 11 through 15.

Line 11: Enter the amount of your tax. That's line 41 for 1040 filers and line 28 for Form 1040A taxpayers.

Line 12: Here is where you subtract other tax credits, such as the foreign tax credit (line 44), credit for child- and dependent-care expenses (line 45), credit for the elderly (line 46), education credits (line 47), and retirement savings contribution credit (line 48). Total these credits and enter that amount here in box 10.

Line 13: Here's yet another yes or no question. If the amount on line 10, for example, is $3,000 or more (that's 3 kids × $1,000 and you didn't receive any advance of the credit in 2003) and you aren't claiming an adoption credit (Form 8839), mortgage interest credit (Form 8396), or the D.C. first-time homebuyer credit (Form 8859), check no and enter the amount from box 12 in box 13. If you checked yes, you have to complete the worksheet for this line, which is found on page 5 of Publication 972, *(Child Tax Credit)*. Our suggestion: Let a good tax software program do the number crunching for you.

Line 14: Subtract line 13 from 11.

Line 15: Finally, the last line, and luckily it's another yes or no question. If line 10 (your child tax credit) isn't more than line 14 (your tax), check no and enter the amount from line 10 in box 15. This is the amount of the credit that reduces your tax. Enter this amount on line 49 of Form 1040 or line 33 of Form 1040A. If line 10 is more than line 14, enter the amount from line 14 on line 15. This is your reduced child tax credit. Enter the amount on line 15 on line 49 of your 1040 or line 33 of 1040A.

If you checked yes on line 15, you may be entitled to take the additional child tax credit (Form 8812). So don't overlook this opportunity. The additional child tax credit is claimed on line 65.

Line 50: Adoption credit (Form 8839)

In 2003, both the adoption credit and the exemption from income for employer reimbursed adoption expenses were adjusted for inflation to $10,160 from $10,000. The income phase-out range in which the credit starts getting whittled away also went up slightly and is now from $153,390 to $192,390 (up from $150,000 to $192,000 in 2002). Starting in 2003, if you adopt a child with special needs, you can claim the credit even if you don't incur adoption expenses (see Chapter 25).

You're entitled to a credit of up to $10,160 against your tax for adoption expenses. A *child with special needs* means someone with a medical, physical, mental, or emotional handicap; a child whose age makes him or her difficult to adopt; or a member of a minority group. A foreign child can't be considered a child with special needs. Here are the rules:

- ✔ If your AGI is $152,390 or less, you're entitled to the full credit. Between $153,390 and $192,390, the credit is phased out. At $192,391, it's gone. If you claimed a foreign income exclusion or housing deduction (Form 2555 or Form 2555-EZ) because you're working abroad, because you're claiming an income exclusion from Puerto Rico, or because you're a resident of American Samoa (Form 4563), you have to add these amounts to your income per line 35, Form 1040 or line 22, Form 1040A when figuring whether your income is more than the income threshold.

✔ The child must be younger than 18 or physically or mentally incapable of self-care.

✔ Adopting your spouse's child doesn't qualify, nor does a surrogate parenting arrangement.

✔ Adoption expenses can't be paid with funds received from any federal, state, or local adoption program.

✔ The credit can't exceed your tax minus any credits claimed on lines 44 through 49 on Form 1040 or lines 29 through 33 on Form 1040A.

✔ Any unused credit can be carried forward for five years until you use it up.

✔ Married couples must file a joint return. However, if you're legally separated for the last six months of the year, you're eligible to file a separate return and claim the credit.

The types of expenses that qualify for the credits include adoption fees, court costs, attorney fees, and other expenses directly related to adopting an eligible child.

In addition to the adoption credit, you exclude up to $10,160 from your income for adoption expenses paid by your employer under an adoption assistance program. For example, you incur $20,320 in adoption expenses. You pay $10,160, and your employer pays $10,160 as part of an adoption assistance program. You're entitled to a $10,160 credit for the expenses you paid, and you're not taxed on the $10,160 paid by your employer.

As a practical matter, owners or principal shareholders of a business aren't eligible to participate in an employer adoption assistance program.

If you pay adoption expenses in any year prior to the year the adoption becomes final, the credit is taken in the year following the year the expenses are paid. If you pay adoption expenses in the year the adoption becomes final you claim the credit in that year. If you pay adoption expenses in a year after the adoption becomes final you claim the credit for those expenses in the year of payment.

Here is how the above rule works: You incur $10,000 of adoption expenses in 2003 but pay $8,000 in 2003 and $2,000 in 2004 when the adoption is finalized. You have to wait until 2004 to claim the credit for the $8,000 of expenses which is added to the $2,000 you paid in 2004. Had the adoption become final in 2003, you could claim the credit based on the $8,000 you paid in 2003. In 2004 you base the credit on the $2,000 paid that year.

For expenses paid before 2002 that weren't deductible because the adoption wasn't finalized until 2003, you are limited to the $5,000 ($6,000 for a child with special needs) limits that prevailed before 2002.

With a foreign adoption, you can't claim the credit or the exclusion until the adoption becomes final. Adoption expenses paid in an earlier year are considered paid in the year the adoption becomes final.

Regardless of the year paid, your adoption expenses or adoption exclusion can't exceed $10,160 for any child.

Both the credit and the exclusion are computed on **Form 8839, Qualified Adoption Expenses.** The amount of the credit (line 18) gets entered on line 50 (Form 1040) or line 34 (Form 1040A). Any unused credit that can be carried forward to 2004 gets entered on line 13 of Form 8839. The phase-out income limits don't apply to carryovers. The phaseout is applied only once in the year that generated the credit.

The amount of taxable employer-provided adoption expenses is computed in Part III of Form 8839. The taxable portion, if any, on line 31, gets reported on line 7 whether you're filing Form 1040 or 1040A. Next to line 7, write AB for adoption benefit. How could you have a taxable benefit? Say your employer paid $7,000 in benefits, but you were entitled to only a $4,000 exclusion because your income exceeded $152,390. In that case, $3,000 of the benefit would be taxable.

You can claim the adoption credit for expenses on an unsuccessful adoption. On Line 1 of Form 8839 where the child's name goes enter `See page 2`. At the bottom of page 2 of Form 8839, indicate the name and address of the agency or attorney that assisted in the attempted adoption. Then complete the form as if the adoption had taken place. We know that this probably is painful, and we wish we knew what to say to ease that pain.

Line 51: Credits from box (a) Form 8396 box (b) Form 8859

Form 8396 is for claiming the Mortgage Interest Credit. You may be eligible for this credit if you were issued a mortgage credit certificate by a state or local government agency. This is a state and local governmental program to provide taxpayers with financing to help them purchase a principal residence. Home purchasers are issued a Mortgage Credit Certificate (MCC), which entitles them to a tax credit equal to between 10 percent and 50 percent of the amount of the mortgage interest they paid. If the MCC has a rate that exceeds 20 percent, the maximum credit is limited to $2,000. Amounts of more than $2,000 can be carried over to future years but are subject to the $2,000 annual limit. You must reduce your home mortgage interest deduction on Schedule A by the amount of the credit. A good mortgage broker can assist you in qualifying for a state-sponsored mortgage loan so you can qualify for this credit.

Form 8859 is for residents of Washington, D.C. First-time homebuyers in the district are entitled to a tax credit of up to $5,000 of the cost of the residence. This credit took effect August 5, 1997, and is good until December 31, 2003. *First-time homebuyer* means that you didn't own a home within one year of the purchase of your new home. The credit is claimed on **Form 8859, District of Columbia First-Time Homebuyer Credit.** The amount of the credit is reduced if your income is more than $70,000 ($110,000 for joint filers). For every $1,000 above the threshold, the credit is reduced by $250.

Line 52: Other credits

The application of the following credits is extremely limited, and few people are eligible for them. So, if you want to explore them further, you need to call the IRS (800-829-3676) and ask for the forms and instructions. Sorry! Here is what boxes a through c on line 52 refer to:

a **Form 3800, General Business Credit:** This form includes a number of credits that qualify as general business credits. If you're claiming more than one of these general business credits, check the Form 3800 box on line 52 of your 1040, and then fill in and attach Form 3800, as well as the forms for the types of credits you are claiming. If you're claiming just one of these general business credits, check the box c Form (specify) on line 52, fill in the form number, and attach that specific form. The following list includes the general business credits on **Form 3800:**

- **Form 3468, Investment Credit**
- **Form 5884, Work Opportunity Credit**
- **Form 6478, Credit for Alcohol Used for Fuel**
- **Form 6765, Credit for Increasing Research Activities**

- Form 8586, Low-Income Housing Credit
- Form 8820, Orphan Drug Credit
- Form 8826, Disabled Access Credit
- Form 8830, Enhanced Oil Recovery Credit
- Form 8835, Renewable Electricity Production Credit
- Form 8845, Indian Employment Credit
- Form 8846, Credit for Employer Social Security and Medicare Taxes Paid on Certain Employees' Tips
- Form 8847, Credit for Contributions to Certain Community Development Corporations
- Form 8861, Welfare-To-Work Credit
- Form 8874, New Markets Credit (this is a credit for an investment in or a loan to small businesses in low-income communities)
- Form 8881, Small Employer Pension Plan Start Up Costs
- Form 8882, Employer Provided Child Care Facilities and Services

The Small Employer Pension Plan Start Up Costs Credit allows employers with fewer than 100 employees who didn't have a plan in the three immediate past years to claim a credit of 50 percent of the start-up costs to establish a company pension. The maximum amount of the credit is $500 and can be claimed for costs incurred for up to three years. The maximum amount of expenses that can be used to compute the credit is $1,000. Start-up expenses above the amount used to compute the credit may be deducted as a business expense.

To claim the start-up credit, the pension plan must cover at least one employee who is not an owner or who makes less than $90,000 (the 2003 amount).

Credits carried over from previous years also are entered on Form 3800.

b **Form 8801, Credit for Prior Year Minimum Tax — Individuals and Fiduciaries.** If you paid the alternative minimum tax in the prior year, you may be entitled to a credit for past payments.

c **Form (specify)_____:** If you're claiming only one of the credits listed above, enter the form number and the amount of the credit on this line. If you're claiming more than one of the listed credits, you have to fill out Form 3800 that we just mentioned and enter the total of the credits on line a.

Form 8834, Qualified Electric Vehicle Credit — for all you environmentalists. Electric cars come with a maximum $4,000 per-car credit. To claim the credit, enter the form number (8834) on the line by box c and enter the credit to which you're entitled per line 20 of Form 8834 on line 52. In 2004, the credit drops to $3,000.

The electric vehicle credit doesn't apply to hybrid gas/electric vehicles produced by Toyota and Honda. They aren't 100 percent electric powered. However, those cars qualify for the $2,000 clean fuel–burning deduction. See Line 33, Chapter 7.

Line 53: Total credits

Add lines 44 through 52 and put the sum on line 53. (If you make a mistake, your grade will suffer.)

Line 54: Subtract line 53 from line 43

If line 53 is greater than line 43, just enter -0- on line 54.

Other Taxes

What! More taxes? Could be. Read the following sections to see whether any of these taxes apply to you.

Line 55: Self-employment tax (Schedule SE)

If you earn income from being self-employed and from other sources, Schedule SE is used to figure another tax that you owe — the Social Security tax and Medicare tax. The first $87,000 of your self-employment earnings is taxed at 12.4 percent (this is the Social Security tax part). There isn't any limit for the Medicare tax; it's 2.9 percent of your total self-employment earnings. For amounts of $87,000 or less, the combined rate is 15.3 percent (adding the two taxes together), and above $87,000, the rate is 2.9 percent. See Chapter 15 for information about filling out Schedule SE.

Line 56: Social Security and Medicare tax on unreported tip income (Form 4137)

If you worked in a restaurant that employed at least ten people and didn't report your share of at least 8 percent of the restaurant's income as tip income, your employer will do it for you. This amount (the difference between what you reported as tip income to your employer and your share of 8 percent of the restaurant's income), which otherwise is known as your allocated tips, is entered on box 8 of your W-2. The amount in box 8 isn't included in box 1 of your W-2 and has to be added to your total wages on Form 1040 (line 7). The Social Security tax that you owe on the amount in box 8 is computed on **Form 4137, Social Security and Medicare Tax on Unreported Tip Income** and is entered on line 56.

When we say "your share of 8 percent of the restaurant's income," that doesn't mean that you're entitled to this income. It means that the IRS arbitrarily claims that the restaurant generated tip income equal to 8 percent of the restaurant's income. Box 8 of your W-2 is for your share of the total amount of tips. The IRS can always audit the restaurant and determine, for example, that the tip rate was really 14 percent. Ouch!

If your employer wasn't able to collect from you all the Social Security and Medicare tax you owe on your reported tip income, box 12 of your W-2 will show that amount. Code A next to the amount in box 12 is for Social Security tax, and Code B next to the amount in box 12 is for Medicare Tax. Enter the amounts in box 12 on the dotted line to the left of line 60, Form 1040, and to the left of the amount, write UT, which stands for uncollected tax on tips. Don't forget to enter the amount on the dotted line in the total on line 60.

Line 57: Tax on IRAs, other retirement plans, and other tax-favored accounts (Form 5329)

The IRS should simply list **Form 5329** by the name **"IRA and Pension Penalties."** Remember, if you take money out of an IRA or pension before you're 59½, you may owe a

10 percent penalty in addition to the tax on the amount that you withdraw. If you took out too little after reaching 70½, the penalty is 50 percent of the amount that you should have taken — based on your life expectancy — and what you actually withdrew or failed to withdraw. A 6 percent penalty also takes effect whenever you contribute more than you're allowed to an IRA or a retirement plan. This penalty is owed annually until the excess contribution and the earnings on it are withdrawn. These penalties are computed on Form 5329 and entered here for "other taxes." Refer to Chapter 6, "Lines 15a and 15b: Total IRA distributions," for details on how to escape this penalty. You have a whole bunch of ways to escape, such as withdrawals for first-time homebuyers and certain education expenses. To read more about pension plans, see Chapter 6, the section, "Line 16a and 16b," which also shows a number of ways to avoid this penalty. Withdrawals and excess contributions to other tax-favored accounts such as the Archer Medical Savings Accounts (Line 23, Chapter 7) and Education IRAs (Coverdell Education Savings Accounts) — see line 24 in Chapter 7.

Line 58: Advance earned income credits

Enter the amount from box 9 of your W-2. If you're entitled to an EIC, you can file Form W-5 with your employer and up to $1,528 (the 2003 amount) can be added to your paycheck throughout the year. This advance payment is available only if you have at least one qualifying child. That way, you don't have to wait until you file your tax return after the end of the year to get a refund (refer to Chapter 6, "Box 9: Advance EIC payment," and the later section, "Line 63: Earned income credit").

The reason you add your Advanced Earned Income Payments on this line is because you followed the instructions in Chapter 6 and had part of the tax credit to which you were entitled added to your paycheck throughout the year. Now when you file your return and compute the Earned Income Tax Credit to which you are entitled on line 63, you have to give back what you already received during the year. Otherwise, you'd be double dipping. The IRS doesn't like that.

Line 59: Household employment taxes (Schedule H)

Even if you don't expect to hold high political office — or low political office — the provisions of the nanny tax can save you a tidy sum and simplify the number and type of returns that you have to file. The law covers housekeepers, babysitters, and yard-care workers, as well as nannies.

The nanny tax is figured on **Schedule H,** and the amount you owe is entered on line 59. If you didn't pay cash wages of $1,400 or more in 2003, or $1,000 or more in any calendar quarter, or didn't withhold any federal income tax, you can skip this form. If you paid more than $1,400 in wages in 2003 but less than $1,000 in any calendar quarter, you only have to fill out page 1 and enter the amount from line 8 of Schedule H onto line 59. If you paid more than $1,000 in any quarter, you must fill out page 2 of the form and enter the amount from line 27 of Schedule H onto line 59. See Chapter 15 for more about filling out Schedule H.

Line 60: IRS pop quiz

Find your total tax by adding lines 54 through 59 and placing the amount here.

Payments

This section of the return is where you finally, thankfully, get to tally up how much actual federal tax you paid during the year.

Line 61: Federal income tax withheld

Enter the amounts from box 2 of your W-2s and your W-2Gs, 1099-DIVs, and 1099-INTs, and from box 4 of your Form 1099-Rs, 1099-DIVs, 1099-INTs, and 1099-MISCs on line 61. Make sure that you don't overlook any tax withheld on any other Form 1099.

Line 62: Estimated tax payments

If you made estimated tax payments toward your 2003 tax, fill in the total amount of the payments here. If you applied last year's overpayment to this year's return, don't forget to enter that amount, too! The IRS isn't kind enough to send you a reminder; you have to keep track yourself.

Remember, the IRS doesn't want to wait until April 15, 2005, to collect your 2004 tax. So, if you expect to owe money come next April 15, you must file quarterly estimates if 90 percent of your tax isn't being withheld from your income and you'll owe more than $1,000.

Estimated tax payments are made on **Form 1040-ES, Estimated Tax for Individuals.** The form requires only your name, address, Social Security number, and the amount you're paying. For 2004 estimated payments, make sure that you use the 2004 1040-ES. See Chapter 15 if you need help filling out Form 1040-ES.

Line 63: Earned income credit (EIC)

The earned income credit is a special credit for lower-income workers. The credit is refundable — which means that if it exceeds your tax or if you don't owe tax, the IRS will send you a check for the amount of the EIC.

Claiming the EIC won't disqualify you from receiving welfare benefits.

Unlike other credits, the EIC is no small piece of change. The credit can be as high as $4,204 for a married couple with two kids. To qualify for the credit, your AGI (Line 35 on Form 1040 or Line 21 on Form 1040A) or earned income must be less than the following amounts:

- ✔ $29,666 ($30,666 for married filing jointly) if you have one child
- ✔ $33,692 ($34,692 for married filing jointly) if you have two or more children
- ✔ $11,230 ($12,230 for married filing jointly) if you don't have any children and you are at least 25 (but younger than 65) and are not being claimed as a dependent by anyone else

Net self-employment income for the purposes of the EIC is your net earnings reduced by one-half of your self-employment tax on Schedule SE that you deducted on Form 1040 (line 28). If you lost money in your business as reported on Schedule C, you have to deduct your loss from your other earned income.

Earned income doesn't include the following:

- Interest and dividends
- Social Security benefits
- Pensions or annuities
- Veterans' benefits
- Alimony or child support
- Unemployment insurance
- Welfare benefits
- Taxable scholarships or fellowships that were not reported on your W-2

Rules that everyone must follow include the following:

- You need a valid Social Security number.
- Your filing status can't be married filing separately.
- You must be a U.S. citizen or resident alien for the entire year.
- You can't file Form 2555 or 2555-EZ (see Chapter 6).
- Your investment income must be $2,600 or less.
- You must have earned income.

Rules that must be met if you have a child include the following qualifying child tests:

1. **Relationship test:** The child must be your:

   - Child, adopted child, stepchild, or foster child placed by an authorized agency.

   - Your brother, sister, stepbrother, stepsister, or the child or the grandchild of one of these relatives if you care for the individual as you would your own child.

   Your child doesn't have to be your dependent unless he, she, or they are married. A great-grandchild and even a great-great-grandchild passes the relationship test. Congratulations, you would have to be well past 100 to have great-great descendents.

2. **Residency test:** Your child must have lived with you in your main home in the U.S. for more than six months. For a child who was born or died during the year, the residency test is met if the child lived with you for part of the year. Military personnel stationed outside the U.S. are considered to be residing in the U.S. A child who was kidnapped or missing (there were 725,000 such cases in 2001) is treated as having met the residency test. However, the last year the child is considered to have lived with you is the year in which the child would have turned 18. The rules for claiming a kidnapped or missing child as a dependent in Chapter 4 are the same for considering that child as a qualifying child for the EIC. Brief absences such as being hospitalized or away at school are ignored in determining the six-month residency.

3. **Age test:** Your child must be younger than 19 (or younger than 24 if a full-time student) or any age if permanently and totally disabled.

4. **Qualifying child test:** Your qualifying child (meaning he or she meets the tests in 1, 2, and 3) can't be the qualifying child of another person. Similarly, you can't be the qualifying child of another person when you have a child who qualifies.

Figuring the earned income credit

If you meet all of the requirements, figuring the earned income credit is easy. No math is required. The credit to which you're entitled usually is based on the lower of your earned income and adjusted gross income (AGI). However, if these two amounts are the same, just look up that amount for the corresponding income bracket in the Earned Income Credit Table and read across to the appropriate column: No qualifying child, one child, or two children under your filing status, single or head of household, or married filing jointly. For example, if your earned income and AGI is $12,240, and you have one qualifying child and are filing as a head of household, you're entitled to an EIC of $2,547. If your earned income and AGI are not the same, your earned EIC is based on the lower of these two figures. However, if your AGI is less than $6,240 ($7,240 for married filing jointly), and you don't have any children, or if your AGI is less than $13,730 ($14,730 for married filing jointly), and you have one or more children, then you base your EIC on your earned income. Attach the EIC Schedule to your return and enter the credit on Form 1040 (line 63).

A nice feature of this credit is that you don't have to wait until you file your return to claim it. If you're eligible for the credit, you can file **Form W-5, EIC (Advance Payment Certificate)** with your employer, and a portion (up to $1,528, the 2003 amount) of the credit will be added to your weekly paycheck. The advanced credit you received during the year is entered on box 9 of your W-2. You must enter the amount in box 9 on Form 1040 (line 58) and the EIC to which you're entitled on line 63. For example, if you're entitled to an EIC of $1,200 and you received $500 throughout the year from your employer, $500 will be entered in box 9 of your W-2. The $500 is subtracted from your EIC of $1,200, and $700 will be refunded. However, the IRS does the math a different way. The $500 advance EIC payment is added to your tax and $1,200 is subtracted as a payment. The IRS always has its own mysterious way of doing things. You must have at least one child to qualify for the advance payment EIC program.

You can also take the easy way out and let the IRS figure your EIC. Attach Form 1040 EIC to your return and write EIC to the right of line 63. Make sure that you complete all the other lines on your return.

Sometimes a child meets the rules to be the qualifying child for two people. How can this happen? Say your sister and her 4-year-old son lived with you for the entire year. You care for your nephew as you would your own child. Who gets to claim the EIC? You or your sister? Tiebreaking rules govern. Here they are. The EIC goes to the parent of the child, in this case your sister. If neither is the child's parent, the EIC is claimed by the person with the highest AGI. If both parents seek to claim the credit, but don't file jointly, the parent with whom the child resided longest during the year receives the EIC. If a tie still results, the EIC goes to the parent with the highest AGI. I bet you thought only tennis had tiebreakers.

In addition to the income limit, the rules for individuals without children say you must have maintained a home in the U.S. for more than six months, file a joint return if married, not be a dependent of another, and be at least 25 but younger than 65.

To compute the credits, go to the EIC Table in your tax-instruction booklet. Based on your income and the number of qualifying children, read across for your earned income line to the amount of credit that you can claim.

Your earned income

Generally your earned income includes your wages and salaries, what you earned from being self-employed less 50 percent of the Social Security and Medicare Tax, tips, and union strike benefits. (If you retired on disability, union strike benefits payments are considered earned income until you meet the minimum retirement age.) This is a drastic change from the old way of figuring your earned income.

If you don't list your dependent's Social Security number on the EIC form, you get NO CREDIT. If investment income exceeds $2,600, you get NO CREDIT. Investment income includes capital gains, interest, dividends, and tax-exempt interest. If you are married filing separately, you are not entitled to the credit.

Your investment income

Because you can't claim the EIC whenever your investment income exceeds $2,600, here's how to determine whether you're under or over that limit.

Taxable interest (line 8a of Form 1040 or 1040A) $_____

Tax-exempt interest (line 8b of Form 1040 or 1040A) $_____

Dividends (line 9a of Form 1040 or 1040A) $_____

Capital gains (line 13a of Form 1040 or line 10a Form 1040A) $_____

If line 13a shows a loss enter -0- $_____

Rental and royalty income line 26, Schedule E $_____

If line 26 shows a loss enter -0- $_____

Total $_____

Anyone who fraudulently claims the EIC is ineligible to claim it for ten years. For those who are reckless or intentionally disregard the rules, the penalty is two years. This year the IRS initiated a program in which 25,000 filers must precertify that their children lived with them for more than six months to be eligible for the credit. The IRS wanted to contact twice as many, but Congress wouldn't allow it.

Line 64: Excess Social Security and RRTA tax withheld

Line 64 applies only if you worked for two employers and your total wages were $87,000 or more. The maximum Social Security tax you are required to pay for 2003 is $5,394. So if $5,694 was reported withheld on your W-2s, $300 is entered on line 64. Box 4 of your W-2s contains the amount of Social Security tax that was withheld from your salary. If you worked for only one employer and more than $5,394 was withheld, skip line 64; you have to get the excess back from your employer.

Line 65: Additional child tax credit (Form 8812)

This credit is the refundable portion of the Child Tax Credit that we explained on line 49. To have part of the credit refunded, you have to file **Form 8812, Additional Child Tax Credit.**

Line 66: Amount paid with extension request (Form 4868)

If you requested a four-month extension of time by filing **Form 4868, Application for Automatic Extension of Time to File U.S. Individual Income Tax Return,** enter the amount that you paid when you requested the extension. (You can find this form in the back of this book. Unbelievably, despite the millions of taxpayers who file for extensions each year, the IRS still doesn't include this form in the Form 1040 instruction booklet.) See the section, "When to file" in Chapter 4 for more about how to obtain an extension of time to file.

Line 67: Other payments

Here are a couple of the more obscure forms to wonder about:

a **Form 2439, Notice to Shareholders of Undistributable Long-Term Capital Gain:** You will receive this form if you invested in a mutual fund where the company did not distribute your share of the long-term capital gains that you were entitled to receive. Enter the amount from line 2 of this form on line 67 and attach a copy of the form to your 1040. See Chapter 12 for information on how to handle the capital gains retained by the fund.

b **Form 4136, Credit for Federal Tax Paid on Fuels:** This form is for claiming a refundable credit for the tax paid on gasoline and gasohol for off-highway use. Bulldozers, forklifts, generators, and compressors used in your business qualify for the credit. Fuel used in motorboats doesn't qualify. Tax paid on undyed kerosene used in home heaters also qualifies for the credit.

c **Form 8885, Health Coverage Tax Credit for Eligible Recipients:** This tax credit allows dislocated workers and uninsured retirees who are receiving pension benefits from the federal government's Pension Benefit Guarantee Corporations (PBGC) to claim a refundable credit equal to 65 percent of their health insurance expenses. This group of people is by no means small. In 2002, the PBGC took over the responsibility for paying the pensions of 95,000 retirees of Bethlehem Steel. Individuals can elect to forego the credit and instead have the government pick up the tab directly for 65 percent of their health insurance premiums.

To be eligible for the credit or the advance payment, you have to be receiving Trade Adjustments Assistance (TAA) allowances under the Trade Act or Alternative Trade Adjustments Assistance (ATAA), or be an uninsured retiree between 55 and 65 who is receiving pension benefits from the PBGC. TAA allowances are paid to workers who lost their jobs because of foreign trade. ATAA benefits are paid to displaced workers under the Trade Acts alternative program. The credit and the advance payment may very well become the prototype for all unemployed workers.

TAA or ATAA allowances can be obtained by submitting a request for determination of eligibility with the U.S. Department of Labor. A special hot line has been set up for the TAA and ATAA programs at 866-628-4282. The Health Coverage Tax Credit (HCTC) Web site is at `www.irs.gov/individuals/article/0,,id=109915,00.html`.

The credit isn't available to individuals who are unemployed and paying health insurance premiums under COBRA unless they meet the eligibility requirements for receiving TAA, ATAA, or PBGC benefits. Coverage under a spouse's health insurance counts toward determining the credit. Individuals covered by Medicare aren't eligible.

Line 68: Total payments

You enter the total of the payments (lines 61 through 67) on line 68 and hold your breath (or your nose).

Refund or Amount You Owe

Okay, this is it. Now comes the moment you've worked so hard for. Do you get money back? Do you pay? Read on and find out.

Line 69: The amount that you overpaid

If the amount of your total payments (line 68) is more than your total tax (line 60), subtract line 60 from line 68 (see Figure 8-2). The remainder is the amount you overpaid. Do you like that word "overpaid"?

Refund	69	If line 68 is more than line 60, subtract line 60 from line 68. This is the amount you **overpaid**	69	
Direct deposit?	70a	Amount of line 69 you want **refunded to you** ▶	70a	
See page 56 and fill in 70b, 70c, and 70d.	▶ b	Routing number ☐☐☐☐☐☐☐☐☐ ▶ c Type: ☐ Checking ☐ Savings		
	▶ d	Account number ☐☐☐☐☐☐☐☐☐☐☐☐☐☐☐☐☐		
	71	Amount of line 69 you want **applied to your 2004 estimated tax** ▶ 71		
Amount You Owe	72	**Amount you owe.** Subtract line 68 from line 60. For details on how to pay, see page 57 ▶	72	
	73	Estimated tax penalty (see page 58) 73		

Third Party Designee	Do you want to allow another person to discuss this return with the IRS (see page 58)? ☐ **Yes.** Complete the following. ☐ **No**
	Designee's name ▶ Phone no. ▶ ( ) Personal identification number (PIN) ☐☐☐☐☐

Sign Here Joint return? See page 20. Keep a copy for your records.	Under penalties of perjury, I declare that I have examined this return and accompanying schedules and statements, and to the best of my knowledge and belief, they are true, correct, and complete. Declaration of preparer (other than taxpayer) is based on all information of which preparer has any knowledge.			
	Your signature	Date	Your occupation	Daytime phone number ( )
	Spouse's signature. If a joint return, **both** must sign.	Date	Spouse's occupation	

Paid Preparer's Use Only	Preparer's signature ▶		Date	Check if self-employed ☐	Preparer's SSN or PTIN
	Firm's name (or yours if self-employed), address, and ZIP code	▶		EIN	
				Phone no. ( )	

Form **1040** (2003)

Figure 8-2: The rest of the Form 1040. Fill it in and you're done! (Hope you get to fill in the refund line!)

Line 70a: Amount that you want refunded to you

You can speed up the receipt of your refund by almost three weeks by having your refund wired to your account. That way, you can ensure that it won't be lost or stolen. To do so, enter your routing number on line 71b. That's the nine-digit number at the bottom left in Figure 8-3. On line 71c, check the type of account: checking or savings. On line 71d, enter your account number. That's the number to right of the routing number in Figure 8-3.

PAUL MAPLE
LILIAN MAPLE
123 Main Street
Anyplace, NY 10000

1234
15-0000/0000

_____ 20 ___

PAY TO THE
ORDER OF _____ $ ☐☐☐☐

SAMPLE

_____ DOLLARS

ANYPLACE BANK
Anyplace, NY 10000

For _____

I:250000005I :200000"86" 1234

Routing Number (line 71b)   Account Number (line 71d)

Figure 8-3: A sample check.

Line 71: Amount of line 69 you want applied to your 2004 estimated tax

Here you indicate what amount of your refund you want applied to your 2004 (next year's) estimated tax. After you make this selection and file your return, you can't change your mind and ask for it back. You have to claim it as a credit on your 2004 return.

Line 72: The gosh darn AMOUNT YOU OWE line

If your total tax (line 60) is larger than your total payments (line 68), subtract line 68 from line 60. This is the amount you owe. Sorry. Fill out **Form 1040-V, Payment Voucher,** that the IRS sends you.

If you want to charge what you owe on a credit card, go back to line 12 of the 1040EZ for the ins and outs of how to do this (see Chapter 5). The IRS now has a host of alternate payment options. The "new" IRS never stops thinking of ways to separate you from your money.

If you want to pay what you owe the old-fashioned way, by check, see the section "Finishing Up," which follows.

Line 73: Estimated tax penalty (Form 2210)

If you owe more than $1,000 and haven't paid 90 percent of your tax liability in either quarterly estimates or in withholding, you will be assessed an underestimating penalty. A number of exceptions either excuse or reduce this penalty. You calculate this penalty on **Form 2210, Underpayment of Estimated Tax.** See Chapter 19 on penalties to see whether one of the exceptions applies to you. Chapter 15 gives you all the facts on the 1040-ES, the estimated tax form, and the penalties that may apply if you don't fill it out. If you got socked for the penalty this year, learn the rules so it won't happen again next year.

Remember, the IRS doesn't want to wait until April 15, 2005, when you file your 2004 tax return, to collect your 2004 tax. You should have paid at least 90 percent of your tax by having tax withheld from your salary, pension, or IRA distributions — or by making estimated quarterly tax payments. If you don't calculate this penalty yourself, the IRS does and will bill you for it. You don't want the IRS to prepare this form, because the IRS will prepare it on the basis of your paying the maximum!

A good tax software program will breeze through this form to see whether you are eligible to have the penalty reduced or eliminated by one of the exceptions. The ability to calculate this form alone is worth the price of the software package.

Finishing Up

Attach your W-2s, W-2Gs, 1099s where federal tax was withheld, and all schedules. If you owe money, make sure you write your Social Security number on the front of the check along with the notation 2003 Form 1040. Sign your return and mail it to the IRS Service Center for the area in which you live. (See the IRS Web site for the correct address.) If you have to send a check, make it out to the United States Treasury.

Part III
Filling Out Schedules and Other Forms

The 5th Wave   By Rich Tennant

"I put an extension on my tax return like you suggested, but I still don't think it's going to get there on time."

In this part . . .

The plain old 1040 isn't just the plain old 1040 — it's really a souped-up version that rides around with a number of schedules and forms, tailored to your specific tax situation. Naturally, these schedules and forms take after the 1040 in their complexity and potential for causing confusion. This part walks you through the schedules and forms that affect most taxpayers, with ways you may be able to take advantage of new tax cuts and tips that help you pay only what you really owe.

Chapter 9

Itemized Deductions: Schedule A

••

In This Chapter

▶ Standard deductions versus itemizing

▶ Deductions for medical and dental expenses

▶ Deductions for taxes and interest you paid

▶ Deductions for gifts to charity and casualty and theft losses

▶ Deductions for job expenses and miscellaneous expenses

••

If *Hamlet* were to be written today, we wonder whether Shakespeare would have him lament, "To itemize or to take the standard deduction, that is the question." Forgive the Shakespearean reference, but that is indeed the question that must be answered.

The Decision: You've reached that point in preparing your return where this decision must be made. You've totaled your income and subtracted your allowable adjustments to income. Now to arrive at your taxable income, you have to subtract your standard deduction and exemptions — or take the more difficult road and subtract your itemized deductions.

The Standard Deduction

If you're younger than 65, the standard deductions are as follows:

▸ Married filing jointly or a qualifying widow(er) — $9,500

▸ Head of household — $7,000

▸ Single — $4,750

▸ Married filing separately — $4,750

If you're married filing separately, you may claim the standard deduction only if your spouse also claims the standard deduction. If your spouse itemizes, you also must itemize. If you decide not to itemize your deductions, enter the standard deduction for your filing status on line 37.

A March 2002 General Accounting Office report revealed that 1 million taxpayers overpaid the IRS by using the standard deduction instead of itemizing their deductions.

Older than 65 or blind

If you're 65 or older, you get to increase your standard deduction by $1,150 if you are single or a head of household, and it's increased by $950 if you are married filing jointly or a qualifying widow(er). If you're blind, you're entitled to an extra $1,150 if single, and $950 if married. For example, if you're single, over 65 and blind, the standard deduction of $4,750 increases by $2,300 for a total of $7,050.

Instead of adding this extra deduction to your regular, standard deduction, just check the appropriate blanks in the chart (see Table 9-1).

Table 9-1	Standard Deduction Chart for People Age 65 or Older or Blind		
Check the appropriate boxes below and total. Then go to the chart.			
You		65 or older ❏	Blind ❏
Your spouse, if claiming spouse's exemption		65 or older ❏	Blind ❏
Total number of boxes you checked		_____	
If Your Filing Status Is:	*And the Total Number of Boxes You Checked Above Is:*		*Your Standard Deduction Is:*
Single	1		$5,900
	2		$7,050
Married filing joint return	1		$10,450
or qualifying widow(er)	2		$11,400
with dependent child	3		$12,350
	4		$13,300
Married filing separate return	1		$5,700
	2		$6,650
Head of household	1		$8,150
	2		$9,300

If you're claiming an increased standard deduction, you can't use Form 1040EZ; you must use Form 1040A or Form 1040.

Standard deduction for dependents

If you can claim your child or dependent on your own or if someone else can claim that dependent on his or her tax return, the dependent's standard deduction is limited to either $750 or to the individual's 2003 earned income plus $250 for the year (whichever amount is larger — but not more than the regular standard deduction amount of $4,750). So if you're helping your son or daughter prepare his or her return, use the worksheet in Table 9-2 to compute the standard deduction. If your dependent is 65 or older or blind, however, this standard deduction may be higher. Also use Table 9-2 to determine your dependent's standard deduction. Whether you're preparing your own return (as a child being claimed on your parent's return, for example) or you're preparing a return for a dependent that you're claiming, you must complete this worksheet. Otherwise, use the regular standard deduction.

Earned income includes wages, salaries, tips, professional fees, and other compensation that you received for services performed. It also includes anything received as a scholarship that counts as income.

An illustrated example of how to fill out the worksheet in Table 9-2 is provided in Chapter 5 under 1040EZ, line 5.

Table 9-2	Standard Deduction Worksheet for Dependents	
If you are 65 or older or blind, check the boxes below. Then go to the worksheet.		
You	65 or older ❏	Blind ❏
Your spouse, if claiming spouse's exemption	65 or older ❏	Blind ❏
Total number of boxes you checked	_____	
1. Enter your earned income. If none, go on to line 3.	1. _____	
1a. Additional amount allowed in 2003	1a.	$250
1b. Add lines 1 and 1a	1b. _____	
2. Minimum amount	2.	$750
3. Compare the amounts on lines 1b and 2. Enter the larger of the two amounts here.	3. _____	
4. Enter on line 4 the amount shown below for your filing status. Single, enter $4,750. Married filing separate return, enter $4,750. Married filling jointly or qualifying widow(er) with dependent child, enter $9,500. Head of household, enter $7,000.	4. _____	
5. Standard deduction 5a. Compare the amounts on lines 3 and 4. Enter the smaller of the two amounts here. If under 65 and not blind, stop here. This is your standard deduction; otherwise, go on to line 5b.	5a. _____	
5b. If 65 or older or blind, multiply $1,150 by the total number of boxes you checked; if married or qualifying widow(er) with dependent child, use $950. Enter the result here.	5b. _____	
5c. Add lines 5a and 5b. This is your standard deduction for 2003.	5c. _____	

Itemized Deductions

Some taxpayers simply compute their tax by using the standard deduction. If you have any doubt about being able to itemize and take more than the standard deduction, try itemizing, and then use the higher of the two amounts. Does this advice make sense, or what? That is, of course, unless you *want* the government to have more of your money.

Here's your itemized deduction shopping list:

✔ Medical and dental expenses that exceed 7.5 percent of your adjusted gross income (AGI)

✔ Taxes you paid

- Interest you paid
- Gifts to charity
- Casualty and theft losses
- Job-related, investment, and tax-preparation expenses that exceed 2 percent of your AGI
- Other miscellaneous itemized deductions not subject to the 2 percent limit. See the section on line 27 later in this chapter for an in-depth analysis of these types of deductions.

You claim these deductions on Form 1040 with Schedule A. You carry the total on line 28 over to Form 1040 (line 37), where you subtract it from your AGI.

Separate returns and limits on deductions

If you're married and filing separately, both spouses have to itemize their deductions. One spouse can't use the standard deduction while the other itemizes. If you're divorced or legally separated, you're considered single, and you can itemize your deductions or claim the standard deduction no matter what your former spouse does. However, in itemizing your separate expenses, you can claim only those expenses for which you or your spouse are personally liable. For example, if a residence is in your former spouse's name and you paid the property taxes and the mortgage interest, you can't deduct them. Depending on the terms of your divorce or separation agreement, these could possibly qualify as deductible alimony.

Generally, if your home is jointly owned and your divorce or separation agreement requires that you make the mortgage payments, then one half of the payments can be deducted as alimony. Your former spouse reports one half of the payments as taxable alimony and is allowed to deduct one half of the mortgage interest if they itemize their deductions. You get to deduct one half of the mortgage interest paid if the home is your residence (which isn't very likely). Payments to a third party (a bank, for example) are treated as received and then paid by your ex. The general rule we just recited for mortgage payments also applies to real estate taxes, provided the title to the home isn't held as *tenants by the entirety* or in *joint tenancy*. Because you aren't a lawyer (be thankful for small favors), we explain the meaning of these legal terms in the alimony section in Chapter 7 and in the sidebar "Separate returns and real estate taxes," later in this chapter. But if you hold title in this manner, here are the rules: None of the payments for real estate taxes are considered alimony payments, and you get to deduct all the real estate taxes.

Deciding who gets to deduct what when a couple divorces is almost as bad as dividing the property. The alimony rules in Chapter 7 explain who gets to claim various deductions. To dig into this further, take a look at IRS Publication 504 *(Divorced or Separated Individuals)*. If you live in a community property state, the rules we just recited are different, so you may want to take a look at IRS Publication 555 *(Federal Tax Information on Community Property)*.

If you and your spouse are separated but don't have a decree of divorce or separate maintenance, you may be able to itemize or use the standard deduction and file as either single or head of household. You can do this if you didn't live with your spouse during the last six months of 2003, and if you maintained a home for more than half of 2003 for you and a child that you are entitled to claim as a dependent, you can use the head of household filing status.

But if you change your mind

Oops! Suppose that you discover you should have itemized after you already filed. Or even worse, suppose that you went to all the trouble to itemize but shouldn't have done so. Just amend your return by filing **Form 1040X, Amended U.S. Individual Income Tax Return.** But if you're married and you filed separately, you can't change your mind unless both you and your spouse make the same change. And if either of you must pay additional tax as a result of the change, you both need to file a consent. (Sorry, dear!) Remember that if one of you itemizes, the other no longer qualifies for the standard deduction.

Lines 1–4: Medical and Dental Costs

Your total medical and dental expenses (after what you were reimbursed by your health insurance policy) must exceed 7.5 percent of your AGI (line 35 of your Form 1040). Line 35 is your AGI that you copied from line 34. Lines 34 and 35 should be the same amount. If they aren't, your math is off. This detail knocks many people out of contention for this deduction. For example, if your AGI equals $30,000, you need to have at least $2,250 in medical and dental expenses. If you don't, you can cruise past these lines. (Because the threshold is so high, we hope, for your health's sake, that this is one deduction you *can't* take.)

You can deduct medical and dental expenses for you, your spouse, and your dependents, as well as the medical expenses of any person who is your dependent, even if you can't claim an exemption for this person because he or she had income of $3,050 or more or filed a joint return, or your ex-spouse is claiming him or her as a dependent. You fill in the amounts on lines 1 through 4 on Schedule A (see Figure 9-1). This rule means you can deduct the medical expenses you paid for your child, even though your ex-spouse is claiming him or her. For the purposes of the medical deduction, the child is considered the dependent of both parents (see the sidebar "Special cases — who gets the deduction?" later in this chapter).

Medical and dental expense checklist

When you calculate your medical and dental expenses for 2003, this handy checklist will help you know what to deduct and what not to deduct. Be sure to note the following new additions to the eligible deductible expenses as of 2003:

- ✔ Weight-loss programs rooted in a diagnosis of obesity or another disease. However, the restriction against deducting weight reduction costs for purely cosmetic reasons hasn't been lifted. That means you can't deduct the cost of going to Weight Watchers so you'll look amazing at your 25th class reunion.

- ✔ Breast reconstruction surgery after a mastectomy.

- ✔ Laser eye surgery, including corrective procedures such as LASIK and radial keratotomy. This surgery is deductible because it corrects an eye problem even though a pair of glasses would, arguably, cost considerably less.

- ✔ Medical equipment and supplies, crutches, bandages, and diagnosis devices such as blood sugar kits sold over-the-counter, even though over-the-counter medicines aren't deductible.

- ✔ Expenses in obtaining an egg donor.

Adoption and medical expenses

If you adopted a child, you can deduct the medical expenses you paid before the adoption if the child qualified as your dependent when the medical expenses were incurred or paid. If you have an agreement to pay an adoption agency or other persons for medical expenses they paid on behalf of the child, you can deduct the payment as a medical expense. But — bet you knew a *but* was coming — if you pay back medical expenses incurred and paid before the adoption negotiations began, sorry, no deduction.

The following is a list of other things that are deductible, so remember to save all those bills:

- Medical services (doctors, dentists, opticians, podiatrists, registered nurses, practical nurses, psychiatrists, and so on).

- Hospital bills.

- Medical, hospital, and dental insurance premiums that you pay (but you can't deduct premiums paid by your employer); don't overlook premiums deducted from your paycheck. This includes a portion of your long-term health-care premiums (flip ahead to insurance premiums for the amounts).

- Guide dog.

- Electric wheelchairs (nonelectric ones as well) and electric carts such as *The Rascal* that you see advertised on TV, including their upkeep and operating cost, are deductible medical expenses. The cost of hand controls or special equipment for a car so a handicapped person can operate it may also be deducted.

- Wages and Social Security tax paid for worker providing medical care.

- Birth control pills.

- Legal abortion.

- Special items (artificial limbs, contact lenses, and so on).

- Wages for nursing service.

- Oxygen equipment and oxygen.

- Part of life-care fee paid to a retirement home designated for medical care.

- Treatment at a drug or alcohol clinic.

- Special school or home for a mentally or physically handicapped person.

- Ambulance service.

- Transportation for medical care.

- Drugs and medicines prescribed by a doctor.

- Costs for medical equipment or modifications to your home for needed medical care.

- Laboratory fees and tests.

- Childbirth classes (but if your husband attends the classes as your coach, his portion of the fee isn't deductible).

- Stop-smoking programs. The cost of prescription drugs to alleviate nicotine withdrawal also qualifies as a medical expense, but over-the-counter nicotine gum and patches do not. When will the IRS ever stop making these types of distinctions? A foolish question, we guess, because the IRS is in the business of splitting hairs.

- Sexual dysfunction treatment.

SCHEDULES A&B		Schedule A—Itemized Deductions	OMB No. 1545-0074

SCHEDULES A&B
(Form 1040)

Department of the Treasury
Internal Revenue Service   (99)

Schedule A—Itemized Deductions

(Schedule B is on back)

► Attach to Form 1040. ► See Instructions for Schedules A and B (Form 1040).

OMB No. 1545-0074

20**03**

Attachment
Sequence No. **07**

Name(s) shown on Form 1040

Your social security number

Medical and Dental Expenses	1	**Caution.** Do not include expenses reimbursed or paid by others. Medical and dental expenses (see page A-2)	1	
	2	Enter amount from Form 1040, line 35	2	
	3	Multiply line 2 by 7.5% (.075)	3	
	4	Subtract line 3 from line 1. If line 3 is more than line 1, enter -0-	4	

Taxes You Paid (See page A-2.)	5	State and local income taxes	5	
	6	Real estate taxes (see page A-2)	6	
	7	Personal property taxes	7	
	8	Other taxes. List type and amount ►	8	
	9	Add lines 5 through 8	9	

Interest You Paid (See page A-3.)	10	Home mortgage interest and points reported to you on Form 1098	10	
	11	Home mortgage interest not reported to you on Form 1098. If paid to the person from whom you bought the home, see page A-3 and show that person's name, identifying no., and address ►	11	
Note. Personal interest is not deductible.	12	Points not reported to you on Form 1098. See page A-3 for special rules	12	
	13	Investment interest. Attach Form 4952 if required. (See page A-4.)	13	
	14	Add lines 10 through 13	14	

Gifts to Charity If you made a gift and got a benefit for it, see page A-4.	15	Gifts by cash or check. If you made any gift of $250 or more, see page A-4	15	
	16	Other than by cash or check. If any gift of $250 or more, see page A-4. You **must** attach Form 8283 if over $500	16	
	17	Carryover from prior year	17	
	18	Add lines 15 through 17	18	

Casualty and Theft Losses	19	Casualty or theft loss(es). Attach Form 4684. (See page A-5.)	19	

Job Expenses and Most Other Miscellaneous Deductions (See page A-5.)	20	Unreimbursed employee expenses—job travel, union dues, job education, etc. Attach Form 2106 or 2106-EZ if required. (See page A-5.) ►	20	
	21	Tax preparation fees	21	
	22	Other expenses—investment, safe deposit box, etc. List type and amount ►	22	
	23	Add lines 20 through 22	23	
	24	Enter amount from Form 1040, line 35	24	
	25	Multiply line 24 by 2% (.02)	25	
	26	Subtract line 25 from line 23. If line 25 is more than line 23, enter -0-	26	

Other Miscellaneous Deductions	27	Other—from list on page A-6. List type and amount ►	27	

Total Itemized Deductions	28	Is Form 1040, line 35, over $139,500 (over $69,750 if married filing separately)? ☐ **No.** Your deduction is not limited. Add the amounts in the far right column for lines 4 through 27. Also, enter this amount on Form 1040, line 37. ☐ **Yes.** Your deduction may be limited. See page A-6 for the amount to enter.	► 28	

For Paperwork Reduction Act Notice, see Form 1040 instructions.   Cat. No. 11330X   Schedule A (Form 1040) 2003

Figure 9-1: Use Schedule A to determine the itemized deductions that you can claim.

Special cases — who gets the deduction?

Sometimes, when two or more people support someone, special rules apply to determine who can claim the medical expenses that were paid.

One tricky case is that of divorced and separated parents. A divorced or separated parent can deduct the medical expenses he or she paid for a child's medical costs — even if the child's other parent is entitled to claim the child as a dependent.

For the purposes of claiming medical expenses, a child is considered the dependent of both parents if all the following conditions are met:

✔ The parents were legally separated or divorced or were married and living apart for the last six months of 2003.

✔ Both parents provided more than half the child's support in 2003.

✔ Either spouse had custody of the child for more than half of 2003.

Just like alcohol or drug treatment addiction programs, where an individual often has to travel away from home to seek treatment, the limited $50 a day deduction for lodging can be claimed for a stay at a weight-reduction clinic. Reduced-calorie diet foods aren't deductible. They are considered a substitute for a person's normal diet.

What about deducting health clubs? Here's the general rule: health club costs are only considered a deductible medical expense when prescribed by a physician to aid in the treatment of a specific disease or ailment.

Be aware that many medical and dental expenses can't be deducted. Surprisingly, a number of expenses that you make to improve your health, which should reduce your medical expenses, aren't deductible. You can't deduct these things:

✔ Diaper service

✔ Funeral expenses

✔ Health club or spa dues for activities and services that merely improve your general health

✔ Household help (even if recommended by a doctor)

✔ Life insurance premiums

✔ Maternity clothes

✔ Medical insurance included in a car insurance policy covering all persons injured in or by the car

✔ Social activities (such as swimming or dancing lessons)

✔ Trips for general health improvement

✔ Nursing care for a healthy baby

✔ Over-the-counter medicines (except insulin); aspirin to relieve pain; toothpaste; toiletries; and cosmetics

✔ Surgery for purely cosmetic reasons (such as face-lifts, tummy tucks, and so on) — plastic surgery required as the result of an accident *is* deductible

✔ Teeth-whitening — to the IRS, it merely improves a person's attractiveness and doesn't serve to treat an ailment

Deductible travel costs

The cost of traveling to your doctor or a medical facility for treatment is deductible. If you use your car, you can deduct a flat rate of 12 cents a mile (down from 13 cents in 2002. Talk about pinching pennies when the price of gas has been skyrocketing!), or you can deduct your actual out-of-pocket expenses for gas, oil, and repairs. You can also deduct parking and tolls. You can't deduct depreciation, insurance, or general repairs.

Deductible travel costs to seek medical treatment aren't limited to just local auto and cab trips — a trip to see a specialist in another city also qualifies for the deduction. Unfortunately, though, transportation costs incurred when you're not going to and from a doctor's office or a hospital are a deduction the IRS likes to challenge (maybe because many taxpayers tried to deduct as a medical expense travel to a warm climate, claiming health reasons!). The cost of transportation to a mild climate to relieve a specific condition is deductible — but the airfare to Arizona, for example, for general health reasons is not.

Trips to visit an institutionalized child have been allowed when a doctor prescribed the visits.

Travel expenses of a nurse or another person who has to accompany an individual to obtain medical care because he or she can't travel alone are deductible.

In a recent ruling, the IRS said it would allow the deduction for the cost of a medical conference and the travel to get there. This stipulation is a victory for anyone with a chronic illness, or worse, anyone with a child with a chronic illness who knows the frustration of trying to find answers that are often beyond the knowledge of the physician treating the illness. Now if you need to go to a medical conference to find out about the latest treatment options, the cost of the conference and the travel to get there are deductible. Meals and lodging aren't.

Another complicated case is that of a *multiple-support agreement* in which two or more people together provide more than half of a person's total support — but no one on his or her own provides more than half. Such an agreement allows *one* and only one of the individuals to claim the exemption for the person (even without providing more than half the support). If you are the person entitled to claim the exemption under the agreement, you can deduct the medical expenses you pay. But any other taxpayers who also paid medical expenses can't deduct them.

Special medical expense situations

The deductibility of a medical expense depends on the nature of the services rendered and not on the qualifications, title, or experience of the person providing the service. This means that payments to an unlicensed medical provider are deductible if the provider renders medical care that isn't illegal.

When an expense is generally considered nonmedical, the burden falls on the taxpayer to prove that it meets the definition of a medical expense. This is especially true for expenses incurred for massages, yoga lessons, water filtration systems, and health centers.

Just like every other section of our tax laws, what qualifies as a medical deduction can get hopelessly complex. Here are a few examples:

- ✔ Marijuana used for medical purposes in violation of federal law cannot be deducted, even though you obtained a prescription for it as required under state law.

- ✔ The cost of a wig purchased on the advice of a doctor to benefit the mental health of a patient who lost all hair as the result of a disease can be deducted.

✔ Vitamins can be deducted only when prescribed by a doctor as part of a treatment for a specific ailment and not merely for nutritional needs.

✔ Special foods that serve as supplements to a regular diet qualify as a medical expense only when prescribed by a doctor to treat a specific ailment. A special diet is not deductible if it is part of the regular nutritional needs of a person. For instance, diabetics cannot deduct the cost of food that doesn't contain sugar. Their sugarless diet merely acts as a substitute for the nutritional needs of a normal diet.

Get the picture? The IRS gives nothing away.

Meals and lodging

Your bill at a hospital or similar institution is fully deductible. That's the *whole* bill, including meals and lodging. You may be able to deduct as a medical expense the cost of lodging not provided in a hospital while you're away from your home if you meet all the following requirements:

✔ The lodging is necessary for your medical care.

✔ The medical care is provided by a doctor in a medical facility.

✔ The lodging is not extravagant.

✔ No significant element of personal pleasure, recreation, or vacation is involved in the travel.

The amount that you can deduct as a medical expense for lodging can't exceed $50 a night for you and $50 a night for anyone accompanying you. Only meals that are part of a hospital bill are deductible.

Insurance premiums

Health insurance premiums that cover hospital, medical, and dental expenses; prescription drugs; and eyeglasses and the replacement of lost or damaged contact lenses are deductible as medical expenses. So is the monthly *Part B Medicare* premium that gets deducted from your Social Security check. Based on your age, a limited portion of the premium for long-term healthcare also is deductible.

Here are the deductible amounts for long-term health-care premiums:

Age	Deductible
40 or less	$250
More than 40, but not more than 50	$470
More than 50, but not more than 60	$490
More than 60, but not more than 70	$2,510
More than 70	$3,130

Reimbursements and damages

You must reduce your medical expenses by what you were reimbursed under your health insurance policy and from Medicare. Payments that you received for loss of earnings or damages for personal injury or sickness aren't considered reimbursement under a health insurance policy and don't have to be deducted from your medical expenses. If the total reimbursement you received during the year is the same as or more than your total medical expenses for the year, you can't claim a medical deduction.

If you are reimbursed in a later year for medical expenses you deducted in an earlier year, you must report as income the amount you received up to the amount you previously deducted as a medical expense. If you didn't deduct the expense in the year you paid it because you didn't itemize your deductions or because your medical expenses weren't more than 7.5 percent of your AGI, the reimbursement isn't taxable.

If you receive an amount in settlement of a personal injury suit, the part that is for medical expenses deducted in an earlier year is taxable if your medical deduction in the earlier year reduced your income tax.

In 1997, the IRS ruled that medical expenses or premiums paid by an employer for an employee's domestic partner or the domestic partner's dependent(s) are taxable to the employee and not a tax-free employee fringe benefit.

Special schooling

You can deduct as a medical expense the cost of sending a mentally or physically handi-capped child or dependent to a special school to help him or her overcome a handicap. The school must have a special program geared to the child's specific needs. The total costs, transportation, meals and lodging, and tuition qualify. The types of schools that qualify are ones that do the following things:

- ✔ Teach Braille or lip reading
- ✔ Help cure dyslexia
- ✔ Treat and care for the mentally handicapped
- ✔ Treat individuals with similar handicaps

Nursing home

You can include in medical expenses the cost of medical care in a nursing home or home for the aged for yourself, your spouse, or your dependents. This deduction includes the cost of meals and lodging in the home if the main reason for being there is to get medical care. But you cannot deduct nonmedical care expenses. For example, if a person enters a nursing home because he or she can't prepare meals or take care of personal needs, then that person cannot take a deduction.

You can't deduct the cost of meals and lodging if the reason for being in the home is personal and nonmedical (such as taking up residence in a retirement home). You can, however, include as a deductible medical expense the part of the cost that is for medical or nursing care.

Improvements to your home

You can deduct as a medical expense the cost of installing equipment and making improvements to your home to help treat a disease or ailment. For example, you can deduct the cost of an air conditioner because you suffer from allergies or asthma. But if the equipment or improvement increases the value of your home, your deduction is limited to the cost of the equipment or improvement minus the increase in the value to your home.

Be prepared to have a battle when making a large improvement to your home for medical reasons. Unless you arrive at the audit in a wheelchair with tears streaming down your cheeks, don't expect an overly sympathetic IRS. On the other hand, deductions for swimming pools have been allowed as a form of therapy in treating a severe ailment or disease. But improvements that merely help improve someone's general health (such as a hot tub or workout room) aren't deductible.

The increase-in-value test for a home doesn't apply to handicapped persons. Modifying stairs and doorways; building ramps, railings, and support bars; and adapting a home to the special needs of the handicapped are allowed. Chairlifts, but not elevators, are also part of the no-increase-in-value category.

Figuring your medical and dental deduction

Your deductible medical and dental expenses equal the total expenses that you've paid minus what you were reimbursed by your insurance policy. The result is then reduced by 7.5 percent of your AGI.

For example, suppose that your medical and dental expenses for the tax year were $4,500 and that your health insurance company reimbursed $500 of that amount. Thus, you had $4,000 of unreimbursed medical expenses. Enter $4,000 on line 1 of Schedule A. On line 2, you enter your AGI from Form 1040 (line 35). On line 3, you enter 7.5 percent of your AGI (suppose that your AGI is $40,000; you would enter $3,000 — that's $40,000 × 0.075). Subtract this amount from the medical expenses reported on line 1 of Schedule A and stick the remainder on line 4.

Lines 5–9: Taxes You Paid

As a general rule, you may deduct only the following tax payments made during the tax year:

- ✔ State and local income taxes
- ✔ Local real estate taxes
- ✔ State and local personal property taxes
- ✔ Other taxes (such as foreign income taxes)

Federal income and Social Security taxes are not deductible.

Line 5: State and local income taxes

This deduction consists of two elements: the amount of state and local taxes withheld from your salary (boxes 17 and 19 of your W-2), and what you paid in 2003 when you filed your 2002 state tax return. If you made estimated state and local income tax payments in 2003, they are also deductible. You can also deduct taxes relating to a prior year that you paid.

If you applied your 2002 refund on your state return as a payment toward your estimated 2003 state tax, that's also considered a deductible tax payment. However, you also have to report the amount as taxable income on Form 1040 (line 10).

Enter the total of your state and local tax payments from boxes 17 and 19 of your W-2(s) on line 5 of Schedule A. Also enter on this line your state and local estimated income tax payments that you made in 2003. And don't forget to add the balance that you paid on your 2002 return. For residents of California, New Jersey, or New York, mandatory payments that you made to your state's disability fund are also deductible. So are disability payments to Rhode Island's temporary fund or Washington State's supplemental workers' compensation fund.

Line 6: Real estate taxes

You can deduct real estate taxes you paid during the year. If your monthly mortgage payment also includes an amount that's placed in escrow by the bank, you can't claim a deduction for that amount until the bank actually pays the local tax authorities. At the end of the year, the bank will send you a statement — probably called your Annual Mortgage Statement — indicating the amount that was paid to the local property tax collector. The statement usually lists the dates of the payments.

If you don't have a mortgage or you aren't escrowing your tax, you won't be making payments to the bank. You'll be making payments directly to the tax collector. So add up your canceled checks to figure the amount of tax you paid and enter the amount on this line. (And if you don't have canceled checks, your problems are more serious than filling out Schedule A.)

Cooperative apartment

Tenants or stockholders of a cooperative housing corporation may deduct their share of the real estate taxes paid by the corporation. The corporation will furnish you with a statement at the end of the year, indicating the amount of the deduction you're entitled to claim.

Special assessments

Water, sewer, and garbage pickup aren't deductible because they're considered nondeductible personal charges — and so are charges by a homeowners' association. Assessments by the local tax authorities to put in a new street, sewer system, or sidewalks aren't deductible. These types of assessments are added to the tax basis of your home. Either your annual mortgage statement from your bank or the tax collector's bill will indicate whether you're paying a special assessment or a real estate tax.

When you buy or sell real estate

When real estate is bought or sold, the buyer and the seller apportion the real estate taxes between them. This stuff is done at the closing when the buyer and seller are furnished a settlement statement. For example, suppose that you paid $1,000 in real estate taxes for the year on January 1. On June 30, you sell the property. At the time of the sale, your settlement statement should reflect a payment or credit from the buyer for the property taxes you already paid for the remainder of the year. This is how the buyer pays you for the taxes you've effectively paid on his or her behalf for the remainder of the year when the buyer will be in the home. Therefore, you can deduct only the taxes you paid ($1,000) minus what the buyer reimbursed you ($500). That means you deduct only $500 in real estate taxes for the year on line 6 of Schedule A.

You can find this information on your settlement statement and in box 5 of **Form 1099-S, Proceeds from Real Estate Transactions.** The 1099-S is normally issued to you when you sell your home. However, under the new law not all home sales have to be reported on 1099-S. See Chapter 12 for more about this issue.

If the buyer pays *back taxes* (in other words, taxes that the property seller owed from the time he or she actually owned the home) at the closing or at a later date, they can't be deducted. They are added to the cost of the property. The seller can deduct back taxes paid by the buyer from the sales price when computing the profit that has to be reported on Schedule D (Form 1040). See Chapter 12 for information about handling the sale of your home.

The downside of property tax refunds and rebates

If you receive a refund or rebate in 2003 for real estate taxes you paid in 2003, you must reduce your itemized deductions that you're claiming for real estate taxes by the amount refunded to you. For example, if you paid $2,000 in property taxes during the year and also received a $300 refund because of a reduction in your tax that was retroactively granted, you may claim only $1,700 as the deduction for real estate taxes.

If you received a refund or rebate in 2003 for real estate taxes that you took as an itemized deduction on Schedule A in an earlier year, you must include the refund or rebate as income in the year you receive it. Enter this amount on your 1040 (line 21). In the unlikely event that your refund exceeds what you paid in taxes during the year, you need to include only the portion of the refund up to the amount of the deduction you took in the earlier year. For example, if you claimed a $500 deduction in 2002 and received a $600 rebate in 2003, only $500 of the rebate is taxable. If you didn't itemize your deductions in 2003, you do not have to report the refund as income.

Line 7: Personal property taxes

Personal property taxes, both state and local, are deductible if the tax charged is based on the value of the personal property. Usually, you pay personal property taxes based on the value of your car and motorboat.

In most states, a registration fee is assessed on cars. These fees are not deductible unless the fees are based on the value of the car. The state agency that invoices you for this fee should state what portion, if any, of the fee, is based on the car's value.

Don't get confused. This section doesn't cover business taxes; they belong on Schedule C. And if you pay sales tax on the purchase of equipment, you can't deduct the sales tax separately; it's added to the cost of the asset, which is depreciated on Schedules C and E. And, finally, as much as you'd like to deduct your Social Security tax here, you can't.

Line 8: Other taxes (foreign income taxes)

You can deduct foreign taxes you paid (along with your state or local income taxes) as an itemized deduction on Schedule A, or you can claim a credit for foreign taxes by filing **Form 1116, Foreign Taxes.** *Note:* If your foreign income wasn't subject to U.S. tax (because it was excluded under the $80,000 foreign earned income allowance), you can't claim a deduction or a credit for any foreign taxes paid on the income that you didn't pay U.S. tax on.

Separate returns and real estate taxes

When a couple decides to file separate returns, deducting real estate taxes becomes a complicated matter. That's because the deduction is based on how title to the property is held. If the title is in your spouse's name and you paid the real estate taxes, neither of you can claim a deduction. If your payment is required as a result of your divorce or separation decree, the payment may qualify as an alimony deduction (see Chapter 7).

If property is owned by a husband or wife as tenants by the entirety or as joint tenants (which means the survivor inherits the other's share), either spouse can deduct the amount of taxes paid. If the property is held as tenants in common (each owner's share goes to his or her heirs at his or her death), each spouse may deduct his or her share of the taxes paid. However, the rules are somewhat different in community property states; see IRS Publication 555 *(Federal Tax Information on Community Property)*.

In case you're asking yourself what foreign taxes have to do with you, the answer is that if you invested in a mutual fund that invests overseas, the fund may end up paying foreign taxes on some of your dividends. It seems more people are investing in these types of funds than ever before. If your mutual fund paid any foreign taxes, you'll find that information in box 6 of **Form 1099-DIV** that you received.

You can either deduct the foreign tax you paid on this line of Schedule A or claim a credit on Form 1040 (line 44). A deduction reduces your taxable income. A credit reduces the actual tax you owe. So if you're in the 25 percent tax bracket, claiming a deduction for $100 of foreign taxes will reduce your tax bill by $25. On the other hand, if you claim the $100 you paid as a foreign tax credit, you reduce your tax liability by $100, because credits are subtracted directly from the tax you owe.

So to the unsuspecting, claiming a foreign tax payment as an itemized deduction would appear to be a poor choice, because claiming the payment as a credit produces a greater tax saving. But have you ever tried to tackle Form 1116? The IRS estimates that it should take you over six hours to read the instructions and fill out the form.

If the foreign tax you paid isn't more than $600 if married or $300 if single, and the only foreign income that you have is from investments, you can bypass Form 1116. Enter the foreign tax you paid on line 44. On the other hand, if the foreign tax you paid is more than these amounts, try a tax software program or seek advice.

Lines 10–14: Interest You Paid

The IRS allows you to deduct interest on certain types of loans. According to the IRS, acceptable loans include some (but not all) mortgage loans and investment loans. Interest incurred for consumer debt, such as on credit cards and auto loans — so-called *personal interest,* isn't deductible. Business interest isn't deducted as an itemized deduction; it's deducted from your business income on Schedule C (see Chapter 11).

You can't deduct interest on taxes you owe. It's worth noting, however, that corporations can deduct interest on tax assessments. Doesn't it seem that everyone is allowed a special tax break but you?!

Lines 10–11: Home mortgage interest and points reported to you on Form 1098

You can deduct mortgage interest on your main home and a second or vacation home. Why two? We think it's because most representatives in Congress own two homes — one in Washington and one in their district! It doesn't matter whether the loan on which you're paying interest is a mortgage, a second mortgage, a line of credit, or a home equity loan. The interest is deductible as long as your homes serve as collateral for the loan.

Where is the data?

If you paid mortgage interest of $600 or more during the year on any one mortgage, you will receive a **Form 1098, Mortgage Interest Statement,** from your mortgage lender, showing the total interest you paid during the year. Enter the amount from Box 1 of Form 1098 on line 10 of your Schedule A. Enter mortgage interest not reported on a 1098 on line 11. If you purchased a main home during 2003, Form 1098 reports the deductible points you paid. If you paid points that weren't reported on Form 1098, enter the amount on line 12. (If you paid less than $600 in mortgage interest, see your lender.) If the points were reported on Form 1098 (Box 2), add this amount to the interest you are deducting on line 10. The tax treatment of points paid when refinancing a mortgage is discussed on the next page.

You can deduct late payment charges as home mortgage interest. You find these charges on your annual mortgage statement.

If you can pay down your mortgage more quickly than required, don't assume that doing so is not in your best financial interests just because of the deductions allowed for it (see Chapter 24). If you are charged a prepayment penalty you can deduct that as additional interest.

Limitations on deductions

In most cases, you will be able to deduct all your home mortgage interest. Whether all of it is deductible depends on the date you took out the mortgage, the amount of the mortgage, and how the mortgage loan was used.

Interest on mortgage loans of up to $1 million taken out after October 13, 1987, to buy, build, or improve a first or second home is deductible. Your main home is the home you live in most of the time. It can be a house, a condominium, a cooperative apartment, a mobile home, a boat, or similar property. It must provide basic living accommodations including sleeping space, toilet facilities, and cooking facilities. Your second or vacation home is similar property that you select to be your second home.

In addition, interest on a home equity loan of up to $100,000 taken out after October 13, 1987, is deductible regardless of how the money is used. (Cut these amounts in half if you are married and file a separate return.) The proceeds of a home equity loan don't have to be used to buy, build, or improve your home. They can be used to pay off bills, pay college tuition, or take a vacation.

Interest on a home-improvement loan isn't deductible if it isn't a mortgage loan. The rule is simple: no mortgage, no interest deduction. So if a relative lends you money to buy a home, any interest that you pay isn't deductible unless the relative obtains a mortgage on the house.

Interest on mortgages of any size is tax deductible if you took out your mortgage before October 14, 1987, and you still retain that mortgage. If you've refinanced into a new mortgage since this magical date, you may be out of luck if you refinanced the mortgage for more than you owed prior to refinancing.

Interest on refinanced loans

If you refinanced a mortgage on your first or second mortgage for the remaining balance of the old mortgage, you're safe. If the interest on the old mortgage was fully deductible, the interest on the new mortgage is also fully deductible. To the extent of the remaining balance of the old mortgage, the new mortgage is considered a mortgage used to acquire, build, or improve a home.

But, if you refinanced your old mortgage for more than its remaining balance, the rules on whether you can deduct all the interest on your new mortgage are crazy — the deductibility of the mortgage interest on the new loan depends on how you use the excess funds and the amount you refinanced. If the excess is used to improve, build, or buy a first or second home, and the excess plus all other mortgage loans is under $1 million, the interest on the new loan is fully deductible. If any of the excess of a new mortgage loan isn't used to build, buy, or improve your home, the excess is applied to your $100,000 home equity limit. If the excess is under $100,000, you're safe and it's fully deductible. The interest on the part that exceeds $100,000 is not deductible.

Mixed-use mortgages

You don't need one mortgage to meet the requirement that the mortgage was taken out to buy, build, or improve your home and then one to meet the $100,000 home equity requirement. One mortgage can be considered both, hence the term mixed-use.

Points

The term *points* is used to describe certain upfront charges that a borrower pays to obtain a mortgage. One point equals 1 percent of the loan amount financed. For example, if the loan is for $200,000, two points equal a $4,000 charge. You can deduct the amount you paid in points in 2003 if the loan was used to buy or build your *main* residence. The points you pay on a second home have to be deducted over the term of the loan.

Points are sometimes referred to as *loan origination fees, processing fees, maximum loan charges,* or *premium charges.* Look for these charges on the settlement statement that the lender (by law) has to provide you.

Points on refinancing

The points paid to refinance a mortgage on a main home aren't usually deductible in full in the year you pay them — even if the new mortgage is secured by your main home. However, if you use part of the refinanced mortgage to improve your main home and you pay the points instead of paying them from the proceeds of the new loan, you can deduct in full (in the year paid) the part of the points related to the improvement. But you must deduct the remainder of the points over the life of the loan. For example, suppose that the remaining balance of your mortgage is $100,000. You take out a new mortgage for $150,000 and use $25,000 for improvements to your home, $25,000 for personal purposes, and $100,000 to pay off the old loan. The points on the $25,000 used for improvements are deductible in 2003. The points on the $100,000 used to pay off the remaining $100,000 balance of the old mortgage have to be written off over the term of the new loan. The points on the $25,000 used for personal purposes can't be deducted. The $25,000 wasn't used to buy, build, or improve your home. The only way the interest on this $25,000 can be deducted is if it's applied toward your allowance to deduct interest on the first $100,000 on a home equity loan.

But here's a tip: Say that you refinanced your home three years ago and you're writing off the points you paid over the 25-year term of the mortgage. If you refinance your mortgage again in 2003, the points remaining to be written off on your old mortgage can be written off in full in 2003. Enter this amount on line 12. The points on your new refinanced loan have to be deducted over the term of the new mortgage.

A penalty for paying off a mortgage early is deductible if the loan qualified for the mortgage interest deduction (the mortgage loan was used to buy, build, or improve your main home).

Seller-paid points

Sometimes, desperate times call for desperate measures. So if the seller pays the points that the buyer normally does, the buyer gets a double windfall. The buyer not only gets the seller to pay the points, but the buyer also gets to deduct them. The buyer also has to subtract the points deducted from the tax basis of the home. Although the seller paid the points, the seller can't deduct them. The points the seller paid are deducted from the selling price.

So if you are a buyer who had the seller pay the points on the purchase of your home but didn't deduct them, you can still do so by filing a **Form 1040X, Amended Return.** But you have to take this step before the three-year statute of limitations expires (see Chapter 19), or you can kiss any refund goodbye. When you file Form 1040X, write `SELLER PAID POINTS` on the upper-right corner of the form.

Line 12: Points not reported to you on Form 1098

If the points you paid, for some reason, were not reported on the 1098, based on the rules in the two preceding sections, you'll have to compute this amount on your own. If the points were for the purchase or improvement of your principal residence, you can deduct the points in 2003. If they were for refinancing or for your second home, you have to deduct them over the term of the mortgage. Hunting for this information isn't all that difficult. When the loan was made, you were given a settlement statement by the lender indicating the points you paid.

Line 13: Investment interest

When you borrow against the value of securities held in a brokerage account, the interest paid on what is referred to as a *margin loan* is deductible. This deduction, however, can't exceed your total investment income. If it does, the excess is carried forward and deducted from next year's investment income — or carried over to future years until it can be deducted. You use **Form 4952, Investment Interest,** to compute the deduction and carry over the result to Schedule A (line 13).

Investment income is income from interest, dividends, annuities, and royalties. It doesn't include income from rental real estate or from a *passive activity* (a passive activity — see Chapter 13 — is IRS jargon for a business deal or venture in which you are a silent partner). The following are not usually considered investment income:

- ✔ If you borrow money to buy or carry tax-exempt bonds, you can't deduct any interest on the loan as investment-interest expense. If 20 percent of your portfolio consists of tax-exempt bonds, 20 percent of your margin interest on your security account isn't deductible.

- ✔ Capital gains aren't usually considered investment income, but you can choose to treat capital gains as investment income. There is a trade-off, however. You have to reduce the amount of your capital gains that are eligible for the maximum long-term capital gain rate — which can be either 20 percent (8 percent or 10 percent if you're in the 10 percent or 15 percent bracket) for gains before May 6, 2003, or you can use the 5 percent (if you're in the 10 percent or 15 percent bracket) or 15 percent for gains after May 5, 2003, 25 percent (for real estate), or 28 percent (for collectibles) — by the amount of your capital gains you are treating as investment income. Did you follow that? Say you have $1,000 of investment interest and $10,000 of capital gains and want to consider $1,000 of your capital gains as interest income so you can deduct your $1,000 of investment interest. If you make this choice, then only $9,000 of your capital gains is eligible for the reduced capital gain tax rates.

The same rule that applies to capital gains now applies to *qualified dividends* (which are those dividends that qualify for the same reduced rates as capital gains, see line 9b, Chapter 8) when you elect to include qualified dividends in the amount of investment income that you use to compute the maximum permissible investment interest deduction.

For example, suppose that you have interest income of $3,000, nonqualified dividend income of $2,000, investment interest expense of $10,000, a $20,000 long-term capital gain on stock you sold, and qualified dividends. You can deduct only $5,000 of your $10,000 of investment interest expense. The balance is carried over to 2004. However, if you elect to treat $5,000 of your capital gain or qualified dividend income as investment income, you can deduct your entire investment interest expense of $10,000. But the amount of your $20,000 capital gain and qualified dividends that is eligible for the maximum rates on long-term capital gains and qualified dividends is reduced to $15,000. Make this election on Form 4952, lines 4e and g. If this election isn't made, the IRS assumes that the reduced rates on capital gains and qualified dividends apply.

✔ Interest expense incurred in a passive activity such as rental real estate, a limited partnership, or an S Corporation isn't considered investment-interest expense. It can be deducted only from your passive-activity income.

You can deduct up to $2,500 of student loan interest even if you don't itemize your deductions. The deduction is claimed as an adjustment to your income along with the other adjustments we discuss in Chapter 7, in the section on line 25.

Here's the fine print on student loan interest: Your income can't exceed $50,000 ($100,000 for joint filers); above these amounts, the deduction gets phased out. So at the $65,000 income level if you're single, and the $130,000 income level if you're married, you can kiss this deduction goodbye.

Don't overlook your out-of-pocket expenditures

A commonly overlooked deductible charitable expense is your out-of-pocket expenses (money spent) incurred while doing volunteer work for a charity.

For example, you can deduct out-of-pocket expenses (such as gas and oil, but probably not rest-stop candy bars!) that are directly related to the use of your car in charitable work. You can't deduct anything like general repair or maintenance expenses, tires, insurance, depreciation, and so on. If you don't want to track and deduct your actual expenses, you can use a standard rate of 14 cents a mile to figure your contribution. You can deduct actual expenses for parking fees and tolls. If you must travel away from home to perform a real and substantial service, such as attending a convention for a qualified charitable organization, you can claim a deduction for your unreimbursed travel and transportation expenses, including meals and lodging. If you get a daily allowance (per diem) for travel expenses while providing services for a charitable organization, you must include as income the amount that is more than your travel expenses. Of course, you can deduct your travel expenses that are more than the allowance.

There's one restriction on these deductions: They're allowed only if there is *no significant amount* of personal pleasure derived from your travel. What is the limit the IRS sets on personal pleasure? Well, we can't find an IRS chart, but we can at least assure you that the IRS allows you to enjoy your trip without automatically disqualifying you from this deduction. The IRS doesn't mind if you decide to do some sightseeing, but you can't deduct expenses for your spouse or children who may accompany you. If you go to a church convention as a church member rather than as a representative of the church, you can't deduct your expenses.

You can deduct the cost and upkeep of uniforms that you must wear while doing volunteer work — as long as these uniforms are unsuitable for everyday use. A Boy or Girl Scout uniform, for example, would not be the type of clothing you would wear just anywhere!

Lines 15–18: Gifts to Charity

You can deduct your charitable contributions, but the amount of your deduction may be limited, and you must follow a number of strict rules. One good turn doesn't always deserve another!

After you understand the types of things you can and cannot deduct, completing this section is a snap. Qualifying contributions that you make by cash and check are totaled and entered on line 15, and those made other than by cash and check (for example, you donate your old *Taxes For Dummies* books to charity when new editions come out) are entered on line 16.

If you make out a check at the end of the year and mail it by December 31, you can deduct your contribution even if the charity doesn't receive the check until January. If you charge a contribution on your credit card, you get to deduct it in the year you charged it — even if you don't pay off the charge until the following year.

If you signed up for a program where a percentage of your credit-card purchases is donated to charity, remember to deduct what the credit-card company paid on your behalf.

Qualifying charities

You can deduct your contributions only if you make them to a *qualified* organization. To become a qualified organization, most organizations (other than churches) must apply to the IRS. To find out whether an organization qualifies, just ask the organization for its tax-exemption certificate.

If for some reason you doubt that an organization qualifies, you can check IRS Publication 78 *(Cumulative List of Organizations)*. Most libraries have Publication 78. You also can call the IRS toll-free tax help telephone number (800-829-3676) to request this publication. If you're Internet-savvy, you can visit the IRS Web site at www.irs.gov and type Publication 78 in the window "Search for Forms and Publication." Click on Publication 78 and then "Search Now," where you can find out whether the charity is a qualified one. Nearly all the tax-exempt charities are listed. If that doesn't work, search www.guidestar.org.

Contributions that you make to the following charitable organizations are generally deductible:

- Religious organizations, including churches, synagogues, mosques, and so on
- Public park and recreational facilities
- Nonprofit schools
- Organizations such as CARE, the Red Cross, the Salvation Army, Goodwill Industries, the Girl and Boy Scouts, and so on
- War veterans' groups
- Your federal, state, and local government — if your charitable contribution is only for public purposes

The records you need: Part I

For contributions of $250 or more, you need a receipt from the charity — otherwise, you could have your deduction tossed out in the event of an audit. The receipt should indicate either the amount of cash you contributed or a description (but not the value) of any property you donated. The receipt must also indicate the value of any gift or services you may have received and you must have the receipt by the time you file your return.

For cash contributions below $250, a canceled check will suffice. But remember, if you donate cash or property valued at $250 or more, you also need a receipt. If you donate property, you need a receipt from the charity listing the date of your contribution and a detailed description of the property. Every donation is treated as a separate donation for applying the $250 threshold. You don't need a receipt for two $150 checks to the same charity.

If you contribute property worth more than $500, you have to attach **Form 8283, Noncash Charitable Contributions.** On the form, you list the name of the charity, the date of the gift, your cost, the appraised value, and how you arrived at the value. If the value of the property you contributed exceeds $5,000, you need a written appraisal, and the appraiser has to sign off on Part III in Section B of Form 8283. The charity has to complete and sign Part IV of the form. A written appraisal isn't needed for publicly traded stock or nonpublicly traded stock worth $10,000 or less.

Nonqualifying charities

Generally speaking, contributions or donations made to causes or organizations that just benefit the organization, as opposed to the greater society, are not deductible. The following are examples of organizations or groups for which you can't deduct contributions:

- ✔ Individuals

  Big surprise here! So don't try to deduct what you gave to your brother-in-law, because he doesn't count in the eyes of the IRS! The contribution can be to a qualified organization that helps needy and worthy individuals — like your brother-in-law.

- ✔ Social and sport clubs

- ✔ Members of the clergy who can spend the money as they want

- ✔ Labor unions

- ✔ Groups that lobby for law changes (such as changes to the tax code!)

- ✔ The IRS does not want you to deduct contributions to organizations from which you may benefit — so include bingo and raffle tickets in this forbidden group.

- ✔ Political groups or candidates running for public office

- ✔ Foreign charities (but you can deduct contributions to a U.S. charity that transfers funds to a foreign charity — if the U.S. charity controls the use of the funds). Contributions to charities in Canada, Israel, and Mexico are deductible if the charity meets the same tests that qualify U.S. organizations to receive deductible contributions.

- ✔ Homeowners' associations

- ✔ Lottery ticket costs (gee, we wonder why not?)

- ✔ Dues paid to country clubs, lodges, orders, and so on

  But union dues are deductible as an itemized deduction subject to the 2 percent AGI limit on Schedule A.

- ✔ Tuition to attend private or parochial schools

This list can go on and on — didn't you suspect that a list of nonqualifying charities would be longer than a list of qualifying ones? — but we think you get the idea. So don't try to deduct the value of your blood donated at a blood bank, and don't even think about trying to deduct your contribution to your college fraternity or sorority!

Contributions of property

Generally, you can deduct the *fair market value* (FMV) of property given to a charity. FMV is the price at which property would change hands between a willing buyer and a willing seller. So if you bought a painting for $2,000 that's worth $10,000 when you donate it to a museum, you can deduct $10,000.

You can use the FMV only if — on the date of the contribution — the property would have produced a long-term capital gain or loss if it had been sold (property held more than one year). If you donate property you held for one year or less, or you donate *ordinary income property,* your deduction is limited to your cost. Ordinary income property is inventory from a business, works of art created by the donor, manuscripts prepared by the donor, and capital assets held one year or less. Following are guidelines for deducting contributions of property:

- **If you contribute property with a fair market value that is less than your cost or depreciated value:** Your deduction is limited to fair market value. You can't claim a deduction for the property's decline in value since you acquired it.

- **If you have an asset that has declined in value:** Sell that asset to lock in the capital loss deduction (see Chapter 12) and donate the cash for an additional deduction.

    For example, suppose that you paid $12,500 for shares of a mutual fund that invested in Russia that are now worth only $6,000. If you donate the shares, all you can claim is a $6,000 charitable deduction. By selling the shares and donating the cash, not only will you be entitled to a $6,000 charitable deduction, you also will have a $6,500 capital loss that you can deduct.

- **If you have an asset that has appreciated substantially in value:** Give the asset to the charity rather than sell the asset, get stuck for the tax, and donate the cash you have left. If you donate the asset itself, you get to deduct the full value of the asset, thereby escaping the tax.

Used clothing and household goods

Clean out those closets for next year so that you can save on your taxes! Hey, even Bill and Hillary Clinton took a deduction for this one! Used clothing — even used underwear, preferably washed — and household goods usually have a fair market value that is much less than the original cost. For used clothing, you claim the price that buyers of used items pay in used-clothing stores. See IRS Publication 561 *(Determining the Value of Donated Property — Household Goods section)* for information on the value of items such as furniture and appliances and other items you want to donate.

What's used clothing or furniture worth? You can get a $25 publication, updated annually, called *Cash For Used Clothing* by William R. Lewis, published by Client Valuation Service (call 800-875-5927), that can serve as a guide. Many charities offer a free printed guide to estimated values. *The Salvation Army Valuation Guide* can be downloaded off the Internet (www.salvationarmy-usaeast.org/help/valuation_guide.htm).

Contributions that are both qualified and nonqualified

If you receive a benefit from making a valid deductible contribution, you can deduct only the amount of your contribution that is more than the value of the benefit. For example, if you pay to attend a charity function such as a ball or banquet, you can deduct only the amount that is more than the fair market value of your ticket. You can also deduct unreimbursed expenses such as uniforms and actual automobile expenses, or use a standard rate of 14 cents per mile. Just subtract the value of the benefit you received from your total payment. Ask the charity for a receipt that details the actual amount you contributed. Most charities are happy to provide this information. In fact, if the value of your contribution is $75 or more and that is partly for goods and services, the charity must give you a written statement informing you of the amount you can deduct. If you can't easily obtain a receipt, use an estimate based on something the IRS can't disagree with — common sense.

Cars, boats, and aircraft

If you contribute a car, a boat, or an aircraft, you may be able to determine its fair market value by using guides such as *blue books* that contain dealer sale or average prices for recent model years. These guides also give estimates for adjusting values to take into account mileage and physical condition. The prices aren't official, however, and you can't consider a blue book as an appraisal of any specific donated property. But the guides are a good place to start.

Charitable deduction limits

All cash and noncash gifts are subject to some limits. Depending on whether you contributed cash or property, the amount of your deduction may be limited to either 30 percent or 50 percent of your AGI. Contributing cash to churches, associations of churches, synagogues, and all public charities, such as the Red Cross, for example, is deductible up to 50 percent of your AGI. Gifts of ordinary income property qualify for this 50 percent limit.

A 30 percent limit applies to gifts of capital gain property that has appreciated in value. In such instances, you can use the 50 percent limit — if you limit your deduction to your cost instead of using the FMV. For example, suppose you donate a painting to a museum that cost you $10,000. It's currently worth $20,000. If you use the $20,000 value, your deduction for 2003 can't exceed 30 percent of your AGI. If you use the $10,000 cost, you can deduct up to 50 percent of your AGI. The contribution has to be to a church or public charity, and you have to have owned the gift for more than a year. See Chapter 12 for the rules on how the one-year (holding period) is calculated.

Line 17: (For the world's great humanitarians)

Line 17 is a pretty obscure line. The general rule for cash contributions is that they can't exceed 50 percent of your AGI. For gifts of property like stocks, bonds, and artwork, the amount can't exceed 30 percent of your AGI. So if you contribute more than the IRS permits as a deduction in one year, you can carry over the amount you couldn't deduct and deduct it within the next five years. Enter on line 17 the amount that you couldn't deduct from the last five years and want to deduct this year.

Line 19: Casualty and Theft Losses

We hope that you don't need to use this one. But if you do, and if you've come to view the Internal Revenue Service as heartless, this line may correct that impression. It's not — well, not completely. If you've suffered a casualty or theft loss, you will find that the IRS can be somewhat charitable. Unfortunately, as is the case with any unusual deduction, you've got to jump through quite a few hoops to nail it down.

After you determine whether your loss is deductible, get a copy of IRS **Form 4684, Casualties and Thefts,** on which you list each item that was stolen or destroyed. If your deduction ends up being more than your income — and it does happen — you may have what's known as a *net operating loss*. You can use this type of loss to lower your tax in an earlier or in a later year. This rule is an exception (of course!) to the normal rule that you must be in business to have a net operating loss. See "More expenses than income," in Chapter 19.

When a casualty loss occurs in a presidentially declared disaster area, a taxpayer has the choice of deducting the loss in the year that it occurred or in the preceding year. By electing to go the prior year route, you can obtain an immediate refund (usually within 45 days) instead of having to wait until the end of the year to receive the full benefit of the loss. Use Form 1040X to claim the loss in the prior year. You have up until the time you file (including extensions) for the year of the loss to make this decision. Remember, the earlier you make it, the quicker you will get your hands on the refund the loss entitled you to. This maneuver also makes sense if you were in a higher bracket in the prior year.

Victims of Terrorist Attacks

In addition to the casualty loss deduction, a number of tax relief provisions are available for victims of September 11, Oklahoma City, and the anthrax attacks. For those who died in the September 11 and the anthrax attacks, their 2000 and 2001 income taxes were forgiven. For Oklahoma City, the qualifying years are 1994 and 1995. By filing Form 1040X, the taxes paid in those years will be refunded. Victims are entitled to a minimum refund of $10,000. In addition, the following types of payments are exempt from tax: The Victim Compensation Fund of 2001, qualified disaster relief payments, death benefits paid by an employer, and debt cancellations between September 10, 2001, and December 31, 2001.

Families of the victims of Oklahoma City had until January 22, 2003, to file amended returns. For families of September 11 victims, the deadline for filing an amended return for 2000 runs out April 15, 2004. For 2001, it's April 15, 2005.

The income tax forgiveness also applies to those killed in the rescue and recovery operations. If someone didn't die instantly in these attacks, but in a later year as the result of their injuries, their income taxes were forgiven for the two years mentioned above as well as all years up to and including the year of death. The IRS can postpone the filing deadline for up to one year.

IRS Publication 3920 *(Tax Relief for Victims of Terrorist Attacks)* has the details.

Do you have a deductible loss?

Strange as it may seem, the Tax Court has haggled extensively over what is and isn't a casualty. The phrase to remember is *sudden, unexpected, and unusual.* If property you own is damaged, destroyed, or lost as the result of a specific event that is sudden, unexpected, and unusual, you have a deductible casualty. Earthquakes, fires, floods, and storms meet this strict legal test.

The insurance effects

You've got casualty insurance? Great. But there are a couple of things you need to watch out for. First, if you expect to be reimbursed by your insurer but haven't seen any cash by tax-filing time, you've got to subtract an estimate of the expected reimbursement from your deductible loss. Second — and this sounds strange — you must reduce the amount of your loss by your insurance coverage even if you don't file a claim. Suppose that your loss is 100 percent covered by insurance, but you decide not to ask for a reimbursement for fear of losing your coverage. You can't claim a deduction for the loss. Only the amount of your loss that's above the insurance coverage would be deductible in that case.

If you're reimbursed by insurance and decide not to repair or replace your property, you could have a taxable gain on your hands. That's because the taxable gain is calculated by subtracting your cost from the insurance proceeds and not the property's fair market value. For example, imagine that your summer cottage, which cost $150,000 (the cost here refers to the cost of the building and excludes the land costs), burned to the ground. You get $190,000 in insurance money (the house's current FMV), giving you a fully taxable $40,000 gain.

To postpone the gain, you have to replace the property with a similar one, and it must be worth at least as much as the insurance money you received. If the new place is worth less than that, you must report the difference as a capital gain. In addition, you've got to replace the property within two years. The two-year period begins on December 31 of the year you realize the gain. If your main home is located in a federally declared disaster area, you have four years, and you can generally get a one-year extension beyond that, if necessary.

For property destroyed in the New York Liberty Zone as the result of the events of September 11, 2001, the replacement period is five years.

But if you dropped a piece of the good china, if Rover chewed a hole in the sofa, if moths ate your entire wardrobe, or if termites gobbled up your brand-new backyard deck, you're doubly out of luck. You've suffered a nondeductible loss. These incidents don't meet the sudden-unexpected-unusual test.

Figuring the loss

Unfortunately, the amount of your deduction isn't going to equal the amount of your loss because the IRS makes you apply a deductible just as your auto insurer does. The IRS makes you reduce each individual loss by $100 and your total losses by 10 percent of your AGI. So if your AGI is $100,000 and you lost $11,000 when the roof caved in, your deduction is only $900. (That's $11,000 minus $100 minus 10 percent of your adjusted gross, or $10,000.)

That stipulation effectively wipes out a deduction for plenty of people. For those whose losses are big enough to warrant a deduction, though, the fun is just beginning. That's because your deduction is limited to either the decrease in the fair market value of your property as a result of the casualty, or the original cost of the property — whichever is lower.

Suppose that you bought a painting for $1,000 that was worth $100,000 when damaged by fire. Sorry. Your loss is limited to the $1,000 you paid for it. Now reverse it. You paid $100,000 for the painting, and thanks to the downturn in the market for black-velvet portraits of Elvis, it's worth only $1,000 right before it's destroyed. Your deductible loss is limited to $1,000. And you must apply this rule to each item before combining them to figure your total loss. (One exception is real estate. The entire property, including buildings, trees, and shrubs, is treated as one item.)

The reduction rule ($100 and 10 percent of your income) doesn't apply to property used in a business. It applies only to personal items. Neither is a business casualty limited to the value of the property at the time of the loss. Normally, the loss is what you paid less the depreciation to which you were entitled.

Casualty losses? You be the judge

Listen to this. A loss as the result of water damage to wallpaper and plaster seems like it ought to be deductible. Not according to the Tax Court, which ruled on such a case in the 1960s. The homeowner failed to prove that the damage came after a sudden, identifiable event. The water had entered the house through the window frames, and the damage could have been caused by progressive deterioration. Now suppose that a car door is accidentally slammed on your hand, breaking the setting of your diamond ring. The jewel falls from the ring and is never found. That lost diamond qualifies as a casualty. On the other hand, if your diamond merely falls out of its setting and is lost, there is no deduction. The number of cases like this is endless. Proving a theft loss can be just as complex. The mere disappearance of cash or property doesn't cut it. You have to prove an actual theft occurred. The best evidence is a police report — and your failure to file one could be interpreted as your not being sure something was stolen.

You should know that theft losses aren't limited to robbery — they also include theft by swindle, larceny, and false pretense. This very broad definition includes fraudulent sales offers or embezzlement. In one case, a New Yorker was even able to get a theft-loss deduction after handing over a bundle of money to fortune-tellers. The reason? The fortune-tellers were operating illegally.

Because your loss is the difference between the fair market value of your property immediately before and after the casualty, an appraisal usually is the best way to calculate your loss. The only problem: The appraiser can't see your property before the casualty, and any photographs or records you may have had probably went up in smoke or floated away. Therefore, it makes sense to videotape both the outside of the property and its contents, including expensive jewelry, and keep the tape in a safe-deposit box, for example. You're not totally out of luck if you don't have before-and-after photos, though. A picture after the casualty and one showing the property after it was repaired comes in very handy when trying to prove the dollar value of your loss. See Chapter 3 for what you should do in case all your tax records went up in smoke, for instance.

Normally, you can't deduct the cost of repairing your property because the cost of fixing something isn't really a measure of its deflated fair market value. As with nearly every IRS rule, however, this one has exceptions. You can use the cost of cleaning up or making a repair under the following conditions:

- The repairs are necessary to bring the property back to its condition before the casualty, and the cost of the repairs isn't excessive.

- The repairs take care of the damage only.

- The value of the property after the repairs is not — because of the repairs — more than the value of the property before the casualty.

Another point is worth knowing: With leased property, such as a car, the amount of your loss is in fact the amount you must spend to repair it.

Although appraisal fees aren't considered part of your loss, they count as miscellaneous itemized deductions. The IRS is required to accept appraisals to get a government-backed loan in a disaster area as proof of the loss.

The IRS can extend the deadline for filing tax returns for up to one year in a presidentially declared disaster area. When the IRS declares a postponement to file and pay, it publicizes the postponement in your area and on its Web site. The postponement also delays the time for making contributions to IRAs. Neither interest nor penalties are charged during the postponement period.

If your casualty or theft loss exceeds your income, you may have a net operating loss (see Chapter 11). This loss enables you to obtain a refund for taxes paid in prior years by carrying it (the loss) back to those years. An amended return has to be filed to accomplish this.

If you have a casualty loss from a disaster that occurred in a presidentially declared disaster area, you can choose to deduct the loss on your return in the year in which the casualty occurred or on an amended return for the preceding year. Say you have a casualty loss of $25,000 that occurred in a presidentially declared disaster area as the result of the tornadoes and flooding that devastated 11 Ohio counties between July 21 and August 25, 2003. You can deduct the loss on your 2002 return and obtain an immediate refund. Because tax rates where higher in 2002 than in 2003, the $25,000 deduction will result in a larger tax savings by deducting the loss on an amended 2002 return.

Lines 20–26: Job Expenses and Most Other Miscellaneous Deductions

Everybody likes to see a deduction that says something about "other." Oh goody, you think, here's my opportunity to get some easy deductions. Unfortunately, if you're like the vast majority of taxpayers, you won't get the maximum mileage out of these deductions. Why? Because the allowable items in this category tend to be small-dollar items. And you have to clear a major hurdle: You get a deduction only for the amount by which your total deductions in this category exceed 2 percent of your AGI. Here's how it works: If your AGI is $50,000 and you have $1,500 of job-related expenses, only $500 is deductible. That's $1,500 minus $1,000 (2 percent of $50,000).

Line 20: Unreimbursed employee expenses

Even if you're not employed by Scrooge International — famous for offering few fringe benefits and not reimbursing job-related expenses — there's a good chance that you're spending at least some out-of-pocket money on your job. Ever take an educational course that helped you get ahead in your career? How about that home fax machine you bought so customers could reach you after hours? If your employer didn't pick up the tab, all is not lost. You can deduct those expenses — or at least a portion of them — from your taxes.

One word of caution: Just about every IRS rule regarding job-related expenses is subject to varying interpretations, which has made the IRS extremely inflexible as to what is and isn't deductible. On the other hand, the Tax Court, which ultimately decides disputes of deductibility, has a tendency to be more liberal than the IRS.

Job search expenses

Job search expenses are deductible even if your job search isn't successful. The critical rule is that the expenses must be incurred in trying to find a new job in the same line of work. So if you're looking to make a career change or seeking your first job, you can forget about this deduction. A taxpayer who retired from the Air Force after doing public relations for the service was denied travel expenses while seeking other employment in public relations. The way the IRS sees the world, any job he sought in the private sector would be considered a new trade or business.

Here are job search expenses that are considered deductible:

- Employment-agency and career-counseling fees
- Cost for placing situation-wanted ads

- ✔ Telephone calls

- ✔ Printing, typing, and mailing of resumes

- ✔ Travel, meals, and entertaining

Another time, the IRS held that, because a taxpayer had incurred a "substantial break" of more than a year between his previous job and his hunt for a new one, there was a lack of continuity in the person's line of work. No deduction. The IRS is unyielding when it comes to interpreting this rule. Fortunately, the Tax Court sees things differently, tending to consider such gaps as temporary.

If you're away from home overnight looking for work, you can deduct travel and transportation costs, hotels, and meals. The purpose of the trip must be primarily related to searching for a job, though. A job interview while on a golf outing to Palm Springs won't cut it. The IRS looks at the amount of time spent seeking new employment in relationship to the amount of time you are away.

Normally, you deduct job-related expenses on **Form 2106, Employee Business Expenses.** However, unless you're claiming job-related travel, local transportation, meal, or entertainment expenses, save yourself some trouble. You can enter the most basic job-hunting expenses directly on Schedule A (line 20) instead of having to fill out Form 2106. You can use the shorter Form 2106-EZ if you weren't reimbursed for any of your expenses and you simply claim the 36 cents per mile rate for your job-related auto expenses.

Job education expenses

If you find that your employer demands greater technical skills, or the fear of being downsized has sent you back to the classroom, the cost of those courses is deductible (even if they lead to a degree) under the following conditions:

- ✔ You are employed or self-employed.

- ✔ The course doesn't qualify you for a new line of work.

- ✔ You already have met the minimum educational requirements of your job or profession.

- ✔ The course is required by your employer or state law, or the course maintains or improves your job skills.

Up to $5,250 under an employer-paid educational assistance program is a tax-free fringe benefit that you shouldn't overlook. This tax-free benefit even applies to graduate level courses.

Like many other tax terms, "maintains or improves job skills" has consistently placed the IRS and taxpayers at odds. The intent of the law was to allow a deduction for refresher courses, such as the continuing education classes tax advisors have to take every year.

For example, an IRS agent was denied a deduction for the cost of obtaining an MBA, while an engineer was allowed to deduct the cost of his degree. The rationale: A significant portion of the engineer's duties involved management, interpersonal, and administrative skills. The court felt the engineer's MBA didn't qualify him for a new line of work and was directly related to his job. The IRS agent flunked this test. (There's something strangely satisfying about seeing the IRS turn on its own, isn't there?)

The general rule is that you must be able to prove by clear and convincing evidence how the course is helpful or necessary in maintaining or improving your job skills. So if you can clear that hurdle, here's what's deductible:

- ✔ Tuition and books
- ✔ Local transportation
- ✔ Travel and living expenses while away from home

Travel expenses are allowable if you must go abroad to do research that can only be done there. Travel and living expenses also are deductible when taking a course at a school in a foreign country or away from your home, even if you could have taken the same course locally. Unfortunately, you can't claim a deduction for "educational" trips. Let's say you're a French teacher who decided to spend the summer traveling in the south of France to brush up on your language skills. Nice try, says the IRS, but no deduction.

Instead of claiming a deduction for education expenses, the Hope Scholarship Credit and the Lifetime Learning Credit allow you to take a direct credit against your tax for those expenses. Although the rules you have to meet to qualify for the credits are rather lengthy, we explain them in Chapter 8.

Up to $3,000 in higher-education expenses can be deducted, even if you don't itemize your deductions. The nifty thing about this deduction is you don't have to show a business need to claim it. The only bummer is that the deduction starts fading away when your income reaches $65,000 ($130,000 filing jointly). See line 26, Chapter 7 for the rest of the rules. Amounts above $3,000 can be deducted as a miscellaneous itemized deduction if you meet the "maintaining or improving job skills" criteria for the portion above $3,000. Bear in mind that the $3,000 deduction covers only tuition and fees, and not room and board or transportation. The deduction isn't allowed if you are claiming an education credit on line 47, Form 1040 or line 31, Form 1040A for yourself or the same student.

Miscellaneous job expenses

Just because your job requires you to incur certain expenses doesn't mean they are automatically deductible. Here's a rundown on what generally is deductible:

- ✔ Professional and trade-association dues
- ✔ Books, subscriptions, and periodicals
- ✔ Union dues
- ✔ Unreimbursed travel and entertainment (covered in detail in the next section)
- ✔ Uniforms and special clothing
- ✔ Medical exams to establish fitness
- ✔ Commuting expenses to a second job (moonlighting, are you?)
- ✔ Small tools and equipment
- ✔ Computers and phones

Deductions for computers and cellular phones are hardest to nail down. You must prove you need the equipment to do your job because your employer doesn't provide you with it or because the equipment at work isn't adequate or available. A letter from your employer stating that a computer is a basic requirement for your job isn't good enough. You must also establish that its use is for your employer's convenience and not yours.

For example, suppose that you are an engineer who, rather than staying late at the office, takes work home. You have a computer at home that is similar to the one in the office. Because the use of your computer isn't for the convenience of your employer, you can't claim a deduction. On the other hand, if you need a computer to use while traveling on business, it would be deductible because you now meet the convenience-of-your-employer requirement.

Fax machines, copiers, adding machines, calculators, and typewriters aren't subject to this rigid rule. You must, however, be able to prove that this equipment is job-related and not merely for your own convenience. Although the law requires that you keep a diary or record that clearly shows the computer's or cellular phone's percentage of business use, you don't have to keep a similar record for other office equipment. Be prepared, however, to prove that it is used mainly for business. With a fax machine, for example, it's worth keeping those printouts showing where your calls have been going and where they've been coming from.

We know, this is a crazy thing to ask; after all, are you going to write down every time you use a copier if the copies are for work or personal reasons? But that behavior is exactly what the law requires. Write your representative in Congress and tell him or her what you think. (You'll probably get a reply that says: "Really? When was that law passed?")

Just because your employer requires that you be neatly groomed doesn't mean the cost of doing so is deductible. An airline pilot can't deduct the cost of his haircuts, even though airline regulations require pilots to have haircuts on a regular basis.

Meeting the requirements and keeping the necessary records to deduct job-related expenses can become a part-time job. Unpleasant as it is, though, doing so will almost certainly slash your taxes and save you in the event you're audited.

Job travel (and entertainment!)

Probably no other group of expenses has created more paperwork than travel and entertainment expenses. Taxpayers may spend more time on the paperwork accounting for a business trip than they do planning for it. Unfortunately, this situation can't be changed. But at least we can help you deduct every possible expense in this area. So let's begin with the three basic rules regarding travel and entertainment expenses:

- ✓ You have to be away from your business or home to deduct travel expenses. (Makes sense, doesn't it?)
- ✓ You can deduct only 50 percent of your meal and entertainment expenses.
- ✓ You need good records.

Travel expenses that are deductible include taxi, commuter bus, and limousine fare to and from the airport or station — and between your hotel and business meetings or job site. You can also deduct auto expenses, whether you use your own car or lease (see "Line 9: Car and truck expenses," in Chapter 11), and the cost of hotels, meals, telephone calls, and laundry while you're away. Don't forget tips and baggage handling. Finally, remember the obvious deductions on airplane, train, and bus fare between your *tax home* and business destination.

Your tax home and travel expenses

Yes, we said tax home. This is where the situation gets a little tricky because, to be able to deduct travel expenses, you must be traveling away from your tax home on business. You are considered to be traveling away from your tax home if the business purpose of your trip requires that you be away longer than an ordinary working day — and you need to sleep or rest so you can be ready for the next day's business. Wouldn't it be nice if the law simply stated that you have to be away overnight?

Your *tax home* isn't where you or your family reside. Of course not. It's the entire city or general area in which you work or where your business is located. For example, suppose that you work in Manhattan but live in the suburbs. You decide to stay in Manhattan overnight because you have an early breakfast meeting the next morning. You aren't away from your tax home overnight; therefore, you can't deduct the cost of the hotel. The only meal expense you can deduct is the next morning's breakfast — if it qualifies as an entertainment expense.

At this point, you probably want to know how far away from your tax home you have to be. Unfortunately, there isn't a mileage count. When it comes to determining whether you're away from home overnight, the IRS uses that famous U.S. Supreme Court definition: "I can't define it, but I know it when I see it."

Also, your tax home may not be near where you live. For example, if you move from job to job without a fixed base of operation, each place you work becomes your tax home. And travel expenses aren't deductible. And if you accept a temporary assignment that lasts for more than a year, you have moved your tax home to the place of the temporary assignment. Sorry, no deduction. Guess what? It gets worse. Say your assignment is expected to last more than a year but then it doesn't. That sort of assignment isn't considered a temporary assignment (one year or less) that makes your travel and living expenses deductible. It's considered a permanent assignment that doesn't allow you to deduct your travel expenses.

Trips that mix business with pleasure

For travel within the U.S., the transportation part of your travel expenses is fully deductible even if part of it is for pleasure. For example, perhaps the airfare and cabs to and from the airport cost $700 for you to attend a business convention in Florida. You spend two days at the end of the convention playing poker with some old friends. Your transportation costs of $700 are fully deductible, but your meals and lodging for the two vacation days aren't.

Transportation costs for travel outside the U.S. have to be prorated based on the amount of time you spend on business and vacation. Suppose that you spend four out of eight days in London on business. You can deduct only 50 percent of your airfare and four days of lodgings and meals. Any other travel costs (such as taxis and telephone calls while you were conducting business) are deductible.

But this general rule for transportation expenses on travel abroad doesn't apply if you meet any of the following conditions:

- ✔ The trip lasts a week or less.
- ✔ More than 75 percent of your time outside the U.S. was spent on business. (The days you start and end your trip are considered business days.)
- ✔ You don't have substantial control in arranging the trip.

You are considered not to have substantial control over your trip if you are an employee who was reimbursed or paid a travel expense allowance, are not related to your employer, and are not a managing executive. Oh well, *c'est la vie.*

The records you need: Part II

You need a receipt for every travel and entertainment expense that exceeds $75. No receipt, no deduction if you're audited. And a canceled check just won't cut it anymore. The receipt — or a separate diary entry — must also show the business purpose. Although you don't need a receipt if the amount is below $75, you still need an entry in your diary to explain to whom, what, where, when, and why. This $75 rule doesn't apply to your hotel bill. A hotel bill is required, regardless of the amount. For entertainment, you need the name and location of the restaurant or the place where you did the entertaining; the number of people served or in attendance; the date and amount of the bill; and the business purpose, such as "Bill Smith, buyer for Company Z."

A hotel receipt has to show the name and location of the hotel, the dates you stayed there, and the separately stated charges for the room, meals, telephone calls, and so on.

Weekends, holidays, and other necessary standby days are counted as business days if they fall between business days. Great! But if these days follow your business activities and you remain at your business destination for personal reasons, they are not business days.

For example, suppose that your tax home is in Kansas City. You travel to St. Louis where you have a business appointment on Friday and another business meeting on the following Monday. The days in between are considered tax-deductible business-expense days — you had a business activity on Friday and had another business activity on Monday. This case is true even if you use that time for sightseeing (going up in the Arch!) or other personal activities.

Trips primarily for personal reasons

If your trip was primarily for personal reasons (such as that vacation to Disney World), some of the trip may be deductible — you can deduct any expenses at your destination that are directly related to your business. For example, calls into work are deductible, as well as a 15-minute customer call in Fantasyland. But spending an hour on business does *not* turn a personal trip into a business trip to be deducted.

Convention expenses

You can deduct your convention-travel expenses if you can prove that your attendance benefits your work. A convention for investment, political, social, or other purposes that are unrelated to your business isn't deductible. Nonbusiness expenses (such as social or sightseeing costs) are personal expenses and aren't deductible. And you can't deduct the travel expenses for your family!

Your selection as a delegate to a convention doesn't automatically entitle you to a deduction. You must prove that your attendance is connected to your business. For conventions held outside North America, you must establish that the convention could be held only at that site. For example, an international seminar on tofu research held in Japan would qualify if that seminar was unique.

Entertainment: The 50 percent deduction

You can deduct only 50 percent of your entertaining expenses — and that includes meals. People in the transportation industry get a special break, so read on.

You may deduct business-related expenses for entertaining a client, customer, or employee. To be deductible, an entertainment expense has to meet the *directly related or associated test.* That is, the expense must be directly related to or associated with the business you conduct. Under the directly related test, you must show a business motive related to your business other than a general expectation of getting future business (what does the IRS think business entertainment is all about?). Although you don't have to prove that you actually received additional business, such evidence will help nail down the deduction. Don't panic! You can deduct goodwill entertaining and entertaining prospective customers under the associated test. You or your employee has to be present, and your entertaining has to be in a business setting. Because the IRS considers distractions at nightclubs, sporting events, and cocktail parties to be substantial, such events don't qualify as business settings. They do under the associated test.

If you have a substantial business discussion before or after entertaining someone, you meet the associated test. For example, suppose that after meeting with a customer, you entertain him and his spouse at a theatre and nightclub. The expense is deductible. Goodwill entertaining and entertaining prospective customers falls under the associated test. But handing a customer two tickets to the Super Bowl and telling him to have a good time doesn't cut it. The reason: There was no business discussion within a reasonable amount of time before or after the game. In such an event the tickets could qualify as a gift.

Entertainment includes any activity generally considered to provide amusement or recreation (a broad definition!). Examples include entertaining guests at nightclubs (and social, athletic, and sporting clubs), at theaters, at sporting events, on yachts, and on hunting or fishing vacations. If you buy a scalped ticket to an entertainment event for a client, you usually can't deduct more than the face value of the ticket. Country club dues aren't deductible; only the cost of entertaining at the club is. Meal expenses include the cost of food, beverages, taxes, and tips.

You can't claim the cost of a meal as an entertainment expense if you are also claiming it as a travel expense (this activity is known as *double-deducting*). Expenses are also not deductible when a group of business acquaintances take turns paying for each other's checks without conducting any business.

With regard to gifts, you can't deduct more than $25 for a business gift to any one person during the year. A husband and wife are considered one person. So if a business customer is getting married, you can't give a $25 gift to each newlywed-to-be and expect to deduct $50.

Standard meal and hotel allowance — or "my city costs more than your city"

Instead of keeping records for your actual meal and incidental expenses (tips and cleaning), you can deduct a flat amount. You don't need to keep receipts with this method. But you do have to establish that you were away from home on business. If you use the high-low method and travel to what the IRS considers a high-cost area, you can use $45 a day. For all other areas, the rate is $35 per day. (IRS Publication 463 lists high-cost areas.) Instead of using the simplified high-low method, you can use the city-by-city rate listed in IRS Publication 1542. For any location not listed in Publication 1542, the rate is $30. Employees and self-employed taxpayers can use the standard meal allowance. Taxpayers in the transportation industry (those involved in moving people and goods) can use a flat rate of $40 a day in the United States and $45 outside the United States. These per diem rates are from January 1, 2003, through September 30, 2003. For the period October 1, 2003, through December 31, 2003, the $35 daily rate increased to $36. The $45 rate jumped to $46, and the transportation industry rates of $40 and $45 respectively increased to $41 and $46. Whether you use the city-by-city or high-low method, you have to use it consistently throughout the year. For example, you can't use the high-low method for the period before October 1, 2003 and switch to the city-by-city after that date because the rates went up for that city.

People in the transportation industry covered by the U.S. Department of Transportation work rules get to deduct 65 percent of their meal expenses instead of the normal 50 percent limit. In later years, it will gradually increase to 80 percent (in 2008). Airline pilots, the flight crew, ground crews, interstate bus and truck drivers, railroad engineers, conductors, and train crews are eligible for this break.

If your employer reimburses you at a flat rate of $125 a day for your hotel and meal and incidental expenses, you don't have to keep records for those expenses. You only need to show that the trip was for business. If you are traveling in what the IRS considers a high-cost location area, you are allowed $204 per day. Both rates are in addition to your transportation expenses, of course. The rates for the period October 1 to December 31, 2003, are $206 for high-cost areas and $126 for others.

Unfortunately, self-employed taxpayers can't use the flat per diem rates listed for hotel-and-meal expenses; only employees can. They can, however, choose to use the part of the rate that applies to meals and incidentals. If you are self-employed, you can compute your travel expense deduction based on $35 and $36 a day for meals and incidentals plus your hotel bills. If you are traveling in a high-cost area, it's $45 and $46 a day.

Once upon a time, when it came to per diem travel rates, the IRS tried to keep things simple. In 2001, they decided to make their per diem rates for travel as complicated as everything else. The per diem rates now are no longer effective for the entire calendar year. The rates now change every October 1. The reason? The federal government is on a fiscal year that starts on October 1, and because the feds set the per diem travel rates, the IRS switched to the federal way of doing things. So, now two rates exist in a given tax year, one for the period January 1, 2003, through September 30, 2003, and another set for the period October 1, 2003, through December 31, 2003. As the result of all this, you have two choices. You can use the per diem rates from January 1 to September 30 we cited above for all of 2003, or you can use the rates for travel up to September 30, 2003, and when the new high/low and city-by-city rates come out, you can use those rates from October 1, 2003, through the end of the year.

Instead of using the high/low rates, you can use the per diem rates in effect for a specific locality. For example, say you went to Chicago on business. The per diem rate before October 1, 2003, was $205. After September 30, 2003, it jumped to $206. The hotel rate before and after October 1, 2003, included in these two amounts remained at $155. It was the $1 increase in the Chicago meal and incidental rate from $50 to $51 that pushed the total per diem rate to $205 from $201. These rates are posted on the government's Web site at www.policyworks.gov/perdiem. The site also links you to the State Department's Web site where international per diem rates are posted. The IRS announced this change by stating that it was trying to make things as "painless" as possible for taxpayers.

If your employer's per diem reimbursement rate is equal to or less than the standard rate above, no paperwork is necessary. That's what the standard rate is all about — to keep you from having to attach an accounting of your expenses when you file your return. If your actual expenses or your expenses using the standard meal allowance (your hotel bill plus the standard meal allowance) is more than your per diem allowance, you enter your actual expenses and per diem allowance on **Form 2106, Employee Business Expenses.** Your expenses that are in excess of your per diem allowance per Form 2106 are deducted on Schedule A. If your actual expenses are less than the standard per diem rate don't look a gift horse in the mouth. You need do nothing. Just say thanks.

If your per diem allowance is more than the standard rate, the excess gets reported in box 1 (Wages) of your W-2. The standard rate, say it was $204 a day, is entered in box 12 of your W-2 with the code L. If your actual expenses are more than the standard rate, you can deduct the excess. Enter your actual expenses on lines 1 through 5 of Form 2106. Enter the amount shown in box 12 of your W-2 on line 7 of Form 2106. The difference between these two amounts gets deducted on Schedule A. If your actual expenses are less than the standard rate in box 12, you are not entitled to any deduction and you don't have to file Form 2106. What you do get stuck for is the tax on the excess above the standard rate that was included in box 1 (Wages) of your W-2.

You can find all the per diem rates on the IRS Homepage on the World Wide Web at www.irs.gov, or at www.policyworks.gov/perdiem.

The standard meal and hotel allowances don't apply to Alaska, Hawaii, Puerto Rico, or foreign locations, however. A separate schedule can be found at the site for those places and for foreign travel.

You can't use the standard meal and hotel per diem allowances if you're traveling for medical, charitable, or moving-expense purposes. Self-employed people can't use this per diem rate. They are, however, allowed to use the meal per diem rates but have to substantiate their actual hotel expense. The rate also can't be used if your employer is your brother or sister, half brother or half sister, ancestor, or lineal descendent. Finally, you can't use the standard allowance if your employer is a corporation in which you hold 10 percent or more ownership. So many details!

What IRS form to use

What other form you attach to your Form 1040 depends on whether you are an employee or are self-employed:

> ✔ **If you're self-employed:** You deduct travel on line 24a, meal and entertainment expenses on line 24b and the deductible portion on line 24d of Schedule C.

> ✔ **If you're employed:** You must use Form 2106, Employee Business Expenses, or 2106-EZ.

For example, if you are paid a salary with the understanding that you will pay your own expenses, you claim these expenses on Form 2106 and then carry over the amount from line 10 of Form 2106 or line 6 of Form 2106-EZ to Schedule A (line 20) of your Form 1040, where the amount is claimed as an itemized deduction. Form 2106 also allows you to claim travel and entertaining costs that exceed your travel allowance or the amount for which you were reimbursed.

If you received a travel allowance, your employer adds the amount of the allowance to your salary, and it will be included in box 1 of your W-2. So if you received a travel allowance of $10,000 and spent $10,000, the $10,000 is not completely deductible because it's reduced by 2 percent of your AGI. For example, if your income is $100,000, you can deduct only $8,000 ($10,000 minus 2 percent of $100,000) of your travel expenses. If your income exceeds $139,500, or $69,750 if you are married filing separately, a portion of these deductions is reduced again.

Here's a neat hint: Instead of getting an allowance, have your employer reimburse you for actual expenses that you submit on an expense report. You won't have to file Form 2106, and you won't have to pay tax on the money that you never earned and lose part of your deductions due to silly rules like the 2 percent rule. Neat, huh?

Line 21: Tax preparation fees

You can deduct the fees paid to a tax preparer or advisor! You may also deduct the cost of being represented at a tax audit and the cost of tax-preparation software programs, tax publications, and any fee you paid for the electronic filing of your return. You can also deduct travel expenses when you have to go to a tax audit. This is probably one deduction you wish you weren't entitled to.

Fees paid to prepare tax schedules relating to business income (Schedule C), rentals or royalties (Schedule E), or farm income and expenses (Schedule F) are deductible on each one of those forms. The expenses for preparing the remainder of the return are deductible on Schedule A. That way, more of the fee is deductible, because most of it isn't subject to the 2 percent of AGI rule.

Ready for another tax surprise? *Taxes For Dummies* is deductible!

Line 22: Other expenses — investment, safe-deposit box, and so on

You may be scratching your head as to how the IRS can throw in a line item here called "other expenses," when we're within the miscellaneous deduction category. The expenses that are most likely to help you on this line to build up to that 2 percent hurdle are fees you incur in managing your investments. Here's a rundown of deductible investment expenses:

✔ Financial periodicals.

✔ Accounting fees to keep track of investment income.

✔ Investment fees, custodial fees, trust administration fees, and other expenses you paid for managing your investments.

✔ Investment fees shown in box 5 of Form 1099-DIV.

✔ Safe-deposit box rentals.

✔ Trustee's fees for your IRA, if separately billed and paid.

✔ Investment expenses of partnerships, S Corporations, and mutual funds. (You will receive a Schedule K-1 that will tell you where to deduct those expenses.)

You can't deduct expenses incurred in connection with investing in tax-exempt bonds. If you have expenses related to both taxable and tax-exempt income but can't identify the expenses that relate to each, you must prorate the expenses to determine the amount that you can deduct.

One of the benefits of having so many lawyers here in America is that when you hire one for a variety of personal purposes, you may qualify to write off the cost. For example, you can deduct a legal fee in connection with collecting taxable alimony and for tax advice related to a divorce if the bill specifies how much is for tax advice and if the bill is determined in a reasonable way.

Part of an estate tax planning fee may be deductible. That's because estate planning involves tax as well as nontax advice. A reasonable division of the bill between the two usually supports a deduction for the portion attributable for tax advice. Legal costs in connection with contesting a will or suing for wrongful death aren't deductible. The same goes for financial planner fees that you pay. The part that applies to tax advice is deductible.

You may deduct legal fees directly related to your job, such as fees incurred in connection with an employment contract or defending yourself from being wrongfully dismissed. You can deduct legal expenses that you incurred if they are business related or in connection with income-producing property.

The payment of a contingent fee where an attorney gets a percentage of a settlement has created problems for a number of taxpayers. We know what you're probably thinking — the IRS *and* lawyers are problems! In a number of instances (back wages is an example) where a contingent fee was paid and the recovery was taxable, the taxpayer reported only the net amount. Then the IRS stepped in and made the taxpayer report the entire recovery as income and the legal fee as a miscellaneous itemized deduction. Doing it this way caused the deduction to trigger the Alternative Minimum Tax (See Chapter 8), and the taxpayer ended up owing additional tax. Appeals courts in four Federal circuits have upheld the IRS; three others haven't. This controversy won't be resolved until one of these cases goes before the Supreme Court, if ever. As it now stands, how you handle a matter like this depends on the state where you reside.

If you receive a taxable settlement, for age discrimination or sexual harassment for example, and part of the settlement reimbursed you for medical expenses you incurred to alleviate the symptoms of emotional distress, make sure the settlement agreement accounts for the medical expenses separately. That way you can deduct the medical expenses from the settlement and pay tax on only the net amount.

A legal fee paid to collect a disputed Social Security claim also is deductible to the extent that your benefit is taxable. For example, suppose you paid a $2,000 fee to help collect your Social Security benefits. If 50 percent of your Social Security is taxable, you can deduct $1,000 (50 percent of the fee).

Lines 23–26: Miscellaneous math

Congratulations! You've slogged through one of the parts of the tax return that clearly highlights how politicians and years of little changes add up to complicated tax laws. We know you've spent a lot of time identifying and detailing expenses that fit into these ridiculous categories. As we warned you in the beginning of this section on job expenses and other miscellaneous deductions, you can deduct these expenses only to the extent that they exceed 2 percent of your AGI. Lines 23 through 26 walk you through this arithmetic.

Line 27: Other Miscellaneous Deductions

More miscellaneous deductions? You bet. These "other miscellaneous deductions" are different from those on lines 20 through 26 in that they aren't subject to the 2 percent AGI limit. Hooray, no convoluted math! These are 100 percent Grade A, no-fat deductions!

- ✔ **Gambling losses to the extent of gambling winnings:** Enter on line 27 of Schedule A.

- ✔ **Estate tax on income you received as an heir:** Enter on line 27 of Schedule A. You can deduct the estate tax attributable to income you received from an estate that you paid tax on. For example, suppose that you received $10,000 from an IRA account when the owner died. You included this amount in your income. The owner's estate paid $2,000 of estate tax on the IRA. You can deduct the $2,000 on line 27. It's called an *IRD deduction.* That's IRS lingo for *income in respect of a decedent,* which means that because the IRA owner never paid income tax on the money in the IRA, guess what? You have to! But you get to deduct a portion of estate tax.

- ✔ **Repayment of income:** If you had to repay more than $3,000 of income that was included in your income in an earlier year, you may be able to deduct the amount you repaid or take a credit against your tax. This is known as a "claim of right." (See Chapter 6 for help tackling this little gem.) However, if the repayment is less than $3,000, you must deduct it on line 22 of Schedule A.

- ✔ **Unrecovered investment in a pension:** If a retiree contributed to the cost of a pension or annuity, a part of each payment received can be excluded from income as a tax-free return of the retiree's investment. If the retiree dies before the entire investment is returned tax free, the unrecovered investment is allowed as a deduction on the retiree's final return. See line 16 in Chapter 6.

- ✔ **Work expenses for the disabled:** If you have a physical or mental disability that limits your being employed or that substantially limits one or more of your activities (such as performing manual tasks, walking, speaking, breathing, learning, and working), your impairment-related work expenses are deductible.

- ✔ **Impairment-related work expenses:** These expenses are allowable business expenses of attendant care services at your place of work and expenses in connection with your place of work that are necessary for you to be able to work. See IRS Publication 907 *(Tax Highlights for Persons with Disabilities)* for more information.

  If you're an employee, enter your impairment-related work expenses on line 10 of Form 2106. This amount is also entered on line 27 of Schedule A. And the amount that is unrelated to your impairment is entered on line 20 of Schedule A.

Line 28: Total Itemized Deductions

You've (thankfully) reached the end of Schedule A. Warm up that calculator again because you need to do some adding. Sum up the totals that you've written in the far right column on the schedule. You should be adding the amounts on lines 4, 9, 14, 18, 19, 26, and 27.

But wait! You can't just go ahead and enter that total on line 28. Why would the IRS allow you to do that after plowing through this difficult schedule? If your adjusted gross income (listed on line 35 of Form 1040) exceeded $139,500 for the year (or was above $69,750 if you're married filing separately), you're going to have to jump through more hoops, because the IRS wants to limit your itemized deductions if you make this much money.

If your AGI is $139,500 or less for the year ($69,750 or less if married filing separately), you can call it quits now and simply write the total you calculated on line 28 of your Schedule A. Then you can enter this amount on line 37 of your Form 1040. Just make sure that the total of your itemized deductions is greater than the standard deduction (see the amounts at the beginning of the chapter).

If your income is above these limits, you've got more work to do. Read on. (We'd never accuse the IRS of living by that adage, "You can never have enough of a good thing.")

Limit on itemized deductions

If your AGI exceeds $139,300 (or $69,750 if you are married filing separately), you have to reduce your total itemized deductions by 3 percent of your income above $139,500. Here's how it works: Say that your income is $159,500 and your total itemized deductions are $30,000. Because your income exceeded $139,500 by $20,000, you have to reduce your itemized deductions by $600 ($20,000 × 3 percent). Although you started with itemized deductions of $30,000, you can deduct only $29,400.

The 3 percent rule won't completely eliminate your itemized deductions because your deductions can't be reduced by more than 80 percent. So, in the preceding example, if your income was $1 million, you would still get to deduct $6,000, because your $30,000 in deductions can't be reduced by more than $24,000 ($30,000 × 80 percent).

So let's put this on paper to make it easier to do the math. Use the worksheet in Table 9-3 if your AGI exceeds $139,500 (married filing jointly) or $69,750 (married filing separately) to figure your allowable deductions.

Table 9-3	Itemized Deduction Worksheet	
	Sample	*Your Computation*
1. AGI line 35 (1040)	$167,900	1. _____
2. Enter $139,500 ($69,750 if filing separately)	$139,500	2. _____
3. Subtract line 2 from line 1	$ 28,400	3. _____
4. Total itemized deductions (Schedule A)	$ 20,000	4. _____
5. From Schedule A enter: Medical (line 4) Investment interest (line 13) Casualty loss (line 19) Gambling losses (line 27)	$ 10,000	5. _____

	Sample	*Your Computation*
6. Subtract line 5 entries from line 4	$ 10,000	6. _____
7. Multiply line 6 by 80%	$ 8,000	7. _____
8. Multiply line 3 by 3%	$ 852	8. _____
9. The smaller of lines 7 and 8	$ 852	9. _____
10. Your reduced itemized deductions: line 4 less line 9	$ 19,148*	10. _____

*This is the amount you're allowed to deduct. Now you can enter this amount on line 28 of Schedule A and carry it over to line 37 of your Form 1040. Just make sure that the total of your itemized deductions is greater than the standard deduction (see amounts at the beginning of this chapter).

You may be wondering why your medical and dental expenses, investment interest, casualty and theft losses, and gambling losses don't have to reduce these itemized expenses. The IRS doesn't limit or reduce your ability to write off these expenses so that they aren't subject to the 3 percent reduction rule. The IRS *does* want to limit your ability to deduct too much in the way of state and local taxes (including property taxes paid on your home), home mortgage interest, gifts to charity, job expenses, and miscellaneous deductions.

The net effect of the IRS tossing out some of these write-offs is that it raises the effective tax rate that you're paying on your income higher than the IRS tables indicate. This may encourage you, for example, to spend less on a home or to pay off your mortgage faster (see Chapter 24), because you don't merit a full deduction.

What your neighbors are deducting

Table 9-4 shows the IRS statistics of the average deductions taken by taxpayers on their 2001 tax returns.

Table 9-4	Average Itemized Deductions (2001)			
AGI ($000)	*Medical*	*Taxes*	*Contributions*	*Interest*
Under $15	$7,281	$2,134	$1,329	$6,884
$15–30	$5,616	$2,311	$1,875	$6,406
$30–50	$5,489	$3,052	$1,906	$6,783
$50–100	$5,532	$5,108	$2,429	$8,330
$100–200	$10,780	$9,713	$3,761	$11,817
$200 & above	$35,927	$38,931	$17,842	$23,260

Source: Statistics of Income Bulletin, The Internal Revenue Service

But you can't simply go ahead and claim the amounts listed in Table 9-4 — the IRS imposes penalties for doing that! And if your deductions exceed these amounts, you stand a greater chance of being audited. But at least you can see how your deductions match up with the norm. Remember, the IRS computer scans returns to check that the mortgage interest that you deduct agrees with the amount of interest your bank reported to the IRS as being paid.

Chapter 10

Interest and Dividend Income: Schedule B

● ●

In This Chapter
▶ Interest income stuff
▶ Understanding your 1099-INT
▶ Dividend income stuff
▶ Understanding your 1099-DIV
▶ Foreign accounts and trusts

● ●

Ah! More income — bring it on, you say? Remember that you're going to add it to the taxable income section. In this chapter, we go through Schedule B (see Figure 10-1). Can you find the form? It's a little IRS trick — Schedule B is on the back of Schedule A. After you do the math, transfer the interest income from line 4 on Schedule B to line 8a of the trusty Form 1040; the dividend income from line 6 on Schedule B goes on line 9a of Form 1040.

If your interest or dividends is $1,500 or less, you don't have to fill out and attach Schedule B — Interest and Ordinary Dividends — to Form 1040, and 1040A filers don't have to file Schedule 1. Remember: The threshold is $1,500 or less of interest and $1,500 or less of dividends.

Even though you may not have to attach Schedule B to your return , you do have to keep track of your total interest and dividends somewhere, and Schedule B is as good a place as any. So why not continue to use it as a worksheet?

If you have a foreign bank account or are involved in a foreign trust, we get into that near the end of the chapter, Schedule B has to be filed. Sorry!

Year after year, many taxpayers dutifully complete Schedule B, file it with the rest of their return, and forget about it until they need to complete their next return. This particular schedule is a potential gold mine for reducing your future taxes. Why? Because you report on this schedule all the taxable interest and dividend income that you received during the year. If you complete this schedule and you're in the higher tax brackets, many investments are tax-friendly. Be sure to check out Chapter 23 to find out all about them.

What you need to complete Schedule B are those 1099s (1099-INT and 1099-DIV) that banks, corporations, brokerage firms, and mutual fund companies send by January 31 of the following year. Make sure that you have one of these forms for each and every nonretirement account that you held money in during the tax year. If you're missing a form, get on the horn to the responsible financial institution and request it.

If you don't report all your interest or dividend income (or don't furnish the payer with your Social Security number), your future interest and dividend income is subject to backup withholding of 28 percent! To add insult to injury, about a year after filing your taxes, you'll receive a nasty notice called a CP-2000 listing the interest and dividends that you didn't report. You'll end up owing interest and penalties in addition to the tax.

Although becoming ensnared in backup withholding is unpleasant, don't worry that the amounts withheld by financial institutions from your accounts and sent to the IRS are for naught. They simply represent a forced payment of your expected tax on your interest and dividends. You get "credit" for it on line 61, "Federal income tax withheld," on your Form 1040 (see Chapter 8 for more details). On Form 1040EZ, it's line 7; on Form 1040-A, it's line 39.

Schedules A&B (Form 1040) 2003		OMB No. 1545-0074	Page **2**

Name(s) shown on Form 1040. Do not enter name and social security number if shown on other side. | **Your social security number**

Schedule B—Interest and Ordinary Dividends

Attachment Sequence No. **08**

Part I
Interest

(See page B-1 and the instructions for Form 1040, line 8a.)

1 List name of payer. If any interest is from a seller-financed mortgage and the buyer used the property as a personal residence, see page B-1 and list this interest first. Also, show that buyer's social security number and address ▶

Amount

Note. If you received a Form 1099-INT, Form 1099-OID, or substitute statement from a brokerage firm, list the firm's name as the payer and enter the total interest shown on that form.

2 Add the amounts on line 1 . . . . **2**

3 Excludable interest on series EE and I.U.S. savings bonds issued after 1989. Attach Form 8815 . . . . **3**

4 Subtract line 3 from line 2. Enter the result here and on Form 1040, line 8a ▶ **4**

Note. If line 4 is over $1,500, you must complete Part III.

Part II
Ordinary Dividends

(See page B-1 and the instructions for Form 1040, line 9a.)

5 List name of payer ▶

Amount

Note. If you received a Form 1099-DIV or substitute statement from a brokerage firm, list the firm's name as the payer and enter the ordinary dividends shown on that form.

6 Add the amounts on line 5. Enter the total here and on Form 1040, line 9a . ▶ **6**

Note. If line 6 is over $1,500, you must complete Part III.

Part III
Foreign Accounts and Trusts

(See page B-2.)

You must complete this part if you **(a)** had over $1,500 of taxable interest or ordinary dividends; or **(b)** had a foreign account; or **(c)** received a distribution from, or were a grantor of, or a transferor to, a foreign trust.

	Yes	No

7a At any time during 2003, did you have an interest in or a signature or other authority over a financial account in a foreign country, such as a bank account, securities account, or other financial account? See page B-2 for exceptions and filing requirements for Form TD F 90-22.1 . . .

b If "Yes," enter the name of the foreign country ▶

8 During 2003, did you receive a distribution from, or were you the grantor of, or transferor to, a foreign trust? If "Yes," you may have to file Form 3520. See page B-2 . . . .

For Paperwork Reduction Act Notice, see Form 1040 instructions. | Schedule B (Form 1040) 2003

Figure 10-1: Had a good year with your investments? Report your interest and dividend income on Schedule B.

Part 1, Lines 1–4: Interest Income

In this first part of the schedule, you need to declare interest income that you earned during the tax year. Although this income can come from a variety of sources, as you'll soon realize, most of it is reported by large, impersonal financial institutions that will send you a computer-generated **Form 1099-INT, Interest Income.**

Before you complete the lines on Schedule B, we'd like to explain how to read your 1099-INT forms.

Understanding Form 1099-INT

You receive Form 1099-INT from the financial institution, such as a bank, that pays you interest. These forms aren't too difficult to read. The following are brief descriptions of little boxes and other stuff you find on your 1099-INT (see Figure 10-2).

9292	☐ VOID	☐ CORRECTED		
PAYER'S name, street address, city, state, ZIP code, and telephone no.	Payer's RTN (optional)	OMB No. 1545-0112		
		20**03** Form **1099-INT**	**Interest Income**	
PAYER'S Federal identification number	RECIPIENT'S identification number	**1** Interest income not included in box 3 $		**Copy A** **For** **Internal Revenue Service Center** **File with Form 1096.**
RECIPIENT'S name		**2** Early withdrawal penalty $	**3** Interest on U.S. Savings Bonds and Treas. obligations $	For Privacy Act and Paperwork Reduction Act Notice, see the
Street address (including apt. no.)		**4** Federal income tax withheld $	**5** Investment expenses $	**2003 General Instructions for**
City, state, and ZIP code		**6** Foreign tax paid	**7** Foreign country or U.S. possession	**Forms 1099, 1098, 5498, and W-2G.**
Account number (optional)	2nd TIN not. ☐	$		

Form **1099-INT**   Cat. No. 14410K   Department of the Treasury - Internal Revenue Service

Do Not Cut or Separate Forms on This Page — Do Not Cut or Separate Forms on This Page

Figure 10-2: You receive Form 1099-INT from institutions that pay you taxable interest.

Don't assume that your 1099-INT forms are all correct. Big companies make mistakes, and they often cause taxpayers to pay more tax. Check your 1099-INT forms against the statements that you received throughout the year from the financial firm where you had the account paying the interest. If you receive an incorrect 1099-INT, ask the payer to issue a corrected one on the double! Form 1099-INT lists the telephone number of the person you need to contact in case it has to be revised.

One problem with filing too early is that you may receive a corrected 1099-INT, which means that you'll have to amend your return. And filing one return per year is more than enough for most of us!

The amount in box 1 and box 3 of the 1099-INT is the taxable interest that you have to report on line 1 of this schedule. But if you don't have more than $1,500 of total interest income for the tax year, you need not complete this part of Schedule B (you have to complete Part II, "Dividend Income," if you had more than $1,500 in dividend income). If you don't have more than $1,500 in interest, skip Part I and enter the total of your interest income on line 8a of Form 1040. Don't concern yourself with the rest of the boxes on your 1099-INT right now. As we breeze through this chapter, we'll let you know what to do with them.

Completing lines 1–4

Now that you've located and understand Form 1099-INT, you're ready to complete Part I of Schedule B.

Line 1: Taxable interest

Taxable interest includes interest you receive from bank accounts, interest income on loans you made to others, and interest income on loans from most other sources (anything except for municipal bond interest).

Taxable interest does not include interest on insurance dividends you leave on deposit with the Department of Veterans Affairs (for people who were in the armed services).

Interest that is taxed as dividends

In the past, savings and loans, credit unions, savings banks, and money market funds often reported the interest you earned as dividends. Now that qualified dividends (we explain this term in Part II, Lines 5 and 6: Dividend Income) are taxed at a reduced rate, these financial institutions have to clean up their dividend-labeling act. You have to report these so-called dividends as interest even though the interest was reported on a **1099-DIV, Dividends and Distributions** by the financial institution instead of Form 1099-INT. Don't you think, sometimes, that everyone out there is trying to confuse you?

Gifts for opening an account

The value of that toaster you received is reported as interest on Form 1099-INT. Enjoy your toast! A gift valued at $10 or less for a deposit of less than $5,000 or $20 for a deposit of $5,000 or more isn't taxable, thanks to a kinder and gentler IRS.

Interest on life insurance dividends

This interest is taxable, but the dividends you receive aren't taxable until the total of all dividends received exceeds the total of all the premiums paid. Keep your annual dividend statements from your company in a file so that you can track that amount versus the premiums you paid.

Interest on EE U.S. Savings Bonds

If you don't have EE bonds, you may happily skip this line. (If you want to know about them, be sure to read Chapter 25.) You report the interest on EE bonds when you cash in the bonds. You can choose to report the interest every year instead of waiting to report all the interest earned on the bond when it is cashed in. Whatever method you choose as to when you have to report the interest, you must use the same method for all E, EE, and I bonds that you own.

Reporting the interest every year may make sense if you have a child who has little or no income, because the first $750 of interest is exempt from tax (see Chapter 25). Attach a statement to your child's return saying that you elect to report the interest annually. If the interest is under $750, you're going to have to file a return even if one isn't required, so that you can make this election for the initial year. After that, as long as the interest is under $750 (an amount that periodically is increased for inflation) and your child doesn't exceed earned income limits, you don't have to file.

Series E bonds stop earning interest after 40 years; Series EE bonds stop earning interest after 30 years. (Series E were issued before 1980, and Series EE were issued after that.) You can avoid paying the tax on the accumulated interest at or before maturity by exchanging these bonds for HH bonds (see the next section, "U.S. H and HH bonds").

Joint returns, minors, and interest stuff

If your Social Security number is the one that's reported on the 1099-INT, the computers at the IRS check to see whether the interest from the 1099-INT is on your return. On a joint return, either your SSN or your spouse's number can be on the account because you're filing jointly.

But what about an account owned by you and someone other than your spouse (or if you're merely holding the money for someone else)? Suppose that only 50 percent of the $1,200 reported under your SSN is yours. Report the $1,200 on Schedule B, and on the line below, subtract the $600 belonging to the other person. In the space for the name of the payer, write NOMINEE Distribution.

Enter the $600 as a negative number <$600>. This is how you subtract the $600 from the total that you must report but that doesn't belong to you. The rules also require that you issue that person Form 1099-INT for their $600. What a pain!

When a minor has an account, make sure that the minor's Social Security number is on the account. If he or she has more than $750 in interest, the minor must file a return. If the minor is under the age of 14, with interest and investment income exceeding $1,500, the excess is taxed at the parent's tax rate (find out more about the Kiddie Tax in Chapter 15).

When the owner of an E or EE bond dies, the heir pays the tax when the bond is cashed in — unless the interest was reported on the decedent's final return. This choice makes sense if the owner of the bond died at the beginning of the year and had little or no income (and was in a lower tax bracket than the heir).

For example, if the owner died on January 10 and filed a return reporting the accumulated EE bond interest of $4,000, no tax would be added because the decedent is entitled to a standard deduction of $4,750 (if single) and a personal exemption of $3,050. On the other hand, if the heir is in the 25 percent tax bracket and had to report the $4,000 of accumulated interest when cashing in the bond, the tax would be $1,000.

Say you or the person you inherited a bond from had been reporting the interest on a savings bond annually and you redeem the bond. Guess what. You will receive a 1099-INT for the entire amount of interest the bond earned through the years. Here's what to do so you don't pay tax on interest you don't have to. Report the entire amount of interest on line 1 of Schedule B and then enter, on the line below, the amount previously reported as a <negative number>. In the space for the name of the payer, write U.S. Savings Bond Interest Previously Reported. This is how you subtract the interest on which you previously paid tax from the total interest you have to report.

A distribution of savings bonds from a retirement gets reported as a retirement distribution. The amount you report is the cost of the bond plus the interest up to the time of distribution. When you cash in the bond you will receive a 1099-DIV for all the interest earned through the years. No problem! Just follow the instructions in the preceding paragraph on how to deal with "U.S. Savings Bond Interest Previously Reported."

Here are the rules when you buy a savings bond with someone or in someone else's name. If you buy a bond in the name of another person who is the sole owner, the owner reports the interest. If you buy a bond jointly with your money, you report the interest. If each of you put up the dough, the interest is reported in proportion to what each of you paid. In a community property state, if the bond is community property and you file separately, generally, each spouse reports half the interest.

U.S. H and HH bonds

H and HH bonds are issued only in exchange for E and EE bonds. Interest is paid semiannually, and you receive a Form 1099-INT from the government showing the amount of interest you must report. H bonds have a 30-year maturity, and HH bonds have a 20-year maturity. (In case you really want to know, H bonds were issued before 1980, and HH bonds were issued after that time.)

The amount of interest earned on the E or EE bonds that you exchanged is stated on the H or HH bonds. You report this amount when you cash in the H or HH bonds.

U.S. Treasury bills

U.S. Treasury bills are short-term obligations of the U.S. government, issued at a discount. These bills mature in 1, 2, 3, 6, or 12 months. You report the interest in the year the bill matures, not when you purchase it.

For example, suppose that you purchase a $10,000, 6-month T-bill for $9,700 in December 2003. You report the $300 of interest you earned when the bill matures in 2004. This maneuver is an excellent way to defer income to the next year.

Interest on U.S. Treasury bonds, notes, and bills is exempt from state tax.

I-bonds

I-bonds are similar to EE bonds. The difference is that the interest that is paid at maturity (30 years) or when the bond is cashed in is linked to inflation. I-bonds are issued in denominations as low as $50.

How do I-bonds stack up against regular inflation-indexed Treasury bonds? A regular inflation-indexed bond carries a fixed rate of interest, with the principal adjusted annually to keep up with inflation. Whereas I-bond holders don't pay tax until the bond is cashed in, holders of regular inflation-indexed bonds have to pay tax every year on the interest payment and the capital gains tax on the inflation-index increase in the value of the bond. Unlike I-bonds, regular inflation-indexed bonds can be purchased only in $1,000 denominations.

Zero-coupon bonds

Zero-coupon bonds don't pay annual interest, but they are issued at a discount very similar to U.S. Savings Bonds. Each year, the bond increases in value equal to the amount of interest it is considered to have earned. In tax lingo, this is referred to as *original issue discount* (OID). Each year, the issuer or your broker will compute the amount of interest you have to report and send you a Form 1099-OID.

Interest on bonds bought or sold

When you buy a bond between the interest payment dates, you pay the seller the interest that was earned up to the sale date.

For example, suppose that on April 30 you buy a bond that makes semiannual interest payments of $600 on June 30. You must pay the seller $400 for the interest earned up to April 30. You report the $600 in interest that you received for the bond on Schedule B. On the line below, subtract the $400 of interest you paid the seller, and to the left of the $400 amount, write ACCRUED INTEREST PAID. Enter the $400 as a negative amount, <$400>. That's how you subtract the $400 of interest that you paid from the total interest reported.

✔ Sales and purchases between interest dates: Say you sold a bond for $1,040, $25 of which represents interest on the bond that was earned but not yet paid. Here's how this plays out:

1. In the year of the sale, $25 is reported as interest income. Next, you reduce the $1,040 you received by the $25. $1,015 is your selling price for computing your gain or loss. If you paid $1,000 for the bond, you have a $15 gain.

2. When the buyer receives the next interest payment, he is entitled to reduce the payment by the $25 of interest he paid to you. Next, he makes a reduction in his tax basis. He reduces the $1,040 by $25 and uses $1,015 as his tax basis (cost) when he sells the bond to determine whether he has a profit or loss.

✔ Bond premiums and discounts: Say you purchase a bond for $1,000 that pays 6 percent ($60) that matures in 10 years at a $100 premium. You can elect to deduct $10 ($100 ÷ 10 years) of the premium each year, so you have to pay tax on only $50. Enter $60 on line 1 of Schedule B. On the next line, enter <$10>, as a negative number. Next to this amount, write ABP Adjustment, which stands for *amortized bond premium*. Here's a plain English definition of amortization: It's the $10 deduction you are entitled to. Additionally, every year you have to reduce the $1,100 you paid by the $10 you get to deduct. This is a current deduction that many investors fail to claim. If you don't make this election in the year of purchase, you treat the $100 as part of the cost of the bond in determining your profit or loss on its sale or maturity.

Let's reverse the above example. Say you purchased a $1,000, 6 percent bond that matures in 10 years at a $100 discount for $900. When the bond matures, you report the $100 as interest. Suppose you sell the bond for $950 before it matures; you don't have a capital gain of $50. Instead, you have interest income of $50. Let's add a different twist to the example. You sell the bond after 5 years for $960. You report $50 as interest income ($10 × 5 years) and $10 as a capital gain. Instead of doing it this way, you can elect to report a portion of the $100 as interest income ratable over 10 years at a rate of $10 a year. You make this election in the year of purchase by simply reporting the $10 as interest. If you make the election, every year you add the $10 to your tax basis of the bond. You may want to report the income annually because you have a lot of investment interest expense that can't be deducted because you don't have enough investment income to offset the interest expense (see investment interest in Chapter 9, line 13). This rule, which requires that part of the discount be reported as interest instead of capital gain, applies to bonds issued after July 19, 1984, regardless of when you bought them. For tax-exempt bonds, which we will get to in a moment, this rule applies to bonds purchased after April 30, 1993, regardless of when the bond was issued.

Tax refunds

Interest on tax refunds is taxable. The amount of your state and local refund is reported on line 10. Federal tax refunds aren't taxable. Interest on them is.

Tax-exempt bonds (muni)

Interest on city and state bonds is exempt from tax. But you still must report it on Form 1040A (line 8b) or on Form 1040 (line 8b). Although the entry on line 8b is not added to your taxable income, it is used to determine the amount of your Social Security that may be subject to tax.

Most states have a provision that tax-exempt bonds are exempt from state income tax only if the bonds are issued by that state. For example, a New York State resident pays state tax on a tax-exempt bond issued by Ohio but doesn't pay state tax on a tax-exempt bond issued by New York.

If you purchase a *muni* at a discount — for example, a $1,000, 10-year, 6 percent bond for $900 — you have $100 of taxable interest at maturity. This is not a misprint. The $100 is taxable. Say you sell the bond after 5 years for $960. $50 is reported as interest and $10 is a capital gain. Here's the math on how this nasty bit of business is computed. Every year during the 10 years until the bond matures, $10 of the discount is considered interest ($100 ÷ 10). This amounts to $50 during the five years you owned the bond. The $50 is reported as interest and is added to the $900 you paid to figure your capital gain. All this probably comes as a surprise to you because you more than likely thought that 100 percent of the income on a muni was tax-exempt. Just like a taxable bond, you can elect to report the discount annually. The interest the bond earns every year is tax-exempt, but not the discount you receive when either the bond matures or is sold.

Line 2: Total interest

Add all the amounts on line 1.

Line 3: U.S. Savings Bonds — education program

One tax shelter that most people are unaware of is that Uncle Sam wants you to put money aside for the education of your children and provides you with a tax exemption to boot. All or part of the interest on U.S. Savings Bonds used to pay college tuition is exempt from tax under the following conditions:

- ✔ The U.S. Savings Bonds (Series EE) were issued after December 31, 1989.

- ✔ You're 24 years of age or older before the month in which you buy the bonds.

- ✔ The total redemption proceeds — interest and principal — don't exceed the tuition and fees paid for the year. (Room and board aren't considered tuition.) The tuition and fees paid have to be reduced by any nontaxable scholarships.

- ✔ The tuition is for you, your spouse, or your dependents.

- ✔ The exclusion isn't available if you are married filing separately.

- ✔ The bond must be issued in either your name or in your name and your spouse's name as co-owners.

The amount of interest that can be excluded is reduced if your 2003 adjusted gross income meets the following requirements:

- ✔ Unmarried taxpayers with an income of $58,500 or less are entitled to a full interest exclusion. Between incomes of $58,500 and $73,500, the exclusion is gradually phased out.

- ✔ For married people filing jointly, there is a complete interest exclusion if your income is under $87,750 with a phaseout range between $87,750 and $117,750.

- ✔ The above income limits are based on your AGI (line 21, Form 1040A or line 34, Form 1040), adding back any student loan interest deduction (line 25, Form 1040), foreign earned income and housing exclusion (Form 2555 or 2555-EZ), the exclusion from income for employer-provided adoption assistance (line 30, Form 8839), and the tuition and fees deduction (line 26, Form 1040).

The amount of interest that you can exclude is computed on **Form 8815, Exclusion of Interest from Series EE U.S. Savings Bonds Issued after 1989.** The amount of excludable interest is entered on Schedule B, line 3, and the total interest is listed on line 1. For example, suppose you earned $500 of interest, all of which is excludable interest. You enter the $500 on lines 3 and 1.

You can't redeem a bond and exclude the interest because you're paying higher education expenses and at the same time use those expenses to compute a Hope or Lifetime Learning Credit. It's one or the other. Double dipping isn't allowed!

As long you don't use the same education expenses to compute the exclusion and either of the education credits, you can do both; claim the exclusion as well as an education credit. For example, you have $5,000 in higher education expenses and you want to pay off $1,000 with the interest you have received from a Series EE Savings Bond. If you limit the amount of education expenses you use to compute either the Hope or the Lifetime Learning Credit to $4,000, you can exclude $1,000 of the interest you received.

Interest-free loans

Say you make an interest-free loan to someone. Guess what. The IRS assumes that the borrower paid you interest anyway. This is called *imputed interest*. The IRS *imputes* (states) what the minimum rate should be. The borrower can deduct the interest he or she is considered to have paid if he or she uses the money to make an investment that produces income. You have to report as income the minimum amount of interest the IRS claims you should have charged. There's a second leg to this transaction: You're also considered to have made a gift of the interest you should have charged but didn't for gift tax purposes. For the applicable minimum rates, go to the IRS Web page (www.irs.gov). Loans with below-market rates of interest are also subject to this rule.

As with every other IRS rule, there are exceptions to this rule. Here they are:

- Loans under $10,000 aren't subject to the rule.

- For loans between $10,000 and $100,000, interest isn't imputed (that is, assumed to have been made) if the borrower's investment income for the year doesn't exceed $1,000. If the borrower's income exceeds $1,000, the imputed interest is limited to that amount of the person's investment income. Say you lend your son $50,000. If his investment income is under $1,000, no interest is imputed (considered to have been paid). If his investment income is $1,200, that's all the interest you have to report, even if you should have charged him $4,000.

- Certain employee relocation loans to buy a new residence aren't subject to the interest-free loan rule that requires that a minimum rate be charged. See your company's employment benefits office or a tax advisor.

- If the loan exceeds $100,000, you have to deal with the imputed interest rule in its full glory.

Interest-free or below-market-rate-of-interest loans usually occur when a family member taps you for money. In many cases, loans like these end up not being repaid (see Chapter 12, the section on "Nonbusiness bad debts"). If scaring someone off with the imputed interest rules doesn't work, try Shakespeare's "neither a borrower nor a lender be."

A lender reporting imputed interest or a borrower claiming an interest deduction must attach a statement to his return indicating how the interest was computed, the loan balance, the name of the borrower or lender, and the borrower's or lender's Social Security number. (If you're the borrower, it's the lender's, and vice versa.) That should also frighten most would-be borrowers off. As a general rule, when the parties to a below-market-rate-of-interest loan don't make the imputed interest calculations, the IRS ends up drooling over doing it when an audit of the lender uncovers the loan. The lender usually is someone's employer.

Part II, Lines 5 and 6: Dividend Income

Well, we hope that you made a good bit of extra dough in Part I. Part II provides another opportunity to count your silver coins — er, we mean dividends. You find out about your dividends from another version of a 1099. You'll receive **Form 1099-DIV, Dividends and Distributions** (see Figure 10-3) from the payer by January 31, 2004. If your 1099-DIV is incorrect, get the payer to correct it; otherwise, you may pay tax on income you never earned. Getting an incorrect 1099 corrected isn't as much of a headache as it used to be; the telephone number of the person you need to contact is listed on the form.

9191		☐ VOID	☐ CORRECTED			
PAYER'S name, street address, city, state, ZIP code, and telephone no.			**1a** Total ordinary dividends $	OMB No. 1545-0110	**Dividends and Distributions**	
			1b Qualified dividends $	20**03** Form **1099-DIV**		
			2a Total capital gain distr. $	**2b** Post-May 5 capital gain distr. $	**Copy A** **For** **Internal Revenue** **Service Center**	
PAYER'S Federal identification number		RECIPIENT'S identification number	**2c** Qualified 5-year gain $	**2d** Unrecap. Sec. 1250 gain $	**File with Form 1096.**	
RECIPIENT'S name		S	**2e** ection 1202 gain $	**2f** Collectibles (28%) gain $	For Privacy Act and Paperwork Reduction Act Notice, see the **2003 General Instructions for Forms 1099, 1098, 5498, and W-2G.**	
			3 Nontaxable distributions $	**4** Federal income tax withheld $		
Street address (including apt. no.)				**5** Investment expenses $		
City, state, and ZIP code			**6** Foreign tax paid $	**7** Foreign country or U.S. possession		
Account number (optional)		2nd TIN not. ☐	**8** Cash liquidation distributions $	**9** Noncash liquidation distributions $		

Form **1099-DIV**   Cat. No. 14415N   Department of the Treasury - Internal Revenue Service

Do Not Cut or Separate Forms on This Page — Do Not Cut or Separate Forms on This Page

Figure 10-3:
Form 1099-DIV shows you the dividends you reaped in 2003.

To report the income from jointly owned stock, follow the rules explained for reporting interest on a joint bank account in the sidebar "Joint returns, minors, and interest stuff," earlier in this chapter.

Watch out for corrected 1099s. If you file really early, you may need to file an amended return. (April 15 comes only once a year; it's best that way.)

Line 5: Name, payer, and amount

Schedule B, Part II, has a column for the name of the payer and a column for the amount of the dividend you received. Enter the name of the payer in the column that says to list the name of the payer. Enter the amount of the dividend you received in the column that says *amount*. For each 1099-DIV you received, enter the name of the payer and the amount received.

Line 6: Total dividends

This is the easy part. Total all the dividends you listed on line 5 and enter that amount on line 9a of your 1040.

Your 1099-DIV: Decoding those boxes

Here's what all those boxes on your 1099-DIV mean:

✔ **Box 1a: Total ordinary dividends.** Enter the total amount of your ordinary dividends on line 5. Make sure you list the payer's name to the left of the amount column.

If the total of your ordinary dividends doesn't exceed $1,500, skip Part II and enter the total on line 9a of Form 1040.

✔ **Box 1b: Qualified dividends.** These dividends are eligible for either the 15 percent or 5 percent rates. Enter this amount on line 9b. The portion of your total dividends (line 9a) less your qualified dividends (line 9b) ends up getting taxed at whatever bracket your taxable income (line 40) places you in. Now that couldn't be simpler, could it?

✔ **Boxes 2a–2f: Capital gain distributions.** Capital gains, although reported on Form 1099-DIV, aren't entered on Schedule B. Enter them on Schedule D.

- Box 2a has the total capital gain distributions. Enter this amount on Schedule D, line 13 (column f) — see Chapter 12. If the only amounts you have to report on Schedule D are capital gain distributions from boxes 2a and 2b, because you have no other capital gains or losses and no amounts are entered in boxes 2c through 2f, you don't have to file Schedule D. Enter the amounts from box 1a on Form 1040, line 13a and the amounts from box 2b on line 13b.

- Box 2b has the amount of the capital gain distribution received after May 5, 2003. That's when the new law kicked in, making these distributions eligible for the reduced rates. Enter this on line 13 (column g), Schedule D. If you are not required to file this schedule, enter the amounts from box 2c on line 13b of Form 1040.

- Box 2c applies only to sales before May 6, 2003. An entry in this box alerts you that the gain is eligible for the special 8 percent capital gains rate because it was held for 5 years. This reduced rate applies if your taxable income without your capital gains places you in either the 10 percent or 15 percent tax bracket — see Chapter 12 for the special reduced capital gains rates. The new law did away with this special 8 percent rate. After May 5, 2003, it no longer applies.

- Box 2d is for real estate capital gain dividends. The instructions to Box 2d direct you to a mind-numbing worksheet in your 1040 Instruction Booklet entitled "Unrecaptured Section 1250 Gain Worksheet." This amount also gets entered on line 19 of Schedule D.

- Box 2e indicates the amount of a gain from a small business start-up and specialized small business investment companies; 50 percent of these types of gains can be exempt from tax. The investment has to be in an economically depressed area designated as an *Empowerment Zone* by the government.

- Box 2f indicates the amount of the total gain in box 2a that gets taxed at 28 percent instead of the lower capital gain rate. This is the rate for the gain on the sale of collectibles (art, antiques, and so on). Also enter this amount on line 20, Schedule D.

To make sure you don't overpay the tax on capital gain distributions, flip back to line 41 in Chapter 8, where we show you how to prevent that from happening.

✔ **Box 3: Nontaxable distributions.** Nontaxable dividends and distributions aren't entered on your return. *Nontaxable* means exactly that. You don't currently pay tax on these dividends. These distributions reduce the basis of your shares when figuring your gain or loss when the shares are sold. For example, suppose that you purchased shares in a company or a mutual fund for $10,000, and you received $500 in nontaxable dividends. Your basis for determining gain or loss when you sell the shares is $9,500.

✔ **Box 4: Federal tax withheld.** Report your federal tax withheld on Form 1040 (line 61). On Form 1040A, it's line 39.

✔ **Box 5: Investment expenses.** This box refers to shares you own in funds not available to the public, so it doesn't apply to most people. We have yet to see a 1099-DIV with an entry in this box! (But it must be there for a reason!) If this box applies to you, it means that you own shares in a nonpublicly traded fund. You can deduct this expense as a miscellaneous itemized deduction on line 22 of Form 1040, Schedule A (see Chapter 9). Publicly traded funds don't pass investment expenses on to shareholders.

✔ **Box 6: Foreign tax paid.** If you own shares in a company or fund that was required to pay tax in a foreign country, your share of the tax is recorded in box 6. You can claim this amount as a credit against your tax or as an itemized deduction. We discuss how to handle this in the section "Other taxes" in Chapter 9.

✔ **Box 7: Foreign country or U.S. possession.** This is easy. It states the country or U.S. possession where the tax was paid. You need this information when you fill out **Form 1116, Foreign Tax Credit.** See Chapter 8.

✔ **Boxes 8 and 9: Liquidating distributions.** You report these amounts (cash and non-cash) on Schedule D (Capital Gains and Losses). If you have entries in these two boxes, see a tax advisor. And check out Chapter 12 to find out more about Schedule D.

Reduced tax rates on dividends

The reduced 15 percent and 5 percent rates (for those individuals whose taxable incomes, line 40, places them in the 10 percent or 15 percent tax bracket) maximum tax rates don't apply to all dividends. Only qualified dividends are entitled to this reduced rate of tax.

Qualified dividends are those dividends paid by

✔ U.S. Corporations

✔ A corporation incorporated in a U.S. possession

✔ Foreign corporations traded on a U.S. stock exchange

✔ A foreign corporation whose shares are not traded on a U.S. market, from a country that has a comprehensive tax treaty with the U.S. that includes a program providing for the exchange of tax information. Because not many countries have such a comprehensive treaty with the U.S., this will probably cause many investors in international funds to rethink whether it makes sense to continue to hold shares that don't entitle them to preferred tax treatment on their dividends.

Not only do you have to know where qualified dividends come from, but you also have to know what dividends aren't considered qualified and eligible for the reduced rates. These are dividends paid by

✔ Credit unions

✔ Mutual insurance companies

✔ Savings banks and savings and loans

✔ Money market funds

✔ Banks on certificates of deposits

✔ Bond funds

✔ Farmers' cooperatives

✔ Real Estate Investment Trusts (REITs)

✔ Tax-exempt corporations

When is a dividend NOT a dividend?

Stock dividends and splits

Stock dividends and splits aren't taxable. You now own more shares!

For example, suppose that you own 100 shares. If the stock is split two for one, you now own 200 shares. If you receive a 10 percent stock dividend, you now own 110 shares. Chapter 12 explains how you treat the shares that you received when they are sold.

Life insurance dividends

Life insurance dividends aren't taxable until the total dividends received exceed the total premiums paid.

Savings dividends

So-called dividends from savings and loans, credit unions, savings banks, and bond and money market funds have to be reported as interest.

Three other categories of dividends that aren't considered qualified are

✔ Dividends paid on stock purchased with borrowed funds, if the dividend was included in investment income in claiming a deduction for investment interest (line 13, Chapter 9 provides a plain English explanation of what this is all about)

✔ Payments in lieu of a dividend on a short sale (see Chapter 12)

✔ Dividends on stock owned less than 60 days in the 120-day period surrounding the *ex-dividend date,* or the date the stock trades without the announced dividend, which is normally two days before the *record day,* the day when the company determines who is the record owner of the stock. You need to have owned the stock 60 days out of the 120-day period beginning 60 days before the ex-dividend day.

Qualified dividends that mutual funds receive (from stockholdings) and in turn distribute to you remain qualified and are eligible for the reduced rates. Because qualified dividends received by IRAs, 401(k)s, and retirement accounts are paid in a tax-free environment, you will not pay tax on these dividends as long as the stock is held in one of these accounts.

Part III, Lines 7–8: Foreign Accounts and Trusts

If you have a foreign bank or security account, you have to check "yes" on line 7a of Schedule B and enter the name of the foreign country. However, if the average balance in the account in 2003 was under $10,000, you can check "no." But if you had more than $10,000 in a foreign bank or security account during the year, then you have to file **Form TD F 90-22.1, Report of Foreign Bank and Financial Accounts,** by June 30, 2004. On this form, you have to list where your account(s) are located, including the name of the bank, security firm, or brokerage firm; its address; and the account number.

If you're unique enough to have to deal with line 8, it means that you have a foreign trust. You have to check "yes" and complete **Form 3520, Annual Return to Report Transactions With Foreign Trusts and Receipt of Certain Foreign Gifts,** or **Form 926, Return by a U.S. Transferor of Property to a Foreign Corporation** (the trustee completes Form 3520-A). Good luck! (These forms are complicated; consider using a tax advisor.)

If you received a distribution from a foreign partnership or corporation in excess of $11,827 (this amount gets adjusted for inflation every year) that you have treated as a gift, you have to report it to the IRS. If you receive a gift or inheritance from a foreign individual or estate above $100,000, you also have to provide the IRS with the foreigner's name and address. Report this information on Form 3520. You also have to file Form 3520 if you are an owner of a foreign trust or if you received a distribution from one regardless of the amount. The penalty for not filing is 5 percent for each month the return is not filed, up to a maximum of 25 percent of the amount received. Evidently, a lot of people were claiming that what they earned abroad was a gift or bequest. The amount you report to the IRS as a gift or inheritance isn't taxable. The IRS does, however, want to know about it. A distribution from a foreign trust, partnership, or corporation more than likely is taxable.

The due date for filing Form 3520 is April 15. File the form separately and don't attach it to your return.

Taxpayers with interest earned in Canadian Registered Retirement Savings Plans are probably unaware that they must file Form 3520. If you haven't been doing this, the good news is that the IRS has pardoned all those who haven't filed the form for all years before 2002. Starting with 2002, you either have to file Form 3520 or attach a statement to your return every year that you're claiming the benefit of Article XVIII (7) of the treaty, including the name of the trustee of the savings plan, the account number, and the balance in the account at the beginning of the year. The amount in the plan isn't taxable until distributions are made.

Chapter 11

Profit or Loss from Business: Schedule C

· ·

In This Chapter

▶ Using Schedule C-EZ

▶ Using Schedule C

▶ Reporting income

▶ Tallying and categorizing expenses

· ·

*R*unning your own firm really can be the American dream. In fact, the only thing better than working for yourself is knowing how to keep more of what you earn. It's like giving yourself an immediate raise at tax time.

If you're self-employed, you must report your income on Schedule C (or C-EZ), along with your business expenses. You subtract your expenses from your income to arrive at your profit, on which you have to pay tax.

Schedule C-EZ

Schedule C-EZ is a three-line form that's relatively EZ to complete. The only catches are that your deductible expenses can't exceed $2,500, you don't have an inventory of items for sale, you operate only one business as a sole proprietor, and you use the cash method of accounting (we will explain in a moment). You also can't use the C-EZ if you have a net loss from your business, you're claiming expenses for the business use of your home, you had employees, or you're required to file **Form 4562, Depreciation and Amortization** (see our discussion about line 13, later in this chapter, where we explain who has to file this form).

If you qualify, have a go at it. After you fill in the easy background information in Part I, figure your net profit. So we don't have to constantly repeat ourselves, take a gander two paragraphs down on the form at Basic Information (A–E) on how to obtain the information for items B and D. Here's how to fill out this form:

> ✔ **Line 1:** Fill in your income.
>
> ✔ **Line 2:** Fill in your expenses. There is an optional worksheet on page 2, where you can list and total your expenses.
>
> ✔ **Line 3:** Subtract line 2 from line 1; this amount is your net profit.

You're done. Carry the profit over to Form 1040 (line 12). Unless you're a statutory employee (see Chapter 6), also carry the profit to Schedule SE to calculate your self-employment tax.

Okay, okay, you caught us. If you're deducting automobile expenses on line 2, you have to fill out Part III and answer six (maybe seven) more questions so the IRS can be sure that your expenses are legitimate. Four of those questions are Yes/No questions. Don't you wish all IRS forms were like this?

On the other hand, knowing what's taxable and what's deductible can, at times, be confusing. So read on. We take you by the hand to make sure that you don't miss a thing.

Schedule C

This schedule is not so EZ, but it isn't as bad as it looks (see Figure 11-1). In the rest of this chapter, we take you through the line-by-line instructions.

SCHEDULE C
(Form 1040)

Department of the Treasury
Internal Revenue Service   (99)

Profit or Loss From Business
(Sole Proprietorship)

Partnerships, joint ventures, etc., must file Form 1065 or 1065-B.

▶ **Attach to Form 1040 or 1041.**   ▶ **See Instructions for Schedule C (Form 1040).**

OMB No. 1545-0074

2003

Attachment
Sequence No. **09**

Name of proprietor

Social security number (SSN)

A   Principal business or profession, including product or service (see page C-2 of the instructions)

B   Enter code from pages C-7, 8, & 9 ▶

C   Business name. If no separate business name, leave blank.

D   Employer ID number (EIN), if any

E   Business address (including suite or room no.) ▶
City, town or post office, state, and ZIP code

F   Accounting method: (1) ☐ Cash   (2) ☐ Accrual   (3) ☐ Other (specify) ▶

G   Did you "materially participate" in the operation of this business during 2003? If "No," see page C-3 for limit on losses   ☐ Yes   ☐ No

H   If you started or acquired this business during 2003, check here   ▶ ☐

Part I   Income

1	Gross receipts or sales. **Caution.** If this income was reported to you on Form W-2 and the "Statutory employee" box on that form was checked, see page C-3 and check here ▶ ☐	1
2	Returns and allowances	2
3	Subtract line 2 from line 1	3
4	Cost of goods sold (from line 42 on page 2)	4
5	**Gross profit.** Subtract line 4 from line 3	5
6	Other income, including Federal and state gasoline or fuel tax credit or refund (see page C-3)	6
7	**Gross income.** Add lines 5 and 6 ▶	7

Part II   Expenses. Enter expenses for business use of your home **only** on line 30.

8	Advertising	8	19 Pension and profit-sharing plans	19
9	Car and truck expenses (see page C-3)	9	20 Rent or lease (see page C-5):	
10	Commissions and fees	10	a Vehicles, machinery, and equipment	20a
11	Contract labor (see page C-4)	11	b Other business property	20b
12	Depletion	12	21 Repairs and maintenance	21
13	Depreciation and section 179 expense deduction (not included in Part III) (see page C-4)	13	22 Supplies (not included in Part III)	22
14	Employee benefit programs (other than on line 19)	14	23 Taxes and licenses	23
15	Insurance (other than health)	15	24 Travel, meals, and entertainment:	
16	Interest:		a Travel	24a
a	Mortgage (paid to banks, etc.)	16a	b Meals and entertainment	
b	Other	16b	c Enter nondeductible amount included on line 24b (see page C-5)	
17	Legal and professional services	17	d Subtract line 24c from line 24b	24d
18	Office expense	18	25 Utilities	25
			26 Wages (less employment credits)	26
			27 Other expenses (from line 48 on page 2)	27

28	**Total expenses** before expenses for business use of home. Add lines 8 through 27 in columns ▶	28
29	Tentative profit (loss). Subtract line 28 from line 7	29
30	Expenses for business use of your home. Attach **Form 8829**	30
31	**Net profit or (loss).** Subtract line 30 from line 29.
● If a profit, enter on **Form 1040, line 12,** and **also** on **Schedule SE, line 2** (statutory employees, see page C-6). Estates and trusts, enter on Form 1041, line 3.
● If a loss, you **must** go to line 32.	31
32	If you have a loss, check the box that describes your investment in this activity (see page C-6).
● If you checked 32a, enter the loss on **Form 1040, line 12,** and **also** on **Schedule SE, line 2** (statutory employees, see page C-6). Estates and trusts, enter on Form 1041, line 3.
● If you checked 32b, you **must** attach **Form 6198.**	32a ☐ All investment is at risk.
32b ☐ Some investment is not at risk.

For Paperwork Reduction Act Notice, see Form 1040 instructions.   Cat. No. 11334P   Schedule C (Form 1040) 2003

Figure 11-1:
Schedule C,
page 1.

Basic Information (A–E)

Lines A through D are pretty easy background stuff. Employer ID Numbers can now be obtained instantly by applying online at www.irs.gov, click on "Businesses," then click on "More Topics" (both these buttons are on the left of the screen) and you'll be taken to Employer ID Numbers. You can also call 800-829-4933 or go the paper route by sending a completed **Form SS-4, Application For Employer Identification Number,** to the IRS. You can pick up your business code from the list on pages C-7, C-8, and C-9 in your instruction booklet. On line E, simply fill in your business address.

Accounting Method Stuff (F–H)

The two methods to report income are *cash* and *accrual.* With the cash method, you report income when it's actually received, and you deduct expenses when they're actually paid. However, there is (of course) one exception to this rule: If you charge an expense on a credit card, you deduct this expense in the year charged, even if you pay the charge in a later year. (So don't leave home without it!)

Does your business take in $10 million or less? We knew that would get a smile out of you. If that is the case, then you can use the cash method of accounting, but only if a bunch of restrictions don't apply. If you're in a purely service business, then you don't have to worry about these restrictions. You're eligible to use the cash method. You're also eligible to skip the following paragraph.

Here are the folks who can't use the cash method — anyone whose line of business is in the wholesale or retail trade, manufacturing, information services, or mining. Now for the exceptions to this rule: Even if you're in one of these businesses that disqualifies you from using the cash method, you still can use it if providing a service is the main thing you do. For example, you are a publisher (information services) whose main activity is the sale of advertising space. You can use the cash method even though information services is not one of the businesses normally allowed to use the cash method. The reason? The sale of advertising space is considered a service. When will the IRS ever stop making such distinctions? Similarly, businesses that manufacture or modify a product to a customer's specifications and design can also use the cash method even though manufacturing isn't an eligible business.

A small business whose average annual income (the current and two previous years) is $1 million or less can use the cash method regardless of its line of business. However, it can deduct the purchase of merchandise for resale only when it's sold and not when it's purchased, so read on.

Even though some people are permitted to use the cash method, if they use materials and supplies that are not incidental to the services they perform, they face a hitch. Roofing contractors are an example. Even though they use the cash method, they are not allowed to deduct the cost of the materials they purchase until the later of either when it is used on the customer's job or when they pay for it. Say a contractor paid $5,000 for shingles in December 2003, but didn't install them until January 2004. Sorry, it's a 2004 tax deduction. The amount the contractor charges the customer is reported in the year it is received because the contractor is using the cash method.

Say you must use the accrual method because you operate a clothing store; you report income in the year that sales are made — even when the sales are billed or collected in a later year. You deduct expenses in the year that they're incurred, even if those expenses aren't paid until a later year. Under both cash and accrual methods, you report all income and expenses for the calendar year ending December 31.

A hybrid method of accounting also exists. Even if you have to use the accrual method to report income and deduct merchandise sold, you nevertheless can use the cash method for the rest of your expenses, rent, telephone, wages, and so on. Doing so should make your bookkeeping less complicated.

"Did you 'materially participate' in the operation of the business?" is a trick question designed to limit losses that someone can deduct as a silent partner. If you put up the dough, but someone other than your spouse operated a business that lost money, then *you* can't deduct the loss. The reason? *You* didn't materially participate in the operation of the business, and (as a result) you're considered to be operating a tax shelter — see the tax shelter rules in Chapter 13. Seven criteria determine *material participation*. Page C-2 of your 1040 instruction booklet has them all. The basic criteria include whether you meet either the 500- and 100-hour rules regarding material participation, whether you were the only one who did the work, or whether you participated on a regular, continuous, and substantial basis. Pass any one of the seven and you're okay.

If you're filing Schedule C to report a working interest in an oil or gas well, you automatically get to check the "Yes" box. Why? Ever heard of the oil and gas lobby?

If you have the choice, the cash method of accounting gives you more control over when your business sees a profit from year to year. For example, if next year looks like a slower year for you, perhaps because you plan to take a sabbatical, you may elect to push more income into next year. This plan will likely save you tax dollars, because you should be in a lower tax bracket that next year. You legally can do this by delaying the sending of invoices until January, for example, that you normally would have mailed in December. Likewise, you can pay more of your expenses in December instead of waiting until January. The general rule is if you're selling merchandise, you have to comply with the accrual method rules. Even though your business involves the sale of merchandise, you still can use the cash method if your average income is $1 million or less. However, you can't deduct your merchandise purchases until you sell those goods. If you're providing a service, you can use the cash method.

The tax cut we just cited is the general rule. It may not apply to everyone. For example, if you operate a business that receives large cash advances from customers before you undertake the work, you would be better off using the accrual method. That way the cash advances wouldn't have to be reported until you actually did the work.

Part 1, Lines 1–7: Income

Time to tally. This section wants you to find some gross things: gross sales, gross profits, and gross income.

Line 1: Gross receipts or sales

If you operate a service business, enter the income from fees (that's the amount from box 7, Form 1099-MISC) that you actually collected (because you're reporting income under the cash method).

If you are filing this form because you are a statutory employee (see Chapter 6, the section about line 7), enter the amount from box 1 of your W-2 and check the "Statutory employee" box on this line. Next, enter your business expenses on lines 8 through 27, and you can ignore our instructions on line 31 about paying Social Security tax, because you already paid it (see lines 4 and 6 of your W-2).

If you're required to use the accrual method, enter the total of all the sales that you billed to your customers on this line.

Line 2: Returns and allowances

If you had to return any fees, enter that amount here. If any customers returned merchandise, that amount also goes on this line, along with any discounts that those customers took.

Line 3: Subtraction quiz

All that you need to do on this line is subtract your returns and allowances (line 2) from your gross receipts and sales (line 1).

Line 4: Cost of goods sold

The IRS must think that you're an accountant; otherwise, the agency would simply tell you to subtract the cost of the merchandise that you sold from your sales to arrive at this figure. Services and other businesses that don't sell products don't have to put an amount on this line.

But because you're not an accountant — thank heavens, you say? — you have to compute the cost of the merchandise that you sold in Part III (on the back of Schedule C). Part III is an eight-line schedule where you enter your beginning inventory, the merchandise that you purchased, the salary that you paid to your production workers (if you manufacture the product that you sell), and the cost of production supplies. You total all these expenses on line 40. From this total, you subtract your ending inventory to arrive at the cost of the goods that you sold. This amount goes back to line 4 (where you are right now!).

Remember, you can't deduct the cost of all the merchandise that you purchased during the year. You can deduct only the cost of merchandise that you sold. That's why you have to subtract your ending inventory, which is the stuff that you didn't sell. You get to deduct what's on hand when it's sold. You enter the amount of the merchandise that you didn't sell (it's called *ending inventory*) on line 41. Your ending inventory gets carried over to your 2004 return. So don't forget to enter the amount from line 41, which becomes your inventory at the beginning of the year, on line 35 of your 2004 return.

The following example explains what this inventory business is all about. Say you own a retail furniture store. In 2003, you purchased two identical chairs, one for $1,200 and the other for $1,000. You sold only one chair (we hope business is better next year). Which one did you sell? The inventory method that you select determines that.

Under the *FIFO method* — First In, First Out — the first chair purchased is deemed the first one sold. If that's the $1,200 chair, then enter the cost of the $1,000 chair on line 41, because that's the one considered on hand at the end of the year. Under the *LIFO method* — Last In, First Out — the chair purchased last is deemed to be sold first. Under this method, the $1,000 chair is considered to be sold first, so enter $1,200 on line 41, because that's the cost of the chair that's considered the unsold one. Which method is better? In a period of rising costs, it's the LIFO method. FIFO is better when costs are declining.

Line 33 also requires you to select the method that you used to value your inventory. Three methods are available — cost (box a), lower of cost or market (box b), and other (box c). Skip box c, because it's too complicated. Most people check box a, because it's the easiest. Although using the lower of cost or market method can increase deductions if your inventory declines in value (you get to deduct the amount of the decline), it requires you to revalue your inventory every year.

After you select a valuation method, you can change it only with permission from the IRS.

Writing off what a customer doesn't pay

When you use the accrual method to report income, you can write off losses when customers don't pay. However, when you use the cash method, you can't — because you never recorded the income and paid tax on the money that your client owes. The rules regarding when cash-method taxpayers can write off bad debts on loans that they make are similar to the rules regarding when you can write off a personal loan that goes bad. We explain such things in "Nonbusiness bad debts" in Chapter 12.

When you're using the accrual method and want to write off what your deadbeat customers owe, these amounts can be claimed on line 27.

Line 5: Gross profit

Hey, here's where you put the profit that you made on the merchandise that you sold. (It is hoped that this is a pleasant reminder of a successful year.) Subtract line 4 from line 3.

Line 6: Other income

Just do what the schedule orders you to do — see page C-3 of the 1040 booklet if you have any questions about other income. Some of the more common — and more obscure — examples of other income include the following:

- ✔ Federal and state gasoline or fuel tax credit
- ✔ Interest on accounts receivable
- ✔ Scrap sales
- ✔ Fee for allowing a company to paint an advertisement on the side of your building

Line 7: Gross income

This amount *usually* is the same as the amount on line 5. But if you had other items of income, such as a refund of a prior year's expense, enter that amount on line 6 and add it to the amount on line 5 to arrive at your gross income.

Part II, Lines 8–27: Expenses

Take a breath and get ready for all those wonderful lines that are split into two columns — so they'd all fit on one page!

Line 8: Advertising

On this line, enter the cost of any advertising that your business does to promote itself — for example, an ad in the Yellow Pages and other forms of advertising, including radio, newspaper, and promotional brochures and mailers.

Line 9: Car and truck expenses

If you plan to make an entry on this line, be sure to answer questions 43 through 47b in Part IV on the other side of Schedule C, commonly referred to as Page 2.

When you use your car for business, the expenses of operating your car are deductible. But remember that "using it for business" is the key phrase. You can compute this deduction by using either a flat rate per business mile (see the standard rate sidebar), or you can keep track of actual expenses (gas, oil, repair, insurance, depreciation, and so on). Regardless of which method you use, you're supposed to keep a log or diary so that you can record the business purpose of your trips as well as the mileage ("Dear Diary . . ."). You also have to record the odometer reading at the beginning and end of the year. You need all this information to be able to divide your expenses into personal and business use. But here's a word of caution: Whether you use the flat rate or tabulate your actual expenses, proving that you use your car 100 percent for business is just about impossible. Unfortunately, there's always some personal use!

You don't have to write down the miles that you travel every time you get in and out of your car. Making entries in your diary on a weekly basis meets the IRS requirement that you keep a record of your car's business use near or at the time of its use.

No help from Uncle Sam with commuting expenses

Commuting expenses between your home and office aren't deductible. These expenses are considered personal commuting expenses, no matter how far your home is from your office or place of work. And making telephone calls from your car while commuting or having a business discussion with a business associate who accompanies you doesn't turn your ride into a deductible expense (besides, you should be watching the road). And using your car to display advertising material on your way to the office doesn't count as business use of your auto, either. Finally, the cost of parking at your place of business isn't deductible — but the cost of parking when you visit a customer or client is.

If you use your car to call on clients or customers and don't have a regular office to go to, the mileage between your home and the first customer that you call on — and the mileage between the location of the last customer that you call on and your home — is considered commuting. If your office is in your home, you can deduct all your auto expenses for calling on clients or customers. Line 44 on the back of Schedule C asks you about the *first-and-last-customer-of-the-day rule,* but the IRS refers to it as commuting. The IRS wants you to enter on this line (44) the number of miles that you use your car when commuting.

Second job

If you moonlight after work, you can deduct the cost of getting from one job to the other. But transportation expenses going from your home to a part-time job on a day off from your main job aren't deductible. A meeting of an Armed Forces Reserve unit is considered travel to a second job, however. If the meeting is held on the same day as your regular job, it's deductible.

Temporary job site

If you have a regular place of business and commute to a temporary work location, you can deduct the cost of the daily round trip between your home and the temporary job site.

If you don't have a regular place of work (but ordinarily work at different locations in the general area where you live), you can't deduct the daily round trip between your home and your temporary job site. But if you travel to a job site outside your general area, your daily transportation is deductible. Sounds like a distinction without a difference, right? But if this exception applies to you, don't look a gift horse in the mouth.

Standard mileage rate

Instead of figuring your actual expenses with those maddening depreciation computations, you can use a flat rate of 36 cents for every business mile.

If you drove your car 15,000 miles for business, you'd be entitled to a $5,400 deduction (15,000 × 36 cents). You can claim this deduction on page 2 of **Form 2106, Employee Business Expenses.**

Although Form 2106 is intended for employees who are deducting auto expenses, self-employed Schedule C filers will find Part II of the form helpful in computing their deductible automobile expenses.

On Form 2106, you multiply the business miles on line 13 by 36 cents and enter the total on line 22. Carry over this amount to line 1 of form 2106, which, naturally enough, is on page 1. If you were reimbursed for any of your car expenses that weren't included in box 1 of your W-2 as taxable wages, a code L appears next to the amount of the reimbursement in box 12 of your W-2. You must deduct this amount from your auto expenses and enter it on line 7 of Form 2106.

If you choose the flat-rate method, you can't claim any of your actual expenses, such as depreciation, gas, oil, insurance, and so on. If you want to use this method, you must choose it the first year that you start using your car for business. If you don't use the standard mileage rate in the first year, you can't use the standard mileage rate in a subsequent year. But if you use the standard mileage the first year, you can switch to deducting your actual expenses, but you probably won't want to after you take a look at the rules in the IRS Publication 463 *(Travel, Entertainment, Gift, and Car Expenses).*

If you trade in your car, you can use the flat rate for both cars because you owned them at different times.

You can use the standard mileage rate whether you own or lease a vehicle.

If you sell your car, you have to reduce its tax basis by the amount of depreciation built into the flat rate so that you can determine whether you made a taxable profit or loss. A table (of course) in IRS Publication 463 shows you how to make this computation.

You can deduct the business portion of the following: depreciation, leasing and rental fees, garage rent, licenses, repairs, gas, oil, tires, insurance, parking, and tolls.

If you're self-employed, you can deduct the business portion of interest on a car loan; if you're an employee, you can't. Fines for traffic violations aren't deductible, either — so slow down!

Sales tax can't be deducted separately — it's added to the car's tax basis for the purposes of determining the amount of depreciation that you're entitled to claim. If you're an employee, you can deduct personal property tax on your car if you itemize your deductions on Schedule A. (See "Line 7: Personal property taxes" in Chapter 9 for more info.) If you're self-employed, you deduct the business portion of your personal property tax on line 23 and the personal part on Schedule A.

Standard mileage rate or actual expenses?

You can deduct either the business portion of your actual expenses or use the standard mileage rate for your business miles (see the "Standard mileage rate" sidebar). The standard mileage method relieves you of the task of keeping track of your expenses. It only requires that you track your miles. Deducting your actual expense requires both. Whichever method you use, Part II of Form 2106 (although intended for employees) contains an excellent worksheet to help you compute your deduction.

Depreciation

Computing the amount of depreciation on your car is mind-numbing. Unfortunately, the only way around this exercise in frustration is to use the standard 36-cent flat rate.

The IRS lumps automobiles into the listed property category of assets (they're subject to the 50 percent business use test) and gives cars a whole bunch of rules and regulations. *Listed property* is an IRS term for autos, telephones, computers, boats, and airplanes — items that the IRS suspects you may use more for pleasure than for business. The IRS considers cars to have a useful life of five years, which is the starting point to determine the amount of depreciation on the auto that you can deduct. Ready for the computation? Here goes.

If the business use of your car is more than 50 percent of its total use, you compute your depreciation (under *MACRS — Modified Accelerated Cost Recovery System*) according to what is known as the *half-year convention* (see Table 11-1). The half-year convention means that assets, in the year of purchase, regardless of the month they were acquired, are considered to have been purchased on July 1, and you're, therefore, entitled to a half-year's depreciation. In subsequent years, you're entitled to a full-year's depreciation for that year.

New cars purchased in 2003 before May 6th

For new cars purchased before May 6, 2003, $7,660 is the maximum amount of depreciation you can deduct. For light trucks and SUVs, the limit is $7,950.

New cars purchased in 2003 after May 5th

For new cars purchased after May 5, 2003, the maximum deduction is $10,710. For light trucks and SUVs, the limit is $11,010.

These increased limits are available only for the purchase of new autos. If you purchased a used car, the 2003 depreciation limit is $3,060.

The effect of the depreciation limits is that the days of being able to write off a $90,000 car in three years are gone. If, for example, you purchased a new car in 2003 for $30,000, the maximum amount of depreciation that you can claim in 2003 is either $7,660 or $10,710 for sedans, or $7,950 and $11,010 for light trucks and SUVs depending on whether you bought the vehicle before May 6, 2003, or on or after May 5, 2003, and then $4,900 in 2004, $2,950 in 2005, and $1,775 a year until the $30,000 is fully depreciated (which takes about 11 years). This formula, however, assumes that you use your car 100 percent for business. So if the business use of your car is less, the maximum yearly limits are reduced.

Table 11-1		Half-Year Convention for Auto Depreciation			
Year	Yearly Percent	For a $30,000 Car if No Limit Is Applied		Maximum Yearly Limit	
		Before May 6th	After May 5th	Before May 6th	After May 5th
1-2003	20.00	$13,200	$18,000	$7,660	$10,710
2-2004	32.00	$6,720	$4,800	$4,900	$4,900
3-2005	19.20	$4,032	$2,880	$2,950	$2,950
4-2006	11.52	$2,419	$1,728	$1,775	$1,775
5-2007	11.52	$2,419	$1,728	$1,775	$1,775
6-2008	5.76	$1,210	$864	$1,775	$1,775
	100.00	$30,000	$30,000	$1,775*	$1,775*

*and $1,775 in each succeeding year

If your car is used less than 100 percent for business, the yearly maximums must be reduced accordingly. For example, if a car is used only 80 percent of the time for business, the yearly maximum depreciation for a car acquired after May 5, 2003, is $8,568 ($10,710 × 80 percent).

September 11, 2001, changed many things, and the way depreciation is computed is no exception. The law entitles taxpayers to an additional first-year depreciation deduction of 30 percent on the amount of new business assets purchased after September 10, 2001, and before September 11, 2004, that they start using in their businesses before January 1, 2005. The law was written in this convoluted manner to allow the additional first-year deduction for items ordered before September 11, 2004, but not delivered until after that date, as long as taxpayers start using them in their businesses before January 1, 2005. Why couldn't the IRS say that in the first place?

In 2003, the rule regarding the 30 percent additional first-year depreciation changed. The 30 percent first-year rate increases to 50 percent. Unfortunately, the change wasn't made retroactive to January 1, so the higher rate applies only to depreciable items acquired after May 5, 2003; otherwise, the 30 percent rate still applies.

The 30 percent or 50 percent additional first-year depreciation deduction is in addition to regular depreciation. Along with this additional first-year depreciation deduction came a provision that bumped up the maximum first-year depreciation that can be claimed on an auto used for business by $4,600 for cars purchased before May 6, 2003, and by $7,650 for cars purchased after May 5, 2003. That means the maximum first-year depreciation amount went to $7,660 from $3,060 for cars purchased before May 6, 2003, and to $10,710 from $3,060 for cars purchased after May 5, 2003. The $4,600 and $7,650 amounts aren't adjusted for inflation, but the $3,060 is. Another hitch is that you must claim the extra 30 percent or 50 percent. It is not automatic; it is not built into the depreciation tables. So claim it! We explain how to claim the extra depreciation in the next paragraph entitled, "September 11 additional first-year depreciation." As we already noted, there are different allowable depreciation amounts for light trucks and SUVs, which we discuss later in this section.

September 11 additional first-year depreciation — New autos purchased before May 6, 2003

Here's what the 30 percent extra depreciation is all about. The automobile must be a new one. Used ones don't qualify. The auto's original use had to begin with you. You have to reduce what you paid for the car by the 30 percent before you figure your regular 2003 depreciation. For example, if a car cost $20,000, your additional first-year depreciation is $6,000. Next you reduce the car's cost by that amount to $14,000 ($20,000 – $6,000). Your regular depreciation of $2,800 is computed by multiplying $14,000 by 20 percent (Table 11-1). Your total depreciation before applying the maximum limit of $7,660 comes to $8,800 ($6,000 + $2,800). But, remember you can deduct only the $7,660 maximum. That's how our screwy tax law makes you do the math so that you nail down the additional first-year September 11 depreciation deduction.

Had you not claimed the extra 30 percent, your depreciation for the year would come to $4,000 ($20,000 × 20 percent) limited to a maximum of $3,060. The $7,660 maximum is only available when you claim the extra 30 percent. How do you claim it? By computing the amount to which you are entitled and entering it on of **Form 4562, Depreciation and Amortization** (don't forget to attach it to your return).

In future years, if you don't compute the additional first-year 30 percent deduction and you don't elect not to claim it, you nevertheless have to reduce the cost of the auto as if you *had* claimed the 30 percent depreciation deduction. Who says the IRS is not out to trap you? A virtual minefield is out there for the unsuspecting. To inform the IRS that you don't want to claim the additional first-year depreciation deduction, simply write: `I choose not to claim the additional first-year 30 percent depreciation on the auto I purchased in 2003.`

For those who just learned about this 30 percent business, who purchased a car for business use after September 10, 2001, and who didn't claim the additional first-year deduction on their 2001 or 2002 returns (or attach a statement to the return indicating that they didn't want to claim it), here's what to do. You can claim the deduction and obtain a refund by filing an amended return on Form 1040X (see Chapter 19). Across the top of the form write, FILED PURSUANT TO REG. 301.9100-3. This regulation allows the IRS to grant relief to taxpayers who fail to make a timely election to claim or not to claim (sounds like something from Shakespeare) a deduction or tax credit. In Part II on page 2 of Form 1040X, be sure to state that the fact that the law allowing 30 percent additional first-year depreciation is so new and complex that you just became aware of it and you are taking immediate action to correct your error. State that you are now claiming the additional first-year depreciation deduction and that you are making this statement under the penalties of perjury (they want blood, don't they?). If you're electing not to claim the deduction, then state that and send your 1040X off to IRS central. You will be surprised how (don't laugh) generous the IRS can be when it wants to.

Not claiming the extra depreciation might make sense if 2003 was a lousy year, which it seems to have been for many folks. If your income was down, the extra deduction would be wasted or not as valuable as it might be if it was claimed in a high-income year.

Just when you thought all this rigmarole was bad enough, Congress, many years ago — in its infinite wisdom — enacted the 40 percent rule. Under this rule, if you purchased more than 40 percent of all your business assets (including your auto) in the last quarter of 2003 (October to December), you don't use the depreciation percentages in Table 11-1. Instead, you must use the depreciation percentages known as the mid-quarter convention (see Table 11-2). *Mid-quarter convention* means that you start computing depreciation in the quarter it was acquired. Thankfully, you can ignore this rule in computing either the 30 percent or 50 percent additional first-year depreciation, but not in computing your regular depreciation.

September 11 additional first-year depreciation — New autos purchased after May 5, 2003

Guess what? The law was changed again. Instead of claiming a deduction for additional first-year bonus depreciation of 30 percent, you now can claim a 50 percent deduction. The hitch? The car has to be a new one, purchased after May 5, 2003, and you must start using it in your business before January 1, 2005. However, if 30 is your lucky number, you can elect to continue to use the 30 percent rather than the 50 percent rate. Additionally, where purchases made after May 5, 2003, are concerned, the requirement that the vehicle be acquired before September 11, 2004, no longer is in effect regardless of whether you're using the 30 percent or 50 percent rate. January 1, 2005, is now the date that counts.

If you want to continue using the 30 percent rate, simply compute your auto depreciation using that rate instead of 50 percent. If you choose to use neither simply write across the top of Form 4562, Depreciation and Amortization: I choose not to claim the additional first-year 30 percent or 50 percent depreciation on the auto that I purchased in 2003.

Say you purchased a car after May 5, 2003, for $20,000. Here's how you compute your depreciation for 2003. Your additional first-year depreciation is $10,000. Next, you reduce the cost of the car by that amount to $10,000 ($20,000 – $10,000). Your regular depreciation of $2,000 is computed by multiplying $10,000 by 20 percent (Table 11-1). Your total depreciation before applying the maximum limit of $10,710 comes to $12,000 ($10,000 + $2,000). But remember, you can deduct only the $10,710 maximum. That's how our screwy tax law makes you do the math to nail down the additional first-year September 11 depreciation deduction. It gets screwier. The $1,290 that you couldn't deduct ($12,000 – $10,710) can't be deducted until the end of the depreciation period (Table 11-1), which would be 2008.

Table 11-2	Mid-Quarter Convention for Auto (and Computer) Depreciation			
Year	**First Quarter**	**Second Quarter**	**Third Quarter**	**Fourth Quarter**
1	35.00%	25.00%	15.00%	5.00%
2	26.00	30.00	34.00	38.00
3	15.60	18.00	20.40	22.80
4	11.01	11.37	12.24	13.68
5	11.01	11.37	11.30	10.94
6	1.38	4.26	7.06	9.58

For example, you purchased a car for $20,000 in December (fourth quarter) and a computer for $10,000 before May 6 (second quarter). Because computers and autos are considered to have a five-year life for depreciation purposes, Table 11-2 shows the depreciation rates for both items. The percentage that you use to depreciate the computer in 2003 is 25 percent. Your auto depreciation schedule, however, looks like something else (see Table 11-3). Why? Because Table 11-3 alerts you that your yearly auto depreciation can't exceed the maximum amount in the table.

Table 11-3	Mid-Quarter Convention for Auto Depreciation		
Year	**Yearly % per 4th Quarter Chart in Table 11-2**	**For a $20,000 Car**	**Maximum Yearly Limit**
1-2003	5.00	$10,500	$10,710
2-2004	38.00	$3,800	$4,900
3-2005	22.80	$2,280	$2,950
4-2006	13.68	$1,368	$1,775
5-2007	10.94	$1,532	$1,775
6-2008	9.58	$1,094	$1,775
	100.00	$20,000	$1,775 in each succeeding year

As a result of the 40 percent rule, your regular auto depreciation (in the previous example) comes to only $500 ($10,000 × 5 percent), because you started using the car in the fourth quarter. When you add that amount to the 50 percent additional first-year depreciation of $10,000, ($20,000 × 50 percent), your total auto depreciation for the year comes to $10,500. This amount is $210 less than the maximum allowed. So doing all this math pays off. But you need to remember two things:

- ✔ You have to reduce the cost of the car by the $10,000 extra depreciation to which you're entitled before you figure your regular depreciation for the year.

- ✔ The 40 percent rule doesn't apply to the extra 50 percent deduction. You can claim it regardless of what part of the year the auto was purchased.

The depreciation for the computer amounts to $6,250. Here is how it's figured. The additional first-year depreciation comes to $5,000 ($10,000 × 50 percent). To figure regular depreciation, you must reduce the cost of the $10,000 computer by the $5,000 additional first-year depreciation. Additionally, because you purchased the computer in the second quarter, you get to deduct 25 percent (per Table 11-2) of its reduced $5,000 cost or $1,250. In subsequent years, the yearly depreciation percentages would be 30 percent, 18 percent, 11.37 percent, and so on (refer to Table 11-2).

In 2004, you'd use 38 percent for the auto, which is applied to the $10,000 figure. Because 38 percent comes to $3,800 and is less than the 2003 limit of $4,900, you can deduct the entire amount. (See Tables 11-4 and 11-5 for SUVs and light trucks.)

Table 11-4				Annual Depreciation Ceiling for Cars					
Year	1994	1995	1996	1997	1998	1999	2000	2001	2002	2003
1994	$2,960									
1995	$4,700	$3,060								
1996	$2,850	$4,900	$3,060							
1997	$1,675	$2,950	$4,900	$3,160						
1998	$1,675	$1,775	$2,950	$5,000	$3,160					
1999	$1,675	$1,775	$1,775	$3,050	$5,000	$3,060				
2000	$1,675	$1,775	$1,775	$1,775	$2,950	$5,000	$3,060			
2001	$1,675	$1,775	$1,775	$1,775	$1,775	$2,950	$4,900	3,060**		
2002	$1,675	$1,775	$1,775	$1,775	$1,775	$1,775	$2,950	$4,900	$7,660	
2003	$1,675	$1,775	$1,775	$1,775	$1,775	$1,775	$1,775	$2,950	$4,900	$10,710***
2004	$1,675	$1,675	$1,775	$1,775	$1,775	$1,775	$1,775	$1,775	$2,950	$4,900
2005	$1,675	$1,675	$1,775	$1,775	$1,775	$1,775	$1,775	$1,775	$1,775	$2,950
2006*	$1,675	$1,675	$1,775	$1,775	$1,775	$1,775	$1,775	$1,775	$1,775	$1,775

*and later years
**$3,060 before September 11, 2001 and $7,660 after September 10, 2001
***$10,710 after May 5, 2003, and $7,760 before May 6, 2003

To compute your annual depreciation deduction, first figure the maximum depreciation that you're allowed, assuming your car was used 100 percent for business. Then multiply that amount by the business-use percentage. For example, for a car that you started using in 2003, the maximum depreciation amount is $7,660. If you used your car 75 percent of the time for business, you can deduct $5,745 ($7,660 × 75 percent). If the maximum limit is $10,710, because it was acquired after May 5, 2003, your deduction is $8,033 ($10,710 × 75 percent).

SUVs

Here's a bit of a break regarding light trucks, vans, and SUVs. If the vehicle has been specially modified for business use so as to preclude the likelihood of personal use, the maximum limits on auto depreciation do not apply. What the IRS means by *specially modified* is that after the modification, personal use will be negligible. The modifications the IRS is referring to are, the vehicle only has a front bench for seating, permanent shelving fills most of the cargo area, merchandise and equipment constantly are being carried, and the vehicle has been painted with advertising or the company's logo. Not much of gift, but it's enough of a break to enable you to use the vehicle to get to and from work without the IRS limiting the amount of the depreciation deduction that can be claimed.

SUVs and light trucks with a gross vehicle weight of more than 6,000 pounds are not subject to the maximum depreciation limit that vehicles weighing less than 6,000 pounds are. *Gross vehicle weight* is the total weight including passengers and cargo. This means that people who purchase vehicles — such as the GMC Yukon weighing 6,500 pounds, the larger Ford Expedition at 6,900 pounds, and the Hummer, for example — for business use between 2003 and 2005 can write off the entire cost in the year of purchase. This is the result of a change that took effect in 2003 that allows the first $100,000 of business equipment to be written off in the year of purchase. But, as this edition of *Taxes For Dummies* goes to press, the Senate Finance Committee slashed the write-off to $25,000 from $100,000 for these behemoths of the road. Although the jury is still out on the fate of this provision, there seems to be a lot of support for its passage.

Table 11-5	Annual Depreciation Ceiling for SUVs and Light Trucks			
Year	Yearly Percent	Maximum Yearly Limit Before May 6th	After May 5th	Used Less than 50% for Business
1-2003	20.00	$7,960	$11,010	$3,360
2-2004	32.00	$5,400	$5,400	$5,400
3-2005	19.20	$3,250	$3,250	$3,250
4-2006	11.52	$1,975	$1,975	$1,975
5-2007	11.52	$1,975	$1,975	$1,975
6-2008	5.76	$1,975	$1,975	$1,975
	100.00			

*and $1,975 in each succeeding year

If the business use of your car is 50 percent or less, you must depreciate it using the *straight-line method* under the *alternative depreciation system (ADS)* (see Table 11-6). Straight-line depreciation is relatively easy, right? Wrong . . . in this case. Remember, this calculation is for a car with a business use of less than 50 percent, so the IRS makes you reduce the amount of depreciation that you're allowed under the straight-line method by the percentage of personal use.

The additional first-year 30 percent or 50 percent depreciation deduction, which entitles you the maximum first-year-of-use deduction of $7,660 or $10,710 in 2003, doesn't apply to a car that is used 50 percent or less for business.

Table 11-6	Straight-Line Method under ADS for Auto Depreciation	
Year	5-Year Property	Maximum Yearly Limit*
1	10%	$3,060
2	20%	$4,900
3	20%	$2,950
4	20%	$1,775
5	20%	and $1,775 each succeeding year
6	10%	and $1,775 each succeeding year

*Remember that this is the maximum deduction if your car was used 100 percent for business.

So if you used your car for business 40 percent of the time, the maximum depreciation allowed by law in the first year is $1,224 ($3,060 × 40 percent).

In coming years, you calculate your depreciation deduction the same way. In years 2 through 5, you use a depreciation rate of 20 percent according to Table 11-6, and then 10 percent for year six. Any depreciation that you can't claim in years 1 through 6 (because of the yearly maximum limits) is deducted in subsequent years at $1,775 a year, less your personal use, until your car is fully depreciated.

All this auto depreciation stuff is almost enough to make you start using your feet to call on clients. But then, there's no depreciation allowance for shoes.

A tax software program can save you from all this mind-numbing number crunching.

If you started depreciating your car prior to 2003, Table 11-4 shows you the maximum yearly depreciation limits.

Electric vehicles

The maximum annual depreciation limits for electric vehicles are substantially more than the limits for gas-powered ones. The first year maximum for an electric vehicle purchased before May 6, 2003, is $22,880, if you are claiming the additional first-year September 11 depreciation. If not, it's $9,080. For electric vehicles purchased after May 5, 2003, the maximum limit jumped to $32,030. Regardless of when the vehicle was purchased, the year two depreciation is $14,600; year three, $8,750; and then $5,225 a year until the car is fully depreciated.

A vehicle has to be 100 percent electric powered to qualify for the increased limits. The Toyota and Honda hybrid gas/electric vehicles don't qualify. They do, however, qualify for the clean fuel–burning vehicle deduction of $2,000 (see Chapter 7). Whenever one of these vehicles is used for business, the $2,000 deduction is claimed on line 27 of Schedule C and not on line 33 of Form 1040. In figuring your annual depreciation deduction, subtract the $2,000 from the cost of the car.

Don't forget that an electric vehicle also qualifies for the Electric Vehicle Credit, which can be as high as $4,000 (see line 52, Form 1040). The government is willing to pay you to become an environmentalist.

Leased autos

If you lease a car rather than buy it, you're probably asking yourself why we waited so long to discuss how leased autos are deducted. The reason: A special rule applies. This is your lucky day!

If you lease a car, you can deduct rental payments. If the rental payments are, for example, $700 a month, enter $8,400 on line 24a of Form 2106, Employee Business Expenses. This sounds like a great deal, right? Why buy a car if the most that you can deduct in depreciation for a car purchased in 2003 (before May 6th) is $7,660, when you can deduct $8,400 in rental payments? Well, don't celebrate just yet.

Here's how the IRS gets back at you. Look at the line directly below line 24a on Form 2106. Yes, you see line 24b is for the *inclusion amount*. Based on the value of the car that you're leasing, you must reduce your rental payments by this inclusion. If you lease a car that's worth $35,000, you have to reduce your lease payments by $70. Every year of the lease, this amount increases. What's an inclusion amount? You don't want to know. But, fortunately, IRS Publication 463 *(Travel, Entertainment, Gift, and Car Expenses)* has a chart of the annual lease-inclusion amounts that are adjusted for inflation each year. In fact, it has three annual lease-inclusion charts — one for autos, a second for SUVs and light trucks, and a third for electric vehicles. The IRS thinks of everything. (Call 800-829-3676 to obtain a free copy of this publication.)

As you probably already realize, even though you reduce your rental payments by the lease-inclusion amount, leasing still provides you with a larger deduction than purchasing. But remember, lease payments that are payments toward the purchase price of a car aren't deductible. The IRS considers such leases a purchase contract, because you end up owning the jalopy at the end of the lease. If you have such a lease agreement, you must depreciate the car based on its value, and that sends you right back to the annual limit that you can claim for auto depreciation.

Line 10: Commissions and fees

The fees that you paid to sell your merchandise or to bring in new clients (as in referral fees) go on this line.

However, if you pay someone who isn't your employee more than $600 in a year, you have to file **Form 1099-MISC** with the IRS and send the person that you paid a copy of the form by January 31. IRS Publication 334 *(Tax Guide for Small Business)* explains how to comply with this requirement.

Line 11: Contract labor

This line is new for 2003 and it's meant to clearly identify businesses using independent contractors. The IRS is zeroing in on businesses that pay workers as independent contractors instead of as employees where the employer is obligated to withhold and pay Social Security and Medicare Taxes on their salaries. If someone works on your premises and under your control, he or she is probably your employee, and the rules about withholding taxes and Social Security apply. However, if treating these types of workers as independent contractors is standard in your industry (that is, at least 25 percent of your industry treats them this way) and you issue these workers a Form 1099 at the end of the year, you may have an escape hatch. IRS Publication 1779 *(Independent Contractor or Employee)* and IRS Publication 15-A *(Employer's Supplemental Tax Guide)* address the independent contractor issue in greater detail.

Line 12: Depletion

This line applies if your business deals with properties such as mines, oil and gas wells, timber, and exhaustible natural deposits. You can compute depletion two ways, and, of course, you want to use the one that produces the larger deduction. To be on the safe side, take a look at IRS Publication 535 *(Business Expenses)*.

Line 13: Depreciation

Depreciation is the annual deduction that enables you to recover the cost of an investment (that has a useful life of more than one year) in business equipment or in income-producing real estate. The word *depreciation* is itself enough to send most readers to the next chapter, we know, but just think of depreciation as a way of reducing your tax! Now, are you more excited about depreciation possibilities? If it's a vehicle that you want to depreciate, flip back to line 9. Unless you elect the special provision that allows you to deduct the first $100,000 (up from $24,000 in 2002) of equipment or furniture used in your business (we explain this provision later in the chapter in "Your buying bonanza: The $100,000 deduction"), you have to write off your purchase of these assets over their respective useful lives — as established by the IRS (see Table 11-7). You can't depreciate land and works of art. (So you can't depreciate your Van Goghs!) See Chapter 22 for a discussion of the pros and cons of depreciating versus taking an outright deduction.

If you're an employee claiming auto expenses, you claim the depreciation for the auto on **Form 2106, Employee Business Expenses;** Form 4562 isn't required. For rental income reported on Schedule E, use Form 4562 for property that you started renting in 2003. For property that you started renting before 2003, you don't need to file Form 4562.

To file (or not to file) Form 4562

You compute your depreciation deduction for business property that you started using in 2003 on **Form 4562, Depreciation and Amortization.** Carry the amount of depreciation that you calculate on this form over to line 13 of Schedule C.

The depreciation you normally can deduct every year is determined by an item's useful life. Based on that, you then take a percentage of the item's cost as a deduction. Before we get into explaining how that works, you need to know about two depreciation deductions that you can take right off the bat, "Your buying bonanza: The $100,000 deduction," and the "September 11 additional first-year depreciation deduction."

The $100,000 deduction

You can deduct up to $100,000 of the cost of business equipment that you purchased and started to use in 2003. You don't have to fuss with the standard depreciation tables to claim this depreciation deduction. We show you the ins and outs of this in just a moment. It doesn't matter whether what you purchased is new or used. It only has to be used more than 50 percent of the time in your business.

September 11 additional first-year depreciation — Purchases before May 6, 2003

You are also entitled to an additional first-year 30 percent depreciation for new equipment, machinery, office furniture, and so on purchased after September 10, 2001, and before September 11, 2004, that you start using in your business before January 1, 2005. Used items don't qualify. The law was written in this convoluted manner to allow the additional first-year deduction for items ordered before September 11, 2004, but not delivered until after that date, as long as taxpayers start using them in their businesses before January 1, 2005. Why couldn't the IRS say that in the first place? The 30 percent is in addition to your regular depreciation and up to $100,000 of the special bonus depreciation. You are allowed these three depreciation deductions, but you have to buy something new every year to claim the 30 percent additional first-year depreciation deduction and the special bonus depreciation.

You can't buy something and keep claiming the 30 percent every year.

Another hitch: You have to claim the extra 30 percent; it isn't automatic (meaning that the deduction is not built into the depreciation tables). So claim it! Before we explain how, you need to know what qualifies for the deduction and what doesn't. Real estate doesn't. Leasehold improvements do, if the building is more than three years old. Computer software also qualifies.

Here's how you compute the two special depreciation deductions and your regular depreciation deduction. Say you purchase computer equipment (which has a 5-year useful life) for $150,000 before May 6, 2003. How do you know what its useful life is? You, of course, looked it up in Table 11-7. If you *don't* claim the two special depreciation deductions, your depreciation for 2003 comes to $30,000 ($150,000 × 20 percent — see Table 11-8). By claiming your $100,000 buying bonanza and the additional first-year September 11 depreciation deduction, your 2003 depreciation deduction comes to $122,000. Quite a difference!

Here is the math. First you claim your buying bonanza depreciation of $100,000. This deduction requires that you reduce the $150,000 by the $100,000 to $50,000. This is the figure you use to compute the additional first-year 30 percent September 11 depreciation, which amounts to $15,000 ($50,000 × 30 percent). Now for your regular 2003 depreciation: You guessed it? You have to reduce the $50,000 by the $15,000 September 11 depreciation, which comes to $35,000 ($50,000 – $15,000). Stay with us, we are almost there. Your regular 2003 depreciation is $7,000 ($35,000 × 20 percent). Now tally the three amounts, $100,000, $15,000 and $7,000. That's how you come to your total depreciation deduction for 2003 of $122,000. Enter that amount on Form 4562 and don't forget to attach it to your return. In future years you base your depreciation on $35,000. Phew! Hey, no one said minimizing what you have to fork over to Uncle Sam was a walk in the park.

In future years, if you don't compute the additional first-year 30 percent deduction and you do not elect not to claim it, you nevertheless have to reduce the cost of the computer equipment as if you *had* claimed the 30 percent depreciation deduction. Who says the IRS is not out to trap you? A virtual minefield awaits the unsuspecting. To inform the IRS that you don't want to claim the additional first-year depreciation deduction, simply write: `I choose not to claim the additional first-year 30 percent depreciation on the computer equipment I purchased in 2003.`

For anyone who just learned about this 30 percent business, who also purchased a depreciable asset for business use after September 10, 2001, and neither claimed the additional first-year deduction on your 2001 and 2002 returns nor attached any statement to the return indicating that you didn't want to claim it, here's what to do. You can (don't laugh) throw yourself at the mercy of the IRS by filing an amended return. Flip back to line 9 and the next-to-last paragraph in the "September 11 additional first-year depreciation" section. We wouldn't advise doing this if we thought it wouldn't work.

Not claiming the extra depreciation may make sense if 2003 was a lousy year, which is the way it seems like it's been for many folks. If your income was down, the extra deduction would be wasted or not as valuable as it would be if it was claimed in a high-income year.

If the equipment, machinery, or office furniture that you purchased for your business didn't exceed $100,000, you can forget all the computation we just went through. Simply deduct what you spent on Form 4562 and on line 13.

September 11 additional first-year depreciation – Purchases after May 5, 2003

For purchases made after May 5, 2003, the additional first-year bonus depreciation deduction was bumped up to 50 percent. The hitch? Only purchases of new items qualify. The purchase has to be after May 5, 2003, and you have to start using it in your business before January 1, 2005. But if 30 is your lucky number, you can elect to continue using the 30 percent rather than the 50 percent rate. Additionally, where purchases made after May 5, 2003, are concerned, the requirement that the item be acquired before September 11, 2004, no longer is in effect regardless of whether you're using the 30 percent or 50 percent rate. January 1, 2005, is now the date that counts.

If you want to continue to use the 30 percent rate, simply compute your asset depreciation using that rate instead of 50 percent. If you choose to use neither simply write across the top of Form 4562, Depreciation and Amortization: `I choose not to claim the additional first-year 30 percent or 50 percent depreciation on the asset(s) I purchased in 2003.`

Assuming the same facts regarding equipment purchases of the $150,000 computer that we cited in the "Purchases before May 6, 2003" section earlier, except that you made the purchase after May 5, 2003, and that you claimed the 50 percent additional first-year September 11 depreciation, your deduction for 2003 would come to $130,000. That amount includes the $100,000 special depreciation, the 50 percent depreciation of $25,000 ($150,000 – $100,000 or $50,000 × 50 percent) and the regular depreciation of $5,000 ($50,000 – $25,000 × the 20 percent amount from Table 11-8).

So we won't have to repeat ourselves, flip back to "Purchases before May 6, 2003," if you neglected to claim the 30 percent additional first-year depreciation in either 2001 or 2002.

Table 11-7	Useful Life
Type of Property	*Useful Life (Years)*
Computers and similar equipment	5
Office machinery (typewriters, calculators, copiers)	5
Autos and light trucks	5
Office furniture (desks, files)	7
Appliances (stoves, refrigerators)	7
Shrubbery	15
Residential buildings	27.5
Nonresidential buildings after 5/12/93	39
Nonresidential buildings before 5/12/93	31.5
Goodwill, customer lists, franchise costs, and covenants not to compete	15

For property that you started using prior to 2003, Form 4562 isn't required. On line 13 of Schedule C, just enter the amount to which you're entitled based on the useful life of the asset from the applicable schedule that we provide in this chapter. For example, if you want to depreciate an asset that has a five-year useful life, use Table 11-8. If you're depreciating cars, computers, or cellular phones, however, you must use Form 4562, because you can depreciate only the business portion of those kinds of items.

IRS depreciation percentages

To calculate the amount of depreciation that you're entitled to claim, glance at the IRS depreciation tables (Tables 11-8 through 11-12). For business property other than real estate, you'll notice that each table has two categories: *half-year convention* and *mid-quarter convention*. Usually, you use the half-year convention, because the mid-quarter convention comes into play when the business assets you acquired and started using in the last three months of the year exceed 40 percent of all business assets that you placed in service during the year. Got that? Read on and follow the examples for both types of depreciation conventions.

Table 11-8	MACRS (Modified Accelerated Cost Recovery System): 5-Year Property				
Year	*Half-Year Convention*	*Mid-Quarter Convention*			
		First Quarter	*Second Quarter*	*Third Quarter*	*Fourth Quarter*
1	20.00%	35.00%	25.00%	15.00%	5.00%
2	32.00	26.00	30.00	34.00	38.00
3	19.20	15.60	18.00	20.40	22.80
4	11.52	11.01	11.37	12.24	13.68
5	11.52	11.01	11.37	11.30	10.94
6	05.76	01.38	04.26	07.06	09.58

Table 11-9 — **MACRS: 7-Year Property**

| Year | Half-Year Convention | Mid-Quarter Convention | | | |
		First Quarter	Second Quarter	Third Quarter	Fourth Quarter
1	14.29%	25.00%	17.85%	10.71%	3.57%
2	24.49	21.43	23.47	25.51	27.55
3	17.49	15.31	16.76	18.22	19.68
4	12.49	10.93	11.97	13.02	14.06
5	8.93	8.75	8.87	9.30	10.04
6	8.92	8.74	8.87	8.85	8.73

Table 11-10 — **MACRS: 15-Year Property**

| Year | Half-Year Convention | Mid-Quarter Convention | | | |
		First Quarter	Second Quarter	Third Quarter	Fourth Quarter
1	5.00%	8.75%	6.25%	3.75%	1.25%
2	9.50	9.13	9.38	9.63	9.88
3	8.55	8.21	8.44	8.66	8.89
4	7.70	7.39	7.59	7.80	8.00
5	6.93	6.65	6.83	7.02	7.20
6	6.23	5.99	6.15	6.31	6.48

Table 11-11 — **Residential Rental Property (27.5-Year)**

Use the row of the month of the taxable year that the property was placed in service.

Month	Year 1	Year 2	Year 3	Year 4	Year 5	Year 6
Jan.	3.485%	3.636%	3.636%	3.636%	3.636%	3.636%
Feb.	3.182	3.636	3.636	3.636	3.636	3.636
Mar.	2.879	3.636	3.636	3.636	3.636	3.636
Apr.	2.576	3.636	3.636	3.636	3.636	3.636
May	2.273	3.636	3.636	3.636	3.636	3.636
Jun.	1.970	3.636	3.636	3.636	3.636	3.636
Jul.	1.667	3.636	3.636	3.636	3.636	3.636
Aug.	1.364	3.636	3.636	3.636	3.636	3.636
Sept.	1.061	3.636	3.636	3.636	3.636	3.636
Oct.	0.758	3.636	3.636	3.636	3.636	3.636
Nov.	0.455	3.636	3.636	3.636	3.636	3.636
Dec.	0.152	3.636	3.636	3.636	3.636	3.636

Residential real estate is depreciated over 27½ years. Nonresidential real estate, a factory or office building for example, placed in use after May 12, 1993, is depreciated over 39 years. If it was *placed in service* (that's the IRS term for when you started using it) after 1986 and before May 13, 1993, it's depreciated over 31½ years. You can get the depreciation rates for these two periods from IRS Publication 946 *(How To Depreciate Property)*. For prior periods, you have to use the rates in IRS Publication 534 *(Depreciating Property Placed in Service before 1987)*.

Table 11-12	Commercial Property (31½ Years and 39 Years)			
Use the row of the month of the taxable year that the property was placed in service.				
Month	*(31½ Years)*		*(39 Years)*	
	Year 1	*Later Years*	*Year 1*	*Later Years*
Jan.	3.042%	3.175%	2.461%	2.564%
Feb.	2.778	3.175	2.247	2.564
Mar.	2.513	3.175	2.033	2.564
Apr.	2.249	3.175	1.819	2.564
May	2.273	3.175	1.605	2.564
Jun.	1.720	3.175	1.391	2.564
Jul.	1.455	3.175	1.177	2.564
Aug.	1.190	3.175	0.963	2.564
Sept.	0.926	3.175	0.749	2.564
Oct.	0.661	3.175	0.535	2.564
Nov.	0.397	3.175	0.321	2.564
Dec.	0.132	3.175	0.107	2.564

For example, say you purchased the building where you operate your business in March 2003 for $225,000. Because it is nonresidential property purchased after May 12, 1993, you have to depreciate it over 39 years. You make a reasonable determination that the land is worth $25,000, so you have a depreciable basis of $200,000. Next you look up the rate in the 39-year column for March (2.033 percent). Your depreciation for 2003 is $4,066 ($200,000 × 2.033 percent). In later years, it is $5,128 ($200,000 × 2.564 percent).

Real estate isn't eligible for the special $100,000 depreciation or the 30 percent or 50 percent additional first-year depreciation deduction.

Additions or improvements to property

An addition or improvement that you make to your property is treated as a separate item for the purposes of depreciation — regardless of how you depreciate the original asset. For example, you own a house that you've rented since 1984 and have been depreciating over 19 years (you were allowed to use that short of a useful life back then). And in 2003, you added a new roof. The roof has to be depreciated over 27½ years and at the rate in the IRS depreciation tables for residential real estate. The depreciation tables reproduced in this chapter go up to only six years. For tables that go beyond six years, send for IRS Publication 946 *(How to Depreciate Property)*.

If you're a tenant and make improvements to the space you occupy, you get to deduct the improvements over the remaining term of the lease. Say, for example, that the improvements amount to $10,000 and the balance of the lease is five years. Every year for the remainder of the lease you can deduct $2,000. This deduction is called *amortization* not depreciation. Why? Don't ask us.

Suppose that you're depreciating a computer that you purchased for $5,000 in 2003. First, you must look up its useful life (Table 11-7). Computers have a useful life of five years, so use the depreciation percentages for five-year property. Okay, easy enough so far.

Under the half-year convention for five-year property (Table 11-8, you find 20 percent as the amount. For 2003, you're entitled to a $1,000 depreciation deduction ($5,000 × 20 percent). In 2004, you'd multiply the $5,000 cost by 32 percent, for a deduction of $1,600. And then you use 19.20 percent, 11.52 percent, 11.52 percent, and 5.76 percent in each of the succeeding years. You have to make these calculations after you reduce the cost of the asset for the special $100,000 and the additional first-year September 11 depreciation, or if you decided not to claim these deductions to figure your regular depreciation for 2003 and for future years. Fun calculations, right? Based on the convention rules, the write-off period for stuff is one year longer than its useful life. That's because in the first year you're entitled to only a half-year's worth of depreciation. The half-year convention rule means that all assets are considered to have been purchased on July 1 — which entitles you to only half the normal amount of depreciation in the first year.

Mid-quarter convention depreciation

Remember that you must use the mid-quarter convention if the business property that you placed in service during the last three months of the year exceeds 40 percent of all your business property placed in service during the year.

For example, say you bought a calculator for $500 on February 1, 2003, and a copier for $1,000 on October 1, 2003, and chose not to claim the two special depreciation deductions. Under the half-year convention, you're entitled to a depreciation deduction of $300 ($1,500 × 20 percent). But because more than 40 percent of all your business property was bought and placed into service the last three months of the year, you have to switch to the mid-quarter convention for each asset. So here's how you have to separately compute the depreciation for these two pieces of equipment.

Under the mid-quarter convention for five-year property (see Table 11-8), for an asset purchased in the first quarter, the depreciation rate is 35 percent. Therefore, you're entitled to a $175 depreciation deduction ($500 × 35 percent) for the calculator. For the copier, you have to use the 5 percent rate for property bought during the fourth quarter ($1,000 × 5 percent), which entitles you to a $50 deduction.

The long and the short of all this is that by using the mid-quarter convention, you can claim only half the depreciation that you normally would. At this point, you're probably scratching the back of your head and wondering who thinks of these things. We must confess that we don't know either. Just play along.

You can save yourself the headache that this mid-quarter convention causes and get a larger deduction to boot by claiming your *$100,000 buying bonanza deduction,* which we point out in the next section.

Your buying bonanza: The $100,000 deduction

Instead of computing depreciation by using the standard depreciation tables, you can elect to deduct up to $100,000 of the cost of business equipment that you purchased and started using in your business in 2003. Actually, this isn't a one-time deduction; you can do this every year. One taxpayer that we know of liked this deduction so much that he deducted the same amount every year. Remember, however, that you must have actually spent up to $100,000 in 2003 to get the write-off. If you spend another $100,000 in 2004, you get to write that off in one shot on your 2004 tax return. This bonanza is known in IRS terms as Section 179 depreciation. If you think that they use these terms to confuse people, guess what. You're right!

Unlike the additional first-year 30 percent and 50 percent deductions, used business equipment qualifies for this first-year depreciation deduction.

Be aware that the Community Renewal Tax Relief Act of 2000 allows businesses in economically depressed areas called Empowerment Zones to expense the first $135,000 of business property. IRS Publication 954 *(Tax Incentives for Empowerment Zones and Other Distressed Communities)* has the lowdown on this extra depreciation deduction and on a number of tax credits that are available in these zones. Publication 954 lists the areas designated as Empowerment Zones and Communities. To see if your exact business location falls within one of these general areas, call the Department of Housing and Urban Development (HUD) at 800-998-9999 or check out their Website at www.ezec.gov.

If you buy a few items, you can pick and choose which ones you want to write off completely and which ones you don't. If, for example, you spend $130,000 for equipment, $80,000 of which has a seven-year life and is eligible for only the 30 percent additional first-year September 11 depreciation, and $50,000 of which has a five-year life that is eligible for the 50 percent additional first-year September 11 depreciation, you have a larger deduction when you choose to use your special $100,000 deduction to write off the $80,000 with a seven-year life and then $20,000 of the remaining $50,000 of equipment with the five year life. By doing it this way, you're entitled to depreciation of $118,000. If you did it the other way around, so that after deducting the $100,000 you were left with a balance of $30,000 worth of seven-year equipment, your depreciation would only amount to $112,001. This example demonstrates that when you have two assets of equal value, but one depreciates over five years and the other over 15 years, you should write off the one with the longer depreciation first.

Now for the fine print (there always has to be some — this *is* a tax book, after all). If you're married filing separately, you can deduct only $50,000, unless you and your spouse agree upon how much of the $100,000 buying bonanza each of you is entitled to deduct. If you buy equipment costing more than $400,000, the $100,000 that you're entitled to deduct is reduced dollar for dollar by the amount over $400,000. So if the total cost is $500,000 or more, you can kiss any part of your $100,000 write-off good-bye. Here's how this works: Say you purchased equipment costing $424,000. You have to reduce the maximum $100,000 you can write-off by $24,000. The beauty of the $100,000 limit (besides the immediate deduction) is that it keeps you from having to wade through the depreciation tables to compute your depreciation. The second rule regarding the $100,000 expensing is that this deduction can't produce a loss from all your business activities. Suppose that your consulting income — after all other expenses — is $10,000, and you bought $24,000 worth of equipment. You can expense only $10,000. The $14,000 balance carries over to the next year. If you have enough consulting income after your other expenses, you can deduct it then. If you don't, keep carrying it over until you do.

But there is a pleasant surprise. You can count all your earned income to determine whether you pass the *no-loss test*. So in the preceding example, if you or your spouse had at least $14,000 in wages (in addition to your $10,000 consulting income), you can deduct the whole $24,000 of the equipment you purchased.

Line 14: Employee benefit programs

Enter here the premiums that you paid for your employees' accident, health, and group term life insurance coverage — but don't count the cost of your own insurance benefits here. See "Line 29: Self-employed health insurance deduction" in Chapter 7 to find out how you may be able to deduct 100 percent of your personal health insurance premiums. In 2002, only 70 percent of self-employed individuals' health insurance premiums were deductible.

Line 15: Insurance (other than health)

Enter on this line the premiums that you paid for business insurance, such as fire, theft, robbery, and general liability coverage on your business property.

Line 16a: Mortgage interest

If you own the building in which you operate your business, deduct any mortgage interest you paid on line 16a. If you're claiming a deduction for the business use of your home, the mortgage interest you paid is deducted on line 10 of **Form 8829, Expenses for Business Use of Your Home.** The amount of the deduction is stated on **Form 1098, Mortgage Interest Statement** that you should receive in January 2004 from your bank.

Line 16b: Other interest

Here you can deduct interest on business loans. If you took out a mortgage on your house and used the proceeds of the loan to finance your business, deduct the interest here — and not on Schedule A. If you borrowed money for your business from other sources, such as a bank or even your credit card, deduct the interest on those loans here as well.

You can't deduct the interest you paid on the taxes you owed on your personal tax returns. You can, however, deduct late interest paid on employment taxes (Social Security, Medicare and withholding taxes) that as an employer you paid. See "Interest You Paid," in Chapter 9.

Line 17: Legal and professional services

On this line, enter any fees that you paid for tax advice, for preparing tax forms related to your business, and for legal fees regarding business matters.

Professional services include fees for accounting and engineering work that you pay for. Garden variety consulting work gets entered on line 10, contract labor.

If you pay someone more than $600 (your accountant or lawyer, for example), you have to provide them with Form 1099-MISC by January 31 — just like we told you to do with commissions and contract labor that you deducted on lines 10 and 11.

The IRS must love lawyers. You must report all payments that you made to your lawyer — even for the reimbursement of expenses that you were billed. Additionally, the present exemption saying that payments made to corporations don't have to be reported to the IRS on Form 1099 no longer applies to lawyers. Know any good lawyer jokes?

Line 18: Office expense

Enter your costs for stationery, paper supplies, postage, printer toner, and other consumable items that you use in the operation of your office or business.

Line 19: Pension and profit-sharing plans

Enter your contribution to your employees' Keogh, SIMPLE, or SEP account(s). As for your own Keogh or SEP, enter that amount on Form 1040 (line 30). See Chapter 7.

Employers with fewer than 100 employees may establish what's known as SIMPLE retirement plans. These plans have none of the mind-numbing rules to follow or forms to file that regular retirement plans have. A SIMPLE plan can also cover the owner(s) of a farm (see Chapter 21 for more about SIMPLE plans and other small business retirement plans).

Lines 20a and b: Rent or lease

If you rented or leased an auto, machinery, or equipment, enter the business portion of the rental payments on line 20a. But if you leased a car for more than 30 days, you may have to reduce your deduction by an amount called the *inclusion amount* if your leased car's value exceeded the following amounts (see Table 11-13) when you started leasing it.

Table 11-13	Inclusion Amounts
Year Lease Began	*Amount*
2003	$18,000
2002	$15,500
2001	$15,500
2000	$15,500
1999	$15,500
1998	$15,800
1997	$15,800
1996	$15,500

See the earlier section, "Line 9: Car and truck expenses," to compile the inclusion amount. IRS Publication 463 *(Travel, Entertainment, Gift, and Car Expenses)* has the lease inclusion table.

On line 20b, enter your office rent, for example.

Line 21: Repairs and maintenance

Enter the cost of routine repairs — such as the cost to repair your computer — on this line. But adding a new hard disk isn't a repair; that cost must be depreciated over five years, unless it qualifies for the special election to write off the first $100,000 of business assets.

A repair (as opposed to an improvement) keeps your equipment or property in good operating condition. A repair that also prolongs the life of your equipment has to be depreciated, so make the most of the $100,000 deduction instead of depreciating the cost over its useful life.

If you're confused about what qualifies as a repair and what qualifies as an improvement, you're not alone. Through the years, the Tax Court has been clogged with cases dealing with repairs as current write-offs versus improvements that have to be depreciated. We suggest that you contact a tax advisor to evaluate your specific situation. The new $100,000 immediate write-off should solve this problem.

Line 22: Supplies

If your company manufactures a product, you report factory supplies here. In other words, you deduct the cost of supplies that contribute to the operation of the equipment that you use in your office or business. For example, if you operate a retail store, you enter the cost of mannequins, trim, packaging, and other such items on this line.

Line 23: Taxes and licenses

Here you deduct your business taxes, such as Social Security and unemployment insurance taxes for your employees. You also enter the costs of permits and business licenses. You don't deduct on this line the Social Security tax that you pay because you're self-employed; you can deduct half of this tax on line 28 of your 1040 (see Chapter 7 for more on how this deduction works).

Lines 24a–d: Travel, meals, and entertainment

To find out what you can deduct for travel, meals, and entertainment, see the explanation in Chapter 9 (in the "Lines 20–26: Job Expenses and Most Other Miscellaneous Deductions" section). No point repeating all that stuff here!

Because you can deduct only 50 percent of your meals and entertainment expenses, enter 50 percent of the amount on line 24b on line 24c. Subtract line 24c from line 24b and enter the result on line 24d.

If you're in the transportation industry and are subject to the Department of Transportation restrictions on the number of hours you can work, you're allowed to deduct 65 percent of your meals, so enter 35 percent (that's the nondeductible portion) of your meals and 65 percent of your entertainment on line 24c.

Line 25: Utilities

Can you imagine what this line is for? If you're thinking of electric and telephone bills, for example, you hit the nail on the head. However, if you're claiming a home office deduction (discussed in further detail later in this chapter), your utility costs belong on **Form 8829, Expenses for Business Use of Your Home,** and not here.

Line 26: Wages

Enter here the wages that you paid your employees. Payments to independent contractors, however, should be deducted on line 11. Deduction of independent contractor expenses is a hot issue with the IRS. So flip back to line 11.

Line 27: Other expenses

On the reverse side of Schedule C is Part V, a schedule where you list your expenses whose descriptions defy the neat categories of lines 8–26. Here you can enter dues, subscriptions to related business periodicals, messenger services, overnight express fees, and so on. If you have more than nine items in the other expense category just add another Part V page, but enter the grand total on line 48 of only one of the forms.

Line 28: Total expenses

Addition time — add lines 8–27. This is what it costs to operate your business.

Line 29: Tentative profit (loss)

Subtract line 28 from line 7. If line 28 is more than line 7, you have a loss, and you enter it as a negative number. For example, if you lost $10,000, enter it as <$10,000> (a negative number).

Line 30: Form 8829

Yes, you can deduct home office expenses. If you work out of your home, the rules for claiming a deduction for a home office are now more lenient. That's the good news. The bad news? You must use **Form 8829, Expenses for Business Use of Your Home,** to claim the deduction for the portion that you use for business. You can find a copy of this form in the back of this book. Detailed instructions for filling it out and other rules you must follow to nail down this deduction are found in Chapter 15. You can't take a loss because of the home office deduction. You can, however, carry over an excess deduction amount to another year's tax return.

Because only a portion of your total mortgage interest and real estate taxes are deducted as part of your home office expenses, don't forget to deduct the balance of your total mortgage interest that you entered on line 10(b) of Form 8829, and the balance of your total real estate taxes from line 11(b) of this form. Your mortgage interest balance goes on line 10 of Schedule A; the real estate taxes balance goes on line 6 of Schedule A. These two amounts represent your mortgage interest and taxes related to the portion of the house you live in.

Line 31: Net profit (or loss)

After you arrive at your net profit or loss, copy it onto Form 1040 (line 12) and then on Schedule SE (line 2) so that you can compute the amount of Social Security tax that you have to pay. See Chapter 8 to find out how to complete Schedule SE.

Lines 32a and b: At-risk rules

Suppose that you borrow money to go into business. The at-risk rules limit the amount of business losses that you can deduct on borrowed money that you're personally not liable to repay. For example, you need $20,000 to go into business. You invest $10,000, and your rich uncle gives you $10,000. You lose the entire $20,000. You can deduct only the $10,000 that you personally invested in your business. See Chapter 13 (Lines 27 and 28) for more details on the at-risk rules. Basically, if you're personally responsible for all the liabilities of your business, check box 32a. If you are, you can deduct all your losses. If you're not at risk for all the investment that was made in your business, check 32b. Guess what? You have to fill out **Form 6198, At Risk Limitations.** This form determines how much of your loss you are allowed to deduct.

If you aren't personally responsible, see a tax professional, because the rules in this area are anything but clear or simple.

Start-up expenses

These are the expenses incurred in getting into business before the business actually starts operating. The types of expenses usually incurred during this period are market studies, consulting and professional services, and travel in securing prospective suppliers, customers, and feasibility studies. Whether you can deduct these expenses depends on whether you actually start the business.

If you go into business, you can elect to deduct these expenses over 60 months. You make the election in the year that you start the business by attaching a statement to your return describing the expenditures, the dates incurred, the month the business opened, and the number of months you are electing to deduct the expenditures. You can elect more than 60 months but not less. The deduction is computed on Form 4562, Part VI, Depreciation and Amortization.

If you don't go into business, you can deduct some of your start-up expenses in the year that your attempt to go into business failed. Now you are probably asking, which ones? The answer isn't all that clear. You can deduct your business start-up expenses but not investigatory expenses. What's the difference, you ask? Here's what the IRS says the difference is. *Investigatory expenses* are costs incurred in reviewing a prospective business prior to reaching a final decision to acquire or enter the business. Start-up expenses are costs incurred after you decide to go into business but prior to the time the business actually begins to operate. If you guessed that a lot of taxpayers end up in Tax Court as the result of how they decided to separate the two, you're right. Start-up expenses are deducted on Schedule C.

Operating Loss

Suppose that you start a business and it produces an operating loss. In other words, your costs — not just equipment, but rent, salaries, and other expenses — exceed your income. You may write off that loss against any other income that you and your spouse made that year.

And get this. If the loss is greater than your combined income in the current year, you have what is known in IRS jargon as a *net operating loss (NOL)* that you can carry back over each of the past two years and obtain a refund on the tax that you paid at that time. Whenever the loss still isn't used up by carrying it back, you can carry it forward to offset your income during the next 20 years. The carryback is mandatory unless you elect to carry it only forward. Making the election is simple. Just attach a statement to your return, indicating: `I choose to carry my loss forward.` After you've made this election, you can't change your mind. See Chapter 19 for information about amending a prior year's return and carrying back losses.

Losses incurred before January 1, 1998, could be carried back three years and forwarded for only 15 years. The three-year carryback still applies to the NOLs incurred by small businesses in presidentially declared disaster areas. A small business is one that earned $5 million or less of income in each of the three preceding years. Farmers get to carry back losses five years (see Chapter 14).

NOLs incurred in 2001 and 2002 had to be carried back five years. This was mandatory unless you informed the IRS in a written statement attached to your return that you wanted to either carry back the NOL two years, three years if you qualified, or if you wanted to carry it forward instead. This action had to be taken when you filed your return, which could have been extended to October 15 if you had a valid extension of time to file until then. If you didn't attach such a statement to your return stating what you wanted to do, the NOL had to be carried back five years.

Keep in mind, however, that you can't operate a part-time business, for example, that continually loses money. This situation is known as a *hobby loss.* If you don't show a profit in at least three of every five consecutive years, you may have a fight — with the IRS — on your hands. You must show a profit in at least three of every five consecutive years, or the IRS can declare your business a hobby and disallow your losses. The IRS doesn't consider your enterprise a business when you have continuing losses. No business, no business deductions. Some taxpayers have challenged this rule in Tax Court and won. They were able to prove that they ran their enterprises like a business and anticipated making a profit but didn't. The three-out-of-five-year rule was established to keep the IRS off your back. If you meet this requirement, the IRS can't claim that the losses in the two other years can't be deducted because the business is a hobby. Not making a profit in three out of five years doesn't automatically make the venture a hobby, but it is a strong indication that it may be.

Chapter 12

Capital Gains and Losses: Schedule D

· ·

In This Chapter

▶ Tax basis background stuff

▶ Your introduction to Schedule D

▶ Short-term and long-term capital gains and losses

▶ How to handle Form 4797 (if you need to)

▶ How to deal with the sale of your home, worthless securities, stock options, and bad debts

· ·

*I*f you sell a security, such as a stock, bond, or mutual fund (or another investment held outside of a tax-sheltered retirement account), and you sell it for more than you paid for it, you owe capital gains tax on the profit. Conversely, when you sell an investment at a loss, the loss is tax deductible. Although it may seem unfair, a loss on the sale of your home, auto, jewelry, art, and furniture isn't deductible. That's a cruel reality regarding the sale of personal items.

Schedule D is the place where you plug in your profit or loss on the following examples:

- ✔ Your coin or stamp collection
- ✔ Jewelry and art
- ✔ Stocks and bonds
- ✔ Your home (if you can't exclude all the gain)
- ✔ Household furnishings

The maximum capital gains rates were lowered in 2003. So for 2003 we have two sets of rates, one for gains realized before May 6, 2003 and another for gains on or after May 6, 2003.

Gains before May 6, 2003: If the investment sale took place before this date, the maximum capital gains rate is 20 percent (10 percent for those in the 10 or 15 percent bracket), which is the rate that normally applies when you sell a stock or bond. Taxpayers in the 10 or 15 percent tax bracket who've owned the asset sold for five years pay tax at a reduced 8 percent rate. The maximum rate on the sale of collectibles is 28 percent and the portion of a gain attributable to the depreciation that was deducted through the years when real estate is sold is taxed at 25 percent.

The special 18 percent lower rate provision for assets purchased after 2000 and held for five years was done away with. Taxpayers wouldn't have been eligible for this provision until 2006 anyway. See the "The 18 percent offer that evaporated" later in this chapter.

Gains on or after May 6, 2003: For gains after May 5, 2003, the maximum rate dropped from 20 to 15 percent. For those taxpayers in the 10 or 15 percent tax brackets the maximum rate decreased to 5 percent. Here's some more good news for these folks, in 2008 the rate will be zero. A zero tax rate is IRS jargon for *tax-free*. The 28 percent maximum rate on the gain from the sale of collectibles and the 25 percent maximum rate on the portion of a gain attributable to the depreciation that was deducted through the years when real estate is sold didn't change.

If you made a sale prior to May 6, 2003, say in 2001 for example, and are collecting the payments in installments, any payment received after May 5, 2003, is eligible for the reduced rates of 15 or 5 percent.

Collectibles and Real Estate

The maximum rate on the sale of collectibles (art, antiques, stamp collections, memorabilia, and so on) is 28 percent regardless of the year it was sold.

One additional capital gains rate of 25 percent kicks in when you sell depreciable real estate. In that case, part of the profit — equal to the depreciation that you deducted through the years — is taxed at 25 percent, and the balance of the profit is taxed at the lower capital gains rate. Taxing all the depreciation at 25 percent relates only to real estate that you started to depreciate after 1986. If you started to depreciate it prior to 1987, part of the depreciation gets taxed at 25 percent and part at regular tax rates. Our advice: If you sell real estate that you started depreciating before 1987, see a tax pro.

Tax Basis Background

Before we jump into completing Schedule D, a little background is necessary on gains and losses and how to figure them. When you understand these concepts, Schedule D shouldn't be too difficult. If you already understand these key concepts, you can cruise on ahead to the instructions for completing Schedule D.

To determine whether you sold something at a taxable gain or deductible loss, you first must compute its tax basis. *Basis* is the tax system's way of measuring what you paid for your investment in stocks, bonds, or real estate, for example. In addition to helping you to calculate your capital gains and capital losses, your basis also is used to figure deductions for depreciation, casualty losses, and sometimes even charitable gifts.

For example, if you purchase 100 shares of the Informed Investor's Mutual Fund at $40 per share, your cost basis is considered to be $4,000, or $40 per share. Simple enough. Now suppose that this fund pays a dividend of $2 per share (so you receive $200 for your 100 shares) and that you choose to reinvest this dividend to purchase more shares of the mutual fund. If, at the time of the dividend payment, the fund has increased to $50 per share, your $200 dividend purchases four more shares. Now you own 104 shares. At $50 per share, your 104 shares are worth $5,200. But what's your basis now? Your basis is your original investment ($4,000) plus subsequent investments ($200) for a total of $4,200. Thus, if you sold all your shares now, you'd have a taxable profit of $1,000 (current value of $5,200 less your original investment and your reinvested dividends).

Property defined

Definitions are the spice of life for IRS agents. Here's an important one.

When most people refer to property, they mean real estate. But when the IRS talks about property, it can be anything that you own, such as stocks, bonds, cars, boats, or computers. So when you see the term *property* on a form, the government is talking about more than the old homestead. For example, a landlord's payment to a tenant to give up a rent-controlled apartment is considered the sale of property subject to lower capital gain tax rates.

With a home, the basis works the same way. The tax basis of your home is increased for any improvements you made and costs connected with purchasing the property — such as the fee that you paid the title company and your attorney. Any real estate broker's commission that you paid when you sold your home, as well as any attorney and closing fees that you paid, is subtracted from the selling price to arrive at what is called the *net selling price*. To determine your profit (we hope that you had one), subtract your basis from the net selling price. Make sure that you take more than a peek at "Use Schedule D When You Sell Your Home," later in this chapter, to see whether you qualify for a $500,000 (couples) or $250,000 (singles) exemption from tax on the profit that can be claimed on the sale of a home.

If you own rental real estate, depreciation and any casualty losses that you may have deducted (see Chapter 13 for more details) reduce your basis. Here's how to figure the tax basis depending on how you acquired the property:

- ✔ **Property you purchased:** This tax basis usually is your cost increased by improvements or decreased by depreciation and casualty losses.

- ✔ **Property received as a gift:** To figure the basis of property that you received as a gift, you must know the donor's basis at the time the gift was made, its *fair market value* (FMV) at the time the gift was made, and any gift tax that the donor paid.

  - If the FMV at the time of the gift was *more than* the donor's basis, then your basis for figuring a gain or loss is the donor's basis.

    For example, suppose that your father gives you a gift of stock that cost him $5,000 but was worth $12,000 when he gave it to you. Your basis for figuring a gain or loss is $5,000.

  - If the FMV at the time of the gift was *less than* the donor's basis, your basis for figuring a gain is the donor's basis, and your basis for figuring a loss is the fair market value at the time of the gift.

    In other words, the IRS says, "Heads, we win; tails, we win." For example, suppose that your father gave you stock that cost him (basis) $10,000, but was worth (FMV) $8,000 when he gave it to you. (Nice gift, huh?) If you sell the stock for $12,000, you have a $2,000 gain (sale price of stock $12,000 – $10,000 donor's basis). If you sell the stock for $7,000, you have a $1,000 loss (sale price of stock $7,000 – $8,000 FMV). If the sale price is between the FMV and the donor's cost ($8,000 and $10,000, in the example), you have neither a gain nor a loss. If your father paid a gift tax when he gave you the gift, a portion of the gift tax that he paid is added to your basis.

- ✔ **Property that you inherited:** Your basis for figuring a gain or loss is usually the fair market value on the decedent's date of death. Sometimes — to save on taxes — the executor of an estate is allowed to use an alternative valuation date, which is six months after the date of death. When you inherit something, make sure that the executor gives you the estate tax valuation, because when you sell the asset, that figure will be your tax basis.

- ✔ **Property received for services:** The amount that you're required to include in your income becomes your basis. Suppose that for putting a deal together you receive 100 shares of stock valued at $10,000. Because you had to pay tax on the value of the shares, your tax basis for the 100 shares is $10,000.

- ✔ **Property received in a divorce:** You use your spouse's basis. Generally, neither spouse is required to pay tax on property transferred as part of a divorce settlement.

See Chapter 3 for what to do if you received property or a stock as a gift or by inheritance and you don't have a clue as to its tax basis or FMV, or if you believe the values the donor or executor gave you are off the mark.

Details for figuring short term or long term

In most cases, whether you've held a security or other asset for more than 12 months is obvious. Here are some details that may help in less-clear cases. For securities traded on an established securities market, you begin counting the days in your holding period the day after the trading date on which you bought the securities, and stop on the trading date on which you sold them. For holding-period purposes, ignore the *settlement date* — this is the date when you actually pay the broker for a purchase or get paid from the broker for a sale.

For property that you received as a gift, you're considered to have purchased the property on the same day that the donor did — and not on the date of the gift — if you use the donor's tax basis as your basis. However, the holding period starts on the date of the gift if you sell it at a loss, and you're required to use the fair market value of the property when it was given to you. Property inherited via someone's estate is treated as a sale of a long-term capital asset, even if you sold the shares or property the day after you received them. The more-than-12-months-rule is ignored.

When you purchase assets such as stocks or bonds by exercising an option, the holding period starts the day after the option is exercised — and not on the day that you received or purchased the option.

What Part of Schedule D?

The 2003 changes to the maximum capital gain rates wreaked havoc with this form. Whereas last year's Schedule D had 40 lines (which was bad enough), the 2003 version has a mere 53 (see Figure 12-1). That's if you have gains that are subject only to the 5, 8, 10, 15, or 20 percent capital gain rates. If you have a capital gain that is subject to the 25 percent or 28 percent rates, you must use the worksheet in your instruction booklet in addition to Parts I, II, and III of Schedule D. Fortunately, most people don't have these types of capital gains and have to deal only with Schedule D. Schedule D is structured into four major parts. Part I is for reporting short-term gains and losses. Part II is for reporting long-term gains and losses. Part III summarizes the short- and long-term gains and losses. Part IV computes the maximum 5, 8, 10, 15, or 20 percent capital gains tax that you have to pay. The IRS includes a Schedule D-1, which is a continuation sheet for those of you with lots of gains and losses.

If you hold property for one year or less, the gain or loss is *short term*. If you hold property for more than a year, the gain or loss is *long term*.

You list all your individual capital gains and losses on line 1 or 8. Line 1 is for short-term gains and losses, and line 8 is for long-term gains and losses.

Why the distinction? Because the IRS wants to make life complicated. The tax rates for long-term and short-term gains and losses differ. If your net capital gain is a long-term gain, depending on the type of asset and your tax bracket, the tax on the gain may be as low as 5, 8, 10, 15, or 20 percent, depending on whether it occurred before May 6, 2003, and it can't exceed 28 percent on collectibles, for instance. If the capital gain is short term, the tax on it can be as high as the income tax brackets go (currently 35 percent at the federal level).

Schedule D: Columns

After you determine whether the security that you sold goes in the short-term (Part I) or long-term (Part II) section, you're ready to work your way across the page. We must say that Schedule D is one of the least attractive IRS schedules. We'll walk you through an example and then explain how to complete the remaining line numbers.

Suppose that you sold 100 shares of General Motors stock for $4,000 on April 17, 2003. You had paid $6,000 for the shares on April 16, 2002. Therefore, you have a capital loss of $2,000. To figure out whether the loss is long term or short term, start counting on April 17. The 17th of each month starts the beginning of a new month. Because you sold the shares on April 17, 2003 — one day more than 12 months — the loss is long term. (Had you sold them on April 16 — exactly 12 months after buying them — the loss would have been short term.) Now plug the loss into Schedule D on line 8.

SCHEDULE D **(Form 1040)** Department of the Treasury Internal Revenue Service (99)	**Capital Gains and Losses** ▶ Attach to Form 1040. ▶ See Instructions for Schedule D (Form 1040). ▶ Use Schedule D-1 to list additional transactions for lines 1 and 8.	OMB No. 1545-0074 20**03** Attachment Sequence No. **12**
Name(s) shown on Form 1040		Your social security number

Part I Short-Term Capital Gains and Losses—Assets Held One Year or Less

(a) Description of property (Example: 100 sh. XYZ Co.)	(b) Date acquired (Mo., day, yr.)	(c) Date sold (Mo., day, yr.)	(d) Sales price (see page D-6 of the instructions)	(e) Cost or other basis (see page D-6 of the instructions)	(f) Gain or (loss) for the entire year Subtract (e) from (d)	(g) Post-May 5 gain or (loss)* (see below)
1						

2 Enter your short-term totals, if any, from Schedule D-1, line 2	**2**				
3 **Total short-term sales price amounts.** Add lines 1 and 2 in column (d)	**3**				
4 Short-term gain from Form 6252 and short-term gain or (loss) from Forms 4684, 6781, and 8824	**4**				
5 Net short-term gain or (loss) from partnerships, S corporations, estates, and trusts from Schedule(s) K-1	**5**				
6 Short-term capital loss carryover. Enter the amount, if any, from line 8 of your 2002 Capital Loss Carryover Worksheet	**6**	( )		
7a Combine lines 1 through 5 in column (g). If the result is a loss, enter the result. Otherwise, enter -0-. **Do not** enter more than zero	**7a**			( )
b **Net short-term capital gain or (loss).** Combine lines 1 through 6 in column (f) .	**7b**			

Part II Long-Term Capital Gains and Losses—Assets Held More Than One Year

(a) Description of property (Example: 100 sh. XYZ Co.)	(b) Date acquired (Mo., day, yr.)	(c) Date sold (Mo., day, yr.)	(d) Sales price (see page D-6 of the instructions)	(e) Cost or other basis (see page D-6 of the instructions)	(f) Gain or (loss) for the entire year Subtract (e) from (d)	(g) Post-May 5 gain or (loss)* (see below)
8						

9 Enter your long-term totals, if any, from Schedule D-1, line 9	**9**				
10 **Total long-term sales price amounts.** Add lines 8 and 9 in column (d)	**10**				
11 Gain from Form 4797, Part I; long-term gain from Forms 2439 and 6252; and long-term gain or (loss) from Forms 4684, 6781, and 8824	**11**			
12 Net long-term gain or (loss) from partnerships, S corporations, estates, and trusts from Schedule(s) K-1	**12**			
13 Capital gain distributions. See page D-2 of the instructions	**13**			
14 Long-term capital loss carryover. Enter the amount, if any, from line 13 of your 2002 Capital Loss Carryover Worksheet	**14**	( )		
15 Combine lines 8 through 13 in column (g). If zero or less, enter -0-	**15**			
16 **Net long-term capital gain or (loss).** Combine lines 8 through 14 in column (f) **Next:** Go to Part III on the back.	**16**			

*Include in column (g) all gains and losses from column (f) from sales, exchanges, or conversions (including installment payments received) **after** May 5, 2003. However, **do not** include gain attributable to unrecaptured section 1250 gain, "collectibles gains and losses" (as defined on page D-8 of the instructions) or eligible gain on qualified small business stock (see page D-4 of the instructions).

For Paperwork Reduction Act Notice, see Form 1040 instructions.   Cat. No. 11338H   Schedule D (Form 1040) 2003

Figure 12-1:
Schedule D,
page 1.

Column (a) Description of the property
100 shares of General Motors

Column (b) Date acquired
4-16-02

Column (c) Date sold
4-17-03

Column (d) Sales price
$4,000

Column (e) Cost or other basis
$6,000

Column (f) Gain or <loss> for entire year
<$2,000>

Column (g) Post–May 5 percent gain or <loss>
Because the $2,000 loss occurred before May 6, 2003, leave column (g) blank. If you sold a collectible (art, for instance) or depreciable real estate, also leave column (g) blank, regardless of whether it was sold after May 5.

When you leave column (g) blank, you inform the IRS that either the old 8, 10, or 20 maximum rates apply to the gain reported in column (f). If you make an entry in column (g), you're telling the IRS that the reduced capital gains rates of 5 or 15 percent apply to the gain in column (f). For example, because column (f) has a $2,000 loss, and column (g) is blank, the loss is applied to any long-term gains (taxed at 20 percent) that occurred before May 6, 2003, before it's applied to any gains that occurred after May 5, 2003, which would be taxed at 15 percent.

If you need more spaces because lines 1 and 8 accommodate only four stock transactions, use Schedule D-1 to list the rest of your stock trades.

Figuring Your Profit or Loss

Now that you understand where the numbers go on the form, where the heck do you get the numbers? The following list tells you where:

- **Stocks and bonds:** If you sold a stock or bond, you will receive a **Form 1099-B, Proceeds from Broker and Barter Exchange Transactions,** or an equivalent, from your broker by January 31, 2004. The IRS also gets a copy of this form. Form 1099-B lists the date of every sale and the amount after the broker's commission has been deducted. You enter this information on Schedule D. The IRS checks to see whether it's correct. Just another friendly service by the folks at the IRS.

  A redemption or retirement of bonds or notes at their maturity is also considered a sale or trade and must be reported on Schedule D, regardless of whether you realized a gain or loss on the redemption. Your tax basis is generally your purchase price plus the broker's commission.

- **Stock dividends and splits:** If you receive additional stock as part of a nontaxable stock dividend or stock split, you must reduce the per-share basis (but not the total basis) of your original stock. You make this computation by dividing the cost of the stock by the total number of shares that you now have. You must, however, reduce your basis when you receive nontaxable cash distributions, because this transaction is considered a return on your investment.

For example, suppose that in 1991 you bought 100 shares of ABC stock for $500, or $5 a share. In 1992, you bought 100 shares of ABC stock for $800, or $8 a share. In 1993, ABC declared a 2-for-1 stock split. You now have 400 shares, 200 shares with a basis of $2.50 a share ($500 cost ÷ 200 shares) and 200 shares with a basis of $4 a share ($800 cost ÷ 200 shares).

Or suppose that you purchased shares for $10,000 and received a $500 nontaxable cash dividend. Your tax basis is now $9,500 ($10,000 – $500).

✔ **Identifying shares:** If you buy and sell securities at different times in varying quantities and you can't definitely identify the securities that you sell, the basis of those sold is figured under the *first-in-first-out method* — the first securities that you acquired are considered the first ones sold.

If you bought 100 shares of GM at $30 and 100 at $50 and then sold 100 shares at $60, you would pay less tax if you used the shares that you purchased for $50 as your cost. You make this choice only if you specifically tell your broker to sell the shares purchased for $50; otherwise, you're deemed to have sold the 100 shares you bought at $30 per share.

✔ **Mutual fund shares:** When you sell shares of a fund, you can average the cost of the shares sold if they were bought at different times — or you can specifically identify the shares that you sold. Remember that the dividends used to purchase additional shares on which you paid tax every year increase your tax basis for determining a gain or loss when the shares are sold.

For example, suppose that you bought 1,000 shares of a fund for $10,000. Through the years, you received $5,000 in dividends that you used to buy additional shares. Your tax basis is $15,000 ($10,000 original cost plus the $5,000 of dividends received) for the shares that you now own.

You can use three methods to determine your tax cost, and your choice of which method to use depends on how your fund has performed and whether you want to pay taxes now (if you're in a lower bracket this year, for example) or later.

- The first way to determine your tax cost is the specific-share identification method. You simply decide which of your shares you want to sell, and make sure the fund notes it on the confirmation slip. For example, you bought 100 shares at $10 a share and another 100 shares for $20 a share. If you sell 100 shares, you can designate the 100 shares that cost $20 as being sold, thereby reducing your profit and the tax that you have to pay.

- The second method is called the first-in, first-out method, meaning that you always sell the shares that you've owned for the longest period of time.

- The third and most complex option is the average-cost method. You must select either the single- or double-category option. With the single-category, you divide the amount you paid for your shares (including reinvested dividends) by the number of shares that you own. Eureka! Average cost. Under this method, you're considered to have sold your long-term holdings first. After you select this method, you must use it for all accounts in the same fund. However, you can use a different method for figuring the cost of other funds, even for funds within the same family of funds.

  The double-category method enables you to sell either your short-term or long-term holdings. You divide your shares into short- and long-term holdings at the time of the sale, and then you compute the average cost for each category.

✔ **Undistributed capital gains:** Here's an oddity that you shouldn't overlook. If your fund had capital gains that it didn't distribute to its shareholders, you can increase the tax cost of your fund's shares, which in turn reduces the tax that you eventually have to pay when you sell. We often see undistributed capital gains with technology and biotech funds. You'll be sent **Form 2439, Notice to Shareholders of Undistributed Long-Term Capital Gains.** You report your share of the undistributed gains and get a credit for the tax paid by the fund (entered on line 67, Form 1040). Your tax basis in the fund is increased by the difference between the capital gain that was retained by the fund and the actual tax paid by the fund on your behalf. We bet that you thought that mutual funds represented the simplest way to invest in the market. This way of reporting the gain and the tax paid by the fund on your behalf puts you in the same position as if you actually received the entire capital gain, paid the tax, and reinvested the difference.

For capital gains retained by a mutual fund before August 6, 1997, you increase your *tax cost* (basis, in IRS jargon) by a flat 65 percent of the capital gains retained by the fund. Here is the rule for dividends retained after August 6, 1997: Suppose that your fund retains $1,000 of your capital gain and pays a $350 tax. You report the $1,000 as a capital gain dividend and get a $350 credit on your return for the tax paid by the fund. You also get to increase the tax basis of your fund shares by the $650 difference between the $1,000 capital gain you reported and the $350 credit you claimed.

Now you have all the information that you need to tackle your 2003 Schedule D.

Part 1, Lines 1–7a and b: Short-Term Capital Gains and Losses — Assets Held One Year or Less

Line 1 should be a breeze if you fine-tuned your form skills in the preceding General Motors example. Now you use your own short-term financial gains and losses as examples and complete the columns for line 1. If you have more than four items, you can list more on Schedule D-1.

Only make an entry in column (g) in this part of the form if the gain or loss occurred after May 5, 2003; leave this column blank if you have a gain from the sale of a collectible or real estate, even if the gain occurred after May 5, 2003.

Line 2: Enter your short-term totals, if any, from Schedule D-1, Line 2

Why is Schedule D-1 needed? Because line 1 has space for only four trades. If you had more, enter them on Schedule D-1, add them all up, and enter the total sales price from Schedule D-1 in column (d) of this line. Enter the profit or the <loss> that you computed on Schedule D-1 in column (f) on this line as well.

Line 3: Total short-term sales price amounts

Follow the instructions. Add column (d) of lines 1 and 2. Why? The IRS wants to compare the stock trades that you're reporting with the trades that your broker said you made and reported to the IRS on Form 1099-B.

Line 4: Short-term gain from Form 6252, and short-term gain or <loss> from Forms 4684, 6781, and 8824

All these form numbers! Because these forms rarely apply to most people, you may as well use them to play the lottery. Seriously, most people are going to deal with only **Form 4684, Casualties and Theft,** at some specific point in their lives. We cover this form in Chapter 9.

For those of you who are curious, **Form 6252** is for installment sales, **Form 8824** is for like-kind exchanges, and **Form 6781** is for commodity straddles. You can find more on Form 6252 later in this chapter; if the other two forms apply to you, we suggest that you consult a tax advisor. Enter the short-term gains or losses from these forms on line 4 of Schedule D.

Line 5: Net short-term gain or <loss> from partnerships, S Corporations, estates, and trusts from Schedule (s) K-1

Short-term gains or losses from a partnership, an S Corporation, an estate, or a trust are reported on a schedule called a K-1. On line 5, enter the short-term gain or loss as indicated on the K-1 (short-term gains and losses only; long-term gains and losses go to line 12). See line 4 of the K-1 for the information that goes on this line.

Line 6: Short-term capital loss carryover

If you had more short-term losses than gains in previous years, the balance is called a *carryover.* If your short-term losses exceeded your long-term gains, you're allowed to deduct up to $3,000 of those losses against your other income and carry over the balance to future years. If you have no gains next year, you may deduct $3,000 on next year's Schedule D. You can keep carrying over losses until they're used up. For example, suppose that you had a $10,000 short-term loss in 2002 and no long-term gains or losses. You were allowed to write off $3,000 in 2002, and the $7,000 balance you are allowed to carry over to 2003 is entered on line 6.

Lines 7a and b: Net short-term gain or <loss>

On line 7a, combine lines 1 through 5 in column (g) and enter the total. If the result produces a loss, enter -0-.

On line 7b, combine lines 1 through 6 in column (f) and enter the total. Just a little more addition and subtraction to make your day complete.

Part II, Lines 8–16: Long-Term Capital Gains and Losses — Assets Held More than One Year

You want long-term capital gains because the government taxes them at lower rates.

Line 8: Columns (a), (b), (c), (d), (e), (f), and (g)

As you did in Part I, fill in the columns for your long-term gains and losses. Schedule D-1 is available to list all your trades in case you had more than can fit on line 8 of this form.

When you leave column (g) blank, you inform the IRS that either the old 8, 10, or 20 maximum rates apply to the gain reported in column (f). If you make an entry in column (g), you're telling the IRS that the reduced capital gains rates of 5 or 15 percent apply to the gain in column (f). Don't enter post-May 5, 2003, column (f) gains or losses from the sale of collectibles or real estate in column (g).

When estates or heirs sell property that they inherited, they automatically get the long-term rate.

Line 9: Enter your long-term totals, if any, from Schedule D-1, Line 9

Just like you did on line 2 for short-term gains or losses, enter the totals of your long-term gains or losses from Schedule D-1 here. The total sales price goes in column (d). Enter your gain or <loss> in column (f) and the amount of your gain or loss from column (f), but not gains from collectibles and real estate, in column (g). This column (g) is important because it lets the IRS know whether your capital gain is subject to the 15 percent rate or the 5 percent rate (if you're in the 10 or 15 percent tax brackets).

Line 10: Total long-term sales price amounts

Add column (d) of lines 8 and 9. The IRS compares this figure to determine whether you reported all the sales that your broker reported to the IRS. If this number doesn't agree with what your broker reported on Form 1099-B, you can expect to hear from the IRS in about 12 months that you didn't report all your sales and that you owe additional tax and interest.

Line 11: Gain from Form 4797, Part 1; long-term gain from Forms 2439 and 6252; and long-term gain or <loss> from Forms 4684, 6781, and 8824

Here are some more lottery numbers. Everything that we said in our discussion of line 4 applies here — plus **Form 2439, Notice to Shareholder of Undistributed Capital Gains,** and **Form 4797, Sales of Business Property.**

If you received a Form 2439, don't overlook the tax benefits that you're entitled to in the section on mutual funds in this chapter.

Form 4797, Sales of Business Property

The odds of having to complete any of those other nasty forms thankfully are small. But just in case you sell a business property, such as a building or an office copier, and have to deal with Form 4797, here are some tips to help you get through that form.

First of all, you should know that the reason for a separate form is that the tax treatment of this type of sale is extremely complex. So what's new? Long-term gains can be taxed as low as 5 percent, 8 percent, 10 percent, 20 percent, 25 percent, or 28 percent, (depending on your tax bracket and the type of asset and whether it was sold on or after May 6, 2003, or before that date) instead of at the regular rates, which can be as high as 35 percent. The government believes that the new maximum rates are too good of a deal — many taxpayers were claiming a depreciation deduction on the real estate they owned, and having any gain when they sold the property taxed at the lower capital gains rate. So the maximum rate for the part of the profit equal to the depreciation deducted through the years is taxed at 25 percent. The balance of the profit is taxed at 15 or 20 percent (or perhaps 5 percent, 8 percent, or 10 percent) depending on whether it made the May 6, 2003, cut-off.

Here's how this depreciation rule for real estate works. Say you sold a building for $400,000 that you originally paid $200,000 for. Through the years, you claimed depreciation of $100,000, which reduces your tax basis for figuring your profit to $100,000. You have a $300,000 profit — $400,000 minus your cost ($200,000) reduced by your depreciation ($100,000). Of the $300,000 profit, the $100,000, representing deductions that you took for depreciation, is taxed at 25 percent, and the $200,000 balance is taxed at either 15 or 20 percent, depending on whether the sale took place before May 6, 2003, or on or after that date (a portion of the $200,000 may even be taxed at 5 percent, 8 percent, or 10 percent, if your taxable income after subtracting the $300,000 profit places you in the 10 or 15 percent bracket). And you thought being Donald Trump was easy.

If you think *this* sounds complicated, you need to remember that this is the rule for real estate that you started to depreciate after 1986. For depreciation claimed before 1987, part is taxed at the regular rate and part at 25 percent. Which part? See a tax professional.

The previous example explains why Form 4797 was invented. Generally, if you sell a business asset for a profit, the part of the gain that equals the depreciation deductions that you took through the years isn't taxed as a capital gain; it's taxed at your regular tax rate. The rule is worth repeating. With real estate, the part of the profit relating to the depreciation that you claimed is taxed at 25 percent. For all other property, depreciation is taxed at whatever your tax bracket is. To make this calculation, first you must figure out your tax basis of the property. Your basis is the price that you paid minus the total depreciation that you've taken over the years.

For example, suppose that you purchased machinery for $10,000 and that you used it in your business. In the three years that you owned it, you took depreciation deductions totaling $7,120. This step reduces your tax basis to $2,880 ($10,000 cost – $7,120 depreciation). Then you figure your profit. Your profit is the price that you sold the property for minus your tax basis. The next step is to figure out what part of that profit is to be taxed at regular rates and what part is to be taxed at capital gains tax rates. This procedure is known as *depreciation recapture* — IRS jargon for getting taxed at regular tax rates (as opposed to the capital gains tax rates) on the part of the profit that equals the depreciation deductions that you took in previous years. Any amount of profit that's left over is taxed at the capital gains tax rates.

Perhaps you sold that same machinery (in the preceding example) for $5,880. Your profit is $3,000 ($5,880 sale price – $2,880 tax basis). You then subtract the depreciation deductions that you took ($3,000 – $7,120 = –$4,120). If you come up with a negative number, the full profit ($3,000) is taxed at your regular tax rate. On the other hand, if you sold the machinery for $11,000, your profit would be $8,120 ($11,000 sale price – $2,880 tax basis). Subtract the amount of depreciation that you claimed ($8,120 profit – $7,120 depreciation = $1,000). The $7,120 (the amount of depreciation that you claimed) is taxed at your regular tax rate, and the $1,000 that's left over is taxed as a long-term capital gain (if you owned the machinery for more than one year).

For the purposes of depreciation, business property is divided into two types:

- Auto, business equipment, and machinery
- Real estate

All the depreciation deducted in the first category is recaptured if the property is sold at a gain. For real estate, depreciation is recaptured if there's a profit when it's sold, depending on whether you started to depreciate it before 1981 or between 1982 and 1986. Real estate that you started to depreciate after 1986 isn't subject to the recapture rules (taxed at regular rates). The depreciation is taxed at 25 percent. The depreciation recapture rules don't apply to business property sold at a loss. The loss is deductible from your income without limitation. The part of the profit that's recaptured and taxed at your regular tax rate is carried over from Form 4797 to Form 1040 (line 14). The long-term capital gain portion is carried over from Form 4797 to Schedule D (line 11). Use the long-term capital gain worksheet in Chapter 8 (in "Line 41: Tax") to make sure that you don't overpay.

This stuff may be more than you care to know about the sale of business property. But before you even contemplate the sale of business property, seek advice. If the amount involved is large, make sure that you get the best advice possible. See Chapter 2 for information about how to pick a good tax specialist.

Form 6252, Installment Sale Income

Here's the story on **Form 6252, Installment Sale Income.** Suppose that you sold a parcel of land for $60,000 in 2003. You paid $15,000 for it and will receive $10,000 in 2003 — and $10,000 a year for the next five years. You don't report the $45,000 profit that you made in 2003. You report a percentage of the profit as each installment is received.

You report the $10,000 that you receive every year on Form 6252, but you pay tax on only $7,500 of it, or 75 percent of what you received. (Your $45,000 profit is 75 percent of your $60,000 selling price.) The $2,500 that you don't pay tax on is the recovery of your cost. The $7,500 profit that you owe tax on is transferred to Schedule D.

When an asset is sold under an arrangement where the payments are made in installments, the date that the payments are *received* governs whether the new capital gain rates apply — not the date of the sale. For example, say you made an installment sale in 2002. Any payments received after May 5, 2003, are eligible for the reduced 5 or 15 percent rates.

Additionally, you can elect out of the installment method and report the entire gain in the year of sale. You may want to go this way if you have a great deal of itemized deductions that would be wasted because they're more than your income (or if you're in an Alternative Minimum Tax situation). See line 42, Chapter 8, for more about this tax.

The "Accounting Method Stuff (F–H)" in Chapter 11 contains the new rules regarding the reporting of capital gains on the *installment method*. The installment method can't be used for sales of merchandise to customers. And, if you charge an unrealistically low rate of interest on the sale, the IRS will impute a rate of interest equal to the *Applicable Federal Rate* (AFR) that it publishes monthly on its Web site. Say you make a sale of $100,000 that's due in one year and you don't charge the buyer interest when the AFR should have been 5 percent. The IRS will recast the sale as follows: $5,000 will be considered interest, and $95,000 will be considered the amount of the sale that qualifies as a capital gain.

If you have more deductions than income, you'll waste those excess deductions. Don't throw them out like you do with the garbage. For example, say that you have $10,000 in salary income, and personal exemptions and itemized deductions come to $55,000. You could report another $45,000 of income before you have to pay a dime in tax. So reporting all the income from an installment sale in the year of the sale would make sense in this example.

Line 12: Net long-term gain or <loss> from partnerships, S Corporations, estates, and trusts from Schedule(s) K-1

Line 12 is similar to line 5. You report any long-term gains and losses, as indicated on Schedule K-1, from partnerships, S Corporations, estates, and trusts on line 12. We discuss these entities in Chapter 13. See line 4 of the K-1 for the information that goes on this line.

Line 13: Capital gain distributions

Mutual fund distributions are reported on Form 1099-DIV, boxes 2a–2f. Capital gain distributions received from a partnership, an S Corporation, or an estate or trust are reported on a schedule called a K-1. You enter these distributions on line 13.

Say that you have two capital dividends — one for $800 and one for $200 that is subject to the 28 percent maximum rate. Enter $1,000 in column (f) and $800 in column (g), if the $800 was also entered box 2b of Form 1099-DIV. This lets the IRS know that, of the $1,000 gain, $800 can't be taxed at a rate higher than 15 percent or perhaps 5 percent. Enter the $200 along with the rest of your 28 percent gains on line 20 of Schedule D, Page 2.

If all you have are capital gain distributions from mutual funds and no other capital gains or losses, you can skip Schedule D. If you qualify under this rule, tally all your capital gain distributions and enter the total on lines 13a and b of Form 1040, which is titled "Capital gain or (loss)." See lines 13a and b in Chapter 8 on how to capture the information in boxes 2a and b from Form 1099-DIV. Also check the box to the left of line 13 instructing you that Schedule D is not required. Also, see line 41 in Chapter 8 to make sure you don't overpay your capital gains tax.

Line 14: Long-term capital loss carryover

Enter your long-term capital losses that you couldn't deduct in previous years because you didn't have any capital gains in those years on this line. "Line 6: Short-term capital loss carryover" explains how to handle carryovers.

Line 15: Combine lines 8–14 in column (g)

Just follow the instructions. Add lines 8–14 in column (g). It couldn't be easier, and besides, you're almost finished. If you have gains in column (g) line 15, enter the total of these gains in column (g). Remember, column (g) is for capital gains that took effect after May 5, 2003. If the total of these lines produces a loss, enter -0-.

Line 16: Net long-term gain or <loss>

Combine the amounts from lines 8–14 in column (f). The addition and subtraction never seem to end.

Part III, Lines 17–20: Summary of Parts I and II

Hey, this part should be easy, right?

Line 17a: Combine lines 7b and 16

If this line is a loss, enter -0- on line 17b and enter the <loss> on line 18. If it's a gain, enter the gain on Form 1040, line 13a.

Line 17b: Combine lines 7a and 15

If the result is a loss, enter -0-.

Line 18: Capital losses

If your capital losses exceed your capital gains as reported on line 17a of Schedule D, you can deduct up to $3,000 of that loss ($1,500 if you're married and filing separately) from your other income. Any remaining loss after deducting the $3,000 is carried over to the next year and applied to capital gains. If you don't have any gains in 2004, you can deduct $3,000 in 2004 and carry any remaining balance over to future years, until you use up the loss.

For example, you and your spouse sold securities in 2003 that resulted in a capital loss of $7,000. You had no other capital transactions. On your joint 2003 return, you can deduct $3,000. You can carry over the unused part of the loss — $4,000 ($7,000 – $3,000) — to 2004. If your capital loss had been only $2,000, your capital loss deduction would have been $2,000 for 2003. You would have no carryover to 2004.

Note: Capital losses can't be carried over after a taxpayer's death. They're deductible only on the decedent's final income tax return. The capital loss limits ($3,000 a year) apply in this situation, too. A decedent's estate or heirs can't deduct his or her unused capital loss.

Lines 19 and 20

Remember all the cautions about your gains or losses from the sale of collectibles and real estate that you entered in column (f), Parts I and II on Page 2, about not entering them again in column (g)? Line 19 is where you should record them. So make that entry now. Enter the depreciation portion of the gain that's recaptured when real estate is sold (see **Form 4797, Sales of Business Property** at the beginning of the chapter) on line 19. Page D-6 of your 1040 instruction booklet has a worksheet on how to compute the amount that you have to plunk down on line 19.

On line 20, enter the gain on the sale of collectibles.

If you have an entry on either line 19 or 20, you can't use Part IV of Schedule D to compute your maximum capital gains tax. Instead, the IRS refers you to a 51-line worksheet on page D-10 of your 1040 instruction booklet. If you find yourself in this predicament, see a tax professional.

Don't overpay your capital gains tax

You can end up paying more than the maximum tax rate for long-term capital gains if you're not careful. If this occurs, your only defense is whether the computer at the IRS picks up on it, recomputes your tax, and sends you a refund. But if the computer is lazy, that may not happen. If you discover that you made an error in paying this tax on a prior year's return, see Chapter 19 for information on how to file an amended return and get a refund.

So if you don't want to pay more than the 5, 8, 10, 15, 20, 25, or 28 percent rates on your long-term gains, check to see whether your taxable income for your filing status is more than the amounts shown in Tables 8-1 and 8-2 in Chapter 8, line 41. If your income is more than the amounts in these tables, you'll overpay your capital gains tax unless you use the appropriate worksheet in Table 8-1 or Table 8-2. You compute your tax on line 41.

If you don't use the worksheets in either Table 8-1 or Table 8-2, you'll overpay the tax on your capital gain.

The 8 percent rate

If your taxable income, without your taxable gain, places you in the 10- or 15-percent bracket, and you owned the asset that you sold before May 6, 2003, for more than five years, the part of the gain that normally would be taxed at 10 or 15 percent if the gain were treated as ordinary income is taxed at 8 percent. Table 8-2 in Chapter 8 provides an example of how this works.

This should really be titled *old law,* because this rate on assets held more than five years only applies if the sale took place before May 6, 2003. After May 5, 2003, the five-year holding period rule no longer applies. Now only the five percent capital gain rate applies for taxpayers in the 10 or 15 percent tax brackets.

The new 5 percent rate that took effect regarding sales of appreciate investments after May 5, 2003, offers a unique tax savings opportunity for a parent, for example, to give an investment to a child and have the child make the sale. If the child is older than 14, and therefore not subject to the Kiddie Tax (see Chapter 25 and line 41 in Chapter 8), up to $28,400 of the gain may be taxed at only 5 percent. That's a tax of $1,420. If, on the other hand, the parent reported the gain, the tax at the 15 percent rate would amount to $4,260. This works because the time the parent owned the stock is added to the child's ownership period when determining whether the more-than-one-year ownership requirement has been met in order to be considered a long-term capital gain.

The 18 percent offer that evaporated

Since May 6, 2003, this rate no longer exists. When the maximum rate for most was 20 percent, a special 18 percent rate applied to investments purchased after December 31, 2000, that were held for five years. Because of the five-year holding period and the fact that the property had to have been purchased or deemed purchased after 2000, this rate wouldn't have kicked in until 2006.

We warned our readers that holding an investment for five years so they could shave their capital gains tax on a potential profit by 2 percentage points was risky business.

In 2001, the IRS made taxpayers an offer we advised the readers of *Taxes For Dummies* to reject. It concerned investments owned as of January 1, 2001. Taxpayers could have elected to treat the investment as being sold and repurchased on that date. Doing so enabled them to start the clock running on the five-year holding period for any asset owned on January 1, 2001. But there was a hitch. They had to pay tax on any appreciation as of January 1, 2001, but losses on this deemed sale and repurchase were not deductible. Those who accepted the offer paid tax at the rate of 20 percent, which is now 15 percent, on their paper profit as of December 31, 2000, even if they didn't cash in their investment.

Now for an even sadder part of the tale: Some saw this provision as a loophole to receive a tax benefit by realizing a gain on the deemed sale and repurchase that they wouldn't have to pay tax on. Say a married couple paid $500,000 for their home that was worth $1 million on January 1, 2001. Their scheme was built around the exemption from tax on the first $500,000 of profit on the sale of a principal residence that is allowed couples filing jointly. No tax would have to be paid and their home would now have a tax basis of $1 million in computing the gain on any future sale (the original cost of $500,000 and the $500,000 deemed profit on January 1, 2001, that they thought would be exempt from tax). You guessed it. They thought wrong. The $500,000 ended up being taxable, and they couldn't file an amended return to undo what they did. Some people with tax shelter losses that couldn't currently be deducted also tried the same deemed sale and repurchase scheme. Early in 2002, Congress, retroactive to 2001, slammed the door on this maneuver.

Using Schedule D When You Sell Your Home

A married couple can exclude up to $500,000 of the profit they make on the sale of their home. A single person is entitled to a $250,000 exclusion from the capital gains tax.

To qualify:

- You or your spouse must have owned the residence within two of the past five years, and both of you must have used it as your primary residence for two out of the past five years; a vacation home can't meet this test.

- If you're single, the two-year ownership-and-use rule also applies; you must have owned and used the residence as your primary residence for two of the past five years.

Here's how the two-out-of-the-past-five-years rule works. The look-back starts on the date of the sale. For example, suppose that you sold your home on July 1, 2003. Between July 1, 1998, and July 1, 2003, you must have owned and used your home as your principal residence for any two years during this period. The periods don't have to be consecutive as long as they add up to two years.

Say you shuttle between two residences, one in New Jersey and one in Florida, the one that you use most of the time will ordinarily be considered your primary residence. Where it's a close call, the IRS looks at these factors to determine which residence is the primary one:

- The taxpayer's place of employment

- Where the taxpayer's family lives most of the time

- The address listed on tax returns, driver's license, auto registration, and a voter registration card

- The mailing address for bills and correspondence

- The location of the taxpayer's religious institutions and recreational clubs he or she is a member of

- Location of the taxpayer's bank

Tips for the newly widowed, married, or divorced

The ownership and use as a primary residence includes the period that a deceased spouse used and owned the residence.

The exclusion is available on an individual basis, which means that the $250,000 exclusion is available for the qualifying principal residence of each spouse for those who file jointly but live apart — not an uncommon arrangement these days. If you should marry someone who used the exclusion within the two-year period before your marriage, you're entitled to your $250,000 exclusion and vice versa.

If a residence is transferred in a divorce, the time period that the ex-spouse owned the residence is taken into account to determine whether the ownership-and-use tests have been met.

If you're a surviving spouse and owned your home jointly, your basis for the half-interest owned by your spouse is one-half of the fair market value on your spouse's date of death. (Don't let the term basis throw you. For a quick, one-sentence explanation, check out the sidebar "Property defined," earlier in this chapter.) The basis in your half-interest is one-half the tax basis of the house as computed in the next paragraph (usually the cost plus improvements).

For instance, if your home cost $200,000 and was worth $400,000 when your spouse died, your new basis is $300,000 (½ of the $200,000 cost plus ½ of the $400,000 FMV).

In community property states, when a spouse dies, the fair market value at the date of death becomes the tax basis of the entire house. So in the previous example, the surviving spouse's tax basis is $400,000 (the FMV) and not $300,000.

The $500,000/$250,000 exclusion replaces the old once-in-a-lifetime $125,000 exclusion that was available only to taxpayers over 55. Age no longer matters. In addition to raising the exclusion limits, the new provision is more generous in another way: You may use it repeatedly, but not more often than every two years.

The two-year rule is waived for both singles and couples when they have to sell their homes within two years because a new job requires them to move (the new place of employment must be 50 miles farther from the old home than the old home was from the old workplace — see the moving expense deduction in Chapter 9 for more about the 50-mile rule), they move for health reasons (it must be a specific illness and not just for general health), or they move for other unforeseen circumstances (more details in this section). The sale for health reasons must involve the health of:

- ✔ The taxpayer, his or her spouse, or the co-owner
- ✔ A member of the taxpayer's household
- ✔ Members of the taxpayer's family — children, their descendants, brothers and sisters and their descendents and their children, parents, aunts, uncles, stepchildren, stepbrothers, stepsisters, stepparents, and in-laws, as well as descendants of the taxpayer's grandparents. I bet you thought this list would never end!

Here is the official IRS list of "unforeseen circumstances":

- ✔ Death
- ✔ Divorce or legal separation
- ✔ Becoming eligible for unemployment insurance
- ✔ A change in employment that leaves you unable to pay your mortgage or basic living expenses
- ✔ Multiple births resulting from the same pregnancy
- ✔ Damage to the residence resulting from a natural or man-made disaster or an act of war or terrorism

For example, say you buy a house on August 1, 2002, for $350,000, and you sell it for $550,000 on August 1, 2003 (if we're going to make up a story, why not make it a good one?), because you're moving from New York to Los Angeles to start a new job. You're single. Because you owned the house for only 12 months of the required 24-month period, you're entitled to one-half of the $250,000 exclusion, or $125,000. That means that only $75,000 of your $200,000 profit is subject to tax.

The $500,000/$250,000 exclusion may have given you the idea that, because of the increased exclusion amount, you no longer have to keep records of your purchases or improvements. Although this premise may be true for many people, it doesn't necessarily apply to everyone. Suppose that you're single and buy a house for $300,000. Because you don't know what you'll sell the house for in 20 years, you'd better hang on to the receipts for any improvements that you paid for. Suppose that you sell your house for $600,000 — a $300,000 profit — but you're entitled to only a $250,000 exclusion. Good records can help you reduce the profit even further.

The sale of vacant land adjacent to a principal residence qualifies for the $250,000/$500,000 exclusion if it's used as part of the principal residence. This is so even if the land is sold separately, as long as the land sale occurs within the 2-year period before or after the sale of the dwelling place. Say the land was sold in 2002, and the dwelling was sold in 2003. Because the adjacent land had to be reported on your 2002 return, you have to file an amended return for 2002 if the sale of the land and the dwelling are less than the exclusion. You are entitled to obtain a refund for the tax you paid on the land in 2002.

Computing your profit

Computing the profit on the sale of your home is simple.

From the sales price, subtract the following expenses in connection with the sale:

- ✔ Real estate broker's commission
- ✔ Attorney fees
- ✔ Title closing costs
- ✔ Advertising costs

From the sales price after the expenses of the sale, subtract the following:

- ✔ Original cost of your castle
- ✔ Closing costs and attorney fees at the time of purchase
- ✔ Improvements

What constitutes an improvement? Anything that adds to the value of your house or prolongs its life. Drapery rods, Venetian blinds, termite proofing, and shrubbery all fit the bill. If you own a condo or co-op, your cost basis also includes special assessments to improve the building, such as renovating the lobby or installing a new heating system. Co-op owners get an additional boost, because the part of their maintenance charges that goes to paying off the co-op's mortgage also is added to their cost.

From your profit, subtract the exclusion that you're entitled to. If you're single, it's $250,000; for couples, it's $500,000. If this exclusion exceeds your profit, you can stop right there because there's nothing more to do. You need not report the sale on your return; the entire profit is tax-free. If your profit exceeds the exclusion, you owe tax and have to report the sale on Schedule D. For example, your profit is $410,000, and you're entitled to only a $250,000 exclusion. You have to report the sale and pay tax on $160,000.

On the other hand, if your profit is $410,000 and you're entitled to a $500,000 exclusion, you need not report the sale on your return.

If you have a loss, it isn't deductible. Profits above the exclusion amounts are. We're sure that you've heard this before: "Heads, they win; tails, you lose."

You can find an excellent worksheet in the IRS Publication 523 *(Selling Your Home)* that can guide you through your profit computation. This publication also has a nifty list of examples of the types of improvements that increase the tax basis of a home. So don't overlook it.

Reporting a profit that exceeds the exclusion

You report the sale of your residence on Schedule D only if the profit exceeds the exclusion you're entitled to.

Normally, the purchaser (typically via the title company) reports the sale on **Form 1099-S, Proceeds from Real Estate Transactions.** If you're single and the sale is for $250,000 — or $500,000 or less for couples — and you meet the other requirements such as the two-year principal residence test, you can sign a certificate at the time of the sale so that a Form 1099-S doesn't have to be sent to the IRS.

Here's how you compute the profit on the sale of your home and report the profit on Schedule D if you are required to:

1. **Figure your tax basis by adding your original cost, closing costs, and cost of improvements.**

2. **Compute your net selling price.**

   That's your selling price less your selling and closing expenses.

3. **Subtract your tax basis from your net selling price.**

For example, you sold your home for $610,000. Your closing costs were $10,000, and the original cost of your home plus improvements and closing costs was $400,000.

Congratulations, you made a $200,000 profit ($610,000 – $10,000 – $400,000). If you're single or married, you don't have to report the profit on Schedule D, because your exclusion ($250,000 for singles or $500,000 if married) exceeds your profit.

If your profit exceeds your exclusion, you have to report the profit on Schedule D. Here's how you do it. Report the entire gain on line 8, filling out columns (a) through (f). Because you qualify for the exclusion, enter it on the line directly below the line where you reported the gain. Write `Section 121 exclusion` in column (a) and the amount of the exclusion in column (f) as a loss (in parentheses). For example, $250,000 is written as `<$250,000>` in column (f). If you are married, enter `<$500,000>`. If the sale occurred after May 5, 2003, enter the amount of the profit in column (g) as well as the ($250,000 or $500,000) exclusion amount. This informs the IRS that the maximum capital gain tax on the sale is at the 15 percent rate. If the sale took place prior to May 6, 2003, leave column (g) blank. Leaving this column blank means the sale is subject to the 20 percent rate.

If you used part of your home as an office or rented out your home, the exclusion doesn't apply to any depreciation that you claimed after May 6, 1997. For example, if you claimed $10,000 in depreciation after May 6, 1997, and you're entitled to a $500,000 exclusion and the gain on the sale of your home is $400,000, you can exclude only $390,000 of that gain. You owe tax on the $10,000 of depreciation claimed after May 6, 1997.

Following the home office and rental rules

Under the old rule, the IRS considered a taxpayer's home sale (where the home was partially used for business) the sale of two pieces of property — the portion used as the residence that qualified for the $250,000 or $500,000 exclusion, and the portion used for business that didn't. For example, if someone used 20 percent of his or her home for business and then sold the home at a $150,000 profit, $30,000 would be considered the sale of business property that has to be reported on **Form 4797, Sales of Business Property** and would be taxed. The remaining $120,000 would be considered the gain on the sale of a principal residence that is exempt from tax because it is less than the exclusion. At the end of 2002, the IRS had a change of heart!

Under the new rule, only the depreciation claimed after May 6, 1997, is taxable. The rest of the profit on the sale is eligible for the $250,000/$500,000 exclusion. You report the depreciation on **Form 4797, Sales of Business Property,** and carry it over to line 11 of Schedule D. This profit is subject to the 25 percent maximum capital gains tax, even if it occurred after May 5, 2003.

If under the old rule you paid tax on the part of the profit from the sale of your in-home office, file an amended return and get your money back (see Chapter 19 to find out how to file an amended return).

If the portion of your home that's used for business is separate from the dwelling unit, the new rule doesn't apply, and you are to considered to have sold two parcels: the business portion, which is taxable, and the residence, which is eligible for the exclusion. The clearest example of this is of a townhouse with a finished basement that you convert into a separate unit and close off by removing the interior stairway that leads to the rest of the house.

Use Schedule D for Other Issues Involving Stocks (Worthless and Otherwise)

You can use Schedule D to handle such issues as worthless securities, wash sales, stock options, stock for services, and appreciated employer securities.

Worthless securities

Suppose that you felt certain that Company X was going to make a comeback, so you invested $15,000. But you were wrong. Not only has Company X failed to make this comeback, but its shares are no longer even being quoted in the morning paper.

Great! So at least $15,000 is a write-off, right? No. The problem with this scenario is that you must be able to prove — with an identifiable event — that your investment is in fact *completely worthless.* Being partially worthless won't cut it. In one case, bondholders in a company canceled 30 percent of the face value of their bonds to keep the company afloat. But they couldn't deduct the portion of the debt they canceled because their investment hadn't become completely worthless. Likewise, the fact that the shares of a company are no longer being quoted doesn't make them worthless.

We wish that we could tell you that convincing the IRS that you're entitled to write off your $15,000 investment is as easy as losing it. It's not — and this is an area of the law that's more confusing than most. You may think that bankruptcy, going out of business, liquidation, the appointment of a receiver, or insolvency indicates that your investment no longer had any value. But these events only prove that the company is in financial trouble, not that its shareholders won't receive anything in liquidation. In order to claim a deduction for worthless securities, your investment must be completely worthless.

When is an investment worthless? As a general rule, you can say that an investment is worthless when a company is so hopelessly insolvent that it ceases doing business or it goes into receivership, leaving nothing for its stockholders. If you're not sure, one source worth checking is CCH Incorporated (which also does the technical editing of this book). This outfit publishes an annual list of worthless securities as part of its "Capital Changes Reports." Most major brokerage firms and public libraries subscribe to this service, or you can reach the company directly at 800-TELL-CCH (800-835-5224).

If proving when unmarketable shares in a company actually became worthless is so difficult, why not lock in a loss by finding some accomplice — the broker who sold them to you, for example — to take the shares off your hands for a penny apiece? Nice try, but no go. A number of taxpayers have attempted to "structure sales" in this fashion, but both the IRS and the Tax Court have denied the losses because these sales weren't considered legitimate. Instead, the taxpayers were told to hang on to their investments and deduct them only when they became certifiably worthless. In other words, they were back to square one.

Securities that became worthless in a given tax year are considered to have become worthless on the last day of that year and reported in the short-term section of Schedule D. Enter your cost and -0- for the sales price because the investment is worthless. So, as you can see, Schedule D has a few other handy uses as well.

Wash sales

Suppose that you own a stock that has declined in value. You think that it will recover, but you want to deduct the money that you lost. If you sell the stock and buy back the shares within 30 days of the sale, you can't deduct the loss. This type of trade is called a *wash sale*. The loss can't be deducted in the year of the trade. The loss is deducted when you sell the new shares.

Here is an example of how the wash sale rule works. You paid $15,000 for a stock that has declined in value to $6,000. You sell it incurring a $9,000 loss. Unfortunately this has been happening a lot these days. The stock starts to rebound. Isn't that what usually happens and you get that loving feeling that it is going to stage a comeback? Two weeks later you buy the stock back for $7,000. You can't deduct your $9,000 loss, because you sold and repurchased shares of the same company within a 30-day period. Your $9,000 loss is added to the $7,000 you paid for the new shares. $16,000 is now the cost you use to determine any gain or loss when the new shares are sold.

Small business stock

You can deduct up to $50,000 ($100,000 if filing jointly) of a loss from the sale, or from worthlessness of *small business stock* (more commonly called "Code Section 1244 stock"). A corporation qualifies as a "1244 corp." if at the time its stock is issued, the amount of money it receives does not exceed $1 million. That means if you are married and sustained a $150,000 "1244 loss," you can deduct $100,000 from your income. The $100,000 loss is computed on Form 4794, line 10. The $100,000 is then carried over to line 14 of Form 1040 as a negative number. The $50,000 balance is considered a capital loss and is entered on Schedule D. How do you know whether the company you invested in is a "1244 corp."? Find out before you put up your dough. But, if you are reading about this for the first time, track down the company's accountant or attorney. You must be the original owner of the shares. Additional contributions of capital do not qualify as "Section 1244 stock."

Stock options

Stock options usually come in two varieties: *statutory options,* which have to meet certain IRS rules to qualify for special tax advantages, and *nonstatutory stock options,* which are also subject to special rules even though the tax savings aren't as great. Statutory stock options include incentive stock options and options under an employee stock purchase plan.

Incentive stock options (ISOs)

You aren't subject to tax when an *incentive stock option* is granted. You realize income or loss only when you sell the stock that you acquired by exercising the ISO.

You must exercise the option within 10 years from the date that it was granted. The option price has to be at least equal to the value of the stock on the day that the option was granted. For example, you can't receive an option to buy shares for $10 a share when the shares are selling for $18 a share. In any one year, you can't receive an option to buy shares that are worth more than $100,000 on the date that the option was granted. If you go over $100,000, the excess isn't considered an ISO, so read on until you get to the section "Nonstatutory stock options."

When you sell stock that you acquired by exercising an ISO, you have a long-term capital gain if you held the shares for more than one year from the date when you exercised the option and more than two years after the ISO was granted. For example, say you exercise an option for $15,000. You later sell the shares for $25,000. You have a long-term capital gain of $10,000 if you meet the one- and two-year rules. If you don't meet these rules, the $10,000 gain is divided into two parts. The difference between the exercise price and the value on the day that you exercised the option is taxed as ordinary income. The difference between the value on the day that you exercised the option and the value on the day that you sold the stock is treated as a capital gain (either short- or long-term). In the previous example, if the shares were worth $20,000 on the day that you exercised the option, then $5,000 of the gain would be taxed as ordinary income, and $5,000 (the difference between the sales price, $25,000, and the $20,000 value on the day the option was exercised) is taxed as a long-term capital gain.

Although the spread between the option price and the value on the day that you exercised the option isn't subject to tax for regular tax purposes, it is subject to the fiendish Alternative Minimum Tax (AMT). So take a peek at the section about line 42 (AMT) in Chapter 8, or better yet, speak to a good tax pro.

The holding period for determining long- or short-term capital gains on shares acquired by exercising a stock option starts on the day after you exercise the option. We explain the holding period rules at the beginning of this chapter, in the sidebar "Details for figuring short term or long term."

If an ISO is transferred, say in a divorce, it loses its special tax treatment. An ISO transferred at death doesn't.

Employee stock purchase plans

Employee stock purchase plans allow you to buy your company's stock at a discount. The discount isn't taxed until you sell the shares. If you hold the shares for more than two years after the option was granted and more than one year after you acquired the shares, the discount is taxed as ordinary income, and the difference between the value on the day that you acquired the shares is a capital gain (either short- or long-term) and what you sold the shares for. For example, you sold shares for $25,000 that you had purchased under an employee plan for $16,000. On the day that the options were granted, the shares were worth $18,000. Of the $9,000 gain, $2,000 ($18,000 − $16,000) is taxed at ordinary rates, and $7,000 ($25,000 − $18,000) is taxed as a capital gain, either short- or long-term.

If you sold the shares before the end of the two-year period, substitute the value of the shares on the day that you purchased them in place of the value when the option was granted to determine the ordinary income portion of the $9,000 gain. Suppose that the value of the shares on the day that you purchased them was $20,000. Of the gain, $4,000 ($20,000 – $16,000) is taxed as ordinary income, and the $5,000 balance ($25,000 – $20,000) is taxed as a capital gain. Is there a way around these maddening rules? Hold the shares for more than two years.

Nonstatutory stock options

Because nonqualified stock options don't have to meet any IRS rules, there are no restrictions on the amount of these types of options that may be granted. If a nonstatutory stock option doesn't have an ascertainable value when it's issued (which is usually the case for options that aren't traded on a stock exchange), no income is realized when you receive the option. When you exercise the option, you're taxed on the spread. For example, you exercise a $4,000 option to purchase stock trading at $10,000; you realize ordinary income of $6,000. Your tax basis for figuring a gain or loss when you sell the shares is $10,000. If the option has an ascertainable value, the value of the option is taxed as additional salary. For example, you receive an option to buy 100 shares that you can sell for $1,000 on the day that you receive the option. The bad news: You owe tax on the $1,000. The good news: When you exercise the shares, the $1,000 is added to the cost of the shares when determining whether you have a profit or loss when you sell the shares.

Unlike an ISO, a nonstatutory stock option can be transferred tax-free in a divorce.

Options that have expired

Say you paid $1,500 in December 2002 to purchase an option to buy 1,000 shares of a stock for $60 a share that was good for 60 days, and you let the option expire in 2003 because you lost your bet when the stock never increased in value. You have a $1,500 short-term loss that you can deduct in 2003.

The reason we are warning you about this situation is because options that have expired aren't reported on the year-end tax statement that your broker is required by law to send. Only sales are reported, and consequently, many people tend to overlook this deduction. Don't be one of them.

Short sales

Not many people get involved with short sales, but we thought you should know about them. When an investor believes a stock is going to tank and wants to take advantage of that fact, he or she "shorts" the stock by selling it. How can you sell, you say, something that you don't own? You borrow the shares you sell from your broker. If you are right and the stock goes down, you can buy the stock down the road for much less than you sold it for and replace the shares you borrowed from the broker. Doesn't everybody wish they had done this before the market took a nosedive?

With a short sale, your gain or loss is reported when you buy the shares you have to return to the broker. Only, the normal rule (that you always use the trade date and not the settlement date) doesn't apply to short sales. If you made a profit, it's the trade date. If you have a loss, it's the settlement date. This rule is important at the end of the year. For example, you make a short sale and then buy the shares you are going to return to the broker on December 31, but that purchase doesn't settle until January 4. If you made a profit, you report it in 2003. A loss, on the other hand, gets reported in 2004.

If, at the end of the year, you have an open short position (you hadn't returned the shares to the broker), your year-end tax statement (remember the IRS gets a copy of it) will probably report the short sale as a regular one. Report the sale on your return so that you and the IRS are in synch. By using the sales price as your cost, you obtain the net effect of showing a zero gain or loss on your Schedule D. That way you won't be reporting any actual income, and the IRS won't start up with you by claiming you failed to report all your sales. Report the sale when you buy the shares that you owe the broker.

Short sales are considered short-term because with a short sale your holding period starts with the day you purchase the shares that you return to the broker, which usually is one day.

If your short position was open for more than 45 days, and your broker charged you for any dividends that you owed to the owner of the shares you borrowed, that charge gets deducted on line 13 of Schedule A as investment interest. See why keeping good records is so important?

Stock for services

Stock for services is taxed as additional salary or fee income if you're an independent contractor. However, special rules apply as to when you have to report the income. If the stock is subject to restrictions, you report as income the value of the stock when the restrictions are lifted. For example, a restriction may be that you have to work for the company for three years; otherwise, you forfeit the shares.

Even if the shares are subject to restrictions, you can elect to report the value of the shares as income in the year you receive them. This is known as a *Section 83(b) election.* Why would you want to do this? Say you receive shares in a start-up venture that have little value at the time you receive them. If you wait to report the value of the shares as income five years from now, when the restrictions are lifted and the shares are worth a great deal, you could be taxed at rates which currently are as high as 35 percent, or 39.6 percent when rates are scheduled to revert back to that rate in 2010, on the value at that time. On the other hand, if the shares currently are worth only a few thousand dollars, reporting the income now and paying a small amount of tax makes sense, because when you sell the shares after they've increased dramatically in value, the profit will be subject to the maximum 15 percent (or perhaps the lower 5 percent) capital gain rate. Remember, such a tactic is a gamble. If the company goes bust, you'll have paid tax on shares that ended up being worthless, but you will have a worthless stock deduction for the amount of income you paid tax on when you made the Section 83(b) election.

Appreciated employer securities

Many taxpayers overlook a special rule that applies when shares of the company where they work are distributed to them as part of a lump-sum distribution from a retirement plan. The value of the shares isn't subject to tax at the time you receive them. Only the cost of the shares when they were purchased is. For example, shares of your employer's stock that you bought through your employer's retirement plan for $50,000 now are worth $200,000. Only the $50,000 is subject to tax when you receive the shares. If you sell the shares the following year for $225,000, you have to report a $175,000 capital gain that year.

If you don't hold the shares for more than one year, part of the gain is taxed as a short-term sale. In the previous example, if you didn't hold the shares for more than a year after they were distributed, $25,000 of the gain is short-term, and $150,000 is long-term. The difference between the cost and the value on the day that they were distributed is treated as long-term ($200,000 – $50,000), and the difference between the sales price and the value on the date of distribution is short-term ($225,000 – $200,000).

Using Schedule D for Nonbusiness Bad Debts

Suppose that you lent your best friend $2,500 on New Year's Eve, and you haven't seen him since New Year's Day. All is not lost. You can deduct the $2,500. This news comes as a surprise to many people, because you can usually deduct losses only on investment and business transactions. But you must be able to prove that a valid debt existed, that the debt is worthless, and that you previously paid tax on the money that you lent.

- ✔ **What is worthless?** As with securities, there must be some identifiable event — such as bankruptcy, legal action, or the disappearance of the debtor — to prove that you can't collect what you're owed. You don't necessarily have to sue the debtor or even threaten to take legal action. This is one of the few instances where the IRS is on your side, not your lawyer's!

- ✔ **The right to sue:** To prove that you have a valid debt, you should be able to show that you have a right to sue. This situation creates a special problem with loans to family members. The IRS tends to view such loans as gifts. So if you had your brother sign a promissory note and put up collateral when you lent him money, you could prevail if the IRS ever questioned whether it was a valid debt. Yet, as you probably know, most dealings between family members are done a little more casually than that. See Chapter 10 for more on this painful subject.

- ✔ **Is the debt deductible?** Finally, to establish that a debt is deductible, you must have paid tax on what you lent. Suppose that you worked in a local bookstore in anticipation of being paid later. The bookstore went out of business, and you weren't paid. Sorry. Because you never received the bookstore income and didn't report it on your tax return, you're not entitled to a deduction if it's not paid.

You deduct nonbusiness bad debts on good old Schedule D as a short-term loss, regardless of how long the money was owed. If you don't have capital gains to offset the deduction, you can deduct up to $3,000 of the loss and carry over the balance to next year, just like with other investment losses. Additionally, you must attach a statement to your return explaining the nature of the debt, name of the debtor and any business or family relationship, date the debt became due, efforts made to collect the debt, and reason for determining that the debt is entirely worthless (only business debts can generate a deduction if they're partially worthless).

Don't confuse nonbusiness bad debts with business-related bad debts that can be deducted on your business tax returns. Refer Chapter 11.

Day traders

There are tax advantages to being considered a trader rather than a mere investor. Vast sums, however, have been lost day trading and the tax impact has been significant (see Chapter 23 for more on investing and taxes). Most people are investors because they purchase securities they hold for a long time in anticipation the investment will appreciate in value and produce income (dividends). An investor reports gains and losses on Schedule D. If losses exceed gains, they are limited to an annual deductible of $3,000 with a lifetime to carryover to future years to offset gains. Investment expenses are deducted as miscellaneous itemized deductions. A home office deduction isn't allowed no matter how much time investors spend analyzing their investments because they're not carrying on a trade or business.

A trader, on the other hand, typically tries to capture short-term swings in the market. A trader reports his expenses on Schedule C and trading gains and losses on Schedule D. Traders can claim a home-office deduction because they're carrying on a trade or business. A trader can deduct all margin interest on Schedule C. Investors deduct theirs on Schedule A, provided it doesn't exceed their investment income. Gains aren't subject to Self-Employment Tax, nor can a deduction for a contribution to an IRA or retirement plan based on the gain be claimed, because the gain isn't considered earned income. Traders are subject to the same $3,000 annual limit on trading losses that exceed gains. The wash sale rule also applies. To be a trader, your trading has to be, in IRS jargon, "sufficiently frequent and substantial." Like so many IRS definitions it falls under the heading of, "I can't define it, but I know it when I see it." The IRS tends to take the position that you can't be a trader if you have another regular job. They like to reserve trader status for people who trade on a full-time basis to the exclusion of other activities. This is plainly wrong. You can be a part-time trader. The New York Stock Exchange defines a trader as someone who buys and sells a stock in the same trading session at least four times a week.

Mark-to-market traders

A mark-to-market trader elects to treat any stocks he or she holds at the end of the trading day on December 31 as being sold on that day. Any of these deemed gains or losses are reported on the mark-to-market trader's return. For true day traders, this requirement shouldn't be of any consequence, because they typically don't own securities at the end of any day. A position trader, on the other hand, who has an open position December 31, and who makes a mark-to-market election, loses the ability to use the year-end tax strategy of selling the losers and holding the winners. On the following January 1, a mark-to-market trader must adjust the tax bases of the securities deemed to have been sold. Gains that were reported because of the election are added to the basis of the securities held on December 31 and losses are subtracted from its basis.

A mark-to-market trader reports expenses on Schedule C and trading activity as ordinary gains and losses on Form 4797. The wash-sale rule doesn't apply to this type of trading. If net losses occur, all these losses can be used to offset other income; the $3,000 limit doesn't apply. If the losses produce a net operating loss (exceeding your other income), they can be carried back to a prior year to obtain a refund and then forward to future years. A regular trader can't do this. Because a day trader only has short-term gains, it is irrelevant that the gains are treated as ordinary income. Trading gains aren't subject to Self-Employment Tax, and no IRA or retirement deduction can be claimed.

That the gains are treated as ordinary income doesn't mean that mark-to-market traders can't have long-term capital gains taxed at the favorable lower rates. They can accomplish this by holding their investment securities in a separate account.

It's too late to make the mark-to-market election for 2003. The election has to be made a year in advance. To be effective for 2004, it has to be made on your tax return (2003) or on an extension of time to file (Form 4868) that is filed by April 15, 2004. After you make the election, it applies to all future years unless you obtain IRS permission to change. Make the election by attaching the following signed statement to your return or extension request:

```
I hereby elect to use the mark-to-market method of accounting under
Section 475(f) of the Internal Revenue Code for my trade and business
of trading securities. The first year for which this election is
effective is the taxable year beginning January 1, 2004.
```

_____(Signed)

(Your name and date)

Chapter 13

Supplemental Income and Loss: Schedule E

- -

In This Chapter

▶ Defining supplemental income

▶ Completing Schedule E

▶ Discussing tax shelter

- -

Don't let the words *supplemental income* throw you. That's just IRS-speak for the income you receive from rental property or royalties, or through partnerships, S Corporations (corporations that don't pay tax; the owners report the corporations' income or loss on their personal tax returns), trusts, and estates. To report your rental or royalty income, you use Schedule E, which is laid out in the form of a profit or loss statement (income and expenses). From your income, you subtract your expenses. The remainder is your *net income*, the income that you have to pay taxes on. If you have a loss, the rules get a little sticky as to whether you can deduct it. (Isn't that a surprise?)

Remember that if you're a self-employed taxpayer receiving royalties, such as a musician, you use Schedule C. The information in this chapter applies to people who receive royalties and are not self-employed. For example, George Gershwin received royalties from *Porgy and Bess* and reported them on Schedule C. But he has passed away, and now his heirs receive royalties that must be reported on Schedule E.

First-time authors get a break. They aren't subject to self-employment tax (Social Security tax on royalties), because being an author, at this point, isn't considered their regular line of work. Thanks to a Tax Court case, first-time authors don't become subject to self-employment tax until their particular book is revised or they start on a second one.

Part 1: Income or Loss from Rental Real Estate and Royalties

If you receive rent or royalties, you should receive Form 1099-MISC. Box 1 is for rent, and box 2 is for royalties. (Even if you rent your summer home to the Queen of England, you report your rent and royalties separately.)

Line 1: Kind and location of each real estate property

On line A, enter the location. For example: Two-family home, Albany, New York. The line provides enough room for listing three properties. If you have more than three properties, enter the additional properties on another Schedule E, but use the total column on only one Schedule E to enter the total of all the properties.

Line 2: Vacation home questions

Here, you're asked whether you used any of the properties listed on line 1a, 1b, or 1c, and for how long. For example, you may have rented out your beach home for July and August, but you used it in June and September. See the "Vacation homes" sidebar later in this chapter for information about vacation home expenses you can and can't deduct.

Lines 3–4: Income

Copy the amounts from box 1, rent, and box 2, royalties, of your 1099-MISC onto lines 3 and 4 of Schedule E.

You may wonder whether some unusual cases of rent are counted as income. Rent paid in advance, for example, is counted as rent. If you sign a lease in December 2003 and collect January's rent of $1,000, this amount is included in 2003's rent income on this schedule, even though it applies to 2004's rent. Security deposits that you must return are not rental income. And if your tenant pays you to cancel the lease, the amount you receive is rent — it isn't considered a tax-free payment for damages. Although expenses paid by the tenant are considered rental income, you're entitled to deduct those expenses. Finally, if you're a Good Samaritan and charge a relative or friend less than the fair rental value, your deductions for depreciation and maintenance expenses can't exceed the rent you collect.

Lines 5–18: Expenses

On these lines, you tabulate the amounts that you're allowed to deduct. Now don't you wish that you were a better bookkeeper? If you have good records, you can save a tidy sum. The expense lines apply to both royalties and rents.

If you rent out half of a two-family house and you occupy the other half, for example, you can deduct only 50 percent of your expenses. If it's a three-family unit and you occupy one of the units, you can deduct only 66 percent of the expenses. Get the picture? But remember that the portion of your mortgage interest and property taxes that relates to the part you occupy gets deducted on Schedule A (see Chapter 9).

Line 5: Advertising
You're allowed to deduct the cost of newspaper ads, for example, if you had to run ads to find renters for your property. The same goes if you had building signs made.

Line 6: Auto and travel
Travel to inspect your rental property is deductible. But if you live in Buffalo and go to Florida in January to inspect a vacation home that you rent out part of the time, be prepared for a battle with the IRS. Refer to the guidelines for deducting travel in Chapter 9 ("Line 20: Unreimbursed employee expenses") and your auto expenses in Chapter 11 ("Line 9: Car and truck expenses").

Line 7: Cleaning and maintenance
You can deduct your costs for cleaning and maintenance, such as your monthly fee for the window washer and your payment to the guy who tunes up your furnace before the cold weather sets in.

Line 8: Commissions

You can deduct commissions paid to a real estate broker to find a tenant. The norm is 5 percent to 10 percent.

Line 9: Insurance

We hope that you carry insurance to protect against your building burning down, lawsuits, and other perils such as floods and earthquakes. You can deduct the cost of these policies. One tricky area to be aware of is if you pay for an insurance premium that covers more than one year. In that case, you deduct only the portion of the premium that applies to each year's Schedule E. For example, suppose that in 2003 you pay a $900 premium that covers a three-year period. You deduct $300 in 2003, another $300 in 2004, and the final $300 in 2005.

Line 10: Legal and other professional fees

Legal fees incurred in the purchase of the property must be added to the cost of the building and deducted as part of your depreciation deduction (coming later). Legal fees for preparing a lease are deductible. And the part of your tax-preparation fee used to prepare this Schedule E is deductible. See line 17, Chapter 11, about having to issue Form 1099.

Line 11: Management fees

You can deduct the costs of managing the property — collecting the rent, seeing to all repairs, paying a management company (if you have one), and so on.

Line 12: Mortgage interest paid to banks (Form 1098)

This amount comes right off of **Form 1098, Mortgage Interest Statement,** which you get from the bank that holds the mortgage. The bank sends you this statement by January 31. A copy goes to the IRS so it can check whether you're deducting the correct amount.

Line 13: Other interest

If the person from whom you purchased the property provided the financing and holds a mortgage on the property, the interest is entered here because this is where the interest that wasn't paid to financial institutions goes. All the fees you paid when you took out the mortgage are deducted over the duration of the loan. You also put the interest on a second mortgage here, as well as the interest on short-term installment loans for the purchase of appliances and other assets.

Unlike with a personal residence, points and fees to obtain a mortgage on rental property aren't deductible in the year that you pay them. You must write off these amounts over the term of the loan and deduct them on this line. If you didn't receive a Form 1098, enter the interest you paid on this line.

Interest paid on an income tax bill can't be deducted. Interest on employment taxes that you were late in paying can.

Line 14: Repairs

Repairs are deductible in full. Improvements may be deducted over 27½ years for residential property and over either 31½ or 39 years, depending on when it was acquired, for commercial or nonresidential property (refer to Chapter 11 to obtain the rate of depreciation that you can claim every year). A *repair* — such as fixing a leaky roof — keeps your property in good operating condition. It doesn't materially add to the value of the property or prolong its life. An *improvement,* such as adding an entire new roof, on the other hand, adds to the property's value or prolongs its life and thus is written off over its useful life.

Line 15: Supplies

You can deduct such things as cleaning supplies, light bulbs, and small items that you buy at a hardware store.

Line 16: Taxes

This line includes real estate taxes on the property. Additionally, if you employ a superintendent or a janitor, this is where you enter the Social Security and unemployment taxes that you must pay. The bank holding the mortgage sends you an annual mortgage statement that gives you the tax information. The Social Security and unemployment taxes will be listed on your quarterly payroll tax return.

Line 17: Utilities

Why don't you just go ahead and enter your electric, gas, fuel, water, sewer, and phone costs for your property here? We would.

Line 18: Other

This is one of those catchall lines for things whose descriptions don't fit on the preceding lines, such as gardening and permits.

Lines 19–26

Add lines 5 through 18 and enter the total on line 19. Then you get to do more figuring. Read on.

Line 20: Depreciation expense or depletion (Form 4562)

The tax law allows you to claim a yearly tax deduction for depreciation. You can't depreciate land. So, for example, you can depreciate only 85 percent of your cost (because, as a rule, at least 15 percent of a building's purchase price must be allocated to land). You can make this allocation based on the assessed value for the land and the building or on a real estate appraisal. You compute your depreciation deduction on **Form 4562, Depreciation and Amortization,** and you attach this form to your 1040 only if you first started to claim a deduction for a particular item in 2003. If you started claiming depreciation on an asset in an earlier year, the form isn't required. Compute the depreciation and enter the amount here. An annual depreciation rate schedule for residential real estate is available in Chapter 11 (Table 11-11). IRS Publication 946 *(How to Depreciate Property),* has the complete depreciation schedule for commercial real estate. Also in Chapter 11 we have an abridged schedule (see Table 11-12), for commercial property, which must be depreciated over either 31½ or 39 years. We provide a detailed example of exactly how depreciation is computed.

Even though an apartment building must be depreciated over 27½ years, furniture and appliances used in the building must be depreciated over only seven years.

Line 21: Total expenses

Add lines 19 and 20 and place the total on this line.

Line 22: Income or loss from rental real estate or royalty properties

The first part is just basic arithmetic. Subtract line 21 from your income from line 3 or 4. If your number is positive, you have, as the title of Schedule E announces, supplemental income; if your total is negative, you have a loss. On line 22, you'll notice a reference to Form 6198. This refers to the wonderful at-risk rules. Don't concern yourself with these rules unless you were lucky enough to get a mortgage for which you aren't personally liable for the payments. We get to the at-risk rules on line 27.

Line 23: Deductible rental real estate loss (Form 8582)

If your real estate property showed a loss for the year (on line 22), you may not actually be able to claim that entire loss on your tax return. If you didn't show a loss, skip ahead to the next line.

Line 23 is where you enter how much of the loss on line 22 can be deducted. Rental real estate is considered a passive activity, and you normally have to complete **Form 8582, Passive Activity Loss Limitations,** to determine the portion, if any, that you're allowed to deduct. However, if you meet all the following conditions, you're spared from Form 8582 (keep your fingers crossed):

- ✔ Rental real estate is the only passive activity you're involved in. (Remember that passive activity is a business or investment where you act as a silent partner — you aren't actively involved.)

- ✔ You actively participated in making management decisions or arranged for others to provide services, such as repairs.

- ✔ Your rental real estate loss did not exceed $25,000 — or $12,500 if you're married and filing separately.

- ✔ You didn't have rental or passive activity losses that you could not deduct in a prior year.

- ✔ If you're married and filing separately, you must have lived apart from your spouse for the entire year.

- ✔ Your modified adjusted gross income (see the following worksheet) is less than $100,000 (or $50,000 if you are married and filing separately).

If you meet all six of the above criteria, congratulations, you can skip the dreaded Form 8582 and write your deductible real estate loss right here on line 23.

If you have to fill out Form 8582 to compute your rental losses on Schedule E (line 22) because your modified AGI (adjusted gross income) is more than the limit (or you were involved in other passive activities), you have to be familiar with tax-shelter and other rules that allow you to deduct up to $25,000 of losses from rental real estate that you actively manage. If Form 8582 applies to you, oh taxpayer, you need a tax advisor! *Note:* You don't necessarily need professional tax help every year, but you do need to consult with an advisor in the year that you purchase the property to make sure you understand all the tax rules that you must obey. As long as nothing monumental changes in the future, you'll do perfectly fine on your own with just *Taxes For Dummies*. If we went into the tax-shelter rules in complete detail we'd need a second volume to this book.

Worksheet to determine whether you need to use Form 8582

This little worksheet helps you compute your modified AGI so that you can determine whether it exceeds the limits that we just mentioned. If it does, off you go to Form 8582.

1. AGI from Form 1040 (line 34) $_____

2. Taxable portion of Social Security (line 20b of Form 1040) $_____

3. Subtract line 2 from line 1 $_____

4. Your IRA deductions (line 24 of Form 1040) $_____

5. Student loan interest (line 25) $_____

6. Tuition and fees deduction (line 26) $_____

7. One-half of self-employment tax (line 28 of Form 1040) $_____

8. Passive activity losses (line 17 of Form 1040) $_____

9. Interest from Series EE and I Savings Bonds used to pay education expenses (Form 8815) $_____

10. Exclusion for adoption assistance payments, Form 8839, line 30 $_____

11. Add lines 4–10 $_____

12. Add line 11 to line 3; which equals your modified AGI $_____

Vacation homes

Determining the expenses you can deduct on a vacation home is no fun in the sun because you have to allocate the operating expenses based on how many days you rent your home and on how many days you use it. What's deductible and what's not are based on the following three mind-numbing rules:

✔ **Rule 1:** If you rent your home for fewer than 15 days, you don't have to report the rent you collected, and none of the operating expenses are deductible. Your mortgage interest and real estate taxes still are deducted as itemized deductions.

✔ **Rule 2:** If you rent your home for 15 or more days and your personal use of your home is more than the greater of 14 days or 10 percent of the total days it's rented, then the property isn't considered rental property, and the expenses allocated to the rental period can't exceed the rental income. Expenses that are allocated to the rental period but can't be deducted are carried forward to future years. These expenses can be deducted to the extent of your future rental income or until you sell the property. If you have a profit on the rental of a vacation home, this rule doesn't apply. Tax shelter rules apply only to losses.

In figuring the rental days, count only the days the home actually was rented. The days that you held the property out for rent, but it was not rented, don't count as rental days. After making this computation, you allocate your rental expenses based on the total number of days rented divided by the total number of rented days plus the days you used it. For example, suppose that your beach cottage was rented for 36 days and you used it for 36 days. In such a case, 50 percent of the operating expenses for the year would be allocated to the rental period, 36 days rented ÷ 72 days (36 rented and 36 personal days). Don't count any days that you worked full-time to repair the property as personal days.

The Tax Court is on your side when it comes to deducting mortgage interest and taxes, which don't have to be allocated under the preceding formula. You can allocate this stuff on a daily basis. So, in the example, 10 percent (36 rental days ÷ 365) of your taxes and mortgage interest would have to be allocated to the rental period. This process means that a larger amount of your other rental expenses can be deducted from your rental income, and (better yet) you get to deduct 90 percent of your mortgage interest and taxes as an itemized deduction rather than just 50 percent.

✔ **Rule 3:** If the personal use of your residence doesn't exceed 14 days or 10 percent of the total days it's rented, then your vacation home is treated as rental property. If the total amount of your rental expenses exceeds your rental income, your loss is deductible if you have other passive income (or if the $25,000 special allowance permits). You still have to allocate the expenses of running the property between personal and rental days.

Have a nice vacation.

If line 12 is less than $100,000, or less than $50,000 if you are married and filing separately, you don't have to use Form 8582 (as long as you meet the other six criteria we mentioned earlier). If you have only rental or royalty income or losses, you don't need to turn the page of your Schedule E. You're done! After you follow all those little instructions about what lines to add, take the amount from line 26 over to your 1040 (line 17). But, if you must continue, bear up. You're halfway there.

The $25,000 special allowance

Here's why that $100,000 modified AGI figure is so important. You can deduct up to $25,000 of the losses you incurred in rental real estate if you actively participate in the management of the property and own at least 10 percent — which means that you have to make management decisions regarding the approval of new tenants and rental terms, approving expenditures, and other similar decisions. So if you turn an apartment or home that you own over to a real estate agent to rent and manage, the $25,000 loss-deduction rule doesn't apply. You may be able to pull off this deduction, however, if you reserve the right to approve all expenditures and improvements that have to be made.

Now for the ever-present exception to the general rule: If your income exceeds $100,000, the $25,000 limit is reduced by 50 cents for every dollar of income you earn that's more than $100,000. When your income reaches $150,000, the $25,000 allowance is completely phased out. The loss that's phased out (the portion that you can't deduct in any year) doesn't just disappear. You carry it over and enter it on line 1c of **Form 8582, Passive Activity Loss Limitations** (this is IRS-speak for a tax shelter) to determine the amount of the carryover that's deductible in a future year. When you eventually sell the property, all your suspended losses can be deducted in the year of the sale. We explain all this in greater detail in the section "The tax shelter rules" later in this chapter. A *passive activity* is an investment in which you don't materially participate in its management — See Chapter 11 for the material participation rules. Real estate is considered a passive activity, even if you materially participate in its operation. That's why the $25,000 real estate exception is important.

The $25,000 figure is reduced to $12,500 if you're married, filing separately, and living apart from your spouse for the entire year; the phaseout begins at $50,000 of your AGI (not $100,000) and is completely phased out at $75,000. If you lived with your spouse at any time during the year and you are filing separate returns, you can't use the $12,500 exception (half of $25,000). Please don't ask us about the reason for this one. On Form 8582, you compute the portion of the $25,000 allowance to which you're entitled.

IRS math quiz

Complete Part I of Schedule E by adding the positive amounts on line 22 and entering them on line 24. Line 24 is where you gather your profits. So, if you have a profit in column A of Line 22 and a loss in column B the profit is entered on line 24 and the loss on line 25. For reasons we can't explain, the IRS form makes you snake your way through line 22 and separate the profits from losses. After you complete this process add any royalty losses from line 22 to your real estate losses from line 23 and enter the total on line 25. Finally, add the amounts on lines 24 and 25 and enter that total on line 26. Carry this total over to line 17 of Form 1040.

Think twice before converting a residence you lived in to a rental, because you'll be forfeiting the $250,000 ($500,000 for couples) exclusion on your potential profit if you do. Because a residence must be your principal residence for two of the five years looking back from the date of the sale (see Chapter 12 for the rules on sales of a residence), once you've rented your former home for more than three years, you can kiss the exclusion goodbye.

The tax shelter rules

If you rent out your vacation home or part of a two-family house, you're operating a tax shelter — and you always thought that tax shelters were something that only movie stars and high-income athletes were involved with!

In 1986, Congress decided to kill tax shelters and passed an anti-tax-shelter law. As a result, you can deduct a loss from a *passive activity* (that's what a tax shelter is now called in IRS jargon) only if you have income from another passive activity. If you don't, the loss is *disallowed*. Disallowed losses are suspended and carried over to future years. If you have passive income (that's income from a shelter) next year, you can deduct the loss. If you don't have passive income next year, you keep carrying over the loss until you do, or until you sell the property or your interest in the tax shelter.

For example, suppose that you have a rental loss of $5,000 in 2003 and no other passive income. You can't deduct any of the $5,000 loss in 2003 (but see "The $25,000 special allowance" earlier in this chapter). The loss is carried over to 2004. If in 2004 the property generates a $4,000 profit, you can deduct $4,000 of the suspended loss and carry over the $1,000 balance to 2005. If you sell the property in 2005, the $1,000 can be deducted — even if you don't have a rental income in 2005.

If you have two or more passive activities, you combine them to determine whether a loss in one can be used to offset a profit in another. For example, suppose that you own one building that you rent out at a $6,000 loss and another building that produces a $5,000 profit. You can use $5,000 of the $6,000 loss to offset the $5,000 profit from the second building, and the $1,000 balance is carried over to the next year.

If you have a passive activity loss, you compute the amount of the loss that can be deducted or that has to be carried over to future years on **Form 8582, Passive Activity Loss Limitations.** On this form, you combine your passive activity losses and income. If income exceeds losses, you have a deduction. If it doesn't, you have a suspended loss. But remember: If you sell the property, the loss, together with any suspended losses, is deductible.

When isn't a loss a loss? When you have a sweetheart deal. In a recent Tax Court case, a tax-payer was denied a rental loss deduction because she gave her brother a big break on the rent. The court considered the days she rented to her brother as personal use. She there-fore ran afoul of the 14 days or 10 percent of the days rented rule (see the "Vacation homes" sidebar in this chapter). And it doesn't end there: Any loss on a subsequent sale of the house isn't deductible. The low rent she charged shows she lacked a profit motive. No profit motive, no deductible loss.

Part II: Income or Loss from Partnerships and S Corporations

The average taxpayer finds page 2 of Schedule E the most daunting. You report income and losses from partnerships, S Corporations, estates, and trusts on that page. Instead of the nice, long, symmetrical columns of page 1, Schedule E's flip side looks as if it was designed to confuse rather than clarify.

Partnerships and S Corporations aren't taxable entities. The income, gains, losses, and deductions of a partnership or an S Corporation are passed through to each partner or shareholder based on ownership percentage. Instead of a 1099, each partner or shareholder receives a form called a K-1 that reflects the income, loss, or deduction that belongs on the return. For a partnership, it's **Form 1065 K-1;** for an S Corporation, it's **Form 1120S K-1.**

Line 27: The at-risk and other tax shelter rules

You can hardly consider line 27 a simple yes or no question. Here you are asked whether you're reporting losses that were not allowed in prior years because of at-risk or basis limi-tations, passive losses not reported on Form 8582, Passive Activity Loss Limitation (the name alone is enough to frighten most people), or unreimbursed partnership expenses.

The purpose of the at-risk rules is to prevent investors from deducting losses in excess of what they actually stand to lose. This rule prevents you from investing $10,000 and deduct-ing $30,000 when the partnership loses an additional $20,000 on money it borrows and you aren't personally responsible for any portion of that debt. The K-1 that you receive indicates what your risks are (see item F). At-risk rules are extremely complex and are an area where we recommend that you consult a tax advisor for help. Typically, the at-risk rule comes into play when you invest $30,000: $10,000 in cash and you sign a *promissory note* for $20,000 bearing the language "without recourse against the maker (you)." Because you can't be forced to pay the $20,000, you're not at risk and, therefore, you can deduct losses only up to your $10,000 cash investment.

The basis limitation rule prevents you from limiting the amount you can lose when you make an investment and deduct more than that amount. Say you invest $25,000 . . . that's all you can deduct regardless what your share of the entities' loss amounts to.

The question about passive losses not reported on Form 8582 is new for 2003. Its purpose is to flush out taxpayers who are deducting losses they claim are not passive when they actually are. For a quick refresher, passive losses are those losses in which you didn't materially participate. Why couldn't the IRS simply say, "silent partner"?

Haven't you noticed? The IRS is getting snoopier and snoopier, and we're not just referring to the cartoon character? What this question is all about is that sometimes, when a tax shelter entity runs out of dough, partners are called upon to pay some of the expenses personally to keep the business afloat. When partners try to deduct these expenses the IRS invariably claims they can't. The question on line 27 is an attempt to bring these expenses out in the open instead of burying them along with other deductions. However, a court case states that when an investor and a partner are essentially in the same type of business any unreimbursed expenses that the investor pays on behalf of the partnership are deductible.

Lines 28–32: Name . . . and so on!

Now you have to deal not only with line numbers but also with letters! Here's what you enter in the following columns of line 28:

(a) Enter the name of the partnership or S Corporation.

(b) Enter P for partnership or S for S Corporation.

(c) Put a check here if it's a foreign partnership.

(d) Scribble in the identification number for the partnership or S Corporation. (Hey, this is pretty easy so far!)

(e) This column is the easiest of all. Place a check mark here if you're not at-risk for any of the liabilities of the entity.

Passive income and loss

Enter in column (f) what the K-1 shows as a passive activity with a little check in the box — limited partner or publicly traded partnership. If you have a passive activity loss, enter the loss on Form 8582. You compute your allowable passive loss on Form 8582, and then enter that amount in this column.

In column (g), enter the income from the passive activity in this lovely column.

Refer to "The tax shelter rules," described earlier in this chapter, for the definition of passive income and losses.

Nonpassive income and loss

Column (h) deals with nonpassive income and losses. If you're a working partner in a partnership or a shareholder in an S Corporation, line 1 of the K-1 shows the share of the loss you're entitled to deduct. Enter that amount here.

For column (i), the wonderful K-1 also shows the amount of the partnership's or S Corporation's special depreciation that you get to deduct — line 9 of the K-1 for partnerships and line 8 for S Corporations. Enter it here.

In column (j), enter the amount of income from Schedule K-1 in this column — it's the amount on line 1.

Lines 29 through 32 are strictly addition. What a relief!

Part III: Income or Loss from Estates and Trusts

In this part, you enter income or loss from an estate or trust of which you're a beneficiary. You should receive a K-1 from either the estate or the trust, and the K-1 also indicates income such as dividends, interest, and capital gains. Interest and dividends go on Schedule B (see Chapter 10), and capital gains go on Schedule D (see Chapter 12). The ordinary income or loss reported on the K-1 is what goes on in this section of Schedule E. Maybe that's why the IRS gives us only two lines to work with in this part of the form — and that's down from *three* lines a couple of years back!

Lines 33–37: Name . . . and so on!

In column (a), carefully enter the name of the estate or trust.

In column (b), enter the identification number for the trust or estate.

Passive income and loss

In column (c), you put the passive loss allowed from Form 8582.

In column (d), you enter passive income from the K-1s and Form 8582.

Nonpassive income and loss

Columns (e) and (f) are mostly for show, because most heirs or beneficiaries don't participate in the management of the estate or trust, and so it is rare for an heir or beneficiary to have nonpassive income or loss.

Lines 34 through 36 are the simple part of this section. All it requires is simple addition.

Part IV: Lines 38–39: Income or Loss from Real Estate Mortgage Investment Conduits (REMIC)

If you've invested in an REMIC, which is a company that holds a pool of mortgages, you'll most likely receive interest on **Form 1099-INT, Interest Income,** or **Form 1099-OID, Original Issue Discount.** But if you received **Form 1066, Schedule Q,** from the REMIC, enter the amounts, names, and so on from that form on line 38. Add columns (d) and (e) and enter the total on line 39.

Part V: Summary

Unless you're a farmer and file Form 4835 (line 40) or a real estate professional (line 43), everything on Schedule E is pulled together on line 41. Do the math and transfer the amount to Form 1040 (line 17) and take a break. You deserve it.

If you rent out your farm, you report your rental income and expenses on **Form 4835, Farm Rental Income and Expenses.** Donald Trump — or rather, his accountant — is an example of one who has to fill out line 43, Reconciliation for Real Estate Professionals.

Chapter 14

Profit or Loss from Farming: Schedule F

. . . .

In This Chapter

▶ Figuring out Schedule F

▶ Reporting your income

▶ Tallying and categorizing all those expenses

▶ Understanding the special rules that apply only to farming

. . . .

*P*art of the responsibility of running a farm is reporting to the government how much income you receive when you sell your crop or livestock. Schedule F is the form that you use to report this income, whether from operating a farm that produces livestock, dairy, poultry, fish, aquaculture products, bee products, fruit, or a truck farm (because produce isn't the only thing farmers raise and harvest). Even though Schedule F is titled "Profit or Loss from Farming," this form also is used to tell the IRS what you took in from operating a plantation, ranch, nursery, orchard, or oyster bed. Schedule F is not as bad as it looks. In this chapter, we take you through it, line by line.

Once upon a time, all taxpayers could reduce their taxes by averaging their incomes over a number of years whenever their incomes suddenly shot up. However, all that ended in 1986. In 1998, farmers, but not other taxpayers, got a lucky break. If farmers' incomes suddenly shoot up, they can once again reduce their taxes by averaging their incomes over the past three years.

When you get to line 41 of your Form 1040 — the line where you compute your tax — use **Schedule J, Form 1040, Farm Income Averaging,** when computing your tax. Make sure that you attach this schedule to your return.

Basic Information (Lines A–E): Accounting Method Stuff

The first few lines of Schedule F look at your accounting method.

Lines A and B: Product and code. Lines A and B are the simplest part of the form. Suppose that you're a dairy farmer. On line A: Principal product, you write Milk. On line B: Principal agricultural activity code, write 112120. You may be asking where the number on line B came from. It's derived from the list of Principal Agricultural Activity Codes found in Part IV on the reverse side of Schedule F. Code 112120 indicates that you're a dairy farmer.

Line C: Accounting method. The two accounting methods used to report income are the cash and the accrual methods. With the *cash method,* you report income at the time it actually is received, and you deduct expenses at the time they're actually paid. However, one exception to this rule exists (of course): If you charge an expense on a credit card, you can deduct this expense in the year you charged the purchase, even if you *pay* the charge in the following year. (So don't leave home without it.)

Most farmers use the cash method because it's the easier of the two methods. You total what you received and subtract what you paid. You don't need to figure out what you owe and who owes you. You don't need to determine your inventory at the end of the year (for crops or animals that you didn't sell). A slight exception to this rule also exists, however. If you bought livestock or other items for resale, you must keep a separate record of the items that you didn't sell. These purchases can't be deducted until they're sold. And thanks to depreciation rules, farm structures and equipment can't be deducted in the year you paid for them. They have to be depreciated over their useful lives.

Under the *accrual method,* you report income in the year sales are made — even if the sales are billed or collected in a later year. You deduct expenses in the year in which the expenses are incurred, even if you don't pay these expenses until later.

Under both cash and accrual methods, you report all income and expenses for the calendar year ending December 31. You choose one of the two accounting methods in the year that you file your first Schedule F. Once selected, an accounting method can't be changed without IRS permission.

The cash method of accounting gives you more control over when your farm sees a profit from year to year. For example, if next year looks like a slower year for you, you may elect to claim more of your income in that next year. Doing so will likely save you tax dollars, because you're more likely to be in a lower tax bracket that year (if it is, in fact, a less profitable year for you). You can legally shift your income by deferring sales or by delaying sending out bills until January (bills that you otherwise would have mailed in December, for example). Likewise, to lower your taxable income this year, you can pay more of your expenses in December instead of waiting until January.

Another reason for selecting the cash method of accounting is that you don't have to fill out lines 38 through 51 in Part III of Schedule F. That part is for accrual method folks. Isn't that reason enough?

If you're operating a farm and aiming to produce a tax deduction (commonly referred to as a *tax shelter*) rather than a profit, you're *required* to use the accrual method.

Line D: Employer ID number. Enter your employer ID number on line D. If you don't have a number, you can obtain one instantly by applying online at the IRS Web site, www.irs.gov. Click on "Businesses" and then "More Topics" — both buttons are on the left side of the screen — scrolling down to and clicking on "Employer ID Numbers." You can also call 800-829-4933 or go the paper route by sending a completed **Form SS-4, Application For Employer Identification Number,** to the IRS.

Line E: Did you "materially participate"? If the sun isn't up when you start working on the farm each day, check "yes." If you show up only on holidays and weekends to go horseback riding, check "no." If you check no, you're operating a tax shelter and probably won't be able to deduct any loss if the farm isn't profitable. In such cases, we advise consulting a tax advisor, and make sure that you see a good one. See Chapter 2 for more information about choosing a competent tax advisor. Chapter 13 explains how the tax-shelter rules operate. The material-participation rules are explained at item G at the beginning of Chapter 11.

Accounting for when your crops sell

Before leaving accounting methods, you need to know about the crop method of accounting. If you don't harvest your crop in the same year that you plant it, you can, with advance IRS approval, use the crop method. Using this method, you deduct the entire cost of producing the crop in the year that you sell it. This method is a variation of the accrual method, and unless you want to set up a special bookkeeping department, stay away from it. You can't use this method for timber.

Part 1, Lines 1–11: Income

Time to tally up your income. This section describes, line by line, the types of income that you need to enter on each line and how to complete the Income section of Schedule F. Wouldn't it be nice if you could just write down one simple number on one single line? No such luck. Hey, but who said farming (or paying taxes) was easy?

Line 1: Sales of livestock and other items you bought for resale

If you sold livestock that you bought for resale, enter the income you received on line 1. (For income you received from the sale of livestock that you raised yourself, just hold your horses. You'll have a chance to pony up that income amount on line 4, which we discuss momentarily.)

Line 2: Cost or other basis of livestock and other items reported on line 1

You must keep a careful record of when the animals you bought for resale were purchased (because the only time you can deduct the purchase price of those animals is in the year that you sell them). For example, suppose that in 2002 you bought 10 cows for a total purchase price of $10,000, and you then sold the cows in 2003. You couldn't deduct the purchase price on your 2002 tax return; you deduct the $10,000 cost of these animals in 2003, because that's when they were sold — enter that amount on line 2.

You're allowed to defer income to the next year on sales caused by a weather-related condition, such as a flood. See the sidebar "Livestock sales caused by weather-related conditions," later in this chapter.

Matching the cost with sales for resale reported on line 1 sounds much easier than it really is. For some types of livestock, figuring out which animals you purchased when can be tough. Think about it. Suppose that you're a poultry farmer who is continually buying baby chicks and raising others. When you sell 50 chickens, it's impossible to tell whether the chickens you sold are the ones you raised or the ones you purchased (unless you're on a first-name basis with your chickens, or you use a teeny-tiny little branding iron on them). For this reason, poultry, fish, or other hard-to-differentiate livestock are exempt from the which-critter-was-purchased-when requirement. You can keep it simple — enter the income from the sale of this type of livestock on line 4. On line 34, enter the cost of the poultry, fish, and other such livestock that you purchased.

Don't use Schedule F to report income from the sale of animals held for draft, breeding, or sport. Income from the sale of these types of animals is reported on **Form 4797, Sales of Business Property.** And because these animals are classified as business property, you can depreciate that Clydesdale, stud bull, or racehorse just as if it were a John Deere tractor.

Line 3: Subtraction quiz

All you do is subtract line 2 from line 1 and enter the total on line 3. So do it.

Line 4: Sales of livestock, produce, grains, and other products you raised

Line 4 is where you report the income from the sale of the products that you raise, grow, or produce. So if you're a dairy farmer, enter what you received from the sale of milk. If you also sold your corn and hay crop, tally up all your income and enter the total right here.

Lines 5a and 5b: Total cooperative distributions (Form 1099-PATR)

If you purchase farm supplies from a cooperative, you may receive income in the form of *patronage dividends,* which is fancy jargon for a *distribution of the cooperative's profits.* These payments are reported to you on Form 1099-PATR. You report patronage dividends on line 5a of Schedule F. However, dividends received from the purchase of personal family living items aren't taxable because the supplies weren't used in your business (that is, on your farm).

Sometimes, a cooperative doesn't issue a dividend in the form of cash. It may issue a written *Notice of Allocation* or a *Per-Unit Retain Certificate* that can be redeemed in the future. If these certificates are qualified ones, you report them as income in the year you receive them; if they're nonqualified, you report the income in the year you redeem them.

Although you normally report dividends and distributions on Schedule B of Form 1040, Interest and Dividend Income, reporting cooperative distributions is an exception to this rule; you enter them on line 5. Enter the amounts from Form 1099-PATR (boxes 1, 2, 3, and 5) on line 5a; use 5b for the taxable amount. Remember, if the cooperative dividend was paid on purchases for nondeductible family living expenses, don't enter it on 5b. It isn't taxable. For example, say you received a $1,000 dividend of which $800 relates to farm supplies and $200 to personal items. Enter $1,000 on line 5a and $800 on line 5b.

Lines 6a and 6b: Agricultural program payments

Normally, most payments you receive from the government under agricultural programs are taxable in the year you receive them. However, you don't have to pay tax on some of the payments you receive under certain cost-sharing conservation programs. The rules are rather nightmarish. Therefore, our advice is to seek the help of a tax professional who is experienced in this area. But for you die-hard do-it-yourselfers, IRS Publication 225 *(Farmer's Tax Guide),* which you can order by calling 800-829-3676, walks you through the rules on this issue. It is not a light read, however.

If you received payments under a governmental agricultural program, that income is reported to you in box 7 on **Form 1099-G,** which you should receive by January 31, 2004.

These payments may have come from a conservation program or payment-in-kind certificates. If you receive a payment-in-kind, you're entitled to a deduction for the material or supplies that you receive (because you use those materials to operate your farm). Because you can sell commodity credit certificates and use them to pay price-support loans or other federal debts, you report the certificates as income in 2003, even if you don't use them until 2004.

No additional tax breaks are allowed for money received under feed assistance programs — all money you receive for feed assistance is taxable. If you didn't receive any cost-sharing payments, you need to enter the same amount on line 6b that you entered on 6a.

Not all payments that you receive from the government are taxable. For example, soil and water conservation payments aren't taxable. Farmers and ranchers who use special conservation practices are eligible to receive up to $50,000 under this program.

Lines 7a–c: Commodity Credit Corporation (CCC) loans

Normally, you report income when you sell something such as your crop. However, if you pledge part of or your entire crop to receive a CCC loan, you can elect to report the loan proceeds in the year you receive the loan rather than in the year you sell the crop. We don't recommend doing this, however, because you can end up paying tax on a higher amount than the actual payments you receive.

Our advice is to stay clear of electing to pay the tax on loan payments you receive in advance of selling a crop.

Lines 8a–d: Crop insurance proceeds and certain disaster payments

Crop insurance and disaster payments are taxable in the year they're received. But (there is always a but) because you're using the cash method of accounting, you can elect to postpone reporting income received from crop insurance or disaster payments until 2004 by attaching a statement to your 2003 return that includes the following items:

- ✔ The statement that you're making this election pursuant to section 451(d) of the Internal Revenue Code

- ✔ A description of crops that were destroyed or damaged, the cause, and the date the damage was incurred

- ✔ What you received for each crop and from whom it was received

On lines 8a through 8d, you enter the following information about any income you receive from crop insurance or disaster payments:

- ✔ **8a:** Enter the amount received.

- ✔ **8b:** Taxable amount: This is usually the same as 8a. But remember, as previously explained, you can elect to report the payment next year.

- ✔ **8c:** If you decide to defer reporting the insurance or disaster payment until 2004, check this box.

- ✔ **8d:** Enter the amount that you deferred from 2002. Next year, the difference between lines 8a and b gets entered here. The difference between lines 8a and 8b is the amount you're deferring to 2004.

Livestock sales caused by weather-related conditions

If you sold more livestock (which includes poultry) than you usually do because of a weather-related condition such as a drought, you can postpone reporting some of your earnings until next year. Suppose that you normally sell 100 head a year, but because of a drought you sell 200 head of livestock for $300 a head. Of the $60,000 you receive, $30,000 can be reported in 2004 instead of reporting the entire $60,000 in 2003. The $30,000 you're allowed to postpone consists of the extra 100 head that you sold at $300 a head.

To qualify for this postponement, the weather-related area must be eligible for federal assistance. The income postponement includes sales that you made before the area became eligible for federal assistance, as long as the weather-related condition caused the sale. You have to be in the area; the animals don't.

To claim a postponement, list the following items in a statement:

✔ That an election under 451(e) of the Internal Revenue Code to postpone a part of the income you received is being made

✔ The date and location of the area eligible for federal assistance

✔ The number of animals sold in each of the three preceding years

✔ The number of animals you would've sold had it not been for the weather-related condition

✔ The total number of animals sold because of the weather-related condition

✔ A statement showing how you computed the amount you're postponing (as shown earlier in this sidebar)

Attach this statement to your tax return.

Line 9: Custom hire (machine work) income

If you receive cash, services, or merchandise as payment for plowing your neighbor's field or renting out your tractor, jot down this amount on line 9 — the value of those items or services is taxable.

Line 10: Other income

Line 10 is where you enter every last dollar you earned from a whole bunch of miscellaneous activities, such as the following:

✔ **Cancellation of Debt:** For tax purposes, almost any debt that is canceled or forgiven must be included as income (see the sidebar "Canceled or forgiven debts that aren't taxable," later in this chapter, for exceptions). Yes, the IRS is so hard up that it even wants to collect from people who can't pay their bills. If the amount of canceled debt is more than $600, you should receive **Form 1099-C, Cancellation of Debt,** by January 31, 2004.

✔ **Bartering:** Suppose that you help a neighbor build a barn and you receive a horse in return for your work. The value of the horse must be reported as income. Even poor Jack of Beanstalk fame had taxable income when he traded his cow for those beans.

✔ **Refunds and reimbursements:** If you receive a refund on an item for which you took a deduction in a prior year, sorry — it's taxable. For example, suppose that you purchased feed in 2002 and took a deduction in that year. In 2003, however, you received a $500 refund. This refund also gets reported as income on line 10.

✔ **Soil, natural deposits, or timber sales:** If you remove and sell timber, topsoil, fill dirt, gravel, or sand, you don't have to guess at all on this one — the proceeds on the sale of those items are taxable. Normally when you use up a natural resource by mining, quarrying, drilling, and felling, you're entitled to a depletion deduction, based on the theory that you've used up something and you're entitled to a deduction. However, farmers who cut timber on their land to sell as firewood, logs, or pulpwood, usually have no cost or other basis on which to figure a depletion deduction. These sales usually constitute a minor part of their farm income. Even if you can't claim a depletion deduction, you can claim a deduction for expenses incurred in cutting, hauling, and so on.

Here is a second however: If sales of natural resources amount to more than a casual sale, seek professional advice, because a number of exceptions to the normal depletion rules may apply and you may otherwise be missing out on them.

✔ **Rents and crop shares:** If you pasture someone else's cattle and take care of the cattle for a fee, include that income on line 10. But if you simply rent your pasture, the rent goes on **Form 4835, Farm Rental Income and Expenses.** This form is similar to Schedule E, Supplemental Income and Losses that we discussed in Chapter 13.

If you find it confusing knowing when to use Schedule F or Form 4835 when it comes to farm rental income, you're not alone. Follow this rule. If you materially participate in the rental as in the above example of renting a pasture and caring for the animals, the rent that you receive in cash or in a share of the crop or part of the increase in the herd is reported on Schedule F. Rental income from merely renting something you own without being involved in the business where your rental item is being used is reported on Form 4835. By reporting rental income on Schedule F, you get to pay more Social Security and Medicare tax (lucky you!). However, paying more now probably means that you'll be able to collect more when you're old and gray.

If the rent you receive is paid as a share of the crop (rather than cash), you don't have to report the crop as income until you sell it or feed it to your animals, which are good ways of deferring income to a later year.

✔ **Fuel tax credit and refunds:** If you claimed the cost of fuel as a deduction on line 21 during a prior year, any refund of federal excise taxes on that fuel is taxable. What the government has given now gets taken away.

✔ **Prizes:** If you win a cash prize at the county fair, include that income on line 10. The blue ribbon, however, isn't taxable.

Line 11: Gross income

The IRS couldn't have picked a better name for this line, especially after forcing you to snake your way through all the preceding lines. Add the amounts on lines 3 through 10 and enter the total amount on line 11. Because you're reporting income and expenses under the cash method, you can ignore the instruction to add the amount from page 2, line 51. That's for taxpayers using the accrual method of accounting.

Part II, Lines 12–34: Expenses

This part of Schedule F usually brings tears to your eyes as you take a hard look at what things cost.

Line 12: Car and truck expenses

One method you can use to deduct vehicle expenses is taking a standard per-mile deduction for every mile you use your car or truck in running your farm. For 2003, you can use 36 cents per mile. However, this standard mileage deduction can be taken only on cars or light trucks — and even then only if you're claiming expenses on a single vehicle. If you're like most farmers, you have expenses on multiple light vehicles. Therefore, if you're using two cars or trucks, you can't use this simplified method. You're required instead to deduct your actual car and truck expenses. Sorry. See the sidebar "Standard mileage rate" in Chapter 11, for a detailed illustration of how the standard 36 cents per mile works.

Canceled or forgiven debts that aren't taxable

Guess what? Although most canceled debt must be claimed as income, a whole bunch of other canceled or forgiven debts are *not* taxable. Here's the list:

- **Gifts:** Suppose that your father lends you $7,500 and then a year later tells you to forget it. A "loan" from a relative can be considered as a gift — and gifts aren't subject to income tax — they're subject to gift tax paid by the donor.

- **Debt wiped out in a bankruptcy.**

- **Price reductions:** Suppose that you buy seed and (after it's delivered to you) the seller then reduces the price — and sends you a rebate. Or perhaps your accountant reduces her bill because you may be having financial trouble. Even though you aren't bankrupt or insolvent, this type of debt forgiveness is not considered as income. Because you use the cash method of accounting, the payment of a business service would've been deductible if it had been paid.

- **Debt cancellation when you're insolvent:** Insolvency is when your liabilities exceed the value of your assets (even by one penny). If you're insolvent, you don't have to claim a portion of canceled debt as income — but only to the extent that you're insolvent. (Huh?) Well, here's where the math gets a bit tricky. Suppose you're fortunate enough to get someone to cancel a $7,500 debt. Immediately before the cancellation, your assets are worth $75,000, and your liabilities total $80,000, which makes you insolvent to the tune of $5,000. In the case of the $7,500 canceled debt, you're not required to report the $5,000 (the amount of insolvency) as income. Unfortunately, you must pay tax on the remaining $2,500. (Not an uncommon situation to be in these days.)

Because the amount of income that you have to report is based on the value of your assets, an accurate appraisal can save you a bundle. And it isn't unusual for two appraisals on the same property to be as different as night and day. When seeking an appraisal, always remember — if you ask an appraiser how much two and two is and the appraiser responds, "Am I buying or selling?" that's the guy you want to hire.

- **Farm debt:** Cancellation of farm debt isn't subject to tax either, provided that at least 50 percent of your income for the preceding three years came from farming, and the person forgiving the debt is not related to you, not the person from whom you acquired the farm, and not related to the person from whom you bought the farm.

- **Contested liability:** The settlement of a contested liability is not considered income. For example, suppose that you're billed $10,000 for supplies that are so badly damaged you can't use them. If you contest that, you owe nothing (because you're not liable for the cost of supplies you can't use), any cancellation of what you were billed is not considered as income.

If you receive a **Form 1099-C, Cancellation of Debt,** for debt that isn't subject to tax, our advice is to indicate the canceled debt on **Form 982, Reduction of Tax Attributes Due to Discharge of Indebtedness.** That way, the amount indicated on the 1099-C gets included on your return without your having to report it on any of the income lines on Schedule F. Everyone ends up happy — you and the IRS. When business or farming debt is canceled, the nontaxable portion of the cancellation must reduce any operating losses, tax credits, passive activity losses, capital losses, and the tax basis of your depreciable property. Our recommendation: See a tax professional when it comes to debt cancellation.

As a general rule, claiming your actual expenses provides a larger deduction, because you can deduct your expenses on the following items:

- Gas
- Oil
- Repairs
- License tags and fees
- Insurance
- Depreciation

You can deduct only vehicle expenses connected with actual business use, regardless of whether you take the standard mileage deduction or keep track of your expenses. For example, if a van is used 80 percent of the time for farm business and 20 percent for personal use, you can deduct only 80 percent of your actual expenses (or 80 percent of the miles you drove during the year, if you're using the standard 36-cents-per-mile rate). See Chapter 11 for more discussion on tracking expenses connected to car and truck use.

Line 13: Chemicals

On line 13, enter the total amount you paid for pesticides and herbicides.

Line 14: Conservation expenses

Want to see a farmer get really mad just before April 15? Just tell him that the $10,000 he spent to clear a pasture or cut diversion channels can't be deducted until he sells the land. Thankfully, though, these types of expenses *are* deductible, if they're consistent with a government conservation program. But limits do exist. Conservation expenses can't exceed 25 percent of your total farming income. The 75 percent you can't deduct is carried over to 2004 and subject to that year's 25 percent limit. You can deduct the following conservation expenses:

- Leveling
- Grading
- Conditioning
- Terracing
- Contour furrowing
- Restoration of soil fertility
- Construction of diversion channels, drainage ditches, irrigation ditches, earthen dams, outlets, or ponds
- Eradication of brush
- Planting of windbreaks

Line 15: Custom hire (machine work) expenses

If you paid someone to spray your crop, plow a field, or harvest a crop, enter the amount you paid here. Tax auditors are trained to investigate this deduction to find out whether you're deducting land-clearing expenses or paying someone to build structures that have to be depreciated.

Remember two things: Land-clearing can be deducted only as a conservation expense and is subject to the limit explained on line 14. And if you pay a custom hire more than $600, you have to file Form 1099-MISC with the IRS by February 28, 2004, and furnish a copy to the person you paid by January 31, 2004.

Line 16: Depreciation and Section 179 expense deduction

Depreciation is the annual deduction that allows you to recover the cost of your investment (which has a useful life of more than one year) in farm equipment and structures. The word depreciation in itself is enough to send most readers to the next chapter. We know, but just think of depreciation as a way of increasing your after-tax income. Now, are you more excited about depreciation possibilities?

Unless you elect the special provision that allows you to deduct the first $100,000 of equipment used on your farm (see the section on "Your Buying Bonanza: The $100,000 Deduction" in Chapter 11), you have to write off your purchase of these assets over their useful life — as established by the IRS (see Table 14-1). In Table 14-1, notice the GDS and ADS columns. GDS stands for *General Depreciation System.* ADS stands for *Alternative Depreciation System.*

As you can readily see from Table 14-1, the GDS system uses much shorter useful lives, and that means you can claim your depreciation deductions more quickly than with the ADS system. So why would anyone not want to use the ADS system? People who are subject to the *uniform capitalization rules,* that's who. Talk about wanting to tear out your hair. Under these rules, the cost of growing a citrus tree until it starts bearing a marketable fruit, for example, has to be depreciated over 20 years as per Table 14-1.

If you raise a crop that takes less than two years to harvest, then thankfully, the uniform capitalization rules don't apply, and you can use the GDS system that everyone else uses, and you have no need to delve further into this uniform capitalization business.

The two-year rule

The uniform capitalization rules must be used if you're raising a fruit-bearing crop, ornamental trees, sod, or other crop that takes more than two years to bear fruit or bring to market. Some of those kinds of crops are listed here:

Uniform Capitalization Crops

Almonds	Apples	Apricots	Avocados
Blackberries	Blueberries	Cherries	Chestnuts
Coffee Beans	Currants	Dates	Figs
Grapes	Grapefruit	Guavas	Kumquats

Lemons	Limes	Macadamia Nuts	Mangoes
Nectarines	Papayas	Peaches	Pears
Pecans	Persimmons	Pistachio Nuts	Plums
Pomegranates	Prunes	Olives	Oranges
Raspberries	Tangelos	Tangerines	Walnuts

Even if you're involved in growing one of the crops we've listed above, you can elect not to have the uniform capitalization rules apply. You make the election by simply deducting your planting, cultivation, and development expenses in the year of your first growing season. Once you make this election it binds you until judgment day. You can make a change only with IRS permission. With citrus or almond groves, you can't make this election during the first four years after planting. Why? Don't ask us!

If you elect not to use the uniform capitalization rules, then you're required to use ADS depreciation with its longer useful lives. Not only that, you're not permitted to claim the additional September 11 depreciation that we explain in just a bit for your autos and farm equipment. Not only that, you aren't allowed to use the depreciation percentages in the tables we provide in this chapter. You divide the cost of the farm equipment you purchased by its useful life to arrive at your depreciation deduction. This is known as the straight-line way of computing depreciation. What you get to deduct every year never varies. With the GDS system, your deductions in the first few years are larger than with the ADS system, but then they start tapering off. At the end of an asset's useful life, the total depreciation deductions under both systems are the same. The difference is that with the GDS system, you get to claim your depreciation deductions faster, and doing so produces a quicker tax savings.

Table 14-1   Farm Property Recovery Periods (Useful Lives)

Type of Property (Assets)	Useful Life (Years)	
	GDS	*ADS*
Agricultural structures (single purpose)	10	15
Airplanes (including helicopters)[1]	5	6
Automobiles	5	5
Calculators and copiers	5	6
Cattle (dairy and breeding)	5	7
Communication equipment[2]	7	10
Computers and peripheral equipment	5	5
Cotton-ginning assets	7	12
Drainage facilities	15	20
Farm buildings[3]	20	25
Farm machinery and equipment	7	10
Fences (agricultural)	7	10
Goats and sheep (breeding)	5	5

(continued)

Table 14-1 *(continued)*

Type of Property (Assets)	Useful Life (Years)	
	GDS	ADS
Grain bin	7	10
Hogs (breeding)	3	3
Horses (age when placed in service)		
Breeding and working (12 years or less)	7	10
Breeding and working (more than 12 years)	3	10
Racing horses (more than 2 years)	3	12
Horticultural structures (single purpose)	10	15
Logging machinery and equipment[4]	5	6
Nonresidential real property[5]	39	40
Office equipment (not calculators, copiers, or typewriters)	7	10
Office furniture or fixtures	7	10
Residential rental property	27½	40
Tractor units (over-the-road)	3	4
Trees or vines bearing fruits or nuts	10	20
Truck (heavy duty, unloaded weight 13,000 lbs. or more)	5	6
Truck (weight less than 13,000 lbs.)	5	5
Typewriter	5	6

[1] Not including airplanes used in commercial or contract carrying of passengers
[2] Not including communication equipment listed in other classes
[3] Not including single-purpose agricultural and horticultural structures
[4] Used by logging and sawmill operators for cutting of timber
[5] GDS is for property placed in service after May 12, 1993; for property placed in service before May 13, 1993, the recovery period is 31½ years.

Livestock that you *purchase* for draft, breeding, dairy, or sport must be depreciated. If you raise this type of livestock, you can't depreciate them because you incurred no purchase cost.

Normally, buildings don't qualify for the $100,000 "Buying Bonanza." (See Chapter 11 to determine whether you qualify for the increased maximum amount allowed of $135,000 allowed in certain low income areas.) However, single-purpose agricultural or horticultural structures do qualify. An agricultural structure is one that is used to raise and feed livestock, breed chickens or hogs, or produce milk, feeder cattle, pigs, broiler chickens, or eggs. A greenhouse used for the commercial production of plants or mushrooms qualifies as a horticultural structure.

The structure must be used only for the single purpose for which it was designed. For example, a hog pen will not qualify for the $100,000 maximum deduction if it is also used to house poultry. Using part of a greenhouse to sell plants also disqualifies you from claiming the deduction. But if you can't claim the immediate write-off under this rule, you're entitled to depreciation over the structure's useful life as explained in the following paragraphs. Land can't be depreciated. See Chapter 22 for a discussion of the pros and cons of depreciating versus taking an outright deduction.

Depreciating your car

Computing the amount of depreciation on your car can be mind-numbing. Unfortunately, the only way around this exercise in frustration is using the 36-cents-per-mile flat expense rate.

The IRS lumps automobiles into the listed property category of assets (they're subject to the 50 percent business-use test), and gives cars a whole bunch of rules and regulations. *Listed property* is an IRS term for assets for automobiles, telephones, computers, boats, and airplanes — items that the IRS suspects you may be using more for pleasure than for business. The IRS lists cars as having a useful life of five years, which means that the IRS deems them to have a useful life of five years. Ready for the computation? Here goes.

If the farm/business use of your car is 50 percent or more, you compute your depreciation as under the *MACRS (Modified Accelerated Cost Recovery System),* according to what is known as the *half-year convention* (see Table 14-2). The table also shows the limits that can be claimed for auto depreciation in any year.

Straight-line depreciation is relatively easy, right? Wrong . . . at least in this case. Remember, this calculation is for a car with a business use of less than 50 percent, so the IRS makes you reduce the amount of depreciation that you're allowed under the straight-line method by the percentage of that personal use.

Table 14-2	Half-Year Convention for Auto Depreciation				
Year	**Yearly Percent**	**For a $30,000 Car if No Limit is Applied**		**Maximum Yearly Limit**	
		Before May 6th	**After May 5th**	**Before May 6th**	**After May 5th**
1–2003	15.00%	$12,150	$17,250	$7,660	$10,710
2–2004	25.50%	$5,355	$3,825	$4,900	$4,900
3–2005	17.85%	$3,748	$2,678	$2,950	$2,950
4–2006	16.66%	$3,499	$2,499	$1,775	$1,775
5–2007	16.66%	$3,499	$2,499	$1,775	$1,775
6–2008	8.33%	$1,749	$1,249	$1,775	$1,775
Total	100%	$30,000	$30,000	$1,775	$1,775*

*and $1,775 in each succeeding year

If your car is used less than 100 percent for business, the yearly maximums have to be reduced accordingly. For example, if a car is used only 80 percent of the time for business the yearly maximum depreciation for a car acquired after May 5, 2003, is $8,568 ($10,710 × 80 percent).

The effect of the depreciation limits is that the days of being able to write off a $90,000 car in three years are gone. If, for example, you purchased a new car in 2003 for $30,000, the maximum amount of depreciation that you can claim in 2003 is either $7,660 or $10,710, depending on whether you bought the car before May 6, 2003, or on or after May 5, 2003, and then $4,900 in 2004, $2,950 in 2005, and $1,775 a year until the $30,000 is fully depreciated (which takes about 11 years). This formula, however, assumes that you use your car 100 percent for business. So if the business use of your car is less, the maximum yearly limits are reduced.

These increased limits are available only for the purchase of new autos. If you purchased a used one the 2003 depreciation limit is $3,060.

SUVs

Here's a bit of a break regarding light trucks, vans, and SUVs. If the vehicle has been specially modified for business use so as to preclude the likelihood of personal use, the maximum limits on auto depreciation do not apply. What the IRS means by *specially modified* is that after the modification, personal use will be negligible. The modifications the IRS is referring to are the vehicle has only a front bench for seating, permanent shelving fills most of the cargo area, merchandise and equipment is being constantly carried, and the vehicle has been painted with advertising or the company's logo. Not much of a gift, but it's enough of a break to enable you to use of the vehicle without having to worry about the maximum depreciation limits. However, this rule applies only to light trucks and vans placed into business use on or after July 7, 2003.

SUVs and light trucks with a gross vehicle weight of more than 6,000 pounds are not subject to the maximum depreciation limit that vehicles weighing less than 6,000 pounds are. Gross vehicle weight is the total weight including passengers and cargo. This means that people who purchase vehicles such as the GMC Yukon weighing 6,500 pounds, the larger Ford Expedition at 6,900 pounds, and Hummers for business use, for example, between 2003 and 2005 can write off the entire cost in the year of purchase. This is the result of a change that took effect in 2003 that allows the first $100,000 of business equipment to be written-off in the year of purchase. But, as this edition of *Taxes For Dummies* goes to press the Senate Finance Committee slashed the write-off to $25,000 from $100,000 for these behemoths of the road. Although the jury is still out on the fate of this provision there seems to be a lot of support for its passage.

Table 11-5 in Chapter 11 has the limit for SUVs and light trucks. Also see Chapter 11 for the depreciation limit on electric vehicles.

New cars purchased in 2003 before May 6

For new cars and light trucks purchased before May 6, 2003, $7,660 is the maximum amount of depreciation that can be deducted. For light trucks and SUVs the limit is $7,950.

New cars purchased in 2003 after May 5

For new cars and light trucks purchased after May 5, 2003, the maximum deduction increased to $10,710. For light trucks and SUVs the limit is $11,010.

September 11 changed many things, and the way depreciation is computed is no exception. The law entitles taxpayers to an additional first-year depreciation deduction of 30 percent on the amount of new business assets purchased after September 10, 2001, and before September 11, 2004, that they start using in their businesses before January 1, 2005. The law was written in this convoluted manner to allow the additional first-year deduction for an item ordered before September 11, 2004, but not delivered until after that date, as long as taxpayers start using them in their businesses before January 1, 2005. Why couldn't the IRS say that in the first place?

In 2003 the rule regarding the 30 percent additional first-year depreciation changed. The 30 percent first-year rate was increased to 50 percent. Unfortunately, the change wasn't made retroactive to January 1, so the higher rate applies only to depreciable items acquired after May 5, 2003; otherwise, the 30 percent rate still applies.

The 30 percent or 50 percent additional first-year depreciation deduction is in addition to regular depreciation. Along with this additional first-year depreciation deduction came a provision that bumped up the maximum first-year depreciation that can be claimed on an auto used for business by $4,600 for cars purchased before May 6, 2003, and by $7,650 for cars purchased after May 5, 2003. That means that the maximum first-year depreciation amount went to $7,660 from $3,060 if the car was purchased before May 6, 2003, and to $10,710 from $3,060 for cars purchased after May 5, 2003. The $4,600 and $7,650 amounts aren't adjusted for inflation, but the $3,060 is. Another hitch is that you must claim the extra 30 percent or 50 percent. The additional first-year depreciation isn't automatic; it isn't built in to the depreciation tables. So claim it! We explain how to claim the extra depreciation in the next paragraph entitled, "September 11 additional first-year depreciation."

September 11 additional first-year depreciation — New autos purchased before May 6, 2003

Here's what the 30 percent extra depreciation is all about. The automobile must be new. Used ones don't qualify. The auto's original use had to begin with you. You have to reduce what you paid for the car by the 30 percent before figuring your regular 2003 depreciation. For example, if a car cost $20,000, your additional first-year depreciation is $6,000. Next you reduce the cost of the car by that amount to $14,000 ($20,000 – $6,000). Your regular depreciation of $2,100 is computed by multiplying $14,000 by 15 percent (Table 14-2). Your total depreciation before applying the maximum limit of $7,660 comes to $8,100 ($6,000 + $2,100). But, remember you can deduct only the $7,660 maximum. That's how the screwy tax law makes you do the math so that you nail down the additional first-year September 11 depreciation deduction. The $440 you couldn't deduct ($8,100 – $7,660) can't be deducted until the end of the depreciation period (Table 14-2), which would be 2008.

Had you not claimed the extra 30 percent, your depreciation for the year would come to $3,000 ($20,000 × 15 percent) limited to a maximum of $3,060. The $7,660 maximum is only available when you claim the extra 30 percent. How do you claim it? By computing the amount to which you're entitled and entering it on of **Form 4562, Depreciation and Amortization** (don't forget to attach it to your return).

In future years, if you don't compute the additional first-year 30 percent deduction and you don't elect not to claim it, you nevertheless must reduce the cost of the equipment as though you had claimed the 30 percent depreciation deduction. Who says the IRS is not out to trap you? A virtual minefield awaits the unsuspecting. To inform the IRS that you don't want to claim the additional first-year depreciation deduction, simply write: I choose not to claim the additional first-year 30 percent depreciation on the auto I purchased in 2003.

For anyone who just learned about this 30 percent business, who purchased a car for business use after September 10, 2001, and who didn't claim the additional first-year deduction on their 2001 or 2002 returns (or attach a statement to the return indicating that they didn't want to claim it), here's what to do. You can claim the deduction and obtain a refund by filing an amended return on Form 1040X (see Chapter 19). Across the top of the form write, FILED PURSUANT TO REG. 301.9100-3. This regulation enables the IRS to grant relief to taxpayers who fail to make a timely election to claim or not to claim (sounds like something from Shakespeare) a deduction or tax credit. In Part II on page 2 of Form 1040X, be sure to state that the fact that the law allowing 30 percent additional first-year depreciation is so new and complex that you just became aware of it and that you're taking immediate action to correct your error. State that you're now claiming the additional first-year depreciation deduction and that you're making this statement under the penalties of perjury (they want blood, don't they?). If you're electing not to claim the deduction then state that and send your 1040X off to IRS central. You'll be surprised how (don't laugh) generous the IRS can be when it wants to.

Not claiming the extra depreciation may make sense if 2003 was a lousy year, which it seems to have been for a lot of folks. If your income was down, the extra deduction would either be wasted or not as valuable as it might otherwise be, if it was claimed during a high-income year.

Just when you thought all this rigmarole was bad enough, Congress many years ago — in its infinite wisdom — enacted the 40 percent rule. Under this rule, if you purchased more than 40 percent of all your business assets (including your auto) during the last quarter of 2003 (October to December), you don't use the depreciation percentages in Table 14-2. Instead, you must use the depreciation percentages known as the mid-quarter convention (see Table 14-3). *Mid-quarter convention* means that you start computing depreciation in the quarter in which a depreciable item is acquired. Thankfully, you can ignore this rule in computing either the 30 percent or 50 percent additional first-year depreciation, but not in computing your regular depreciation.

September 11 additional first-year depreciation — New autos purchased after May 5, 2003

Guess what? The law was changed again. Instead of claiming a deduction for additional first-year bonus depreciation of 30 percent, you now can claim a 50 percent deduction. The hitch? The car has to be a new one, purchased after May 5, 2003, and you must start using it in your business before January 1, 2005. However, if 30 is your lucky number, you can elect to continue to use the 30 percent rather than the 50 percent rate. Additionally, where purchases made after May 5, 2003, are concerned, the requirement that the vehicle be acquired before September 11, 2004, no longer is in effect regardless of whether you're using the 30 percent or 50 percent rate. January 1, 2005, is now the date that counts.

If you want to continue using the 30 percent rate, simply compute your auto depreciation using that rate instead of 50 percent. If you choose to use neither, simply write across the top of **Form 4562, Depreciation and Amortization:** I choose not to claim the additional first-year 30 or 50 percent depreciation for the auto I purchased in 2003.

Say you purchased a car after May 5, 2003, for $20,000. Here's how you compute your depreciation for 2003. Your additional first-year depreciation is $10,000. Next you reduce the cost of the car by that amount to $10,000 ($20,000 − $10,000). Your regular depreciation of $1,500 is computed by multiplying $10,000 by 15 percent (Table 14-2). Your total depreciation before applying the maximum limit of $10,710 comes to $11,500 ($10,000 + $1,500). But, remember you can deduct only the $10,710 maximum. That's how the screwy tax law makes you do the math in order to be able to nail down the additional first-year September 11 depreciation deduction. It gets screwier. The $790 that you couldn't deduct ($11,500 − $10,710) can't be deducted until the end of the depreciation period (Table 14-2), which would be 2008.

To file (or not to file) Form 4562

You compute your depreciation deduction for business property that you started using in 2003 on **Form 4562, Depreciation and Amortization.** Carry the amount of depreciation you calculated on this form over to line 16 of Schedule F.

For property you started using prior to 2003, Form 4562 isn't required. Just enter the depreciation you are entitled to deduct on line 16 of Schedule F. However, if you are depreciating cars, computers, or cellular phones, you must fill out and attach Form 4562 to your return every year.

How to compute the additional September 11 depreciation

Before we explain how to compute this deduction, you need to know what items qualify for it and which ones don't. Real estate doesn't. Leasehold improvements do, if the building is more than 3 years old, and so does computer software.

Here's how you compute your $100,000 buying bonanza and the additional September 11 and regular depreciation deductions. Say you purchase breeding cattle that have a 5-year useful lifetime for $150,000 after May 5, 2003. How do you know what useful life is? You looked it up in Table 14-1. If you don't claim these two special depreciation deductions, your depreciation for 2003 comes to $22,500 ($150,000 × 15 percent — from Table 11-4). By claiming your $100,000 buying bonanza and the additional September 11 depreciation deduction, your 2003 depreciation comes to $128,750. Quite a difference!

Here is the math. First you claim your buying bonanza depreciation of $100,000. This deduction requires you to reduce the $150,000 by $100,000 to get $50,000, which is the figure you use to compute the additional 50 percent depreciation, or $25,000 ($50,000 × 50 percent). Now, for your regular 2003 depreciation, you guessed it, you have to reduce the $50,000 by the $25,000 September 11 depreciation, which comes to $25,000 ($50,000 – $25,000). Stay with us, we're almost there. Your regular 2003 depreciation is $3,750 ($25,000 × 15 percent). Now tally all three amounts, $100,000, $25,000 and $3,750, to arrive at your total depreciation deduction for 2003 of $128,750. Enter that amount on Form 4562 and don't forget to attach it to your return. In future years, you base your depreciation on $25,000. Phew! Hey, no one said minimizing what you have to fork over to Uncle Sam was a walk in the park.

If you don't compute the additional 30 percent deduction and don't elect not to claim it, you must reduce the cost of the cattle as though you had claimed the September 11 depreciation in future years. So flip back to the "September 11th additional depreciation" section to learn how to elect not to claim this additional depreciation deduction or what to do if you just learned about this 30 percent business and filed your 2001 or 2002 without coming to grips with it.

You can claim up to $100,000 on the purchase of either new or used equipment regardless of whether you claim the additional 30 percent or 50 percent additional first-year September 11 depreciation. For the fine print and the special situations when this special depreciation can't be claimed flip back to "Your buying bonanza: The $100,000 deduction" in Chapter 11. The beauty about this special deduction is that not only do you get to claim a deduction of up to $100,000 but you also don't have to cope with all the maddening depreciation rules.

IRS depreciation percentages

To figure the amount of depreciation that you're entitled to claim, glance at the IRS depreciation tables (see Tables 14-2 through 14-7). For business property other than real estate, notice that each table has two categories: *half-year convention* and *mid-quarter convention*. Usually you use the half-year convention. The mid-quarter convention comes into play when the farm assets you acquired and started using during the last three months of the year exceed 40 percent of all the business property that you placed in service during the year. Got that? Read on and follow the examples for both types of depreciation conventions.

Half-year convention depreciation

Suppose that you're depreciating a computer that you purchased for $5,000 in 2003. First you must look up its useful life in Table 14-1. Computers have a useful life of five years, so use the depreciation percentages for five-year property. Okay, easy enough so far, right?

Under the half-year convention for five-year property (see Table 14-4), you find 15 percent as the amount. For 2003, you're entitled to a $750 depreciation deduction ($5,000 × 15 percent). In 2004, you'd multiply the $5,000 cost by 25.5 percent for a deduction of $1,275. And then you use 17.85 percent, 16.66 percent, 16.66 percent, and 8.33 percent in each of the succeeding years. Fun calculations, right? Based on the convention, note that the write-off period for an asset is one year longer than its useful life. That's because in the first year you're entitled to only a half-year's worth of depreciation. The half-year convention means that all assets are considered to have been purchased on July 1 — which entitles you to only half the normal amount of depreciation.

Regardless of whether you use the half-year or are required to use the mid-quarter convention, you must reduce the cost of the item you are depreciating, as we explained earlier, by the 30 percent or 50 percent additional September 11 depreciation that you claimed as your buying bonanza depreciation of up to $100,000. You don't have to reduce the cost if you elected not to claim any of these extra depreciation deductions this year.

Mid-quarter convention depreciation

You must use the mid-quarter convention whenever the business property that you placed in service during the last three months of the year exceeds 40 percent of all your business property placed in service during the year.

For example, suppose you bought a calculator for $500 on February 1, 2003, and a copier for $1,500 on October 1, 2003. Under the half-year convention, you're entitled to a depreciation deduction of $300 ($2,000 × 15 percent). However, because more than 40 percent of all your business property was bought and placed into service during the last three months of the year, you have to switch to the mid-quarter convention. So here's how you must compute the depreciation for these two pieces of equipment.

Under the mid-quarter convention for five-year property (see Table 14-4), the depreciation rate is 26.25 percent for an asset purchased in the first quarter. Therefore, you're entitled to a $131.25 depreciation deduction ($500 × 26.25 percent) for the calculator. For the copier, you have to use the 3.75 percent rate for property bought during the fourth quarter ($1,500 × 3.75 percent), which entitles you to a $56 deduction. In 2004, you can use 22.13 percent for the calculator and 28.88 percent for the copier.

The long and the short of all this is that if you're forced into using the mid-quarter convention, you get less than half the depreciation in the first year that you normally would.

For farm property that you started depreciating in 1987 and 1988, you must use different depreciation tables than the ones shown here. The other tables allow you to take larger deductions in the earlier years and smaller ones in the later years. Whatever depreciation rate you're required to use, at the end of three, five, seven, or ten years, and so on, you get to write off the entire asset. You can obtain the depreciation tables for assets you started to depreciate before 1989 by calling the IRS for Publication 946 (*How To Depreciate Property*).

Table 14-3		MACRS: Three-Year Property			
Year	**Half-Year Convention**	**Mid-Quarter Convention**			
		First Quarter	**Second Quarter**	**Third Quarter**	**Fourth Quarter**
1	25.00%	43.75%	31.25%	18.75%	6.25%
2	37.50%	28.13%	34.38%	40.63%	46.88%
3	25.00%	25.00%	25.00%	25.00%	25.00%
4	12.50%	3.12%	9.37%	15.62%	21.87%

Table 14-4		MACRS: Five-Year Property			
Year	**Half-Year Convention**	**Mid-Quarter Convention**			
		First Quarter	**Second Quarter**	**Third Quarter**	**Fourth Quarter**
1	15.00%	26.25%	18.75%	11.25%	3.75%
2	25.50%	22.13%	24.38%	26.63%	28.88%
3	17.85%	16.52%	17.06%	18.64%	20.21%
4	16.66%	16.52%	16.76%	16.56%	16.40%
5	16.66%	16.52%	16.76%	16.57%	16.41%
6	8.33%	2.06%	6.29%	10.35%	14.35%

Table 14-5		MACRS: Seven-Year Property			
Year	Half-Year Convention	Mid-Quarter Convention			
		First Quarter	Second Quarter	Third Quarter	Fourth Quarter
1	10.71%	18.75%	13.39%	8.04%	2.68%
2	19.13%	17.41%	18.56%	19.71%	20.85%
3	15.03%	13.68%	14.58%	15.48%	16.39%
4	12.25%	12.16%	12.22%	12.27%	12.87%
5	12.25%	12.16%	12.22%	12.28%	12.18%
6	12.25%	12.16%	12.22%	12.27%	12.18%
7	12.25%	12.16%	12.23%	12.28%	12.19%
8	6.13%	1.52%	4.58%	7.67%	10.66%

Table 14-6		MACRS: Ten-Year Property			
Year	Half-Year Convention	Mid-Quarter Convention			
		First Quarter	Second Quarter	Third Quarter	Fourth Quarter
1	7.5%	13.13%	9.38%	5.63%	1.88%
2	13.88%	13.03%	13.59%	14.16%	14.72%
3	11.79%	11.08%	11.55%	12.03%	12.51%
4	10.02%	9.41%	9.82%	10.23%	10.63%
5	8.74%	8.71%	8.73%	8.75%	9.04%
6	8.74%	8.71%	8.73%	8.75%	8.72%
7	8.74%	8.71%	8.73%	8.75%	8.72%
8	8.74%	8.71%	8.73%	8.74%	8.72%
9	8.74%	8.71%	8.73%	8.75%	8.72%
10	8.74%	8.71%	8.73%	8.74%	8.71%
11	4.37%	1.09%	3.28%	5.47%	7.63%

Table 14-7		MACRS: Twenty-Year Property			
Year	Half-Year Convention	Mid-Quarter Convention			
		First Quarter	Second Quarter	Third Quarter	Fourth Quarter
1	3.75%	6.563%	4.688%	2.813%	0.938%
2	7.219%	7.088%	7.148%	7.289%	7.430%
3	6.677%	6.482%	6.612%	6.742%	6.872%
4	6.177%	5.996%	6.116%	6.237%	6.357%

(continued)

Table 14-7 (continued)

Year	Half-Year Convention	Mid-Quarter Convention			
		First Quarter	Second Quarter	Third Quarter	Fourth Quarter
5	5.713%	5.546%	5.658%	5.769%	5.880%
6	5.285%	5.130%	5.233%	5.336%	5.439%
7	4.888%	4.746%	4.841%	4.936%	5.031%
8	4.522%	4.459%	4.478%	4.566%	4.654%
9	4.462%	4.459%	4.463%	4.460%	4.458%
10	4.461%	4.459%	4.463%	4.460%	4.458%

For years 11 through 21, see IRS Publication 946 (*How To Depreciate Property*). For property with a 27½-year life (residential real estate), see Chapter 11.

Line 17: Employee health and benefit programs

Enter on line 17 the premiums you paid for your employees' accident, health, and group term life insurance coverage — but not the cost of your *own* health insurance. Your health insurance premiums plus the premium for your spouse and dependents are deducted on Line 29: Self-employed health insurance deduction. Chapter 7 has the lowdown on this deduction. In 2002, only 70 percent of a self-employed individual's health insurance premiums were deductible. Now it's the entire amount.

Line 18: Feed purchased

On line 18, enter the total cost of livestock feed you purchased during the year.

Your expenses for prepaid feed (along with other prepaid farm supplies) can't exceed 50 percent of your other deductible farm expenses. Doesn't it seem these rules never end? They do, and quicker than you realize, so hang in there. For example, suppose that in 2003, you spent $10,000 on fertilizer, feed, and seed that you plan to use in 2004. Your other deductible farm expenses in 2003 total $18,000. Therefore, your allowable 2003 deduction for prepaid farm supplies can't exceed $9,000 (that's 50 percent of $18,000). The other $1,000 that you can't deduct in 2003 can be deducted in 2004, when you actually use the supplies.

The 50 percent rule doesn't apply if a change occurred in your farming operation that was caused by an extraordinary event such as a flood, a drought, or other catastrophe. Prepaid farm supplies include feed, seed, fertilizer, similar farm supplies not consumed during the year, and poultry that you purchased. Even if your prepaid expenses were more than 50 percent of your other expenses this year, but less than 50 percent of your other farm expenses for the three preceding years, you're still okay. The 50 percent rule for 2003 doesn't apply, and all your prepaid expenses can be deducted.

Livestock feed is an exception to the prepaid farm supplies rule. An advance payment for livestock feed can be deducted in full if:

- The prepayment isn't a deposit that can be refunded.
- The prepayment has a business purpose and wasn't made merely to avoid paying tax
- By deducting the prepayment, you didn't materially distort your income.

If the prepayment doesn't reduce your income and tax by more than 20 percent, you shouldn't have a problem. Even though the IRS may have it's own opinion as to when a distortion of income occurs, 20 percent is a reasonable position.

Line 19: Fertilizer and lime expenses

Although you have to report as income the value of fertilizer and lime that you receive under a government program, the good news is: Because you're using these items on your farm, you're also entitled to claim the value of these items as a deduction. Enter the expenditure for these items on line 19. The rule for prepaid items (discussed in the preceding section) also applies to fertilizer and lime and so does the exemption from the rule.

Line 20: Freight and trucking expenses

You don't have to be a tax expert to figure out what goes here. The cost of operating your own truck goes on line 12. You can't deduct fines for overloading a truck, even if unintentional. Here's where you deduct the freight bills for moving items off and onto your farm.

Line 21: Gasoline, fuel, and oil

Gasoline for operating a car or truck goes on line 12. This line is for tractor gas, grease, oil, antifreeze, kerosene and coal for heaters, brooder stoves, lanterns, and tank heaters. This is what the IRS means by *fuel*. Fuel to heat your personal residence isn't deductible, unless you use part of it for business. Don't overlook the chance to claim a credit on your return for some of the tax you pay when you buy gas. But more on that later under the heading "Fuel Credits."

Line 22: Insurance (other than health)

Insurance premiums to protect your buildings, livestock, grain, crops, equipment, and supplies from loss or damage are deductible. Premiums for workers' compensation insurance and liability insurance also are included on line 22.

Suppose that a horse wanders onto your property, falls down a drainage ditch, and has to be destroyed. If you don't have liability insurance, guess who would need to hire a lawyer? Our advice is to protect yourself with liability insurance and to carry adequate fire, theft, robbery, and crop insurance. Although you can't deduct the insurance premiums paid for your residential insurance, if you use a portion of your home for business purposes, you can deduct that portion of the premium.

Insurance premiums that you pay in advance can be deducted only in the year that they apply. For example, suppose that on January 1, 2003, you paid a three-year insurance premium of $1,500. Of that prepaid amount, $500 gets deducted in tax year 2003, $500 in 2004, and $500 in tax year 2005. Business interruption insurance can also be deducted. But any amount paid under the policy is fully taxable.

Lines 23a and 23b: Interest expense

Most farm interest is deductible; that includes interest on the mortgage on your farm and the interest on loans used to buy farm equipment and farm supplies. As a general rule, the IRS divides interest into the following categories:

> ✔ Trade or business interest
>
> ✔ Investment interest
>
> ✔ Interest on a residence
>
> ✔ Personal interest

Deductible interest includes mortgage interest and interest on other business debts that you may incur while running your farm.

Of the other types of interest, investment interest is deducted on **Schedule A, Itemized Deductions.** What's investment interest? Suppose that you open a margin account at Merrill Lynch to trade commodities. The interest that you pay is categorized as investment interest. Investment interest can be deducted only to the extent of your investment income. However, if you trade farm commodities as part of your farm operation, the investment interest rules don't apply. Interest on a residence is also deducted on Schedule A.

Personal interest, such as credit card interest and personal loans, can't be deducted. But what if you borrow $30,000 and use $10,000 to buy farm equipment and $20,000 to buy a car that is strictly for personal use? You have to make an allocation. The interest on the $10,000 used to buy farm equipment is deductible; the interest on the $20,000 used to buy the car is not deductible. For more information on deducting interest, see Chapter 9.

Line 24: Labor hired (less employment credits)

On line 24, enter the amount you paid in cash wages — that is, the total amount you pay your employees *before* you withhold income tax, Social Security, and Medicare taxes. The cost of any meals and lodging that you provide is not considered wages, which means that employees don't have to pay tax on it. However, *you* are allowed to deduct those costs as a valid "other expense." On line 34, you can deduct the cost of food you buy for your employees.

Any cash allowance that you give employees to buy meals is considered part of their wages. Normally, you can deduct only 50 percent of the cost of meals. (See entertainment expenses in Chapter 11.)

If more than half of all the employees to whom you provide meals are furnished the meals for what the law calls "the convenience of the employer," then all the meals you furnish your employees are fully deductible. No 50 percent "haircut" for farmers who meet this "convenience" test.

If you pay your employees *in-kind,* you can deduct (as a labor expense) the value of the goods they received. For example, suppose that you give an employee a horse worth $1,500 as payment for painting your barn. You can then deduct the $1,500 as a labor expense. However, remember that you must also report (as income) the $1,500 as if you sold the horse to your employee, because bartering is a taxable event.

The wages you paid and the income tax, Social Security, and Medicare taxes that you're required to withhold are reported to the government on **Form 943, Employer's Annual Tax Return for Agricultural Employees.** This form must be filed by January 31, 2004. If you withheld less than $2,500 for the year, you can pay what you owe when you file Form 943. But once you withhold $2,500 or more, you have to turn over to the government what you withheld for the month by the 15th of the following month. If you withheld $50,000 or more during 2002, you must remit your withholding taxes electronically (directly from your bank by wire transfer on a semiweekly basis). You'd think that if you're required to wire your withholding taxes in 2004, you'd have to do so because you withheld more than $50,000 in 2003 and not 2002. Guess what? You'd be wrong. If you operate more than a mom-and-pop family farm, get your hands on IRS Publication 51 (Circular A, *Agricultural Employer's Tax Guide*). More than you want to know about this subject is explained in all its glorious detail.

You have to reduce your deduction for the wages you paid by the amount of any employment credits you claimed on line 52 of Form 1040 (see Chapter 8). You didn't ask, but here they are: the Indian Employment Credit (Form 8845), the Welfare-to-Work Credit (Form 8861), the Empowerment Zone Employment Credit (Form 8844), and the Work Opportunity Credit for qualified employees (Form 5884).

The wages you pay to a child under the age of 18 are not subject to Social Security and Medicare taxes. So, as long as the child's wages total less than $4,750 (the standard deduction for tax year 2003), the child won't have to pay any tax at all (as long as that $4,750 is the child's *only* source of income). And better still, you get to deduct the $4,750 as a labor expense. The only requirement is that the amount you pay for the child's services must be reasonable. For example, you can't claim that you paid your 3-year-old $4,750 to clean out the barn. And because the standard deduction is tied to the rate of inflation, every year it goes up by about $100 or so.

Line 25: Pension and profit-sharing plans

On line 25, enter the amount you contributed to your employees' Keogh and SEP (Simplified Employee Pension) account(s). As for your own Keogh or SEP, enter that amount on Form 1040, line 30 (see Chapter 7 for information on deducting your own contributions to your retirement accounts). A relatively new type of retirement plan called a SIMPLE retirement plan is available to employers with fewer than 100 employees. These plans have none of the mind-numbing rules to follow or forms to file that regular retirement plans have. A SIMPLE plan can also cover the owner(s) of a farm. See Chapter 21 for more information on retirement accounts.

Lines 26a and 26b: Rent or lease expense

On line 26a, enter the amount that you paid to rent farm machinery and tractors.

If you lease equipment under the condition that you own the equipment at the end of the lease, the IRS considers this *a conditional sales contract,* which isn't really a lease. A conditional sales contract is considered a purchase — you must depreciate the cost of this equipment instead of deducting the lease payments as a business expense.

If you rent a farm, you can deduct the rental payments that cover the land, buildings, and so on, but you can't deduct the amount that represents the fair rental value of the farmhouse in which you live. However, if you use part of your home for business, you *can* deduct that portion. For more on deducting home office expenses, see Chapter 11.

If you pay rent in the form of crop shares, you can't deduct the value of the crops as rent, even though you are required to send the landlord a Form 1099-MISC (if the value of what you paid was more than $600). The reason for this is that you get to deduct the expenses in planting, cultivating, growing, and harvesting the crop. One set of deductions per customer. That's IRS policy. Only the rent that you paid in cash gets deducted on line 26.

If you happen to be leasing a vehicle, flip back to line 9 in Chapter 11 for the special rule that governs these rentals.

Line 27: Repairs and maintenance

Repairs are deductible in full. Improvements must be depreciated. How can you tell the difference between a repair and an improvement? An *improvement* extends the useful life of something. A repair doesn't. Fixing a leak is a repair. Replacing a roof is an improvement. When does a repair move into the category of an improvement? This is something the IRS and taxpayers often go to court over. There is no easy answer.

Line 28: Seeds and plants purchased

Line 28 is one of the simplest lines on the form — just enter the amount you paid for seed and plants. If you prepaid for seed or plants that you'll use the following year, you may be able to deduct only a portion of that expense this tax year. See the rules regarding prepaid seed in the "Line 18: Feed purchased" section, earlier in this chapter.

Even if you're a cash-basis taxpayer and permitted to deduct expenses as they're paid, you can't currently deduct the costs incurred to grow plants and trees that take more than two years to produce a marketable crop. The IRS lists 36 fruit trees (see line 16) that are included in the more-than-two-years-to-bear-fruit category. Per depreciation Table 14-1 earlier in this chapter, trees have a 10-year write-off period. Just in case an IRS agent is lurking behind the fruit tree you just planted, you'd better know that the rules get even more complex: Your fertilizer and soil and water conservation expenses aren't currently deductible until the first marketable crop is grown. Expenses incurred prior to the period the tree starts bearing fruit have to be depreciated along with the cost of the tree or plant. Remember, just about every IRS rule has an exception to it. Flip back to line 16 to learn about this one.

Line 29: Storage and warehousing

Nothing tricky here. Enter the amount you paid the grain elevator operator and other storage and warehousing expenses.

Line 30: Supplies purchased

Baling wire, oil for lamps, shovels, and other types of supplies used around a farm get deducted here.

Line 31: Taxes

Line 31 is where you deduct real estate, your share of the Social Security and Medicare taxes that *you* had to fork over on the wages that you paid (not the amount you *withhold* from the employee's check — that withholding gets reported on Form 943, Form W-3, and the employee's Form W-2), and personal property taxes on farm business assets. You can deduct half the amount that you pay on your own Social Security tax. However, that amount is deducted on line 28, Form 1040, not on Schedule F. See Chapter 7 for more information on how to pay your Social Security tax.

The real estate taxes you paid on the part of your farm that you use as your home are deducted on **Schedule A, Itemized Deductions,** and not on this line. State income taxes also get deducted there. Sales taxes paid on the purchase of farm equipment can't be deducted separately. Sales taxes are added to the total cost of the equipment, which then gets depreciated.

Some states grant a sales tax exemption for farm equipment and supplies. Check with your state's revenue office.

Line 32: Utilities

On line 32, deduct your utility expenses. For example, you can deduct your water expenses for irrigation and other farm uses, electricity to run farm equipment, and your telephone (to the extent it's used for business). However, if some of these items are used for your farm residence as well, that portion of your utility bill is considered a personal expense and can't be deducted.

Line 33: Veterinary, breeding, and medicine

On line 33, tally up your expenses for veterinary and breeding fees, medicines, vaccines, culling chickens, dehorning, and testing cattle.

Lines 34a–f: Other expenses

Congratulations! You made it to the last line on which you have to make entries. On line 34, put deductions for expenses that you couldn't find a home for on lines 12 through 33, such as accounting, dues, bookkeeping, commissions, office supplies, government milk assessments, business travel, and entertainment. Only 50 percent of your entertainment can be deducted. See Chapter 9 for the lowdown on entertainment rules.

Personal clothing isn't deductible. The IRS has been known at times to disallow a deduction for overalls or work clothes because a farmer couldn't convince the tax auditor that it wouldn't be appropriate to wear the overalls into town. If you get to line 34f and run out of space, attach a schedule of additional expenses, write `See expenses from attached schedule`, and enter the total of those expenses on line 34f.

Line 35: Total expenses

Time for an addition quiz: Add up lines 12 through 34f; then enter the amount of your total farm expenses on line 35.

Line 36: Net farm profit or loss

An additional math test: Subtract your total expenses (line 35) from your total income (line 11). If you come up with a positive number, guess what? You've made a profit! Enter the amount of your net profit on line 36, copy the amount onto Form 1040, line 18, and also onto Schedule SE, line 1. (Schedule SE is used to compute your Social Security and Medicare tax.)

If you have a loss (line 35 is larger than line 11), then subtract line 11 from line 35. Enter this amount in brackets. For example, enter a $10,000 loss as `<$10,000>`. Enter this amount on Form 1040, line 18, and on Schedule SE, line 1.

Lines 37a and 37b: At risk

If you have a loss and are personally liable to pay back every dime that you borrowed to go into business, check line 37a. If not, check line 37b and flip over to the Seek Advice icon by line 27 in Chapter 13 to find out what this is about. The rules are complex regarding the deduction of losses when you have no economic risk.

Tax Issues Specific to Farmers

Unfortunately, you still have to cope with a few additional things that we explain in the following sections.

Estimated taxes

The IRS doesn't want to wait until April 15 to collect what you owe. If two-thirds of your income was from farming in 2002 or 2003, you have to make an estimated income tax payment by January 15, 2004, for what you owe for 2003, or file your return (including your full tax payment) by March 1, 2004. If you don't make an estimated payment, you'll be charged a penalty equal to current market interest rates. The penalty is computed on **Form 2210-F, Underpayment of Estimated Tax by Farmers and Fishermen.**

The amount of your required estimated tax payment is 66⅔ percent of your 2003 actual tax *or* 100 percent of your 2002 tax, whichever is the smaller amount. For example, suppose that your 2003 tax is $10,000 and your 2002 tax was $1,000. Because your 2002 tax of $1,000 is smaller than $6,667 (⅔ of your 2003 tax of $10,000), you needed to have paid only $1,000 on January 15, 2004. The $9,000 balance can be paid when you file on April 15.

If you file your return by March 1, 2004, and pay what you owe, you can skip having to make the January 15 payment.

Even though you file your return by March 1, 2004, you have until April 15, 2004, to make and deduct your IRA contribution (see Line 24, Chapter 7).

If two-thirds of your income in 2002 or 2003 wasn't from farming, then the regular estimated tax rules apply. See Chapter 15.

If you're hearing about all this for the first time — sorry. Mark your January 2005 calendar so this won't happen again when you file your 2004 return.

Operating at a loss

When operating any business, you must show a profit in at least three of every five consecutive years, or the IRS will term your business a hobby and disallow your losses, a situation known as *hobby losses*. If you're breeding horses, training, showing, or racing them, however, you must make a profit in *two out of seven years* to keep the tax collector away. The IRS does not consider your enterprise a business if you have continuing losses — no business, no business deductions.

The three-out-of-five rule was established to keep the IRS off your back. If you meet this requirement, the IRS can't claim that the losses in the two other years can't be deducted because the business is a hobby. Not making a profit in three out of five years or two out of seven years doesn't automatically make the venture a hobby, but it is a strong indication that it may be.

However, if your farm does incur a net loss in 2003, you can write off that loss against any other income you and your spouse made that year. And get this — if the loss is greater than your combined income in the current year, you can carry the loss back over each of the past five years and obtain a refund on the tax you paid at that time. If the loss still isn't used up by carrying it back, you can carry it *forward* to offset your income in the *next* 20 years. You can also choose not to carry the loss back and use it only in future years instead. See Chapter 19 for more information on amending a prior year's return and carrying losses back as well as forward.

For losses incurred before 1998, the carryback was three years. If the losses weren't used up by offsetting income in the three preceding years, they were carried forward for 15 years. For nonfarmers and for casualty losses, a mishmash of rules governs whether the carryback is limited to two years as opposed to three years. For losses incurred in 2001 and 2002, the five-year carryback also is the rule for nonfarmers. You also can choose to carry your loss back two or three (if applicable) years instead of five years. See Chapter 19 for more details.

Your Social Security tax

This tax is commonly referred to as the self-employment tax. See the section explaining line 55 in Chapter 8 to find out how to compute this amount and take a deduction for half of what you pay in Social Security tax.

Farmers have an optional method for computing this tax. The computation is made in Part II of Schedule SE.

Here's how it works. If your gross income (from line 11 on Schedule F) is $2,400 or less, or your net income (line 36) was less than $1,733, you can report two-thirds of your gross income as your *net farm income from self-employment*. Remember, you use this amount to compute your Social Security tax (not for figuring the amount on which you pay income tax). For example, suppose that your gross income was $1,800 and your net income (profit) was $500 — you can elect to report $1,200 (⅔ of $1,800) as your self-employment income, for the purpose of computing your Social Security tax. (However, you pay income tax on only the $500 of net income that you earned.) Why do all this?

- ✔ You receive credit for Social Security coverage.

- ✔ Your dependent child-care deduction and earned income credit increase with this method.

The IRS considers dividends from a farm cooperative income that's subject to self-employment tax and not investment income, which is what most other dividends are, and therefore not subject to this tax. If you receive part of a crop from a tenant farmer, it's considered rental income, which isn't subject to self-employment income if you didn't materially participate in overseeing your tenant's activities.

Investment credits

The law allows an *investment credit,* which is similar to a direct payment of tax, for what you spent on reforestation or to rehabilitate historic structures and buildings placed in service before 1936. For reforestation, the law allows a credit for up to $10,000 of these expenditures. If you rehabilitate a historic structure, you can take an investment credit equal to 20 percent of your expenses. The *energy credit* equals 10 percent of what you spend installing solar or geothermal energy-producing equipment. These credits are computed on **Form 3468, Investment Credit.** Also check out the tax incentives for empowerment zones and other distressed communities in IRS Publication 954 *(Tax Incentives for Empowerment Zones and Other Distressed Communities),* and **Form 8850, Work Opportunity and Welfare-to-Welfare Credits.**

Fuel credits

You can claim a credit for the off-highway use of fuels on your farm. The credit is computed on **Form 4136, Credit for Federal Tax Paid on Fuels.** *Note:* The definition of *off-highway* use doesn't apply to pleasure boats. The credit is equal to 18.4 cents for every gallon of gas used on your farm.

You can buy dyed diesel fuel tax-free for use on a farm. Ask the vendor for an exemption certificate. Fill it out, hand it back to him, and watch the price drop 24.4 cents a gallon.

You can now claim a credit or refund for the excise tax on undyed kerosene or diesel fuel for home use.

Electric and clean fuel–burning vehicles

Don't overlook the electric car credit (line 52, Chapter 8) and the deduction for the Toyota and Honda hybrid gas/electric clean fuel–burning deduction (line 33, Chapter 7).

Sale of a farm or equipment

The sale of a farm or farm equipment gets tricky — you must consider many different factors, such as recapture of depreciation, credits, and basis (cost) adjustments to the property being sold. These types of sales are reported on **Form 4797, Sales of Business Property.** For more information on capital gains, see Chapter 12.

Installment sales

Cash-method farmers who use the installment method for reporting the sale of farm property don't have to take installment sales into account when determining whether they're subject to the Alternative Minimum Tax. See information in Chapter 8 if you're subject to this fiendish tax because you're claiming too many deductions.

Chapter 15

Other Schedules and Forms to File

∙ ∙

In This Chapter

▶ Form 1040-ES (the estimated tax)

▶ Forms 2441 and 3903 (kids of working parents, and moving away)

▶ Forms 8606, 8615, 8814, and 8829 (IRAs, kiddie taxes, and home office expenses)

▶ Form W-4 (tax withholding)

▶ Schedules H, R, and SE (for nannies, the elderly and disabled, and the self-employed)

∙ ∙

*M*ost taxpayers need to file a variety of other tax schedules and forms to accompany their 1040s. These documents are tailored to specific tax situations. For example, for nondeductible IRAs, you need Form 8606. We know it's a chore, but think of the process this way: As a general rule, the yuckier the schedules, the more you reduce the amount of tax you pay. This chapter presents a brief overview of the major forms that taxpayers need to file, with tips for filling out the trickier lines. We discuss them in alphabetical and numeric order.

Form 1040-ES, the Estimated Tax Form

If you're self-employed or have income, such as retirement benefits, that isn't subject to withholding, you should be making quarterly estimated tax payments on Form 1040-ES. On average, a third of what you earn isn't yours. (It's depressing, we know.) You're only its temporary custodian until mid-April. But if you keep too much in custody — that is, you don't have enough withheld — that "third of what you earn" is subject to a penalty if you don't pay in enough. What's enough? Read on.

You must pay in at least 90 percent of your tax during the year. But if not paying in 90 percent leaves a balance of less than $1,000, you don't need to make quarterly estimates. For example, your 2003 tax is $3,000. Ninety percent amounts to $2,700. Your withholding comes to $2,600, which is less than 90 percent of your tax. Because you owed less than $1,000 when you filed, no estimated payments were required. For 2004, you'll have to make quarterly estimated payments if you expect to owe more than $1,000 when you file in 2005.

You make estimated tax payments on **Form 1040-ES, Estimated Tax for Individuals.** The form requires only your name, address, Social Security number, and the amount that you're paying. For 2004 estimated payments, make sure that you use the 2004 1040-ES. Enter the estimated payments you made for 2003 on line 62 of Form 1040.

Here's how it works. Suppose that you're self-employed. Your 2003 tax is $7,000, and your self-employment tax is $3,000 — a total of $10,000. The law requires that you make estimated tax payments of 90 percent of your estimated 2004 tax or 100 percent of your 2003 tax. So if you expect your 2004 total tax to be the same amount that it was in 2003 (that is,

$10,000), you must make quarterly estimates of $2,250 (90 percent of $10,000 ÷ 4), with 10 percent, or $1,000, coming due in April 2005. However, if you make quarterly estimates of $2,500 (100 percent of your 2003 tax) and your actual 2004 tax comes to $25,000, no penalty will be assessed. Why? Because you paid 100 percent of your 2003 tax ($10,000), you can wait until April 15, 2005, to pay the $15,000 balance.

If your 2003 income is more than $150,000, you have to make estimated tax payments equal to 110 percent of your 2003 tax to escape a 2004 underestimating penalty if your 2004 tax turns out to be substantially more than your 2003 tax. For example, suppose that your 2003 tax was $100,000. Because your 2003 income was more than $150,000, you have to make estimated payments of at least $110,000 for 2004. Now, suppose your 2004 tax turns out to be $200,000. Because you made estimated payments of at least $110,000 (110 percent of your 2003 tax), you can wait until April 15, 2005, to pay the $90,000 balance without incurring any penalty. This rule doesn't apply to farmers or fishermen.

The only way that you can escape the penalty for not making the quarterly payments is to know the rules. If you were burned by this penalty on your 2003 return, don't let it happen in 2004. When you file your 2003 return on April 15, 2004, you also need to make your first quarterly estimated payment for 2004. The three additional payments are due June 15, 2004; September 15, 2004; and January 15, 2005.

Use Form 1040-ES (2004) to compute your 2004 estimated tax payments. It comes with four vouchers that must accompany your checks so you get credit for your payments.

But before you fill in the vouchers that are due April 15, 2004; June 15, 2004; September 15, 2004; and January 15, 2005; you have to figure out how much you have to pay. That's why the first part of the form contains a worksheet. It's sort of a mini tax return, so you can figure out your 2004 tax and how much you have to pay in quarterly installments. Because you're making an estimate, you can adjust future estimated payments if your income for the balance of the year moves up or down.

If your income has been pretty consistent and you end up paying the same amount of tax every year, enter the amount of tax from line 60 of your 1040 (or line 38 of your 1040A) on line 13c of the worksheet that comes with Form 1040-ES less any tax withheld from your salary or pension, for example. Divide this amount by four and enter the resulting amount on line 17. That amount is what you have to pay every quarter. But if you want to keep a little more money in your pocket, you can get away with paying only 90 percent of this amount. Say your 2003 tax was $10,000. As we explained previously, a fail-safe method is to pay 100 percent of that amount. Then, no matter what your tax turns out to be, the IRS can't assess a penalty if your estimate of your 2004 tax is off by a mile. If your 2004 tax turns out to be $100,000, you can wait to pay the $90,000 balance on April 15, 2005, without incurring a penalty. However, if your 2003 income is more than $150,000, this "fail-safe" method works only if you pay in 110 percent of your 2003 tax when making your 2004 estimated payments.

If you can't base your 2004 estimated income on what you earned in 2003 because your earnings are too up and down, the IRS provides an estimated tax worksheet. Where can you get your hands on this worksheet? Try page 4 of Form 1040-ES.

Here's help when filling out the 1040-ES:

Line 1: Enter your 2003 income or what you expect to earn in 2004.

Line 2: Enter your standard deduction or your itemized deductions for 2004. If you expect them to be the same as 2003, enter the amount from line 37 of your 1040.

Line 3: Subtract line 2 from line 1.

Line 4: Enter your exemptions. Multiply the amount that you claimed on line 6(d) of your 1040 by $3,100. This amount will actually be a little higher in 2004 because exemptions are increasing every year by the annual inflation rate. Your exemptions are whittled away if your income is too high (see the phaseout of personal exemptions in Chapter 4). Remember, this figure is an estimate; we're trying to take you through this form in the quickest and simplest way.

Line 5: Subtract line 4 from line 3. This figure is your taxable income.

Line 6: Figure your tax on line 5 by using the tax rate schedules that come with the 1040-ES for 2004. Figure your tax the same way that you did when you prepared your 2003 return. For a quick refresher course, go back to line 41 in Chapter 8.

Line 7: Alternative minimum tax. See line 42 in Chapter 8.

Line 8: Add lines 6 and 7. It's getting easier.

Line 9: Enter the tax credits that you're entitled to — child tax credit, child-care, earned income, and foreign tax credits are the most common ones. The child tax credit for 2004 is $1,000 per child.

Line 10: Subtract line 9 from line 8.

Line 11: Enter your 2004 self-employment tax. We cover how to compute this tax later in this chapter, so jump to "Schedule SE: Self-Employment Tax Form" if you need a quick review. (That's how you pay your Social Security tax if you're self-employed.) Line 11 of the worksheet has the 2004 self-employment tax rates and the amount of income subject to it.

Line 12: Additional taxes. On this line, enter the 10 percent penalty that you expect to pay because you're under 59½ and plan to tap into your IRA in 2004, for example. If you don't expect to have any weird kind of financial transactions, enter a zero (-0-) on this line. See lines 55 to 59 in Chapter 8 for a crash course in what these might be.

Line 13a: Add lines 10 through 12.

Line 13b: We took care of this credit on line 9, so you can ignore this line.

Line 13c: Subtract line 13b from 13a. You should end up with the same amount as on line 13a. **This figure is your 2004 estimated tax.**

Lines 14a and 14b: Here's where you have an option. You can pay either 100 percent of your 2003 tax (line 38 of your 2003 Form 1040A or line 60 of your 2003 Form 1040) or 90 percent of line 13c. The choice is yours. Using your 2003 tax is the fail-safe method because you pay no penalties if you're off by a mile. Remember, if your 2003 income was more than $150,000, you have to pay 110 percent of your 2003 tax to use this fail-safe method.

Line 14c: Enter the amount that you want to pay — the 90 percent amount from line 14a, or 100 percent (or 110 percent if your 2003 income was more than $150,000) of your 2003 tax from line 14b.

Line 15: Enter the amount of tax that you expect to have withheld from your salary or pension.

Line 16: Subtract line 15 from line 14c. **This amount is what you have to pay.**

Line 17: Divide line 16 by four to figure out what you have to pay every quarter. However, if you skipped the first payment on April 15, 2004, you have to divide line 16 by three because now you have to make three payments: June 15, September 15, and next January 15. If you're making two payments because you missed both the April 16 and June 15 payments, divide line 16 by two and get your money in on September 15 and January 15.

The payment vouchers: Enter your name, address, Social Security number, and the amount you're paying on the voucher that you submit. Also, put your Social Security number on your check with the notation 2004 1040 ES. Make your check out to the U.S. Treasury and mail it, along with the voucher, to the address on the back page of the 1040-ES. Instead of cutting a check and mailing vouchers, you can use your credit card to make these payments or wire transfer the money from your bank account — see line 12 in the 1040-EZ of Chapter 5.

Don't mail your payment to the Service Center where you file. Use the preaddressed envelopes that the IRS sent you. If you're using your own envelopes, be sure to mail your check and payment voucher to the address shown on the Form 1040-ES instructions for the place where you live.

Form 2441, Child and Dependent-Care Expenses

If you hire someone to take care of your children so you can work, you're entitled to the credit that you figure on **Form 2441.** Nursery school and day-care expenses also qualify for the credit. To qualify for the credit, your child must be under the age of 13 or a dependent of any age who is physically or mentally handicapped. You're also entitled to the credit if your spouse is handicapped or is a full-time student and you incur expenses getting care for your kids so that you can work. Here are the ins and outs of the Child and Dependent-Care Credit:

- You can claim child-care expenses while you're working or looking for work, as long as you have some earned income.

  What constitutes earned income? Wages, tips, strike benefits, disability pay reported as wages, voluntary salary deferrals such as for a 401(k) plan, meals and lodging furnished for the convenience of the employer (regardless of whether these fringe benefits are subject to tax), and earnings from being self-employed after deducting expenses — add all these up and that's what's called *earned income*. Want a shorter definition? What were you paid for working? But, because this is a tax book, we have to give you every last item.

- Working includes looking for work. However, if you don't find a job and don't have earned income, you can't claim a credit for your child-care expenses.

- If you're married, both of you must work or be looking for work.

  Your spouse is considered to be working and having earned income if he/she is a full-time student or unable to care for himself or herself.

- For your expenses to be considered work-related, they must help to enable you to work or look for work.

- Sleep-away camp does not qualify as a child-care expense.

- Payments to relatives count even if they live in your home, provided they're not your dependent. If the relative providing the care is your child, the child must be 19 by the end of the year and not your dependent for the payment to count as child-care expenses.

- Although nursery school counts as a child-care expense, after the child enters the first grade, the tuition must be allocated between the schooling expenses and the expenses incurred for childcare.

- Expenses incurred while you're out sick don't qualify. They weren't incurred for the purpose of enabling you to work. You incurred the expenses because you were sick and couldn't take care of your kids.

- Medical expenses incurred on behalf of a spouse or dependent who is unable to care for himself or herself count as work-related expenses. But, you can't claim these expenses as both medical and work-related. You must claim one or the other. Claim medical expenses on Schedule A, Form 1040. (See Chapter 9.)

To claim this credit, you can be single, a head of household, qualifying widow(er) with dependent child, or married filing jointly. Here's how to fill out this form:

- **Line 1** of Form 2441 requires that you report the name, address, Social Security number, or Employer Identification Number (EIN) of the person or organization providing the care, and the amount that you paid to the provider. If your nanny or baby sitter is off the books, you can't claim this credit. However, if your annual payment to any one individual is less than $1,400, you're not liable for the payment of Social Security taxes for your child-care provider. See "Schedule H: Nanny Tax," later in this chapter, for the nanny tax rules.

  If you didn't receive dependent-care benefits from your employer, you need to complete only Part II in addition to line 1. If you did receive these benefits, you have to complete Part III on the back of the form. Employer-provided dependent-care benefits are noted in box 10 of your W-2.

- **On line 2,** enter the qualifying person's name (that's IRS speak for your child), the child's Social Security number, and what it cost to care for the child so that you could work. However, you can't enter more than $3,000 for one child or $6,000 for two or more children.

- **On line 3,** enter the amounts from line 2, keeping in mind the $3,000 limit for one child and $6,000 limit for two or more kids. If you completed Part III, enter the amount from line 26.

- **On line 4,** enter your earned income.

- **On line 5,** enter your spouse's earned income. If your spouse doesn't have any income you can't claim this credit. However, an exception exists for a spouse who is either a full-time student or unable to care for himself. Spouses are considered to have earned income even if they didn't receive any wages. Under this deemed-to-have-income rule, your spouse is considered to have earned $200 per month if you have one qualifying child or dependent and $400 a month if there are two qualifying children or dependents. A second rule linked to this deemed-income business. Your credit is based on the lower of your spouse's income or your allowable child-care expenses. If this sounds more complex than most rules, here's how it works. Say your spouse was a full-time student for six months, and you have $3,000 in child-care expenses for caring for your two-year-old daughter. Your spouse is deemed to have earned $1,200, six months times $200. Because this amount is lower than your actual expenses, it is the amount the credit is based on.

- **On line 6,** enter the smaller of lines 3, 4, or 5.

- **On line 7,** enter your adjusted gross income (AGI) from line 35 of your 1040.

  Based on your AGI, use the chart below line 8 to find out what percentage of line 6 can be claimed as a credit. For example, if your amount on line 7 was more than $43,000, you're entitled to a credit equal to 20 percent of the amount you entered on line 6. Enter that percentage on line 8, and do the math to get the figure on line 9. For example, if line 6 is $6,000 (you have two kids), your credit is $1,200 ($6,000 × 20 percent).

✔ **On line 10,** you have to do a little comparing. Your credit for child- and dependent-care expenses can't exceed your tax on line 43 of Form 1040 minus the amount on line 44 of Form 1040. Enter that amount on line 10.

✔ **On line 11,** enter the smaller of line 9 or 10. Copy that number over to line 45 on the 1040. 1040A filers have a separate form for this credit — **Schedule 2, Form 1040A** — and should enter the credit on line 29 of the 1040A.

Many states also allow a credit for child- and dependent-care expenses. New York, for example, bases its tax credit on the amount of the federal credit. Check with the tax office in your state to find out what credit, if any, you can take.

Looking ahead, find out whether your employer offers you the ability to have money deducted from your paycheck — before taxes — into a dependent-care spending account. You may be able to do this in the future and save even more tax dollars instead of taking this credit (you can't do both).

If your employer has a day-care plan or provides day-care services under a qualified plan, the reimbursement paid to you or your care provider may not be completely tax-free. To determine whether any portion is taxable, you have to complete Part III of Form 2441. The amount your employer paid for day-care costs or the value of the day-care services that your employer provides is indicated in Box 10 of Form W-2. The amount that is excludable from tax is limited to the smallest of

✔ The amount in Box 10 Form 1040

✔ The total of your child- and dependent-care expenses

✔ Your earned income

✔ Your spouse's earned income

✔ $5,000 ($2,500 if married, filing separately)

The portion of tax-free child-care benefits that you received reduces the amount of child- and dependent-care expenses eligible for the child-care credit.

Form 3903, Moving Expenses

If you incur moving expenses because you have to relocate for your job, you can deduct moving expenses for which your employer didn't reimburse you. Self-employed individuals may also deduct their moving expenses. And, unlike other deductible expenses, this deduction isn't subject to varying interpretations. It's subject to two mathematical tests. The first one: The distance between your new job location and your former home must be at least 50 miles more than the distance between your former home and your former job location. Let us run this by you one more time:

A. Miles from your old home to new workplace

B. Miles from your old home to old workplace

C. Subtract line B from line A.

If line C is at least 50 miles, you're entitled to a moving-expense deduction. For someone just entering the workforce, the new job must be at least 50 miles from his or her old residence.

The second test requires that you remain employed on a full-time basis at your new job location for at least 39 weeks during the 12-month period immediately following your arrival. You don't have to work for the same employer. In other words, you can't claim a deduction unless you pass the distance test and satisfy the employment-duration requirement.

The rule is even tougher on self-employed people. To get the deduction, you must work full time in the general area of your new workplace for 78 weeks (that's a year and a half) during the 24 months after your arrival. To save you this bit of math, a part-time job doesn't satisfy the 39- or 78-week test.

If you work outside the U.S., you're eligible for a special exemption: You can deduct expenses for a move to a new home in the U.S. when you permanently retire. The move doesn't have to be related to a new job. This exemption also applies to a survivor of someone who worked outside the U.S.

Members of the Armed Forces aren't subject to either the distance or length-of-employment requirements at the new location.

You can deduct moving expenses in either the year in which they're incurred or the year in which they're paid. When you consider that moving companies demand payment in advance or COD, this deduction option sounds better than it really is.

Meals, temporary living expenses, and expenses incurred in the sale or lease of a residence are no longer deductible. You may deduct only the cost of moving and storage of your household goods and personal effects from your former residence to your new one, plus travel and lodging costs for you and members of your household while traveling to your new residence. The cost of storing and insuring your household goods and personal effects can be deducted for any 30 consecutive days after the day your possessions were removed from your former home and before they are delivered to your new home. You can deduct lodging on the day of your arrival and lodging within the area of your former home within one day after you could not live in your former home because your furniture had been removed. Deductible moving expenses include connecting and disconnecting utilities, shipping an auto, and transporting household pets — so don't forget Fido. Meals are never deductible, even while traveling from one area to another. These are the federal rules. Some states allow a deduction for moving expenses — your state rules may or may not be similar to the federal rules.

The place to deduct moving expenses is **Form 3903, Moving Expenses.** If you haven't met the 39- or 78-week test by the time that you file your return, don't worry. You're still allowed to claim the deduction if you expect to meet the test. However, if it turns out that you fail the 39- or 78-week test, you must report the deduction as income on next year's tax return. No fun at all.

You've lucked out with Form 3903; it's only five lines to get through! Here's what you do:

Line 1: Enter the cost of transporting and storing your household and personal goods plus the other deductible moving expenses we discussed earlier.

Line 2: Enter the travel and lodging expenses you're allowed for you and members of your household that you incurred in traveling from your old home to your new home, plus the one-day lodging expenses on the day of arrival and departure. This is limited to a single trip from your old residence to your new one. If you use your car, you can claim 12 cents a mile plus tolls and parking.

Line 3: Add lines 1 and 2 (your total moving expenses). All these expenses must be incurred within one year from the time you start to work at the new location. Expenses incurred beyond a year are deductible for reasons such as allowing a child to finish school.

Line 4: Enter the amount that your employer reimbursed you for your moving expenses. Here is where things can become confusing and you can end up not deducting all that you are entitled to deduct or paying tax on part of the moving expenses that you were reimbursed. When your employer reimburses you for moving expenses of the type that you could deduct if you had paid them directly, the reimbursement will be noted in box 12 of your Form W-2 with a `code P` next to it. If you didn't incur deductible moving expenses in excess of what you were reimbursed, you have nothing to deduct and need not file Form 3903.

If, on the other hand, your employer gave you a specific amount, say $15,000, to cover your moving expenses, that amount will be reported in box 1 of your W-2 as taxable wages. Nothing will be entered in box 12 of your W-2. If that is the case, you couldn't be making a bigger mistake by believing that because you were reimbursed you have nothing to deduct. Because the $15,000 shows up as taxable wages, you are entitled to claim *your* deductible moving expenses. If you don't find out from your employer how the $15,000 was reported to the IRS, it's going to cost you dearly, because you'll pay more tax than you have to by not deducting the moving expenses to which you're entitled. Enter your deductible moving expenses on lines 1 and 2, and don't enter what you were reimbursed, because it's already been included in your taxable wages.

If your employer reimbursed you for moving expenses of the type that you could have deducted if you had paid them directly and for moving expenses that you can't deduct, the reimbursement for the deductible expenses will be noted in box 12 of your Form W-2 with a `code P`. The nondeductible moving expenses included in the reimbursement are included in box 1 of your W-2 as taxable wages. Temporary living expenses paid by your employer are the type that can't be deducted if you had paid them. Sorry, you owe tax on this amount. If this situation occurred, enter all your deductible moving expenses on lines 1 and 2 of Form 3903 and what your employer reimbursed you as indicated in box 12 of your W-2 on line 4.

If you weren't reimbursed by your employer, box 12 will have nothing in it, and nothing will be added to your taxable wages. Enter your deductible moving expenses on lines 1 and 2 and put a zero (-0-) on line 4 of Form 3903.

Line 5: Subtract line 4 from line 3. The result is the amount of your deductible 2003 moving expenses. Now enter this amount on your Form 1040 (line 27).

If line 3 is less than line 4, subtract line 3 from line 4 and include the amount on line 7, Form 1040, labeled "wages, etc." The reason? If you receive a reimbursement from your employer that's larger than your deductible moving expenses, you have to pay tax on the difference and cannot enter any amount on line 5 of Form 3903.

Form 8606, Nondeductible IRAs

This form is divided into three parts:

- Part I: Traditional IRAs (Nondeductible Contributions, Distributions, and Basis)
- Part II: Conversions from Traditional IRAs to Roth IRAs
- Part III: Distributions from Roth IRAs

Here are line-by-line instructions for Parts I, II, and III. (See Chapter 6 for the complete rules on all three IRAs in the list above.)

Contribution limits for traditional and Roth IRAs is $3,000, and if you're older than 50, you can put away an additional $500 — see Chapters 6 and 21 for more about this subject. The financial institution handling your investment reports your contribution to either a regular, nondeductible, or Roth IRA to the IRS on **Form 5498, IRA Contribution Information.**

The taxable portion of distributions from a Coverdell Education Savings Account (ESA) is no longer computed on Form 8606. Report a contribution to a Coverdell on **Form 5498 ESA.** Withdrawals on Form 1099-Q and the taxable portion of the withdrawals, if any, are computed on Worksheet 5-3 provided in Publication 970 *(Tax on Benefits for Education).* Report the taxable portion, if any, on line 21 of Form 1040.

Part 1: Traditional IRAs

This section is important if you made or are making nondeductible contributions or if you're taking money out of a traditional IRA to which you've made nondeductible contributions. This form tells you how much money you have to pay tax on every time you withdraw money from your nondeductible IRA account.

Line 1: Enter your 2003 nondeductible IRA contribution, including the dough that you put in between January 1, 2004, and April 15, 2004. Enter your $3,000 (or $3,500 if you are over 50) contribution on this line if you meet any of the following criteria:

- ✔ You're contributing the $3,000 (or $3,500) maximum, and you're covered by a pension plan where you work and earned more than $70,000, if married, or $50,000, if single.

- ✔ You can't make any part of a Roth IRA contribution because your income exceeds $160,000 for couples or $110,000 if single.

If only a portion of your contribution qualifies for an IRA deduction or a Roth IRA and you elect to have the remaining balance treated as a nondeductible contribution, enter that amount here. Say, for example, you want to put away $3,500 because you're over 50, you're single and covered by a plan at work, your income is $45,000, and, under those circumstances, only half of your $3,500 qualifies for the deduction. So, on line 24 of Form 1040 or line 17 of Form 1040A, enter $1,750. Now enter the $1,750 balance here on line 1 of Form 8606. In this example, however, you have more than one choice when selecting an IRA. You can contribute $1,750 to a deductible IRA and $1,750 to either a Roth IRA or a nondeductible IRA, or you can contribute the entire $3,500 to a Roth IRA. Flip back to Chapter 6 for a refresher on how to make this computation.

Line 2: Here's where you enter the total of all the nondeductible IRA contributions that you made in prior years. Where do you get this info? It was reported on line 14 of your 2003 Form 8606.

Line 3: This is the really easy part of the form. Add lines 1 and 2, and enter the total here.

If you didn't withdraw any money from this IRA, enter the amount from line 3 on line 14. Sign and date the form, and attach it to your return. Nothing else is required.

If you withdrew any money from your nondeductible IRA, you have to tackle lines 4 through 13. They may look complicated, but they really aren't — just a lot of adding and subtracting, so get your calculator ready.

Line 4: If you withdrew money from your nondeductible IRA, and you made your nondeductible contribution for 2003 between January 1, 2004 and April 15, 2004, you have to enter that amount again on this line. Why? To determine how much of your withdrawal is taxable, you must compare the total of all of the nondeductible contributions that you made through December 31, 2003, with the value of your IRA on that date. You know the rules. Apples to apples!

Line 5: Subtract line 4 from line 3. This amount is the total of all your nondeductible contributions through December 31, 2003.

Line 6: Enter the value of all your IRAs on December 31, 2003.

Line 7: Enter what you withdrew only in 2003.

Line 8: Enter the amount you converted, if any, from a regular IRA (we hope you took our advice in Chapter 7 about not converting a traditional IRA to a Roth IRA). The IRS allows you to make this conversion if you pay the tax on the entire conversion in the year that you make it in exchange for their promise that when you start making withdrawals from the Roth, they won't be taxed. You know the line from the movie about someone being made an offer they couldn't refuse? Refuse this one. If you converted to a Roth, you can undo it by converting it back to your original IRA as long as it's done by the date you file (including filing extensions).

Line 9: Add lines 6, 7, and 8. This is the amount that your IRAs would've been worth on December 31, 2003, if you hadn't withdrawn any money.

Line 10: Get out your calculator. Divide the amount on line 5 by the amount on line 9. Don't panic; we don't leave you dangling over this computation. Here's a hypothetical situation: Say your nondeductible contributions on line 5 is $10,000. The value of your IRAs on line 6 is $90,000, and according to line 7, you withdrew $10,000 in 2003. Line 9 is $100,000 (the total of lines 6, 7, and 8). Now divide line 5 ($10,000) by line 9 ($100,000). The answer: 10 percent. Enter that amount on line 10.

Line 11: Because you took our advice about not doing a conversion, you can skip this line. If, however, you converted your regular IRA to a Roth IRA, you also have to complete lines 16, 17, and 18 in Part II of this form. That's where you compute how much income you have to pay tax on because of the conversion. See our instruction for these three lines in the following section.

Line 12: Multiply line 7 (the $10,000 that you withdrew in 2003) by line 10 (10 percent). In the example, if you came up with $1,000, you got it right. This amount is the portion of the $10,000 that you withdrew that you *don't* have to pay tax on.

Line 13: Add lines 11 and 12. This is the nontaxable portion of what you withdrew.

Line 14: Subtract line 13 ($1,000) from line 3 ($10,000). In our example, this amount is $9,000. The IRS refers to this amount as your *tax basis,* which is nothing more than IRS lingo for the remaining balance of the nondeductible money that you put into your IRA that you don't have to pay tax on when it comes out. Whoo!

Line 15: Subtract line 12 ($1,000) from line 7 ($10,000) and enter the difference ($9,000) here. This amount is the portion of your withdrawal that you have to pay tax on. Enter this amount on line 15b, Form 1040, or on line 11b, Form 1040A.

Sign and date the form if you are not attaching it to your return.

Recharacterizations

Recharacterization is a fancy word for changing your mind and undoing the IRA–to–Roth IRA conversion. You should consider recharacterization if the value of your Roth dropped after you made the conversion. You have to do a recharacterization if you misfigured your 2003 income and it ended up being more than $100,000, which is the permissible limit.

Chapter 7 explains how recharacterizations are treated on your return.

You must file Form 8606 to report nondeductible contributions even if you don't have to file a tax return for the year. If you file a Form 1040, you must attach Form 8606 to your 1040. There is a $50 penalty for not filing your 8606! Also, if your IRA contributions are more than permissible amounts, you may be subject to a 6 percent penalty, and you must withdraw the overpayment.

Part II: Conversions from traditional IRAs to Roth IRAs

See Chapters 7 and 21 for information about why converting a traditional IRA to a Roth IRA may not be the best of ideas. But because you already made this conversion, here is how you fill out Part II.

Line 16: Enter the amount you converted from your traditional (simple) IRA to your Roth IRA.

Line 17: Enter the amount from line 11 if you converted a nondeductible IRA.

Line 18: Subtract line 17 from 16 and carry it over to line 15b of your 1040 or line 11b of 1040A. This is the amount for which you have to pay tax because you made a conversion.

Part III: Distributions from Roth IRAs

In this part, you compute the portion of what you took out of your Roth that you have to pay tax on. For a quick review on how a Roth is taxed, sprint back to Chapter 7. Remember, you have to keep money in a Roth for at least five years in order to have the entire withdrawal escape tax.

Line 19: Enter the amount you withdrew from your Roth IRA.

Line 20: Enter the basis (what you contributed to your Roth) of what you withdrew. Here is how you do that. This sounds like a killer computation, but it isn't. That's because you don't start paying tax on Roth withdrawals until you get back tax-free all the money that you put in. For example, say you withdrew $3,000 in 2003 and contributed $8,000 since 1998 (the year Roths came into being). Enter $8,000 on this line. Because what you contributed exceeded what you withdrew, your withdrawal isn't subject to tax. Keep in mind, however, that if you made a withdrawal in a prior year, you also must subtract that withdrawal from what you enter on this line.

Line 21: Subtract line 20 from 19. Enter -0- if line 20 is more than line 19.

Line 22: Thankfully, you followed our advice in Chapter 7 and didn't do a conversion from a regular IRA to a Roth, so enter -0 .

Line 23: Subtract line 22 from line 21. If line 22 is more than line 21, enter -0-. If not, carry this amount over to line 15b of your 1040 or line 11b of 1040A. This is the amount on which you have to pay tax. If you're under age 59½, this amount may also be subject to a 10 percent penalty.

Forms 8615 and 8814, the Kiddie Tax

If you have children under age 14 who have investment income, you may need to complete Form 8615 or Form 8814. Once a child reaches age 14, the kiddie tax doesn't apply — the child pays whatever his or her tax rate is.

Form 8615 is the form that you use when your child files his or her own return; use **Form 8814** when you elect to report your kids' investment income on your return. See the sidebar "Why your 3-year-old may be in the 35 percent tax bracket" for more on making this election.

Here's how the kiddie tax works. If a child has $2,500 in interest income, for example, the first $750 is exempt from tax. The next $750 is taxed at the child's tax rate (10 percent), which comes to $75. The remaining $1,000 is taxed at the parent's rate. So if the parent is in the 30 percent tax bracket, the kiddie tax amounts to $300 ($1,000 × 30 percent), plus the child's portion of $75, for a total bill of $375.

Children whose investment income is more than $750 must file a return, but if their income is less than $1,500, they can file their return by using the less complicated Form 1040A. If they don't have any taxable investment income (you invested the money that their grandparents gave them in tax-exempt bonds), they don't have to file a return until their earned income, such as income from a part-time job, exceeds $4,750. Unless your child was 14 by the end of 2003, here's how to compute the kiddie tax. Enter your Social Security number and taxable income on Form 8615. Add the amount of your child's investment income that's in excess of $1,500 to your taxable income. Recompute your tax, and the difference between the tax on your return and the recomputed figure is the kiddie tax. A good tax software program can save you all this math (see Chapter 2).

But if you don't have a tax software program and your child's investment income in excess of $1,500 is $1,000, add the $1,000 to your taxable income. Now compute your tax on this amount. For example, if the tax on this amount is $9,305 and the tax on your return is $9,000, the $305 difference is the kiddie tax. Enter that amount plus $75 (the tax on the $750 that isn't exempt from tax, per the tax tables) on your child's return on Form 1040 (line 41).

If your kid gets stuck for the kiddie tax, you have to use Form 1040 when filing his or her return. The computation of the kiddie tax on Form 8615 doesn't affect the tax that you have to pay. Your taxable income is used only to determine the tax rate to apply to your kid's income above $1,500. It only feels like you're being taxed twice.

But there's more. (There always is.) If you and your spouse file separate returns, you enter the larger of either your or your spouse's taxable income on Form 8615. If you're separated or divorced, the parent who has custody of the child for the greater part of the year uses his or her taxable income when completing Form 8615. But if you and your spouse live apart and qualify to file as unmarried (single or head of household), the custodial parent's taxable income is used on Form 8615.

And it gets worse (as it always seems to)! If you have two or more kids, you enter the total of all their investment income on Form 8615. The kiddie tax is computed and allocated among them. For example, suppose that your daughter's investment income in excess of $1,500 is $3,000, and your son's is $2,000; you enter $5,000 on each child's Form 8615. Then each child's share of the total kiddie tax is allocated. Your daughter's share is three-fifths of the tax, and your son's share is two-fifths.

By now you're looking for a way to avoid having to file a separate tax return because your child has $1 more than $750. Is there a way, you ask? Yes. If your child has investment income of only $7,500 or less and it's all from interest and dividends, you can report the income on your return by filing Form 8814. That's $7,500 for each child. But we don't recommend this course of action because the kiddie tax is higher on your return than it would be on the child's return, and your tax could also be higher. To learn more about the smartest ways to invest in your child's name, read Chapter 25. The $7,500 threshold is indexed for inflation.

Why your 3-year-old may be in the 35 percent tax bracket

Once upon a time, if you were in the 70 percent tax bracket (rates were that high before 1981), it made sense to make a gift of investment property to your children, because the income the property produced would be taxed at the child's tax rate — which could have been as low as 11 percent. But that was back in the good old days (that is, if you think anything is nostalgic about 70 percent tax rates). This tax savings scheme ended in 1986. Nowadays, if a child is under the age of 14, all investment income over $1,500 is taxed at the parent's tax rate — which can be as high as 35 percent. The reason for the change is to remove the incentive for higher-income earners to transfer lots of money to their kids just to save tax dollars by benefiting from lower tax brackets.

Form 8829, Expenses for Business Use of Your Home

Your home office no longer has to be the place where you meet customers or the principal place where you conduct business. You're entitled to claim a home office deduction, even if it is used only to conduct administrative or management activities, provided there is no other location where you can conduct these activities. So if you're a lawyer who likes to take work home because it's more convenient to work there, sorry. Your home office still has to be used exclusively and on a regular basis as the place where you conduct administrative or management activities. Working occasionally on your dining room table won't cut it, either. A separate room isn't necessary. A dedicated portion of a room that you use exclusively as your office is good enough.

The rule allowing taxpayers to claim a deduction for the portion of their home they use to perform administrative and management activities was designed to help doctors who perform their primary duties in hospitals, salespeople who spend most of their time calling on customers at their customers' offices, and house painters and other tradespeople who spend their time at job sites but use an office in their home to do all their paperwork.

Form 8829, Expenses for Business Use of Your Home, is used to claim the deduction. You can find a copy of this form in the back of this book.

If you use part of your residence for business, you can deduct the mortgage interest, real estate taxes, depreciation, insurance, utilities, and repairs related to that part of your house. Renters get to deduct their business portion of the rental expenses.

If you use a portion of your home to store inventory or samples, you are also entitled to deduct your home office expenses. Say that you sell cosmetics and use part of your study to store samples. You can deduct expenses related to the portion of your study used to store the cosmetics, even if you use the study for other purposes.

A home office deduction can't produce a loss. For example, suppose that your business income is $6,000. You have $5,000 in business expenses and home office expenses of $1,500 (of which $1,000 is for the percentage of your mortgage interest and real estate tax allocated for the use of the office). First, you deduct the interest and taxes of $1,000, which leaves a balance of $5,000 for possible deductions. Then you deduct $5,000 of business expenses, which brings your business income to zero. The remaining $500 of your home office expenses can't be deducted, but you can carry it over to the next year. If you don't have sufficient income to deduct the $500 next year, you can carry it over again.

If you're a renter, filling out Form 8829 correctly means that you first have to determine your total rent — including insurance, cleaning, and utilities. Then you deduct the portion used for business. If you rent four rooms and one room is used for business, you're entitled to deduct 25 percent of the total. (If the rooms are the same size, you can use this method. If not, you have to figure out the percentage on a square-footage basis.)

For homeowners, you compute the total cost of maintaining your home, depreciation, mortgage interest, taxes, insurance, repairs, and so on. Then deduct the percentage used for business.

Measuring your home office

Complete lines 1 through 7 on Form 8829 to find out how much of your home you used *exclusively* for your business.

- ✔ **Line 1:** Enter the area, in square feet, of the part of your home that you used for business: for example, 300 square feet.

- ✔ **Line 2:** To determine the percentage of your home that you used for business, enter the total area, in square feet, of your home: for example, 1,500 square feet.

- ✔ **Line 3:** Divide line 1 by line 2 and enter the result as a percentage here. In the earlier example, you would enter 20 percent (300 ÷ 1,500). Keep this percentage handy; it's the percentage of the expenses for the whole house — such as interest, real estate taxes, depreciation, utility costs, and repairs — that you use on Form 8829 to determine your deduction.

- ✔ **Line 7:** Unless you use your home as a day-care facility, you can skip lines 4 through 6 and enter your deduction percentage from line 3 onto line 7.

Figuring your allowable home office deduction

Lines 8 through 34 on Form 8829 involve megacomputations, much more than our space allows. In this section, we take you through the basics that apply to most people. Take a peek at IRS Publication 587 *(Business Use of Your Home)* for additional information.

- ✔ **Line 8:** Enter the amount from line 29 of your Schedule C (this is what you earned after expenses). Your home office deduction can't exceed this amount.

- ✔ **Lines 9 through 20, column (a):** Expenses that apply exclusively to your office go in this column. Repairs and maintenance, such as painting your office, are two such items.

- ✔ **Lines 9 through 20, column (b):** Enter your expenses that apply to the entire house on these lines. The IRS refers to them as *indirect expenses*.

  If you rent, instead of owning your home, the rent that you paid goes on line 20, column (b).

- ✔ **Lines 21 through 34:** It's number-crunching time — enough to make us wonder who came up with this form!

- ✔ **Line 34:** This is your allowable deduction. Carry it over to line 30 on Schedule C.

Determining your home office's depreciation allowance

You also have to apply your home office deduction percentage (from line 7 of Form 8829) to your home's depreciation allowance. This section includes a line-by-line breakdown of the appropriate part on Form 8829.

Line 35: Your home's value

Here's where you compute your depreciation deduction. You get to write off the percentage of your home that you claim as a home office (in our earlier example, 20 percent) over either 31½ or 39 years, depending on when you set up your office. Residential property usually is written off over 27½ years, but because the office is used for business, it's considered business property and has a longer life.

On line 35, enter the smaller of what you paid for your home (including the original and closing costs, as well as any improvements you've made to the property) or its fair market value at the time you first started to use it for business. You don't have to make this comparison every year — only when you started claiming a home office deduction.

Line 36: Land not included

Because you can't deduct land, you have to subtract the value of the land that your home sits on from the cost of your home so that you calculate the net cost of the house. A value of 15 percent for the land is a safe subtraction.

Line 37: Basis of building

Subtract line 36 from line 35. This amount is the basis of your home after subtracting the value of the land that you can't depreciate.

Line 38: Business portion of your home

Multiply line 37 by your home office deduction percentage from line 7. In our continuing example, that's the 20 percent of the house used for business that you can write off.

Line 39: Depreciation percentage

If you set up your office before May 12, 1993, it's a 31½-year write-off. Use Table 15-1 to determine your depreciation percentage.

Table 15-1   31½-Year Depreciation Schedule for Business Use of Home (%)

Use the column for the month of the year that you set up your office.

Year	Jan	Feb	Mar	Apr	May	Jun	Jul	Aug	Sep	Oct	Nov	Dec
1	3.042	2.778	2.513	2.249	1.984	1.720	1.455	1.190	0.926	0.661	0.397	0.132
2–7	3.175	3.175	3.175	3.175	3.175	3.175	3.175	3.175	3.175	3.175	3.175	3.175

For years 8 and beyond, use the depreciation table in IRS Publication 587 (*Business Use of Your Home*).

If you set up your office after May 12, 1993, the write-off is over 39 years. Use Table 15-2 to determine your depreciation percentage.

Table 15-2			39-Year Depreciation Schedule for Business Use of Home (%)								
Use the column for the month of the year you set up your office.											
Year	Jan	Feb	Mar	Apr	May	Jun	Jul	Aug	Sep	Oct	Nov	Dec
1	2.461	2.247	2.033	1.819	1.605	1.391	1.177	0.963	0.749	0.535	0.321	0.107
2–39	2.564	2.564	2.564	2.564	2.564	2.564	2.564	2.564	2.564	2.564	2.564	2.564

For example, if you set up your office in June 2003, enter 1.391 percent on line 39 of Form 8829. Every year thereafter you use 2.564 percent.

Line 40: Depreciation allowable

Multiply line 38 by line 39. This is your depreciation deduction, based on the business use of your home. Enter this amount on lines 40 and 28 of this form.

Deducting what's left

Remember that you can't take a loss because of the home office deduction. You can, however, carry over an excess deduction amount to another year's tax return.

On lines 41 and 42, compute the amount of your home office deduction that you couldn't deduct. You get to deduct it in future years, provided that you have enough income.

On Schedule A, don't forget to deduct the balance (in our example, 80 percent) of your total mortgage interest that you entered on line 10(b) of Form 8829, and the balance of your total real estate taxes from line 11(b) of this form. Your mortgage interest balance goes on line 10 of Schedule A; the real estate taxes balance goes on line 6 of Schedule A.

Form W-4, Employee Withholding

If you owe a bundle to the Internal Revenue Service for 2003, chances are you aren't withholding enough tax from your salary. Unless you don't mind paying a lot on April 15, you need to adjust your withholding in order to avoid interest and penalties if you can't pay what you owe when it's due. We include a worksheet to help you through the morass of IRS instructions on the back of your W-4 (see Table 15-3).

Table 15-3	Worksheet for Completing Your 2004 W-4	
		Amount
1.	Enter your 2004 estimated itemized deductions. If you're claiming the standard deduction, enter 0 on lines 1 and 3, and go to line 4.	$
2.	Enter $9,700 if you're filing jointly, $7,150 if head of household, $4,850 if single married filing separately.	$
3.	Subtract line 2 from line 1.	$
4.	Enter adjustments to your income (IRA contributions, alimony, and so on).	$
5.	Add lines 3 and 4.	$

	Amount
6. Enter your 2004 non-wage income, such as interest and dividends where no tax is being withheld.	$_____
7. Subtract line 6 from line 5.	$_____
8. Divide line 7 by $3,100 (drop fractions). For example, if line 7 is $9,775, dividing that by $3,100 gives you 3.153, so enter 3 on line 8.	$_____
9. Child tax credit. If you're single and your income is less than $50,000 ($63,000 if married), enter 1 on line 9 for each child that you can claim the credit for. If you're single and your income is between $50,000 and $80,000 ($63,000 and $115,000 if married), enter 1 if you have one kid, if you have two kids enter 2, if you have three kids enter 3, or if you have four kids or more enter 4. Every exemption you claim assumes you are entitled to a $3,100 deduction. On this line, you convert the child tax credit to its equivalent deduction. A $1,000 credit equals a $3,100 deduction but tapers off as your income increases.	$_____
10. Enter the number of personal exemptions you are entitled to claim for yourself, your spouse, and your dependents. For example, if you are married and have two kids, enter 4.	$_____
11. Add lines 8, 9, and 10. This is the number of exemptions that you're entitled to claim on line 5 of your W-4.	$_____

As you fill out this worksheet, remember: If you're married and both you and your spouse work, you need to factor in the *marriage penalty*, which assures that together you'll owe more than two unmarried people who have the same incomes. The marriage penalty is one of those family unfriendly facts of the tax code, and in our experience, it's the single greatest cause of underwithholding.

To make sure that your W-4 reflects the marriage penalty, you have to adjust your withholding allowances.

First, on a sheet of paper, write down the salary of the lower-paid spouse. Next to the salary figure, write the number of allowances that you show on line 11 of the worksheet in Table 15-3.

Too many exemptions

If you claimed more than ten withholding exemptions on your **Form W-4, Withholding Allowance Certificate,** or if you earned more than $200 per week and claimed an exemption from all withholding, your employer must submit the W-4 to the IRS.

If the IRS determines that you overstated the number of exemptions to which you're entitled, it will either notify your employer that your withholding certificate is inaccurate or ask you for written verification of why you believe you're entitled to the extra exemptions that you claim. If the IRS asks you for this information, it sends you the **Form 6355, Worksheet to Determine Withholding Allowances.** The three-page Form 6355 is more detailed than the W-4 that you completed.

If, after reviewing Form 6355, the IRS determines that you aren't entitled to the number of exemptions that you claimed, it notifies your employer to disregard your W-4 and to withhold tax based on the number of exemptions it says you're entitled to. This edict remains in effect until the IRS approves a new W-4. To get approval to change the number of your exemptions, you must file a new W-4 with your employer, who again submits the W-4 to the IRS. You also must attach a written statement explaining why you're requesting a change.

If you don't have reasonable basis for the number of exemptions that you claim, you'll be assessed a $500 penalty. A simple error or an honest mistake won't result in penalty. Phew!

✔ For every $5,000 of wages (up to $60,000), you subtract one allowance. The lower-paid spouse makes $40,000? You cut eight allowances.

✔ For every $10,000 of wages between $60,000 and $110,000, you slice another allowance.

The IRS Web site, www.irs.gov, has a nifty W-4 calculator. After you enter the Web site, type "W-4 Calculator" in the box labeled "Search IRS Site for" and hit "Go."

Schedule H: Nanny Tax

You figure the nanny tax on Schedule H, and enter the amount that you owe on line 60 of the 1040.

✔ If you paid cash wages of $1,400 or more during the year to any one person, or withheld federal income tax (you're not required to withhold tax, but you may want to accommodate your employee's request to do so), you have to fill out only page 1 and enter the amount from line 8 of Schedule H onto line 59 of Form 1040.

✔ If you paid more than $1,000 in any quarter, don't carry the amount from line 8 over to line 59 of your 1040. In addition to page 1, you have to fill out page 2 of the form and then enter the amount from line 27 of Schedule H onto line 60 of Form 1040.

Even if you don't expect to hold high political office — or low political office — the provisions of the nanny tax can save you a tidy sum and simplify the number and type of returns that you have to file. The law covers housekeepers, baby sitters, yard-care workers, and nannies.

Prior to the nanny tax, which is retroactive to January 1, 1994, household employers had to file quarterly reports and pay Social Security taxes if they paid household help more than $50 in a quarter. Now you don't have to withhold and pay Social Security taxes unless you pay a domestic worker more than $1,400 during the year. If you're just learning about the change in the law and didn't pay more than $1,200 in 2000, or $1,300 in 2001 and 2002, but filed quarterly returns, you can get your money back by filing **Form 843, Claim for Refund and Request for Abatement.** After April 15, 2004, you can no longer get back any 2000 tax you incorrectly overpaid. See Chapter 19 to find out more about the statute of limitations on refunds.

Here are two important provisions of the nanny tax that you should be aware of:

✔ You don't have to pay Social Security tax for domestic employees under the age of 18, regardless of how much you pay them. *Under the age of 18* means that the employee is under that age for any portion of the year. The exemption doesn't apply if the principal occupation of the employee is household employment.

✔ You don't have to file quarterly payroll tax forms. Any Social Security, Medicare, or federal unemployment (FUTA) taxes, and income taxes that you choose to withhold can be paid when you file your return in April.

If your withholding or estimated tax payments are not enough to cover the Social Security, Medicare, and FUTA (we explain these taxes later in this section) taxes that you owe, a penalty will be assessed. So make sure that you pay in enough.

Although the nanny tax simplifies your IRS filings, you still have to keep filing quarterly state unemployment tax returns, unless your state elects to conform to the IRS method of filing annually.

Schedule H looks more formidable than it really is. Here's the lowdown on what it's really about:

✔ If you paid your household help less than $1,400 in 2003 and didn't withhold any income tax, you don't have to file this form.

✔ If you paid someone more than $1,400, but no more than $1,000, in any one quarter (that's a three-month period — January, February, and March, and so on), you only have to fill out Part I.

For example, suppose that you pay someone $60 a week. That's $780 a quarter and $3,120 for the year. You only have to answer questions A, B, and C on the form and fill out the eight lines in Part I. It's strictly simple math stuff. You have to multiply the $3,120 in cash wages that you paid by the 12.4 percent Social Security rate and the 2.9 percent Medicare tax rate. Add both of these taxes together on line 8 of the form and carry this amount over to line 59 of Form 1040. Sign and date the form at the bottom of page 2 if you are not attaching it to your return.

Don't forget that you also have to furnish your employee with a W-2 stating the amount that you paid, as well as the amount of Social Security, Medicare, and income tax that you withheld. Withholding income tax is optional on your part. One further chore: You have to file a copy of the W-2 and Form W-3 (if more than one W-2 is being filed) with the Social Security Administration in Wilkes-Barre, Pennsylvania by February 28, 2004. Your employees must get their W-2s by January 31.

✔ If you paid someone employed in your home more than $1,000 in any quarter, you have to fill out Parts II and III because not only do you owe Social Security and Medicare taxes, you also have to pay federal unemployment tax. This tax is commonly referred to as FUTA.

Check with your state tax department to find out whether you have to register and pay state unemployment tax on a quarterly basis. Also check with your insurance broker to see whether your homeowner's insurance covers domestic employees or whether you need a separate workers' compensation policy. Don't play fast and loose in this area. If your nanny gets hurt or injured, you may have to pay a bundle if you don't have insurance coverage.

The immigration law requires that you verify that every new employee is eligible to work in the U.S. You do this by completing **Form I-9, Employment Eligibility Verification.** You can get this form from the Immigration Service (800-521-1504). The form doesn't get filed. Hang onto it in case someone from the Immigration Service knocks on your door.

Schedule SE: Self-Employment Tax Form

If you earn income from being self-employed, as well as from other sources, use Schedule SE to figure another tax that you owe — the Social Security tax and Medicare tax. The first $87,000 of your self-employment earnings is taxed at 12.4 percent (this is the Social Security tax part). The Medicare tax doesn't have any limit; it's 2.9 percent of your total self-employment earnings. For amounts of $87,000 or less, the combined rate is 15.3 percent (adding the two taxes together), and for amounts above $87,000, the rate is 2.9 percent. If your self-employment earnings are under $400, you are not subject to this tax.

Your self-employment earnings may be your earnings reported on the following:

✔ **Schedule C** (line 31)

✔ **Schedule C-EZ** (line 3)

✔ **Schedule K-1** (line 15a), **Form 1065** — if you're a partner in a firm

✔ **Schedule F** (line 36)

✔ **Form 1040** (line 21) — your self-employment income that you reported as miscellaneous income

You can use Section A of Schedule SE, called the *short worksheet,* if you have only self-employment income. If you're self-employed and also are employed by someone else, you have to use the long form; otherwise, you'll pay more Social Security than you're required to pay because Social Security tax has already been withheld from your salary. To prevent this disaster, enter the total of the amounts from boxes 3 and 7 of your W-2 on line 8a of page 2 of Schedule SE. (And if you file **Form 4137** on unreported tips, enter the amount from line 9 of that form on line 8b of Schedule SE.)

Now for some good news! (Yes, occasionally there is some good news when it comes to taxes.) Half of your self-employment tax is deductible. Complete Schedule SE and note the following: The amount on line 5 of Schedule SE is the amount of tax that you have to pay; you carry it over to Form 1040 (line 55) and add it to your income tax that's due. Enter half of what you have to pay — the amount on line 6 of Schedule SE — on Form 1040 (line 28).

Wouldn't it be nice if this form simply said, "If you are self-employed, use this form to compute how much Social Security and Medicare tax you have to pay"? Paying this tax ensures that you'll be entitled to Social Security when you're old and gray.

You have three choices when filling out this form:

- ✔ **Section A — Short Schedule SE:** This section is the shortest and easiest one to complete — 6 lines. But if you were employed on a salaried basis and had Social Security tax withheld from your wages, you will pay more self-employment tax than required if you use the short schedule . Moonlighters beware.

- ✔ **Section B — Long Schedule SE:** Use this part of the form if you received wages and are self-employed. Suppose that you have wages of $40,000 and have $55,000 in earnings from your business. If you use the Short Schedule SE, you'll end up paying Social Security tax on $95,000 when the maximum amount of combined earnings that you're required to pay on is only $87,000. You pay Medicare tax, however, on the entire $95,000.

  This section is not all that formidable. Make use of it so you don't end up paying more Social Security tax than you have to.

- ✔ **Part II — Optional method:** If your earnings are less than $1,600, you can elect to pay Social Security tax on at least $1,600, so you'll build up Social Security credit for when you become 65.

Here's the lowdown on Section A — Short Schedule SE:

Line 1: If you're not a farmer, you can skip this line. If farming is your game, enter the amount from line 36 of Schedule F (F is for farming) or line 15a, Form 1065, Schedule K-1 for farm partnerships.

Line 2: Enter the total of the amounts from line 31, Schedule C (line 3, Schedule C-EZ) and line 15a, Schedule K-1 (for partnerships). This is how each partner pays his or her Social Security and Medicare tax. You also have to pay Social Security and Medicare tax on the miscellaneous income reported on line 21. What kind of income do you have to pay on? The answer: directors' fees, finders' fees, and commissions.

What is not subject to self-employment tax? Jury duty, notary public fees, forgiveness of a debt even if you owe tax on it, rental income, executor's fees, prizes and awards, lottery winnings, and gambling winnings — unless gambling is your occupation.

Line 3: A breeze. Add lines 1 and 2.

Line 4: Multiply line 3 by 92.35 percent (0.9235). Why? If you were employed, your employer would get to deduct its share of the Social Security tax that it would have to pay, and so do you. Or you can think of it this way: Paying self-employment tax of 15.3 percent on 92.35 percent of your earnings is a lot better than having to pay on 100 percent. So don't ask any more questions. Do the math and be thankful for small favors.

Line 5: If line 4 is $87,000 or less, multiply line 4 by 15.3 percent (0.153) and enter that amount on line 55 of Form 1040. For example, if line 4 is $10,000, multiply it by 15.3 percent, and you get $1,530.

If line 4 is more than $87,000, multiply that amount by 2.9 percent (0.029) and add that amount to $10,788. (This amount is the maximum Social Security tax that you're required to pay.) For example, if line 4 is $90,000, multiply that amount by 0.029, which comes to $2,610. Now add this amount ($2,610) to $10,788 for a grand total of $13,398. Enter this amount on line 55 of Form 1040. (The 2.9 percent is your Medicare tax.)

Line 6: Multiply line 5 by 50 percent. You can deduct this amount ($6,699) on line 28 of your 1040.

Schedule R: Credit for the Elderly or the Disabled

You use (and attach!) Schedule R for this credit. You're entitled to claim this credit (which could amount to as much as $1,125) if you're married and both you and your spouse are 65 or older — or both of you are disabled and any age. For single taxpayers, the maximum credit is $750.

But wait, some requirements may make most people ineligible for this credit: You have to reduce the amount of the income that's eligible for the credit by the nontaxable portion of your Social Security and other pension and disability benefits. Also, if your income is more than $7,500 if you're single (or $10,000 if you're married), the amount of your income that's eligible for this credit is reduced further. Yup. The long and short of all this interesting information is that after completing this two-page form, most people discover that they aren't entitled to claim this credit.

If you find that your credit is zero, try this step: Instead of struggling with the form, you can have the IRS figure the credit for you. Fill out page 1 of the form, which asks questions about your age, filing status, and whether you're disabled. Attach the form to your return, and on Form 1040 (line 46), write CFE (an acronym for "credit for the elderly") on the dotted line. *Remember:* Always check the computation for a form that you asked the IRS to calculate to make sure that the IRS's computation is right. The IRS isn't infallible.

The amount of the credit is 15 percent of the following base amounts:

- ✔ $5,000 if you're single, head of household, or a qualifying widow(er)
- ✔ $5,000 if you're filing jointly and only one of you is over 65 or disabled
- ✔ $7,500 if you're filing jointly and both of you are over 65 or disabled, or one of you is over 65 and the other is under 65 and disabled
- ✔ $3,750 if you're married filing separately and are 65 or older (or disabled) and didn't live with your spouse in 2003

Additionally, the base amount is reduced by the amount of your Social Security income that isn't subject to tax and one-half of the excess of your AGI that exceeds one of the following:

- $7,500 if you're single, head of household, or a qualifying widow(er)

- $10,000 if you're married, filing jointly

- $5,000 if you're married, filing separately, and lived apart from your spouse for all of 2003

For example, suppose that your AGI is $20,000, you have nontaxable Social Security of $2,000, and you and your spouse are older than 65.

Base amount	$7,500
Nontaxable portion of Social Security	$2,000
AGI	$20,000
Reduction limit	$10,000
Excess	$10,000
One-half of excess	$5,000
Reduced base amount ($7,500 – $5,000 – $2,000)	$500
Credit (15 percent of $500)	$75

Enter the $75 credit on line 46 of Form 1040. The credit can't exceed your tax. So if your tax is $60 and the credit is $75, the $15 difference isn't refundable. If you're claiming the credit because you're under 65 and disabled, your doctor must complete and sign the physician's statement on page 4 of the Schedule R instructions. You don't have to attach the statement to your return. Keep it filed in case the IRS ever audits you.

Part IV
Audits and Errors: Dealing with the IRS

The 5th Wave   By Rich Tennant

"You know that mail order company that promised to show you how to avoid a tax audit? Well, their package just arrived."

In this part . . .

Good news and bad news arrives via the U.S. Postal Service. One letter that you hope doesn't find its way to you is an official, thin envelope from the IRS announcing that you've won its special drawing. Perhaps you were hoping that the return that you hadn't filed wouldn't be missed. Maybe you're a law-abiding citizen and can't understand why the tax folks are hassling you again. You could choose to ignore the IRS's queries, but we don't recommend making the IRS angry.

In this part, you learn how to deal with just about everything the IRS can throw at you during the year. If you didn't file in time or couldn't pay all of your taxes, we provide a shoulder to cry on as well as sound counsel for how to make things better.

Chapter 16

The Dreaded Envelope I: IRS Notices

reetings!

Now that the military draft is over, Americans no longer receive notices from their government bearing such a salutation. A different government agency, the Internal Revenue Service, now provides you with equally unpleasant news. Did you know that you have a 35 percent chance of receiving a notice from the IRS stating that you failed to report all your income, filed late, didn't pay what you owed, or made an error in preparing your return? Maybe you even committed a combination of these infractions!

Getting an envelope in the mail from the IRS strikes fear in the hearts and souls of even the most confident and honest taxpayers. In some cases, the mistakes taxpayers make are easily fixed. An IRS computer, in one of the IRS's ten regional service centers, automatically generates a notice when it spots an inaccuracy. The good news is that this system is cost-effective for the IRS because it brings in billions more tax dollars. The bad news for you is that these notices are often ambiguous, intimidating, and (in some cases) wrong!

Finding Strength in Numbers

If you think that you received an IRS notice simply because you're unlucky, you may be mistaken. Winning the IRS notice lottery is easy, and you're hardly in exclusive company! Each year, the Internal Revenue Service issues the following items:

- ✔ 28.3 million penalty notices
- ✔ 1.5 million notices informing taxpayers that they didn't report all their income
- ✔ 2 million notices to taxpayers stating that they failed to file a tax return
- ✔ 8.3 million notices citing math or clerical errors
- ✔ Tens of millions of notices to taxpayers, the exact number not being quantifiable, that they failed to pay what they owed

Every year, millions of beleaguered taxpayers write back saying that the notices they received are either incorrect or unclear. Shortly before he recently left office, former IRS Commissioner, Charles Rossotti, admitted that the IRS is "still sending over 100 million notices per year to taxpayers that often only a tax lawyer could decipher or love."

In dealing with the IRS, or with any large bureaucracy, persistence and patience count. The importance of this strategy can't be stressed enough. The only thing that you must not do is give up or become discouraged. "I shall overcome" should be your motto. It works. In 1998, the IRS reversed 46 percent of its decisions to reduce or disallow the earned income credit after taxpayers provided the corrected information that the IRS claimed they failed to supply with their original return.

One of the biggest headaches in dealing with the IRS is that the agency can be big and impersonal. That's why this part of this book provides you with suggested strategies and sample response letters developed from the decades of experience that have helped our clients deal with those daunting IRS notices. These strategies and letters work. When an IRS form can work better and faster than a letter, we include that form and suggest using it.

All the letters and IRS forms contained in this book may be copied for your personal use. On the sample letters, items that you must fill in are enclosed in brackets.

Understanding the IRS Notice Process

If you've never had a pen pal, you have one now. And you don't even have to write back — the letters just keep coming. However, this pen pal doesn't like being ignored. This pen pal doesn't get mad — this pal (the IRS) just takes your money.

Receiving your typical notice

The notice system usually starts with the issuance of a notice of adjustment: a **CP-2501** (an income verification notice); a **CP-2000, Notice of Proposed Adjustment for Underpayment/ Overpayment;** a **CP-13, We Changed Your Account;** or a 30-day letter (notifying you of the results of an audit). If you fail to respond to this notice, if the IRS isn't satisfied with your reply, or if you fail to exercise your appeal rights, a Statutory Notice of Deficiency is issued. Remember that adjustments merely correcting a math or processing error — or assessing a penalty — don't require the issuance of a Statutory Notice. Why the big deal over this kind of notice? The law requires a Statutory Notice if the IRS is demanding more than your return revealed that you owed. We get into what you should do when you receive a Statutory Notice in "Receiving a Statutory Notice of Deficiency," later in this chapter.

When the IRS makes an assessment, the amount of that assessment — plus penalties — is entered into the service center's computer under your Social Security number. The service center then sends four notices; the first three come at approximately five-week intervals, over a 15-week period. All three notices ask for payment within ten days. The fourth notice announces that things are about to hit the fan.

The first notice is either a notice informing you that there is a balance due (you filed but didn't pay what you owed), that there was a math error, or that an adjustment was made to your account (for example, you didn't make all the tax payments you claimed). The notice explains the reason(s) for the change plus any penalties that are being assessed. Unfortunately, interest is always charged when a balance is owed. The second notice is **Form 503.** It's marked, **IMPORTANT immediate action is required.** If that doesn't get your attention the third notice, **Form CP-504,** bears the legend, **Urgent! We intend to levy certain assets. Please respond NOW.** The fourth notice is sent by certified mail 30 days after the third notice (the law requires that it be sent this way before the IRS can start seizing someone's property or wages). This notice bears the legend **Final Notice of Intent to Levy and Notice of Your Right to a Hearing.** This notice informs you that if payment isn't received within 30 days or you don't request a collection hearing within that period, the IRS has the right to seize your property and garnish your wages. (Remember, the IRS defines property as more than just your residence; it likes to drool over your car, boat, and investments, too.) Ouch! You can expect to receive this type of notice (letter) about 20 weeks after the first notice.

Now for some good news: You can now appeal a notice of intent to levy or a notice that a lien has been filed. When you do, the IRS must stop all collection activity while your appeal is pending. Thanks to the 1998 law that overhauled the IRS, a separate notice is now sent informing you of your appeal rights. For more information, see "Appealing a lien or levy," later in this chapter.

If you receive a Final Notice and can't pay what you owe, see Chapter 19 to review your options. If you haven't paid the balance or contacted the IRS to arrange payment within ten days after receiving a Final Notice, the contact section of the Automated Collection System (ACS) takes over, unless the IRS has what's known as *levy source information* — that is, the IRS knows where it can get your cash; it knows where to find your property or income. In that case, a Notice of Levy will be issued against your salary and bank accounts, for example. The contact section handles cases where the payment of tax can't be satisfied by levy. The ACS contacts you by telephone, and if it can't get you to pay, the ACS turns the case over to a revenue officer.

Business taxpayers in arrears will be contacted by phone after receiving two bills over a period of 11 weeks.

Deciphering a notice

Don't panic! If you're like most taxpayers, you'll look at the notice, see a dollar figure, and decide it's too painful to look at again. Do yourself a favor, take a peek at it again; the dollar figure might be a refund — but it isn't likely.

One critical bit of advice: The computers at the service centers won't tolerate being ignored. Maybe they hooked you by error, but there's no satisfying them until they reel you in, or until you convince the IRS that their computer made an error. To do so, you must respond quickly to a notice. Otherwise, you severely prejudice your appeal rights and end up with no recourse but to pay the tax and forget the whole thing — or to pay the tax and then try to get your money back. The latter isn't as impossible as it sounds. We tell you how to get back what is rightfully yours in Chapter 18.

Every notice contains the following:

- Date of the notice.
- Taxpayer Identification number — your Social Security or Employer Identification number for businesses (make sure that it's yours).
- The form number you filed — 1040 is your tax return.
- Tax period — the year.
- A control number. Evidently your name, address, and Social Security number aren't enough.
- Penalties charged.
- Interest charged.
- Amount owed.
- Tax payments you made.

Both you and the IRS are able to track any missing tax payment by a long series of numbers printed on the back of your check. The first 14 numbers make up the IRS's control or tracking number; the next nine are your Social Security number, followed by a four-letter abbreviation of your name. The next four numbers are the year the payment was applied (0312 means the year ending December 2003), and the last six digits record the date on which the payment was received.

Be careful about making a payment with a check drawn on a money market or line of credit account. These checks may not be returned with your monthly statement; therefore, you won't have a canceled check with all the IRS data stamped on the back of it to help the IRS locate the payment and prove the payment was made. Getting a copy from the bank usually is as difficult as getting the bank to raise its passbook savings account interest rate.

Unfortunately, not every notice provides all the information necessary to precisely determine what went wrong — IRS notices are famous for their lack of clarity. Our favorite is a client's notice that indicated that either an error was made, an outstanding balance existed, not all the payments listed on the return were made, or a penalty was being assessed. The notice went on to promise that the IRS would send a separate notice (which, by the way, never came) stating which explanation applied.

All is not lost if you receive an IRS notice that, after careful inspection, is not understandable. Call the IRS at the telephone number indicated on the notice, or at 800-829-1040, and request a Record of your Tax Account Information, which takes about seven to ten days to arrive. This printout lists every transaction posted to your account. With this additional information, you should be able to understand why you were sent the notice.

If the transcript of your tax account fails to clarify why you received the notice in the first place, write to the IRS and ask it to provide a better or more exact explanation. See Chapter 18 to find out more about getting a better explanation.

Assessing Assessment Notices

Assessment notices usually inform you of one of the following situations:

- ✓ You weren't given credit for all the tax payments that you claim you made.
- ✓ You made a math error or used the wrong tax table or form.
- ✓ You filed a return but neglected to pay what you owed.
- ✓ You agreed to the results of a tax examination.
- ✓ You owe a penalty.

General assessment notices — the CP series forms

The IRS uses one of the CP series forms to inform you that your refund is being reduced or eliminated. This may be the case if your refund is being applied to other taxes you owe, which will be announced on Form CP-49. Or it may be the result of one of the reasons from the list in the preceding section. The IRS also intercepts refunds to pay nontax governmental debts, such as defaults on student loans and nonpayment of child support. The IRS refund interception program is discussed in greater detail in Chapter 18.

The IRS also sends a general assessment notice to assess a penalty for filing or paying late, failing to make timely estimated tax payments, failing to report all your income, or overstating credits or deductions on your return. Watch out!

Income verification notice — Form CP-2501

A few years ago, a convict serving prison time sent the IRS 1099s stating that the prosecutor and judge who sentenced him received $900,000 in income. Can you imagine the face of the prosecutor when he found out the IRS wanted another $400,000 in taxes? You can now sue in Federal Court if something like this happens. The lesson: Don't believe that the IRS is automatically correct in its assessment of your income. As an example, here's what happened to one of the authors of this book: A 1099 for $820 was wrongly entered into the IRS's computer as $82,000. Based on that entry, the IRS issued a bill for additional tax, interest, and penalties totaling $50,000. One of our form letters in Chapter 18 corrected the error in a matter of weeks. No one is immune from such errors. Getting a notice from the IRS that you owe $50,000 doesn't exactly make your day, even if you happen to be a tax expert.

Generally, each 1099 must include the name, address, and telephone number of whom to contact in case the 1099 is incorrect, and the IRS must investigate the disputed 1099.

Income verification notices ask you to explain differences between the income and deductions you claimed on your return — such as mortgage interest — and the income and deductions reported to the IRS by banks, your employer, and brokerage firms. Your salary is reported to the IRS on Form W-2, and all other income is reported to the IRS by the payer on Form 1099. The IRS *assumes* that the information reported to it on these forms is correct and that you made a mistake on your return. If you ignore an income verification, you will receive a notice adjusting your account and billing you for penalties, interest, and additional tax. If income tax was withheld, the notice will reflect that and reduce what you owe by that amount. Usually, the IRS won't send an income verification notice; it simply assumes that the information about you in its computer is correct and sends **Form CP-2000, Notice of Proposed Adjustment for Underpayment/Overpayment.**

One of the quickest ways we know to become separated from your money is to ignore one of these nice little notices. If the notice you receive is wrong or unclear, you need to notify the IRS. To find out how to do this, see Chapter 18.

In 2002, the IRS sent out 1.5 million CP-2000 notices that picked up a cool $2.5 billion from taxpayers who didn't report all their income. If you fail to report all your income, you can expect to receive a CP-2501 or CP-2000 within 12 to 15 months after filing your return.

CP-515 and 518 are reserved as nonfilers' first notice and then final notice of overdue return. These notices went to 2 million people last year asking why they didn't file. (You can't refer to these 2 million nonfilers as taxpayers.)

An IRS notice can be wrong for many reasons:

- ✔ The income that the IRS says you didn't report is exempt from tax.

- ✔ The income that the IRS says you failed to report is not yours. For example, you opened a bank account for your child or for a relative, and you inadvertently gave the bank your own Social Security number.

- ✔ The IRS counted the income twice. Perhaps you reported interest income on a schedule other than the proper one. Or your broker reported your total dividends to the IRS as having been paid by the broker, while you reported those dividends on your return according to the names of the corporations that paid them.

- ✔ You reported income in the wrong year. Maybe someone paid you at the end of the year, but you didn't receive this income until the beginning of the next year — and you reported it in that year.

- ✔ You made a payment to the IRS for which you were not given credit.

If you think that the IRS's conclusions about your return are wrong, turn to Chapter 18 to find out how to respond to the various types of IRS notices.

We are proposing changes to your tax return — CP-2000

This form cuts right to the chase. It assumes the information that the government received regarding your income and that doesn't appear on your return is correct. No questions are asked about whether this information is correct or not. The IRS assumes it's correct, and you're billed for additional tax and interest.

Backup withholding notice

As a trade-off for repeal of the short-lived mandatory withholding on interest and dividends, Congress enacted a system of backup withholding if you fail to furnish a payer of taxable income with your Social Security number. The IRS also notifies the payer that backup withholding should be started if you failed to report interest and dividend income on your tax return.

If the IRS determines that backup withholding is required, the payer is informed to withhold tax at the rate of 28 percent. What type of income most often gets hit for this type of withholding? Interest and dividends, payments of more than $600 per year to independent contractors, sales of stocks and bonds, and annual royalties in excess of $10 are usually targeted.

Backup withholding usually applies only to interest and dividend income. Other payments, however, are subject to withholding if you fail to provide the payer with your Social Security number. The IRS doesn't notify you that you're subject to backup withholding — it instead notifies the payer, who is required by law to notify you.

By notifying your local *Taxpayer Advocate* — the IRS problem-solving official (see Chapter 18) — you can stop backup withholding under certain circumstances:

- ✔ You did not underreport your income.

- ✔ You did underreport — but you paid the tax, interest, and penalties on the unreported income.

- ✔ The backup withholding will cause you undue hardship, and the underreporting probably will not happen again.

If you get hit with backup withholding, file all your returns for delinquent years, start reporting all your income, or pay what you owe. If you do this, the IRS will automatically stop backup withholding on January 1 if everything is in order by the preceding October 15.

Withholding allowances notice — Form 6355

We have to be a little technical here, but please stay with us through this bit of IRS paperwork. If you claimed more than ten withholding exemptions on your **Form W-4, Withholding Allowance Certificate,** or if you earned more than $200 per week and you claimed an exemption from all withholding, your employer *must* submit the W-4 to the IRS. If the IRS determines that you overstated the number of exemptions you're entitled to, or if you are not exempt from withholding, it will either notify your employer that your withholding certificate is inaccurate or ask you for written verification of why you believe you're entitled to the extra exemptions you claimed.

Hardship, IRS style

If backup withholding creates a hardship — that is, you need the dough to live on — you can request that it be stopped. IRS regulations state that undue hardship exists in several forms. For example, you are under hardship if backup withholding — when combined with other withholding and estimated tax payments — produces a substantial overpayment of tax. Or perhaps your ability to pay medical expenses might be affected. Maybe you rely upon interest and dividend income to meet basic living expenses, or you live on a modest fixed income. You're also a hardship case if you've filed a bankruptcy petition or if you're an innocent spouse who had no knowledge of your mate's failure to report all income.

See Chapter 4 for more information on the latter topic. Every October 15, the IRS makes a determination on whether backup withholding should be stopped, such as where there is no underreporting of interest and dividends or the underreporting has been corrected. If the IRS decides in your favor, backup withholding stops on January 1 of the following year. The two exceptions to the January 1 rule: If the IRS determines that there was no underreporting or that you would suffer undue hardship, it notifies you and informs the payer either not to start backup withholding or to stop backup withholding within 45 days of its determination.

If the IRS asks you for this information, it will send you **Form 6355, Worksheet to Determine Withholding Allowances.** Form 6355 is three pages long and is more detailed than the W-4 that you completed.

If, after reviewing Form 6355, the IRS determines that you aren't entitled to the number of exemptions claimed, it will notify your employer to disregard your W-4 and to withhold tax based on the number of exemptions you're entitled to. This edict remains in effect until the IRS approves a new W-4. To get approval to change the number of your exemptions, you must file a new W-4 with your employer, who again submits the W-4 to the IRS. You also must attach a written statement explaining the reason for requesting a change.

If you don't have a reasonable basis for the number of exemptions claimed, you will be assessed a $500 penalty. A simple error or an honest mistake will not result in a penalty. Phew!

The IRS receives about 600,000 W-4s annually claiming either more than ten exemptions or a complete exemption from withholding. All these W-4s get screened, of course. The IRS contacts about 42 percent of the taxpayers submitting these W-4s and sends them a Form 6355 or **Form 6450, Questionnaire to Determine Exemption From Withholding.**

Are you still with us? To bring you back to life after that stuff, here's the story of why we have all these forms for withholding. A few years back, all the workers from an assembly line in a Michigan auto plant claimed an exemption from withholding; they didn't file returns for that year. It took some time, but the IRS put a stop to those shenanigans!

Federal tax lien notice — Form 668 (F)

A *statutory lien* automatically goes into effect when you neglect or refuse to pay the tax the IRS demands. This type of lien attaches to all property that you own. A statutory lien is sometimes referred to as a *secret lien* because its validity doesn't depend on its being filed as a matter of public record. *Statutory* simply means that, under the law, the IRS has the right to do it. They don't have to prove that you failed to pay what you owe before they file a lien. Guilty unless proven innocent! Yup!

Because a statutory lien places the rights of only the IRS ahead of yours, the IRS will usually file a Notice of Lien so that it places itself first in line before your other creditors. (No cutting in line, please!) A federal tax lien covers all of a taxpayer's property, including real estate, cars, bank accounts, and personal property. These liens are filed in accordance with state law, usually with the county clerk, town hall, or court where the taxpayer lives.

You should be aware that credit agencies routinely pick up liens that have been filed against you. After a credit agency has this information, your credit is marked as lousy. Even if paid, a lien stays on your credit history for seven years.

Although the law requires that the IRS release a lien within 30 days after it has been paid, the IRS doesn't always comply. Upon paying the tax, you can obtain a release of the lien by either contacting the revenue officer who filed the lien or by following the procedure in **Publication 1450, A Certificate of Release of Federal Tax Lien.**

Collection Due Process Hearing

When the IRS files a Notice of Tax Lien or issues a Levy Notice, the law requires it to inform you of your right to a hearing before the IRS's Appeals Office, where you can protest the filing of the lien, the amount of tax the lien or levy is for, request an installment agreement, make an offer in compromise, or request innocent spouse relief. This is called a Collection Due Process Hearing. You'll receive **Form 12153, Request for Collection Due Process Hearing,** along with the lien or levy notice. You have 30 days from the date you receive the notice to make the request. The Taxpayer Bill of Rights (discussed in Chapter 18) tells you what to do when the IRS fails to release a lien. The IRS is liable for damages if it fails to release an erroneous lien or a lien that has been paid.

What you can't do at these hearings is reargue the same issue that you addressed at previous hearing. The law considers such actions a stalling tactic and allows no second chances when you're caught stalling. You can challenge the underlying amount of tax due only if you never received a Statutory Notice of Deficiency (explained in "Receiving a Statutory Notice of Deficiency" later in this chapter) or if you had no prior opportunity to dispute the tax liability.

If your appeal is rejected, you can appeal to the U.S. Tax Court. If, for some reason, the Tax Court lacks jurisdiction, you can appeal to a federal district court.

Property levy notice — Form 668-A (c)

A Notice of Levy is used to seize your property, and that includes your bank and brokerage accounts. You can kiss your money good-bye 30 days after this levy is served. A Notice of Levy usually isn't issued until after the IRS has exhausted all other possible collection procedures, however. The IRS makes an effort to contact you to try to arrange a payment schedule, and it usually sends at least four prior notices. Remember, you filed a tax return indicating where you work, where you bank, and where you have other assets!

Whenever the IRS issues a Levy Notice, you have the right to request a Collection Due Process Hearing. So flip back to that heading. You can't miss it; it's only a few paragraphs back.

You may be interested in knowing that some assets are exempt from levy:

- A taxpayer's principal residence — if the amount of the levy doesn't exceed $5,000. When a levy exceeds this limit, the IRS can't grab a residence unless it has the written consent of a U.S. district court judge. Property used in a taxpayer's business can't be seized unless approved by a district director or an assistant district director (the head IRS official for your district), or if the collection of tax is in jeopardy.

- 85 percent of unemployment benefits.

- Tools and books of a taxpayer's trade, business, or profession up to a value of $3,440. (This amount is for 2003. It's adjusted every year for inflation.)

✔ Schoolbooks. (The IRS doesn't want you to stop studying!)

✔ Court-ordered child-support payments.

✔ Wearing apparel.

✔ $6,890 worth of furniture and personal effects, livestock, and poultry. (This amount is for 2003. It's adjusted every year for inflation.)

✔ Undelivered mail.

✔ 85 percent of worker's compensation and non–means-tested welfare payments.

✔ Military service disability payments.

Although pension, Keogh, and IRA benefits aren't exempt from levy, it's IRS policy that they will be levied upon judiciously — these plans were established for a taxpayer's future welfare. This policy statement also mandates that pension benefits totaling less than $6,000 annually will not be levied upon. Although Social Security benefits aren't exempt from levy, the IRS generally doesn't go after these benefits unless they are dealing with a real deadbeat.

Wage levy notice — Form 668-W(c)

Form 668-W(c), Notice of Levy on Wages, Salary, and Other Income, is used to seize wages. It's a six-part form served on your employer. Whereas a Notice of Levy (see the preceding section) attaches only to property held by a third party (such as a bank) at the time the levy is issued, a wage levy is a continuing one — it applies to all wages, salaries, and commissions owed and to future wages, salaries, and commissions.

Continuous levies that apply to what you'll receive in the future not only cover your salary, but they also cover 15 percent of any unemployment, worker's compensation benefits, and non-means-tested welfare payments you are scheduled to receive. The meek won't inherit the world; the IRS will.

But part of every taxpayer's wages is exempt from levy. This exemption is equal to a taxpayer's standard deduction plus the number of personal exemptions he or she is entitled to, divided by a 52-week year. Therefore, in 2003, a married taxpayer entitled to four exemptions (husband, wife, and two children) would be entitled to a weekly exemption of $417, computed as follows:

Standard deduction	$ 9,500
Personal exemptions (4 × $3,050)	$12,200
Total	$21,700

$21,700 ÷ 52 = $417 per week

The $21,700 is the 2003 amount. In 2004, it will be adjusted for inflation, and the $417 exemption from levy in the example will probably be increased to about $425. Don't spend it all in one place. IRS Publication 1494 *(Table for Figuring Amount Exempt From Levy on Wages Salary, and Other Income)*, has the exemption amounts.

A taxpayer claims the amount of the exemption from levy to which he or she is entitled on **Form 668-W(c), Part 6, Statement of Exemptions.** If you don't fill out Part 6 and return it to your employer, so it can be sent to the IRS, your employer is required to compute your exemption as married filing separately with one exemption, which works out to only $150 a week. (Yikes — better fill out Part 6!) The amount of wages that can be exempted can be increased for the amount of court-ordered child support payments.

If, by levying your wages, the IRS pushes you below the poverty level, or you wind up not being able to meet your basic living expenses, see Chapter 19 to free yourself from this forced slavery.

Handling Nonassessment Notices

The IRS usually issues a nonassessment notice to inform you of one of the following situations:

- ✔ You forgot to sign a return.
- ✔ You failed to attach a W-2.
- ✔ You omitted a form or schedule.
- ✔ You didn't indicate filing status.

If you receive a nonassessment notice, simply write across it in bold lettering: INFORMATION REQUESTED IS ATTACHED. Then attach the requested information to the notice and return it to the IRS in the envelope provided. After you provide the IRS with the requested information, the matter usually is closed — unless the information you submit conflicts with information previously reported on your return. If this situation occurs, the IRS will send a notice that assesses additional tax, interest, and possibly a penalty, or that instructs you to contact a particular person at the IRS.

A notice correcting a refund due to you (usually made on Form CP-49) shouldn't be viewed as a nonassessment notice. Just because a notice doesn't demand that you write a check, don't think that the IRS isn't billing you for something. Quite often, the IRS reduces a refund when it assesses additional tax or penalties.

But I never got Part 6 of Form 668-W(c)!

If your employer fails to furnish you with Part 6 of Form 668-W(c), send the following statement to the IRS revenue officer (you can find the agent's name, address, and telephone number on the notice, or your employer can give you this information):

{date}

RE: {your name}

{Social Security number}

Dear {revenue officer's name}:

In connection with the Notice of Levy that was served on my employer, please be advised that I am married and entitled to claim the following personal exemptions on my tax return:

1. Myself

2. My spouse {his or her name and Social Security number}

3. My children {their names, ages, and Social Security numbers}

4. My court-ordered child support payments that amount to {$} weekly

Please adjust your notice accordingly.

Very truly yours,

{your name}

Paying interest on additional tax

The IRS must send a notice of additional tax due within 18 months of the date when you file your return. If the IRS doesn't send such a notice before the 18 months are up, it can't charge interest after this 18-month period. Nor can the IRS resume charging interest until 21 days after it gets around to sending a notice.

This provision doesn't cover all notices, so here's what you should know about this 18-month rule:

- Your return had to be filed on time — otherwise, you're not entitled to this suspension of interest.

- The failure to file or to pay penalties isn't covered by this rule.

- Additional tax due as the result of an audit isn't covered.

So what is covered? Suppose that you forgot to report $1,000 of income on your 2003 return that you filed August 15, 2004 (assuming that you obtained a four-month extension), and the IRS didn't send a notice until September 1, 2006. You owe interest from April 15, 2004 (filing an extension doesn't stop the running of interest from the original due date) through February 15, 2006 (18 months from August 15, 2004). However, interest is suspended from February 15, 2006, through September 21, 2006 (21 days from the September 1, 2006, notice date).

Receiving a delinquent tax return notice

A word of caution: You should treat a delinquent tax return notice as seriously as it sounds. If your tax return is delinquent, you may be contacted by mail, by telephone, or in person. Remember that the IRS has the right to issue a summons commanding you to appear with your tax records and explain why you didn't file a tax return.

Any taxpayer who receives a delinquent return notice should consider seeking the services of a qualified tax advisor (see Chapter 2).

Failure to file a tax return or returns can involve possible criminal violation of the Internal Revenue Code. Usually, the IRS isn't terribly interested in prosecuting individuals who haven't filed and who don't owe a substantial amount of tax. The IRS is, however, very interested in prosecuting prominent individuals because these prosecutions make good headlines. Extra! Extra! Read all about it!

If you file late returns — even in response to an IRS inquiry — and don't owe a substantial amount of tax (what's considered substantial is known only to the IRS), the IRS probably will accept the return and assess a penalty for late payment and possibly fraud.

If you don't reply to a delinquent return notice, the IRS can take one of the following steps:

- Refer the case to its Criminal Investigation Unit.

- Issue a summons to appear.

- Refer you to the Audit Division.

- Prepare a "substitute" return.

If the IRS decides to prepare a *substitute return* for you, it will use the information that it has on you in its master file, using the married-filing-separately or filing as single tax table, the standard deduction, and one exemption. Having the IRS prepare your return is the quickest way we know to become separated from your money. Although no fee is involved, you're likely to pay unnecessary tax. Remember, the IRS isn't interested in saving you money.

Why not beat the IRS to the punch? The IRS has an official policy of usually not prosecuting anyone who files a return prior to being contacted and makes arrangements to pay what is owed. Penalties and interest, however, will be assessed. This procedure is called a *voluntary disclosure*. The IRS wants customers back in the fold so badly that it lists voluntary disclosures in a prominent location on its Web site.

Appealing the results of an audit

The IRS issues **Form 4549-A, Income Tax Examination Changes,** and **Form 1902-B, Report of Individual Tax Examination Changes,** after an audit has been completed. Form 4549-A spells out any adjustments to income and expenses that have been made and any penalties and interest that are due.

These notices often are referred to as *30-day letters*. Within 30 days after receipt of an audit notice, you must agree to the adjustment, submit additional information explaining why an adjustment shouldn't be made, or request a hearing before the Appeals Division.

If you disagree with the proposed adjustment, and the amount of tax is more than $25,000, a written protest must be filed. IRS Publication 5 *(Your Appeal Rights and How To Prepare a Protest If You Don't Agree)* is extremely helpful in preparing a protest. Consider retaining a tax advisor when protesting large sums. This written protest is akin to a legal brief lawyers submit in outlining a case.

Appeals, you guessed it, are made to the Appeals Office, whose purpose is to settle disputes. The IRS agent who examined your return has no authority to take into account the time and expense to the IRS and the possibility that the IRS may lose in court. An appeals officer can. Approximately 90 percent of all cases referred to the Appeals Office are settled.

If the amount involved is not more than $25,000, a formal written protest isn't required. A simple statement explaining the changes you don't agree with and why you feel your deduction should be allowed is all that is necessary.

The IRS also issues a 30-day letter if you fail to show up for an audit. In such an instance, the examining agent will review your return and make adjustments to both income and deductions that he or she deems warranted.

If you receive a 30-day letter because you failed to show — even if you missed the audit because you never received the original notice scheduling it — contact the agent at the number given on the letter and schedule an audit appointment. If you make a new appointment within 30 days, the examining agent or appointment clerk will place a hold on your adjusted return (that is, it won't be processed), pending the outcome of the rescheduled audit.

After completing the audit, the IRS issues a new notice of income tax changes that supersedes the preceding one. If you agree to the audit changes and sign off on them, you can pay what you owe at that time, or you can wait to be billed.

Receiving a Statutory Notice of Deficiency

Although a notice (such as one proposing income tax changes) informs a taxpayer that additional tax is due, the IRS can't legally enforce the collection of additional tax until a Statutory Notice of Deficiency — often referred to as a *90-day letter* — is sent to a taxpayer by certified mail at the taxpayer's last known address.

A Statutory Notice of Deficiency isn't required if additional tax is due because of a math error. Statutory Notices are generally required only if additional tax is due as the result of the IRS adjusting a taxpayer's income, deductions, or credits from what was originally reported on the tax return the taxpayer filed. Unless a petition is filed with the U.S. Tax Court in Washington within 90 days of receipt of a Statutory Notice, the IRS can initiate collection action at the end of the 90-day period. If you file a petition with the Tax Court, all collection action is delayed until 60 days after the court renders its decision. If you live outside the United States, the 90-day period for filing a petition is extended to 150 days. The address of the Tax Court is included on the notice, but we give it to you here anyway, just in case:

400 Second Street, N.W.
Washington, DC 20217

The notice will indicate when the 90-day period expires. If your petition gets lost in the mail or arrives late, you're out of luck. However, a certified mail, FedEx, DHL, Airborne, or UPS receipt showing that the petition was sent to the Tax Court within the 90-day period will save the day.

Chapter 17

The Dreaded Envelope II: Audits

On a list of real-life nightmares, most people would rank tax audits right up there with having a tooth pulled without Novocain. The primary trauma of an audit is that it makes many people feel like they're on trial and are being accused of a crime. Don't panic.

First of all, you may be one of the tens of thousands of taxpayers whose return is audited at random. No, the IRS isn't headed by sadists. Random audits help the IRS identify common areas on tax forms where taxpayers make mistakes or fail to report income. Second, you may be audited simply because a business that reports tax information on you, or someone at the IRS, made an error regarding the data on your return.

About 15 percent of audited returns are left unchanged by the audit — that is, the taxpayers don't end up owing more money. In fact, if you're the lucky sort, you may be one of the rare individuals who actually gets a refund because the audit finds a mistake in your favor! Unfortunately, it's more likely that you'll be one of the roughly 85 percent of audit survivors who end up owing more tax money. The amount of additional tax that you owe in interest and penalties hinges on how your audit goes.

What You Should Know about Audits

Most people would agree that not knowing what to expect in a situation is what's most terrifying about it. This is even truer when dealing with the IRS. Here's what you need to know about audits:

✔ You needn't attend your audit. An EA, CPA, or attorney can go in your place.

✔ If at any time during the audit you feel hopelessly confused or realize that you're in over your head, you can ask that the audit or interview be suspended until you can speak to a tax pro. When you make this request, the IRS must stop asking questions and adjourn the meeting so you can seek help and advice.

✔ The burden of proof is on you. You're considered to be guilty until proven innocent. Unfortunately, that's how our tax system operates. However, if you and the IRS end up in court, the burden of proof switches to the IRS, provided you meet the IRS's substantiation and recordkeeping requirements and present credible evidence. What all this means is that you can't just sit in court and say, "Prove it" to the IRS.

✔ Unless a routine examination reveals the likelihood of unreported income, the IRS can't conduct a financial status audit by demanding that you fill out **Form 4822, Statement of Annual Estimated Personal and Family Expenses** so the IRS can determine how you lived on the income reported on your return.

- ✔ While it's true that fewer people are being audited than ever before, that's only part of the story. The IRS's computers constantly compare the information received from employers, banks, and brokers with the information reported on people's returns. As a result of this matching, 3.4 million taxpayers were sent bills totaling $5 billion.

- ✔ Through a major shift of its audit priorities, the IRS is now targeting high-income earners, self-employed taxpayers, small businesses, and workers who receive tip income, because it believes that these groups possess the greatest ability to not report all their income. Low-income taxpayers haven't escaped the wrath of the IRS, though. This year, 25,000 of them will be asked to document their eligibility for the Earned Income Tax Credit.

Surviving the Four Types of Audits

Thankfully, only four types of audits exist: office audits, field audits, correspondence audits, and random statistical audits, more commonly referred to as the audits from hell. With all four types of audits, maintaining good records is the key to survival. (Chapter 3 tells you what to do if you're audited and can't produce the needed evidence. If you haven't already taken out the trash and lost all your evidence, you can also refer to Chapter 3 for help filing and organizing the documents you may need.)

Office audits

An office audit takes place at an IRS office. The IRS informs a taxpayer that it is scheduling an office audit by sending a notice numbered 904. The front of this notice lists the date of the audit, and the back lists the items that the IRS wants to examine.

The audit date isn't chiseled in granite. If you can't gather the information necessary to substantiate the items the IRS is questioning, you can request a postponement. As a general rule, the IRS grants only two postponements unless you can demonstrate a compelling reason for an additional delay, such as an illness or the unavailability of certain tax records.

If you need more time but can't get an additional postponement, go to the audit with the records you have, put on your most confident face, and calmly inform the tax examiner that you need more time to secure the documents you need so that you can substantiate the remaining items the IRS is questioning. The tax examiner then prepares a list of the additional items the IRS needs to complete the audit, together with a mailing envelope so you can mail copies of the requested documents to the IRS.

Never, ever, mail originals. If the additional documents don't lend themselves to easy explanation through correspondence, then schedule a second appointment to complete the audit.

Most office audits are concerned with employee business expenses, itemized deductions such as medical expenses, charitable contributions, tax and interest expense deductions, miscellaneous itemized deductions, deductions for personal exemptions, and moving-expense deductions. Lately, the IRS has expanded office audits to include small-business returns, income from rental property, and income from tips and capital gains.

If the IRS is trying to verify your income, it may want to know about your lifestyle.

How will the IRS find out about your lifestyle? You'll tell them, that's how. Auditors are trained to control the interview. They feign ignorance, use appropriate small talk, use "silence" and "humor" appropriately, and avoid overtly taking notes so as not to distract the taxpayer, and they pay attention to the taxpayer's nonverbal language. The IRS even has a form to flush out lifestyle information, **Form 4822, Statement of Annual Estimated Personal and Family Expenses,** which — thank heaven — the IRS can now only spring on you when a routine examination has established the likelihood of unreported income. The form asks all about your expenses, from groceries to insurance — anything you and your family would spend money for as consumers. We don't know what it is about this form, but when the IRS shoves it under someone's nose, many taxpayers can't resist the urge to respond, "I'll show them what it costs to live in this country." What most people are unaware of is that you're under no obligation to fill out this form. The law only requires you to fill out and file a tax return. Statistical research has revealed that the IRS can collect more tax by examining sources of income than by examining deductions. If you operate a small business or have rental income, be prepared to explain where every deposit into your bank account came from.

Field audits

Field audits are conducted at a taxpayer's place of business. These audits focus on business returns and complex individual returns. If you file Form 1040, Schedule C, you're a likely candidate for a field audit.

Again, be prepared to verify the source of every deposit into your bank account. Field agents are required to survey both your preceding and subsequent years' tax returns to determine whether similar items were treated in a consistent manner. If an audit results in a significant increase in tax, you are now suspect, and the tax examiner will audit your subsequent years' tax returns (which normally are only surveyed).

Deciding where your audit happens

Both field and office audits are conducted in the district where a return was filed. This practice may create a burden if you live in one district and are employed or have your business located in another. For example, if you work or your business is located in Manhattan and you live in Connecticut, you normally would be contacted by the examination branch in Connecticut. If your tax records are in Manhattan or you spend most of your time there, you can request that the examination be transferred to the Manhattan District.

Besides gaining the convenience of having the audit conducted where your records, your advisor, or your business is located, you also get a little more time to pull together your tax data.

To transfer an audit from one district to another, call the IRS auditor and tell him or her why you want to transfer the audit to a different district. The transfer usually takes two to three months. The IRS also requires that you request the transfer in writing.

The following note will suffice when requesting that a tax examination be transferred from one IRS district to another:

[your address]

[date]

District Director

[address of district that issued exam notice]

Re: [your name and your Social Security number]

[exam year]

Dear District Director:

Because my tax records are located in [for example, Manhattan] and I spend most of my time there, I respectfully request that the audit you have scheduled be transferred to the [for example, Manhattan] District.

You may contact me during business hours at [telephone number]. Thank you in advance for your prompt attention to this request.

Very truly yours,

[your name]

Enclosed: Copy of exam notice

An office audit specifies what items will be examined from the very beginning of the process. Not so with a field audit — tax examiners have a great deal of discretion as to what items they review and to what depth they review the items. Count on having to verify your total income, travel and entertainment expenses, gifts, automobile expenses, commissions, payments to independent contractors, and any expenses that appear large in relation to the size of your business.

A tax examiner may examine each and every deduction or merely select a month or two of expenses and examine them on a sample basis. If they don't turn up any discrepancies, the examiner will accept the rest of the expenses for that category as correct.

Correspondence audits

Correspondence audits are exactly what the name suggests. The IRS conducts correspondence audits completely by mail and limits them to a few key areas of individual returns, such as itemized deductions, casualty or theft losses, employee business expenses, IRA and Keogh plan payments, dependency exemptions, childcare and earned income credits, deductions for forfeited interest on early withdrawals from savings accounts, and exclusion from income of disability payments. Income items may also be examined by a correspondence audit.

If you're ever the proud subject of a correspondence audit, the IRS gives you a return envelope in which to submit your documents, canceled checks, bills, and statements to substantiate the items the IRS questions. Again, *never* send original documents — only copies. Retaining the originals is crucial in case you have to stare down further inquiries.

When it comes to substantiating any deduction, the burden of proof is on you. If what you must substantiate is complex or requires a detailed explanation, you can ask for an interview in which you can explain in person.

Random Statistical audits

They're back! The IRS announced that over a one-year period it will subject 49,000 randomly selected taxpayers to audits under its National Research Program. The IRS conducts these audits to gather statistical information that can be used to determine pockets of tax cheating. The IRS, however, never uses that word. It refers to failing to report income or inflating deductions as "noncompliance."

How the IRS selects returns for audit

A computer program called the Discriminant Function System (DIF) selects returns for audits. This program scores each return for potential error based on IRS criteria. IRS personnel then screen the returns and select those most likely to have mistakes. They also look for returns that will result in significant additional taxes being assessed when they're audited.

Some returns are selected for audit as the result of an IRS project, such as one targeting waiters not reporting all their tip income, or another focusing on tax shelters. Small businesses and businesses where a high percentage of the income is in cash are currently hot audit areas.

Returns are also selected by examining claims for refunds and by matching information documents, such as Forms W-2 and 1099, with returns.

Location, as strange as it may seem, plays a role in who gets audited. IRS audit statistics reveal that someone in Pennsylvania has less than half the chance of being audited than someone living in Manhattan, who, in turn, has half the audit risk of someone living in Los Angeles.

Three tax-audit myths debunked

#1. If you file at the last minute or get an extension of time to file, you won't be audited because your return will get lost in the crowd.

Wrong! The audit selection, unseen by human eyes, is done by computer.

#2. Don't use the adhesive mailing label showing your name and address that the IRS sends. If you do, you will increase your chances of being audited.

Wrong! The weird numbers on this label are used by the IRS for data processing purposes only, not for deciding whether your return should be audited.

#3. The IRS audits fewer returns each year, so I can take chances.

Although fewer face-to-face audits occur each year, in this golden age of computers, the IRS has the ability to check if you reported all your income and properly claimed a number of deductions based on the information that your employer, banks, and others furnish them. Big Brother is watching!

Under its research program , the IRS randomly selects 1,000 freelance writers (or any other group of individuals or businesses), for example, so it can measure the degree of tax compliance for that industry, trade, or profession. It then moves on to another group until the total reaches its 49,000 total. On the basis of these audits, the IRS National Office determines which areas require stricter or greater enforcement efforts. In this post-Enron environment, no storm of protest has swelled to have the IRS suspend its current research audit program, as was the case a few years back.

Under the new audit research program, some taxpayers will be audited by means of the IRS having its computer check the correctness of their returns, others solely by correspondence, and the balance, some 30,000, will have select parts of their tax return examined in great detail. Birth certificates of a taxpayer's kids might be requested to prove the parent is entitled to claim kids as dependents. If something smells fishy or doesn't look right, you can count on being questioned in detail about the matter. The IRS looks under every rock, including matching up cash settlements you may have received in a personal injury lawsuit, for example.

Questioning Repetitive Audits

It is IRS policy *not* to examine an individual's tax return if the taxpayer has been examined for the same issue(s) in either of the two preceding years and the audit resulted in no (or only a small) tax change.

If you receive a notice of an audit questioning the same item(s) questioned in a previous audit, call the agent and inform him or her that the IRS audited the same issue(s) in one of the two prior years with little or no change in tax. (And do note that the IRS has never bothered to define *little.* Changes of less than a few hundred dollars in tax, however, should meet this criterion.) The tax examiner will ask you to furnish proof. Mail the examiner a copy of the IRS notice that your prior return was accepted without change, or mail the notice that adjusted your return.

If you can't document that the IRS is questioning items that it *already* questioned — with no change in tax — in one of the two preceding years, the lack of documentation doesn't mean that you can't get the current examination canceled. Just inform the examining agent by telephone about the prior year's tax examination. The tax examiner will postpone the audit and request a Record of your Tax Account Information from the two preceding years. If your tax account supports your contention, the IRS will cancel the audit.

Getting Ready for an Audit

Preparing for an audit is sort of like preparing for a test in school: The IRS informs you of which sections of your tax return the agency wants to examine so that you know what to "study." The first decision you face when you get an audit notice is whether to handle it yourself or to turn to a tax advisor to represent you. Hiring representation costs money but saves you time, stress, and possibly money.

If you normally prepare your own return and are comfortable with your understanding of the areas being audited, represent yourself. If the IRS is merely asking you to substantiate deductions, you'll probably do all right on your own. However, make sure you read "What You Should Know about Audits," earlier in this chapter.

What constitutes substantiation may at times involve a somewhat complicated interpretation of the law and its accompanying regulations. If the amount of tax money in question is small compared to the fee you'd pay a tax advisor to represent you, self-representation is probably the answer. However, if you're likely to turn into a babbling, intimidated fool and are unsure of how to present your situation, hire a tax advisor to represent you.

Even if you choose to represent yourself and find yourself over your head in an audit, you've got a backup. At any time during the examination — such as when you feel a dizzy sensation — the Taxpayer Bill of Rights allows you to request that the audit be suspended until you have time to consult with either an enrolled agent, a certified public accountant, or an attorney. When you make this request, the IRS agent must stop asking questions or requesting documents until you are properly represented.

But if you do decide to handle the audit yourself, get your act together sooner rather than later. Don't wait until the night before to start gathering receipts and other documentation. You may discover, for example, that you can't find certain documents.

You need to document and be ready to speak with the auditor about the areas the audit notice said were being investigated. Organize the various documents and receipts in folders. You want to make it as easy as possible for the auditor to review your materials. *Don't* show up, dump shopping bags full of receipts and paperwork on the auditor's desk, and say, "Here it is — *you* figure it out."

Who can represent you in an audit?

The IRS permits three types of individuals to fully represent taxpayers before the IRS: enrolled agents, certified public accountants, and attorneys. All three are bound by IRS rules of practice. (Tax preparers can represent you at an audit but not in any appeals beyond that.)

Enrolled agents (EAs) become enrolled to practice before the IRS by passing a two-day written examination administered by the IRS in which their knowledge of the tax code is tested. Alternatively, they must have at least five years of experience as an IRS tax auditor. Attorneys and certified public accountants are the other two

groups permitted to represent taxpayers before the IRS. Many states have continuing education requirements for CPAs and attorneys. The IRS requires that EAs also meet continuing education requirements.

Probably the best way to find a qualified tax professional is to ask a relative or friend for a recommendation of someone whose level of service and performance they are more than satisfied with. To figure out which of these tax practitioners may be best suited to help you in an audit, be sure to read Chapter 2.

Don't bring documentation for parts of your return that aren't being audited, either. Besides creating more work for yourself, you're required to discuss only those areas mentioned in the audit letter.

Whatever you do, *don't ignore your audit request letter*. The Internal Revenue Service is the ultimate bill-collection agency. And if you end up owing more money (the unhappy result of most audits), the sooner you pay, the less interest and penalties you'll owe.

Winning Your Audit

Two people with identical situations can walk into an audit and come out with very different results. The loser can end up owing much more in taxes and having the audit expanded to include other parts of the return. The winner can end up owing less tax money. Here's how to be a winner:

- ✔ Treat the auditor as a human being. This obvious advice isn't always practiced by taxpayers. You may be resentful or angry about being audited. You're a busy person with better things to do with what little free time you have, so you might be tempted to gnash your teeth and tell the auditor how unfair it is that an honest taxpayer like you had to spend scores of hours getting ready. You might feel like ranting and raving about how the government wastes too much of your tax money or that the party in power is out to get you.

- ✔ Bite your tongue. Believe it or not, most auditors are decent people just trying to do their jobs. They are well aware that taxpayers don't like seeing them. But you don't have to bow before them, either — just relax and be yourself. Behave as you would around a boss you have to put up with — with respect and congeniality.

- ✔ Stick to the knitting. You're there to discuss *only* the sections of your tax return in question. The more you talk about other areas or things that you're doing, the more likely the auditor will probe into other items.

- ✔ Don't argue when you disagree. State your case. If the auditor wants to disallow a deduction or otherwise increase the tax you owe and you don't agree, state only once why you don't agree. If the auditor won't budge, don't get into a knockdown, drag-out confrontation. He or she may not want to lose face and will only feel inclined to find additional tax money — that's the auditor's job. Remember that you can plead your case with several layers of people above your auditor. If that course fails and you still feel wronged, you can take your case to Tax Court.

- ✔ Don't be intimidated. Just because IRS auditors have the authority of the government behind them, that doesn't make them right or all-knowing. The audit is only round one. If you disagree with the results, you have the right to appeal.

- ✔ Appeal the results of an audit, if necessary. If you're dissatisfied with the results of an audit, refer to the section, "Results of an audit notice: Form 4549," in Chapter 16 to figure out how to make an appeal.

- ✔ Go to Tax Court. If you receive a Statutory Notice of Deficiency (this notice comes after you have exhausted all your appeals within the IRS or if you don't respond to a notice that the IRS wants to audit your return), you have 90 days to appeal your case to the U.S. Tax Court. If you don't appeal, the IRS can enforce collection on the 91st day. Refer to the section "Receiving a Statutory Notice of Deficiency," at the end of Chapter 16.

Understanding the Statute of Limitations on Audits

The IRS must make any assessment of tax, penalties, or interest within three years from the due date for filing a tax return. If the IRS grants you an extension of the filing deadline, the statute of limitations is extended to include the extension period. If the due date falls on a legal holiday or a Saturday or Sunday, the due date is postponed to the next business day.

Here's how the statute of limitations works: The IRS must make an assessment regarding a 2003 tax return by April 15, 2007, three years from the April 15, 2004 due date. After the 2007 deadline, the IRS can make no demand for additional tax. If a return is filed after the due date, the three-year period starts on the date the return is filed. However, if you file your return on or before April 15, 2004, the three-year statute of limitations still expires on April 15, 2007.

If more than 25 percent of the income that you are required to report is omitted from your return, the statute of limitations extends to six years. No statute of limitations runs on a false or fraudulent return. Thus, if a false or fraudulent return was filed, there's no time limit on when the government can assess additional tax. The same goes for *not* filing a return; there's no time limit.

Extending the statute of limitations

If the statute of limitations is about to expire and you haven't resolved your problems with the IRS, you'll be asked to agree to extend the statute of limitations. If you don't agree, the IRS will immediately assess your tax based on the information it has.

The only way to stop the IRS from forcing you to pay the tax is to file a petition with the Tax Court within a 90-day period. Although IRS Publication 1035 (*Extending the Tax Assessment Period*) explains this process, our advice is to see a professional if you ever get into water this hot.

The statute of limitations on tax collection is . . .

Ten years — period. After ten years, the IRS can't collect a dime. The ten-year assessment period starts on the day the IRS receives your return or on April 15, whichever is later. For purposes of the statute of limitations, returns filed early are considered filed on April 15. However, if the government increases your tax or makes an adjustment, the ten years on the additional tax owed starts to run from the date of the additional assessment. The reason the IRS still can go after financier Marc Rich (the second most famous tax evader after Al Capone) after all these years for the hundreds of millions he owes is because the 10-year statute of limitations is suspended when a taxpayer (if you can call him that) is continuously out of the country for more than six months.

If the ten-year period is about to expire, the IRS usually attempts to extend the period by getting you to sign **Form 900, Tax Collection Waiver.** More often than not, the IRS will threaten to seize everything under the sun that you own unless you agree to sign. Here's when you absolutely need professional help — and not just any tax advisor, but someone who is an expert and specializes in these types of cases. Ask people that you trust for suggestions of people to contact.

Your state tax return and the IRS

The IRS and 48 states have an agreement calling for the exchange of information about taxpayers. Only Nevada and Texas haven't signed on. Under these agreements, individual states and the IRS notify each other about taxpayers who failed to file returns and when either a state or the IRS has adjusted a taxpayer's taxable income.

The tax laws of most states provide that if the IRS has adjusted your tax return, you must file an amended state income tax return with that state within 30 to 90 days of the IRS's adjustment. The amended state return must reflect the adjustments made by the IRS, and you must pay any additional tax plus interest. If an amended return isn't filed, your state's tax collector, upon receiving notice of the adjustments from the IRS, will send a demand for additional tax and interest, and possibly a penalty for not notifying the state within the required time frame.

Since January 1, 2000, the IRS is allowed an extension of the 10-year statute of limitations on collection only where it has issued a levy, entered into an installment, or where the IRS has instituted court action. Such suits, however, are rare.

If you have an installment agreement in force, the ten-year period isn't automatically extended until you pay off what you owe. The terms of the agreement at the time you and the IRS entered into it govern how long the government has to collect what you owe. If the agreement is silent as to the collection statute, it's 10 years. So be careful what you sign when you request an installment agreement.

Chapter 18

Fixing Mistakes the IRS Makes

Get out your boxing gloves! Just kidding. Leave your boxing gloves and attitude somewhere else, because you definitely don't want to antagonize the IRS. When you're dealing with bureaucrats, you don't want them to be angry. Remember, they have the power to bring you to your knees, regardless of whether you're dealing with an entry-level clerk, a phone assistant, or a manager.

Most tax problems arrive uninvited, unannounced, and when you least expect them. Unfortunately, most people don't have a clue how to legally, swiftly, and inexpensively get Uncle Sam off their backs. Stay tuned as we explain how to fix a variety of problems caused by the IRS — without breaking a sweat or an IRS employee's limbs!

Although reluctant to admit it, the IRS does make mistakes. In fairness to the IRS, collecting taxes from more than 100 million individuals and businesses under an extraordinarily complex tax system is, to say the least, difficult. The number of errors can appear to be limitless, but most errors occur for simple reasons.

Pointing the Finger: Common IRS Flubs

We wish that we could explain why the IRS can't get it right the first time. We can't. But we can give you an idea of the number of mistakes made, the types of mistakes, and the action that you can take. We also can — and do! — offer tips to keep you away from the IRS paper trail.

The IRS processes more than a billion transactions a year. So, math wizard, what does an error rate of, say, 1 percent translate into? Ten million errors!

That's a whole bunch of errors. The following is a long list of the types of flubs the IRS can make:

▸ **Misapplied payments:** The IRS may not have posted tax payments that you made to your tax account (under your Social Security number). Payments are sometimes posted to the wrong year or type of tax. Perhaps the IRS didn't properly post overpayments from a preceding or subsequent year.

✔ **Misunderstood date:** The IRS may claim that you didn't file or pay tax on time. Computers at a service center may not acknowledge that the due date for filing or paying fell on a legal holiday or on a Saturday or Sunday and may therefore blame you for filing late, when in fact you filed on the first business day following a legal holiday or a Saturday or Sunday. Or perhaps you had a valid extension of time to file, but the IRS said that you filed your tax return late.

✔ **Wrong Social Security/ID number:** A data processing clerk may incorrectly input your Social Security number, or you may have been assigned two numbers. Because all data on a joint return is recorded under the Social Security number of the spouse whose name is listed first, any payments or credits that the other spouse made may not be posted under the first spouse's number. This situation frequently occurs when taxpayers file jointly for the first time or when a taxpayer files separately after having filed jointly in a prior year.

✔ **Wrong income:** Income earned by another person may be inadvertently reported under your Social Security number. This often happens when a taxpayer opens a bank account for a child or another relative.

✔ **Exempt income:** Money you earned on your IRA, Keogh, pension account, or from municipal bond investments was reported to the IRS as being taxable.

✔ **Double-counted Income:** Income earned from a taxpayer's business or profession may be recorded as income from wages — or vice versa — and the IRS moved the income to the line or schedule on the taxpayer's return where it correctly belongs. That's okay, but sometimes the IRS moves the income without removing it from the line or schedule where it first was incorrectly entered!

✔ **Lost return:** The IRS or the U.S. Postal Service may have lost your return and payment, leaving you in the unenviable position of having to prove the timely filing of the return. Hope you made a copy!

✔ **Partially corrected error:** The service center may have corrected only one of the errors that was previously made. For example, an IRS error may be corrected, but the penalties and interest that were incorrectly charged were not removed.

✔ **Data processing error:** A computer bug — or another unexplained phenomenon — may have caused a notice to be issued stating that a math error on your return was made where no error exists. Or someone may have failed to input all the data from the schedules attached to your return into the IRS computer.

Data processing errors are common with **Form 2210, Underpayment of Estimated Tax by Individuals and Fiduciaries,** where a taxpayer claims an exemption from the penalty for underestimating the amount of his or her required estimated tax payments. This type of error usually causes the IRS either to assess a penalty when it shouldn't or to issue a refund for the underestimating penalty that the taxpayer has paid.

✔ **Incorrect 1099:** The IRS may receive an incorrect Form 1099 from a bank or brokerage firm — either the amount of income reported on the form is wrong or the income isn't yours.

Fixing IRS Mistakes: Fight Fire with Fire

There is elegance in simplicity when corresponding with the IRS. Keep to the point. No letter should be longer than one page. A half page gets even quicker results. Remember, the tax examiner reviewing your inquiry could have little experience in the area you're writing about. Such people are, however, extremely conscientious in performing their duties. You stand a better chance of achieving the results you want by making their jobs as easy as possible. Don't succumb to the temptation to go into a narrative on how unfair our tax system is or how you are paying more than your fair share. Save that stuff for your representative in Congress.

Your letter to the IRS should contain the following items — and nothing more:

- ✔ Vital facts: name, mailing address, Social Security number on the tax return, and the year of the disputed tax return.

- ✔ The control number from the notice, type of tax, and a copy of the notice you received — refer to "Deciphering a notice," in Chapter 16, to find out how to get your hands on this information.

- ✔ What type of mistake the IRS made.

- ✔ What action you want the IRS to take.

- ✔ Copies of the documents necessary to prove your case — canceled checks, corrected Form 1099s, mailing receipts — but never send the originals.

Be like that detective on that old TV show *Dragnet,* "Just the facts, ma'am."

Address your letter to the Adjustments/Correspondence (A/C) Branch at the service center that issued the notice. You should note the type of request you are making at the extreme top of the letter — REQUEST TO ADJUST FORM [form number]. Use the bar-coded envelope that was sent with the notice to mail your letter.

Include a simple thank you and the telephone number where you can be reached in case the clerk at the IRS Service Center has any questions. Telephone contact between you and an IRS employee can take weeks off the Adjustments/Correspondence process. See Figure 18-1 for an example of a generic Dear John, er, we mean Dear IRS, letter. This example addresses an adjustment to be made to Form CP-2000.

Upon receipt of your letter, the A/C Branch will stop the computer from sending further notices until the matter is resolved. If your problem can't be resolved in seven days, you will be sent a letter indicating when it can be resolved. If you receive a second notice, don't be alarmed. This delay isn't unusual. The IRS doesn't move all that fast.

Figure 18-1: Here's how to compose a Dear IRS letter that gets right to the point.

Request to Adjust Form CP-2000

[your address]
[date]

Adjustments/Correspondence Branch
Internal Revenue Service Center
[address]

Re: [your name, Social Security number]
[tax year, DLN]

Dear IRS:
I have received your notice dated [date], in which you claim that I failed to report [$] of interest on my tax return.

Please be advised that your notice, a copy of which is enclosed, is incorrect. The interest that you claimed I earned was in fact earned on my daughter's bank account. Her Social Security number is [number], which should have been given to the bank, instead of mine, when the account was opened.

Please adjust your notice to reflect that no additional tax is due. Thank you for your prompt attention to this request. I can be reached at [phone number] should you require any additional information.

Very truly yours,
[your name]

If 30 days go by and you haven't heard from the IRS or you receive a third notice, see the section "Getting Attention When the IRS Ignores You," later in this chapter.

Sending a Simple Response to a Balance Due Notice

If you receive a balance due notice for a tax that already has been paid, simply mark the front of the notice: THIS BALANCE HAS BEEN PAID. ENCLOSED IS A COPY, FRONT AND BACK, OF MY CANCELED CHECK THAT YOU FAILED TO GIVE ME CREDIT FOR HAVING PAID. PLEASE REMOVE ALL PENALTIES AND INTEREST CHARGES THAT WERE ASSESSED.

The information that the IRS requires to properly credit your payment can be obtained from the back of your canceled check. On the back of the check, you'll notice the date, the location of the IRS service center, where it was endorsed, and the serial number stamped on it. See Chapter 16 to find out what these numbers relate to.

If any of this information isn't legible or you can't readily cull it from the back of the check, simply photocopy the check (front and back) and send the photocopy — along with the notice — in the envelope provided. Write across the notice: THIS HAS BEEN PAID — COPY OF CHECK ENCLOSED.

Sending Generic Responses to Generic Notices

If you're like us, you probably dislike form letters with a passion. At times, however, you have no choice but to fight fire with fire. To simplify things, we have included an all-purpose generic response letter (see Figure 18-2).

You can use this letter simply by inserting any one of the following responses to frequent IRS errors. To keep it simple, we list the IRS error you want to address as the heading, and the response you can use appears right below it in a different typeface between quotation marks. We also include some explanatory text without quotes.

Misapplied payments

"Enclosed is a copy of my canceled check, front and back, showing that the tax was paid."

Misunderstood due date

Here are several solutions to common problems with due dates.

Due date for filing or paying fell on Saturday, Sunday, or legal holiday

"Please be advised that your notice incorrectly penalizes me for filing/paying late. The due date for filing/paying fell on a [Saturday], and I made payment/filed on the next business day. Enclosed is a copy of my check dated [date], which is dated the date of the extended due date, as allowed by law. The serial number on the back of the check clearly indicates that the IRS negotiated my check on [date].

"Please correct your records to reflect that my return/payment was timely and remove all penalties and interest that were charged."

Figure 18-2:
You can get down-and-dirty with the IRS folks by using this battle-proven generic letter. Just insert the correct generic paragraph from the section where indicated.

Generic Response Letter
Request to adjust Form [number]
[your address]
[date]

Adjustments/Correspondence Branch
Internal Revenue Service Center
[address]

Re: [your name, Social Security number]
[tax year, DLN, Form number]

Dear IRS:

I am in receipt of your notice dated [date] (copy enclosed). Please be advised that your notice is incorrect.

[Insert generic paragraph(s) we have provided pertaining to one of the issues to be corrected.]

I would appreciate your adjusting the notice that you sent me now that you have the information contained in this letter that was previously unknown to you.

I would also appreciate your abating any penalties and interest that were incorrectly assessed.

I thank you in advance for your prompt attention to this request. I can be reached at [number] should you have any questions.

Very truly yours,
[your name]

Enclosed: Notice [number]

If you don't have a mailing receipt and you know your return was mailed on time, you may have to request a copy of the envelope in which you mailed your return from the service center before requesting an adjustment. Your mailing envelope becomes a permanent part of your return.

Valid extension of time to file

"Your notice incorrectly assesses a penalty for late filing. Enclosed is a copy of my extension that granted me an extension of time to file until [date]. I filed my return prior to the expiration of the extension on [date].

"Please correct your records by removing the penalties and interest that were incorrectly assessed."

Enclose a copy of any canceled check that may have accompanied the extension and refer to the check in the letter.

Late filing

If you mailed your return on time with a balance due that you didn't pay — and the IRS sent a notice demanding the balance plus an erroneous late-filing penalty — be prepared for lengthy correspondence with the IRS. If you don't have a postal mailing receipt, you will have to write to the service center and request a copy of the mailing envelope in which your tax return was mailed so that you can check the postmark.

"Your notice incorrectly assessed a late-filing penalty in the amount of [amount]. Please be advised that my return was timely filed on [date].

"By checking the postmark on the envelope in which my return was mailed, you will see that I didn't file late and therefore no penalty should be assessed. I would appreciate your sending me a copy of my mailing envelope when responding to this inquiry."

If the IRS can't locate your envelope (which sometimes happens) or the envelope bears a crazy, illegible postmark date, you have a problem. If this is the only time you were notified that you filed your return late, you will have to request that the penalty be abated because of reasonable cause — and because of your record of always filing on time. (We hope that you've always filed on time.) For more about reasonable cause, see Chapter 19.

If you file on time and enter into an agreement to pay in installments, the late payment penalty gets reduced from 0.5 percent a month to 0.25 percent a month while you're making payments. See "When You Can't Pay Your Taxes" in Chapter 19. The total late payment penalty that can be charged can't exceed 25 percent of the tax owed.

Wrong income

"The income on which you claim I owe additional tax per your notice is not my income. The bank/broker/insurance company [or whatever] incorrectly reported the income that was earned on this account as belonging to me. This account, in fact, belongs to my [mother, for example], who reported it on her tax return for the year in question. Her Social Security number is [123-45-6789].

"Enclosed, please find a copy of my [mother's] tax return and a statement from her stating that the balance in the account you are questioning belongs to her. I have instructed the bank to correct its records. Please correct yours so that my tax account reflects that no tax is owed."

Exempt income

We are constantly amazed when we review returns that clients prepared themselves. One of the things that crops up all the time is how often they pay tax on income when they don't have to. Here are two prominent examples and the appropriate response when the IRS sends a bill for tax due on tax-exempt income.

Keogh — IRA

"The income on which you claim I owe additional tax is income earned from my [Keogh or IRA] account and is exempt from tax. Enclosed is a copy of my year-end statement of that account. Please note that the number of this account is the same as the number that appears on your notice. Please correct your records so my tax account shows that no additional tax is owed your agency."

Municipal bonds

"The income on which you claim I owed additional tax is tax-exempt municipal bond interest. Enclosed is a corrected statement from my broker/bank that clearly identifies that the amount of income reported on your notice is tax-exempt municipal bond interest. Please correct your records so my tax account shows that no tax is owed your agency."

Double-counted income

"The interest income you claim I failed to report on my tax return for the year in question was, in fact, reported on Schedule C of my return (copy enclosed). By adjusting Schedule B

(Interest and Dividend Income) of my tax return without adjusting my Schedule C, you are requiring me to pay tax on the same item of income twice by double-counting it. Please correct your records so my tax account reflects that no tax is owed your agency."

Lost return

This is a tough one. But one secret the IRS closely guards is that it frequently loses or misplaces tax returns. The IRS even has a form letter when this happens. The letter requests that you send a duplicate. Unfortunately, when you do, you're likely to receive a follow-up notice saying that the IRS received the duplicate, but that it was filed late! When you file a duplicate return, always mark the top in bold lettering: `"Duplicate — Original Filed (insert date)."`

Refund return

"Enclosed is a copy of my return that your notice claimed was not filed. Please be advised that this return, which indicated a refund due, was filed on [date]."

If you have a postal mailing receipt, enclose a copy of it.

If someone other than you mailed your return, or if another person saw you mail your return, get a statement to that effect and enclose it. (Of course, if the person you asked to mail your return forgot, you can always try to get him or her to pay your late-filing penalty.)

Balance due return

"Enclosed is a copy of the return that your notice (copy enclosed) dated [date] claimed was not filed. Please be advised that my return was mailed on [date]. However, as of this date, my check number [number] dated [date] that accompanied my tax return hasn't been returned to me by my bank.

"I call your attention to *Estate of Wood,* 92TC No.46 and *Sorrentino,* 171 FSupp2d 1150, cases in which the courts held that a timely mailed return is presumed to have been received by the IRS.

"I would appreciate your correcting your records to reflect that this return was timely filed. If you would be kind enough to send me a bill for the balance I owe without reference to any penalties, I will remit full payment on receipt of your bill."

If, in fact, you included a check for the balance due with your return that has now been lost, don't forget to ask your bank to stop payment on the check. You don't want to have to write the IRS again when it credits two payments to your tax account. Plus, you can send the stop payment order with your letter to the IRS as proof that everything was lost.

Enclose any proof of mailing that you have. In what is known as the "Mailbox Rule," a federal district court in the *Sorrentino* case recently rejected the IRS argument that a taxpayer assumes the risk of nondelivery when they don't send a return by certified or registered mail.

Lost check

"Please be advised that my check, number [number], dated [date], was attached to my return that I filed on [date]. Because my check still hasn't been returned by my bank, I am placing a stop payment on it and have issued a new check for the same amount as the original check. I am enclosing a copy of my bank's stop-payment order. Kindly abate the interest that you charged on your notice. It would be unfair to charge me interest because your agency can't locate my check."

Tax assessed after statute of limitations

By filing a **Form 911, Taxpayer Application for Assistance Order,** or TAO, you put the IRS on notice that it could be liable for damages and costs up to $1,000,000 resulting from its reckless and intentional behavior in dunning you. If the IRS's actions merely are negligent, you can collect damages and costs up to $100,000. TAOs are covered under the Taxpayer Bill of Rights, which we discuss in Chapter 19. This form is filed with the office of the IRS's Taxpayer Advocate in your area. You can get a copy of Form 911 by calling 800-829-3676. The downside of filing this form is that the statute of limitations is extended while this application is pending (see Chapter 17).

To cover all bases, write to the Adjustments/Correspondence Branch at the service center that issued the assessment.

"Please be advised that your assessment for additional tax, penalties, and interest was issued in violation of the statute of limitations. The time for making an additional assessment for the year in question expired on [date].

"Please remove this assessment from my tax account, along with any interest or penalties that were charged. The assessment you made is in direct violation of the law. An assessment must be made within three years after the return is filed. This assessment doesn't comply with that requirement."

Refer to Chapter 17 for more on the statute of limitations.

Partially corrected error

"Please make the following adjustment [insert] as requested in my original letter of [date] (copy enclosed) that your current notice [date] failed to adjust."

At this point, you may want to refer the matter to the local Taxpayer Advocate Office. (See "Getting Attention When the IRS Ignores You," later in this chapter.)

Erroneous refund

Remember what your mother told you about keeping money that doesn't belong to you? She was right, of course — maybe because she had to deal with the IRS. As a practical matter, if you want to save yourself a great deal of time corresponding with the IRS, deposit the check, but don't spend the money (sorry). You ultimately will receive a bill for it. You may be asking, "Why not just return the check?" The problem with doing that is if the IRS doesn't get its paperwork right, you won't have the money, but you will have a bill from the IRS demanding repayment.

You returned a refund check

"Enclosed is a refund check that was incorrectly issued to me."

Return the check to the service center where you filed your return, not to the Treasury Department office that issued the check. Send this letter by certified mail.

You didn't return a refund check sent to you by mistake

"Your notice demanding interest on a refund sent to me in error is assessed in violation of the law. I discovered the error only when I received your notice demanding repayment. I call your attention to the fact that Section 6404(e)(2) of the Internal Revenue Code states that no interest may be charged if a taxpayer who receives an erroneous refund of $50,000 or less repays it when the IRS demands payment. Enclosed please find my check in the amount of the tax that was incorrectly refunded. Please correct your notice by removing the interest that you shouldn't have charged me."

If this approach doesn't work, contact the IRS Taxpayer Advocate in your area.

Data processing error

This problem is probably the most difficult to cope with.

"Your notice incorrectly states that [choose appropriate problem(s)]:

(a)   A mathematical error was made.

(b)   I used the wrong tax table in computing my tax.

(c)   I incorrectly claimed a credit.

"Please be advised that I rechecked my return and do not believe that any error was made. Enclosed is a copy of my return. Please review it and advise me exactly where you believe an error was made.

"I thank you in advance for your prompt attention to this request."

Incorrect 1099

Use (a) or (b) when appropriate.

(a)   "Your notice incorrectly claims that I failed to report all the income I received from [name]."

(b)   "Please be advised that the 1099 information that you received from [name] is incorrect."

"I enclose a copy of a corrected 1099 that [name] has reissued to me."

"I would appreciate your adjusting my tax account to reflect the information contained in the corrected 1099. When this is done, you will readily see that no additional tax is due."

Always try to get the 1099 corrected and send along a copy of the new one. Forms 1099 have to, by law, list the names, addresses, and telephone numbers of whom you can contact when the 1099 is wrong.

Wrong year

"The miscellaneous income your notice claims I failed to report for the year in question was not received until the following year and was reported on that year's return (copy enclosed). Additionally, I am enclosing a copy of my bank statement for the month in which this income was received. You will notice that this bank statement bears the following year's date."

Never received prior notices

"You don't have my correct address, which is probably why I never received your prior notices. Please send me copies of these notices so I can determine whether the most current notice that I enclose is correct. If it is, I will pay the amount I owe upon receipt of the prior notices I never received. If it is not correct, I will contact you. I thank you in advance for your prompt attention to this request."

To speed up the process, call the IRS at the number indicated on the notice and request a copy of the Record of your Tax Account Information. To obtain a copy of your tax account, flip back to "Lost Tax Returns" in Chapter 3. This document reflects all postings made by the IRS for tax, interest, penalties, and payments. Also, send the **IRS Form 8822, Change of Address.**

Getting Attention When the IRS Ignores You

At times, it seems that a black hole ravages every IRS service center, devouring loads of taxpayer correspondence. Naturally, the IRS won't respond right away in these cases. If this happens to you, the IRS has a special office that handles these problems: the office of your local Taxpayer Advocate.

Getting to know your local Taxpayer Advocate

The local Taxpayer Advocate Office is the complaint department of the IRS. There is an advocate in every one of the 33 IRS districts, as well as at each of the 10 service centers. An advocate's function is to resolve taxpayer problems that can't be resolved through normal channels.

The National Taxpayer Advocate, who is appointed by the Secretary of the Treasury, oversees all functions of the local Taxpayer Advocates and their employees. The national and local taxpayer advocates operate independently from the IRS and report directly to Congress. The purpose behind this independence is to provide taxpayers with a "customer-friendly" problem-solving office. Being independent of all other IRS offices enables the office of the local advocate to cut through red tape.

Local Taxpayer Advocates don't interpret tax law, give tax advice, or provide assistance in preparing tax returns. They resolve procedural, refund, notice, billing, and other problems that couldn't be fixed after one or more attempts by a taxpayer. A local advocate can abate penalties, trace missing tax payments, and credit them to a taxpayer's account. An advocate also can approve replacement refund checks for originals that were either lost or stolen, release a lien, and — of greatest importance — stop IRS collection action.

If the Advocate takes your case

Taxpayer Advocate caseworkers are committed to resolving your problem in seven working days. If they can't, you will be informed — usually by telephone — when you can expect the problem to be resolved. Most cases are closed in 30 days or less. If an advocate asks for certain information and it isn't sent, the case won't be held open indefinitely; after two weeks, it will be closed, in which case you must make a new Taxpayer Advocate contact. A caseworker closes a case by writing to the taxpayer and explaining what corrective action has been taken, if any. (If no corrective action can be taken, the advocate's letter offers an explanation.)

Meeting the criteria for a Taxpayer Advocate case

Under its Problem Resolution Program, caseworkers (called Associate and Senior Associate Advocates) working under the local Taxpayer Advocate are the folks that do the actual problem solving. They accept cases for a variety of reasons. The following types of cases are ones that you can cry on their shoulders about:

- ✔ You call or write the IRS about a problem. After 30 days, you contact the IRS again, but the IRS still ignores you.

- ✔ You file your return expecting a nice refund, but after 60 days, you're still waiting. You contact the IRS, but nothing happens.

- ✔ You receive a letter from the IRS promising to respond to your particular inquiry by a certain date, but the IRS forgets about you.

- ✔ You're suffering a hardship or are about to suffer one, such as the loss of your credit or livelihood.

Although an Associate Advocate can be helpful, keep in mind that they don't work for a charitable organization. One thing they are experts at is cutting through red tape. If the advocate won't take your case, he or she will refer it to the IRS office that should have handled it from the start.

Contacting the local Taxpayer Advocate

Except in emergency cases, such as when a levy has been filed and the taxpayer owes no money, taxpayers should write to the advocate in the district where they reside. Your letter should contain the following:

- ✔ A complete description of the problem

- ✔ Copies of the fronts and backs of canceled checks (if applicable)

- ✔ A signed copy of your tax return (if applicable)

- ✔ Copies of all notices received from the IRS

- ✔ Copies of previous letters written to the IRS regarding the problem

- ✔ The number of phone calls you made to the IRS, whom you spoke with, the dates, and what was discussed

- ✔ Any other documents or information that might help the advocate expedite the resolution of this problem

- ✔ A telephone number where you can be reached during the day

In emergency situations, contact the Taxpayer Advocate by phone. When you call, an advocate can immediately take a variety of actions. For example, the advocate can issue a **Taxpayer Assistance Order** (TAO), if a notice of levy has been incorrectly issued. A TAO stops the original IRS action that the IRS never should have undertaken.

The IRS toll-free phone number (800-829-1040) can direct you to the office of your local advocate. If contacting your local advocate didn't resolve your problem, here is the new toll-free help hotline for taxpayers with long-standing problems: 877-777-4778.

Finding Your Refund When It Doesn't Find You

If you didn't receive your refund, you may be one of about 90,000 taxpayers whose refund checks are returned to the IRS by the U.S. Postal Service. According to the IRS, these checks are undeliverable because of incorrect addresses or because the taxpayer moved and failed to leave a forwarding address. So if you move, make sure that you notify the IRS by filing **Form 8822, Change of Address.** That way, you'll be sure to get your refund.

The actual figures on how many taxpayers never receive their refund checks are substantially higher when you take into account the refund checks that are either lost or stolen. There are also a number of other reasons why a taxpayer may not have received a refund. For example, the refund could have been used to offset another year's tax bill or to pay what was owed on a delinquent student loan or past-due child support.

How to locate your refund

Yes, there is a lost-and-found department. You can find out the status of your refund by using the IRS automated TeleTax System. By dialing 800-829-4477 on a touch-tone phone, you're prompted through a series of automated questions — your filing status, the amount of the refund, and your Social Security number. You can also go to the IRS Web site (www.irs.gov) and click on "Where's My Refund."

Refund inquiries shouldn't be made until at least six weeks after your return was filed. It takes about that much time for the IRS to process a tax return and program the information into TeleTax. Only after the IRS inputs the information on your return into its computer can you find out about the status of your refund.

If a mistake was made, the refund may have to be processed manually, which may take an additional four to six weeks. Whatever the reason for the delay, the TeleTax System usually explains it. TeleTax also informs you of the date your refund check was mailed or when it will be mailed.

If more than ten days to two weeks have elapsed since the date that a refund check was scheduled to be mailed, and you still haven't received it, the check probably was lost or stolen. In situations like this, you can do one of three things:

- Fill out **Form 3911, Taxpayer Statement Regarding Refund,** and send it to the service center where you filed. This one-page form asks whether you ever received the check, or whether you received it and lost it. Allow four to six weeks for processing.

- Contact the office of your local Taxpayer Advocate. See "Getting Attention When the IRS Ignores You," earlier in this chapter, for more information.

- Contact the IRS refund section at 800-829-1040. You'll have the opportunity to speak to an IRS employee instead of a machine.

Uncashed refund checks

You have to cash a refund check within 12 months. When your refund check isn't cashed within the required 12-month period, that doesn't mean you're not entitled to your refund. You are. A new refund check must be issued and the uncashed one returned to the IRS. This procedure can be accomplished by filing **Form 3911, Taxpayer Statement Regarding Refund,** with the service center where you filed your return. Across the top of the form, write: THE ENCLOSED REFUND CHECK CANNOT BE CASHED; 12 MONTHS HAVE PASSED SINCE IT WAS ISSUED. PLEASE ISSUE A REPLACEMENT CHECK.

You aren't entitled to additional interest on a replacement check because you failed to deposit or cash your refund. But you are entitled to interest if the IRS is late in issuing your refund. See the very next section.

Interest on refunds

If the IRS doesn't issue your refund within 45 days of filing your return, it must pay you interest. So if you file by April 15 and you don't receive your refund by May 30, interest is due.

Refunds and estimated tax payments

If you requested that your refund be applied to next year's tax, you can't change your mind and subsequently request a refund. You can get your overpayment back only by taking credit for it on next year's tax return. No interest is paid on an overpayment of tax credited to next year's tax bill.

Joint refunds

When married couples divorce or separate, or when a dispute exists as to how much of the refund each is entitled to, Revenue Ruling 80-7 provides a formula for determining each spouse's share of the refund. Again, this is one of those times when consulting a tax advisor is a must. If the parties can't decide how to divide the refund, either spouse may request that the IRS issue a separate refund check by filing **Form 1040X, Amended U.S. Individual Income Tax Return,** and making the computation required by Revenue Ruling 80-7. The IRS will accept a joint 1040X with only one signature from a divorced or separated taxpayer requesting a separate refund check. The worksheet on the back of **Form 8379, Injured Spouse Claim and Allocation,** will guide you through the computation. Attach this form to your amended return. The refund belongs to the spouse whose income, deductions, and tax payments produced the refund. Filing jointly doesn't change who is entitled to the refund. Filing jointly only determines the amount of tax a couple has to pay.

Revenue Ruling 80-7 must be modified for taxpayers residing in community property states (Arizona, California, Idaho, Louisiana, New Mexico, Nevada, Texas, and Washington).

Recently enacted law provides an exception to the joint refund rule that we just cited with regard to the $400 increase in the Child Tax Credit that were mailed to taxpayers last July. Each spouse has a right to half of the payment.

Joint estimated payments

Where joint estimated payments have been made and a husband and wife file separate returns, the estimated payments may be divided in any manner the couple sees fit. However, if a couple can't agree on how estimated payments are to be divided, the payments will be divided in the same manner as joint refunds, as required by Revenue Ruling 80-7.

Deceased taxpayer

If a refund is due a deceased taxpayer, **Form 1310, Statement of Person Claiming Refund Due a Deceased Taxpayer,** must be attached to the return. A surviving spouse who's filing a joint return with the decedent doesn't have to file this form. If the form isn't attached, the

IRS will send back the return along with Form 1310. The refund is processed after the IRS receives the completed Form 1310.

Statute of limitations

To get a refund, you must file a return within three years of its due date, including extensions of time to file (or within two years of the date tax was paid, if that's later). After that time, you can kiss your refund goodbye. A return that's filed before the due date is considered to have been filed on the due date. For example, if the due date for filing a return is April 15, 2004, an amended return must be filed by April 15, 2007. After that date, no refund will be allowed.

If the April 15, 2004, filing date is extended to August 15, 2004, an amended return must be filed by August 15, 2007. Your acceptance of a refund doesn't bar a future claim for a refund if you subsequently discover that you made a mistake in computing the amended return and now realize that you're entitled to an even greater refund than you computed on your amended return.

The statute of limitations is suspended when someone is *financially disabled,* meaning that a disability has rendered you unable to manage your financial affairs. This change in the tax code was brought about by the case of a senile taxpayer who erroneously overpaid the IRS $7,000, and a timely (within three years) refund claim wasn't filed. Assuming that adequate proof of a medical disability can be provided, this taxpayer, under the new law, can still get his $7,000 back.

Given the number of taxpayers who have aging parents, a word of caution is required. This rule doesn't apply when a taxpayer's spouse, or another person such as a guardian, is authorized to act on the disabled taxpayer's behalf regarding financial matters. So where authorized person is handling another's financial affairs, the normal three-year statute of limitations rule prevails regardless of the taxpayer's "financial disability." The IRS believes that the person looking after the disabled person's financial affairs should be bound by the same three-year rule that everyone else has to follow. How disabled does someone have to be? The disability or impairment must be expected to result in death, or expected to last continuously for at least a 12-month period.

Refund offset program

If the IRS or the Treasury Department intercepts a joint refund and only one spouse owes for support, a government debt, or back taxes, the IRS must notify the other spouse of the action that he or she must take to get his or her share of the refund. The government can't keep the entire refund. The IRS intercepts tax refunds for back taxes, and the Treasury grabs tax refunds when you owe nontax federal debts (a student loan, for example) and delinquent child support. Does it make a difference who "gloms" your refund? The nonobligated spouse must file **Form 8379, Injured Spouse Claim and Allocation,** to claim his or her share of the refund. Revenue Ruling 80-7 explains how to divide the refund. In 2002, the IRS intercepted 2.9 million refunds as part of this program. Yes, Big Brother is watching and has long tentacles.

Just remember: To err is human, to forgive divine. And we never accused the IRS of not being human.

Chapter 19
Fixing Your Own Mistakes

• •

In This Chapter
▶ Fixing bad returns
▶ Making a deal with the IRS
▶ Abating penalties and interest
▶ Understanding the Taxpayer Bill of Rights

• •

*W*e all make mistakes. To make them is human; to admit that they're our fault is not, typically, human. In most cases, the sooner you fix a problem, the happier and less poor you'll be. In some cases, you need to complete more paperwork; in others, you have to speak with and cajole IRS employees. Regardless, here's our advice for how to do it now, do it right, and be done with it!

Amending a Return

Through the years, when taxpayers discovered that they failed to claim a deduction or credit in a prior year, they often asked whether they could claim that deduction in the current year. They couldn't, and you can't, either.

If you discover that you forgot to claim a deduction and the statute of limitations hasn't expired, you have to file an amended return. Similarly, if you discover that a deduction was improperly claimed, you must file an amended return and pay any additional tax plus interest.

Not surprisingly, more amended returns are filed when the flow of funds is going in a taxpayer's direction rather than in the government's. Although this discovery isn't a startling one, it has more to do with letting sleeping dogs lie than with people's honesty. It will take a sociologist to properly address this issue, and we aren't quite qualified to pull it off.

If you forgot to claim a deduction in a prior year, you must file an amended return within three years from the date of filing your original return, or within two years from the time the tax was paid, whichever is later. **Form 1040X, Amended U.S. Individual Income Tax Return,** is used to correct a prior year's tax return.

Suppose you filed your 2002 return on April 15, 2003. If you want to amend this return, you must do so by April 15, 2006. However, if you filed your return on or before April 15, 2003, the three-year statute of limitations still expires on April 15, 2006. If you had an extension of time to file until October 15, 2003, the three-year period starts to run from that date.

This three-year rule is suspended for anyone suffering from a disability that renders him or her unable to manage his or her financial affairs. This provision enables such taxpayers to recover tax that was erroneously overpaid in instances where the three-year statute of limitations would normally bar a refund. However, when a taxpayer's spouse or another person such as a guardian is authorized to act on the disabled taxpayer's behalf, this new rule doesn't apply. The IRS believes that the person looking after the disabled person's financial affairs should be bound by the same three-year rule that everyone else has to follow. How disabled does someone have to be? The disability or impairment must be expected to result in death, or it must have lasted or be expected to last for more than a year.

In most cases, filing an amended return doesn't affect the penalty for underestimating your tax. For example, suppose that you were assessed a $1,000 penalty for underpayment of your estimated tax. Your amended return is for half the tax on your original return. The $1,000 underestimating penalty can't be reduced. This is one mistake that can't be amended.

Amended returns also are useful for changing how you reported an item on your original return. You can change your mind in the following situations:

- ✔ You filed separately but now want to file jointly. It is important to note that you *cannot* do this in reverse — you can't switch to filing separately if you originally filed jointly.

- ✔ You want to change from itemizing your deductions to claiming the standard deduction, or vice versa.

- ✔ You reported something incorrectly. This situation may occur if you claimed a deduction or an exemption of income to which you weren't entitled. An example could be when a noncustodial parent incorrectly claimed an exemption for a child or claimed head of household filing status.

Some decisions to treat an item in a certain manner are irrevocable, such as using the straight-line depreciation method and taking a net operating loss forward instead of backward.

More expenses than income

An amended return is permitted whenever you incur a *net operating loss* (NOL). You have an NOL if the amount of money you lost (in a business or profession) exceeds all your other income. You can carry back an NOL to offset your taxable income in the two previous years, and doing so entitles you to a refund for both years. If the NOL isn't completely used up by carrying it back, it can be carried forward for 20 years until it's used up.

Any part of an NOL that the owner of a small business (provided that the person's income for each of the preceding years was under $5 million) resulting from a casualty, or theft loss, and NOLs attributable to losses in a presidentially declared disaster area can be carried back for three years.

NOLs incurred in 2001 and 2002 were allowed to be carried back five years. This mish-mash of rules also provided for a selection process. In these two years you could have chosen whether you wanted to take the loss back five, three, or two years, or not at all. If you didn't select a specific carryback period, then you were bound by the five-year rule for 2001 and 2002 NOLs.

The tax code has returned to the two-year carryback rule, unless the three-year casualty or disaster area loss rules apply.

Telling the IRS what you want to do (we know what you want to tell the IRS) couldn't be easier. Simply attach a statement to your return that indicates whether you want the two- or three-year carryback rule to apply. So for a 2003 loss governed by the two-year carryback rule, the loss is applied against your 2001 income. If the loss exceeds that year's income, the balance is carried over to 2002 and then on to future years. Under three-year rule, your 2000 income would be where your 2003 loss carryback would start.

When filing your return for the NOL year, you can elect to carry the NOL forward instead of having to amend your returns for the preceding years. This choice may make sense when your income or tax rates are rising. The reverse would be true when tax rates are declining the way they currently are. The election to only carry a loss forward to future years would also make sense if you were in a lower tax bracket in prior years. Remember, make sure that you really want to carry the NOL forward, because you can't change this election by filing an amended return. However, if you filed your return and didn't make this election, but now you want to, you have six months from April 15 to file an amended and make the election. See Publication 536, Net Operating Losses (NOLs).

You need **Form 1045, Application for Tentative Refund,** to carry back an NOL. This form can be used only if it is filed within one year of the year you had the NOL. If it isn't, **Form 1040X, Amended U.S. Individual Income Tax Return** must be used.

If you and your spouse were not married to each other in all the years involved in figuring the carryback and carryover, then only the spouse who incurred the loss can carry it back or forward.

The tax benefit rule

Whenever you deduct an expense in one year and part or all that expense is reimbursed in a subsequent year, you usually have to report the reimbursement as income. For example, suppose that you deducted $10,000 in medical expenses in 2002, and were reimbursed $3,000 by your insurance company in 2003. You have to report the $3,000 in 2003.

However, if the original deduction didn't result in a tax savings, you don't have to report the reimbursement. For example, you may receive a state tax refund for a year in which you claimed the standard deduction instead of itemizing your deductions — you don't have to report the refund.

When You Can't Pay Your Taxes

"If you can't pay," goes the old saw, "you can owe." That's certainly the way the Internal Revenue Service looks at things. In 2002, the IRS received 4.8 million returns from taxpayers who couldn't pay what they owed and that amounted to a cool $32 billion.

If you find yourself among the millions of Americans who can't pay all or any part of what they owe, you have four options:

- ✔ You can pay it off in installments, which 2.2 million taxpayers currently are doing.
- ✔ You can put it off until you have more money.
- ✔ You can try to convince the IRS to take less than it wants. In 2002, the IRS accepted 29,000 of the 124,000 offers that it received. The acceptance rate actually is much higher when you consider that a third of the offers can't be processed because they don't contain all the information necessary to make them processible. The average settlement is around 13 percent of what is owed.
- ✔ You can file for bankruptcy in the absolute worst-case scenario.

Whatever you do, don't confuse filing with paying. More people get into hot water because they mistakenly believe that they need to put off filing until they can pay. If you're one of the 2.1 million nonfilers that the IRS currently is looking for, file your return as soon as possible — even if you can pay only part of what you owe. Owing the IRS money is expensive. Four percent interest (the current rate, which is refigured every three months) compounds daily on the balance you owe, in addition to a late-payment penalty of half a percentage point per month. That kind of interest adds up to big bucks! Every month you're late in filing, you have to tack on an extra 5 percent penalty, up to a maximum of 25 percent.

At first, the IRS comes after you through the mail. If you owe money, either from the findings of an audit or because you simply couldn't pay it all on April 15, you'll get four notices from the IRS at five-week intervals.. If you don't pay everything you owe on April 15, the fourth and last letter arrives by certified mail around Labor Day. That's when things start to get ugly.

Suppose that you allow all four notices to go by without paying any money. Your account then is considered delinquent and is forwarded to the IRS Automated Collection System (ACS), which means you'll start getting telephone calls demanding payment — at home and, if the IRS can't reach you at home, at work, at your club, anywhere the IRS has a number for you. Although the IRS is trying to be a friendlier place, the agency is anything but congenial when demanding payment. If the ACS isn't successful in getting you to pay up, your account may be transferred to an IRS revenue officer, who will contact you in person.

Because the IRS usually has what it refers to as *levy source information* about you in its files, it places a levy on your assets or salary, or simply seizes your property. IRS collection agents are especially fond of cars — used or new, they don't discriminate. Keep in mind that from the return you filed the IRS already knows where your income comes from and how much you make and has the right to get additional information about you from credit and governmental agencies, such as the Department of Motor Vehicles, passport agencies, and the U.S. Postal Service. It can make you pay in more ways than one. And every time you make a payment, the IRS makes a permanent record of your bank account.

To avoid that hassle, if there's any way that you can get the money together, send a partial payment when filing your return , a partial payment with the first, second, and third notices, and the balance (including interest and penalties) with the fourth notice.

When the IRS sends a bill for less than $100,000, you have 21 interest-free days to pay it. When the amount you owe is more than $100,000, you have ten *business days* before you're charged interest.

The IRS must notify you of your right to protest a levy of your salary or property. You have 30 days from the date the IRS sends you a Levy Notice by Certified Mail to request what is known as a Collection Due Process Hearing. We explain how to request this type of hearing and what it's all about in Chapter 16.

Requesting an installment agreement

In some cases, people need more time to pay what they owe. If you need more time, you can request to pay in installments by attaching **Form 9465, Installment Agreement Request,** to your return or to any of the notices you receive. Then send it to the IRS Service Center where you file or to the center that issued the notice. You also can request an installment agreement by telephoning the IRS Taxpayer Services office. This number is listed in the telephone directory. It's also printed on the notices that you receive.

The IRS's Web site, www.irs.gov, now features an instant installment payment calculator. Click on "Individuals," then click the "More topics" button, and then click on "Interactive Installment Payment Process," which is where the interactive calculator begins. You're asked the amount that you owe and what you can afford to pay every month. The IRS tacks on an annual interest rate of 5 percent (the current rate — it changes every quarter) and determines whether you can pay off what you owe in five years. If you can, download Form 9465, Installment Agreement, fill it out, and mail it to the IRS. The IRS has a policy of not rejecting requests that pass its Web site calculations. The IRS then sends you a letter that it has accepted your request, and every month thereafter it sends you a payment reminder. By checking the box on line 13 of Form 9465, you can have your monthly payments automatically deducted from your bank account. When you choose this manner of payment, the IRS sends you **Form 433-D, Direct Debit Enrollment.**

If you can't pay what you owe within five years, the IRS calculator asks a series of questions about your monthly living expenses, and then either calculates the monthly payments you must make or suggests that you make an Offer in Compromise (see "Making an offer" later in this chapter).

If you owe less than $10,000 and can pay off what you owe in 36 months, the IRS is required by law to grant your request to pay in installments. However, some strings are attached. During the past five years, you had to have filed and paid your tax on time. Even if this rule knocks you out of contention, the IRS has a new policy that automatically grants installment agreements when the amount owed is less than $25,000 and can be paid off in 60 months. When you request an installment agreement, the IRS mails you an acceptance letter that tells you where to send the money. You won't have to provide a financial statement, and the IRS won't file federal tax lien, which is no small matter, because a tax lien can affect your credit rating for seven years, even if you pay off your tax liability in a shorter period of time. There's a $43 charge for an installment agreement and a $23 charge for reinstating an agreement that's defaulted on. The installment agreement requires that you don't fall behind in filing or paying.

Be careful not to fall behind on your payments, or you may have to apply for an installment plan all over again. If you can't make a payment, contact the IRS. You stand a good chance of being able to skip a payment if you have a plausible reason. Although the IRS isn't all that charitable, it reserves its wrath for taxpayers who ignore the agency.

Installments get trickier when you owe more than $25,000 or want to stretch your payments out for more than 60 months. You can either use Form 9465 or go straight to the IRS, either by mail or by phone. (A representative, such as an enrolled agent, a CPA, or an attorney, can make this request on your behalf.) When you owe this higher amount, you'll need to file a financial statement listing your assets, liabilities, and monthly income and expenses, which is submitted on **IRS Form 433-A, Collection Information Statement for Individuals.** Use Form 433-A if you're self-employed. For a business, use **Form 433-B.**

After reviewing the form, the IRS will recommend one of the following courses of action, or a combination of them. The IRS may tell you to

- ✔ Make immediate payment by liquidating some of your assets.
- ✔ Obtain a cash advance from a credit line.
- ✔ Borrow against the equity in any assets you may have, such as your residence.
- ✔ Make an installment agreement.

There is a fifth option: If there's just no way you can pay, the IRS will stop bothering you for the money. Yes, if you get the fifth option, the IRS will prepare **Form 53, Report of Taxes Currently Not Collectible,** and you'll be off the hook — for a while. However, the IRS will contact you every 9 to 12 months for a new financial statement to find out whether your financial condition has changed. Remember, the IRS has ten years to collect what you owe before the statute of limitations on collections expires.

You can appeal any rejection of a request for an installment agreement to the IRS Appeals Office (see Chapter 16). Although the IRS doesn't have a specific form for this, you can try using **Form 12153, Request for a Collection Due Process Hearing.**

If you filed your return on time and enter into an installment agreement, the late-payment penalty gets reduced from 0.5 percent a month to 0.25 percent a month while you're making your payments. The total late-payment penalty that can be charged can't exceed 25 percent of the tax owed. On $10,000 of tax owed, this reduction amounts to a $25-per-month savings.

Making an offer

What if you think there's no way you'll ever be able to pay it all off? The IRS, believe it or not, often takes partial payment. First, you need to fill out **Form 656, Offer in Compromise.** This nine-line form requires you to complete only three lines in addition to your name, address, and Social Security number. You merely check one of the three boxes in Item 6, which include "Doubt as to Liability" — "I do not believe I owe this amount" — to which you need to attach an explanation, "Doubt as to Collectibility" — "I have insufficient assets and income to pay the full amount" — to which you need to attach a complete financial statement (Form 433-A, or Form 33-B) or "Effective Tax Administration" — "I owe this amount and have sufficient assets to pay the full amount, but due to my exceptional circumstances, requiring full payment would cause an economic hardship or would be unfair and inequitable" — to which the financial statement must be attached. Unlike the application for an installment plan, this financial statement *will be audited,* not merely reviewed.

The 1998 law that restructured the IRS created two additional reasons for submitting an Offer in Compromise. They are known as the *equity offer* and the *hardship offer.* The equity option may be used when the collection of the full liability creates "such an inequity as to be detrimental to voluntary tax compliance." Don't laugh! We're quoting directly from the law. The hardship offer may be submitted when full collection would otherwise create an unreasonable hardship. What qualifies under this provision are situations where seizing or selling your assets or having to make payments would leave you without enough to pay reasonable, basic living expenses.

Underestimating estimated taxes

If you have income that isn't subject to withholding, the IRS doesn't want to wait until April 15 to be paid; it wants you to pay what you owe in quarterly estimates. The penalty kicks in when you owe $1,000 or more when you file your return and you haven't made tax payments equal to 90 percent of your tax during the year.

The penalty for underestimating your tax may be abated because of a casualty, disaster, or another unusual circumstance. It also can be abated by filing **Form 2210, Underpayment of Estimated Tax,** if you meet one of the following conditions:

✔ You paid 100 percent of your 2002 tax. If your 2002 income exceeded $150,000, however, paying 100 percent of your 2002 tax won't cut it. When you've made that much money, you must pay 110 percent of your 2002 tax to escape the penalty for 2003.

✔ You met the 90 percent tax payment requirement.

✔ You filed a return for the preceding year that showed no tax liability.

✔ You retired at age 62 or older, or became disabled, and your underpayment was due to reasonable cause.

If you operate a seasonal business or didn't earn your income evenly throughout the year, you may be able to reduce or eliminate the penalty by using the annualized income installment method. Not many taxpayers use it because of its complexity, but if you think it will save you money, IRS Publication 505 *(Tax Withholding and Estimated Tax)* explains how it works. For example, say you earned nothing for 11 months and then had income in the 12th month. You're required to make only one estimated payment instead of four.

To get the penalty waived, attach an explanation to Form 2210 along with any documentation that will prove you shouldn't be charged a penalty. See Chapter 8 for details about this fiendish penalty.

An Offer in Compromise is a matter of public record and, if accepted, may come with strings attached. You may have to agree that for a period of years, perhaps as many as five, you'll pay more than you offered in the event your financial condition improves. An aging Joe Louis had to accept such terms, just in case he ever started earning millions again by going back into the boxing ring.

Who are candidates for Offers in Compromise? All types of taxpayers: senior citizens with few or no assets or in poor health, spendthrifts who earned large sums of money and squandered it, athletes and actors whose earning potential has diminished, casualties of downsizing, and people whose relatives are reluctant to leave them money because of their tax problems.

You can appeal an offer that is rejected. While an offer is pending, the IRS is prohibited from levying your salary or property. Use Form 12153 to request an appeal.

The IRS now charges a $150 fee for processing an Offer in Compromise application. Don't complain. Instead, be thankful the IRS didn't bring back debtors prison. The fee is waived if the offer is based solely on doubt as to liability or if the income of the person making the offer is below the poverty level.

Don't be fooled by what you may have heard. Making an offer isn't just another version of the old TV programs *The Price Is Right* or *Lets Make A Deal*. The IRS is anything but a pushover when it comes to agreeing to accept less.

Declaring bankruptcy

If things are really dire, you may decide that declaring personal bankruptcy is the only way out. Filing a bankruptcy petition puts a legal stop to all IRS collection action, and the government can no longer garnish your salary or seize your property. Income taxes that are more than three years old are forgiven.

You can recover up to $1 million in damages if the IRS willfully violates the bankruptcy law's prohibition against seizing your salary or property.

Even if your tax liability isn't completely wiped out in bankruptcy court, as often happens, the IRS won't have as much power over you anymore. For example, you don't have to get IRS approval on an installment plan. If the bankruptcy court allows your repayment plan because the bankruptcy judge finds it fair and equitable, the IRS has to accept it.

Remember that bankruptcy is a drastic step and shouldn't be undertaken unless you're guided by an attorney experienced in this area. Bankruptcy damages your credit report, but with all the liens the IRS has filed, your credit is already damaged. Generally, personal income taxes that are more than three years old from the original due date, and more than two years old from the actual filing date, can be wiped out in a bankruptcy and become what is known as *dischargeable debt*. In a Chapter 13 bankruptcy filing, the two-year filing rule doesn't apply. The tax only has to be more than three years old. Proposed bankruptcy reform legislation, pending in Congress, would eliminate this Chapter 13 loophole.

Planning ahead to avoid these problems

Making adequate provisions in the first place is your best defense against not being able to pay your tax bill on April 15. Routinely review your withholding allowances (Form W-4) to make sure that the proper amount of tax is being withheld from your salary. (See Chapter 15 if you need help determining how much to withhold.) If you're self-employed or have income that isn't subject to withholding, you need to make quarterly estimated payments using **Form 1040-ES**.

Abating a Penalty

Although the Internal Revenue Code contains about 150 penalties, some are more common than others. The most common penalties include

- Accuracy errors (the IRS defines accuracy errors as either negligence or disregard of the rules)
- Failure to file
- Failure to pay
- False Withholding Exemption Certificate (Form W-4)
- Underestimating tax

Many taxpayers who receive a penalty notice believe that a penalty wouldn't have been charged unless it was correct, and they simply pay it. After all, penalties are asserted on official-looking documents. Never assume that any notice is correct. Thoroughly reading the notice is the primary requirement for making sure that you don't pay what you don't owe.

In 2002, the IRS assessed 28.3 million penalties that amounted to a total of $18.7 billion. Of those penalties, 4.1 million totaling $9.2 billion were abated for reasonable cause or because they were improperly assessed. Taxpayers can look to several sources — the *Internal Revenue Manual,* court cases, IRS Rulings and Announcements, and regulations to the Internal Revenue Code — to determine whether they meet the definition of reasonable cause. Penalties never are deductible. Because some penalties are additions to the tax you must pay, interest is computed on the total amount due — tax plus penalties.

The Internal Revenue Manual (IRM)

The *Internal Revenue Manual* is the IRS bible. It contains the rules that IRS employees must follow when applying the law (not that it helps you any when they don't). According to the manual, the following situations constitute reasonable cause for abating a penalty:

- Your return was mailed on time but was not received until after the filing date, regardless of whether the envelope bears sufficient postage.
- Your return was filed on time but was received by the wrong IRS office.
- You relied upon erroneous information provided to you by an IRS officer or employee.
- Your return was filed late because of the death or serious illness of the taxpayer or a close family member.
- You were unavoidably away on the filing date.
- Your place of business, residence, or business records was destroyed because of fire or other casualty.
- You applied to the IRS district director for proper tax forms prior to the filing deadline, but these forms were not furnished in sufficient time.
- You presented proof of having visited an IRS office before an IRS expiration date for filing returns to secure information on how to properly complete your return, but you were not able to meet with an IRS representative.
- You were unable, for reasons beyond your control, to obtain the records necessary to determine the amount of tax due, or, for reasons beyond your control, you weren't able

to pay. For example, you couldn't get your money out of a bankrupt Savings & Loan to pay your taxes, or your account was attached by a lien or court order. Perhaps you earned money in a foreign country that you couldn't convert into dollars, or a person who was needed to cosign a check was ill or away.

✔ Your tax advisor incorrectly advised you that you didn't need to file a return, even though you provided him or her with all the necessary and relevant documents, or the advisor prepared the return incorrectly.

Your ignorance of the law may be considered reasonable cause for a late return if other factors, such as a situation in which you are filing a return for the first time, support this contention. However, you must demonstrate that you exercised ordinary care and prudence.

Court cases that define reasonable cause

The following court precedents can be handy to know when dealing with the IRS. Precedents are good things, because they act like rules that the IRS will obey. You can use these arguments when appropriate. The IRS should listen. But be careful: When you start citing court cases (look for the italicized text in the sections that follow so you can identify the court case), the eyes of IRS officials (or anyone else, for that matter) may start to glaze over.

Ignorance

The taxpayer's limited education and business experience, together with his reliance on the advice of an attorney, caused his failure to file to be due to reasonable cause. *C.R. Dexter,* 306 F. Supp 415.

Litigation

The taxpayer's late filing was due to reasonable cause when litigation was necessary to determine the taxability of income received. *F.P. Walker* (CA-9), 326 F. 2nd 261 (Nonacq).

Timely mailed and presumed received

Even though a taxpayer didn't have a certified or registered mailing receipt, the Tax Court held that the IRS is presumed to have received a timely mailed return when a postal official testified that she had accepted and postmarked the envelope prior to the due date of the return. The court found it a mere coincidence that the taxpayer's state return hadn't been received by the state tax authority, either. *Estate of Wood,* 92 TC 793. One could safely infer that the court would have been equally convinced if an employee or other individual had given the same testimony.

A certified or registered mailing receipt isn't necessary to prove a return was mailed. Placing the return in a mailbox is good enough. *Sorrentino,* 171 FSupp2d 1150.

Return executed but misplaced

Tax returns were signed and given to an employee whose duty was to mail the returns. Instead, the employee by error then placed the returns in a file together with copies of the returns of many other corporations. When the IRS sent a notice a year later, the error was discovered and the returns were filed at that time. *Bouvelt Realty,* 46 BTA 45.

Return misplaced by the IRS

The Commissioner failed to refute the taxpayer's evidence that the tax returns were timely filed but misplaced by the IRS. *J.J. Carlin,* 43 TCM (CCH) 22.

Reasonable cause — an important definition

With the exception of fraud penalties, just about every penalty can be abated for what is known as reasonable cause. The IRS defines reasonable cause as follows: "If the taxpayer exercised ordinary business care and prudence and was nevertheless unable to file or pay within the prescribed time, then the delay is due to reasonable cause."

Mailing of return on time

The IRS asserted that a return due on the 15th had not been received for filing until the 17th. The corporate officer who had mailed the return had died, and because of the Commissioner's failure to produce the envelope in which the return was mailed, it was held that no penalty should attach. *Capento Securities Corp.,* 47 BTA 691 (Nonacq) Aff'd CA-1.

Honest belief

The taxpayer's honest but mistaken belief that an extension of time to file allowed him to delay the filing of his tax return until he had sufficient funds to pay his tax constituted reasonable cause for the late filing of his tax return. *M.S. Alba,* DC, East.Dist.MO.No.80-764.

In another case, a taxpayer — while separated from her husband — attached her W-2 to a joint return that she gave back to her husband to file. The honest belief that the return was filed didn't constitute willful neglect. *E. Barker,* 22 TCM 634.

Illness

The taxpayer's illness and hospitalization constituted reasonable cause for failure to file a tax return. *C. Freeman,* 40 TCM 1219, Dec. 37,236 (M).

Reliance on accountant

Where a corporate taxpayer selects a competent tax expert, supplies the expert with all necessary information, and asks the expert to prepare proper tax returns, the taxpayer has done all that ordinary business care and prudence can reasonably demand. *Haywood Lumber & Mining Co. v Comm.,* (CA-2) 178 F.2nd 769.REV'D CA-2.

Excuses that won't fly

The dog-ate-my-taxwork excuse won't work, nor will these.

Delegation of authority

In a landmark case, the Supreme Court held that the reliance on an attorney as to the filing date of a return didn't constitute reasonable cause. *R.W. Boyle,* SCT. 105 S. Ct. 687. The Supreme Court held in this case that a qualified tax advisor's incorrect advice as to whether a tax return should be filed constitutes reasonable cause, but that the tax advisor's mistaken advice as to the correct date a return must be filed does not.

But subsequent to *U.S. v Boyle,* a disabled taxpayer's reliance on an attorney to timely file a return was considered reasonable cause. *C. Brown v U.S.,* 57 AFTR 2d (M.D. Tenn. 1985).

Incarceration

The Tax Court rejected a taxpayer's claim that incarceration constituted reasonable cause. *R. Llorente,* 74 TC 260.

IRS rulings and announcements

Taxpayers are amazed when they discover that most of the rules they must follow are created by the IRS — not by Congress. That's because most tax laws include the following language: "in accordance with rules and regulations to be promulgated by the Secretary of the Treasury" — meaning that the Treasury Department makes and enforces the rules. Therefore, you must pay special attention to IRS rulings and announcements — there's a whole lot of promulgating going on.

Partnership returns — Rev. Proc. 84-35

If a partnership is composed of ten or fewer partners and each of the partners reports his or her share of the partnership's income and deductions, the partnership won't be charged a penalty for either not filing or filing late.

Erroneous advice given by IRS employees over the telephone

According to IRS Information Release IR-88-75, incorrect advice given over the telephone by an IRS employee may constitute reasonable cause. The only problem with this provision is how you prove that you called the IRS and received erroneous advice. The IRS will consider that a taxpayer received incorrect advice over the telephone, if a taxpayer provides the following information:

- Whether the taxpayer tried to find the answer to the question in IRS forms, instructions, or publications.
- The questions asked and the specific facts given to the IRS employee.
- The answer the taxpayer received.
- The IRS employee's name and ID number. Yes, every employee has one.
- The date and time of the call.

If you're reading this provision for the first time, it's probably too late. But the next time you call the IRS for advice, make sure that you jot all this information down.

Erroneous written advice by IRS

Both the tax *and* the penalty attributable to the incorrect written advice can be abated. This is done by filing **Form 843, Claim for Refund and Request for Abatement,** and checking box 4a.

IRS criteria for determining reasonable cause

This IRS ruling spells out the criteria for reasonable cause. Here they are:

- Do the taxpayer's reasons address the penalty that was assessed?
- Does the length of time between the event that caused the late filing and the actual filing negate the fact that the taxpayer attempted to correct the situation in a timely fashion?
- Does the continued operation of a business after the event that caused the taxpayer's noncompliance negate the taxpayer's excuse?
- Should the event that caused the taxpayer's noncompliance or increased liability have been reasonably anticipated?
- Was the penalty the result of carelessness, or does the taxpayer appear to have made an honest mistake?

- Has the taxpayer provided sufficient detail (dates, relationships) to determine whether he or she exercised ordinary business care and prudence? Is a nonliable individual being blamed for the taxpayer's noncompliance? What is the nature of the relationship between the taxpayer and this individual? Is the individual an employee of the taxpayer or an independent third party, such as an accountant or a lawyer?

- Has the taxpayer documented all pertinent facts?

- Does the taxpayer have a history of being assessed the same penalty?

- Does the amount of the penalty justify closer scrutiny of the case?

- Could the taxpayer have requested an extension or filed an amended return?

Critical to getting the IRS to accept your reasons for late filing or paying is the time frame between the event that was clearly beyond your control and the date of your ultimate compliance with your obligation to file or pay. What the IRS considers to be an acceptable amount of time between these two events is based on the facts and circumstances in each case. Figure 19-1 shows a reasonable cause sample letter.

Penalty appeals

If the Adjustments/Correspondence Branch (see Chapter 18) rejects your request to have a penalty abated, you may appeal. Every service center has a penalty appeals unit. The A/C Branch notice informing taxpayers that their request was rejected will also inform them of their appeal rights and how to exercise them.

Payment of the penalty is not a prerequisite to requesting an appeal. No official IRS form exists for requesting this type of appeal. Although some appeals within the IRS need not be in writing, this one must. Your original letter requesting an abatement can be used with one simple modification: Your opening sentence should state that you are requesting an appeal from a tax examiner's determination (which you are enclosing) that you failed to establish reasonable cause.

Some IRS offices require that the tax and interest be paid before they will consider a penalty abatement. No specific law requires this; the IRS is famous for making up its own rules.

You may want to include any additional reasons that constitute reasonable cause, or any proof, such as

- Your passport showing that you were out of the country.

- Medical records stating that you were ill.

- A statement from a third party who saw you mail the return on time.

- A police or insurance report showing that the loss of your records was caused by a theft or other casualty.

These documents, whenever available, need to be sent with the original abatement request. Hold nothing back!

At times, for inexplicable reasons, tax examiners take the position that a taxpayer should have quickly estimated his or her income and filed a return based on this estimate. In such instances, you should point out that the event that took place was the reasonable cause that prevented you from preparing an estimate.

Sample Reasonable Cause Letter

Request to abate penalty
[your name and address]
[today's date]

Adjustments/Correspondence Branch
Internal Revenue Service Center
[address]

Re: [your name]
[Social Security number]
[tax year]

Dear IRS:

I am in receipt of your notice of [date] in which you asserted a late filing and payment penalty in the amount of [penalty $] plus interest on this amount of [interest $].

Please be advised that my late filing and payment were due to reasonable cause and, according to tax law, should be abated.

On [date], I was ill with [illness]. I was hospitalized and didn't recover sufficiently until [date]. When I was well enough to assemble the data necessary to file a return and pay what was owed, I immediately did so. Enclosed is a letter from my physician confirming the nature of my illness and the length of my recovery, as well as the hospital bill.

Regulation 301.6651-1(c) provides that:

> "If a taxpayer exercised ordinary business care and prudence and was nevertheless either unable to file the return or pay within the prescribed time, the delay is due to reasonable cause."

Thank you in advance for your prompt attention to this request. If you require further clarification of any point, I can be reached at [number].

Very truly yours,

[your name]

Enclosed: Form CP-22A (Statement of Change to Your Account)
              Letter from physician and hospital

Figure 19-1:
A sample reasonable cause letter.

The IRS has a policy that no collection action will be taken while a penalty appeal is pending — unless, that is, the case already was assigned to a collection officer who determined that the appeal was requested solely to postpone or delay payment. Whenever you're being bugged for the penalty, contact the office of your local Taxpayer Advocate to get the IRS Collection Division off your back. A Taxpayer Advocate has authority to do this.

Be patient when requesting an abatement of a large penalty or when appealing a penalty abatement decision. The process is not speedy.

Abating Interest

Whereas the IRS has the power to abate a penalty for reasonable cause, it doesn't have — as a general rule — the authority to abate interest. But like every IRS rule, there are some limited exceptions when interest can be abated.

When interest is incorrectly charged

If interest was assessed after the expiration of the statute of limitations or was assessed illegally, then it's probably correct to assume that the underlying tax also was incorrectly assessed. If this is the case, the interest, as well as the tax, can be abated.

Interest and tax that were incorrectly or illegally assessed may be abated in one of two ways. You can use **Form 911, Taxpayer Application for Assistance Order,** or you can write to the Adjustments/Correspondence Branch at the service center (or district office) that issued the notice. Figure 19-2 shows a sample letter with two possible reasons.

You can collect damages when the IRS willfully or negligently collects tax that isn't owed.

Sample Letter
[your name and address]
[today's date]

Internal Revenue Service Center
[address]

                                        Re: [your name]
                                        [Social Security number]
                                        [tax year]

Dear IRS:

I respectfully request that you abate the tax assessment in the amount of [amount] that your agency made by error pursuant to the enclosed notice.

Reason (1): Section 6404(e) specifically allows for the abatement of tax that was assessed as the result of an IRS mathematical or clerical error.

Reason (2): Your assessment was made after the three-year statute of limitations had expired. Such assessments are prohibited by law.

I may be reached by telephone during the day at [number] should you require any further information.

                                        Very truly yours,

                                        [your name]

Enclosed: Copy of notice

Figure 19-2: A sample letter to abate interest.

Erroneous refunds

The IRS is required to abate interest on a demand for repayment of a refund that was issued in error. For this rule to apply, the refund must be less than $50,000, and the taxpayer must in no way be responsible for causing the refund. On an erroneous refund, the IRS can charge interest only from the point in time when it demanded repayment and not for the period prior to the taxpayer being asked to repay it.

For example, suppose that you should have received a $100 refund, but instead, you received a $1,000 refund. No interest can be charged on the $900 for the period of time you held the money. If interest is assessed on the $900, filing **Form 843, Claim for Refund and Request for Abatement,** will get back the interest that you paid.

IRS delays

The Tax Reform Act of 1986 gives the IRS the authority to abate interest on any tax deficiency when an IRS official fails to perform a *ministerial act* and instead moves at a snail's pace in handling routine matters. (In this case, a ministerial act has nothing to do with performing the prescribed rituals of your favorite religious institution; the IRS official must appropriately and in a timely manner perform the prescribed rituals of your "favorite" government agency.) The IRS has the right to abate interest, but it is not compelled to do so. When the failure to perform a ministerial act has occurred, interest is required to be abated from the time when the IRS first contacted you, not from the due date of your tax return, which normally is the case.

Here's how the IRS decided whether interest could be abated in the following cases:

- You moved from one state to another. Your return was selected for audit. You request the audit to be transferred to your new location, and the transfer is approved. But the IRS delays in transferring your case. Interest *can* be abated.
- An audit reveals that additional tax is due. You and the IRS have agreed on the amount of additional tax due, but the IRS delays in sending you a bill. Interest *can* be abated.
- You deducted a loss from a tax shelter that is being audited. The audit of the shelter takes a long time to complete. Interest *can* be abated.
- The agent auditing your return is assigned to a training course, and, during the training course, your audit is neither worked on nor reassigned to a different agent. Interest *can* be abated.

Form 843, Claim for Refund and Request for Abatement, is used to abate interest in situations where the IRS has caused a delay. Check box 4a (Interest Caused by IRS Errors and Delays).

Although delays by the IRS caused by loss of records, transfer of personnel, extended illness, leave, or training now are causes for abating interest, be forewarned that getting interest abated on an IRS delay nevertheless is a tough nut to crack. The IRS has the authority but, again, isn't compelled to abate interest when managerial acts cause delay.

When the IRS doesn't send a bill

When you sign off on the results of a tax examination or notice of proposed adjustments to your return, the IRS must send you a bill for payment within 30 days. If it doesn't, the agency can't charge interest until a bill is sent. Use Form 843 to abate any interest charges after the 30-day period.

When the IRS sends a bill

If the amount that you owe is less than $100,000, you have 21 interest-free days to pay it. If the amount you owe is more than $100,000, you have 10 *business days* before you're charged interest.

The 18-month rule

The IRS must send a notice of additional tax due within 18 months of filing your return. If it doesn't, it has to stop charging interest after 18 months and until 21 days after it sends a notice.

Not all IRS notices are covered by this provision. For example, audit notices aren't. See Chapter 16 for the ins and outs of how this provision works.

The Taxpayer Bill of Rights

This great republic was founded on the principle that taxation without representation is tyranny. But if you've ever had a run-in with the IRS, you know that taxation *with* representation isn't so hot, either. To feed its insatiable appetite for spending, Congress has given the IRS almost unlimited authority to collect taxes — an authority that, sadly, can be abused in all sorts of horrible ways.

A few years ago, lawmakers decided to do something about the monster they had created. Responding to a flurry of taxpayer horror stories, in 1988, Congress enacted its first so-called *Taxpayer Bill of Rights*. The idea was to lay out in writing what the IRS can get away with when collecting your money, and what you can do to fight back.

Now, whenever you get a notice of any kind from the IRS, you get a two-page summary of the taxpayer bill, entitled "Your Rights as a Taxpayer." This remarkably readable document explains how to appeal an IRS decision, suggests where you can get free information, and assures you that you're entitled to "courtesy and consideration" from IRS employees. Reading it, you almost get the impression that the IRS is a friendly place that wants only what's best for you. Following that assumption, of course, would be a terrible mistake.

It's not that the original Taxpayer Bill of Rights is worthless. On the contrary, it contains two significant points:

- At any time during an audit or interview, you may ask to speak with an enrolled agent, attorney, or CPA. Whenever that happens the IRS must stop what it's doing and let you do so.

- The IRS may not take money or property from you on the same day that you comply with a summons. In other words, the IRS can't demand that you appear and then seize your car when you get to its office — something that used to happen a lot.

Despite those important rights, the original Taxpayer Bill of Rights left much to be desired. In too many cases, it allowed the IRS itself to interpret your rights. It's like having the same person as prosecutor, judge, jury, and executioner.

Increased taxpayer rights in a nutshell

In 1998, the IRS received quite a bit of negative press after congressional hearings revealed the abuse taxpayers were routinely being subjected to. It made great headlines, "IRS horror stories." After hearing from individual taxpayers who thought they'd been put through the wringer by the tough guys down at IRS Central, Congress decided to come to the rescue and give taxpayers more protection and rights. We have to chuckle a bit at all this — after all, Congress was the organization that created all these ambiguous and cumbersome tax laws in the first place.

Here are the major provisions that supposedly benefit taxpayers. We say supposedly because the actual benefit often is far, far less than meets the eye:

✔ **Burden of proof falls (more) on the IRS.** Unlike the criminal justice system, which operates under the premise that when charged with a crime, you're presumed innocent until proven guilty, our tax system has operated under the reverse, perverse presumption that you're guilty until proven innocent. However, to benefit from being presumed innocent until the IRS proves otherwise, your tax disagreement must actually land in court, and you must meet other requirements, including having good records and having been cooperative and compliant to that point.

✔ **Taxpayers have new protections regarding collections.** In recent years, the IRS got itself into trouble with the way it handled certain tax collections. In some cases, taxpayers experienced unjustified and confrontational seizure of property and other assets, even for small amounts of tax owed. Now, for example, the IRS needs a court order to sell someone's home and a higher level of approval within the IRS to seize someone's business.

✔ **Innocent spouse rules are enhanced.** As we discuss in Chapter 4, married couples heading toward divorce don't always cooperate about money and taxes. The tax bill passed in 1998 beefs up a spouse's ability to file separately while still married to avoid being held responsible for the other spouse's tax negligence. Although this option may sound attractive, we fear that it will increase total costs for both spouses, especially if you factor in the costs of a divorce lawyer wrangling over tax liabilities. See Chapter 4 for more details.

✔ **Advice given by tax advisors to taxpayers is confidential.** With legal matters, what a client tells his or her attorney is largely confidential. With tax issues, that same standard of confidentiality hasn't been applied to what a taxpayer tells his or her preparer or advisor. Taxpayers can now consult with tax advisors in the same confidential and privileged manner as they do with lawyers. Remember, however, that information disclosed in preparation of a tax return isn't covered by this rule!

The Taxpayer Bill of Rights — Parts 2 and 3

Our complaint with the original Taxpayer Bill of Rights was that it didn't have teeth. Now it does. But not a full set. And, unlike in the *Rocky* movies, the Taxpayer Bill of Rights Part 2 that became law on July 30, 1996, and Part 3, which came about when the IRS was overhauled in 1998, don't see to it that the underdog always wins. Here's what the new-and-improved Taxpayer Bill of Rights does for you:

✔ Abates the penalty for failing to deposit payroll taxes for first-time filers of employment tax returns.

✔ Enables you to file a joint return after a separate return has been filed without having to pay the full joint tax.

✔ Allows the return of levied property, including your salary, if you have an installment agreement to pay what you owe and it would be a hardship (you can't pay your bills) not to return it. Under the old rules, once the IRS "glommed" your dough, it couldn't return it.

✔ Requires that 1099s have the name, address, and telephone number of whom to contact in case the reported amount is incorrect and needs investigating.

✔ Shifts the burden to the IRS to prove that its position was substantially justified when you prevail in a suit with the IRS. If the IRS position was not substantially justified, you can collect for legal fees and court costs from the IRS. Under the old rule, *you* had to prove that the IRS's position was not substantially justified.

✔ Requires that the IRS, upon a taxpayer's request, make every reasonable effort to contact private creditors when a Notice of a Tax Lien has been withdrawn.

The bill also includes the following helpful provisions:

✔ If a few people, namely the owners or officers of a business, are personally responsible for payment of taxes that were withheld from their employees' salaries and one of these individuals pays more than his or her share, that person can sue to recover that amount from the others. The IRS now is obliged to tell what each person paid and what the IRS is doing to collect what is owed from the others. Since the IRS usually goes after the owner where it will have least difficulty in collecting the entire amount that business owes, that poor soul now has the right to know what his partners have paid so he can make them pay their share of what he was forced to pay.

✔ The IRS must notify taxpayers if it receives a payment that can't be applied against what is owed, instead of merely depositing the check and holding it in limbo.

✔ If you owe the IRS, the IRS must send you at least an annual bill so you know where you stand. The statement must include a detailed computation of the interest charged.

✔ For taxes that you and an ex-spouse jointly owe, you can ask the IRS what it is doing to get your ex-spouse to pay the tax, and you have the right to be told how much has been paid. Because of possible hostility toward an ex-spouse, the IRS, however, won't reveal the spouse's home or business addresses.

✔ The *innocent spouse rules* have been made more lenient in a number of ways. Relief can also be obtained on an apportioned basis. See Chapter 4.

✔ If the IRS doesn't send a notice adjusting a taxpayer's return within 18 months, it must stop charging interest after 18 months and until 21 days after a notice *is* sent. See Chapter 16, because not all IRS notices are covered under this rule.

✔ You can collect up to $1 million in damages if the IRS acts with reckless or intentional disregard of the rules in collecting tax. If the IRS is merely negligent, the limit is $100,000. The IRS has the authority — but, again, is not compelled — to abate interest because of delays on its part. Delays caused by loss of records, transfer of personnel, extended illness, leave, or training programs now are causes for abating interest.

✔ If someone issues you a fraudulent 1099, you can sue for damages of up to $5,000.

✔ Proof under the timely-mailing-is-filing rule requires that a document or return had to be sent by either certified or registered mail. Using FedEx, DHL, Airborne, or UPS now is equivalent to sending a return or document by certified or registered mail.

A mailing receipt that you receive from the post office other than for certified or registered mail isn't considered valid proof of meeting the timely-mailing-is-timely-filing rule.

✔ Financial status audits to scrutinize a taxpayer's lifestyle are allowed only when a routine examination has established a likelihood of unreported income. See Chapter 17.

✔ Taxpayers have a 30-day period to appeal a lien or levy. See Chapter 16.

✔ The rejection of an Offer in Compromise or a request for an installment agreement can be appealed.

✔ While an Offer in Compromise or a request for an installment agreement is pending or on appeal, the IRS can't levy against a taxpayer.

✔ Your residence can't be seized unless authorized in writing by a U.S. district court judge. Business assets can't be seized unless authorized by a district or assistant district director.

✔ Shifts the burden of proof from the taxpayer to the IRS in court proceedings.

Part V
Year-Round Tax Planning

The 5th Wave   By Rich Tennant

"And just how long did you think you could keep that pot o'gold at the end of the rainbow a secret from us, Mr. O'Shea?"

In this part . . .

Taxes are not a financial island unto themselves. Just about every major financial decision you make involves a tax angle and has tax consequences. With just a little bit of knowledge and advance planning, you can make your money work much harder for you. In fact, the worse you are at managing your finances, the more money you can put back into your pocket, if you learn how to make tax-wise financial decisions. This part will help you make the most of your money year-round. Just don't forget that it's here!

Chapter 20

Tax-Wise Personal Finance Decisions

You probably work hard for your money. Between actual hours in the office and commuting, you may well spend 50 hours per week on job-related activities. That's about 2,500 hours per year. Think about that number — 2,500 hours per year, *year after year after year,* spanning several decades.

That's a lot of time spent working to earn money.

Now, how much time do you spend learning and figuring out how to make the most of this money? Yeah, we thought so — are you blushing?

Directing your personal finances involves much more than simply investing money. It includes making all the pieces of your financial life fit together. And, just like designing a vacation itinerary, managing your personal finances means developing a strategy to make the best use of your limited dollars.

Taxes are a large and vital piece of your financial puzzle. The following list shows some of the ways that tax issues are involved in making sound financial decisions throughout the year:

✔ **Spending:** The more you spend, the more taxes you'll pay for taxed purchases and for being less able to take advantage of the many benefits in the tax code that require you to have money to invest in the first place. For example, you need money to purchase real estate, which offers many tax benefits (see Chapter 24). And because taxes are a hefty portion of your expenditures (probably one of your top items), a budget that overlooks tax-reduction strategies is doomed to failure. Unless you have wealthy, benevolent relatives, you're resigned to a lifetime of working if you can't save money.

✔ **Retirement accounts:** Taking advantage of retirement accounts can mean tens, perhaps even hundreds of thousands more dollars in your pocket come retirement time. Who says there are no free lunches? See Chapter 21.

✔ **Investing:** Many tax angles factor into wise investing. Merely choosing investments that generate healthy rates of return isn't enough. What matters is not what you *make* but what you *keep* — after paying taxes. Understand and capitalize on the many tax breaks available to investors in stocks, bonds, mutual funds, real estate, and your own business. See Chapter 22 for the details.

✔ **Protecting your assets:** Some of your insurance decisions also affect the taxes you pay. You'd think that after a lifetime of tax payments, your heirs would be left alone when you pass on to the great beyond — wishful thinking. Estate planning can significantly reduce the taxes to be siphoned off from your estate. See Chapter 26 to find out more about estate planning.

Taxes infiltrate many areas of your personal finances. Some people make important financial decisions without considering taxes (and other important variables). Conversely, in an obsession to minimize or avoid taxes, other people make decisions that are counterproductive to achieving their long-term personal and financial goals. Although this chapter shows you that taxes are an important component to factor into your major financial decisions, *taxes should not drive or dictate the decisions you make.*

Taxing Mistakes

Even if some parts of the tax system are hopelessly and unreasonably complicated, there's no reason why you can't learn from the mistakes of others to save yourself some money. With this goal in mind, we list the most typical tax blunders that people make when it comes to managing their money.

Seeking advice after a major decision

Too many people seek out information and hire help *after* making a decision, even though seeking preventive help ahead of time generally is wiser and less costly. Before making any major financial decisions, educate yourself. The book you're holding in your hands can help answer many of your questions.

If you're going to hire a tax advisor to give advice, do so *before* making your decision(s). Read Chapters 2 and 31 for tips about finding a good tax advisor. The wrong move when selling a piece of real estate or taking money from a retirement account can cost you thousands of dollars in taxes!

Underwithholding the right amount of taxes

If you're self-employed or earn significant taxable income from investments outside retirement accounts, you need to be making estimated quarterly tax payments. Likewise, if, during the year, you sell an investment asset at a profit, you may need to make a quarterly tax payment.

Not having a human resources department to withhold taxes from their pay as they earn it, some self-employed people dig themselves into a perpetual tax hole by failing to submit estimated quarterly tax payments. They get behind in their tax payments during their first year of self-employment and thereafter are always playing catch-up. Don't be a "should've" victim. People often don't discover that they "should've" paid more taxes during the year until after they complete their returns in the spring — or get penalty notices from the IRS and their states. Then they have to come up with sizable sums all at once.

To make quarterly tax payments, complete **IRS Form 1040-ES, Estimated Tax for Individuals.** This form and accompanying instructions explain how to calculate quarterly tax payments — the IRS even sends you payment coupons and envelopes in which to mail your checks. We walk you through the essentials of completing this form in Chapter 14.

Although we — and the IRS — want you to keep your taxes current during the year, *we* don't want you to overpay. Some people have too much tax withheld during the year, and this overpayment can go on year after year. Although it may feel good to get a sizable refund check every spring, why should you loan your money to the government interest-free? When you work for an employer, you can complete a new W-4 to adjust your withholding. We're kind enough to include one in the back of the book. Turn the completed W-4 in to your employer. When you're self-employed, complete Form 1040-ES, Estimated Tax for Individuals. (See Chapter 15 for instructions on completing your W-4.)

If you know that you'd otherwise spend the extra tax money that you're currently sending to the IRS, then this forced-savings strategy may have some value. But you can find other, better ways to make yourself save. You can set up all sorts of investments, such as mutual funds (see Chapter 23), to be funded by automatic contributions from your paychecks (or from a bank or investment account). Of course, if you happen to *prefer* to loan the IRS money — interest-free — go right ahead!

Missing out on legal deductions

In most cases, folks miss out on perfectly legal tax deductions because they just don't know about them. Ignorance is not bliss when it comes to your income taxes . . . it's costly. If you aren't going to take the time to discover the legal deductions available to you (you bought this book, so why not read the relevant parts of it?), then spring for the cost of a competent tax advisor at least once.

Fearing an audit, some taxpayers (and even some tax preparers) avoid taking deductions that they have every right to take. Unless you have something to hide, such behavior is costly and silly. Remember that a certain number of returns are randomly audited every year, so even when you don't take every deduction to which you're legally entitled, you may nevertheless get audited! And how bad is an audit, really? If you read Chapter 17, you can find out how to deal with your audit like a pro. An hour or so with the IRS is not as bad as you might think. It may be worth the risk of claiming all the tax breaks to which you're entitled, especially when you consider the amounts you can save through the years.

Passing up retirement accounts

All the tax deductions and tax deferrals that come with accounts such as 401(k)s and IRAs were put in the tax code to encourage you to save for retirement. So why not take advantage of the benefits?

You probably have your reasons or excuses, but most excuses for missing out on this strategy just don't make good financial sense. Most people underfund retirement accounts because they spend too much and because retirement seems so far away. Many people also mistakenly believe that retirement account money is totally inaccessible until they're old enough to qualify for senior discounts. See Chapter 21 to find out all about retirement accounts and why you need to fund them.

Ignoring tax considerations when investing

Suppose that you want to unload some stock so that you can buy a new car. You sell an investment at a significant profit and feel good about your financial genius. But, come tax time, you may feel differently.

Don't forget to consider the taxes due on profits from the sale of investments (except those in retirement accounts) when making decisions about what you sell and when you sell it. Your tax situation also needs to factor in what you invest outside retirement accounts. When you're in a relatively high tax bracket, you probably don't want investments that pay much in taxable distributions such as taxable interest and dividends, which only add to your tax burden. See Chapter 23 for details on the tax considerations of investing and which investments are tax-friendly for your situation.

Not buying a home

In the long run, owning a home should cost you less than renting. And because mortgage interest and property taxes are deductible, the government, in effect, subsidizes the cost of home ownership.

Even if the government didn't help you with tax benefits when buying and owning a home, you'd still be better off owning over your adult life. Why? Because as a renter, all your housing expenses are exposed to inflation, unless you have a great rent-controlled deal. So owning your own abode makes good financial and tax sense. And don't let the lack of money for a down payment stand in your way — methods exist for buying real estate with little money up front. See Chapter 24 to find out about real estate and taxes.

Ignoring the financial aid tax system

The college financial aid system in this country assumes that the money you save outside tax-sheltered retirement accounts is available to pay educational expenses. As a result, families who save money *outside* instead of *inside* retirement accounts qualify for far less financial aid than they otherwise would. So in addition to normal income taxes, an extra financial aid "tax" is effectively exacted. Be sure to read Chapter 25, which covers the best ways to save and invest for educational costs.

Ignoring the timing of events you can control

The amount of tax you pay on certain transactions can vary, depending on the timing of events. If you're nearing retirement, for example, you may soon be in a lower tax bracket. To the extent possible, you need to delay and avoid claiming investment income until your overall income level drops, and you need to take as many deductions or losses as you can *now* while your income still is high. Following are two tax-reducing strategies — income shifting and bunching or shifting deductions — that you may be able to put to good use when you can control the timing of either your income or deductions.

Income shifting

Suppose that your employer tells you in late December that you're eligible for a bonus. You learn that you have the option of receiving your bonus in either December or January (ask your payroll and benefits department if this is an option). Looking ahead, if you're pretty certain that you're going to be in a higher tax bracket next year, you need to choose to receive your bonus in December. (Refer to Chapter 1 to find out about your tax bracket.)

Or suppose that you run your own business and operate on a cash accounting basis and think that you'll be in a lower tax bracket next year. Perhaps business has slowed of late or you plan to take time off to be with a newborn or take an extended trip. You can send out some invoices later in the year so that your customers won't pay you until January, which falls in the next tax year.

Shifting or bunching deductions

When the total of your itemized deductions on Schedule A (see Chapter 9) is lower than the standard deduction, you need to take the standard deduction. This itemized deduction total is worth checking each year, because you may have more deductions in some years than others, and you may occasionally be able to itemize.

Because you can control when you pay particular expenses that are eligible for itemizing, you can *shift* or *bunch* more of them into select years when you're more likely to have enough deductions to take advantage of itemizing. Suppose that because you don't have many itemized deductions this year, you use the standard deduction. Late in the year, however, you feel certain that you'll itemize next year, because you plan to buy a home and will therefore be able to claim significant mortgage interest and property tax deductions. It makes sense, then, to shift and bunch as many deductible expenses as possible into next year. For example, if you're getting ready to make a tax-deductible donation of old clothes and household goods to charity, wait until January to do so.

In any tax year that you're sure you won't have enough deductions to be able to itemize, shift as many itemizable expenses as you can into the next tax year. If you don't know what types of expenses you can itemize, be sure to peruse Chapter 9.

Be careful when using your credit card to pay expenses. These expenses must be recognized for tax purposes in the year in which the charge was made on the card and not when you actually pay the credit card company.

Not using tax advisors effectively

If your financial situation is complicated, going it alone and relying only on the IRS booklets to figure your taxes usually is a mistake. The IRS instructions certainly aren't going to highlight opportunities for tax reductions, and these instructions often are hopelessly complicated. Instead, you can start by reading the relevant sections of this book. You also have the option of hiring a competent tax advisor. You can figure out taxes for yourself, or you can pay someone to figure them out for you. Doing nothing is not an advisable option!

When you're overwhelmed with the complexity of particular financial decisions, get advice from tax and financial advisors who sell their time and nothing else. Protect yourself by checking references, clarifying what advice, analysis, and recommendations the advisor will provide for the fee charged. If your tax situation is complicated, you'll probably more than recoup a preparer's fee, as long as you take the time to hire a good one (see Chapter 2 for tips on hiring help).

Remember that using a tax advisor is most beneficial when you face new tax questions or problems. If your tax situation remains complicated, or if you know that you'd do a worse job on your own, by all means keep using a tax preparer. But don't pay a big fee year after year to a tax advisor who simply plugs your numbers into the tax forms. If your situation is unchanging or is not that complicated, consider hiring and paying someone to figure out your taxes one time. After that, go ahead and try completing your own tax return.

The Causes of Bad Tax Decisions

When bad things happen, it's usually for a variety of reasons. And so it is with making financial blunders that cause you to pay more tax dollars. The following sections describe some common culprits that may be keeping you from making tax-wise financial maneuvers.

"Financial planners" and brokers' advice

Wanting to hire a financial advisor to help you make better financial decisions is a logical inclination, especially if you're a time-squeezed person. But when you pick a poor planner or someone who isn't a financial planner but rather a salesperson in disguise, watch out!

Unfortunately, the majority of people calling themselves financial planners, financial consultants, or financial advisors actually work on commission, which creates enormous conflicts of interest with providing unbiased and objective financial advice. Brokers and commission-based financial planners (who are also therefore brokers) structure their advice around selling you investment and other financial products that provide *them* with commissions. As a result, they tend to take a narrow view of your finances and frequently ignore the tax and other consequences of financial moves. Or they may pitch the *supposed* tax benefits of an investment they're eager to sell you as a reason for you to buy it. It may provide a tax benefit for someone, but not necessarily for you in your specific situation.

The few planners who work on a *fee basis* primarily provide money-management services and charge 1 percent to 2 percent per year of the money they manage. Fee-based planners have their own conflicts of interest, because all things being equal, they want you to hire them to manage *your money*. Therefore, they can't objectively help you decide whether you should pay off your mortgage and other debts, invest in real estate or a small business, or invest more in your employer's retirement plan. In short, they have a bias against financial strategies that take your investment money out of their hands.

Be especially leery of planners, brokers, and money-managing planners who lobby you to sell investments that you've held for a while and that show a profit. If you sell these investments, you may have a hefty tax burden. (See Chapter 23 for more insight on how to make these important investing decisions.)

Advertising

Another reason you may make tax missteps in managing your personal finances is advertising. Although many reputable financial firms with terrific products advertise, the firms that spend the most on advertising often are the ones with inferior or downright lousy offerings.

Responding to most ads usually is a bad financial move, regardless of whether the product being pitched is good, bad, or so-so, because the company placing the ad typically is trying to motivate you to buy a specific product. The company doesn't care about your financial alternatives, whether its product fits with your tax situation, and so on. Many ads try to catch your attention with the supposed tax savings that their products generate.

Advice from publications

You read an article that recommends some investments. Tired of not taking charge and making financial decisions, you get on the phone, call an investment company, and — before you know it — you've invested. You feel a sense of relief and accomplishment — you've done something.

Come tax time, you get all these confusing statements detailing dividends and capital gains that you must report on your tax return. *Now* you see that these investment strategies generate all sorts of taxable distributions that add to your tax burden. And you may be saddled with additional tax forms to complete by April 15. You wish you had known.

Articles in magazines, newspapers, newsletters, and on Web sites can help you stay informed, but they also can cause you to make ill-advised financial moves that overlook tax consequences. Article writers have limited space and often don't think about the big picture or ways their advice can be misunderstood or misused. Even worse is that too many writers don't know the tax consequences of what they're writing about.

Overspending

Far too many tax guides go on and on and on, talking about this tax break and that tax break. The problem is that to take advantage of many of the best tax breaks, you need to have some money to invest. When you spend all that you earn, as most Americans do, you miss out on many terrific tax benefits that we tell you about in this book. And the more you spend, the more taxes you pay, both on your income and on the purchases you make (through sales taxes).

Just like losing weight, spending less *sounds* good, but most people have a hard time budgeting their finances and spending less than they earn. Perhaps you already know where the fat is in your spending. If you don't, figuring out where all your monthly income is going is a real eye-opener. The task takes some detective work — looking through your credit card statements and your checkbook register to track your purchases and categorize your spending.

Financial illiteracy

Lack of education is at the root of most personal financial blunders. You may not understand the tax system and how to manage your finances, because you were never taught how to manage them in high school or college.

Financial illiteracy is a widespread problem not just among the poor and undereducated. Most people don't plan ahead and educate themselves with their financial goals in mind. People react — or, worse, do nothing at all. You may dream, for example, about retiring and never having to work again. Or perhaps you hope that someday you can own a house or even a vacation home in the country.

You need to understand how to plan your finances so you can accomplish your financial goals. You also need to understand how the tax system works and how to navigate within it to work toward your objectives.

If you need more help with important personal financial issues, pick up a copy of the latest edition of *Personal Finance For Dummies* (John Wiley & Sons, Inc.), written by one of us — Eric Tyson.

Chapter 21

Reducing Taxes with Retirement Accounts

Saving and investing through retirement accounts is one of the simplest and best ways to reduce your tax burden. Understanding the myriad account options and rules isn't simple, but we do our best at explaining them in this chapter.

Unfortunately, most people can't take advantage of these plans because they spend too much of what they make. So not only do they have less savings, but they also pay higher income taxes — a double whammy. And don't forget, the more you spend, the more sales tax you pay on purchases. To be able to take advantage of the tax savings that come with retirement savings plans, you first must spend less than you earn. Only then can you afford to contribute to these plans.

Retirement Account Benefits

Retirement may seem like the distant future to young people. It's often not until middle age that warning bells start stimulating thoughts about what money they'll live on in their golden years.

The single biggest mistake people at all income levels make with retirement accounts is *not* taking advantage of them. In your 20s and 30s (and for some in their 40s and 50s), spending and living for today and postponing saving for the future seems a whole lot more fun. But assuming that you don't want to work your entire life, the sooner you start saving, the less painful it is each year, because your contributions have more years to grow.

Each decade that you delay contributing approximately doubles the percentage of your earnings that you need to save to meet your goals. For example, if saving 5 percent per year in your early 20s gets you to your retirement goal, waiting until your 30s may mean socking away 10 percent; waiting until your 40s, 20 percent . . . it gets ugly beyond that!

So the longer you wait, the more you'll have to save and, therefore, the less that will be left over to spend. As a result, you may not meet your goal, and your golden years may be more restrictive than you hoped.

We use this simple lesson to emphasize the importance of considering *now* the benefits you achieve by saving and investing in some type of retirement account.

Contributions are (generally) tax-deductible

Retirement accounts are misnamed. They sound unpalatable to most people, particularly the youngsters among us. Saving for retirement is like eating just plain rice cakes for dinner: It may be healthier and help you to live longer, but you want to live *life* — not live for retirement. Spend money today and you get some instant gratification. Put some of that same money into a retirement account, and you might yawn with excitement and then get a headache figuring where to invest it!

Retirement accounts really should be called *tax-reduction accounts*. If they were, people might be more eager to contribute to them. For many people, avoiding higher taxes is the motivating force that gets them to open the account and start the contributions.

If you're a moderate-income earner, you probably pay about 35 percent in federal and state income taxes on your last dollars of income (see Chapter 1 to identify your tax bracket). Thus, with most of the retirement accounts described in this chapter, for every $1,000 you contribute to them, you save yourself about $350 in taxes in the year that you make the contribution. Contribute five times as much, or $5,000, and whack $1,750 off your tax bill! Thanks to recently passed tax bills, the contribution limits on retirement accounts rise significantly in the years ahead (the details are later in this chapter).

Check with your employer's benefits department, because some organizations match a portion of employee contributions. Be sure to partake of this free matching money by contributing to your retirement accounts.

Special tax credit for lower income earners

In addition to the upfront tax break you get from contributing to many retirement accounts, lower-income earners may receive tax credits worth up to 50 percent on the first $2,000 of retirement account contributions. Like employer-matching contributions, this tax credit amounts to free money (in this case from the government), so you should take advantage!

As you can see in Table 21-1, this new retirement account contribution tax credit phases out quickly for higher-income earners, and no such credit is available to single taxpayers with adjusted gross incomes (AGIs) of more than $25,000 and to married couples filing jointly with AGIs of more than $50,000. (*Note:* This credit is not available to taxpayers who are claimed as dependents on someone else's tax return or who are under the age of 18 or full-time students.)

Table 21-1	Tax Credit for the First $2,000 in Retirement Plan Contributions	
Single Taxpayers Adjusted Gross Income	*Married Couples Filing Jointly Adjusted Gross Income*	*Tax Credit for Retirement Account Contributions*
$0 to $15,000	$0 to $30,000	50 %
$15,001 to $16,250	$30,001 to $32,500	20 %
$16,251 to $25,000	$32,501 to $50,000	10 %

Retirement account penalties for early withdrawals

One objection that some people have to contributing to retirement accounts is the early withdrawal penalties. Specifically, if you withdraw funds from retirement accounts before age 59½, you not only have to pay income taxes on withdrawals, but you also may pay early withdrawal penalties — typically 10 percent in federal and state charges. (There's a 25 percent penalty for withdrawing from a SIMPLE plan within the first two years, which decreases to 10 percent thereafter.)

The penalties are in place for good reason — to discourage people from raiding retirement accounts. Remember, retirement accounts exist for just that reason — saving toward retirement. If you could easily tap these accounts without penalties, the money would be less likely to be there when you need it during your golden years.

If you have an emergency, such as catastrophic medical expenses or a disability, you may be able to take early withdrawals from retirement accounts without penalty. You may withdraw funds from particular retirement accounts free of penalties (and, in some cases, even free of current income taxes) for educational expenses or a home purchase. We spell out the specifics of this loophole in the "Penalty-free IRA withdrawals" section later in this chapter.

What if you just run out of money because you lose your job? Although you can't bypass the penalties because of such circumstances, if you're earning so little income that you need to tap your retirement account, you'll surely be in a low tax bracket. So even though you pay some penalties to withdraw retirement account money, the lower income taxes that you pay upon withdrawal — as compared to the taxes that you would have incurred when you earned the money originally — should make up for most or all of the penalty.

Know also that if you get in a financial pinch while you're still employed, some company retirement plans allow you to borrow against a portion of your cash balance. Just be sure that you can repay such a loan — otherwise, your "loan" becomes a withdrawal and triggers income taxes and penalties.

Another strategy to meet a short-term financial emergency is to withdraw money from your IRA and return it within 60 days to avoid paying penalties. We don't generally recommend this maneuver because of the taxes and potential penalties invoked if you don't make the 60-day deadline.

In the event that your only "borrowing" option right now is a credit card with a high interest rate, you should save three to six months' worth of living expenses in an accessible account before funding a retirement account to tide you over in case you lose your income. Money market mutual funds are an ideal vehicle to use for this purpose.

You may be interested in knowing that if good fortune comes your way and you accumulate enough funds to retire "early," you have a simple way around the pre-age-59½ early withdrawal penalties. Suppose that at age 50 you retire and want to start living off some of the pile of money you've stashed in retirement accounts. No problem. The IRS graciously allows you to start withdrawing money from your retirement accounts free of those nasty early withdrawal penalties. To qualify for this favorable treatment, you must commit to withdrawals for at least five continuous years, and the amount of the withdrawals must be at least the minimum required based on your life expectancy.

Tax-deferred compounding of investment earnings

The tax bill passed in 2003 significantly lowered the tax rate on *long-term capital gains* — investments held more than one year — and stock dividends (see Chapter 23). Even though these new tax rules lowered the tax rate on some investment returns produced outside of retirement accounts, most people will still come out ahead investing through retirement accounts.

After money is placed in a retirement account, any interest, dividends, and appreciation add to the amount of the account without being taxed. You get to defer taxes on all the accumulating gains and profits until you withdraw the money, presumably in retirement. Thus more money is working for you over a longer period of time.

I need *how much* for retirement?

On average, most people need about 70 percent to 80 percent of their pre-retirement income to maintain their standard of living throughout their retirement. For example, if your household earns $40,000 per year before retirement, you'll likely need $28,000 to $32,000 (70 percent to 80 percent of $40,000) per year during retirement to live the way that you're accustomed to living.

Remember that 70 percent to 80 percent is just an average. You may need more or less. If you currently save little or none of your annual income, expect to have a large mortgage payment or growing rent in retirement, or anticipate wanting to travel or do other expensive things in retirement, you may need 90 percent or perhaps even 100 percent of your current income to maintain your standard of living in retirement.

On the other hand, if you now save a high percentage of your earnings, are a high-income earner, expect to own your home free of debt by retirement, and anticipate leading a modest lifestyle in retirement, you may be able to make do with, say, 60 percent of your current income.

If you've never thought about what your retirement goals are, looked into what you can expect from Social Security (stop laughing), or calculated how much you should be saving for retirement, now's the time to do it. The latest edition of *Personal Finance For Dummies* (Wiley, Inc.), written by Eric Tyson, goes through all the necessary details and even tells you how to come up with more to invest and do it wisely.

Your retirement tax rate need not be less than your tax rate during your working years for you to come out ahead by contributing to retirement accounts. In fact, because you defer paying tax and have more money compounding over more years, you can end up with more money in retirement by saving inside a retirement account, even if your retirement tax rate is higher than it is now.

And remember this: You may get an added bonus from deferring taxes on your retirement account assets if you're in a lower tax bracket when you withdraw the money. You may well be in a lower tax bracket in retirement because most people have less income when they're not working. (Also, if you're able to achieve a higher annual investment return than the 8 percent in our example, your retirement tax rate would have to skyrocket even more for you to not be better off having funded your retirement account.)

Note: When you're near retirement and already have money in a tax-sheltered type of retirement account (for example, at your employer), by all means continue to keep it in a tax-favored account if you leave. You can accomplish this goal by rolling the money over into an IRA account. If your employer offers good investment options in a retirement plan and allows you to leave your money in the plan after your departure, consider that option, too.

You can save less money and spend more

That's right! Because of all the terrific tax benefits you get by saving and investing in retirement accounts, you end up with more money now than if you had saved the money elsewhere.

Types of Retirement Accounts

When you earn employment income (or receive alimony), you have the option of putting money away in a retirement account that compounds without taxation until you withdraw the money. In most cases, your contributions are tax-deductible. The following sections discuss the major types of "IRS-approved" retirement accounts and explain how to determine whether you're eligible for them and some other nitpicky but important rules.

Employer-sponsored plans

You should be thankful that your employer values your future enough to offer these benefits and grateful that your employer has gone to the trouble of doing all the legwork of setting up the plan, and in most cases, selecting investment options. If you were self-employed, you'd have to hassle with establishing your own plan and choosing a short list of investment options. All you have to do with an employer plan is save enough to invest and allocate your contributions among the (generally few) investments offered.

401(k) plans

For-profit companies generally offer 401(k) plans. The silly name comes from the section of the tax code that establishes and regulates these plans. A 401(k) generally allows you to save up to $12,000 per year for tax year 2003. Your employer's plan may have lower contribution limits, though, if employees don't save enough in the company's 401(k) plan. Your contributions to a 401(k) generally are excluded from your reported income and thus are free from federal and, in some cases, state income taxes, but not from Social Security and Medicare taxes (and from some other state employment taxes).

The contribution limits of 401(k) and other retirement plans substantially increase in the years ahead. As you can see in Table 21-2, by the year 2006, the 401(k) contribution limit will hit $15,000. Older workers — those at least age 50 — will be able to put away even more — up to $5,000 more per year than their younger counterparts. After 2006, the contribution limit on 401(k) plans (which will be $15,000) and the additional amounts allowed for older workers (which will be $5,000) will rise, in $500 increments, with inflation.

Some employers don't allow you to start contributing to their 401(k) plan until you've worked for them for a full year. Others allow you to start contributing right away. Some employers also match a portion of your contributions. They may, for example, match half of your first 6 percent of contributions (so in addition to saving a lot of taxes, you get a free bonus from the company). Check with your company's benefits department for your plan's details.

Smaller companies (those with fewer than 100 employees) can consider offering 401(k) plans, too. In the past, it was prohibitively expensive for smaller companies to administer 401(k)s. If your company is interested in this option, contact a mutual fund organization, such as T. Rowe Price, Vanguard, or Fidelity, or a discount brokerage firm such as TD Waterhouse (see Chapter 23). In some cases, your employer may need to work with a separate plan administrator in addition to one of these investment firms.

Table 21-2	401(k), 403(b), and 457 Retirement Plan Contribution Limits	
Year	*Contribution Limit for Those Under Age 50*	*Contribution Limit for Those Age 50 and Older*
2003	$12,000	$14,000
2004	$13,000	$16,000
2005	$14,000	$18,000
2006	$15,000	$20,000

403(b) plans

Many nonprofit organizations offer 403(b) plans to their employees. As with a 401(k), your contributions to these plans generally are federal and state tax-deductible. 403(b) plans often are referred to as tax-sheltered annuities, the name for insurance-company investments that

satisfy the requirements for 403(b) plans. For the benefit of 403(b) retirement-plan participants, no-load (commission-free) mutual funds also can be used in 403(b) plans.

Nonprofit employees generally are allowed to contribute up to 20 percent or $12,000 of their
salaries, whichever is less. Employees who have 15 or more years of service may be allowed
to contribute beyond the $12,000 limit. Ask your company's benefits department or the
investment provider for the 403(b) plan (or your tax advisor) about eligibility requirements
and details about your personal contribution limit.

As with 401(k) plans, the contribution limit for 403(b) plans will increase to $15,000 by tax
year 2006 (and to $20,000 for workers age 50 and older). After 2006, the contribution limit
on 403(b) plans (which will be $15,000) and the additional amounts allowed for older work-
ers (which will be $5,000) will rise, in $500 increments, with inflation. Please see Table 21-2.

If you work for a nonprofit or public-sector organization that doesn't offer this benefit, make
a fuss and insist on it. Nonprofit organizations have no excuse not to offer 403(b) plans to
their employees. Unlike 401(k) plans, 403(b) plans have virtually no out-of-pocket setup
expenses or ongoing accounting fees. The only requirement is that the organization must
deduct the appropriate contribution from employees' paychecks and send the money to the
investment company handling the 403(b) plan. If your employer doesn't know where to look
for good 403(b) investment options, send them to Vanguard (800-662-2003), Fidelity
(800-343-0860), or T. Rowe Price (800-492-7670), all of which offer good mutual funds and
403(b) plans.

SIMPLE plans

Employers in small businesses have yet another retirement plan option, known as the
SIMPLE-IRA. SIMPLE stands for Savings Incentive Match Plans for Employees. Relative to
401(k) plans, SIMPLE plans make it somewhat easier for employers to reduce their costs,
thanks to easier reporting requirements and fewer administrative hassles. (However,
employers may escape the nondiscrimination testing requirements — one of the more
tedious aspects of maintaining a 401(k) plan — by adhering to the matching and contribution rules of a SIMPLE plan, as described later in this section.)

The contribution limits for SIMPLE plans will rise to $10,000 by the year 2005 for younger
workers and will be an additional $2,500 more (for a total of $12,500) by 2006. These contribution limits will increase in increments of $500 with inflation after 2006. See Table 21-3.

Table 21-3	SIMPLE Retirement Plan Contribution Limits	
Year	Contribution Limit for Those Under Age 50	Contribution Limit for Those Age 50 and Older
2003	$8,000	$9,000
2004	$9,000	$10,500
2005	$10,000	$12,000
2006	$10,000	$12,500

Employers must make small contributions on behalf of employees, however. Employers can
either match, dollar for dollar, the employee's first 3 percent that's contributed or contribute 2 percent of pay for everyone whose wages exceed $5,000. Interestingly, if the
employer chooses the first option, the employer has an incentive not to educate employees
about the value of contributing to the plan because the more employees contribute, the
more it costs the employer. And, unlike a 401(k) plan, greater employee contributions don't
enable higher-paid employees to contribute more.

After-tax 401(k) and 403(b) contributions

Some employer-based retirement plans allow for after-tax contributions. Historically, it made sense to consider such options after exhausting contributions that provide a tax break. The merit of an after-tax contribution is that it can compound without taxation until withdrawal, at which point you would owe taxes on the investment earnings withdrawn.

Tax legislation passed earlier in this decade introduced another way to make after-tax retirement plan contributions. Specifically, effective tax year 2006, employers can allow employees to make after-tax Roth contributions to both 401(k) and 403(b) plans.

Like Roth IRA contributions, Roth 401(k) and Roth 403(b) contributions not only grow tax-deferred but also allow for tax-free withdrawal of investment earnings. This extra tax break (the Roth tax-free withdrawal of investment earnings) is the new part of being able to make after-tax contributions to 401(k) and 403(b) plans.

Generally speaking, you still will likely be better off making pretax retirement plan contributions before considering after-tax (Roth) contributions. Most people are best served taking the sure tax break than waiting many years for an unspecified tax break. Please see our discussion in the section "To Roth or not to Roth?" later in this chapter for further information.

Self-employed plans

When you work for yourself, you obviously don't have an employer to establish a retirement plan. You need to take the initiative. Although setting up a plan means work for you, you can select and design a plan that meets *your* needs. You can actually do a better job than many companies do; often, the people establishing a retirement plan don't do enough homework, or they let some salesperson sweet-talk them into high-expense (for the employees, that is) investments. Your trouble will be rewarded — self-employment retirement plans generally enable you to sock away more money on a tax-deductible basis than most employers' plans do.

If you have employees, you're required to make contributions comparable to the company owners' (as a percentage of salary) on their behalf under these plans. Some part-time employees (those working fewer than 500 to 1,000 hours per year) and newer employees (less than a few years of service) may be excluded. Not all small-business owners know about this requirement — or they choose to ignore it, and they set up plans for themselves but fail to cover their employees. The danger is that the IRS and state tax authorities may, in the event of an audit, hit you with big penalties and disqualify your prior contributions if you have neglected to make contributions for eligible employees. Because self-employed people and small businesses get their taxes audited at a relatively high rate, messing up in this area is dangerous. The IRS has a program to audit small pension plans.

Don't avoid setting up a retirement savings plan for your business just because you have employees and you don't want to make contributions on their behalf. In the long run, you can build the contributions you make for your employees into their total compensation package — which includes salary and other benefits like health insurance. Making retirement contributions need not increase your personnel costs.

To help small-business owners defray some of the costs of establishing and maintaining a retirement savings plan, Congress established a new tax credit. Eligible small employers can claim 50 percent of the costs to set up and administer a retirement plan (to a maximum of $500 per year) for up to three years with plans begun in 2002 and thereafter. The employer's plan must cover no more than 100 employees and at least one employee who is not deemed highly compensated by the IRS's definition. Highly compensated individuals for 2003 include those who make more than $90,000 per year.

To get the most from your contributions as an employer, consider the following:

Educate your employees about the value of retirement savings plans. You want them to understand how to save for the future, but more important, you want them to value and appreciate your investment.

- ✔ Select a Keogh plan that requires employees to stay a certain number of years to vest in their contributions and allows for "Social Security integration" (see the discussion in the upcoming section on Keogh plans).

- ✔ If you have more than 20 or so employees, consider offering a 401(k) or SIMPLE plan, which allows employees to contribute money from their paychecks.

SEP-IRAs

Simplified Employee Pension Individual Retirement Account (SEP-IRA) plans require little paperwork to set up. Each year, you decide the amount you want to contribute to your SEP-IRA; no minimums exist. Your contributions to a SEP-IRA are deducted from your taxable income, saving you big-time on federal and usually state taxes. As with other retirement plans, your money compounds without taxation until withdrawal.

SEP-IRAs allow you to sock away about 20 percent of your self-employment income (business revenue minus expenses), up to a maximum of $40,000 for tax year 2003. This represents an enormous increase in the contribution limits, which were just 13 percent to a maximum of $25,500 a couple of years back.

Future contribution limits will rise in increments of $1,000 with inflation.

Keoghs

Keogh plans require a bit more paperwork to set up and administer than SEP-IRAs. The historic appeal of certain types of Keoghs was that they allowed you to put away a greater amount of your self-employment income (revenue less your expenses).

Keogh plans now have the same contribution limit ($40,000 and 20 percent of net self-employment income) that SEP-IRA plans do. The future contribution limit of Keogh plans will increase in $1,000 increments with increases in the cost of living, just as with SEP-IRA plans.

So, with Keogh and SEP-IRA plans having the same contribution limits, you may wonder why you should consider a Keogh plan if such plans generally require more paperwork and hassle. Well, an appeal of Keogh plans is that they allow business owners to maximize their contributions relative to employees in two ways that they can't with SEP-IRAs:

- ✔ Keogh plans allow *vesting schedules,* which require employees to remain with the company for a specified number of years before they earn the right to their full retirement account balances. *Vesting* refers to the portion of the retirement account money that the employee owns. After a certain number of years, an employee becomes fully vested and, therefore, owns 100 percent of the funds in his retirement account. If an employee leaves prior to being fully vested, he loses the unvested balance, which reverts to the remaining plan participants.

- ✔ Keogh plans allow for *Social Security integration.* Integration effectively allows the high-income earners in the company (usually the owners) to receive larger percentage contributions for their accounts than the less highly compensated employees. The logic behind this is that Social Security taxes top out after you earn more than $87,000 (for tax year 2003). Social Security integration enables self-employed business owners and key employees earning in excess of this amount to make up for this ceiling.

Retirement account inequities

If you don't have access to a retirement plan through your place of employment, you can try lobbying your employer to set one up — or you can look elsewhere for a job that offers this valuable benefit. Failing these options, you have a right to be displeased about the inequities in terms of access to tax-deductible retirement accounts.

To put everyone on more equal footing, those who work for employers without retirement savings plans should be allowed to contribute more to their IRAs. It isn't fair that people who work for companies that have no retirement savings plans can deduct only $2,000 per year from their taxable income for an IRA. In some cases, they may not be able to deduct anything! Even with recent tax law changes, the IRA contribution limits will rise to just $5,000, and not until tax year 2008.

Consider an example of two households, each of which has an annual employment income of $50,000. One household has access to a 401(k) plan, but the other household has no access to retirement plans other than an IRA. The household with the 401(k) can put away and deduct from its taxable income thousands of dollars more per year than the household with just the IRA. Recent tax bills increased this disparity, because the contribution limits on 401(k) and other similar employer plans rise more than the contribution limits on IRAs do.

The inequality can be even greater with higher-income earners. A self-employed person making $100,000 per year, for example, can sock away a tax-deductible $20,000 per year. Those who earn $200,000-plus per year may be able to save $40,000, perhaps even more, if they establish defined-benefit plans and other types of plans.

Tax deductions for retirement savings are included in the tax system to encourage people to provide for their own retirement. It's hypocritical and inequitable for the government and our tax laws to stress the importance of savings for retirement and not give people equal access to do so.

Just to make life complicated, Keoghs come in several flavors:

- **Profit-sharing plans:** These plans have the same contribution limits as SEP-IRAs. So why would you want the headaches of a more complicated plan when you can't contribute more to it? Profit-sharing plans appeal to owners of small companies who want to use vesting schedules and Social Security integration (described in previous paragraphs), which can't be done with SEP-IRA plans.

- **Money-purchase pension plans**: Historically, you could contribute more to these plans than you could to a profit-sharing plan or a SEP-IRA. Now all these plans have the same maximum tax-deductible contribution limit — the lesser of 20 percent of your self-employment income or $40,000 per year.

- **Defined-benefit plans:** These plans are for people who are able and willing to put away more than the Keogh and SEP-IRA contribution limit of $40,000 per year. Of course only a small percentage of people can afford to do so. Consistently high-income earners older than age 45 to 50 who want to save more than $40,000 per year in a retirement account should consider these plans. If you're interested in defined-benefit plans, you need to hire an actuary to calculate how much you can contribute to such a plan.

Individual Retirement Accounts (IRAs)

A final retirement account option is an Individual Retirement Account (IRA).

Because your IRA contributions may not be tax-deductible, contributing to an IRA generally makes sense only after you've exhausted contributing to other retirement accounts, such as the employer- and self-employed-based plans discussed earlier, which allow for tax-deductible contributions.

After being stuck at $2,000 since 1981, the 2001 tax bill finally increased the contribution limit for IRAs. With prior tax law changes, two types of IRAs — Roth IRAs and Education IRAs (since renamed Education Savings Accounts) — were added and are now among the already-too-long list of Americans' retirement account options. Also in recent years, a variety of existing IRA rules were altered, such as the conditions for making penalty-free withdrawals. You find more on the newer accounts and rules later in this section.

"Regular" IRAs

Anyone with employment (or alimony) income can contribute to a "regular" or "standard" IRA — in other words, the original type of IRA that existed before Congress monkeyed with the laws and created more IRA flavors. You may contribute up to $3,000 each year.

If you don't earn $3,000 a year, you can contribute as much as you'd like (and can afford) up to the amount of your employment or alimony income. If you're a nonworking spouse, you're also eligible to put $3,000 per year into a so-called spousal IRA.

By tax year 2008, the annual contribution limit for IRAs (both regular and the newer Roth IRAs, discussed in the next section) will rise to $5,000. People age 50 and older will be able to contribute even more — an extra $500 now and an extra $1,000 per year starting in 2008 (see Table 21-4).

Table 21-4	IRA (Regular and Roth) Contribution Limits	
Year	**Contribution Limit for Those Under Age 50**	**Contribution Limit for Those Age 50 and Older**
2003–2004	$3,000	$3,500
2005	$4,000	$4,500
2006–2007	$4,000	$5,000
2008	$5,000	$6,000

Your contributions to an IRA may or may not be tax-deductible. For tax year 2002, if you're single and your adjusted gross income (AGI) is $34,000 or less for the year, you can deduct your IRA contribution in full. If you're married and file your taxes jointly, you're entitled to a full IRA deduction if your AGI is $54,000 per year or less. *Note:* These AGI limits will increase in future tax years (more details in a moment).

If you make more than these amounts, you can take a full IRA deduction if and only if you (or your spouse) are not an *active participant* in any retirement plan. The only way to know for certain whether you're an active participant is to look at your W-2 form, that smallish (4-inch by 8½-inch) document your employer sends you early in the year to file with your tax returns. An X mark in a little box in section 13 on the W-2 form indicates that you're an active participant in an employer retirement plan.

Married couples with adjusted gross incomes of $150,000 or less are no longer disqualified from taking a tax deduction for an IRA contribution because one person is an active participant in an employer's retirement plan. At an AGI of between $150,000 and $160,000, a partial deduction is allowed. At an AGI of $160,000 or more, no IRA deduction is allowed for spouses of active retirement account participants.

For tax year 2003, if you're a single-income earner with an adjusted gross income above $40,000 but below $50,000, or part of a couple with an AGI above $60,000 but below $70,000, you're eligible for a partial IRA deduction, even if you're an active participant. The size of the IRA deduction that you may claim depends on where you fall in the income range. For example, a single-income earner at $45,000 is entitled to half ($1,000) of the full IRA deduction because his or her income falls halfway between $40,000 and $50,000.

A couple earning $62,500 loses just a quarter of the full IRA deduction amount because their incomes are a quarter of the way from $60,000 to $70,000. Thus the couple can take a $1,500 IRA deduction. (See Chapter 7 to find out how to calculate your exact deductible IRA contribution.)

Table 21-5 shows how a gradual rise in the AGI ceiling for fully deductible IRA contributions breaks down for future tax years. (Remember that these figures represent the beginning of a $10,000 phaseout range. In 2004, for example, IRA deductibility phases out between $45,000 and $55,000 for single taxpayers.)

Table 21-5	The Adjusted Gross Income Ceiling for Tax-Deductible IRA Contributions	
Tax Year	*Single*	*Married Filing Jointly*
2003	$40,000	$60,000
2004	$45,000	$65,000
2005	$50,000	$70,000
2006	$50,000	$75,000
2007 and beyond	$50,000	$80,000

Nondeductible IRA contributions

Some people think that they can't make the contribution if they can't deduct it. You can contribute to an IRA even if you can't deduct a portion or all of an IRA contribution because you're already covered by another retirement plan and your adjusted gross income is greater than the income limits in Table 21-5.

An IRA contribution that is not tax-deductible is called, not surprisingly, a nondeductible IRA contribution. (We've never accused the IRS of being creative.) To make a nondeductible contribution, you have to have employment income during the year equal to at least the amount of your IRA contribution.

The benefit of this type of contribution is that the money can still compound and grow without taxation. For a person who plans to leave contributions in the IRA for a long time (a decade or more), this tax-deferred compounding may make nondeductible contributions worthwhile. However, before you consider making a nondeductible IRA contribution, be sure to read about the newer Roth IRAs that may offer better benefits for your situation.

If you end up making a nondeductible IRA contribution, you may wonder how the IRS will know not to tax you again on those portions of IRA withdrawals (because you've already paid income tax on the nondeductible contribution) in retirement. Surprise, surprise, you must fill out another form, **Form 8606,** which you file each year with your tax return to track these nondeductible contributions. (Find this form in the back of this book.) If you haven't filed your year 2003 tax form yet, you may still make your IRA contribution.

Roth IRAs

For years, some taxpayers and tax advisors (and book authors and financial counselors) have complained about the rules and regulations on regular IRAs. The income limits that allowed for taking an IRA deduction were set too low. And many people who couldn't take a tax deduction on a contribution were unmotivated to make a nondeductible contribution, because earnings on the contribution still would be taxed upon withdrawal. (Granted, the tax-deferred compounding of earnings is worth something — especially to younger people — but that's a more complicated benefit to understand and value.)

Why so many different types of retirement accounts?

The different types of retirement plans — 401(k)s, 403(b)s, SEP-IRAs, Keoghs, regular IRAs, Roth IRAs, and SIMPLE — and the unique tax laws governing each are enough to drive taxpayers and some tax preparers wacky. The complexity of the different rules is another reason that some folks don't bother with these accounts.

As with the other complicated parts of our tax laws, retirement account regulations have accumulated over the years. Just like the stuff that you toss into your spare closet, attic, basement, or garage, the regulations just keep piling up. No one really wants to deal with the mess.

Our neighbors to the north in Canada have a retirement account system that we could learn from. In Canada, they have but one account — it's called the Registered Retirement Savings Plan (RRSP). Everyone with employment income can establish this account and contribute up to 18 percent, or up to a maximum annual total contribution of $13,500 — simple, equitable, and easy to understand. Why don't we do it? Go talk to the boneheads in Congress who brought us this supposedly "simple, equitable, and easy" tax system you're reading about!

So, rather than addressing these concerns by changing regular IRAs, Congress decided to make things even more complicated by introducing another whole IRA known as the Roth IRA, named after the Senate Finance Committee chairman who championed these new accounts. (Perhaps if congressional representatives couldn't name accounts after themselves, removing some of the incentive to continue creating new retirement accounts, we might someday have real tax reform!)

Understanding the Roth IRA

The Roth IRA allows for up to a $3,000 annual contribution for couples with adjusted gross incomes (AGIs) under $150,000 and for single taxpayers with AGIs under $95,000. The $3,000 limit is reduced for married taxpayers with AGIs above $150,000 ($95,000 if single) and is eliminated for couples with AGIs above $160,000 ($110,000 for singles). As with regular IRAs, the contribution limit for Roth IRAs will rise to $5,000 by 2008 and to $6,000 for those age 50 and older (please refer to Table 21-4).

Although this newer IRA doesn't offer a tax deduction on funds contributed to it, it nevertheless offers benefits not provided by regular IRAs and some other retirement accounts. The distinguishing feature of the Roth IRA is that the earnings on your contributions aren't taxed upon withdrawal as long as you're at least age 59½ and have held the account for at least five years.

An exception to the age-59½ rule is made for first-time homebuyers, who can withdraw up to $10,000 from a Roth IRA to apply to the purchase of a principal residence. Remember, however, that your Roth IRA must be in existence for five years before you're allowed an income tax–free withdrawal for a home purchase.

Another attractive feature of the Roth IRA: For those not needing to draw on all their retirement accounts in the earlier years of retirement, the Roth IRA, unlike a standard IRA, does not require distributions after the account holder passes age 70½.

To Roth or not to Roth?

Before you go running out to contribute to a Roth IRA, keep in mind that the lack of taxation on withdrawn earnings is in no way guaranteed for the future. Congress can giveth tax benefits, and Congress can taketh them away. If the government is running large deficits in future years, turning around and taxing Roth IRA withdrawals would increase tax revenue.

Consider contributing to a Roth IRA if you've exhausted your ability to contribute to tax-deductible retirement accounts and you aren't allowed a tax deduction for a regular IRA contribution because your adjusted gross income exceeds the regular IRA deductibility thresholds. If you find yourself in the fortunate situation that your high income disallows

Should you convert your regular IRA to a Roth IRA?

If the Roth IRA's tax-free withdrawals of accumulated earnings appeal to you, you may be interested in knowing that the tax laws allow taxpayers to transfer money from a regular IRA to a Roth IRA without having to pay any early withdrawal penalties. The catch (you knew there'd be one) is that you must pay income tax on the amount transferred, and such a transfer is available only to taxpayers with adjusted gross incomes of less than $100,000.

Whether you'll come out ahead in the long run by doing this conversion depends largely on your time horizon and retirement tax bracket. The younger you are and the higher the tax bracket you think that you'll be in when you retire, the more such a conversion makes sense. On the other hand, if you drop into a lower tax bracket in retirement, as many retirees do, you're probably better off keeping the money in a standard IRA account. For assistance with crunching numbers to see whether a conversion makes financial sense, visit the investment firm T. Rowe Price's Web site at www.troweprice.com and check out their analytic tools in the "IRA Calculator" section.

Of course, if you can't afford to pay the current income tax you'll owe on the conversion, then don't do it. And again, remember that a future Congress could reverse some of the benefits of the Roth IRA. Thus we generally don't advise many people to convert a regular IRA into a Roth IRA.

you from funding a Roth IRA, then that would be a good reason to contribute to a nondeductible regular IRA (after having maxed out your contributions to other tax-deductible retirement accounts). Sorry, but you can't contribute $3,000 in the same tax year to both a regular IRA and a Roth IRA; the sum of your standard and Roth IRA contributions may not exceed $3,000 in a given year. (If you are so enamored of the Roth IRA's benefits and think you'd rather put your money into a Roth IRA than make a tax-deductible retirement account contribution, check out T. Rowe Price's Web site retirement tools described in the "IRA Calculator" section at www.troweprice.com.

Penalty-free IRA withdrawals

TAX CUT

Except for a few situations having mostly to do with emergencies, such as a major illness and unemployment, tapping into an IRA account before age 59½ (called an *early withdrawal*) triggers a hefty 10 percent federal income tax penalty (in addition to whatever penalties your state charges). Now, however, you're allowed to make a penalty-free early withdrawal from your IRA for two specific expenses. *First-time homebuyers* — defined as not having owned a home in the past two years — may withdraw up to $10,000. Amounts also may be withdrawn for *qualified higher education costs* (college expenses for a family member such as a child, spouse, the IRA holder, or grandchildren).

Early withdrawals from regular IRA accounts still are subject to regular income tax in the year of withdrawal. Withdrawals from a Roth IRA (discussed in the next section) can be both penalty-free and federal income tax-free as long as the Roth IRA account is at least five years old.

Newer Roth IRA accounts also are exempt from the normal retirement account requirement to begin taking minimum distributions at age 70½ if you aren't working.

Education IRAs/Education Savings Accounts

During the 1997 tax law changes, Congress wasn't content to add just Roth IRAs to the new list of IRA flavors, so they created a third type of IRA known as the Education IRA. These accounts are misnamed because they have nothing to do with retirement. They are tax-sheltered vehicles that enable parents to save for their children's educational costs.

Medical savings accounts

In tax year 1997, the government started testing Medical Savings Accounts (MSAs) that allow self-employed people and employers with an average of 50 or fewer employees (during the past two years) to put money away on a pretax basis toward medical expenses.

The maximum amount that eligible employees may contribute each year is limited to 65 percent of that individual's health insurance plan deductible, or 75 percent of the family's deductible. Contributions to an MSA can be made through tax year 2002. A bill currently in Congress would extend and expand MSAs in years ahead.

MSAs have some bizarre limitations and rules. For tax year 2002, contributions to MSAs can be made only for individual health plans with yearly deductibles between $1,700 and $2,500 and maximum out-of-pocket limits not exceeding $3,300, and family plans with deductibles of between $3,350 and $5,050 and maximum out-of-pocket limits not exceeding $6,050.

Unlike healthcare dollars put into an employer's flexible benefit plan, if you don't use the money contributed to the MSA, you can simply let it continue to grow and then use it in the future. However, if you withdraw the money before age 65 and don't use it for medical expenses (unless you have a disability or die), you'll owe a 15 percent federal penalty tax in addition to regular income tax, plus any penalties assessed by your state.

To date, few major investment firms, such as the better mutual fund companies, offer MSAs. As with any other type of investment account, be sure to examine the fees on these accounts and the merits of the investment options each company offers before investing.

For tax years through the end of 2002, seniors on Medicare may be able to establish MedicarePlus Choice MSAs during the pilot program. One caution, however, is that only expenses relating to the medical care of the MedicarePlus Choice MSA holder are considered qualified medical expenses. Distributions used to pay for medical expenses of the account holder's spouse, children, or other dependents would be taxed.

Although Education IRAs, recently renamed Education Savings Accounts (ESAs), offer some benefits, they also come with serious potential drawbacks. Read Chapter 25, which deals with important taxes relating to kids, for an explanation of the pros and cons of ESAs.

Annuities

Annuities, like IRAs, allow your capital to grow and compound without taxation. You defer taxes until withdrawal. Annuities carry the same penalties for withdrawal prior to age 59½ as IRAs do. However, unlike all other retirement accounts except a Roth IRA, you aren't forced to begin withdrawals at age 70½; you may leave the money in an annuity to compound tax deferred for as many years as you desire.

And, unlike an IRA that has an annual contribution limit, you can deposit as much as you want in any year into an annuity — even $1 million if you have it! As with a so-called nondeductible IRA, you get no upfront tax deduction for your contributions. Thus, consider an annuity only after fully exhausting your other retirement account options.

What exactly is an annuity? Well, *annuities* are peculiar investment products — contracts, actually — that are backed by insurance companies. If you, the annuity holder (investor), die during the so-called accumulation phase (that is, prior to receiving payments from the annuity), your designated beneficiary is guaranteed to receive the amount of your original investment.

 Because annuities carry higher fees (which reduce your investment returns) because of the insurance that comes with them, you should first make the maximum contribution that you can to an IRA, even if it isn't tax-deductible. Also, consider annuities only if you plan to leave the money in the annuity for 15 years or more. The reasons are twofold. First, it typically takes that long for the tax-deferred compounding of your annuity investment to make up for the annuity's relatively higher expenses. Second, upon withdrawal, the earnings on an annuity are taxed at ordinary income tax rates, which are higher than the more favorable long-term capital gains and stock dividend tax rates. If you don't expect to keep your money invested for 15 to 20-plus years to make up for the annuities' higher ongoing fees and taxes on the back end, you should simply invest your money in tax-friendly investments in non-retirement accounts (see Chapter 22).

Taxing Retirement Account Decisions

In addition to knowing about the different types of retirement accounts available and the importance of using them, we know from our work with counseling clients that you're going to have other problems and questions. This section presents the sticky issues that you may be struggling with, along with our recommendations.

Prioritizing retirement contributions

When you have access to more than one type of retirement account, prioritize which accounts to use by what they give you in return. Your first contributions should be to employer-based plans that match your contributions. After that, contribute to any other employer or self-employed plans that allow tax-deductible contributions. When you've contributed the maximum possible to tax-deductible plans or don't have access to such plans, contribute to an IRA (read the sections earlier in this chapter about choosing between a regular IRA and a Roth IRA).

If you've maxed out on contributions to an IRA or don't have this choice because you lack employment income, consider an annuity or tax-friendly investments (see Chapter 23).

We hate to bring it up, but some spouses worry about whether the bulk of their retirement account contributions will end up in the other spouse's account. You may be concerned about this situation because of the realities of a potential divorce. In a divorce, money in retirement accounts (regardless of how much is in which person's name) can be divided up like the other assets. But rather than worrying about the possibility of divorce, how about investing in the effort to make your relationship stronger to avoid this problem? If you dislike paying taxes, you're going to hate a divorce wherein you could face a 50 percent "tax rate" — that's the amount of your combined assets your spouse could walk away with!

Transferring existing retirement accounts

With employer-maintained retirement plans, such as 401(k)s, you usually have limited investment options. Unless you are the employer or can convince the employer to change, you're stuck with what is offered. If your employer offers four mutual funds from the Lotsa Fees and Lousy Performance Fund Company, for example, you can't transfer this money to another investment company.

After you leave your employer, however, you generally have the option of leaving your money in the employer's plan or transferring it to an IRA at an investment company of your choice. The process of moving this money from an employer plan to investments of your choice is called a *rollover*. And you thought you weren't going to be reading anything fun today!

When you roll money over from an employer-based retirement plan, don't take personal possession of the money. If your employer gives the money to you, the employer must withhold 20 percent of it for taxes. This situation creates a tax nightmare for you because you must then jump through more hoops when you file your return. You also should know that you need to come up with the extra 20 percent when you do the rollover, because you won't get the 20 percent back that your employer withheld in taxes until you file your tax return. If you can't come up with the 20 percent, you have to pay income tax and maybe even excise taxes on this money as a distribution. Yuck!

After you leave the company, you can move your money held in SEP-IRAs, Keoghs, IRAs, and many 403(b) plans (also known as *tax-sheltered annuities*) to nearly any major investment firm you please. Moving the money is pretty simple. If you can dial a toll-free number, fill out a couple of short forms, and send them back in a postage-paid envelope, then you can transfer an account. The investment firm to which you're transferring your account does the rest. Here's the lowdown on how to transfer retirement accounts without upsetting Uncle Sam or any other tax collector:

1. **Decide to which investment firm you would like to move the account.**

   When investing in stocks and bonds, mutual funds are a great way to go. They offer diversification and professional management, and they're low-cost.

2. **Call the toll-free number of the firm you're transferring the money to and ask for an *account application* and *asset transfer form* for the type of account you're transferring — for example, SEP-IRA, Keogh, IRA, or 403(b).**

   The reason for allowing the new investment company to do the transfer for you is that the tax authorities impose huge penalties if you do a transfer incorrectly. It's far easier and safer to let the company to which you're transferring the money do the transfer for you. If they screw it up (good investment firms won't), they're liable.

3. **Complete and mail back the account application and asset transfer forms to your new investment company.**

   Completing this paperwork for your new investment firm opens your new account and authorizes the transfer. If you have questions or problems, the firm(s) to which you're transferring your account have armies of capable employees waiting to help you. Remember, these firms know that you're transferring your money to them, so they normally roll out the red carpet.

   Transferring your existing assets typically takes a month to complete. If the transfer isn't completed within a month, get in touch with your new investment firm to determine the problem.

   If your old company isn't cooperating, a call to a manager there may help to get the ball rolling. The unfortunate reality is that too many investment firms will cheerfully set up a new account to *accept* your money on a moment's notice, but they will drag their feet, sometimes for months, when it comes time to *relinquish* your money. If you need to light a fire under their behinds, tell a manager at the old firm that you're sending letters to the National Association of Securities Dealers (NASD) and the Securities and Exchange Commission (SEC) if they don't complete your transfer within the next week.

Taking money out of retirement accounts

Someday, hopefully not until you retire, you'll need or want to start withdrawing and enjoying the money that you socked away in your retirement accounts. Some people, particularly those who are thrifty and good at saving money (also known, by some, as cheapskates and tightwads), have a hard time doing this.

You saved and invested money in your retirement accounts to use at a future date. Perhaps you're in a pinch for cash and the retirement account looks as tempting as a catered buffet meal after a day of fasting. Whatever the reason, here's what you need to consider *before* taking the money out of your retirement accounts.

Lower taxes for working seniors

Under prior tax law, some Social Security recipients ages 65 to 69 who were working faced stiff taxes. Specifically, working seniors had to give back $1 of Social Security benefits for every $3 they earned above $17,000 in a tax year. Thus, in addition to owing federal and state income on their earnings, seniors earning in excess of $17,000 annually paid an effective tax rate of 33 percent in lost Social Security benefits!

Now, seniors age 65 and older drawing Social Security benefits can earn as much as they like without being penalized (those under age 65 who are receiving Social Security benefits can earn up to $11,280). Thus working seniors need not end up having to pay back up to half or more of their earnings in excess of $17,000 per tax year.

For seniors needing to continue working for financial reasons, this tax law change is a huge relief. This change also should reduce the number of seniors driven from the workforce because, after paying taxes on their employment earnings, working for pay isn't worth their time.

Increasing numbers of seniors will find that they need to work more years to make financial ends meet. Folks turning age 62 in the years ahead will find that rather than being able to draw full Social Security retirement benefits at age 65, they will have to wait until age 65 years and some number of months. The age at which you can draw full Social Security benefits will gradually rise in the years ahead until it reaches age 67 for those reaching age 62 in the year 2022 and after.

When should you start withdrawing from retirement accounts?

Some people start withdrawing funds from retirement accounts *when* they retire. This option may or may not be the best financial decision for you. Generally speaking, you're better off postponing drawing on retirement accounts until you need the money. The longer the money resides inside the retirement account, the longer it can compound and grow, tax-deferred. But don't wait if postponing means that you must scrimp and cut corners — especially if you have the money to use and enjoy.

Suppose that you retire at age 60 and, in addition to money inside your retirement accounts, you have a bunch available outside. If you can, you're better off living off the money outside retirement accounts *before* you start tapping the retirement account money.

If you aren't wealthy and have saved most of the money earmarked for your retirement inside retirement accounts, odds are you'll need and want to start drawing on your retirement account soon after you retire. By all means, do so. But have you figured out how long your nest egg will last and how much you can afford to withdraw? Most folks haven't. It's worth taking the time to figure how much of your money you can afford to draw on per year, even if you think that you have enough.

Few people are wealthy enough to consider simply living off the interest and never touching the principal, although more than a few people live like paupers so that they can do just that. Many good savers have a hard time spending and enjoying their money in retirement. If you know how much you can safely use, you may be able to loosen the purse strings.

One danger of leaving your money to compound inside your retirement accounts for a long time after you're retired is that the IRS will require you to start making withdrawals by April 1 of the year *following* the year you reach age 70½. It's possible that because of your delay in taking the money out — and the fact that it will have more time to compound and grow — you may need to withdraw a hefty chunk per year. This procedure could push you into higher tax brackets in those years that you're forced to make larger withdrawals.

This forced distribution no longer applies to people who are working for a company, and also does not apply to money held in the newer Roth IRAs discussed earlier in this chapter. Self-employed individuals still have to take the distribution.

If you want to plan how to withdraw money from your retirement accounts so that you meet your needs and minimize your taxes, consider hiring a tax advisor to help. If you have a great deal of money in retirement accounts and have the luxury of not needing the money until you're well into retirement, tax planning will likely be worth your time and money.

Naming beneficiaries

With any type of retirement account, you're supposed to name beneficiaries who will receive the assets in the account when you die. You usually name primary beneficiaries — your first choices for receiving the money — and secondary beneficiaries, who receive the money in the event that the primary beneficiaries also are deceased when you pass away.

The designations aren't cast in stone; you can change them whenever and as often as you desire by sending written notice to the investment company or employer holding your retirement account. Note that many plans require spousal consent to the naming of a beneficiary other than the spouse.

Do the best you can in naming beneficiaries, and be thankful that you don't have to designate someone to raise your children in your absence! You should know that you can designate charities as beneficiaries. If you want to reduce the amount of money that's required to be distributed from your retirement accounts annually, name beneficiaries who are all at least ten years younger than yourself.

The IRS allows you to calculate the required minimum distribution based on the joint life expectancy of you and your oldest named beneficiary. However, you can't use a difference of greater than ten years for a nonspouse. If a nonspouse is named as the beneficiary and is more than ten years younger, for tax purposes of calculating required withdrawals, they are considered to be just ten years younger than you. Maybe that's why some rich, older men like marrying younger women!

Perplexing pension decisions

As discussed earlier in the chapter, if you've worked for a larger company for a number of years, you may have earned what is known as a *pension benefit*. This term simply means that upon attaining a particular age, usually 55 to 65, you can start to receive a monthly check from the employer(s) you worked for. With many pension plans today, you earn *(vest)* a benefit after you have completed five years of full-time work.

Make sure to keep track of the employer(s) where you have earned pension benefits as you move to new jobs and locations. Mail address changes to your previous employers' benefits departments. If they lose track of you and you forget that you've earned a benefit, you could be out a great deal of money.

What age to start?

With some plans, you may be able to start drawing your pension as early as 50 years of age — as long as you've worked enough years somewhere. The majority of plans, however, won't give you payments until age 55 or 60. Some plans even make you wait until age 65.

If you don't have a choice as to what age you want to start drawing benefits, that situation surely simplifies things for you. Before you become perplexed and overwhelmed if you do have options, remember one simple thing: Smart actuaries have created the choices available to you. Actuaries are the kinds of people who score 800s (a perfect score, in case you forgot) on their math SATs. These folks work, eat, breathe, and sleep numbers.

The choices you confront show you that the younger you elect to start drawing benefits, the less you are paid. Conversely, the longer you can wait to access your pension, the more you should receive per month. That said, here are some pointers:

✔ Some pensions stop offering higher benefits after you reach a certain age — make sure that you don't delay starting your benefits until after you've reached this plateau. Otherwise, make your decision as to what age to start drawing benefits based on when you need the money and/or can afford to retire. Run the numbers or hire a competent tax or financial advisor.

✔ If you're still working and earning a healthy income, think twice before starting pension benefits — these benefits are likely to be taxed at a much higher rate. You're probably going to be in a lower income tax bracket after you stop working.

✔ If you know that you're in poor health and will not live long, consider drawing your pension sooner.

Attempting to calculate which age option will lead to your getting more money is not worth your time. So many assumptions, such as the rate of inflation and the number of years you'll live, are beyond your ability to predict accurately. The actuaries have done their homework on these issues, and that's why the numbers vary the way they do.

Which payment option for you married folks?

Besides deciding at what age you'll elect to start receiving benefits, you may have other choices if you're married, such as how much money you'll receive when you begin your pension benefit versus how much your spouse will receive if you pass away.

Before we dig into these choices, remember that actuaries are smart — don't make your selection based on age differences between you and your spouse. For example, if you're married to someone much younger, you may be tempted to choose the pension option that maximizes the amount your spouse receives upon your death because you're likely to pre-decease your spouse. However, each person's pension options already reflect the age differences between spouses, so don't waste your time with this line of thinking. Remember those smart actuaries.

Although the actuaries know your age and your spouse's age, they don't know or care about your ability and desire to accept financial risk. Pension options differ from one another in how much money you can receive now versus how much your spouse is guaranteed to receive in the event that you die first. As with many things in life, there are tradeoffs. If you want to ensure that your spouse continues to receive a relatively high pension in the event of your passing, you must be willing to accept a smaller pension payment when you start drawing the pension.

The actuaries also don't know about your current health. All things being equal, if you're in poor health because of a chronic medical problem when you choose your pension option, lean toward those that provide your spouse with more.

The following are some of the typical options, which are ranked in order of providing the most to the fewest dollars at the beginning of retirement. The first choices, which provide more cash in hand sooner, are the riskiest from the standpoint of surviving spouses. The latter choices, which offer less cash in hand today, are the least risky for surviving spouses:

✔ **Single Life Option:** This option pays benefits only as long as the *pensioner* (the person who earned the pension benefit) is alive. *The survivor receives nothing.* The single life option offers the highest monthly benefits but is also the riskiest option. For example, the pensioner receives $1,500 per month for as long as he or she is alive. The spouse receives nothing after the pensioner's death. Consider this option only if you have sufficient assets for your spouse to live on in the event of your dying early in retirement.

✔ **Ten Years' Certain Option:** This option pays benefits for at least ten years, even if the pensioner passes away within the first ten years of drawing the pension. The pensioner continues receiving benefits for as long as he or she lives, even if he or she lives more than ten years. For example, a pensioner receives $1,400 per month for at least ten years until his or her death. The spouse then receives nothing.

- **50 Percent Joint and Survivor Option:** With this option, the survivor receives 50 percent of the pensioner's benefit after his or her death. For example, a pensioner receives $1,350 per month. Upon the pensioner's death, his or her spouse receives a reduced benefit of $675 per month.

- **Two-thirds Joint and Survivor Option:** With this option, the survivor receives 66 percent of the pensioner's benefit after his or her death. For example, a pensioner receives $1,310 per month. Upon the pensioner's death, his or her spouse receives a reduced benefit of $865 per month.

- **75 Percent Joint Survivor Option:** With this option, the survivor receives 75 percent of the pensioner's benefit after his or her death. For example, a pensioner receives $1,275 per month. Upon the pensioner's death, the spouse receives a reduced benefit of $956 per month.

- **100 Percent Joint and Survivor Option:** With this option, the survivor receives 100 percent of the pensioner's benefit after his or her death. For example, a pensioner receives $1,200 per month. Upon the pensioner's death, the spouse continues to receive $1,200 per month.

Choosing the best pension option for you and your spouse is not unlike selecting investments. What's best for your situation depends on your overall financial circumstances and desire, comfort, and ability to accept risk. The Single Life Option is the riskiest and should be used only by couples who don't really need the pension — it's frosting on the financial cake — and are willing to gamble to maximize benefits today. If the surviving spouse is very much dependent on the pension, select one of the survivor options that leaves a high benefit amount after the pensioner's death.

Beware of insurance salespeople and "financial planners" (who also sell life insurance and are therefore brokers and not advisors) who advocate that you purchase life insurance and take the Single Life Option. They argue that this option enables you to maximize your pension income and protect the surviving spouse with a life insurance death benefit if the pensioner dies. Sounds good, but the life insurance expense outweighs the potential benefits. Choose one of the survivor pension options that effectively provides life insurance protection for your survivor. This method is a far more cost-effective way to "buy" life insurance.

New rules on mandatory retirement account distributions

If you're self-employed or retired from a company, on April 1 of the year following the year you turn 70½, you have to make some important decisions about how the money will come out of your regular IRA. (This policy is not applicable to Roth IRAs.) The first choice: whether you receive yearly distributions based on your life expectancy or based on the joint life expectancies of you and your beneficiary. If your aim is to take out as little as possible, you'll want to use a joint life expectancy. That choice will stretch out the distributions over a longer period.

Next, you have to decide how you want your life expectancy to be calculated.

Sometimes, tax law changes actually make things simpler. You'll be happy to know that recently approved IRS regulations make required minimum distribution calculations much easier.

Under the prior laws, retirees had several confusing methods for calculating their mandated retirement account withdrawal amounts. With the new regulations, in most cases, seniors can simply take their retirement account balances and divide that by a number from an IRS life expectancy table.

Another benefit of these new rules is that the new table generally produces lower required distributions and, therefore, a greater ability to preserve the account tax-free than was possible under the old regulations.

See Chapter 6 for more details.

Chapter 22

Small Businesses and Tax Planning

*W*hether *you* are your entire company or you have many employees for whom you're responsible, running a business can be one of the most frustrating, exhilarating, rewarding — and financially punishing — endeavors of your adult life. Many Americans fantasize about being their own boss. Tales of entrepreneurs becoming multimillionaires and multibillionaires focus our attention on the financial rewards without teaching us about the business and personal costs associated with being in charge.

The biggest challenges business owners face are the personal and emotional ones. It's sad to say, but these challenges rarely get discussed among all the glory tales of rags to riches. Major health problems, divorces, the loss of friends, and even suicides have been attributed to the passions of business owners consumed with winning or overwhelmed by their failures. Although careers and business success are important, if you really think about it, at best these things need be no higher than fourth on your overall priority list. Your health, family, and best friends can't be replaced — but a job or business can.

Business owners know the good and the bad. Consider the myriad activities that your company has to do well to survive and succeed in the rough-and-tumble business world. You have to develop products and services that the marketplace will purchase. You have to price your wares properly and promote them. After you've successfully developed offerings that meet a need, new worries begin: competitors. Your success will likely spur imitators.

With money flowing into and out of your coffers, you need to keep appropriate records documenting your income and expenses. Otherwise, preparing your business's tax returns will be a frustrating endeavor. Being audited under these circumstances can produce a never-ending nightmare. And, unlike working for a corporation, owning a small business makes *you* responsible for ensuring that the right amount of tax is withheld and paid on both the state and federal levels.

This chapter can help you to make tax-wise decisions that will boost your business profits and yet comply with myriad tax regulations that annoy many entrepreneurs like you.

Organizing Your Business Accounting

If you're thinking about starting a business or you're already in the thick of one, you need to keep a proper accounting of your income and expenses. If you don't, you'll have a lot more stress and headaches when it comes time to file the necessary tax forms for your business.

Real versus bogus businesses and hobby loss rules

This chapter is about how small-business owners can make tax-wise decisions while running their businesses. It is not about how to start up a sideline business for the primary purpose of generating tax deductions.

Unfortunately, some self-anointed financial gurus claim that you can slash or even completely eliminate your tax bill by setting up a sideline business. They say that you can sell your services while doing something you enjoy. The problem, they argue, is that — as a regular wage earner who receives a paycheck from an employer — you can't write off many of your other (that is, personal) expenses. These hucksters usually promise to show you the secrets of tax reduction if you shell out far too many bucks for their audiotapes and notebooks of inside information.

"Start a small business for fun, profit, and huge tax deductions," one financial book trumpets, adding that, "The tax benefits alone are worth starting a small business." A seminar company that offers a course on "How to Write a Book on Anything in 2 Weeks . . . or Less!" (we must be doing something wrong) also offers a tax course entitled "How to Have Zero Taxes Deducted from Your Paycheck." This tax seminar tells you how to solve your tax problems: "If you have a sideline business, or would like to start one, you're eligible to have little or no taxes taken from your pay." Gee, sounds good. Where do we sign up?

Suppose that you're interested in photography. You like to take pictures when you go on vacation. These supposed tax experts tell you to set up a photography business and start deducting all your photography-related expenses: airfare, film, utility bills, rent for your "home darkroom," and restaurant meals with potential clients (that is, your friends). Before you know it, you've wiped out most of your taxes.

Sounds too good to be true, right? It is. Your business spending must be for the legitimate purpose of generating an income. According to the IRS, a sideline activity that generates a loss year in and year out is not a business but a *hobby*.

Specifically, an activity is considered a hobby if it shows a loss for at least three of the past five tax years. (Horse racing, breeding, and so on are considered hobbies if they show losses in at least six or more of the past seven tax years.) Certainly, some businesses lose money. But a real business can't afford to do so year after year and still remain in business. Who likes losing money unless the losses are really just a tax deduction front for a hobby?

When the hobby loss rules indicate that you're engaging in a hobby, the IRS will disallow your claiming of the losses. To challenge this ruling, you must convince the IRS that you are seriously attempting to make a profit and run a legitimate business. The IRS will want to see that you're actively marketing your services, building your skills, and accounting for income and expenses. The IRS also will want to see that you aren't having too much fun! When you're deriving too much pleasure from an activity, in the eyes of the IRS, the activity must not be a real business.

The bottom line is this: You need to operate a legitimate business for the purpose of generating income and profits — not tax deductions. If you're thinking that it's worth the risk of taking tax losses for your hobby, year after year, because you won't get caught unless you're audited, better think again. The IRS audits an extraordinarily large number of small businesses that show regular losses.

Besides helping you over the annual tax-filing hurdle, you want accurate records so that you can track your business's financial health and performance during the year. How are your profits running? Can you afford to hire new employees? Analyzing your monthly or quarterly business financial statements can help you answer these important business questions.

Here's a final reason to keep good records: The IRS may audit you, and if that happens, you'll be asked that dreaded question: "Can you prove it?" Small-business owners who file Schedule C, Profit or Loss From Business, with their tax returns are audited at a much higher rate than other taxpayers. Although that dubious honor may seem like an unfair burden to business owners, the IRS targets small businesses because more than a few small-business owners break the tax rules and many areas exist where small-business owners can mess up.

The following sections cover the key tax-organizing things that small-business owners need to keep in mind.

Leave an "audit" trail

When it comes time for filing your annual return, you need the documentation that enables you to figure your business income and expenses. At a minimum, set up some file folders in which you can collect receipts and other documentation — perhaps one folder for tabulating your income and another for compiling your expenses. Computer software (see Chapter 2) also may help you with this chore, but you still must go through the hassle of learning a new program and then continually entering the data.

It doesn't matter whether you use file folders, software, or a good old-fashioned shoebox to collate this important financial information. What does matter is that you keep records of expenses and income.

You'll probably lose or misplace some of those little pieces of paper that you need to document your expenses. Thus one big advantage of charging expenses on a credit card or of writing a check is that these transactions leave a paper trail, which makes it easier to total your expenses come tax time and deal with being audited when you need to prove your expenses.

Just remember to be careful when you use a credit card, because you may buy more things than you can really afford. Then you're stuck with a lot of debt to pay off. On the other hand (as many small-business owners know), finding lenders when you need money is difficult. Using the credit on a low-interest-rate credit card can be an easy way for you to borrow money without shamelessly begging a banker for a loan.

Likewise, leave a trail with your revenue. Depositing all your receipts in one account helps you when tax time comes or if you're ever audited.

Separate business from personal finances

One of the IRS's biggest concerns is that as a small-business owner, you'll try to minimize your business profits (and therefore taxes) by hiding business income and inflating your business expenses. Uncle Sam thus looks suspiciously at business owners who use personal checking and credit card accounts for business transactions. You may be tempted to use your personal account this way (because opening separate accounts is a hassle — not because you're dishonest).

Take the time to open separate accounts. Doing so not only makes the feds happy, it also makes your accounting easier.

Please don't make the mistake of thinking that paying for an expense through your business account proves to the IRS that it was a legitimate business expense. If they find that the expense *was* truly for personal purposes, the IRS then will dig deep into your business's financial records to see what other shenanigans are going on.

Keep current on income and payroll taxes

When you're self-employed, you're responsible for the accurate and timely filing of all your income taxes. Without an employer and a payroll department to handle the paperwork for withholding taxes on a regular schedule, you need to make estimated tax payments on a quarterly basis.

When you have employees, you also need to withhold taxes on their incomes from each paycheck they receive. And you must make timely payments to the IRS and the appropriate state authorities. In addition to federal and state income taxes, you must withhold and send in Social Security and any other state or locally mandated payroll taxes and annually issue W-2s for each employee and 1099-MISCs for each independent contractor paid $600 or more. Got a headache yet?

For paying taxes on your own self-employment income, you can obtain **Form 1040ES, Estimated Tax for Individuals,** from the back of this book. This form comes complete with an estimated tax worksheet and the four payment coupons to send in with your quarterly tax payments. It's amazing how user-friendly government people can be when they want our money! The form itself has some quirks and challenges, but you'll be happy to know that we explain how to complete Form 1040ES in Chapter 15.

To discover all the amazing rules and regulations of withholding and submitting taxes from employees' paychecks, ask the IRS for **Form 941.** Once a year, you also need to complete **Form 940** for unemployment insurance payments to the feds. And, unless you're lucky enough to live in a state with no income taxes, don't forget to get your state's estimated income tax package.

Falling behind in paying taxes ruins many small businesses. When you hire employees, for example, you're particularly vulnerable to multiple tax landmines. If you aren't going to keep current on taxes for yourself and your employees, hire a payroll company or tax advisor who can help you to jump through the necessary tax hoops. (Refer to Chapter 2 for advice on selecting a tax advisor.) Payroll companies and tax advisors are there for a reason, so use them selectively. They take care of all the tax filings for you, and if they mess up, they pay the penalties. Check with a tax advisor you trust for the names of reputable payroll companies in your area.

Minimizing Your Small-Business Taxes

Every small business has to spend money to make money. Most businesses need things like phone service, paper, computers and printers, software, a bottle of extra strength aspirin, and a whole bunch of other things you probably never thought you'd be purchasing.

But don't spend money on business stuff just for the sake of generating tax deductions. In some cases, business owners we know buy all sorts of new equipment and other gadgets at year's end for their business so that they can reduce their taxes. Although we endorse reinvesting profits in your business and making your company more efficient and successful, keep in mind that spending too much can lead to lower profits. Remember that nothing is wrong with paying taxes. In fact, it's a sign of profits — business success!

What follows is an overview of what you can do and what not to do to be a tax-wise spender for your business.

Depreciation versus deduction

When you buy equipment such as computers, office furniture, bookshelves, and so on, each of these items is supposed to be depreciated over a number of years. *Depreciation* simply means that each year, you get to claim as a tax deduction a portion of the original cost of purchasing an item until you depreciate the entire cost of the purchase. Depreciation mirrors the declining value of equipment as it ages.

For example, suppose that you spend $3,000 on computer equipment. According to the IRS, computer equipment is to be depreciated over five years. Thus each year you can take a $600 deduction for depreciation of this computer if you elect straight-line depreciation (which is defined in Chapter 11).

Shifting income and expenses

Many small-business owners elect to keep their business accounting on what's called cash basis. This choice doesn't imply that all business customers literally pay in cash for goods and services or that the business owners pay for all expenses with cash. *Cash basis accounting* simply means that, for tax purposes, you recognize and report income in the year it was received and expenses in the year they were paid.

By operating on a cash basis, you can exert more control over the amount of profit (income minus expenses) that your business reports for tax purposes from year to year. If your income fluctuates from year to year, you can lower your tax burden by doing a little legal shifting of income and expenses.

Suppose that you recently started a business. Assume that you have little, but growing, revenue and somewhat high start-up expenses. Looking ahead to the next tax year, you can already tell that you'll be making more money and will likely be in a much higher tax bracket (see Chapter 1 for the personal income tax brackets and later in this chapter for corporate tax brackets). Thus you can likely reduce your tax bill by paying more of your expenses in the next year. Of course, you don't want to upset any of your business's suppliers. However, some of your bills can be paid after the start of the next tax year

(January 1) rather than in late December of the preceding year (presuming that your business's tax year is on a normal calendar year basis). *Note:* Credit card expenses are recognized as of the date you make the charges, not when you pay the bill.

Likewise, you can exert some control over when your customers pay you. If you expect to make less money next year, simply don't invoice customers in December of this year. Wait until January so that you receive more of your income next year. Be careful with this revenue-shifting game. You don't want to run short of cash and miss a payroll! Similarly, if a customer mails you a check in December, IRS laws don't allow you to hold the check until January and count the revenue then. After you receive the payment, it's supposed to be recognized for tax purposes as revenue.

One final point limits who can do this revenue and expense two-step. Sole proprietorships, partnerships, S Corporations, and personal service corporations (which we discuss later in the chapter) generally can shift revenue and expenses. On the other hand, C Corporations and partnerships that have C Corporations as partners may not use the cash accounting method if they have annual receipts of more than $5 million per year.

By expensing or deducting (by using what's called a Section 179 deduction) rather than depreciating, you can take as an immediate deduction the entire $3,000 you spent on computer equipment (unless it contributes to your business showing a loss or a larger loss). As a small-business owner, you can take up to a $100,000 deduction for tax year 2003 for purchases of equipment for use in your business.

Wanting to expense the full amount of equipment immediately is tempting, but that isn't always the best thing to do. In the early years of your business, for example, your profits may be low. Therefore, because you won't be in a high tax bracket, the value of your deductions is limited. Looking ahead — when you have reason to be optimistic about your future profits — you may actually save tax dollars by choosing to depreciate your purchases. Why? By delaying some of your tax write-offs until future years (when you expect to be in a higher tax bracket because of greater profits), you save more in taxes.

Cars

If you use your car for business, you can claim a deduction. The mistake that some business owners (and many other people) make is to buy an expensive car. This purchase causes two problems. First, the car may be a waste of money that could be better spent elsewhere in the business. Second, the IRS limits how large an annual auto expense you can claim for depreciation (see Chapter 11 for details about business deductions for cars).

The IRS gives you a choice of how to account for business automobile expenses. You can either expense a standard mileage charge (36 cents per mile for tax year 2003) or keep track of the actual operating expenses (such as gas, insurance, repairs, and so on), plus take depreciation costs.

With expensive cars, the mileage expense method will probably shortchange your deduction amounts for auto usage. Now you have another reason not to spend so much on a car! When you buy a reasonably priced car, you won't need to go through the headache of tracking your actual auto expenses (in addition to not wasting money), because the mileage expense method probably will lead to a larger deduction. Tracking mileage and using the mileage expense method is so much easier.

Auto dealers often push automobile leasing. For the auto dealers and salespeople in the showrooms, leases have the marketing appeal of offering buyers a monthly payment that's often lower than an auto loan payment — without the perceived noose around your neck of a large car loan. Don't be fooled. If you do your homework and hunt for a good deal on a car, buying with cash is the best way to go. Borrowing with an auto loan or leasing are much more expensive (leasing generally being the highest cost) choices and tempts car buyers to spend more than they can afford.

Travel, meal, and entertainment expenses

The IRS clamps down on writing off travel, meal, and entertainment expenses because some business owners and employees abused the policy by trying to write off nonbusiness expenses. Some books, seminars, and unscrupulous tax preparers have effectively encouraged this abuse. So, be honest — not only because it's the right thing to do, but also because the IRS looks long and hard at expenses claimed in these areas. Travel must be for a legitimate business purpose. If you take a week off to go to Bermuda, spend one day at a business convention, and then spend the rest of the time sightseeing, you may have a great time — but only a portion of your trip expenses may be deductible.

One exception exists: If you extend a business trip to stay over on a Saturday to qualify for a lower airfare — and you save money in total travel costs by extending your stay — you can claim the other extra costs incurred to stay over through Sunday. If your spouse or friend tags along, his or her costs most definitely are *not* deductible.

Only 50 percent of your business expenses for meals and entertainment are deductible. In addition, the IRS does not allow any deductions for club dues (such as health, business, airport, or social clubs), entertainment facilities (such as executive boxes at sports stadiums), apartments, and so on. Please see Chapter 11 for details.

Home alone or outside office space?

When you have a truly small business, you may have a choice between setting up an office in your home or getting outside office space. You may be surprised to hear us say that the financial and tax sides of the home office decision actually are not important — certainly not nearly as important as many business owners make them out to be. Why? First, the cost of office space you rent or purchase outside your home is an expense that you can deduct on your business tax return. If you own your home, you already get to claim the mortgage interest and property taxes as deductions on your personal tax return. So don't set up a home office thinking that you'll get all sorts of extra tax breaks. You'll qualify for some minor ones (such as deductions for utilities, repairs, and insurance) for the portion of your home devoted to business. Please see Chapter 11 for details.

The one extra home-based office deduction that you can take if you're a homeowner is depreciation. (See Chapter 24 to find out more about the other tips to avoid paying taxes on the profits from the sale of your home.)

If you don't need to move into a larger apartment or home to accommodate your business, then you may feel that your current home provides "free" office space. This situation may be true. However, if your home is larger than you need, you can move to a smaller, less expensive home!

Try as best you can to make your decision about your office space based on the needs of your business and your customers, along with your personal preferences. If you're a writer and you don't need fancy office space to meet with anyone (or to impress anyone), working at home may be just fine. If you operate a retail or service business that requires lots of customers to come to you, getting outside office space is probably the best choice for all involved — and the most legal way to go. Check with governing authorities in your town, city, and county to find out what regulations exist for home-based businesses in your area.

Independent contractors versus employees

If you want to give yourself a real bad headache, read the tax laws applying to the classification of people that a business hires as either employees or independent contractors. When a business hires an employee, the business is required to withhold federal and state taxes and then send those taxes to the appropriate taxing authorities. The government likes the employee arrangement better because independent contractors (as a group) tend to pay less in taxes by underreporting their incomes. Contractors are also entitled to take more business deductions than are allowed for regular employees.

When a business hires independent contractors to perform work, the contractors are responsible for paying all their own taxes. However, business owners now are required to file **Form 1099** with the IRS and some state tax agencies. On Form 1099, you report the amount of money paid to contractors who receive $600 or more from the business. This form enables the IRS to keep better tabs on contractors who may not be reporting all their incomes.

Unless a company offers benefits to an employee (insurance, retirement savings plans, and so on), a hired hand should prefer to be an independent contractor. Contractors have more leeway to deduct business expenses, including the deduction for a home office. Contractors can also tax-shelter a healthy percentage of their employment income in a self-employed retirement savings plan, such as a SEP-IRA or Keogh (see Chapter 21 for details on retirement accounts). However, one additional expense for contractors is their obligation to pay the full share of Social Security taxes (although they can then take half of these Social Security taxes as a tax deduction on their returns). An employer, by contrast, would pay half the Social Security and Medicare taxes on the employee's behalf.

So how do you, as the business owner, decide whether a worker is to be classified as a contractor or as an employee? Some cases are hard to determine, but the IRS has a set of guidelines to make most cases pretty clear-cut.

✔ The classic example of an independent contractor is a professional service provider, such as legal, tax, and financial advisors. These people are considered contractors because they generally train themselves and, when hired, figure out how they can accomplish the job without much direction or instruction from the employer. Contractors usually perform work for a number of other companies and people, and they typically hire any others they need to work with them.

✔ On the other hand, employees usually work for one employer and have set hours of work. For example, a full-time secretary hired by a business would be considered an employee because he or she takes instructions from the employer regarding when, where, and how to do the assigned work. Another indication of employee status is whether the secretary's presence at the work site is important for completing the assigned work.

What do you do if your situation falls between these two types, and you're perplexed about whether the person you're hiring is a contractor or an employee? Ask a tax advisor or contact the IRS for the handy-dandy **Form SS-8, Determination of Worker Status for Purposes of Federal Employment Taxes and Income Tax Withholding.** Complete the form, mail it in, and let the IRS make the call for you. That way, the IRS can't blame you — although you may rightfully feel that you're letting the fox guard the henhouse!

All in the family

When you hire family members to perform real work for fair wages, you may be able to reduce your tax bill. If your children under the age of 18 are paid for work performed, they're probably in a much lower tax bracket than you are. And, if they're working for you, the parent, they need not pay any Social Security tax like you do. You can even get your kids started on investing by taking some of their earnings and helping them to choose some investments or contribute some of their earnings to an Individual Retirement Account.

If you earn more than the family member you're paying does, your child/employee may be in a lower tax bracket. Thus, as a family, you may pay less in total income taxes. But you can't simply pay a family member for the sole purpose of reducing your family's taxes. The family member you're paying must be doing legitimate work for your business, and you must be paying a reasonable wage for the type of work being done.

If you earn more than the $87,000 cap (in 2003) for full Social Security taxes, hiring a family member who isn't your minor child may lead to more Social Security taxes being paid by your family. Why? When you earn more than $87,000, you don't pay Social Security taxes on the amount above $87,000. If you instead pay a family member for working in the business and that person is earning less than the $87,000 threshold, then, as a family, you'll end up paying more in total Social Security taxes. Although it's true that earning more helps you qualify for more Social Security benefits come retirement, given the future of the Social Security system, your family member will be lucky to get back all of what he or she is paying into the system.

Insurance and other benefits

A variety of insurance and related benefits are tax-deductible to corporations for all employees. These benefits include the following:

- ✔ Health insurance
- ✔ Disability insurance
- ✔ Term life insurance (up to $50,000 in benefits per employee)
- ✔ Dependent-care plans (up to $5,000 per employee may be put away on a tax-deductible basis for child care and/or care for elderly parents)
- ✔ Flexible spending or *cafeteria* plans, which allow employees to pick and choose the benefits on which to spend their benefit dollars

For businesses that are *not* incorporated, the business owner(s) can't deduct the cost of the preceding insurance plans for themselves — but they can deduct these costs for employees.

For tax year 2003, self-employed people can deduct 100 percent of their health insurance costs for themselves and their covered family members.

Retirement plans

Retirement plans are a terrific way for business owners and their employees to tax-shelter a healthy portion of their earnings. If you don't have employees, regularly contributing to one of these plans is usually a no-brainer. When you have employees, the decision is a bit more complicated but often is still a great idea. Self-employed people may contribute to Keoghs, Simplified Employee Pension Individual Retirement Accounts (SEP-IRAs), or SIMPLE plans. Small businesses with a number of employees also should consider 401(k) plans.

Recent tax law changes increase the amount of money that both small employers and employees can sock away in retirement plans. A new tax credit also helps small employers recoup some of the costs of establishing and maintaining a retirement plan. We discuss all these plans and the impact of the new tax rules in detail in Chapter 21.

To Incorporate or Not to Incorporate

Starting a business is hard enough. Between mustering up the courage and swinging it financially, many business owners meet their match trying to decide what should be a reasonably straightforward issue: whether to incorporate. Just about every book that addresses the subject (and just about every lawyer or accountant who advises business owners) steers clear of giving definitive answers.

In some instances, the decision to incorporate is complicated, but in most cases, it need not be a difficult choice. Taxes may be important to the decision but aren't the only consideration (Eric Tyson and Jim Schell's *Small Business For Dummies,* published by Wiley, Inc., offers additional information). This section presents an overview of the critical issues to consider.

Liability protection

The chief reason to consider incorporating your small business is for purposes of liability protection. Attorneys speak of the protection of the *corporate veil.* Don't confuse this veil with insurance (or with the veil a bride normally wears on her wedding day). You don't get any insurance when you incorporate — or when you get married! You may need or want to buy liability insurance instead of (or in addition to) incorporating. Liability protection doesn't insulate your company from being sued, either.

When you incorporate, the protection of the corporate veil provides you with the separation or division of your business assets and liabilities from your personal finances. Why would you want to do that? Suppose that your business is doing well and you take out a bank loan to expand. The next year, however, the government enacts a regulatory change that makes your services or product obsolete. Before you know it, your business is losing money and you're forced to close up shop. If you can't repay the bank loan because of your business failure, the bank shouldn't be able to go after your personal assets if you're incorporated, right?

Unfortunately, many small-business owners who need money find that bankers ask for personal guarantees, which negate part of the liability protection that comes with incorporation. Additionally, if you play financial games with your company (such as shifting money out of the company in preparation for defaulting on a loan), a bank may legally be able to go after your personal assets. So, you must adhere to a host of ground rules and protocols to prove to the IRS that you're running a bona fide company. For example, you need to keep corporate records and hold an annual meeting — even if it's just with yourself!

A business can be sued if it mistreats an employee or if its product or service causes harm to a customer. But the owner's personal assets should be protected when the business is incorporated and meets the other tests for being a legitimate business.

Before you call a lawyer or your state government offices to figure out how to incorporate, you need to know that incorporating takes time and costs money. So if incorporating doesn't offer enough benefits to outweigh the hassles and costs, don't do it. Likewise, if the only benefits of incorporating can be better accomplished through some other means (such as purchasing insurance), save your money and time and don't incorporate.

Liability insurance — a good alternative (if you can get it)

Before you incorporate, ask yourself (and perhaps others in your line of business or advisors who work with businesses like yours) what actions can cause you to be sued. Then see whether you can purchase insurance to protect against these potential liabilities. Insurance is superior to incorporation because it pays claims.

Suppose that you perform professional services but make a major mistake that costs someone a lot of money — or worse. Even if you're incorporated, if someone successfully sues you, your company may have to cough up the dough. This situation not only costs a great deal of money but also can sink your business. Only insurance can cover such financially destructive claims.

You can also be sued if someone slips and breaks a bone or two. To cover these types of claims, you can purchase a property or premises liability policy from an insurer.

Accountants, doctors, and a number of other professionals can buy liability insurance. A good place to start searching for liability insurance is through the associations that exist for your profession. Even if you aren't a current member, check out the associations anyway — you may be able to access any insurance they provide without membership, or you can join the association long enough to get signed up. Incorporating, however, doesn't necessarily preclude insuring yourself. Both incorporating and covering yourself with liability insurance may make sense in your case.

Corporate taxes

Corporations are taxed as entities separate from their individual owners. This situation can be both good and bad. Suppose that your business is doing well and making lots of money. If your business is not incorporated, all the profits from your business are taxed on your personal tax return in the year that those profits are earned.

If you intend to use these profits to reinvest in your business and expand, incorporating can potentially save you some tax dollars. When your business is incorporated (as a regular or so-called C Corporation), the first $75,000 of profits in the business should be taxed at a lower rate in the corporation than on your personal tax return (see Table 22-1). One exception to this rule is personal service corporations, such as accounting, legal, consulting, and medical firms, which pay a flat tax rate of 35 percent on their taxable incomes.

Table 22-1	2003 Corporate Tax Rates for Regular (C) Corporations
Taxable Income	*Tax Rate*
$0–$50,000	15%
$50,001–$75,000	25%
$75,001–$100,000	34%
$100,001–$335,000	39%
$335,001–$10,000,000	34%
$10,000,001–$15,000,000	35%
$15,000,001–$18,333,333	38%
Over $18,333,333	35%

Another possible tax advantage for a corporation is that corporations can pay — on a tax-deductible basis — for employee benefits such as health insurance, disability, and up to $50,000 of term life insurance. The owner usually is treated as an employee for benefits purposes. (Refer to the "Insurance and other benefits" section earlier in this chapter for details.) Sole proprietorships and other unincorporated businesses usually can only take tax deductions for these benefit expenses for employees. Benefit expenses for owners who work in the business aren't deductible, except for pension contributions and health insurance, which you can deduct on the front of **Form 1040.**

Resist the temptation to incorporate just so you can have your money left in the corporation, which may be taxed at a lower rate than you would pay on your personal income (see Chapter 1 for the personal income tax rates). Don't be motivated by this seemingly short-term gain. If you want to pay yourself the profits in the future, you can end up paying more taxes. Why? Because you pay taxes first at the corporate tax rate in the year your company earns the money, and then you pay taxes *again* on these same profits (this time on your personal income tax return) when you pay yourself from the corporate till in the form of a dividend.

Another reason not to incorporate (especially in the early days of a business) is that you can't immediately claim the losses for an incorporated business on your personal tax return. You have to wait until you can offset your losses against profits. Because most businesses produce little revenue in their early years and have all sorts of start-up expenditures, losses are common.

S Corporations

Subchapter *S Corporations,* so named for that part of the tax code that establishes them, offer some business owners the best of both worlds. You get the liability protection that comes with being incorporated, and the business profit or loss passes through to the owner's personal tax returns. So if the business shows a loss in some years, the owner may claim those losses in the current year of the loss on the tax returns. If you plan to take all the profits out of the company, an S Corporation may make sense for you.

The IRS allows most — but not all — small businesses to be S Corporations. To be an S Corporation in the eyes of the almighty IRS, a company must meet *all* the following requirements:

- ✔ Be a U.S. company
- ✔ Have just one class of stock
- ✔ Have no more than 75 shareholders (who are all U.S. residents or citizens and are not partnerships, other corporations, or, with certain exceptions, trusts)

Limited liability companies (LLCs)

Just in the past generation, a new type of corporation has appeared. Limited liability companies (LLCs) offer business owners benefits similar to those of S Corporations but are even better in some cases. Like an S Corporation, an LLC offers liability protection for the owners. LLCs also pass the business's profits through to the owners' personal income tax returns.

Limited liability companies have fewer restrictions regarding shareholders. For example, LLCs have no limits on the number of shareholders. The shareholders in an LLC can be foreigners, and corporations and partnerships also can be shareholders.

Compared with S Corporations, the only additional restriction LLCs carry is that sole proprietors and professionals can't always form LLCs (although Texas allows this). All states now permit the formation of LLCs, but most state laws require you to have at least two partners and not be a professional firm.

Other incorporation issues

Because corporations are legal entities distinct from their owners, corporations offer other features and benefits that a proprietorship or partnership doesn't. For example, corporations have shareholders who own a piece or percentage of the company. These shares can be sold or transferred to other owners, subject to any restrictions in the shareholders' agreement.

Corporations also offer *continuity of life,* which simply means that corporations can continue to exist despite the death of an owner — or the owner's transfer of his or her share (stock) in the company.

Don't incorporate for ego purposes. If you want to incorporate to impress friends, family, or business contacts, you need to know that few people would be impressed or even know that you're incorporated. Besides, if you operate as a sole proprietor, you can choose to operate under a different business name ("doing business as" or *d.b.a.*) without the cost — or the headache — of incorporating.

If you've weighed the pros and cons of incorporating and you're still on the fence, our advice is to keep it simple. Don't incorporate. Remember that after you incorporate, it takes time and money to unincorporate. Start off as a sole proprietorship and then take it from there. Wait until the benefits of incorporating for your particular case outweigh the costs and drawbacks of incorporating.

Where to get advice

If you're totally confused about whether to incorporate because your business is undergoing major financial changes, getting competent professional help is worth the money. The hard part is knowing where to turn, because it's a challenge to find one advisor who can put all the pieces of the puzzle together. And be aware that you may get wrong or biased advice.

Attorneys who specialize in advising small businesses can help explain the legal issues. Tax advisors who do a lot of work with business owners can help explain the tax considerations. If you find that you need two or more advisors to help make the decision, it may help to get them together in one room with you for a meeting — which may save you time and money.

Investing in Someone Else's Business

Putting money into your own business (or someone else's) can be a high-risk but potentially high-return investment. The best options are those you understand well. If you hear about a promising business opportunity from someone you know and trust, do your research and make your best judgment. The business may well be a terrific investment. But keep in mind that people are always willing to take more risk with other people's money than with their own — and that many well-intentioned people fail at their businesses.

A relatively new provision in the tax law applies a low 14 percent capital gains rate to profits realized from investments held for five or more years in new stock issued by small businesses (*small* being defined as businesses with gross assets of $50 million or less). With the maximum long-term federal capital gains rate now at 15 percent, this provision offers minor additional relief on small-business investments. So if you have a knack for identifying up-and-coming entrepreneurs, you may be able to make rewarding investments that aren't too taxing. (You may also be able to "roll over" without taxation your profits from one such small-business venture to another — see a good tax advisor for more details.)

Before investing in a project, ask to see a copy of the business plan. Talk to others (who aren't involved with the investment!) about the idea and learn from their comments and concerns. But don't forget that many a wise person has rained on the parade of what turned out to be a terrific business idea.

Avoid limited partnerships and other small-company investments pitched by brokers, financial planners, and the like. They want you to buy limited partnerships because they earn hefty commissions from the sales. If you want a convenient way to invest in businesses and earn tax breaks, buy some stock mutual funds inside a retirement account.

Buying or Selling a Business

When you're buying or selling an existing business, consider getting the help and advice of competent tax and legal advisors. As a buyer, good advisors can help you inspect the company you're buying and look for red flags in the financial statements. Advisors can also help structure the purchase to protect the business you're buying — and to gain maximum tax benefits. When you're a seller, your advisors can help you prepare your business for maximum sale value and minimize taxes from the sale price.

If your business is worth a lot, make sure to read Chapter 26 on estate planning, because hefty taxes may be owed upon your death if you don't structure things properly. Your heirs may be forced to sell your business to pay estate taxes!

For more information about successfully starting, buying, selling, and running a small business, check out the latest edition of *Small Business For Dummies,* by Eric Tyson and Jim Schell (Wiley, Inc.).

Chapter 23

Your Investments and Taxes

....

....

*W*hen you have money to invest or you're considering selling investments that you hold outside the tax-friendly confines of a retirement account, taxes should be an important factor in your decisions. But tax considerations alone should not dictate how and where you invest your money and when you sell. You also should weigh issues such as your desire (and the necessity) to take risks, your personal likes and dislikes, and the number of years you plan to hold on to the investment.

Note: This chapter focuses on tax issues relating to investments in mutual funds, stocks, bonds, and other securities. Other chapters in this part of the book cover tax matters for investing in real estate or small businesses, investing for your children's future, and protecting your assets from estate taxes.

Tax-Reducing Investment Techniques

Lots of folks invest their money in ways that increase their tax burdens. In many cases, they (and sometimes their advisors) don't consider the tax impact of their investment strategies.

For investments that you hold inside *tax-sheltered* retirement accounts such as IRAs and 401(k) plans (see Chapter 21), you don't need to worry about taxes. This money isn't generally taxed until you actually withdraw funds from the retirement account. Thus you should never invest money that's inside retirement accounts in other tax-favored investments, such as tax-free money market funds and tax-free bonds (discussed later in this chapter).

You are far more likely to make tax mistakes investing *outside* of retirement accounts. Consider the many types of distributions produced by nonretirement account investments that are subject to taxation:

✔ **Interest:** Bank accounts, for example, pay you interest that is fully taxable, generally at both the federal and state levels. Bonds (IOUs) issued by corporations also pay interest that is fully taxable. Bonds issued by the federal government, which are known as *Treasury bonds,* pay interest that is *federally* taxable.

✔ **Dividends:** Many companies distribute some of their profits to shareholders of *stock* (shares of company ownership) as dividends.

Thanks to the 2003 tax law changes, there are now significantly lower tax rates applied to stock dividends — just 5 percent for those in the federal 10 and 15 percent tax brackets, and only 15 percent for those in all higher tax brackets.

✔ **Capital gains:** The profit from the sale of an investment at a price higher than the purchase price is known as a *capital gain*. Capital gains generally are federally and state taxable. Lower tax rates apply to capital gains for investments held for the long-term (see the next section).

The following sections detail specific strategies for minimizing your taxes and maximizing your *after-tax returns* — that is, the return you actually get to keep after payment of required taxes.

Buy and hold for "long-term" capital gains

A *long-term* capital gain, which is the profit (sales proceeds minus purchase price) on a security that you own for more than 12 months, is taxed on a different tax-rate schedule. *Short-term* capital gains (securities held for one year or less) are taxed at your ordinary income tax rate.

Effective May 6, 2003, the maximum federal tax rate on long-term capital gains is 15 percent for holding periods of more than 12 months. For investors in the two lowest federal income tax brackets — 10 percent and 15 percent — the long-term capital gains tax is now just 5 percent for assets held more than 12 months.

When investing outside of retirement accounts, investors who frequently trade their investments (or who invest in mutual funds that do the same) should seriously reconsider these strategies and holdings. With longer-term capital gains being taxed at lower tax rates, trading that produces short-term gains (from investments held 12 months or less), which are taxed at ordinary income tax rates, penalizes higher bracket investors the most. The sane strategy of buying and holding not only minimizes your taxes but also reduces trading costs and the likelihood of being whipsawed by fluctuating investment values.

Why, you may wonder, do we have a set of capital gains' tax rates that are different from (lower than) the regular income tax rates presented in Chapter 1? In addition to the possibility that the IRS wants to make our tax lives more difficult, some logic lies behind the lower long-term capital gains tax rates. Some argue that this lower tax encourages investment for long-term growth. However, others complain that it's a tax break that primarily benefits the affluent.

When you buy and hold stocks and stock mutual funds outside of retirement accounts, you can now take advantage of two major tax breaks. As we discuss in this section, appreciation on investments held more than 12 months and then sold is taxed at the low capital gains tax rate. Stock dividends (not on real estate investment trusts) are also taxed at these same low tax rates — just 5 percent for those in the federal 10 and 15 percent tax brackets and 15 percent for everyone else.

Pay off high-interest debt

Many folks have credit card or other consumer debt, such as auto loans costing 8 percent, 9 percent, 10 percent, or more per year in interest. Paying off this debt with your savings is like putting your money in an investment with a guaranteed tax-free return that's equal to the interest rate you were paying on the debt. For example, if you have credit-card debt outstanding at a 15 percent interest rate, paying off that loan is the same as putting your money to work in an investment with a guaranteed 15 percent annual return. Because the interest on consumer debt is *not* tax-deductible, you actually need to earn *more* than 15 percent on your other investments to net 15 percent after paying taxes.

Should you change investment strategies with new tax laws?

Given the recent tax law changes that have reduced the tax rate on dividends (a lot) and capital gains (a little bit more), should you alter your investment strategy?

All things being equal, assets which have appreciation potential (like stocks) and which pay corporate dividends (stocks again) have been given a boost. "Anything which increases the after-tax return of stocks is good for the stock market," says Catharine Gordon, Principal with the Vanguard Group.

Your goals and willingness to take on risk should still drive your overall asset allocation. So, don't skew your asset allocation to dividend-paying stocks instead of income-producing bonds. The fundamental characteristics of stocks compared with bonds haven't been altered by these recent tax law changes. In the short-term, bonds tend to be less volatile than stocks, but in the long run, stocks generally produce higher returns.

You won't benefit from these lower long-term capital gains tax rates and stock dividends tax rates (now just 15 percent and only 5 percent for those in the 10 and 15 percent federal income tax brackets) for investments held inside retirement accounts. When investment earnings are withdrawn from all retirement accounts except Roth IRAs, those returns are taxed as ordinary income. (With a Roth IRA, qualified withdrawals are free of taxation.)

Despite the fact that some of the many tax benefits of retirement accounts have been negated by this new tax bill, an analysis by the investment firm T. Rowe Price shows that investors should still generally take advantage of funding retirement plans that provide for immediate tax reductions. "When taking into account the advantage of investing on a pre-tax basis in the tax-deferred account versus an after-tax basis in the taxable account, the tax-deferred account proves more advantageous, though its relative advantage compared with the taxable account is not as great as it would be under current law," says the T. Rowe Price report.

With regards to funding an annuity or other retirement account which are done on an after-tax basis, T. Rowe Price's analysis found that after factoring in taxes, it takes about 25 years for the non-deductible retirement account to be worth as much on an after-tax basis as an equally funded taxable account.

Christine Fahlund, Senior Financial Planner with T. Rowe Price, adds, "Don't change asset allocation because of these new laws, but you may want to change the location of where you hold some assets. For example, put taxable bond funds inside retirement accounts," because bond interest payments do not receive favorable tax treatment in a non-retirement account. "It may be better to hold dividend-paying stocks outside retirement accounts," says Fahlund, to take advantage of the low tax rate on stock dividends.

Tax rates and laws can and will change again. Don't develop long-term investing strategies based upon short-term tax law changes. Also, be sure to consider your individual situation and goals.

Still not convinced that paying off consumer debt is a great "investment"? Consider this: Banks and other lenders charge higher rates of interest for consumer debt than for debt on investments (such as real estate and businesses). Debt for investments is generally available at lower rates of interest and is tax-deductible. Consumer debt is hazardous to your long-term financial health (because you're borrowing against your future earnings), and it's more expensive.

In addition to ridding yourself of consumer debt, paying off your mortgage quicker may make sense, too. This financial move *isn't always* the best one because the interest rate on mortgage debt is lower than that on consumer debt and is usually tax-deductible (see Chapter 24).

Fund your retirement accounts

Make sure that you take advantage of opportunities to direct your employment earnings into retirement accounts. If you work for a company that offers a retirement savings plan such as a 401(k), try to fund it at the highest level that you can manage. When you earn self-employment income, look into SEP-IRAs and Keoghs. See Chapter 21 for all the details on retirement accounts.

You get three possible tax bonuses by investing more of your money in retirement accounts. First, your contributions to the retirement accounts come out of your pay before taxes are figured, which reduces your overall tax burden. Second, some employers provide matching contributions, which is free money to you. Third, the earnings on the investments inside the retirement accounts compound without taxation until withdrawal. Funding retirement accounts makes particular sense if you can allow the money to compound over many years (at least 10 years, preferably 15 to 20 years or more).

If you need to save money *outside* retirement accounts for short-term purposes such as buying a car or a home, by all means, don't do all your saving inside sometimes-difficult and costly-to-access retirement accounts. But if you accumulate money outside retirement accounts with no particular purpose in mind (other than that you like seeing the burgeoning balances), why not get some tax breaks by contributing to retirement accounts? Because your investments can produce taxable distributions, investing money outside retirement accounts requires greater thought and consideration. This is another reason to shelter more of your money in retirement accounts.

Use tax-free money market and bond funds

A common mistake many people make is not choosing a tax-appropriate investment given their tax bracket. Here are some guidelines for choosing the best type of investment based on your federal tax bracket (please note that the tax brackets referenced may look odd, but are correct because they were changed by the 2003 tax bill):

- ✔ **33 percent or higher federal tax bracket:** If you're in one of these high brackets, you definitely need to avoid investments that produce taxable income. For tax year 2003, the 33 percent federal bracket started at $143,500 for singles and $174,700 for married couples filing jointly.

- ✔ **25 or 28 percent federal tax bracket:** If you invest outside retirement accounts, in most cases, you should be as well or slightly better off in investments that do not produce taxable income. This may not be the case, however, if you're in tax-free money market and bond funds whose yields are depressed because of too high operating expenses.

- ✔ **10 or 15 percent federal tax bracket:** Investments that produce taxable income are generally just fine. You'll likely end up with *less* if you purchase investments that produce tax-free income, because these investments yield less than comparable taxable ones *even after* factoring in the taxes you pay on those taxable investments.

When you're investing your money, it isn't the return that your investment earns that matters; what matters is the return you actually get to keep after paying taxes. The following sections describe some of the best investment choices you can make to reduce your overall tax burden and maximize your after-tax return.

If you're in a high enough tax bracket (federal 33 percent or higher), you may come out ahead with tax-free investments. Tax-free investments yield less than comparable investments that produce taxable earnings. But the earnings from tax-free investments *can* end up being greater than what you're left with from taxable investments *after* paying required federal and state taxes. See the sidebar "Determining whether tax-free funds will pay more," later in this chapter, to find out how to compare the yields.

Tax-free *money market funds,* offered by mutual fund companies, can be a better alternative to bank savings accounts that pay interest (which is subject to taxation). The best money market funds pay higher yields and give you check-writing privileges. If you're in a high tax bracket, you can select a *tax-free* money market fund, which pays dividends that are free from federal and/or state tax. You can't get this feature with bank savings accounts.

Understanding mutual funds

Mutual funds are one of the best, if not the best, investment vehicles ever created. Why? Because good mutual funds take most of the hassle and cost out of figuring out which securities (stocks, bonds, and so on) to invest in. A mutual fund offers tremendous diversification because the fund managers typically invest in dozens of securities from companies in many different industries. Mutual funds allow you to have your money managed by the best money managers in the country — some of the same folks who manage money for the already rich and famous. And mutual funds can help you meet many different financial goals.

Mutual funds, which you can purchase from the comfort of your own living room Barcalounger, can pay you a better rate of return over the long haul than a dreary and boring bank or insurance company account. No-load (no-commission) funds can be bought directly from the mutual fund company without a broker (and therefore without sales commissions). Fund operating fees, which are deducted from your returns, are quite reasonable at the larger and more successful fund companies. You can purchase great funds that charge from 0.1 percent to 1.0 percent (annually) of the amount you have invested. That amount works out to just $2 to $10 per year per $1,000 you invest through the fund.

Mutual funds, like all investments, carry their own unique risks that you need to be aware of before you leave the seemingly safe havens of banks and insurers. For example, funds that invest in stocks and bonds fluctuate in value along with overall changes in the stock and bond markets. If you don't know good funds or how to put together and manage a fund portfolio that meets your needs, pick up a copy of the latest edition of *Mutual Funds For Dummies* by Eric Tyson (Wiley, Inc.).

Unlike bank savings accounts, the FDIC (Federal Deposit Insurance Corporation) doesn't insure money market mutual funds. For all intents and purposes, though, money market funds and bank accounts have equivalent safety. The lack of FDIC insurance should not concern you, because fund companies haven't failed. And in those rare instances when a money fund's investments have lost value, the parent company has infused capital to ensure no loss of principal on the investor's part.

Just as you can invest in a tax-free money market fund, so too can you invest in tax-free bonds via a tax-free *bond mutual fund*. These funds are suitable for higher tax bracket investors who want an investment that pays a better return than a money market fund without the risk of the stock market. Bond funds are intended as longer-term investments (although they offer daily liquidity, they do fluctuate in value).

 Companies offering competitive yields on tax-free money market funds and bond funds are Vanguard (800-662-7447; www.vanguard.com), USAA (800-382-8722; www.usaa.com), and Fidelity (800-343-3548; www.fidelity.com). Fidelity's Spartan series funds generally require higher minimums to open ($10,000 or more versus the other firms' $3,000).

Invest in tax-friendly stock mutual funds

All too often, when selecting investments, people mistakenly focus on past rates of return. We all know that the past is no guarantee for the future. But an even worse mistake is choosing an investment with a reportedly high rate of return without considering tax consequences. Numerous mutual funds effectively reduce their shareholders' returns because of their tendency to produce more taxable distributions (dividends and capital gains).

Historically, however, many mutual fund investors and publications have not compared the tax-friendliness of similar mutual funds. Just as you should avoid investing in funds with high sales commissions, high annual operating expenses, and poor relative performance, you should also avoid tax-unfriendly funds when investing outside of retirement accounts.

When comparing two similar funds, most people prefer a fund that averages returns of 14 percent per year instead of a fund earning 12 percent. But what if the 14 percent-per-year fund causes you to pay a lot more in taxes? What if, after factoring in taxes, the 14 percent-per-year fund nets just 9 percent, while the 12 percent-per-year fund nets an effective 10 percent return? In that case, you'd be unwise to choose a fund solely on the basis of the higher reported rate of return.

Capital gains + dividend distributions = more taxes!

All stock mutual fund managers buy and sell stocks during the course of a year. Whenever a mutual fund manager sells securities, any gain from those securities must be distributed, by year's end, to the fund shareholders. Securities sold at a loss can offset those liquidated at a profit. When a fund manager has a tendency to cash in more winners than losers, significant capital gains distributions can result.

Choosing mutual funds that minimize capital gains distributions, especially short-term capital gains distributions that are taxed at the higher ordinary income tax rates rather than the favored long-term capital gains rates we discuss earlier in this chapter, can help investors defer and minimize taxes on their profits. By allowing their capital to continue compounding, as it would in an IRA or other retirement account, fund shareholders receive a higher total return. (You can find the historic capital gains distribution information on a fund by examining its prospectus.)

Long-term investors benefit the most from choosing mutual funds that minimize capital gains distributions. The more years that appreciation can compound in a mutual fund without being taxed, the greater the value to the fund investor. When you invest in stock funds inside retirement accounts, you need not worry about capital gains distributions.

In addition to capital gains distributions, mutual funds produce *dividends* that are subject to normal income tax rates (except in the case of stock dividends which are taxed at the same low rates applied to long-term capital gains). Again, all things being equal, nonretirement account investors in high tax brackets should avoid funds that tend to pay a lot of dividends. You should hold such funds inside of tax-sheltered retirement accounts.

Timing of fund purchases affects tax bill

Investors who purchase mutual funds outside tax-sheltered retirement accounts should also consider the time of year they purchase shares in funds, so they can minimize the tax bite. Specifically, investors should try to purchase funds *after* rather than just before the fund makes the following types of distributions:

- **Capital gains distributions:** December is the most common month in which mutual funds make capital gains distributions. If making purchases late in the year, investors may want to find out whether and when the fund may make a significant capital gains distribution. Often, the unaware investor buys a mutual fund just prior to a distribution, only to see the value of the fund decline. But the investor must still pay income tax on the distribution. The December payout is generally larger when a fund has had a particularly good performance year and when the fund manager has done a lot of trading that year.

- **Dividend distributions:** Some stock funds that pay reasonably high dividends (perhaps because they also hold bonds) tend to pay out dividends quarterly — typically on a March, June, September, December cycle. Try to avoid buying shares of these funds just before they pay. Make purchases early in each calendar quarter (early in the months of January, April, July, and October). Remember that the share price of the fund is reduced by the amount of the dividend, and the dividend is taxable.

Don't get *too* concerned about when funds make distributions, because you can miss out on bigger profits by being so focused on avoiding a little bit of tax. If you want to be sure of the dates when a particular fund makes distributions, call the specific fund you have in mind.

Determining whether tax-free funds will pay more

If you're in the federal 33 percent tax bracket or higher, you will usually come out ahead in tax-free investments. Making the comparison properly means factoring in federal and state taxes. For example, suppose that you call a fund company and the representative tells you that the company's taxable money market fund currently yields 1.0 percent. The yield or dividend on this fund is fully taxable.

Further suppose that you're a resident of California — home to beautiful beaches and rumbling earthquakes — and that the same fund company's California money market fund currently yields 0.7 percent. The California tax-free money market fund pays dividends that are free from federal and California state tax. Thus you get to keep all 0.7 percent that you earn. The income you earn on the taxable fund, on the other hand, is taxed.

So here's how you compare the two:

Yield on tax-free fund ÷ yield on taxable fund

.007 (0.7%) ÷ .01 (1.0%) = 0.70

In other words, the tax-free funds pay a yield of 70 percent of the yield of the taxable fund. Thus, if you must pay more than 30 percent (1.0 − 0.70) in federal and California state tax, you net more in the tax-free fund (see Chapter 1 for details on how to determine your federal and state tax rate).

If you do this analysis comparing some funds today, be aware that yields do change. The difference in yields between tax-free and taxable funds widens and narrows a bit over time.

Understanding the tax virtues of index funds

Mutual fund managers of actively managed portfolios, in their attempts to increase their shareholders' returns, buy and sell individual securities more frequently. However, this trading increases the chances of a fund needing to make significant capital gains distributions. Index funds, by contrast, are mutual funds that invest in a relatively fixed portfolio of securities. They don't attempt to beat the market averages or indexes. Rather, they invest in the securities to mirror or match the performance of an underlying index.

Although index funds can't beat the market, they have the following advantages over actively managed funds:

- Because index funds trade much less often than actively managed funds, index fund investors benefit from lower brokerage fees.

- Because significant ongoing research need not be conducted to identify companies in which to invest, index funds can be run with far lower operating expenses. All factors being equal, lower brokerage and operating costs translate into higher shareholder returns.

- Because index funds trade less often, they tend to produce lower capital gains distributions. For mutual funds held outside of tax-sheltered retirement accounts, this reduced trading effectively increases an investor's total rate of return. Thus index mutual funds are tax-friendlier.

The Vanguard Group (800-662-7447; www.vanguard.com), headquartered in Valley Forge, PA, is the largest mutual fund provider of index funds.

Tax-Favored Investments to Avoid

Investment and insurance brokers and "financial planners" (who sell products, work on commission, and are therefore salespeople) love to pitch investment products that supposedly save you on your taxes. Salespeople generally don't examine your entire financial situation. Therefore, the salesperson may sell you an inappropriate or lousy investment that pays (the salesperson!) hefty commissions. The following sections discuss the main investments these commission-driven folks try to sell you — along with the reasons why you shouldn't buy them.

Limited partnerships

Avoid limited partnerships (LPs) sold through brokers and financial planners. They are fundamentally inferior investment vehicles. That's not to say that no one has ever made money on one, but they are burdened with high sales commissions and ongoing management fees that deplete your investment. You can do better elsewhere.

Limited partnerships invest in real estate and a variety of businesses, such as cable television and cellular phone companies. They pitch that you can get in on the ground floor of a new investment opportunity and make big money. They also usually tell you that while your investment is growing at 20 percent or more per year, you get handsome dividends of 8 percent or so each year. Sound too good to be true? It is.

Many of the yields on LPs have turned out to be bogus. In some cases, partnerships have propped up their yields by paying back investors' original investment (principal) — without clearly telling them, of course. The other LP hook is the supposed tax benefit. The few loopholes that did exist in the tax code for LPs have largely been closed. (Amazingly, some investment salespeople hoodwink investors into putting their retirement account money — which is already tax-sheltered — into LPs!) The other problems with LPs overwhelm any small tax advantage, anyway.

The investment salesperson who sells you this type of investment stands to earn a commission of up to 10 percent or more — so only 90 cents, or less, of your dollar actually gets invested. Each year, LPs typically siphon off another few percentage points for management fees and other expenses. Most partnerships have little or no incentive to control costs. In fact, the pressure is to charge *more* in fees to enrich the managing partners.

Unlike with a mutual fund (which you can sell if it isn't performing), with LPs you can't vote with your dollars. If the partnership is poorly run and expensive, you're stuck. LPs are *illiquid*. You can't get your money out until the partnership is liquidated, typically seven to ten years after you buy in.

The only thing *limited* about a limited partnership is its ability to make you money. If you want to buy investments that earn profits and have growth potential, stick with stocks (preferably using mutual funds), real estate, or your own business. For income as opposed to longer-term growth potential, invest in bonds.

Cash-value life insurance

Life insurance that combines life insurance protection with an account that has a cash value is usually known as *universal, whole,* or *variable life.* Life insurance should *not* be used as an investment, especially if you haven't reached the maximum allowable limit for contributing money to retirement accounts. Agents love to sell cash-value life insurance for the high commissions.

The cash value portion of such policies grows without taxation until withdrawn. However, if you want tax-deferred retirement savings, you should *first* take advantage of retirement savings plans, such as 401(k)s, 403(b)s, SEP-IRAs, and Keoghs, which give you an immediate tax deduction for your current contributions. These accounts also allow your investments to grow and compound without taxation until withdrawal.

TIP

Reinvesting and dollar-cost averaging tax issues

When you make small purchases in a particular nonretirement account investment over time, you increase your accounting complexity and tax-filing headaches. For example, if you buy shares in a mutual fund, you'll be asked if you want the dividends and capital gains paid out to you as cash or reinvested into buying more shares in the fund. Increasing numbers of individual companies allow you to reinvest dividends on individual stock holdings. These plans are known as dividend reinvestment plans, or DRIPs. Some discount brokers also offer this service for free for individual stocks.

If you're retired or need to live off your investment income, receiving cash payments probably works best. If you don't need the money, reinvesting dividends allows your money to continue compounding and growing in the investment. Although reinvesting complicates your tax situation, because you're buying shares at different times at different prices, the benefits should outweigh the hassles. (But please take note: You still must pay current taxes on reinvested distributions in nonretirement accounts.)

Another investing approach is dollar-cost averaging, which can also cause tax headaches when you sell investments held outside of retirement accounts. Dollar-cost averaging simply means that you're investing your money in equal chunks on a regular basis, such as once a month. For example, if you have $60,000 to invest, you can choose to invest $2,000 per month until it's all invested, which takes a few years. The money that awaits future investment isn't lying fallow. You keep it in a money-market-type account, where it earns a bit of interest while it waits its turn.

The attraction of dollar-cost averaging is that it enables you to ease a large chunk of money into riskier investments instead of jumping in all at once. The possible benefit is that if the price of the investment drops after some of your initial purchases, you can buy more later at a lower price. If you had put all your money at once into an investment and then the value dropped like a stone, you'd kick yourself for not waiting.

The flip side of dollar-cost averaging is that if your investment of choice appreciates in value, you may wish that you had invested your money faster. Another possible drawback of dollar-cost averaging is that you might get cold feet as you continue to invest money in an investment that's dropping in value. People who are attracted to dollar-cost averaging out of fear of buying before a price drop can become scared to continue boarding what may look like a "sinking ship."

Dollar-cost averaging is most valuable when the money you want to invest represents a large portion of your total assets, and you can stick to a schedule. It's best to make your contributions automatic so that you're less likely to be frightened off should prices begin falling after you start investing. If you aren't investing a lot of money, or the amount is a small portion of your total holdings, don't bother with dollar-cost averaging.

When you buy an investment via dollar-cost averaging or dividend reinvestment at many different times and prices, accounting is muddied as you sell portions of the investment. Which shares are you selling: the ones you bought at a higher price or the ones you bought at a lower price?

For record-keeping purposes, save your statements detailing all the purchases in your accounts. Most mutual fund companies, for example, provide year-end summary statements that show all transactions throughout the year. Be sure to keep these statements. For purchases made in recent years, and in the future, fund companies should also be able to tell you what your average cost per share is when you need to sell your shares.

Money paid into a cash-value life insurance policy gives you no upfront tax breaks. When you've exhausted contributing to tax-deductible retirement accounts, you may find that a nondeductible IRA and then, possibly, variable annuities can provide tax-deferred compounding of your investment dollars. Some company retirement plans also allow you to make nondeductible contributions, the benefit of which is that your investment earnings compound without taxation over the years. Recent tax law changes increased the contribution limits for Roth IRA accounts and introduces after-tax Roth contributions for some employer plans. Roth retirement accounts allow for tax-free compounding and tax-free withdrawal of investment earnings, something which cash value life policies don't do. See Chapter 21 for the details on retirement accounts.

The only real financial advantage cash-value life insurance offers is that, with proper planning, the proceeds paid to your beneficiaries can be free of estate taxes. You need to have a fairly substantial estate at the time of your death to benefit from this feature. And numerous other, more cost-effective methods exist to minimize your estate taxes (see Chapter 26 for more details on estate planning).

Load mutual funds and the like

Load simply means sales commission — up to 8.5 percent of your investment dollars are siphoned off to pay some broker a commission. Although mutual funds are good investment vehicles, you don't need to pay a sales commission or load — loads are additional and unnecessary costs that are deducted from your investment money. Load funds don't perform any better than no-load (commission-free) funds. Why should they? Commissions are paid to the salesperson, not to the fund manager.

Another problem with buying load funds is that you miss out on the opportunity to objectively assess whether you should buy a mutual fund at all. For example, maybe you should pay off debt or invest somewhere else. But salespeople almost never advise you to pay off your credit cards or mortgage, or to invest through your company's retirement plan instead of investing through them.

Salespeople who sell mutual funds usually push other stuff as well. Limited partnerships, life insurance, annuities, futures, and options hold the allure of big commissions. Salespeople often don't take the time to educate investors, tend to exaggerate the potential benefits, and obscure the risks and drawbacks of what they sell.

✔ In addition to load mutual funds, you may be pitched to buy a unit investment trust or *closed-end fund.* For the most part, these funds are similar to other mutual funds, and they also pay brokers' commissions.

✔ Beware of brokers and financial planners selling bogus no-load funds, which are actually load funds that simply hide the sales commission.

You may be told something along the line that — as long as you stay in a fund for five to seven years — you won't have to pay the back-end sales charge that would apply upon sale of the investment. This claim may be true, but it's also true that these funds pay investment salespeople hefty commissions. The brokers are able to receive this commission because the fund company charges you high ongoing operating expenses (usually 1 percent more per year than the best funds). So one way or another, these salespeople get their commissions from your investment dollars.

Invest in no-loads and avoid load funds and investment salespeople. The only way to be sure that a fund is truly no-load is to look at the fund's prospectus. Only in the prospectus, in black and white and without marketing hype, must the truth be told about sales charges and other fund fees. Never buy an investment without looking at its prospectus.

Annuities

Annuities are a peculiar type of insurance and investment product — sort of a savings-type account with slightly higher yields that are backed by insurance companies.

Insurance agents and financial planners working on commission happily sell annuities to many people with money to invest. The problem is, annuities are suitable investments for relatively few people. If annuities do make sense for you, you can buy no-load (commission-free) annuities by bypassing salespeople and dealing directly with mutual fund companies.

The major selling hook of annuities is the supposed tax savings. "Why pay taxes each year on your investment earnings?" the agent or financial planner will ask. As in other types of retirement accounts, money that's placed in an annuity compounds without taxation until withdrawal. However, unlike most other types of retirement accounts (discussed in Chapter 21) — 401(k)s, SEP-IRAs, and Keoghs — your contributions to an annuity give no upfront tax deductions. And, unlike Roth retirement accounts, you get no tax break upon withdrawal of your investment earnings from an annuity. The only annuity income tax benefit, as with cash-value life insurance, is that the earnings compound without taxation until withdrawal. Thus it makes sense to consider contributing to an annuity only after you fully fund your tax-deductible and Roth retirement accounts.

Because annuities carry higher annual expenses because of the insurance that comes with them, they generally make sense only if you have many years to allow the money to compound. So annuities are *not* appropriate if you're already in or near retirement. Also, the lower tax rate on long-term capital gains and stock dividends (which we discuss earlier in this chapter) makes investing money in annuities relatively less attractive than simply investing in tax-friendly nonretirement account holdings. All earnings on an annuity are taxed upon withdrawal at ordinary income tax rates, whereas with a nonretirement account investment, much of your profits could be deferred into lower taxed long-term capital gains and lower taxed stock dividends.

Selling Decisions

After you've owned a stock, bond, or mutual fund for a while, you may want to contemplate selling some or all of it. Taxes should factor into the decision when you consider selling investments that you hold outside tax-sheltered retirement accounts. For investments held inside retirement accounts, taxes aren't an issue because the accounts are sheltered from taxation (unless you're withdrawing funds from the accounts — see Chapter 21 for the details). In most cases, you need not waste your money or precious free time consulting a tax advisor. In the sections that follow, we outline issues for you to consider in your selling decisions.

Selling selected shares

Before we get into the specific types of investment decisions you're likely to confront, we must deal with a rather unpleasant but important issue: accounting methods for security sales. Although this stuff gets a little complicated, with some minimal advance planning, you can acquire sound methods to reduce your tax burden. If you sell *all* the shares of a security that you own, you can ignore this issue. Only if you sell a portion of your shares of a security should you consider *specifying* which shares you're selling.

Suppose that you own 200 shares of stock in Intergalactic Computer Software, and you plan to sell 100 shares. You bought 100 of these shares ten years ago at $50 per share, and then another 100 shares two years ago for $100 per share. Today, the stock is worth $150 per share. What a savvy investor you are!

So, which 100 shares should you sell? The IRS gives you a choice, from a tax-accounting standpoint. You can identify the *specific* shares that you sell. In the case of Intergalactic, you would opt to sell the last or most recent 100 shares you bought, which would minimize your tax bill — because these shares were purchased at a higher price. At the time you want to sell the shares through your brokerage account, identify the shares you want to sell by noting the original date of purchase and/or the cost of those shares. So in the case of your Intergalactic stock holdings, simply tell your broker that you want to sell the 100 shares that you bought two years ago (give the date) at $100 per share. (The broker should include this information on the confirmation slip you receive for the sale.) Please note that if these shares had been bought within the past year and you had a gain, you may not want to sell those shares, because the profit *wouldn't* be taxed at the lower long-term capital gains tax rate discussed earlier in this chapter.

The other method of determining *which* shares you're selling is the method the IRS forces you to use if you don't specify *before* the sale which shares are to be sold — the *first-in-first-out (FIFO) method*. FIFO is not a dog with a funny name; it is an accounting term that means that the first shares you sell are the first shares that you bought. Not surprisingly, because most stocks appreciate over time, the FIFO method leads to paying more tax sooner. In the case of Intergalactic, FIFO means that the first 100 shares sold are the first 100 shares that you bought (the ones you bought ten years ago at the bargain-basement price of $50 per share).

Although you'll save taxes today if you specify that you're selling the shares you bought most recently, don't forget (and the IRS won't let you) that when you finally sell the other shares, you'll then owe taxes on the *larger* profit you realize from those shares. The longer you hold these shares, the greater the likelihood that their value will rise, realizing a larger profit for you (although you end up paying more taxes). Of course, the risk always exists that the IRS will raise tax rates in the future or that your particular tax rate will rise. If you sell some of your investments, keep your life simple by considering selling all your shares of a specific security. That way, you don't have to hassle with all this accounting nonsense for tax purposes.

To be able to choose, or *specify*, which shares you're selling, you must select them *before* you sell. If you don't, the IRS says that you must use the FIFO method. You may wonder how the IRS knows whether you specified which shares before you sold them. The IRS doesn't know. But if you're audited, the IRS will ask for proof.

Selling securities with (large) capital gains

Of course, no one likes to pay taxes. But if an investment you own has appreciated in value, someday you will have to pay tax when you sell (unless you plan on passing the investment on to your heirs upon your death — see Chapter 26 on estate planning).

Capital gains tax applies when you sell a security at a higher price than you paid for it. As we explain earlier in this chapter, the long-term capital gains rate is lower than the tax rate you pay on ordinary income (such as from employment earnings or interest on bank savings accounts). Odds are, the longer you hold securities such as stocks, the greater the capital gains you'll accrue, because stocks tend to appreciate over time.

Suppose that your parents bought you 1,000 shares of XYZ company stock ten years ago, when it was selling for $10 a share (your folks probably didn't, but let's pretend). Today, it's selling for $20 per share; but you also vaguely recall that the stock split two-for-one a few years ago, so now you own 2,000 shares. Thus, if you sell XYZ stock for $40,000 today, you'd have a capital gain of $30,000 on which to pay taxes. So why would anyone want to sell?

The answer depends on your situation. For example, if you need the money for some other purpose — buying a home, taking a yearlong trip around the world — and the stock is your only source of funds, go for it. If you can't do what you want to do without selling, don't let the taxes stand in the way. Even if you pay state and federal taxes totaling some 25 percent of the profit, you'll have lots left over. Before you sell, however, do some rough figuring to make sure that you have enough to accomplish what you want.

What if you hold a number of stocks? To diversify and meet your other financial goals, all you need to do is prioritize. Give preference to selling your largest holdings (total market value) that have the smallest capital gains. If some of your securities have profits and some have losses, sell some of each to offset the profits with the losses. (Gains and losses on securities held one year or less are taxed at your ordinary income tax rates — see Chapter 12 for more details.)

Don't expect to obtain objective, disinterested, tax-wise advice regarding what to do with your current investments from a stockbroker or from most financial planners. If they earn commissions on the products they sell, their bias will be to tell you to sell. Even though some financial planners don't get commissions, they can charge fees on what they manage. When you seek objective help with these "sell versus hold" decisions, turn to a competent tax or financial advisor who works on an hourly basis.

Selling securities at a loss

Perhaps you own some turkeys in your portfolio. Should you desire to raise cash for some particular reason, you may consider selling some securities at a loss. Don't hold on to an investment just because its value now is less than what you paid for it. Waiting until its value rises to what you originally paid is a natural, but silly, human desire. Selling a loser now frees up your money for better investments. Losses can also be used to offset gains (investments sold at a profit) — as long as both offsetting securities were held for more than 12 months (long-term) or both were held for 12 months or less (short-term). The IRS makes this delineation because long-term gains and losses are taxed on a different rate schedule than short-term gains and losses.

Both short-term and long-term losses can be deducted against ordinary income, subject to limitations. If you want to sell securities at a loss, be advised that you can't claim more than $3,000 in short-term or long-term losses on your federal tax return in a given tax year. If you sell securities with losses totaling more than $3,000 in a year, the losses must be carried over to future tax years. This situation not only creates more tax paperwork, but also delays realizing the value of deducting a tax loss. So try not to have *net losses* (losses plus gains) exceeding $3,000 in a year.

Some tax advisors advocate doing *year-end tax-loss selling*. The logic goes that if you hold a security at a loss, you should sell it, take the tax write-off, and then buy it (or something similar) back. Sounds good in theory, but when you eventually sell the shares that you bought again at the lower price, you'll owe tax on the increased price anyway. (When you sell other stocks during the year at a profit, tax-loss selling to offset these taxable gains makes more sense.) But many people who sell an investment that has declined in value don't want to buy the same investment again. This reluctance can cause other investment blunders. For example, suppose you had the misfortune to buy some stocks back in 2000. In the next couple of years, your stocks plummeted about 30 percent or more, it wasn't because of your poor stock-picking ability. You simply got caught in the U.S. stock market downdraft. You'll make a bad situation worse by panicking and selling at reduced price levels just to take a tax loss. If anything, under such circumstances you should consider doing the opposite — take advantage of the sale and buy more!

If you do decide to sell for tax-loss purposes, be careful of the so-called *wash sale* rules. The IRS doesn't allow deduction of a loss for a security that you sell if you buy that same security back within 30 days. As long as you wait 31 or more days, no problem. When you're selling a mutual fund, you can easily sidestep this rule simply by purchasing a fund similar to the one you're selling.

When you own a security that has ceased trading and appears worthless (or even if you've made a loan that hasn't been repaid — even if to a friend), you can probably deduct this loss. See Chapter 12 for more information on what situations are deductible and how to claim these losses on your annual tax return.

Mutual funds and the average cost method

In America, you never have a shortage of choices — so why shouldn't it be the same with accounting methods? When you sell shares in a mutual fund, the IRS allows you an additional method — the *average cost method* — for determining your profit or loss for tax purposes. (This information doesn't apply to money market funds, which don't fluctuate in value.)

If you bought fund shares in chunks over time and/or reinvested the fund distributions (such as from dividends) into more shares of the fund, tracking and figuring what shares you're selling can be a real headache. So the IRS allows you to take an average cost for all the shares you bought over time.

Be aware that after you elect the average cost method, you can't change to another method for accounting for the sale of the remaining shares. If you plan to sell only some of your fund shares, and it would be advantageous for you to specify that you're selling the newer shares first, choose that method (as we describe in the "Selling selected shares" section earlier in this chapter).

Stock options and taxes

Some companies grant particular employees *stock options.* If you're the proud holder of this type of option, congratulations! You're either an important employee or work for a company that believes in sharing the success of its growth with its employees.

If you have statutory stock options, sometimes known as *incentive stock options,* you face a number of important decisions that can have significant tax consequences. Basically, stock options grant you the right to buy shares of stock from your employer at a predetermined price. For example, suppose that you take a job with Wal-Mart and the company tells you that, after December 31, 2002, you may "exercise the right" to purchase 1,000 shares of its stock at $50 per share.

In the years ahead, you and other Wal-Mart employees help the company to continue growing and expanding. Suppose Wal-Mart's stock price eventually rises to $75 per share in the next year. Thus, because your options enable you to buy Wal-Mart stock for $50 per share, and it's now at $75 per share, you have a profit on paper of $25,000 (1,000 shares ($25 profit per share)!

To realize this profit, you must first exercise your option (your company benefits department can tell you how). After you are the proud owner of the shares, you can sell them if you want to. However — and this is a big *however* — if you sell the shares within a year of having exercised the options, or within two years after the grant of the option (whichever is later), you will owe ordinary income tax on the profit. If you hold the shares for the required period of time, then you will pay the lowest possible long-term capital gains tax. (You may also be subject to the Alternative Minimum Tax, or AMT — see Chapter 8 to find out more about this tax.)

When you're a high-income earner, it's normally to your advantage to hold on to your exercised stock options for more than 12 months so that you qualify for the favorable capital gains tax treatment. The risk in waiting to sell is that your profits shrink as the stock price drops.

Nonstatutory stock options are a bit different type of option. Unlike incentive stock options, nonstatutory stock options are not given special tax treatment. With nonstatutory stock options, you must pay tax on the options either when you receive them (if you can determine their fair market value) or when you exercise them. You must also pay income tax on the difference between the fair market value of the stock at the time you exercise the option *minus* the value of the option on which you pay tax. After you exercise the option, the decision on when to sell (and the tax consequences) is the same as for incentive stock options. If you don't know which type of option your employer offers, ask the benefits department.

If you aren't a high-income earner, and waiting to sell offers no tax advantage, selling your shares as the shares become exercisable is usually prudent. When the stock market plunged in the early 2000s, a number of employees, especially in high tech companies, got clobbered with taxes on nonstatutory stock options on stock that they held onto that then plummeted in value. So the employees ended up being out a lot of dough in taxes and in some cases holding worthless or near worthless stock. We should also note that it's dangerous to have too much of your wealth tied up in the stock of your employer. Remember that your *job* is already on the line if the company's success wanes.

Selling securities whose costs are unknown

When you sell a security or a mutual fund that you've owned for a long time (or that your parents gave you), you may not know the security's original cost (also known as its *cost basis*). If you could only find the original account statement that shows the original purchase price and amount . . .

If you can't find that original statement, start by calling the firm through which you purchased the investment. Whether it's a brokerage firm or mutual fund company, it should be able to send you copies of old account statements. You may have to pay a small fee for this service. Also, increasing numbers of investment firms (particularly mutual fund companies) automatically calculate and report cost basis information on investments that you sell through them. The cost basis they calculate is generally the average cost for the shares that you purchased. See Chapter 3 for more ideas on what to do when original records aren't available.

Chapter 24

Real Estate and Taxes

● ●

In This Chapter

▶ Home ownership tax breaks

▶ Home-buying and mortgage decisions and taxes

▶ Strategies for keeping the IRS at bay when selling your house

▶ Tax considerations when investing in real estate

● ●

Tax benefits are a significant reason why many people, especially people in the real estate business — such as real estate agents, bankers, mortgage brokers, and others in the lending business — cheerlead for property ownership.

Buying a home or investing in real estate *can* provide financial and psychological rewards. And tax breaks can help reduce the cost of owning real estate. On the other hand, purchasing and maintaining property can be time-consuming, emotionally draining, and financially painful.

Don't make the mistake of looking at someone's property that's worth, say, $200,000 today (bought 30 years ago for $40,000) and assume that real estate investment, and the tax benefits it offers, is the inside track to wealth creation. Consider the expenditures the owner likely made over the years, such as fixing plumbing and electrical problems, updating appliances, replacing the roof, and repainting. And then consider the annual carrying costs — the interest alone over the life of the mortgage can total more than the original purchase price of the property! Of course, when you buy and sell real estate, you have transaction costs, such as a real estate agent's commissions, loan fees, and title insurance. Also, don't forget that $40,000 sounds cheap, but 30 years ago, when the cost of living was much lower, 40 grand bought so much more.

Don't get us wrong — we aren't saying that real estate isn't a good investment. Over the long term, real estate, like stocks, is generally a good investment. However, we don't want you to mistakenly assume that real estate is a better investment than it really is.

Real Estate Tax Breaks

Just as contributing money to retirement accounts (see Chapter 21) yields tax breaks, so does buying a home and investing in other real estate. Our tax system favors property ownership because of the widely held belief that owners take better care of their property when they have a financial stake in its future value. Arguing with this logic is difficult if you have visited almost any government-subsidized tenement.

All the powerful real estate lobbies also contribute to the addition and retention of real estate tax benefits in our tax code. Builders, contractors, real estate agents, the banking industry, and many other real estate–related sectors have an enormous financial stake in the American hunger to own and improve properties.

You should understand the tax aspects of owning a home and investing in other real estate so that you can make the most of these tax-reduction opportunities. Making wise real estate decisions also requires that you know how to fit real estate into your overall financial picture. After all, you have limited income and other options on which to spend your money.

Don't make the mistake of depending on those involved in the typical real estate deal to help you see the bigger picture. Remember that these folks make their livings off your decision to buy real estate, and the more you spend, the more they make.

We know that you can't wait to uncover the real estate tax breaks available for the taking. But before we get to them, we kindly ask that you never forget two important caveats to gaining these property tax advantages:

- ✔ You have to *spend* money on real estate — acquiring property, paying the mortgage and property taxes over the years, and improving the property while you own it — to even be eligible for the tax breaks. As we discuss in this chapter, if you're a high-income earner or make the wrong financial moves, you may not be able to claim some of the real estate tax benefits available.

- ✔ Always remember that you aren't the only one who knows that the U.S. tax code offers these real estate tax breaks. What difference does that make? Remember that the price of real estate in the United States reflects the fact that buyers and sellers know about the tax deductions. This is a major reason why so many people are willing to pay sums with many zeroes for a piece of the American Dream. Other countries that don't offer tax breaks for home ownership, such as Canada, have comparatively lower prices because buyers can't afford to pay higher prices when they can't bank on a tax deduction to help subsidize the cost.

The following sections offer an overview of the tax goodies available to United States homeowners. The benefits are similar to, but different from, the tax benefits for rental or income property owners, which we discuss later in this chapter.

Mortgage interest and property tax write-offs

When you buy a home, you can claim two big ongoing expenses of home ownership as tax deductions on Schedule A of Form 1040. These expenses are your property taxes and the interest on your mortgage.

You're allowed to claim mortgage-interest deductions on a primary residence (where you actually live) and on a second home for mortgage debt totaling $1,000,000. You're also allowed to deduct the interest on a home equity loan of up to $100,000 (see Chapter 9).

What if the politicians took away real estate tax breaks?

If the folks in Washington, who make and forever change our tax laws, yanked away the current tax goodies for real estate, the result would have a depressing effect on U.S. property values. There's not much argument about this outcome. By removing real estate's tax breaks, politicians would effectively raise the cost of property ownership.

In prior years, there's been a movement afoot for "tax reform." Some of the proposals on the table would have disallowed several of the tax deductions currently allowed for real estate. This is not the first time these ideas have been discussed, and it surely won't be the last.

But it's highly unlikely that politicians will take away home-ownership tax breaks and that we'll have major tax reform anytime soon. Property owners, who make up the majority of voters, would likely bounce the offenders out of office, and real estate lobbyists are a powerful force to reckon with.

Dealing with "excess" housing profits

Although the house-sale capital gains tax laws benefit many people, the rules do have a negative twist. If you live in an area with relatively inexpensive real estate, you may find this difficult to believe: Some longer-term homeowners, especially in the higher-cost sections of the country, may have profits in excess of the law's limits ($250,000 for singles and $500,000 for married couples filing jointly).

For those in that admittedly enviable position, the tax laws offer no escape hatch. At the time of sale, single homeowners with accumulated profits (which also include those profits rolled over, under the old tax laws, from previous sales) greater than $250,000 and couples with profits greater than $500,000 must pay capital gains tax on the excess.

When they start to bump up against the maximum amounts that can be shielded from capital gains taxation, long-term homeowners and those buying expensive homes may want to consider selling and moving, even if it's within the same neighborhood.

Those whose homes have appreciated well in excess of the limits may want to consider, if possible, holding their homes until their deaths, at which point, under current tax laws, the IRS wipes the capital gains slate clean (see Chapter 26).

Also keep in mind that although relatively few homeowners today have housing profits in excess of these seemingly high limits, the bounds are fixed and aren't scheduled to increase with inflation. Thus, in the years ahead, increasing numbers of homeowners will be affected by the limits. That's why you should heed our advice to keep receipts for your home improvements which allow you to increase your home's cost basis for tax purposes and thus reduce your potentially taxable capital gain. See the section, "Tracking your home expenditures," later in this chapter.

Property taxes also are fully deductible on Schedule A, whether you purchase a $15,000 one-room shack in an unpopulated rural area without electricity or a multimillion-dollar mansion overlooking the ocean.

Home office deductions

When you run your business out of your home, you may be able to take additional tax deductions beyond the mortgage interest and property taxes that you already claim as a homeowner. Please see the section "Home alone, or outside office space?" in Chapter 22 for a discussion of this issue.

Home ownership capital gains exclusion

Normally, when you make an investment in a stock or business, for example, and you later sell it for a profit (also known as a *capital gain*), you owe tax on the profit. Some real estate, however, receives special treatment in this regard.

The tax laws pertaining to the sale of a primary residence now allow for a significant amount of profit to be excluded from taxation: up to $250,000 for single taxpayers and up to $500,000 for married couples filing jointly. Moreover, to take advantage of this tax break — unlike under the old house-sale rules — house sellers need not be over a particular age or buy a replacement residence of equal or greater value to the one just sold.

So, if you're longing to move to a less-costly housing market, you're largely free of tax constraints to do so. This tax break also benefits empty nesters and others nearing or in retirement who want to buy a less-costly home and free up some of their home equity to use toward retirement.

House losses aren't deductible

Some homeowners have learned firsthand that real estate prices go down as well as up. If it's time for you to sell your house and move on, you may be disappointed to learn that you can't deduct the loss if your house sells for less than what you paid for it. If you lose money investing in the stock market, on the other hand, those losses are usually deductible (see Chapter 23). Although you may think it's unfair that home ownership losses are not tax-deductible, don't forget that you're already getting many tax perks from your home — the mortgage interest and property tax deductions.

Converting rental property to save on taxes

If you want to sell appreciated rental property, the new house-sale rules may benefit you as well. How? By moving into a rental property that you own, and making it your primary residence for at least two years, you can shield the profits from the sale of the property from taxation. (Obviously, this strategy is feasible only for certain types of properties that you would be willing or able to live in. Also, it doesn't apply to depreciation taken after May 7, 1997 — see Chapter 12.)

When you move from your house, rent it out for a period of time, and then sell it, the IRS may consider that you have converted your home from a primary residence to a rental property. Thus you may lose the privilege of excluding tax on the profit from the sale. The only exception: You actively tried to sell the house after you moved and only rented it temporarily to help defray the costs of keeping it until you sold it.

Purchasing Your Own Palace

Why you're thinking of buying a home doesn't really matter. This type of decision seldom is motivated by financial considerations alone. If your five-story walkup has lost its Bohemian appeal or you can't get the paint stains off the kitchen floor, heck, that's a good enough reason to buy a home.

Financially speaking, you really shouldn't buy your own place unless you anticipate being there for at least three years, and preferably five years or more. Many expenses accompany buying and selling a property, such as the cost of getting a mortgage (points, application and credit report fees, and appraisal fees), inspection expenses, moving costs, real estate agents' commissions, and title insurance. And remember, most of these expenses are *not* tax-deductible: (at best, they can only be added to your home's tax basis as we explain in the section, "Tracking your home expenditures" later in this chapter). To cover these transaction costs plus the additional costs of ownership, a property needs to appreciate a fair amount before you can be as well off financially as if you had continued renting. A property needs to appreciate about 15 percent just to offset these expenses, even factoring in the tax benefits that homeowners enjoy.

If you need or want to move in a couple of years, counting on that kind of appreciation is risky. If you're lucky (that is, if you happen to buy before a sharp upturn in housing prices), you may get it. Otherwise, you'll probably lose money on the deal.

Some people are willing to buy a home even when they don't expect to live in it for long because they plan on turning it into a rental when it's time to move on. Holding rental property can be a good long-term investment, but don't underestimate the responsibilities that come with rental property. (Rent the movie *Pacific Heights* and talk to friends and colleagues who've been landlords!)

Keep track of your tax bracket

When you first consider purchasing a home or purchasing a more expensive home, it usually pays to plan ahead and push as many so-called itemizable deductions as you can into the tax year in which you expect to buy your home.

For example, suppose that this year you're using the standard deduction because you don't have many itemized deductions. You decide late in the year that you expect to buy a home next year and therefore will have mortgage interest and property taxes to write off and you'll probably be able to itemize the next year. It makes sense, then, to collect as many deductible expenses as possible and shift them into next year. For example, if the solicitations surrounding the December holidays prompt you to contribute money to charities, you can wait until January to donate. Take a look at the deductible items on Schedule A (discussed in Chapter 9) to determine what else you may want to postpone paying.

Also, be aware that your income tax bracket may change from year to year. Thus, when possible, you can choose to pay more or less of some itemizable expenses in one year versus another. Suppose that you receive your annual property tax bill in the fall of the year, and it's payable in two installments. You must pay one installment before the end of the year, whereas you have until the next spring to pay the other installment. If for some reason you expect to be in a lower tax bracket next year — perhaps you're going to take a sabbatical and will earn less income — you may choose to pay the entire property tax bill before the current year ends. In this case, the property tax deduction has greater value to you in the current year because you're in a higher tax bracket.

Be sure to read Chapter 1, which explains how to figure your current and future expected tax bracket for planning purposes to minimize your taxes.

Exploring the tax savings in home ownership

To quickly estimate your monthly tax savings from home ownership, try this simple shortcut: Multiply your marginal federal tax rate (discussed in Chapter 1) by the total monthly amount of your property taxes and mortgage. (Technically, not all your mortgage payment is tax-deductible; only the portion of the mortgage payment that goes to interest is tax-deductible. However, in the early years of your mortgage, the portion that goes toward interest is nearly all of the payment. On the other hand, your property taxes will probably rise over time, and you can also earn state tax benefits from your deductible mortgage interest and property taxes.)

To figure out more precisely how home ownership may affect your tax situation, try plugging some reasonable numbers into your tax return to guesstimate how your taxes may change. You can also speak with a tax advisor.

When you buy a home, make sure to refigure how much you're paying in income taxes, because your mortgage interest and property tax deductions should help lower your income tax bills (federal and state). Many homebuyers skip this step and end up getting a big tax refund the next year. Although getting money back from the Internal Revenue Service (IRS) and state may feel good, it means that, at a minimum, you made an interest-free loan to the government. In the worst case, the reduced cash flow during the year may cause you to accumulate debt or miss out on contributing to tax-deductible retirement accounts. If you work for an employer, ask your payroll/benefits department for Form W-4 (see Chapter 15 for information about how to fill out this form). If you're self-employed, you can complete a worksheet that comes with Form 1040-ES (turn to Chapter 15 for help filling it out).

Deciding how much to spend on a home

When you fall in love with a home and buy it without looking at your monthly expenditures and long-term goals, you may end up with a home that dictates much of your future spending. Real estate agents and mortgage lenders are more than happy to tell you the maximum that you're qualified to borrow. They want your business, and the more money you spend, the more they make. But that doesn't mean that you should borrow the maximum.

Typical is the advice of this real estate broker who also happens to write about real estate:

> "The first step is to find out what price you can afford to buy. The easiest way to do this is to make an appointment with a loan agent or a mortgage broker."

Easy, yes. Will this get you the right answer? Probably not. Like real estate agents, mortgage brokers tell you the maximum loan you can qualify for. This amount is not necessarily what you can "afford." Remember, mortgage and loan agents get a commission based on the size of your loan. Taking into consideration your other financial goals and needs, such as saving for retirement, isn't part of their job description (nor generally their expertise).

In addition to analyzing your retirement planning, questions you should ask yourself before buying a home may include how much you spend (and want to continue spending) on fun stuff, such as travel and entertainment. If you want to continue your current lifestyle (and the expenditures inherent in it), be honest with yourself about how much you can really afford to spend as a homeowner.

Often, first-time homebuyers are apt to run into financial trouble because they don't know their spending needs and priorities and don't know how to budget for them. Buying a home can be a wise decision, but it also can be a huge burden. Some people don't decrease their spending as much as they should, based on the large amount of debt they incur in buying a home. In fact, many homeowners spend even more on all sorts of gadgets and furnishings for their homes. Many people prop up their spending habits with credit. For this reason, a surprisingly large percentage of people — some studies say about half — who borrow additional money against their home equity use the funds to pay other debts.

Don't let your home control your financial future. *Before* you buy property or agree to a particular mortgage, take stock of your overall financial health, especially in terms of retirement planning if you hope to retire by your mid-60s.

Renting's okay; you're okay if you rent

Don't believe that you aren't a success if you aren't a homeowner. And, as we discuss earlier in this chapter, don't feel pressured to buy a home just because of the tax breaks or because that's what nearly everyone else you know seems to be doing. Remember that the value of those tax breaks is reflected in higher U.S. home prices versus lower home prices in other countries where real estate owners don't receive such tax deductions.

Some financially successful long-term renters include people who pay low rent — because they've made sacrifices to live in a smaller rental, for example, or live in a rent-controlled building. One advantage of low rental costs is that you may be able to save more money. If you can consistently save 10 percent or more of your earnings, you will probably meet your future financial goals, house or no house.

Another advantage of being a long-term renter is that you won't have a great deal of money tied up in your home. Many homeowners enter their retirement years with a substantial portion of their wealth in their homes. As a renter, you can have all your money in financial assets that you can probably tap into far more easily.

Some renters are tempted to invest in a property elsewhere and rent it to others or use it when they want. This decision is neither straightforward nor simple. Make sure that you read the sections later in this chapter that discuss investment property and second homes.

Tracking your home expenditures

Although it may be a bit of a hassle, it's in your best interest to document and track money spent improving your property. For tax purposes, you can add the cost of these improvements to your original purchase price for the home. So, when you sell the property someday, you get to reduce your profit, for tax purposes, accordingly. Keep in mind that under the new tax laws, most people won't owe capital gains tax from the sale of a house. Single people can make a $250,000 profit, and married couples filing jointly can realize $500,000 in profit without paying tax on the proceeds of the sale. However, you still need to track your home improvement expenditures because it's impossible to know while you're living in your home if your future sale, which could be many years off, could trigger capital gains tax. Who knows how much real estate will appreciate in the interim or what changes could happen to the tax laws?

As we discuss later in this chapter, when you sell your house, you may need to report to the IRS, on **Schedule D, Capital Gains and Losses,** the selling price of the house, the original cost of the house, and how much you spent improving it. Therefore, we strongly advise setting up a simple file folder, perhaps labeled "Home Improvements," into which you deposit receipts for your expenditures.

The challenging part for most people is simply keeping the receipts organized in one place. Another challenge is correctly distinguishing between spending on *improvements,* which the IRS allows you to add to your cost of the home, and spending for *maintenance and repairs,* which you can't add to the original purchase price of the home.

Improvements include expenses such as installing an alarm system, adding or remodeling a room, planting new trees and shrubs in your yard, and purchasing new appliances. These improvements increase the value of your home and lengthen its life. Maintenance and repairs include expenses such as hiring a plumber to fix a leaky pipe, repainting, repairing a door so that it closes properly, and recaulking around your bathtub to prevent leaks.

It's interesting to note that if you hire a contractor to do home improvements, the IRS allows you to effectively add the cost of the contractor's time (the labor charges) into the overall improvements that reduce your home's profit for tax purposes. On the other hand, if you elect to do the work yourself, you gain no tax benefit for your sweat. You can't add a cost for the value of your time — the IRS assumes that your time isn't worth anything. You work for free! Now you have another reason for hiring someone to do the work for you.

Also, don't forget to toss into your receipt folder the *settlement statement,* which you should have received in the blizzard of paperwork you signed and received when you bought your home. Don't lose this valuable piece of paper, which itemizes many of the expenses associated with the purchase of your home. You can add many of these expenses to the original cost of the home and reduce your taxable profit when it comes time to sell. You also want to keep proof of other expenditures that the settlement statement may not document, such as inspection fees that you paid when buying your home.

Reporting revenue if you sometimes rent

The IRS allows you to rent your home or a room in your home for up to 14 days each year without having to declare the rental income and pay income taxes on it. Renting your home or a portion thereof for more than 14 days requires that you report the income when you file your annual tax return. You can declare real estate rental income by filing Schedule E. (Refer to Chapter 13 for more information.)

Tread carefully if you purchase a vacation home

Part of the allure of a second or vacation home is the supposed tax and financial benefits. Even when you qualify for some or all of them, tax benefits only partially reduce the cost of owning a property. We've seen more than a few cases in which the second home is such a cash drain that it prevents its owners from contributing to and taking advantage of other attractive investments, including tax-deductible retirement savings plans.

If you can realistically afford the additional costs of a second home, we aren't going to tell you how to spend your extra cash. But please don't make the all-too-common mistake of viewing a second home as an investment. The way most people use them, they aren't.

Investment real estate is property that you rent out. Most homeowners with second homes rent out their other property very little — 10 percent or less of the time. As a result, second homes usually are money pits.

If you don't rent out a second home property most of the time, ask yourself whether you can afford such a luxury. Can you accomplish your other financial goals — saving for retirement, paying for your primary residence, and so on — with this added expense? Keeping a second home is more of a consumption decision than an investment, if you don't rent it out. Most people can't afford such an extravagance.

Also, be aware that if your vacation home appreciates in value, the IRS doesn't allow you to sell this type of home without taxation of your capital gains the way it does with primary residences (see the discussion earlier in this chapter).

Making Tax-Wise Mortgage Decisions

The largest expense of property ownership is almost always the monthly mortgage payment. In the earlier years of a mortgage, the bulk of the mortgage payment covers interest that generally is tax-deductible. In this section, we discuss how to factor taxes and your financial circumstances into making intelligent mortgage decisions.

15-year or 30-year mortgage?

Unfortunately, you have thousands of mortgage options to choose from. Fixed-rate and variable-rate mortgages come with all sorts of bells and whistles. The number of permutations is mind-numbing.

From a tax perspective, one of the most important mortgage selection issues is whether to take a 15-year or 30-year mortgage. To afford the monthly payments, most homebuyers need to spread the loan payments over a longer period of time, and a 30-year mortgage is the only option. A 15-year mortgage requires higher monthly payments because you pay it off more quickly.

Even if you can afford these higher payments, taking the 15-year option may not be wise. The money for making extra payments doesn't come out of thin air. You may have better uses for your excess funds. What you're really asking, if you're considering whether you should take a 30-year or a 15-year mortgage, is whether you should pay off your mortgage slowly or quickly. The answer isn't as simple as some people think.

First, think about *alternative uses* for the extra money you're throwing into the mortgage payments. What's best for you depends on your overall financial situation and what else you can do with the money. When you elect the slow, 30-year mortgage payoff approach and you end up blowing the extra money on a new car, for example, you're better off paying down the mortgage more quickly. In that case, take the 15-year version. (If you want to buy a car in the future, saving in a money market fund so that you don't need to take out a high-cost car loan makes sound financial sense.)

But suppose that you aren't so frivolous with your extra money, and instead, you take the extra $100 or $200 per month and contribute it to a retirement account. That step may make financial sense. Why? Because additions to 401(k)s, SEP-IRAs, Keoghs, and other types of retirement accounts generally are tax-deductible (see Chapter 21).

When you dump that $200 into a retirement account, you get to subtract it from the income on which you pay taxes. If you're paying 35 percent in federal and state income taxes, you shave $70 (that's $200 multiplied by 35 percent) off your tax bill. (You're going to pay taxes when you withdraw the money from the retirement account someday, but in the meantime, the money that would have gone to taxes is growing on your behalf.) You get no tax benefits from that $200 when added to your mortgage payment when you elect a faster payoff mortgage (15-year mortgage).

With kids, you have an even greater reason to fund your retirement accounts before you consider paying down your mortgage faster. Under current rules for determining financial aid for college expenses, money in your retirement accounts is not counted as an asset (see Chapter 25) that you must use towards college costs.

If you're uncomfortable investing and would otherwise leave the extra money sitting in a money market fund or savings account — or worse, if you would spend it — you're better off paying down the mortgage. Take the 15-year approach. If the investments in your retirement account plummet in value, the impact of the tax-deferred compounding of your capital may be negated. Paying off your mortgage quicker, on the other hand, is just like investing your money in a sure thing — but with a modest rate of return.

In most cases, you get to deduct your mortgage interest on your tax return. So if you're paying 7 percent interest, it really may cost you only around 4 percent to 5 percent after you factor in the tax benefits. If you think that you can do better by investing elsewhere, go for it. Remember, though, that you owe income tax from profits on your investments held outside of retirement accounts. You aren't going to get decent investment returns unless you're willing to take risks. Investments such as stocks and real estate have generated better returns over the long haul. These investments carry risks, though, and are not guaranteed to produce any return.

When you *don't* have a burning investment option, it's usually wise to pay down your mortgage as your cash flow allows. If you have extra cash and have contributed the maximum allowed for retirement accounts, you may want to invest in real estate or perhaps a business. You have to decide if it's worth the extra risk in making a particular investment rather than paying down your mortgage.

How large a down payment?

What if you're in the enviable and fortunate position of having so much money that you can afford to put down more than a 20 percent down payment (which generally is the amount needed to qualify for better mortgage terms including not having to take out private mortgage insurance)? Perhaps you're one of those wise people who don't want to get stretched too thin financially, and you're buying a less expensive home than you can afford. How much should you put down?

Some people, particularly those in the real estate business (and even some tax and financial advisors), say that you should take as large a mortgage as you can for the tax deductions — that is, don't make a larger down payment than you have to. This is silly reasoning. Remember that you have to pay out money in interest charges to get the tax deductions.

Again, what makes sense for you depends on your alternative uses for the money. When you're considering other investment opportunities, determine whether you can reasonably expect to earn a higher rate of return than the interest rate you'll pay on the mortgage.

In the past century, stock market and real estate investors have enjoyed average annual returns of around 10 percent per year (just remember, the past doesn't guarantee the future). So if you borrow mortgage money at around 7 percent today, you may come out ahead by investing in these areas. Besides possibly generating a higher rate of return, other real estate and stock investing can help you diversify your investments.

Of course, you have no guarantee that you can earn 10 percent each year. And don't forget that all investments come with risk. The advantage of putting more money down for a home and borrowing less is that paying down a mortgage is essentially a risk-free investment (as long as you have emergency money you can tap).

If you prefer to limit the down payment to 20 percent and invest more elsewhere, that's fine. Just don't keep the extra money (beyond an emergency reserve) under the mattress, in a savings account, or in bonds that provide returns lower than the mortgage is costing you.

Refinancing decisions and taxes

When your mortgage has a higher rate of interest than loans currently available, you may save money by refinancing. To save money by refinancing a mortgage, you have to spend money and time. So you need to crunch a few numbers and factor in taxes to determine whether refinancing makes sense for you.

Because refinancing almost always costs money, determining whether you can save enough to justify the cost can be a bit of a gamble. Ask your mortgage lender or broker how soon you can recoup the refinancing costs, such as appraisal expenses, loan fees and points, title insurance, and so on.

For example, if completing the refinance costs you $2,000 and reduces your monthly payment by $100, the lender or broker typically says that you can save back the refinance costs in 20 months. This estimate isn't accurate, however, because you lose some tax write-offs when your mortgage interest rate and payments are reduced. You can't simply look at the reduced amount of your monthly payment (mortgage lenders like to look at that reduction, however, because lowering your payments makes refinancing more attractive).

To get a better estimate without spending hours crunching numbers, take your marginal tax rate as specified in Chapter 1 (for example, 28 percent) and reduce your monthly payment savings on the refinance by this amount. For example, if your monthly payment drops by $100, you really save only around $72 a month after factoring in the lost tax benefits. So you recoup the refinance costs in 28 months ($2,000 of refinance costs divided by $72) — not 20 months.

If you can recover the costs of the refinance within a few years or less, go for it. If it takes longer, refinancing may still make sense if you anticipate keeping the property and mortgage that long. If you estimate that you need more than five to seven years to break even, refinancing probably is too risky to justify the costs and hassles.

When you refinance, don't forget to adjust the amount of tax you pay during the year. See the section "Exploring the tax savings in home ownership," earlier in this chapter, for more information on how to change your tax withholding.

Besides getting a lower-interest-rate loan, another reason people refinance is to pull out cash from the house for some other purpose. This strategy can make good financial sense, because under most circumstances, mortgage interest is tax-deductible. If you're starting a business or buying other real estate, you can usually borrow against your home at a lower cost than on a business or rental property loan. (If you are a high-income earner, you may lose some of the tax deductibility of your home mortgage interest deductions — refer to the explanation of the limitations on itemized deductions in Chapter 9.)

If you've run up high-interest consumer debt, you may be able to refinance your mortgage and pull out extra cash to pay off your credit cards, auto loans, or other costly credit lines, thus saving yourself money. You usually can borrow at a lower interest rate for a mortgage and get a tax deduction as a bonus, which lowers the effective borrowing cost further. Interest on consumer debt, such as auto loans and credit cards, is not tax-deductible.

Borrowing against the equity in your home can be addictive. An appreciating home creates the illusion that excess spending isn't really costing you. Remember that debt is debt, and you have to repay all borrowed money. In the long run, you wind up with greater mortgage debt, and paying it off takes a bigger bite out of your monthly income. Refinancing and establishing home-equity lines also costs you more in loan application fees and other charges (points, appraisals, credit reports, and so on). For more information and analysis of important mortgage decisions, pick up a copy of *Mortgages For Dummies* by Eric Tyson and Ray Brown (Wiley, Inc.).

Selling Your House

As discussed earlier in this chapter, a homeowner can realize large profits (capital gains) when selling his house. **Schedule D, Capital Gains and Losses,** is filed only when gains exceed the $250,000/$500,000 threshold. You file Schedule D with Form 1040 from the same tax year in which you sell your house.

Form 1099-S must be filed to report the sale or exchange of real estate unless the sale price is $250,000 or less ($500,000 or less for married couples) *and* all the sellers provide written certification that the full gain on the sale is excludable from the sellers' gross income. Neither you nor the IRS receives Form 1099-S from the firm handling the sale of your house unless the gross sale price exceeds $500,000 for married couples or $250,000 for an unmarried seller.

The following sections talk about some common concerns affecting house sales that have important tax angles.

Not wanting to sell at a loss

Many homeowners are tempted to hold on to their properties when they need to move if the real estate market is soft or the property has a lower value than when they bought it, especially because the loss isn't tax-deductible. We don't recommend this strategy. It probably isn't worth the hassle of renting out your property or the financial gamble to hold on to the property.

You may reason that in a few years, the real estate storm clouds will clear and you can sell your property at a higher price. Here are three risks associated with this way of thinking:

✔ You can't know what's going to happen to property prices in the next few years. They may rebound, but they also can stay the same or drop even further. *A property generally needs to appreciate at least a few percentage points each year just to make up for all the costs of holding and maintaining it.* So you're losing more money each year that you hold the property and it doesn't appreciate at least a few percent in value.

✔ If you haven't been a landlord, don't underestimate the hassle and headaches associated with the job. Being a long-distance landlord is even more of a challenge. You can always hire someone to manage your property, but that approach creates costs, too — usually about 6 percent of the monthly rental income.

✔ After you convert your home into a rental property, you need to pay capital gains tax on your profit when you sell (the only exception is if you temporarily rent your home while you're still actively trying to sell it). This tax wipes out much of the advantage of having held on to the property until prices recovered. If your desire is to become a long-term rental property owner, you can, under current tax laws, do a *tax-free exchange* into another rental property after you sell (we discuss this topic in the section, "Rollover of capital gains on rental or business real estate" later in this chapter).

We understand that selling a house that hasn't made you any money isn't much fun. But too many homeowners make a bad situation worse by holding on to their homes for the wrong reasons after they move. No one wants to believe that they're losing money. But remember, the money is already lost. Many people who hold on rub salt into their real estate wounds. If and when the value of the property you're waiting to sell finally increases, odds are that other properties you'd next buy also will have increased. Unless you have sufficient money for the down payment to buy your next home, or you want to keep such a property as a long-term investment, holding on to a home you move from usually is not wise.

Converting a home into rental property

One advantage to keeping your current home as an investment property after you move is that you already own it. Locating and buying a property takes time and money. Also, you know what you have with your current home. When you go out and purchase a different property to rent, you're starting from scratch.

One of the tax benefits of rental real estate is the depreciation deduction. As your property ages, the IRS allows you to write off or deduct from your rental income for the "wearing out" of the building. Although this deduction helps reduce your income taxes, be aware that you may not be able to deduct as much for depreciation expenses when you convert your home to rental property as you can on a rental bought separately. If your home has appreciated since you bought it, the IRS forces you to use your original (lower) purchase price for purposes of calculating depreciation. To make tax matters worse, if your home has declined in value since you originally purchased it, you must use this lower value, at the time you convert the property, for purposes of depreciation.

Don't consider converting your home into a rental when you move unless this decision really is a long-term proposition. As we discuss in the preceding section, selling rental property has tax consequences.

If the idea of keeping the home you move from as a long-term investment appeals to you, take stock of your overall financial situation *before* you make the final call. Can you afford to purchase your next home given the money that's still tied up in the home you're considering keeping as a rental? Can you afford to contribute to tax-deductible retirement plans, or will the burden of carrying two properties use up too much of your cash flow? Will your overall investments be well diversified, or will you have too much of your money tied up in real estate (perhaps in one area of the country)?

House sales, taxes, and divorce

A divorce complicates many personal and financial issues. Real estate is no different. In the past, if ownership of a home that had appreciated in value were transferred between spouses because of a divorce, capital gains tax was owed. This is no longer one of the additional costs of divorce. Transfers of property between spouses aren't taxed if the transfers are made within one year of divorce (and both spouses are U.S. residents or citizens).

If you're selling your house because of a divorce, when you sell the house can have significant tax ramifications. If you agree to sell the house in the divorce settlement, each of you can make up to $250,000 in profit before any tax is levied.

Investing in Real Estate

For most people, the only real estate they own or consider owning is the home in which they live. If that's all you desire, we aren't going to push you into the business of investing in and managing rental property. It's a great deal of work, and other investments are certainly available, such as mutual funds (that own stocks), that are far more convenient and just as profitable.

But some people just have that itch to own something tangible. Real estate is, well, *real*, after all. You can fix it up, take pictures of it, and drive your friends by it!

Deciding whether real estate investing is for you

Whether you should invest in real estate versus other investments, such as stocks, bonds, or mutual funds, depends on many factors. The first and most important question to ask yourself is whether you're cut out to handle the responsibilities that come with being a landlord. Real estate is a time-intensive investment — it isn't for couch potatoes. Investing in stocks can be time-intensive as well, but it doesn't have to be if you use professionally managed mutual funds. Conversely, you can hire a property manager with real estate experience to reduce your workload. But the time required to own and oversee rental property can still be significant.

Good versus bad real estate investments

You can invest in real estate in a number of ways. The traditional and best method is to purchase property in an area that you've researched and are familiar with. Single-family homes and multi-unit buildings generally work best for most investors. Make sure that you do your "due diligence." Have the property professionally inspected and secure adequate insurance coverage.

If you want a stake in real estate but don't want the responsibilities and hassles that come with being a landlord, consider real estate investment trusts (REITs). REITs offer the benefits of property ownership without the headaches of being a landlord. REITs are a collection of real estate properties, such as shopping centers, apartments, and other rental buildings. REITs trade as securities on the major stock exchanges and can be bought through mutual funds such as Vanguard REIT Index, Fidelity Real Estate, and Cohen & Steers Realty Shares.

Be careful, though; some real estate investments rarely make sense because they're near-certain money losers. Many investors get sucked into these lousy investments because of the supposed high-expected returns and tax breaks. Limited partnerships, for example, which are sold through stockbrokers and financial planners who work on commission, are burdened by high sales commissions, ongoing management fees, and illiquidity (see Chapter 23).

Time-shares are another nearly certain money loser. With a time-share, you buy a week or two of ownership, or usage, of a particular unit, usually a condominium in a resort location. If you pay $8,000 for a week (in addition to ongoing maintenance fees), you're paying the equivalent of more than $400,000 for the whole unit year-round, but a comparable unit may sell for only $150,000. All that extra markup pays the salespeople's commissions, administrative expenses, and profits for the time-share development company.

An often-overlooked drawback to investing in real estate is that you earn no tax benefits while you're accumulating your down payment. Rental property also is usually a cash drain in the early years of ownership. Retirement accounts, on the other hand, such as 401(k)s, SEP-IRAs, Keoghs, and so on (discussed in Chapter 21), give you immediate tax deductions as you contribute money to them. Although real estate offers many tax deductions, as we discuss earlier in the chapter, the cost of real estate reflects the expected tax breaks. So don't invest in real estate because of the tax deductions. Exhaust contributing to retirement accounts before considering property as an investment.

A final consideration with regard to whether real estate investing is for you: Do you have a solid understanding of real estate and how to improve its value?

Enjoying rental property tax breaks

When you purchase property and rent it out, you're essentially running a business. You take in revenue — namely rent from your tenants — and incur expenses from the property. You hope that, over time, your revenue exceeds your expenses so that your real estate investment produces a profit (cash flow, in real estate lingo) for all the money and time you've sunk into it. You also hope that the market value of your investment property appreciates over time. The IRS helps you make a buck or two through a number of tax benefits. The major benefits follow.

Operating-expense write-offs

In addition to the deductions allowed for mortgage interest and property taxes, just as on a home in which you live, you can deduct on your tax return a variety of other expenses for rental property. Almost all these deductions come from money that you spend on the property, such as money for insurance, maintenance, repairs, and food for the Doberman you keep around to intimidate those tenants whose rent checks always are "in the mail."

But one expense — depreciation — doesn't involve your spending money. Depreciation is an accounting deduction that the IRS allows you to take for the overall wear and tear on your building. The idea behind this deduction is that, over time, your building will deteriorate and need upgrading, rebuilding, and so on. The IRS tables now say that for residential property, you can depreciate over 27½ years, and for nonresidential property, 39 years. Only the portion of a property's value that is attributable to the building(s) — and not the land — can be depreciated.

For example, suppose that you bought a residential rental property for $300,000 and the land is deemed to be worth $100,000. Thus the building is worth $200,000. If you can depreciate your $200,000 building over 27½ years, that works out to a $7,272 annual depreciation deduction.

If your rental property shows a loss for the year (when you figure your property's income and expenses), you may be able to deduct this loss on your tax return. If your adjusted gross income (as defined in Chapter 7) is less than $100,000 and you actively participate in managing the property, you're allowed to deduct your losses on operating rental real estate — up to $25,000 per year. Limited partnerships and properties in which you own less than 10 percent are excluded. (See Chapter 13 for details.)

To deduct a loss on your tax return, you must *actively participate* in the management of the property. This rule doesn't necessarily mean that you perform the day-to-day management of the property. In fact, you can hire a property manager and still actively participate by doing such simple things as approving the terms of the lease contracts, tenants, and expenditures for maintenance and improvements on the building.

If you make more than $100,000 per year, you start to lose these write-offs. At an income of $150,000 or more, you can't deduct rental real estate losses from your other income. People in the real estate business (for example, agents and developers) who work more than 750 hours per year in the industry may not be subject to these rules. (Refer to Chapter 13 for more information.)

You start to lose the deductibility of rental property losses above the $100,000 limit, whether you're single or married filing jointly. You can carry the loss forward to future tax years and take the loss then, if eligible. This policy is a bit unfair to couples, because it's easier for them to break $100,000 with two incomes than for a single person with one income. Sorry — this is yet another part of the marriage tax penalties!

Rollover of capital gains on rental or business real estate

Suppose that you purchase a rental property and nurture it over the years. You find good tenants and keep the building repaired and looking sharp. You may just find that all that work pays off — the property may someday be worth much more than you originally paid for it.

However, if you simply sell the property, you owe taxes on your gain or profit. Even worse is the way the government defines your gain. If you bought the property for $100,000 and sell it for $150,000, you not only owe tax on that difference, but you also owe tax on an additional amount, depending on the property's depreciation. The amount of depreciation that you deducted on your tax returns reduces the original $100,000 purchase price, making the taxable difference that much larger. For example, if you deducted $25,000 for depreciation over the years that you owned the property, you owe tax on the difference between the sale price of $150,000 and $75,000 ($100,000 purchase price minus $25,000 depreciation).

All this tax may just motivate you to hold on to your property. But you can avoid paying tax on your profit when you sell a rental property by "exchanging" it for a similar or *like-kind property,* thereby rolling over your gain. The section of the tax code that allows rollovers is a 1031 exchange. (You may not receive the proceeds — they must go into an escrow account.) The rules, however, are different for rolling over profits (called *1031 exchanges,* for the section of the tax code that allows them) from the sale of rental property than the old rules for a primary residence.

Under current tax laws, the IRS continues to take a broad definition of what like-kind property is. For example, you can exchange undeveloped land for a multiunit rental building.

The rules for properly doing a 1031 exchange are complex. Third parties are usually involved. Make sure that you find an attorney and/or tax advisor who is expert at these transactions to ensure that you do it right.

Tax credits for low-income housing and old buildings

The IRS grants you special tax credits when you invest in low-income housing or particularly old commercial buildings. The credits represent a direct reduction in your tax bill because you're spending to rehabilitate and improve these properties. The IRS wants to encourage investors to invest in and fix up old or rundown buildings that likely would continue to deteriorate otherwise.

The amounts of the credits range from as little as 10 percent of the expenditures to as much as 90 percent, depending on the property type. The IRS has strict rules governing what types of properties qualify. Tax credits may be earned for rehabilitating nonresidential buildings built in 1935 or before. "Certified historic structures," both residential and nonresidential, also qualify for tax credits. See IRS instructions for Form 3468 to find out more about these credits.

Real estate corporations

When you invest in and manage real estate with at least one other partner, you can set up a company through which you own the property. The main reason you may want to consider this setup is liability protection. A corporation can reduce the chances of lenders or tenants suing you.

Read the discussion in Chapter 22 about incorporating, the different entities under which you may do business, and the pros and cons of each.

Chapter 25

Kids and Taxes

· ·

· ·

Cloth diapers or disposables? Which are better for your baby's bottom? Are you adding to landfills by using disposables? But what about all those harsh chemicals used to clean the cloth diapers?

When should you send your youngster to preschool? And to which school? Should you move to live in a "better" school district? And can you afford to move, or will it cause you to work so many hours that you'll rarely spend time with your child? If you stay put, will your child end up in the junior high like the one in the next town over, where last year a kid brought a gun to school?

And what about toys? You want your baby to be stimulated and have fun, but the toys need to be at least somewhat educational. And then you have to worry about the safety issue. Is your baby going to get hurt when some part comes loose?

Raising children involves many decisions and trade-offs. Many new parents are surprised at the financial and tax consequences of having kids. We wrote this chapter so that you can spend more time enjoying the first smile, first step, first word, and first high-five, and save on your taxes.

Bringing Up Baby

Although kids can cost a bunch of money, the expenses, or the thousands of diaper changes during the infant years, rarely deter people from wanting a family. And for good reason — kids are wonderful, at least most of the time. They're our future. (If you don't have kids, who do you think is going to fund your Social Security and Medicare benefits during your retirement years?)

Raising a family can be the financial equivalent of doing a triathlon. It can stretch and break the budgets of even those who consider themselves financially well off and on top of things. Taxes are an important factor in a number of kid-related issues. Here's our take on some of the important tax issues that you may confront before conception and during the many years you're raising a child.

Getting Junior a Social Security number

When a child is born, he or she may be a bundle of joy to you, but to the federal government and the IRS, Junior is just a number — more specifically, a Social Security number. The IRS allows you to claim your children as dependents on your tax return. For tax year 2003, each child is "worth" a $3,050 deduction as your dependent. So if you're in the 28 percent federal tax bracket, each child saves you a cool $854 in federal taxes ($3,050 × 0.28). Not bad, but the deduction isn't going to cover much more than the cost of diapers for the year. *Note:* As we discuss in Chapter 4, high-income earners have this wonderful deduction reduced or even eliminated.

For you to claim your child as a dependent on your tax return, he or she must have a Social Security number. You also need a Social Security number for your child whenever you want to establish investment accounts in his or her name (although you may not want to after you understand the drawbacks of doing so, which we discuss later in this chapter).

The IRS requires a Social Security number because people were *inventing* children — you know, telling the IRS they'd just had twins when the closest they actually came to becoming parents was baby-sitting their best friend's kid one evening!

If you need **Form SS-5, Application for a Social Security Card,** simply contact the Social Security Administration (800-772-1213; www.ssa.gov) and ask to have one mailed to you. Fill it out and mail it back ASAP. After all, how many times in your child's life do you get to save more than $800 per year just by spending two minutes filling out a government form?

Child-care tax goodies

In addition to the extra personal deduction that you can take with each new child and the tax savings that come with that deduction, you should also be aware of the tax perks (for child-care and related expenditures) that may save you thousands of dollars.

Dependent-care tax credit

When you hire child-care assistance for your youngster(s), you may be able to claim a tax credit on your annual return (which you claim on **Form 2441**). To be eligible for this credit, you (and your spouse, if you're married) must work at least part-time, unless you're a full-time student or you're disabled. Your kid(s) must be younger than the age of 13 or physically or mentally disabled.

Because a credit is a dollar-for-dollar reduction in the taxes you owe, it can save you hundreds of tax dollars every year. And not only do you count child-care expenses toward calculation of the tax credit, but you may also be able to count the cost of a housekeeper, or even a cook, if the expense benefits your kids.

The dependent-care tax credit increases to a maximum of $3,000 per child in tax year 2003, with a $6,000 per family limit. The income threshold at which the credit begins to be reduced increases to $15,000, and the portion of qualifying employment-related expenses for which credits can be claimed increases in tax year 2003 to 35 percent.

As we discuss later in this section, tax and other considerations influence your desire as a parent to work outside the home. Working at least part-time makes you eligible for this tax credit. If you choose to be a full-time mom or dad, unfortunately you aren't eligible for the dependent-care tax credit.

If your employer offers a dependent-care assistance plan (discussed in the following section), you may be able to reduce your taxes by taking advantage of that benefit rather than the dependent-care tax credit. Your tax credit is reduced or eliminated whenever you use your employer's dependent-care plan spending account. To find out more about how to claim this credit on your annual tax return, see Chapter 15.

Dependent-care spending accounts

Increasing numbers of employers offer flexible benefit or spending plans that enable you to choose from among a number of different benefits, such as health, life, and disability insurance; vacation days; and dependent-care expenses.

You can put away money from your paycheck to pay for child-care expenses on a pretax basis. Doing so saves you from paying federal, state, and even Social Security taxes on that money. These flexible benefits plans allow you to put away up to $5,000 per year ($2,500 if you're married filing separately). However, the exact amount that you can put away depends on the specifics of your employer's plan.

Dependent-care spending accounts are a use it or lose it benefit. If you don't spend the money for child-care expenses during the current tax year, the IRS forces you to forfeit all the unused money at the end of the year. So, be careful not to go overboard by contributing more than you're certain to use.

As we mention in the preceding section, participating in your employer's dependent-care assistance plan reduces your tax credit. You can't do both. When you're in the federal 25 percent tax bracket and higher, you should be able to save more in taxes by using your employer's plan than by taking the credit on your tax return. The only way to know for sure is to run the numbers.

The dependent-care tax credit and spending accounts that we discuss in this section also can be used to pay for the costs of taking care of other dependents, such as an ill or elderly parent. Please see Chapter 15 and your employer's employee benefits manual for more information.

Child tax credit

Every child you can claim as a dependent, who is a U.S. citizen and younger than the age of 17 on December 31, can reduce your tax bill by $1,000 for tax year 2003. Many people received the increased portion of this credit as a tax rebate check that was mailed this past summer (see Chapter 8). If you have three or more kids and your total child tax credit exceeds your tax bill, part of the credit may be refundable. The credit is reduced by $50 for every $1,000 or fraction thereof of modified adjusted gross income above $75,000 for singles, $110,000 for married couples filing jointly, and $55,000 for married couples filing separately.

The nanny tax

Someday you may want to run for public office or be nominated for an important position. If you hire a nanny to take care of your child, you're better off to legally withhold and file the taxes necessary for employing such help. A number of candidates for elected or appointed political offices were passed over or rejected because of the bad publicity they received for failing to withhold and file income taxes for their household help.

Even if you aren't planning to run for political office someday, you still need to know that you're legally required to withhold Social Security and other taxes when you have household employees who are earning $1,300 or more in a tax year. You can now do this when you file your annual

tax return, and — surprise, surprise — it requires another form **(Schedule H)**. Refer to the section on household employment taxes in Chapter 15 to find out how to report your so-called nanny tax.

In addition to paying for household help on your annual tax return, you need to pay unemployment tax for any household employee to whom you paid $1,000 or more in a calendar quarter (current or prior tax year). Request **Form 940, Employer's Annual Federal Unemployment Tax Return,** from the IRS to do so. Some states have similar requirements, so be sure to contact your state's employment tax office for information.

Teaching kids about taxes and money

Show your kids your pay stub! Sharing information about what you earn and what you pay in taxes with your children can be highly educational for them. This information gets kids thinking about the realities of living within an income.

Your pay stub helps kids see not only what you earn each month, but also how much goes out for expenses, like taxes. You can then have discussions about the costs of rent and mortgages, utilities, food, and everything else. Your children may better understand your financial constraints, and, as a result, they'll be more responsible for earning money, paying taxes, and meeting monthly bills. You don't do them (or yourself) any favors by keeping them in the dark about financial matters.

In the absence of information, children have no concept of the amount their parents earn. Some have outrageously inflated ideas of how much their parents make — especially children whose parents eagerly fulfill their requests for purchases.

You may be surprised to learn that the child tax credit actually is scheduled to decrease in 2005 to $700, and then increase again in 2009 to $800, and finally reach $1,000 per dependent child in 2010. This quirk is caused by the melding of the provisions of the 2003 and 2001 tax bills. The same income ceilings apply as before for claiming this credit, and no future increases for inflation are planned for the income ceilings. The $1,000 credit will be adjusted for inflation after 2010.

The 2001 tax bill expanded the refundability of the child tax credit for low-income families with one or two children. The credit now is refundable to the extent of 10 percent of the amount that a taxpayer's earned income exceeds $10,500 (which increases with inflation). For tax year 2005 and beyond, the credit will be refundable to the extent of 15 percent of the amount that earned income exceeds $15,000. Families with three or more dependent children face more complicated, although beneficial, calculations. See Chapter 8 for information about how to compute and claim this credit.

Adoption tax credit

Recent tax law changes have substantially increased the tax credits to parents who adopt children. Please see Chapter 5 for all the details.

Costs and benefits of a second income

One of the most challenging decisions that new parents face is whether to work full-time, part-time, or not at all. We mean work at a paying job, that is — parenting is the lowest-paid but potentially most-rewarding job there is. The need or desire to work full-time is obvious — doing so brings more money home.

In addition to less sleep at night and frequent diaper changes, children mean increased spending. At a minimum, expenditures for food and clothing increase. Although you may have less time to shop for yourself, causing your personal spending to decrease, you're likely to spend more on housing, insurance, child care, and education. And don't forget the host of not-so-incidental incidentals. Toys, art classes, sports, field trips, and the like can rack up big bills, especially if you don't control what you spend on them.

You may rightfully feel that working full-time prohibits you from playing as active a role in raising your children as you would like. As you consider the additional expenses of raising children, you may also need to factor in a decrease in income.

Financially speaking, taxes can have a big impact on the value or benefit of working full-time, especially for two-income couples. Remember that the tax brackets are set up so that the last dollars of earnings are taxed at a higher rate (refer to Chapter 1).

Deciding whether to work full-time by counting the salary that your employer quotes you as the total value of that second income leaves you open to making a potentially big personal and financial mistake.

For example, take the case of Ron and Mary, a nice couple who struggled with how to handle their work schedules after the birth of their first child. They both worked full-time. Mary, a marketing manager, earned $55,000 per year, and Ron, a schoolteacher, made $32,000 per year. Ron was considering working part-time or not at all so that he could be at home with their daughter, but because of Ron and Mary's prior financial commitments, such as their mortgage, they believed that they couldn't afford for Ron to work less than full-time.

Ron and Mary took a closer look at their finances and taxes and started to see things a little differently. Taxes took a whopping 40 percent of Ron's income, so his take-home pay was just $19,200 per year, or $1,600 per month. Then they added up all the additional costs of both parents working full-time: day care, a second car, more meals eaten out, and so on. When they totaled up all the extra costs (including taxes) that could be reduced or eliminated if Ron didn't work at all or worked on a greatly reduced basis, they figured that Ron was effectively contributing about $300 per month from his full-time job — or about $1.80 per hour!

Ultimately, because of his low after-tax effective hourly income, Ron decided to quit his job and work part-time at home. This solution gave the family the best of both worlds — a more involved dad and husband and some income without most of the extra costs that come with a second job. And because Ron was able to work part-time, he and his wife were able to earn some tax credits (discussed in the "Dependent-care tax credit" section, earlier in this chapter) for part-time child care for their daughter.

Of course, people enjoy other benefits from working, besides income. Be sure, however, to examine taxes and other expenses on that second income to ensure that you're making your financial decision to work based on complete and accurate information.

Education Tax Breaks and Pitfalls

What, you may ask, do taxes have to do with educational expenses? A surprising amount. How you invest to pay for educating your children can have an enormous impact on your family's taxes, your children's ability to qualify for financial aid, and your overall financial well-being.

The (hidden) financial aid tax system

The financial aid system (to which parents apply so that their children are eligible for college scholarships, grants, and loans) treats assets differently when held outside rather than inside retirement accounts. Under the current financial aid system, the value of your retirement plans is *not* considered an asset. Thus the more of your money you stash in retirement accounts, the greater your chances of qualifying for financial aid and the more money you're generally eligible for.

Most new parents don't place their savings in retirement accounts. Many nonwealthy parents make the mistake of saving and investing money in a separate account for their child (perhaps even in the child's name) or through some other financial product, such as a life insurance policy. Why is this a mistake? Because these products are taxed at a much higher level than if they had employed other savings strategies.

Most important, parents should be saving and investing through retirement accounts that give significant tax benefits. Contributions to a 401(k), 403(b), SEP-IRA, Keogh, and other retirement accounts (described in Chapter 21) usually produce an upfront tax deduction. An additional and substantial benefit is that after the money is placed in these accounts, it grows and compounds without being taxed until you withdraw it.

Therefore, it doesn't make sense to forgo contributions to your retirement savings plans so you can save money in a taxable account for Junior's college fund. When you do, you pay higher taxes both on your current income and on the interest and growth of this money. In addition to paying higher taxes, money that you save *outside* retirement accounts, including money in the child's name, is counted as an asset and reduces your child's eligibility for financial aid. Thus you're expected to contribute more to your child's educational expenses.

Note: As we discuss later in the chapter, if you're affluent enough that you expect to pay for your kid's entire educational costs, investing through custodial accounts, Education Savings Accounts, and Section 529 college savings plans can save on taxes.

College cost tax deductions

Some parents can take a tax deduction of up to $3,000 of college costs. The maximum write-off increases to $4,000 in 2004. Because you claim this write-off on the main part of Form 1040, you need not itemize your deductions on Schedule A to claim this deduction.

However, as with numerous other new tax breaks, you can't claim this deduction if you're a higher-income earner. If your adjusted gross income (AGI) exceeds thresholds — $65,000 for singles and $130,000 for married couples filing jointly — you cannot claim this deduction.

Here are some additional complications to be aware of if you claim this college cost deduction:

- In 2004, single taxpayers with AGIs up to $80,000 and married couples filing jointly with AGIs up to $160,000 can take a partial deduction of up to $2,000 in college costs.

- You can't take a Hope or Lifetime Learning Credit (discussed later in this chapter) in the same tax year that you take this new deduction.

When a millionaire's kid gets more financial aid than a middle-class family's

What's truly amazing and sad about the way the current financial aid system works is that some affluent people who don't really need aid can get more than those who aren't nearly as financially well off. Here's a real case that, although somewhat extreme, is not that unusual. This story highlights the shortcomings of the current procedures used to determine financial need.

Kent, a doctor earning $200,000 per year, and his spouse Marian, a housewife, had a son who applied for and received financial aid. By the time their son was ready to apply to college, Kent had quit working as a physician and was earning little money while doing some part-time teaching. However, he had a seven-figure balance in his retirement savings plan, which he had accumulated over his years of work. Being savvy financial managers, Kent and Marian had little money invested and available outside tax-sheltered retirement accounts. Because the financial aid system ignores retirement accounts in its analysis, and because Kent's income was modest at the time his son applied for aid, the family got significant aid.

On the other hand, Wendy, the daughter of Rick and Liz, full-time employees with a combined income of $60,000, received no financial aid. Why? Because Rick and Liz had been saving money in Wendy's name. By the time she was ready to apply to college, she had about $25,000 saved. Rick and Liz also accumulated some other modest investments outside retirement accounts, but only about $30,000 in retirement accounts. Because of the assets available outside retirement accounts and their current income, they were deemed not needy enough for aid.

The provision allowing for this new tax deduction is set to expire in tax year 2006 unless Congress extends it, which we think it probably will.

Recent tax bills expanded tax breaks to allow for greater ability to deduct the interest paid on student loans. The interest write-off on student loans is no longer restricted to interest paid during the first five years of loan payback. Also, early repayment of interest is now deductible.

The income thresholds for those who can take the student loan interest write-off is now between $50,000 and $65,000 for single taxpayers and between $100,000 and $130,000 for couples and increases annually for inflation.

Education Savings Accounts: Tread carefully

You can establish an Education Savings Account (ESA) for each child and make contributions of up to $2,000 per child per year until the child reaches age 18. Contributions to an ESA, which can be made up until the due date of the income tax return, aren't tax-deductible. However, ESA investment earnings can compound and be withdrawn free of tax as long as the funds are used to pay for college costs. In the year of withdrawal, the new Hope Scholarship and Lifetime Learning Credits may not be claimed for the student — see the next section for more about these credits.

ESA balances can be used for precollege educational costs (in other words, for schooling costs up through and including grade 12). Eligible educational expenses include tuition, fees, books, supplies, computers and other equipment, tutoring, uniforms, extended-day programs, transportation, internet access, and so on. (College room and board expenses qualify only if the student carries at least one-half the normal workload.) Contributions to the accounts of special-needs children are permitted past the age of 18 and balances can continue in those accounts past the age of 30.

Before running out to contribute to an ESA, be aware that college financial aid officers are generally going to treat this type of savings in such a way that it harms a child's financial aid award. Financial aid officers will most likely treat funds placed in an ESA either as a child's asset, which reduces financial aid by 35 percent for each dollar in the child's name, or as a prepaid tuition plan, which reduces aid dollar for dollar.

So, unless you're affluent enough to pay for the full cost of your children's college education without any type of financial aid, hold off on contributing to an ESA until it's clear how financial aid offices are going to treat them. If you're affluent, you may not be eligible to contribute to one anyway. The full $2,000 per child contribution to an ESA may be made only by couples with adjusted gross incomes (AGIs) less than $190,000 and single taxpayers with AGIs less than $95,000. The $2,000 limit is reduced for married taxpayers with AGIs of more than $190,000 ($95,000 if single) and eliminated if the AGI is more than $220,000 ($110,000 for singles).

If you earn more than these thresholds and want your kids to have ESAs, there's a loophole. Simply have someone else who isn't earning more than the threshold amounts, such as a grandparent, make the ESA contribution on your behalf.

Here are some other ESA rules and regulations that you should be aware of:

- The tax-free exclusion of the earnings isn't available on a distribution from the IRA in the same year you claim a Hope Scholarship or Lifetime Earning Credit.

- Contributions to the account must be made before the child reaches 18 unless the child is considered *special needs,* which is defined as "an individual who, because of a physical, mental, or emotional condition (including learning disability), requires additional time to complete his or her education."

✔ The money in the account can't be used to invest in a life insurance policy.

✔ When the beneficiary reaches age 30, any balance must be distributed to him or her, and he or she must include any earnings in his or her income (unless the account holder is considered special needs). However, prior to reaching 30, the beneficiary may transfer or roll over the balance to another beneficiary who is a member of his or her family. The distribution must be made within 30 days of the beneficiary's 30th birthday, or within 30 days of his or her death.

✔ No contribution may be made in a year that a contribution is made to a state tuition program for the child (see "Avoid prepaid and other qualified state tuition programs" later in this chapter for more information).

✔ Any part of a distribution that must be included in income because it wasn't used to pay college expenses is subject to a 10 percent penalty, unless the distribution is paid as a result of death or disability.

Here's an example of how the earnings on an ESA get taxed: Grandma and Grandpa contributed $600 over the years to Chloe's account. It is now worth $1,000; thus the investment earnings total $400 ($1,000 – $600). Because Chloe withdraws the $1,000 but uses only $750 (75 percent) to pay college expenses, of the $400 in earnings, only 75 percent, or $300, is exempt from tax. Chloe must pay tax on the $100 balance. If she had used the entire $1,000 to pay her college expenses, the entire $400 of earnings would be exempt from tax. One additional point: The $100 on which Chloe had to pay tax is subject to a 10 percent penalty.

Chloe can elect to waive the exclusion from tax on her withdrawal from her ESA if she claims the Hope Scholarship or Lifetime Learning Credits instead. In this case, the 10 percent penalty in the preceding example doesn't apply because Chloe includes the earnings from her ESA in her income.

Section 529 plans — state tuition plans

Section 529 plans (named after Internal Revenue Code section 529), also known as qualified state tuition plans, are among the newer tax-advantaged college savings plans around. And recent tax law changes made them even better.

A parent or grandparent can put more than $100,000 into one of these plans for each child. You can put up to $55,000 into a child's college savings account immediately, and that counts for the next five years' worth of $11,000 tax-free gifts (actually, a couple can immediately contribute $110,000 per child) allowed under current gifting laws (see Chapter 26). Money contributed to the account is not considered part of the donor's taxable estate (although if the donor dies before five years are up after gifting $55,000, a prorated amount of the gift is charged back to the donor's estate).

Previously, the biggest attraction of these plans was that the investment earnings, if used to pay for college tuition, room, board, or other related higher education expenses, were taxed at the student's income tax rate at the time the money was withdrawn. In addition to paying college costs, you can use the money in Section 529 plans to pay for graduate school and for the enrollment and attendance expenses of special-needs students.

Thanks to recent tax law changes, Section 529 plan investment earnings can be withdrawn tax-free (that's right — completely free of taxation) as long as the withdrawn funds are used to pay for qualifying higher educational costs.

Some states provide tax benefits on contributions to their state-sanctioned plans, whereas other states induce you to invest at home by taxing profits from out-of-state plans.

Unlike contributing money to a custodial account with which a child may do as he or she pleases when he or she reaches the age of either 18 or 21 (it varies by state), these state tuition plans must be used for higher education expenses. Some state plans even allow you to change the beneficiary or take the money back if you change your mind. (If you do withdraw the money, however, you owe tax on the withdrawn earnings, plus a penalty — typically 10 percent.)

A big potential drawback — especially for families hoping for some financial aid — is that college financial aid offices may treat assets in these plans as the child's, which, as discussed earlier in the chapter, can greatly diminish financial aid eligibility.

Another potential drawback is that you have limited choices and control over how the money in state tuition plans is invested. The investment provider(s) for each state plan generally decides how to invest the money over time within given investment options. In most plans, the more years your child is away from college, the more aggressive the investment mix is. As your child approaches college age, the investment mix is tilted more to conservative investments. Most state plans have somewhat high investment management fees, and some plans don't allow transfers to other plans.

Please also be aware that a future Congress could change the tax laws affecting these plans and diminish the tax breaks or increase the penalties for nonqualified withdrawals. A child can't have contributions to both a Section 529 plan and an Education Savings Account in the same year (even from different contributors).

Clearly, there are pros and cons to Section 529 plans. They generally make the most sense for affluent parents (or grandparents) of children who don't expect to qualify for financial aid.

Do a lot of research and homework before investing in any plan. Check out the investment track record, allocations, and fees for each plan, as well as restrictions on transferring to other plans or changing beneficiaries. These plans are relatively new, and the market for them is changing quickly, so take your time before committing to one of them.

Hope Scholarship and Lifetime Learning Credits

Tax credits assist some parents with the often high costs of education. We say *some* because the credits are phased out for single tax filers with adjusted gross incomes between $40,000 and $50,000 and married couples filing jointly with adjusted gross incomes between $80,000 and $100,000 (these phase-out ranges annually increase with inflation).

The first of the two credits — the Hope Scholarship Credit — allows up to a $1,500 tax credit toward tuition and fees in each of the first two years of college. This credit amount increases (in $100 increments) annually along with inflation.

The second credit — the Lifetime Learning Credit — allows a credit for up to 20 percent of $10,000 in tuition and fee expenses (worth $2,000) per taxpayer. The Lifetime Learning Credit can be used toward undergraduate and graduate education and toward coursework that upgrades job skills.

If you, as a taxpayer, claim either of these credits in a tax year, you are not eligible to withdraw money without taxation from an Education Savings Account, nor can you take the new college cost tax deduction discussed earlier in this chapter. Also, you can't take the Hope Scholarship Credit in the same year that you use the Lifetime Learning Credit.

Minimizing your taxes and paying for college

Socking money away into your tax-sheltered retirement accounts helps you reduce your tax burden and may help your children qualify for more financial aid. However, accessing retirement accounts before age 59½ incurs tax penalties.

So how do you pay for your children's educational costs? There isn't one correct answer, because the decision depends on your overall financial situation. Here are some ideas that can help you meet expected educational expenses and minimize your taxes:

✔ **Don't try to do it all yourself.** Unless you're affluent, don't even try to pay for the full cost of a college education for your children. Few people can afford it. You and your children will, in all likelihood, have to borrow some money.

✔ **Apply for aid, regardless of your financial circumstances.** A number of loan programs, such as Unsubsidized Stafford Loans and Parent Loans for Undergraduate Students (PLUS), are available even if your family is not deemed financially needy. Only Subsidized Stafford Loans, on which the federal government pays the interest that accumulates while the student is still in school, are limited to those students deemed financially needy.

In addition to loans, a number of grant programs are available through schools, the government, and independent sources. Specific colleges and other private organizations (including employers, banks, credit unions, and community groups) also offer grants and scholarships. Some of these have nothing to do with financial need.

✔ **Save in your name.** If you've exhausted your retirement account contributions, it's fine to save money that you're earmarking to pay for college. Just do it in your name. If your children's grandparents want to make a gift of money to them for college expenses, it's generally better if the money is kept in your name; otherwise, have the grandparents keep the money until the kids are ready to enter college.

✔ **Get your kids to work.** Your child can work and save money to pay for college costs during junior high, high school, and college. In fact, if your child qualifies for financial aid, he or she is expected to contribute a certain amount to his or her educational costs from money earned from jobs held during the school year or summer breaks and from his or her own savings. Besides giving the student a stake in his or her own future, this training encourages sound personal financial management down the road.

✔ **Borrow against your home equity.** If you're a homeowner, you can borrow against the equity (market value less the outstanding mortgage loan) in your property. Doing so is usually wise because you can borrow against your home at a reasonable interest rate, and the interest is generally tax-deductible. (Refer to Chapter 9 for information about tax-deductibility rules.) Be careful to borrow an amount you can afford to repay and that won't cause you to default on your loan and lose your home. *Mortgages For Dummies,* which Eric Tyson co-wrote (Wiley, Inc.), can help you with such borrowing decisions.

✔ **Borrow against your company retirement plans.** Many retirement savings plans, such as 401(k)s, allow borrowing. Just make sure that you're able to pay back the money. Otherwise, you'll owe big taxes for a premature distribution.

Taxes on Your Kiddies' Investments

Parents of all different financial means need to be aware of the financial aid implications of putting money into an account bearing a child's name. If you haven't read the section "Educational Tax Breaks and Pitfalls" earlier in this chapter, please read it before investing money in your children's names.

Kiddie taxes for children younger than 14

Prior to reaching the magical age of 14, kids have a special tax system that applies to them. Specifically, the first $750 of *unearned income* (income from interest and dividends on investments) that a child earns is not taxed at all. It's tax-free! In contrast, *earned income* is considered income earned from work. Refer to Chapter 8 to find out when you need to file a tax return for your child.

The next $750 of unearned income for this age set is taxed at the federal level at 10 percent. Everything over $1,500 is taxed at the parents' income tax rate. The system is set up in this fashion to discourage parents from transferring a lot of assets into their children's names, hoping to pay lower taxes.

Because the first $1,500 of unearned income for the child is taxed at such a low rate, some parents are tempted to transfer money into the child's name to save on income taxes. Quite a number of financial books and advisors recommend this strategy. Consider this passage referring to transferring money to your children, from a tax book written by a large accounting firm: "Take advantage of these rules. It still makes sense to shift some income-producing assets to younger children." Wrong! As we discuss in "The (hidden) financial aid tax system," earlier in this chapter, this shortsighted desire to save a little in taxes today can lead to your losing out on significant financial aid later. And what about your limited discretionary income? You don't want to put money in your child's name if it means that you aren't fully taking advantage of your retirement accounts.

Consider putting money into an account bearing your child's name only if

- ✔ You expect to pay for the full cost of a college education and won't apply for or use any financial aid, including loans that aren't based on financial need.

- ✔ You're comfortable with the notion that your child will have legal access to the money at age 18 or 21 (depending on the state in which you live) if the money is in a custodial account in the child's name. At that age, the money is legally your child's, and he or she can blow it on something other than a college education.

After all the caveats and warnings, if you're still thinking about putting money into an account bearing your child's name, consider buying tax-friendly investments that won't generate significant tax liabilities until after the child turns 14. (See Chapter 23 for tax-friendly investment ideas.) As we discuss in the following section, after your kids turn 14, all income they earn is taxed at their rate, not yours.

You also can buy investments in your name and then transfer them to your child after Junior turns 14. (Each parent is limited to gifting $11,000 to each child per year.) That way, if the investment declines in value, you can take the tax loss; if the investment turns a profit, you can save on your taxes by transferring the investment to your child and having your child pay tax on it after turning 14. This strategy won't work if your child is a movie or kid-band star and in a higher tax bracket than you are!

Children 14 and older: Adults to the IRS

Although your gangly teenager may still be wearing braces, using acne cream, and spending two hours a day on the phone, to the IRS, he or she is a warm-blooded, tax-paying adult, just like you, as soon as he or she turns 14. Because most 14-year-olds don't earn a great deal of income, taxes on their investments don't need to be a concern. However, the same negative financial aid consequences that we discuss earlier in the chapter apply to money held in their names versus yours.

Double-what bonds?

Among the many forms of bonds (debt) that our fine government issues are EE (double "E") bonds. These are one of the many classes of Treasury bonds issued by that national organization with a penchant for borrowing money. You may hear about these bonds as a suggested investment for children's college expenses.

EE bonds purchased after 1989 have a unique tax twist if you use the proceeds to pay for educational tuition and fees. (Room and board and other education-related costs are not covered.) The interest earned on the bonds is fully exempt from federal taxation (interest on the Treasury bonds is already state tax–free) as long as two other requirements are met:

- The purchaser of the bond must be at least 24 years of age.

- At the time the bonds were sold to pay for educational tuition and fees, the holder of the bond may not have an adjusted gross income in excess of $73,500 if single or $117,750 if married and filing a joint return. (For single filers with an adjusted gross income between $58,500 and $73,500 and married couples between $87,750 and $117,750, a partial interest–tax exemption applies.)

Even if you're somehow able to know years in advance what your income will be when your toddler has grown into a college-bound 18-year-old, you've gotta file yet another tax form, **Form 8815**, to claim the exclusion of the interest of EEs from federal taxation. And don't forget that not a year goes by without Congress messing with the federal tax laws. So the income requirements for the tax exemptions can change.

You should also know that EE Bonds often pay a lower rate of interest than other, simpler comparable bonds. The yield or interest rate on EE bonds is also a chore to understand. You must hold these bonds for at least five years in order to receive the return. The return is equal to 85 percent of the average yield payable on five-year Treasury notes during the period held, or 4 percent, whichever is higher.

Regardless of how the EE bond proceeds are used, taxation of the interest on them is deferred until they're cashed. Although in most cases this tax deferment is beneficial, don't forget that children younger than age 14 can earn $750 of interest tax-free every year. So, if you buy the bond and register it in your child's name, he or she may end up actually paying more in taxes when the bonds are cashed in, because all the interest income will be recognized at once. Buying the bond in your child's name, however, may hurt his or her chances of obtaining financial aid.

Our advice: Don't waste your time on these complicated bonds. They are testimony to the absurdly complex tax code and government rules. You're better off investing in mutual funds that offer some growth potential. But if we haven't dissuaded you, make sure that you buy these bonds from the Federal Reserve Bank in your area and hold them in an account with the Federal Reserve. Doing so will ensure that you'll always get a statement on your account and won't lose track of the bonds when you're no longer being paid interest!

Tax-wise and not-so-wise investments for educational funds

You hear many sales pitches for "tax-wise" investments to use for college savings. Most aren't worthy of your consideration. Here's our take on the best, the mediocre, and the worst.

Mutual funds are ideal

Mutual funds, which offer investors of all financial means instant diversification and low-cost access to the nation's best money managers, are an ideal investment when you're saving money for educational expenses. See Chapter 23 for a discussion of the tax-wise ways to invest in funds.

Think twice about Treasury bonds

Many tax and financial books recommend investing college funds in *Treasury bonds issued by the federal government*. We aren't enthusiastic about some of these (see the sidebar "Double-what bonds?"). Zero-coupon Treasuries are particular tax headaches. They are sold at a discount to their value at maturity instead of paying you interest each year.

Guess what? You still have to report the effective interest you're earning each year on your tax return. And just to give you a headache or pad your tax preparer's bill, you or your preparer have to calculate this implicit interest. Yuck!

Don't bother with cash-value life insurance

Life insurance policies that have cash values are some of the most oversold investments to fund college costs. The usual pitch is this: Because you need life insurance to protect your family, why not buy a policy that you can borrow against to pay for college? Makes sense, doesn't it? Insurance agents also emphasize that the cash value in the policy is growing without taxation over time. Although this part of their sales pitch is true, you have better alternatives.

The reason you shouldn't buy a cash-value life insurance policy is that, as we discuss earlier in this chapter, you're better off contributing to retirement accounts. These investments give you an immediate tax deduction that you don't receive when you save through life insurance. Because life insurance that comes with a cash value is more expensive, parents are more likely to make a second mistake — not buying enough life insurance coverage. When you need life insurance, you're better off buying lower-cost term life insurance.

Make sure your money grows

An investment that fails to keep you ahead of inflation, such as a savings or money market account, is another poor investment for college expenses. The interest on these accounts is also taxable, which doesn't make sense for many working parents. You need your money to grow so you can afford educational costs down the road.

Avoid prepaid tuition programs

Prepaid tuition plans and other such programs generally should be avoided. A few states have developed plans to enable you to pay college costs at a specific school (calculated for the age of your child) or for any approved college in the state. The allure of these plans is that by paying today, you eliminate the worry of not being able to afford rising costs in the future.

This logic doesn't work for several reasons. First, odds are high that you don't have the money today to pay in advance. If you have that kind of extra dough around, you're better off using it for other purposes (and you're unlikely to worry about rising costs anyway). You can invest your own money — that's what the school's going to do with it anyway. Besides, how do you know which college your child will want to attend (or colleges in what state) and how long it may take him or her to get through it? Also be aware that some states have you forfeit all your investment earnings if you want your original investment back to send your child to an out-of-state college.

Chapter 26

Estate Planning

• •

In This Chapter

▶ Arriving at the ultimate and final insult — taxes for dying?!?

▶ Reviewing strategies for reducing estate taxes

▶ Trusting your estate to trusts, wills, and more trusts

▶ Finding places where you can find help if you need it

• •

Among the dreariest of tax and financial topics is the issue of what happens to your money when you die. Depending on how your finances are structured and when you pass on, you (actually, your estate) may get stuck paying *estate taxes* when you die.

Speaking of timing and when you may pass on, significant tax law changes recently were made to the federal estate tax laws. Just to pique your (morbid) curiosity, you may be interested in knowing that if you have great wealth and have to die, 2010 is a terrific year to do so! In that year and that year alone, the estate tax disappears. Even someone with an estate of tens of billions of dollars may be able to escape estate taxes completely that year. That won't be true if you die in 2009 or 2011 under new absurd rules. In this chapter, we cover the new estate tax laws and the old rules that still apply.

Unfortunately, you can't predict when the grim reaper will pay you a visit. This scenario doesn't mean that we all need to participate in complicated estate planning. On the contrary, if your assets aren't substantial, a few simple moves may be all you need to get your affairs in order.

Estate planning takes time and money, which are precious commodities for most of us. Whether it's worthwhile to spend your time and money on estate planning depends on your personal and financial circumstances, both now and in the near future.

We know that your days are packed with excitement and you bound out of bed most mornings, racing off to a job that you love. Who can blame you for not wanting to plan for the day when you won't see the sunrise? Unlike filing your annual tax return, arranging your financial affairs for your death is easy to put off. Unfortunately, if you don't spend some time on estate planning, your family and others who are close to you will pay the price when you're gone. Do you really want the government to get much of your money?

Figuring Whether You May Owe Estate Taxes

With all the warnings about the enormous estate taxes that you may owe upon your death, you may think that owing estate taxes is a common problem. It isn't, and with the 2001 tax law changes, paying estate taxes will become far less common in the years ahead. But some insurance agents, attorneys, and estate-planning "specialists" use scare tactics to attract prospective clients, often by luring them to free estate-planning seminars. What better way to find people with money to invest!

Understanding the federal estate tax exemption

In tax year 2003, an individual at his or her death can pass $1,000,000 to beneficiaries without paying federal estate taxes. On the other hand, a couple, *if* they have their assets, wills, and trusts properly structured (as discussed later in this chapter), can pass $2 million to beneficiaries without paying federal estate taxes. Because most people still are trying to accumulate enough money to retire or take a trip around the world someday, it's hardly a normal problem for folks to have this much money lying around when they die.

And if those amounts don't seem large enough to you, recent tax law changes significantly increased them in the years ahead (see Table 26-1). By the year 2009, the amount that a deceased person may leave to his or her heirs increases to $3.5 million. Thus married couples making use of bypass trusts eventually will be able to shield $7 million from federal estate taxes.

Table 26-1	Amount That Can Be Passed to Heirs Free of Federal Estate Tax
Year	*Federal Estate-Tax-Free Amount*
2003	$1,000,000
2004–2005	$1,500,000
2006–2008	$2,000,000
2009	$3,500,000

In 2010, your estate could be worth billions of dollars and be passed on to your heirs without any estate tax. In that year and that year alone, the estate tax vanishes. However, in the very next year — 2011 — the allowable amount that can be passed on free of estate tax reverts back to $1,000,000. Does that sound ridiculous, or what?

Although we can't and don't want to predict future tax laws, we believe that you can probably count on the higher exemption amounts in Table 26-1 in large part sticking around. However, we don't think that you should count on the complete repeal of estate taxes in 2010 being made permanent. (Ultimately, what happens with future changes in the estate tax laws will be driven by the composition of Congress and which party holds the presidency. The repeal will be more likely to stick if Republicans have firm control of these branches of government.) We discuss a variety of estate tax–reduction strategies later in this chapter, but first we'll talk about how the IRS figures your taxable estate.

Determining your taxable estate

Unless you die prematurely, whether your assets face estate taxes depends on the amount of your assets that you use up during your retirement, unless you already possess great wealth. How much of your assets you use up depends on how your assets grow over time and how rapidly you spend money.

To calculate the value of your estate upon your death, the IRS totals up your assets and subtracts your liabilities. Assets include your personal property, home and other real estate, savings and investments (such as bank accounts, stocks, bonds, and mutual funds held inside and outside of retirement accounts), and life insurance death benefits (unless properly placed in a trust, as we describe later in this chapter). Your liabilities include any outstanding loans (such as a mortgage), bills owed at the time of your death, legal and other expenses to handle your estate, and funeral expenses.

If you're married at the time of your death, all assets that you leave to your spouse are excluded from estate taxes, thanks to the unlimited marital deduction (which we discuss later in this chapter). The IRS also deducts any charitable contributions or bequests that you dictate in your will from your assets before calculating your taxable estate.

How High Are Estate Taxes?

Under current tax law, if your estate totals more than $1,000,000 at your death, you may owe federal estate taxes. The tax rates are fairly hefty (see Table 26-2).

Table 26-2	Federal Estate Taxes on Estates in Excess of $1,000,000
Value of Estate	*Tax Rate*
$1,000,001–$1,250,000	41%
$1,250,001–$1,500,000	43%
$1,500,001–$2,000,000	45%
$2,000,001–$2,500,000	49%
More than $2,500,000	50%

In addition to raising the amounts that can be passed on free of federal estate taxes (refer to Table 26-1), recent tax law changes lower the tax rates that apply to estates large enough to be subject to estate taxes (see Table 26-3). As we discuss earlier in the chapter, the reason for the abrupt change in 2010 is the repeal of the estate tax that year, but the 2001 tax bill also includes a provision for its reinstatement in 2011. We think that some of the reduction in estate tax rates will stick around for the long-term, but for planning purposes, you shouldn't count on the repeal of the estate tax.

Table 26-3	Top Federal Estate Tax Rate
Year	*Tax Rate*
2003	49%
2004	48%
2005	47%
2006	46%
2007–2009	45%
2010	None — estate tax repealed!
2011	55%

States also can levy additional estate and inheritance taxes. Most states don't; they simply share in the federal taxes that the IRS collects from each estate.

Some states have elected to assess their own estate taxes and, therefore, don't share in the federal estate taxes collected. Not surprisingly, such states opt out of the federal tax—sharing so they can assess and collect an even higher rate of estate tax than they'd receive from the federal government. Thus, if you live in one of those states (listing them would be too complicated because of the uniqueness of each state's system), your estate taxes will be higher because of the additional state levy.

Some states also impose an inheritance tax.

Reducing Expected Estate Taxes (If You're Rich)

You have your work cut out for you as you try to educate yourself about estate planning. You can find many attorneys and nonattorneys selling estate-planning services, and you can encounter many insurance agents hawking life insurance. All are pleased to sell you their services. Most people don't need to do fancy-schmancy estate planning with high-cost attorneys. We give you the straight scoop on what, if anything, you need to be concerned with now and at other junctures in your life, and we tell you the conflicts of interest that these "experts" have in rendering advice.

Thanks to all the changes in the tax laws and the thousands of attorneys and tax advisors working to find new ways around paying estate taxes, a dizzying array of strategies exist to reduce estate taxes — including taking up residence in a foreign country! We start with the simpler stuff and work toward the more complex.

Remember, as we discussed earlier in this chapter, new tax laws substantially increase the amount of assets that you can pass on to your heirs free of estate taxes. Thus, far fewer people will need to engage in complicated or even any estate planning (beyond preparing a will).

Gifting

Nothing is wrong with making, saving, and investing money. But someday, you have to look in the mirror and ask, "For what purpose?" It's easy to rationalize hoarding money — you never know how long you'll live or what medical expenses you may incur. Besides, your kids still are paying off their VISA cards and don't seem to know a mutual fund from an emergency fund. (Not that you'd want to be judgmental of your kids or anything!)

Current tax law allows you to gift up to $11,000 per individual and organization each year to as many people and organizations — such as your children, grandchildren, best friends, or favorite charities — as you desire (no tax forms required). If you're married, your spouse can do the same. The benefit of gifting is that it removes the money from your estate and therefore reduces your estate taxes. Even better is the fact that all future appreciation and income on the gifted money also is removed from your estate, because the money now belongs to the gift recipient. (The current annual tax-free gifting limit of $11,000 per recipient will increase in $1,000 increments in future years with inflation.)

Upon your death, your money has to go somewhere. By directing some of your money to people and organizations now, you can pass on far more now because you'll be saving nearly 50 percent in estate taxes. Plus, while you're alive, you can experience the satisfaction of seeing the good that your money can do.

You can use gifting to remove a substantial portion of your assets from your estate over time. Suppose that you have three children. You and your spouse each can give each of your children $11,000 per year for a total gift of $66,000 per year. If your kids are married, you can make additional $11,000 gifts to their spouses for another $66,000 per year. You also can gift an unlimited amount to pay for current educational tuition costs and medical expenses. Just be sure to make the payment directly to the organization charging the fees.

What should you gift?

You have options in terms of what money or assets you gift to others. Start with cash or assets that haven't appreciated since you purchased them. If you want to transfer an asset that has lost value, consider selling it first; then you can claim the tax loss on your tax return and transfer the cash.

Be careful to avoid gifting assets that have appreciated greatly in value. Why? Because if you hold such assets until your death, your heirs receive what is called a *stepped-up basis*. That is, the IRS assumes that the effective price your heirs "paid" for an asset is the value on your date of death — which wipes out the capital gains tax that otherwise is owed when selling an asset that has appreciated in value.

Starting in 2010, a so-called carry-over basis will apply to your assets, and you won't be able to wipe out capital gains on inherited assets. The inheritor's (heir's) tax basis is the lesser of the deceased's cost basis and the asset's fair market value at the date of death. At this time, an estate's executor will have the power to step up the basis of the estate's assets by up to $1.3 million ($3 million for assets left to a spouse). We believe it's unlikely that this provision will actually be implemented in 2010 (a similar rule change was attempted in 1977 but never took effect).

One other little detail worth noting for year 2010 changes: An estate or heir still may sell the deceased's primary residence and qualify for the capital gains tax exclusion for sale of primary residence discussed in Chapter 24.

A more complicated way to gift money to your heirs and still retain some control over the money is to set up a *Crummey Trust*. (Its name has nothing to do with the quality of the trust!) Although the beneficiary has a short window of time (a month or two) to withdraw money that's contributed to the trust, you can verbally make clear to the beneficiary that, in your opinion, leaving the money in the trust is in his or her best interest. You also can specify in the trust document itself that the trust money be used for particular purposes, such as tuition. Some of the other trusts we discuss later in this chapter may meet your needs if you want more control over the money you intend to pass to your heirs.

Paying some gift taxes now to avoid estate taxes later

You can gift up to $11,000 tax-free per person and per organization per year to as many people or organizations as you like. However, you can gift more than $11,000 in a year to your heirs.

Some people with substantial assets (several million dollars, for example) worry that their advancing age may prohibit them from moving the money out of their estate quickly enough to get down to the estate tax–free limit (refer to Table 26-1). In the past in such a case, we recommended that you could pass on more money to your heirs by transferring a larger sum of money now. This strategy was particularly useful if you wanted to focus your gifting toward one or two people.

Suppose that you want to gift $1.5 million to your heir this year. You'll owe the IRS gift tax. So you write the IRS a check. By doing so, you accomplish two positives for maximizing how much you pass to your son, daughter, and other heirs:

- ✔ You transfer $1.5 million to your heir and avoid accumulating more growth on that money in your estate. (Remember, unless your money is growing inside tax-deductible retirement accounts, that growth is taxable.)

- ✔ Because you pay the gift tax out of your estate, you reduce your taxable estate by the amount of the gift and the gift tax.

Note: Technically, you must live three years following the gift for your heirs to avoid paying estate tax on it.

We no longer recommend considering this strategy, because as Table 26-1 highlights, the amount that you can pass on free of estate tax will greatly increase in the years ahead. Likewise, because of the chance that the estate tax repeal may remain in effect after the year 2010, paying gift tax now to make a large gift to one of your heirs may cause you to pay tax that your estate never will be assessed.

Leaving all your assets to your spouse

Tax laws wouldn't be tax laws without exceptions and loopholes. Here's another one: If you're married at the time of your death, any and all assets that you leave to your spouse are exempt from estate taxes normally due upon your death. In fact, you may leave an unlimited amount of money to your spouse, hence the name *unlimited marital deduction*. Assets that count are those willed to your spouse or for which he or she is named as beneficiary (such as retirement accounts).

Although leaving all your assets to your spouse is a tempting estate-planning strategy for married couples, this strategy can backfire. The surviving spouse may end up with an estate tax problem upon his or her death because he or she will have all the couple's assets. (See the following section for a legal way around this issue, appropriately called a *bypass trust*.) You face three other less likely but potential problems:

- ✔ You and your spouse could die simultaneously.

- ✔ The unlimited marital deduction is not allowed if your spouse isn't a U.S. citizen.

- ✔ Some states don't allow the unlimited marital deduction, so be sure to find out about the situation in your state.

Establishing a bypass trust

As we discussed in the preceding section, a potential estate tax problem is created upon the death of a spouse if all of his or her assets pass to the surviving spouse. When the surviving spouse dies, $1,000,000 (for tax year 2003) can be passed on free of federal estate taxes.

If you have substantial assets, both you and your spouse can take advantage of the $1,000,000 estate-tax-free rule and pass to your heirs a total of $2 million estate-tax-free. By shielding an additional $1,000,000 from estate taxes, you save your heirs more than $400,000 in estate taxes. Thanks to recent tax law changes, the value of this strategy mushrooms as the amount you can pass on free of estate taxes greatly increases. How? Each of you can arrange a *bypass trust* (also known as *credit shelter* or *exemption equivalent*) in your will.

Upon the death of the first spouse, assets held in that spouse's name go into a trust. The surviving spouse and/or other heirs still can use the income from those assets and even some of the principal. They can receive 5 percent of the value of the trust or $5,000, whichever is greater, each year. They also can draw additional principal if they need it for educational, health, or living expenses. Ultimately, the assets in the bypass trust pass to the designated beneficiaries (usually, but not limited to, children).

For a bypass trust to work, you likely will need to rework how you hold ownership of your assets (for example, jointly or individually). You may need to individually title your assets so that each spouse holds $1,000,000 in assets and so that each can take full advantage of the $1,000,000 estate tax–free limit.

Remember, in the years ahead, bypass trusts will become even more valuable. As the amount that an individual can pass on free of estate taxes rises to $3.5 million by the year 2009, a married couple will be able to pass on a total of $7 million free of estate taxes when they use a bypass trust.

Our attorney friends tell us that you need to be careful when setting up a bypass trust so that it's funded up to the full amount of the current federal tax–free exemption amount in Table 26-1. The reason: The surviving spouse may otherwise end up with less than what would've been desired. Be sure to read the section "Getting advice and help," later in this chapter, for how to obtain good legal and tax advice.

Buying cash-value life insurance

Two major types of life insurance exist. Most people who need life insurance — and who have someone dependent on their income — need to buy term life insurance, which is pure life insurance: You pay an annual premium for which you receive a predetermined amount of life insurance protection. If the insured person passes away, the beneficiaries collect; otherwise, the premium is gone. In this way, term life insurance is similar to auto or homeowner's insurance.

The other kind of life insurance, called *cash-value* life insurance, is probably one of the most oversold financial products in the history of Western civilization. Cash-value policies (whole, universal, variable, and so on) combine life insurance with a supposed savings feature. Your premiums not only pay for life insurance, but some of your dollars also are credited to an account that grows in value over time, assuming that you keep paying your premiums. On the surface, a cash-value life policy sounds potentially attractive.

When bought and placed in an irrevocable life insurance trust (which we discuss later in this chapter), life insurance, it's true, receives special treatment with regard to estate taxes. Specifically, the death benefit or proceeds paid on the policy upon your death can pass to your designated heirs free of estate taxes. (Some states, however, don't allow this.)

People who sell cash-value insurance — that is, insurance salespeople and other life insurance brokers masquerading as estate-planning specialists and financial planners — too often advocate life insurance as the best, and only, way to reduce estate taxes. But the other methods we discuss in this chapter are superior in most cases.

Insurance companies aren't stupid. In fact, they're quite smart. If you purchase a cash-value life insurance policy that provides a death benefit of, say, $1 million, you have to pay substantial insurance premiums, although far less than $1 million. Is that a good deal for you? No, because the insurance company invests your premium dollars and earns a return the same way as you otherwise would have, had you invested the money instead of using it to buy the life insurance.

Don't get seduced into buying cash-value life insurance for the wrong reasons

Some insurance salespeople aggressively push cash-value policies because of the high commissions (50 percent to 100 percent of the first year's premium paid by you) that insurance companies pay their agents. These policies are expensive ways to purchase life insurance. Because of their high cost (about eight times the cost of the same amount of term life insurance), you're more likely to buy less life insurance coverage than you need, which, unfortunately, is the sad result of the insurance industry pushing this stuff. The vast majority of life insurance buyers need more protection than they can afford to buy in cash-value coverage.

Agents know which buttons to push to get you interested in buying the wrong kind of life insurance. Insurance agents show you all sorts of projections implying that after the first 10 or 20 years of paying your premiums, you won't need to pay more premiums to keep the life insurance in force. The only reason you may be able to stop paying premiums is that you've poured too much extra money into the policy in the early years of payment. Remember that cash-value life insurance costs eight times as much as term.

Insurance agents also argue that your cash value grows tax-deferred. But if you want tax-deferred retirement savings, you first need to take advantage of retirement savings plans such as 401(k)s, 403(b)s, SEP-IRAs, and Keoghs. These plans, which will have even greater contribution limits in the years ahead thanks to recent tax law changes, give you an immediate tax deduction for your current contributions in addition to growth without taxation until withdrawal. Money paid into a cash-value life policy gives you no upfront tax breaks. When you've exhausted the tax-deductible plans, then variable annuities or a nondeductible IRA can provide tax-deferred compounding of your investment dollars (see Chapter 21).

Life insurance tends to be a mediocre investment anyway. The insurance company quotes you an interest rate for the first year only. After that, the rate is at the company's discretion. If you don't like the future interest rates, you can be penalized for quitting the policy. Would you invest your money in a bank account that quoted an interest rate for the first year only and then penalized you for moving your money in the next seven to ten years?

Through the years, between the premiums you pay on your life policy and the returns the insurance company earns investing your premiums, the insurance company is able to come up with more than $1 million. Otherwise, how could it afford to pay out a death benefit of $1 million on your policy?

Using life insurance as an estate-planning tool is beneficial if your estate includes assets that you don't want to subject to a forced sale to pay estate taxes after you die. For example, small-business owners whose businesses are worth millions may want to consider cash-value life insurance under special circumstances. If your estate will lack the other necessary assets to pay expected estate taxes and you don't want your beneficiaries to be forced to sell the business, you can buy life insurance to pay expected estate taxes.

For advice on whether life insurance is an appropriate estate-planning strategy for you, don't expect to get objective information from anyone who sells life insurance. Please see the section "Getting advice and help," later in this chapter.

Among the best places to shop for cash-value life insurance policies are the following:

- ✔ USAA (800-531-8000)
- ✔ Ameritas (800-552-3553)
- ✔ Waterhouse Insurance (800-622-3699)

Setting up trusts

If estate planning hasn't already given you a headache, understanding the different types of trusts should. A *trust* is a legal device used to pass to someone else the management responsibility and, ultimately, the ownership of some of your assets. We discussed some trusts, such as bypass, Crummey, and life insurance trusts, earlier in this chapter; here, we talk about other trusts you may hear about when planning your estate.

Living trusts

A *living trust* effectively transfers assets into a trust. When you use a *revocable living trust,* you control those assets and can revoke the trust whenever you desire. The advantage of a living trust is that upon your death, assets can pass directly to your beneficiaries without going through *probate,* the legal process for administering and implementing the directions in a will.

Living trusts keep your assets out of probate but in and of themselves do nothing to help you deal with estate taxes. Living trusts can contain bypass trusts and other estate tax–saving provisions.

Property and assets that are owned in joint tenancy or inside retirement accounts — such as IRAs or 401(k)s — and have designated beneficiaries generally pass to heirs without going through probate. (Many states also allow a special type of revocable trust for bank accounts called a *Totten trust,* which also insulates the bank accounts from probate. Such trusts are established for the benefit of another person, and the money in the trust is paid to that beneficiary upon the account holder's death.)

Probate can be a lengthy, expensive hassle for your heirs. Attorney probate fees may approach 5 percent to 7 percent of the estate's value. In addition, the details of your assets become public record because of probate. In addition to saving you on probate fees and maintaining your financial privacy, living trusts are useful in naming someone to administer your affairs in the event you become incapacitated.

Wills

Wills—legal documents that detail your instructions for what you want done with your personal property and assets upon your death—won't save you on taxes or on probate. Wills are, however, an estate-planning basic that most people should have but don't. Most of the world doesn't bother with wills, because laws and customs divvy up a person's estate among the spouse and children or other close relatives.

The main benefit of a will is that it ensures that your wishes for the distribution of your assets are fulfilled. If you die without a will (known in legalese as *intestate*), your state decides how to distribute your money and other property, according to state law. Therefore, your friends, more-distant relatives, and favorite charities will probably receive nothing. For a fee, the state appoints an administrator to supervise the distribution of your assets.

If you have little in the way of personal assets and don't really care who gets your possessions and other assets (state law usually specifies the closest blood relatives), you can forget about creating a will. You can save yourself the time and depression that inevitably accompanies this gloomy exercise.

When you have minor (dependent) children, a will is necessary to name a guardian for them. In the event that you and your spouse both die without a will, the state (courts and social service agencies) decides who raises your children. Therefore, even if you can't decide at this time who would raise your children, you at least need to appoint a trusted guardian who can decide for you.

Living wills and medical powers of attorney are useful additions to a standard will. A living will tells your doctor what, if any, life-support measures you would accept. A medical power of attorney grants authority to someone you trust to make decisions with a physician regarding your medical options. These additional documents usually are prepared when a will is drawn up.

You can't escape the undertaker or the lawyers. Setting up a trust and transferring property in and out costs money and time. Thus living trusts are likely to be of greatest value to people who are age 60 and older, are single, and own assets worth more than $100,000 that must pass through probate (including real estate, nonretirement accounts, and businesses). Small estates actually may be less expensive to probate in some states than the cost and hassle of setting up a living trust.

Charitable trusts

If you're feeling philanthropic, charitable trusts may be for you. With a *charitable remainder trust,* you or your designated beneficiary receives income from assets that you donate to a charity. At the time of your death, or after a certain number of years, the principal is donated to the charity and is thus removed from your taxable estate. A charitable remainder trust makes especially good sense in cases where a person holds an asset that he or she wants to donate that has greatly appreciated in value. By not selling the asset before the donation, a hefty tax on the profit is avoided.

In a *charitable lead trust,* the roles of the charity and beneficiaries are reversed. The charity receives the income from the assets for a set number of years or until you pass away, at which point the assets pass to your beneficiary. You get a current income tax deduction for the value of the expected payments to the charity.

Getting advice and help

The number of people who happily will charge you a fee for or sell you some legal advice or insurance far exceeds the number actually qualified to render objective estate-planning advice. Attorneys, accountants, financial planners, estate-planning specialists, investment companies, insurance agents, and even some nonprofit agencies stand ready to help you figure out how to dispense your wealth.

Most of these people and organizations have conflicts of interest and lack the knowledge necessary to do sound estate planning for you. Attorneys are biased toward drafting legal documents and devices that are more complicated than may be needed. Insurance agents and financial planners who work on commission try to sell cash-value life insurance. Investment firms and banks encourage you to establish a trust account that requires them to manage the assets in the future.

Although the cost of *free* estate-planning seminars is tempting, you get what you pay for — or worse.

Start the process of planning your estate by first looking at the big picture. Talk to your family members about your financial situation. Many people never take this basic but critical step. Your heirs likely have no idea what you're considering or what you're worried about. Conversely, how can you develop a solid action plan without understanding your heirs' needs and concerns? Be careful not to use money to control or manipulate other family members.

For professional advice, you need someone who can look objectively at the big picture. Attorneys and tax advisors who specialize in estate planning are a good starting point. Ask the people you're thinking of hiring whether they sell life insurance or manage money. If they do, they can't possibly be objective and likely aren't sufficiently educated about estate planning, given their focus.

For preparation of wills and living trusts, check out the high-quality software programs on the market. Legal software may save you from the often-difficult task of finding a competent and affordable attorney. Preparing documents with software also can save you money.

Estate planning from the grave

It goes without saying that not everyone does the right type of estate planning before passing on. Some people die before their time, and others just can't seem to get around to the planning part, even when they're in failing health.

Although further planning after you're dead and gone is impossible, your heirs may legally take steps that can, in some cases, dramatically reduce state taxes. Some legal folks call these steps postmortem planning. Here's an example of how it works.

Suppose that Peter Procrastinator never got around to planning for the distribution of his substantial estate. When he died, all of his estate was to go to his wife. No dummy, his wife hired legal help so that she could disclaim, or reject, part of Peter's big estate. Why would she do that? Simple, so that part of the estate could immediately go to their children. If she hadn't disclaimed, Peter would have missed out on his $1,000,000 estate tax exclusion. By disclaiming, she possibly saved her heirs more than $400,000 in estate taxes. (As the estate tax exemption amount increases in the years ahead as per Table 26-1, disclaiming will be a useful and necessary strategy for fewer and fewer estates.)

The person doing the disclaiming, in this case Peter's wife, may not direct to whom the disclaimed assets will go. Peter's will or other legal documents specify who is second in line. Disclaimers are also irrevocable, must be made in writing, and are subject to other IRS rules and regulations. A knowledgeable executor and attorney can help you with disclaiming.

Using legal software is generally preferable to using fill-in-the-blank documents. Software has the built-in virtues of directing and limiting your choices and keeping you from making common mistakes. Quality software also incorporates the knowledge and insights of the legal eagles who developed the software.

As for the legality of documents that you create with software, remember that a will, for example, is made legal and valid by you and your witnesses properly signing the document. An attorney preparing a document is not what makes it legal. If your situation isn't unusual, legal software may work well for you.

For will and living trust preparation, check out *WillMaker Plus* by Nolo Press. In addition to enabling you to prepare wills (in every state except Louisiana), *WillMaker Plus* can help you create a living will, medical power of attorney (as we discuss earlier in the chapter) and a living trust. Living trusts are fairly standard legal documents that serve to keep property out of probate in the event of your death (remember that it doesn't address the issue of estate taxes). The software package advises you to seek professional guidance for your situation, if necessary.

If you want to do more reading on estate planning, pick up a copy of *Plan Your Estate* by Denis Clifford & Cora Jordan (Nolo Press). When you have a large estate that may be subject to estate taxes, it may be worth your time and money to consult an attorney or tax advisor who specializes in estate planning. Get smarter first and learn the lingo before you seek and pay for advice.

Part VI
The Part of Tens

The 5th Wave   By Rich Tennant

Hello. You've reached the IRS help line. Press 1 if you've been slightly negligent and need more time to procrastinate; press 2 if you're not very good at math and made some glaring errors; press 3 if you're a lying cheat and hope we won't notice...

In this part . . .

These short chapters can be read just about anytime you have a few spare minutes, and they're packed with information that needs to stand out. We highlight, for example, the ten most important recent changes in the tax laws. By reading these chapters, you'll also know the ten best ways to avoid an audit, the answers to ten other important tax questions, the top ten ways to reduce your taxes that you or your friends may overlook, and even the ten interview questions you should be sure to ask a tax advisor you're considering hiring.

Chapter 27

Ten Important Tax Law Changes

●●●

Congressional representatives just can't leave the tax laws alone! Only two years ago, lawmakers passed the largest tax cut in a generation as a part of one of the most complicated pieces of tax legislation ever. Hundreds of tax law changes from that bill are being phased in through the year 2010. Then, over Memorial Day weekend, 2003, the U.S. House and Senate put the finishing touches on yet another major tax bill — the *Jobs and Growth Tax Relief Reconciliation Act of 2003*. Although not as large as the package passed in 2001, this new set of tax law changes includes plenty more opportunities for Americans to reduce their federal income taxes.

This chapter highlights the most significant income tax changes that are likely to affect your situation now and in the years ahead. Relevant but smaller changes, are covered in detail elsewhere in this book.

Lowering tax rates for everyone

One of the great misconceptions of the 2003 tax law changes is that they benefit only certain people — wealthy investors, parents with minor children and so on. The reality (and the good news) is that just about everybody who earns taxable income benefits from this new tax bill.

Under the new law, single taxpayers will pay 10 percent on their first $7,000 of taxable income, which is increased from the previous $6,000 level. All taxable income above $28,400 is taxed at least 2 percent lower than the previous rate (see Table 27-1).

For married couples filing jointly, the first $14,000 of taxable income (it was $12,000) is taxed at 10 percent, and income from $14,000 to $56,800 (up from $47,450 previously) is taxed at 15 percent. Taxable incomes that are greater than $56,800 are taxed at least 2 percent lower than the previous rate. See Table 27-2.

Table 27-1	How the 2003 Tax Bill Changed the Tax Brackets and Rates For Single Filers		
Old Law		**New Law**	
2003 Taxable Income	*Tax Rate*	*2003 Taxable Income*	*Tax Rate*
$0–$6,000	10%	$0–$7,000	10%
$6,000–$28,400	15%	$7,000–$28,400	15%
$28,400–$68,800	27%	$28,400–$68,800	25%
$68,800–$143,500	30%	$68,800–$143,500	28%
$143,500–$311,950	35%	$143,500–$311,950	33%
More than $311,950	38.6%	More than $311,950	35%

Table 27-2	How the 2003 Tax Bill Changed the Tax Brackets and Rates for Married Couples Filing Jointly			
Old Law			**New Law**	
2003 Taxable Income	Tax Rate		2003 Taxable Income	Tax Rate
$0–$12,000	10%		$0–$14,000	10%
$12,000–$47,450	15%		$14,000–$56,800	15%
$47,450–$114,650	27%		$56,800–$114,650	25%
$114,650–$174,700	30%		$114,650–$174,700	28%
$174,700–$311,950	35%		$174,700–$311,950	33%
More than $311,950	38.6%		More than $311,950	35%

Getting extra credit for kids

Taxpayers with dependent children will enjoy an increased child tax credit of $1,000 per child in tax year 2003 (up from $600 in 2002). The extra $400 credit per child was mailed out as a tax rebate check this past summer to taxpayers who appeared to be eligible based upon their prior year's tax return.

This credit applies only to dependent children who are U.S. citizens and are younger than 17 on December 31 of the tax year. The credit also phases out for married couples with adjusted gross incomes (AGIs) above $110,000 and singles with AGIs above $75,000. Please see Chapter 8 to determine whether you're eligible for the credit and the amount of the credit to which you're entitled.

You also need to be aware of some of the following tax treats for families claiming the dependent-care credit or adopting:

- **Increased dependent-care credits:** Dependent-care tax credits, which apply to parents who work and hire someone to help care for their children, increase to a maximum of $3,000 per child in tax year 2003, with a $6,000 per-family limit for parents with two or more kids.

  The income threshold at which the credit phases out and the amount of qualifying employment-related expenses for which the credit can be claimed increase in tax year 2003. See Chapter 25 for details.

- **Expanded adoption tax benefits:** The adoption tax credit has been made permanent and increased to $10,160 per child. This credit begins to phase out at $152,390 of modified AGI and is eliminated completely at $192,390. The phase-out will be adjusted in the future with inflation.

  The credit for adopting special-needs kids also increases to $10,160 per child. And beginning with tax year 2003, the adoption tax credit is allowed when adopting special-needs children, even if the taxpayer doesn't actually incur that amount of qualified adoption expenses. Likewise, the maximum exclusion from taxable income of company-paid adoption aid increased to $10,160 per child.

Reducing tax rates for long-term capital gains and stock dividends

Capital gains tax applies when you sell an investment at a higher price than you paid for it. Your capital gains tax rate for securities or mutual funds held more than one year is lower than the tax rate you pay on ordinary income, such as income from employment earnings or interest on bank savings accounts.

Tax cuts: economic booster or boon for the rich?

Tax cuts enable people to keep more of the money they earn and therefore spend and save more, which, in turn, helps the economy. Consider for a moment what would happen if the government took 100 percent of your earnings as taxes. You'd have no money to spend or to save!

Although much has been made of higher income earners reaping greater tax savings from this new tax bill, these greater savings are true only in terms of absolute dollars and not in terms of percentage tax reduction.

Remember that the more affluent pay the lion's share of taxes in the U.S. The top 1 percent of all income earners pay a whopping 30 percent of all personal federal income taxes collected. The top 20 percent of income earners pay nearly 80 percent of all personal federal income taxes paid.

You can pay a federal income tax rate as high as 35 percent on ordinary income, but the maximum federal capital gains tax for long-term gains (investments held more than one year) is now only 15 percent. And, the long-term capital gains tax rate is only 5 percent for taxpayers in the 10 percent and 15 percent federal income tax brackets.

These same lower long-term capital gains tax rates also apply to dividends paid by corporations (domestic or foreign). For people whose incomes place them in the four highest federal income tax brackets (25 percent, 28 percent, 33 percent, and 35 percent), the new tax rate on stock dividends is only 15 percent. Taxpayers in the 10 percent and 15 percent federal income tax brackets will pay a mere 5 percent tax rate on dividends. (The dividend tax rate actually falls to zero for these latter two brackets in 2008.)

Even though the income paid on bond funds and money market funds is referred to as a "dividend," such income doesn't qualify for the new, lower federal income tax rates on stock dividends. Dividend income that you receive from mutual funds holding stocks will qualify for the lower dividend tax rate. Please see Chapter 23 for more details on tax-wise investment strategies.

Greater retirement plan contribution limits

A major change coming out of recent tax bills are the significantly higher amounts that you're allowed to sock away into retirement savings plans. Employer-based plans — 401(k), 403(b), and 457 plans — have a tax year 2003 contribution limit of $12,000. Contribution limits rise to $15,000 by 2006, and after 2006, the contribution limits increase in $500 increments with corresponding increases in the cost of living. If you're older and want to save even more, you're in luck! People aged 50 and older now can put away up to an extra $1,000 in 2003, and up to $5,000 more per year starting in 2006. See Chapter 21 for details.

A newer type of retirement plan, the SIMPLE-IRA, which is used mostly by smaller employers, also will enjoy higher contribution limits in years ahead. The current employee contribution limit of $8,000 gradually rises to $10,000 in 2005. As with other employer-based retirement plans, people 50 and older will be able to put even more into their SIMPLE-IRA plans. The SIMPLE-IRA contribution limits also increase with inflation (in increments of $500) after 2006. See Chapter 21 for more information.

The self-employed also can join in the fun of greater retirement contributions. The contribution limits on SEP-IRA and Keogh plans now are $40,000 annually. Please see Chapter 21 for the specifics.

Last but not least, the contribution limit for Individual Retirement Accounts (IRA), both regular IRAs and Roth IRAs, is now $3,000 and eventually increases to $5,000 in 2008 (and thereafter limits will be adjusted for inflation). People 50 and older can put away even more — an extra $500 for tax year 2003 and an extra $1,000 by 2006. As we discuss in Chapter 21, you generally need to exhaust your contributions to retirement plans offering upfront tax deductions before considering nondeductible IRA contributions.

New retirement plan tax credits

A tax credit of up to 50 percent of qualified retirement plan contributions may be yours if you're a lower-income earner. Like employer matching contributions, this tax credit is like free money — in this case from the federal government — as an incentive to save toward your retirement.

The maximum credit of 50 percent applies to the first $2,000 of retirement plan contributions per year for single taxpayers with AGIs of no more than $15,000 and married couples filing jointly with AGIs of no more than $30,000. Smaller tax credits are available for single taxpayers with AGIs of up to $25,000 and married couples filing jointly with AGIs of up to $50,000. See Chapter 21 for details.

Qualifying small employers who establish a new retirement savings plan likewise may be eligible for a tax credit toward some of the costs of their retirement plans. The credit, which is for a maximum of $500 per year for up to three years, is for 50 percent of the employer's cost of setting up and maintaining the retirement plan. See Chapter 21 for more information.

New (and improved) college cost tax benefits

Some parents who face daunting college bills can enjoy some tax relief starting with a new deduction of up to $3,000 for college costs. The maximum write-off increases to $4,000 in 2004. This provision expires after tax year 2005, unless Congress decides to extend it, which it surely will. Higher-income earners are shut out from claiming this deduction. If your AGI exceeds $65,000 for singles and $130,000 for married couples filing jointly, you can't claim this deduction.

Further complicating matters, single taxpayers with AGIs of up to $80,000 and married couples filing jointly with AGIs of up to $160,000 can take a partial deduction in 2004 — up to $2,000 in college costs. One other little twist on who can and can't claim this tax break: You can't take the Hope or Lifetime Learning credit (see Chapter 25) in the same tax year that you take this deduction.

Some taxpayers will enjoy a tax break enhancement after they start paying back student loans. The interest write-off on student loans no longer is restricted to interest paid during the first five years of loan payback. Also, early repayment of interest now is deductible.

The income thresholds are raised in tax year 2002 for those who can take the student loan interest write-off. The deduction is eliminated for single taxpayers with incomes higher than $65,000, and for couples with incomes higher than $130,000. These thresholds increase annually for inflation.

Finally, tax-free college savings plan withdrawals now are allowed. To qualify, withdrawals must be used to pay for qualified higher education expenses and enrollment and attendance expenses for special-needs students. See Chapter 25 for more information.

Improved Education Savings Accounts

The relatively new Education Savings Accounts (ESAs) are now much better, although, as we've cautioned in the past, you must be careful when contributing to such accounts, because you can suffer reduced financial aid for your kids (see Chapter 25). Here are the recent improvements to ESAs:

✔ The annual contribution limit on ESAs is now $2,000 per child (up from $500).

✔ Balances in ESAs can be used to pay for elementary and secondary school costs (that is, kindergarten through grade 12) in addition to higher education costs.

✔ The modified adjusted gross income limitation for married couples filing jointly is now double (phase-out range of $190,000 to $220,000) that for single taxpayers (phase-out range of $95,000 to $110,000).

✔ You can make contributions for a given tax year until April 15 of the following year.

✔ Contributions may be made for special-needs students older than 18 and allow for the continuation of such accounts past age 30.

For more details on ESA rules, including which educational expenses qualify, see Chapter 25.

Reducing estate taxes

Although higher-income earners are precluded from some of the new tax benefits, a number of estate tax law changes benefit more affluent taxpayers. First, amounts that can be left free of federal estate taxes rise substantially in the years ahead, from the current level of $1,000,000 to a whopping $3.5 million by 2009. In 2010, the estate tax disappears completely but then comes back the next year (2011) with a limit of $1 million! For our thoughts on how to plan your estate in the face of such bizarre changes ahead, see Chapter 26.

The actual tax rate that applies to estates in excess of amounts that can be passed along free of federal estate tax will be reduced slightly in the years ahead. In 2010, additional estate tax law changes that affect capital gains on inherited property and assets take effect. See Chapter 26 for details.

Relieving the marriage penalty

For years, some married couples have found that they pay more in total income taxes as a married couple than they did as two single taxpayers. Recently passed tax laws that address at least some of this inequity include:

✔ Widening the 15 percent tax break for married couples filing jointly beginning in 2005. By 2008, it will be twice the size of the 15 percent bracket for single taxpayers.

✔ Gradually increasing the standard deduction for married couples filing jointly between 2005 and 2009, when it reaches two times the amount allowed a single taxpayer.

✔ Annually increasing the level of income for married couples filing jointly at which the earned income credit (EIC) is phased out.

So if your parents, your in-laws, or your conscience have been pressing you to get married, one drawback has now (at least somewhat) been eliminated!

Yet more retirement plan options

Americans already face a bewildering array of retirement plan options, rules, and regulations. Beginning with tax year 2006, after-tax Roth contributions will be allowed to 401(k) and 403(b) plans. Okay, we're sure you're asking, "What the heck is an 'after-tax Roth contribution'?"

After-tax simply means that unlike regular 401(k) and 403(b) plan contributions, you receive upfront tax break on such contributions. *Roth* means that, as with contributions to a Roth IRA account, investment earnings won't be taxed upon withdrawal during your golden years (at least under the tax laws now on the books). Please read Chapter 21 for the details on these new options and our take on which type of retirement accounts you need to fund first.

And a hodgepodge of other tax law changes . . .

At the beginning of this chapter, we said we'd highlight the most significant and recent tax law changes. We couldn't possibly cover every little change here. For example, beginning in tax year 2006, higher-income taxpayers will begin enjoying the gradual repeal of itemized deductions and personal exemption phaseouts. Higher-income taxpayers currently lose some of their itemized deductions on Schedule A and some or even all of their personal exemptions on Form 1040. The repeal is phased back in beginning in 2006 and completed in 2010, just in time for the new tax laws to expire in 2011.

Throughout this book, we cover as many of these relevant changes as we can. However, because some of these changes are years away from being implemented, may be modified or eliminated with future law changes, and have little impact on your current tax planning, stay tuned to future editions of *Taxes For Dummies* as Congress keeps tinkering.

Chapter 28

Ten Important Tax Questions

• •

*T*hrough the years, many people have asked us all sorts of tax questions. But we've also noted the conspicuous absence of some of the questions people should ask — sometimes you don't know what to ask because you don't know what you don't know!

Plus, we figure that there are some questions you'd really like to ask but don't feel comfortable asking. We answer all these questions for you right now in this chapter.

If I can't make (or already missed) the deadline for filing my return and paying the tax I owe, what do I do?

Don't panic, don't jump off a bridge, and don't get an unlisted home telephone number. However, do get on the stick because unless you lost your records in a fire or some other documented catastrophe (your dog eating them doesn't count), when you miss the April 15 filing deadline, you owe interest and penalties in addition to your taxes. Every day you delay coming clean, the more it's going to cost you as the interest and penalties mount.

Join millions of others and get yourself an additional four months to procrastinate by filing **IRS Form 4868.** (You can find this form in the back of the book — you'd think that the IRS would put this document in its booklet because this form is the one many people realize they need at the last minute.) You need not have a good excuse for the extension — you get it even if you were too busy having fun.

Even if you file an extension, you're still obligated to pay the tax you owe. Because you haven't completed your tax return (that's why you need the extension, right?), you don't know how much you owe. So you're going to have to estimate. Better to overestimate and send the IRS a bit more than you think you need to. Otherwise, you'll owe interest and penalties on past-due tax.

When you don't have the money to pay your taxes, contacting the IRS and explaining is far better than ignoring your situation. The IRS surprisingly is understanding and will work out a payment plan for you (with interest, of course). Refer to Chapter 19 for tips on what to do if you can't pay. If you don't have the necessary records to prepare your return, please see Chapter 3.

How can I know that I'm not overlooking deductions?

Educate yourself. You don't know what you're missing until you know what goodies are available. This book, particularly Parts II, III, and V, can help you see the light. If you're currently working with a tax preparer and aren't confident in his or her capabilities, consider getting a second opinion by taking your past couple of tax returns to another preparer and finding out whether the new preparer uncovers other tax-reduction opportunities. Chapter 2 details other tax resources and provides tips for finding a good tax advisor.

How long should I keep my tax forms?

The quick answer is three years from your official filing date (usually April 15). But check out Chapter 3 for a few exceptions to this rule — remember, the IRS loves exceptions to the rules.

If I forgot to deduct something in a prior tax year, may I go back and fix my mistake now?

It depends on what you forgot and how long ago you filed your return. Unfortunately, one of the best deductions available, the one for retirement accounts, can't be claimed on an amended return (unless the money was legally contributed by the relevant contribution and tax return filing deadline). Other oversights you made in reporting your income, deductions, and expenses generally can be handled on **Form 1040X, Amended U.S. Individual Income Tax Return.** Call the IRS at 800-829-3676 for a copy of Form 1040X, or use the form in the back of this book.

You must file your amendments within three years of April 15 of the year you filed the original return. (If you filed after April 15 because you got an extension, count the amendment due date as three years from the date when you actually filed your completed return.) Refer to Chapter 19 to find out how to amend your return.

Why do I pay so much in taxes?

People in the United States actually pay less in taxes (as a portion of their incomes) than people in most developed countries do. It's easy to overlook all the stuff tax dollars pay for, such as national defense, roads, bridges, schools, libraries, police departments, Social Security income, and retiree health-care benefits.

The best — and legal — way to reduce your taxes is to master the strategies that we discuss in this book, some of which can be applied when preparing your annual return (Parts II and III), and others that involve advance planning (Part V).

You can reduce some taxes, such as sales taxes, simply by spending less money. Besides saving you tax dollars, this approach can boost your investment balances. If you're like most Americans, you probably aren't saving enough, anyway. Now you have another reason to cut your spending — to reduce your taxes.

Blaming the government for high taxes is tempting. Effecting change through government is slow and unlikely. But when you can change your personal financial behavior, you can save big tax dollars. Your ability to take advantage of most tax-saving maneuvers hinges on your consistently spending less than you earn so that you have cash to invest.

Haven't they closed all the tax loopholes?

Tax laws in recent decades eliminated many of the financial schemes concocted to reduce taxes. The closing of these loopholes put a number of investment salespeople and "creative" financial planners out of business. Thankfully, this reduces the likelihood of your being hoodwinked into making some bad investments. Fewer loopholes create a more level playing field. Most of the tax-reduction strategies that we discuss in this book are open to people of any economic means. Read away and slash your taxes!

Why do the wealthy and corporations pay so little in taxes?

This myth is perpetuated by those rare but highly publicized cases where — because of large write-offs — affluent people and mighty corporations appear to slide by without paying their fair share of taxes. Yet the truth is that the highest-income earners typically pay more in taxes than most of us earn in a year! The top 1 percent of income earners pay about 36 percent of all federal taxes. That's why some of these folks moan and complain about how much they pay in taxes. (The polite ones complain to their tax and financial advisors, lest others think that they're ungrateful for their high incomes!)

The only way a person or company with a big income can end up paying less in taxes than a person or company with a smaller income is if they spend a great deal of money on tax-deductible stuff, such as mortgage interest, property taxes, and reinvesting in business. These perfectly legal write-offs are available to anyone, regardless of income. In fact, low-income earners have tax deductions, such as the earned income tax credit, that others can't take. Other deductions — such as for mortgage interest — have limitations ($1.1 million in total mortgage debt) on how much can be claimed.

It's true that the wealthy and corporations can afford to employ tax advisors to keep their tax bills to a minimum, but what they do to reduce their taxes still has to be legal. Cheating is illegal for all taxpayers, and the IRS audits at the highest rate those with the deepest pockets.

Shouldn't 1 buy real estate to reduce my taxes?

You can write off mortgage interest and property taxes on most pieces of real estate (for more details, see Chapter 23). This type of write-off can help, but you shouldn't buy real estate just because of these tax breaks. You should own a home because you need a place to live long-term. Besides, owning should cost you less than paying ever-escalating rent over the years.

Remember that the tax benefits available on homes are factored into the current selling prices. This is one of the reasons that real estate seems expensive.

How can 1 avoid a last-minute scramble for documents?

One of the easiest tax headaches to avoid is the search for tax forms while you're already stressed with getting your tax return done on time. We include, in the back of this book, the tax forms you're most likely to need. (You're welcome.) You can also pick up the forms the next time you're at the local post office or public library, or call the IRS at 800-829-3676 to have them send you the forms you need.

If you have access to the Internet, you can download the tax forms you need (for free!) from the IRS's World Wide Web page (start browsing at www.irs.gov). You need Adobe Acrobat Reader (and you can download it for free from the IRS Web page or from Adobe's Web page at www.adobe.com). Simply download the form you need and print it; the IRS happily accepts the form when you file your return.

Setting up a filing system can be a big time-saver if you experience the missing-form syndrome. If you have limited patience for setting up neat file folders (that is, you haven't saved the receipts that you need for tax purposes throughout the year) and you lead an uncomplicated financial life, you can confine your filing to January and February. During those months, you find in the mailbox your tax booklets from the IRS and your state tax authority, along with tax summary forms on wages paid by your employer (W-2), investment income (1099), and home mortgage interest (1098). Find a file folder or big envelope and label it something easy to remember — "Taxes 2003" may be an appropriate choice — and then dump in all these forms as they arrive. When you're ready to crunch numbers, just open the file or envelope and away you go! See Chapter 3 for more organizing tips.

Why should 1 work so hard just to pay all these taxes?

More people should be asking this question, especially two-income families. Although we don't want to get into trouble by suggesting that someone may not be spending enough time at home with the kids or with other important causes, many couples pay a high effective rate of tax on the second income.

That second-income earner may be making only the minimum wage when you factor in all the commuting costs, lunches out, work-clothing expenses, child-care expenses, and so on. Of course, there are other benefits to working besides money. But you have to ask yourself whether commuting traffic jams and office politics are really worth the minimum wage!

Most people don't make the most of their money. They work hard at earning money but not at educating themselves about how to make it stretch farther. That's why you owe it to yourself to read Part V of this book.

Chapter 29

Ten Tips for Reducing Your Chances of Being Audited

If you've never been audited, you probably fall into one of these categories: You're still young, you haven't made gobs of money, or you're just plain lucky. The fact is that many taxpayers are audited during their adult lives. It's just a matter of time and probability.

Even well-meaning and humble authors of well-meaning and humble tax-advice books aren't exempt. One of us, Eric, has stared down an audit and says that the audit wasn't too bad — sort of like preparing for an exam . . . in a course you aren't taking for credit!

You can take some common-sense steps (honesty being the star of the show) to reduce your chances of having to face an audit. After all, instead of wasting your day in some IRS office, you want to make sure that you have sufficient time for jury duty or to run down to the Department of Motor Vehicles to renew your driver's license. So here are our top tips for lessening your chances of being audited and avoiding all the time and associated costs of an audit.

Double-check your return for accuracy

Audit your own return *before* you send it in. If the IRS finds mistakes through its increasingly sophisticated computer-checking equipment, you're more likely to be audited. They figure that if they find obvious errors, some not-so-obvious ones lurk beneath the surface.

Have you included all your income? Think about the different accounts you had during the tax year. Do you have interest and dividend statements for *all* your accounts? Finding these statements is easier if you've been keeping your financial records in one place. Check your W-2s and 1099s against your tax form to make sure that you wrote the numbers down correctly.

Don't forget to check your math. Have you added, subtracted, multiplied, and divided correctly? Are your Social Security number and address correct on the return? Did you sign and date your return?

Such infractions will not, on their own, trigger an audit. In some cases, the IRS simply writes you a letter requesting your signature or the additional tax you owe (if the math mistake isn't too fishy or too big). In some rare instances, the IRS even sends a refund if the mistake it uncovers is in the taxpayer's favor — really! Regardless of how the IRS handles the mistake, it can be a headache for you to clear up, and, more important, it can cost you extra money.

Declare all your income

When you prepare your return, you may be tempted to shave off a little of that consulting income you received. Who will miss it, right? The IRS, that's who.

Thanks largely to computer cross-checking, the IRS has many ways of finding unreported income. Be particularly careful if you're self-employed; anyone who pays you more than $600 in a year is required to file a Form 1099, which basically tells the IRS how much you received.

When you knowingly hide income, you face substantial penalties and, depending on the amount, criminal prosecution. That wouldn't be a picnic, especially if you can't afford to hire a good defense attorney.

Don't itemize

People who itemize their deductions on Schedule A are far more likely to be audited because they have more opportunity and temptation to cheat. By all means, if you can *legally* claim more total deductions by using Schedule A than you can with the standard deduction (this deduction stuff is all spelled out in Chapter 9), we say "itemize, itemize, itemize." Just don't try to artificially inflate your deductions.

On the other hand, if it's basically a toss-up between Schedule A and your standard deduction, it's safer to take the standard deduction, which the IRS can't challenge.

Earn less money

At first glance, this may seem like an odd suggestion, but there really are costs associated with affluence. One of the costs of a high income — besides higher taxes — is a dramatic increase in the probability of being audited. If your income is more than $100,000, you have about a 1 in 20 chance each year of being audited. But your chance is less than 1 in 100 if your income is less than $50,000. You see, there *are* advantages to earning less!

If you manage to pile up a lot of assets and don't enjoy them in retirement, your estate tax return — your final tax return — is at great risk of being audited. Do you think a 1 in 20 or 1 in 100 chance is bad in the audit lottery? Uncle Sam audits more than 1 in 7 estate tax returns. Nearly half of estate tax returns for estates valued at more than $5 million are audited. Why? Because big bucks are at stake. The IRS collects an average of more than $100,000 for each estate tax return it audits! So enjoy your money while you're alive or pass it along to your heirs in the here and now — otherwise, your heirs may have trouble getting it in the there and later!

Don't cheat

It may have taken the IRS a while to wise up, but now the government is methodically figuring out the different ways that people cheat. The next step for the IRS — after they figure out how people cheat — is to come up with ways to catch the cheaters. Cheaters beware!

The IRS also offers rewards for informants. If you're brazen enough to cheat and the IRS doesn't catch you, you may not be home-free yet. Someone else may turn you in. So be honest — not only because it's the right thing to do but also because you'll probably sleep better at night knowing that you aren't breaking the law.

Tax protesters, take note. The IRS may flag returns that are accompanied by protest notes. Threats are bad, too — even if they're meant in fun (humor is not rife at the IRS, we suspect). The commandment to follow is: *Thou shalt not draw attention to thyself.* The protest issue is interesting. During congressional hearings, tax protesters stand up and tell members of Congress that the income tax is unconstitutional. They say they have proof. If we can get our hands on the proof, we'll include it in the next edition of this book. In the meantime, pay your taxes and resist the temptation to send along a cranky letter with your tax returns and payments. To read the IRS's take on the typical tax protester's arguments, point your Web browser to www.irs.gov/pub/irs-utl/friv_tax.pdf for 32 action-packed pages, including legal citations.

Stay away from back-street refund mills

Although this advice doesn't apply to the majority of tax-preparation firms, unfortunately, some firms out there fabricate deductions. Run away — as fast as you can — from tax preparers who tell you, after winking, that they have creative ways to reduce your tax bill, or those who base their fees on how many tax dollars they can save you. Also beware of any preparer who promises you a refund without first thoroughly reviewing your situation. Please refer to Chapter 2 and Chapter 31 for how to find a top-quality tax preparer.

Be careful with hobby losses

Some people who have full-time jobs also have sideline businesses or hobbies with which they try to make a few bucks. But be careful if you report the avocation as showing a loss year after year on your tax forms. Filers of Schedule C, Profit or Loss from Business, are at greatest risk for audits.

Here's an example. You like to paint surreal pictures, and you even sold one in 1999 for $150. But since then, you haven't sold any paintings (the surreal market has faded). Nevertheless, you continue to write off your cost for canvas and paint. The IRS will take a close look at that record, and you may be a candidate for an audit.

Don't be a nonfiler

The IRS has a special project with a mission to go after the estimated 5 million or more non-filers. Lest you think that the IRS does things in small ways, the IRS assigned hundreds of agents to this project. Again, when you get caught — which is just a matter of time — in addition to owing back taxes, interest, and big penalties, you may also face criminal prosecution and end up serving time in the slammer. So keep a clear conscience, continue to enjoy your freedom, and file your tax returns. And remember, better late than never!

Don't cut corners if you're self-employed

People who are self-employed have more opportunities to make mistakes on their taxes — or to creatively take deductions — than company-payroll wage earners. As a business owner, you're responsible for self-reporting not only your income but also your expenses. You have to be even more honest when dealing with the tax authorities, because the likelihood of being audited is higher than average.

Don't disguise employees as independent contractors. This maneuver is covered by another IRS project. You remember the old barb: You can't put a sign around the neck of a cow that says, "This is a horse." You don't have a horse — you have a cow with a sign around its neck. Okay, we're reaching a bit . . . but the point is this: Just because you call someone an independent contractor doesn't mean that person isn't your employee. If you aren't sure about the relationship, refer to Chapter 22.

Nothing is wrong with being self-employed. But resist the temptation to cheat because you're far more likely to be scrutinized and caught as a self-employed worker.

Carry a rabbit's foot

Try as you may to be an obedient taxpayer, you can be audited simply because of bad luck. Every year, the IRS audits some taxpayers at random. Although such an undertaking may seem like a colossal waste of time to a tax neophyte like yourself, this effort provides the IRS with valuable information about the areas of tax returns where people make the most mistakes — and about the areas where people cheat!

So, if you do get an audit notice, don't assume that you did anything wrong. However, be prepared for your audit — see Part IV of this book.

Chapter 30

Ten Often-Overlooked Tax-Reduction Opportunities

• •

This chapter presents the more commonly overlooked opportunities to reduce individual income taxes.

The income tax you pay is based on your taxable income minus your deductions. We start first with overlooked ways to minimize your taxable income. Then we move on to often-ignored deductions. We don't want you to be like all those people who miss out on perfectly legal tax-reduction strategies simply because they don't know what they don't know.

Move extra savings out of the bank

Out of apathy or lack of knowledge of better options, far too many people keep extra cash dozing away in their neighborhood bank. Yes, the bank has a vault and sometimes-friendly tellers who may greet you by name, but banks also characteristically pay relatively lousy rates of interest. It's fine to keep your household checking account at the local bank, but you're generally throwing away free interest if you keep your extra savings money there.

The better money market mutual funds often pay substantially greater interest than bank savings accounts and offer equivalent safety. And if you're in a high tax bracket, money market funds come in tax-free flavors. Please see Chapter 23 to find out more about tax-friendly investments.

Invest in wealth-building assets

During your working years, while you're earning employment income, you probably don't need or want taxable income from your investments because it can significantly increase your income tax bill. Real estate, stocks, and small-business investments offer the best long-term growth potential, although you need to be able to withstand dips and sags in these markets.

Most of the return that you can earn with these wealth-building investments comes from appreciation in their value, making them tax-friendly because you're in control and can decide when to sell and realize your profit. Also, as long as you hold onto these investments for more than one year, your profit is taxed at the lower, long-term capital gains tax rate. (Stock dividends are also now subject to lower tax rates—see Chapter 23.)

Fund "tax-reduction" accounts

When you funnel your savings dollars into retirement accounts, such as a 401(k), 403(b), SEP-IRA, Keogh, or IRA, you can earn substantial upfront tax breaks on your contributions. If you think that saving for retirement is boring, consider the tens of thousands of tax dollars these accounts can save you during your working years. If you don't use these accounts to save and invest, you may very well have to work many more years to accumulate the reserves necessary to retire. Refer to Chapter 21 to find out more, including how recent tax law changes significantly increased the benefits of these accounts.

Work overseas

You've always wanted to travel overseas. When you go to work in a foreign country with low income taxes, you may be able to save big-time on income taxes. For tax year 2003, you can exclude $80,000 of foreign-earned income (whether working for a company or on a self-employed basis) from U.S. income taxes. To qualify for this income tax exclusion, you must work at least 330 days (about 11 months) of the year overseas or be a foreign resident. You claim this income tax exclusion on IRS Form 2555.

If you earn more than $80,000, don't worry about being double-taxed on the income above this amount. You get to claim credits for foreign taxes paid on your U.S. tax return on **Form 1116, Foreign Tax Credit.** Perhaps to give you more time to fill out this form and others, the IRS gives Americans working abroad two extra months (until June 15) to file their tax returns.

As with many things in life that sound too good to be true, this pot of overseas gold has some catches. First, many of the places you've romanticized about traveling to and perhaps living in — such as England, France, Italy, Sweden, Germany, and Spain — have higher income tax rates than the ones in the U.S. Also, the tax break just discussed is not available to U.S. government workers overseas.

Look at the whole package when deciding whether to work overseas. Some employers throw in a housing allowance and other benefits. Some companies understand the tax breaks and reduce your pay accordingly. Be sure to consider other costs of living overseas, both financial and emotional. Expect to pay sky-high prices for fresh produce in the Middle East, and budget for bigger phone bills to call loved ones in the States.

Check whether you can itemize

The IRS gives you two methods of determining your total deductions. Deductions are just what they sound like: You subtract them from your income before you calculate the tax you owe. So the more deductions you take, the smaller your taxable income — and the smaller your tax bill. You get to pick the method that leads to the largest total deductions — and thus a lower tax bill. But sometimes the choice is not so clear, so be prepared to do some figuring.

Taking the *standard deduction* usually makes sense if you have a pretty simple financial life — a regular paycheck, a rented apartment, and no large expenses, such as medical bills, moving expenses, or loss due to theft or catastrophe. Single folks qualify for a $4,750 standard deduction, and married couples filing jointly get a $9,500 standard deduction for tax year 2003.

The other method of determining your allowable deductions is to itemize them on your tax return. This painstaking procedure is definitely more of a hassle, but if you can tally up more than the standard deduction amounts, itemizing saves you money. Schedule A of your 1040 is the page for summing up your itemized deductions, but you won't know whether you have enough itemized deductions unless you give this schedule a good examination (refer to Chapter 9).

If you currently don't itemize, you may be surprised to learn that your personal property and state income taxes are itemizable. If you pay a fee to the state to register and license your car, you can itemize the expenditure as a deduction (line 8 "Other Taxes" on Schedule A). The IRS allows you to deduct only the part of the fee that relates to the value of your car, however. The state organization that collects the fee should be able to tell you what portion of the fee is deductible. If it's a user-friendly organization, it even shows this figure on your invoice. What service!

When you total your itemized deductions on Schedule A and that amount is equal to or less than the standard deduction, take the standard deduction without fail. The total for your itemized deductions are worth checking every year, however, because you may have more deductions in some years than others, and you may occasionally be able to itemize.

Because you can control when you pay particular expenses for which you're eligible to itemize, you can *shift* or *bunch* more of them into selected years when you know that you'll have enough deductions to take full advantage of itemizing. For example, suppose that you're using the standard deduction this year because you just don't have many itemized deductions. Late in the tax year, though, you feel certain that you'll buy a home sometime during the next year. Thanks to the potential write-off of mortgage interest and property taxes, you also know that you'll be able to itemize next year. It makes sense, then, to shift as many deductible expenses as possible into the next year.

Trade consumer debt for mortgage debt

Suppose that you own real estate and haven't borrowed as much money as a mortgage lender currently allows (given the current market value of the property and your financial situation). And further suppose that you've run up high-interest consumer debt. Well, you may be able to trade one debt for another. You probably can refinance your mortgage and pull out extra cash to pay off your credit card, auto loan, or other expensive consumer credit lines. You usually can borrow at a lower interest rate for a mortgage, thus lowering your monthly interest bill. Plus, you may get a tax-deduction bonus, because consumer debt — auto loans, credit cards, credit lines — is not tax-deductible, but mortgage debt generally is. Therefore, the effective borrowing rate on a mortgage is even lower than the quoted rate suggests.

Don't forget, however, that refinancing your mortgage and establishing home equity lines involve application fees and other charges (points, appraisals, credit reports, and so on). You must include these fees in the equation to see whether it makes sense to exchange consumer debt for more mortgage debt.

Swapping consumer debt for mortgage debt involves one big danger: Borrowing against the equity in your home can be an addictive habit. We've seen cases in which people run up significant consumer debt three or four distinct times and then refinance their homes the same number of times over the years so they can bail themselves out. At a minimum, continued expansion of your mortgage debt handicaps your ability to work toward other financial goals. In the worst case, easy access to borrowing encourages bad spending habits that can lead to bankruptcy or foreclosure on your debt-ridden home.

Consider charitable contributions and expenses

When you itemize your deductions on Schedule A, you can deduct contributions made to charities. For example, most people already know that when they write a check for $50 to their favorite church or college, they can deduct it. Yet many taxpayers overlook the fact that they can also deduct expenses on work done for charitable organizations. For example, when you go to a soup kitchen to help prepare and serve meals, you can deduct your transportation costs to get there. You just need to keep track of your bus fares or driving mileage. You can also deduct the fair market value of donations of clothing, household appliances, furniture, and other goods to charities — many of these charities will even drive to your home to pick up the stuff. Just make sure to keep some documentation: Write a detailed list and get it signed by the charity. Please see Chapter 9 for more on writing off charitable contributions and expenses.

Maximize miscellaneous expenses

A number of so-called *miscellaneous expenses* are deductible on Schedule A. Most of these relate to your job or career and managing your finances. These expenses are deductible to the extent that, in sum, they exceed 2 percent of your adjusted gross income (see Chapter 9):

- ✔ **Educational expenses:** You may be able to deduct tuition, books, and travel costs to and from classes if your education is related to your career. Specifically, you can deduct these expenses if your coursework improves your work skills. Continuing education classes for professionals may be deductible. When the law or your employer requires you to take courses to maintain your position, these courses are also deductible. But educational expenses that enable you to change careers or to move into a new field or career are not deductible.

- ✔ **Job search and career counseling:** After you obtain your first job, you may deduct legitimate costs related to finding another job within your field. For example, suppose that you're a chef in a steakhouse in Chicago, and you decide you want to do stir-fry in Los Angeles. You take a crash course in vegetarian cooking and then fly to L.A. a couple of times for interviews. You can deduct the cost of the course and your trips — *even if you don't ultimately change jobs.* If you hire a career counselor to help you figure everything out, you can deduct that cost, too. On the other hand, if you're burned out on cooking and decide that you want to become a professional volleyball player in L.A., that's a new career. You may get a better tan, but you won't generate deductions from changing jobs.

- ✔ **Unreimbursed expenses related to your job:** If you pay for your own subscriptions to trade journals to keep up-to-date in your field, or if you buy a new desk and chair to ease back pain, you can deduct these costs. If your job requires you to wear special clothes or a uniform, you can write off the cost of purchasing and cleaning them, as long as the clothes aren't suitable for wearing outside of work.

  If you buy a computer for use outside the office at your own expense, you may be able to deduct the cost of the computer if it's for the convenience of your employer, or if it's a condition of your employment (and is used more than half the time for business). Union dues and membership fees for professional organizations are also deductible.

- ✔ **Investment and tax-related expenses:** Investment and tax-advisor fees are deductible, and so are subscription costs for investment-related publications. Accounting fees for preparing your tax return or conducting tax planning during the year are deductible, as are legal fees related to your taxes. If you purchase a home computer to track your investments or prepare your taxes, you may be able to deduct part of that expense, too.

Scour for self-employment expenses

If you're self-employed, you already deduct a variety of expenses from your income before calculating the tax that you owe. When you buy a computer or office furniture, you can deduct those expenses (sometimes they need to be gradually deducted or *depreciated* over time). Salaries for your employees, office supplies, rent or mortgage interest for your office space, and phone expenses are also generally deductible.

Although more than a few business owners cheat on their taxes, some self-employed folks don't take all the deductions they should. In some cases, people simply aren't aware of the wonderful world of deductions. For others, large deductions raise the concern of an audit. Taking advantage of deductions for which you're eligible makes sense and saves you money. It's worth the money to hire tax help — either by using a book like this one and/or by paying a tax professional to review your return one year.

Chapter 31

Ten Interview Questions for Tax Advisors

When you believe that your tax situation warrants outside help, be sure to educate yourself as much as possible beforehand. Why? The more you know, the better able you'll be to evaluate the competence of someone you may hire.

Make sure that you ask the right questions to find a competent tax practitioner whose skills match your tax needs. We recommend that you start with the questions discussed in the following sections.

What tax services do you offer?

Most tax advisors prepare tax returns. We use the term *tax advisors* because most tax folks do more than simply prepare returns. Many advisors can help you plan and file other important tax documents throughout the year. Some firms also assist your small business with bookkeeping and other financial reporting, such as income statements and balance sheets. These services can be useful when your business is in the market for a loan, or if you need to give clients or investors detailed information about your business.

Ask tax advisors to explain how they work with clients. You're hiring the tax advisor because you lack knowledge of the tax system. If your tax advisor doesn't prod and explore your situation, you may be walking into a situation where "the blind are leading the blind." A good tax advisor can help you make sure that you aren't overlooking deductions or making other costly mistakes that may lead to an audit, penalties, and interest. Beware of tax preparers who view their jobs as simply plugging into tax forms the information that you bring them.

Do you have areas that you focus on?

This question is important. For example, if a tax preparer works mainly with people who receive regular paychecks from an employer, that tax preparer probably has little expertise in helping small-business owners best complete the blizzard of paperwork that the IRS requires.

Find out what expertise the tax advisor has in handling whatever unusual financial events you're dealing with this year — or whatever events you expect in future years. For example, if you need help completing an estate tax return for a deceased relative, ask how many of these types of returns the tax preparer has completed in the past year. About 15 percent of estate tax returns are audited, so you don't want a novice preparing one for you.

What other services do you offer?

Ideally, you want to work with a professional who is 100 percent focused on taxes. We know it's difficult to imagine that some people choose to work at this full-time, but they do — and lucky for you!

A multitude of problems and conflicts of interest crop up when a person tries to prepare tax returns, sell investments, and appraise real estate — all at the same time. That advisor may not be fully competent or current in any of these areas.

By virtue of their backgrounds and training, some tax preparers also offer consulting and financial planning services for business owners and other individuals. Because he or she already knows a great deal about your personal and tax situation, a competent tax professional may be able to help in these areas. Just make sure that this help is charged on an hourly consulting basis. Avoid tax advisors who sell financial products that pay them a commission — this situation inevitably creates conflicts of interest.

Who will prepare my return?

If you talk to a solo practitioner, the answer to this question should be simple — the person you're talking to should prepare your return. But if your tax advisor has assistants and other employees, make sure that you know what level of involvement these different people will have in the preparation of your return.

It isn't necessarily bad if a junior-level person does the preliminary tax return preparation that your tax advisor will review and finalize. In fact, this procedure can save you money in tax-preparation fees if the firm bills you at a lower hourly rate for a junior-level person. Be wary of firms that charge you a high hourly rate for a senior tax advisor who then delegates most of the work to a junior-level person.

How aggressive or conservative are you regarding the tax law?

Some tax preparers, unfortunately, view their role as enforcement agents for the IRS. This attitude often is a consequence of one too many seminars put on by local IRS folks, who admonish (and sometimes intimidate) preparers with threats of audits.

On the other hand, some preparers are too aggressive and try tax maneuvers that put their clients on thin ice — subjecting them to additional taxes, penalties, interest, and audits.

Assessing how aggressive a tax preparer is can be difficult. Start by asking what percentage of the tax preparer's clients get audited (see the next question). You can also ask the tax advisor for references from clients for whom the advisor helped unearth overlooked opportunities to reduce tax bills.

What's your experience with audits?

As a benchmark, you need to know that about 1 percent of all taxpayer returns are audited. For tax advisors working with a more affluent client base or small-business owners, expect a higher audit rate — somewhere in the neighborhood of 2 percent to 4 percent.

If the tax preparer proudly claims no audited clients, be wary. Among the possible explanations, any of which should cause you to be uncomfortable in hiring such a preparer: He or she isn't telling you the truth, has prepared few returns, or is afraid of taking some legal deductions, so you'll probably overpay your taxes.

A tax preparer who has been in business for at least a couple of years will have gone through audits. Ask the preparer to explain his or her last two audits, what happened, and why. This explanation not only sheds light on a preparer's work with clients, but also on his or her ability to communicate in plain English.

How does your fee structure work?

Tax advisor fees, like attorney and financial planner fees, are all over the map — from $50 to $300 or more per hour. Many preparers simply quote you a total fee for preparation of your tax return.

Ultimately, the tax advisor charges you for time, so you should ask what the hourly billing rate is. If the advisor balks at answering this question, try asking what his or her fee is for a one-hour consultation. You may want a tax advisor to work on this basis if you've prepared your return yourself and want it reviewed as a quality-control check. You also may seek an hourly fee if you're on top of your tax preparation in general but have some very specific questions about an unusual or one-time event, such as the sale of your business.

Clarify whether the preparer's set fee includes follow-up questions that you may have during the year, or if this fee covers IRS audits on the return. Some accountants include these functions in their set fee, but others charge for everything on an as-needed basis. The advantage of the all-inclusive fee is that it removes the psychological obstacle of your feeling that the meter's running every time you call with a question. The drawback can be that you pay for additional services (time) that you may not need or use.

What qualifies you to be a tax advisor?

Tax advisors come with a variety of backgrounds. The more tax and business experience they have, the better. But don't be overly impressed with credentials. As discussed in Chapter 2, tax advisors can earn certifications such as CPAs and EAs. Although gaining credentials takes time and work, these certifications are no guarantee that you get quality, cost-effective tax assistance or that you won't be overcharged.

Generally speaking, more years of experience are better than less, but don't rule out a newer advisor who lacks gray hair or who hasn't yet slogged through thousands of returns. Intelligence and training can easily make up for less experience.

Newer advisors also may charge less so they can build up their practices. Be sure, though, that you don't just focus on each preparer's hourly rate. Ask each practitioner that you interview how much total time he or she expects your tax return to take. Someone with a lower hourly fee can end up costing you more if he or she is slower than a more experienced and efficient preparer with a higher hourly rate.

Do you carry liability insurance?

If a tax advisor makes a major mistake or gives poor advice, you can lose thousands of dollars. The greater your income, assets, and the importance of your financial decisions, the more financial harm that can be done. We know that you aren't a litigious person, but your tax advisor needs to carry goof-up insurance, sometimes known as *errors and omissions,* or *liability insurance.* You can, of course, simply sue an uninsured advisor and hope the advisor has enough personal assets to cover a loss, but don't count on it. Besides, you'll have a much more difficult time getting due compensation that way!

You may also ask the advisor whether he or she has ever been sued and how the lawsuit turned out. It doesn't occur to most people to ask this type of question, so make sure that you tell your tax advisor that you're not out to strike it rich on a lawsuit! Another way to discover whether a tax advisor has gotten into hot water is by checking with appropriate professional organizations to which that preparer may belong. You can also check whether any complaints have been filed with your local Better Business Bureau (BBB), although this is far from a foolproof screening method. Most dissatisfied clients don't bother to register complaints with the BBB, and you should also know that the BBB is loath to retain complaints on file against companies who are members.

Warning signs that you hired an incompetent tax preparer

✔ He was kicked out of a major accounting firm for not filing his tax return.

✔ He's rarely in his office when you call because his clients' returns are always being audited.

✔ You find a trail of your tax receipts leading from his car to his office.

✔ He scoffs at people who organize their tax records as "anal-retentive."

✔ He wants to complete your tax return on a postcard, even though the flat tax still is just an idea.

✔ When you interview him at his office and he gets out of his chair to shake your hand, there's a copy of somebody's IRS Form 1040 stuck to his butt.

✔ He encourages you to deduct the cost of your trips to visit your in-laws and to write off "laughing at their jokes" as a charitable contribution.

(Of course, the "he" could be a "she." All sorts of folks are tax preparers, and there's no gender-hold on incompetence. See Chapter 2 if you need a competence check.)

Can you provide references of clients similar to me?

You need to know that the tax advisor has handled cases and problems like yours. For example, if you're a small-business owner, ask to speak with other small-business owners. But don't be overly impressed by tax advisors who claim that they work mainly with one occupational group, such as physicians. Although there's value in understanding the nuances of a profession, tax advisors are ultimately generalists — as are the tax laws.

When all is said and done, make sure that you feel comfortable with a tax advisor. We're not suggesting that you evaluate an advisor the way you would a potential friend or spouse! But if you're feeling uneasy and can't understand what your tax advisor says to you in the early stages of your relationship, trust your instincts and continue your search. Remember that you can be your own best tax advisor — finding out the basics will pay you a lifetime of dividends and can save you tens of thousands of dollars in taxes and tax advisor fees!

Appendix

A Little More about the IRS

Einstein was fond of saying that the most complicated thing he ever encountered was the income tax. Evidently, he considered the theory of relativity to be simple mathematics in comparison. So if you go through a bottle of aspirin when filling out your forms, you're in good company. Medical Disclaimer: If you are filling out your tax forms all in one day, don't finish off the bottle!

This appendix is our attempt to give you a little extra information so that you don't have to run all over the place to get what you need. Enjoy!

IRS Tax Forms and Publications

Some of the things that your tax dollars help provide are tax forms and information publications. Only the most commonly used forms come with your annual IRS 1040 booklet. Following this appendix, we provide many more of the forms you'll likely need to complete your tax return. But we also give you a list of other forms that are sometimes needed. So get your money's worth! Call 800-TAX-FORM to get more forms and publications than you ever wanted in your life. (Be prepared for a busy signal. Lots of folks call this number. If you have Internet access, the Web site at www.irs.gov may be faster.)

If you're in a pinch for time and can't wait for some oddball form by mail, you have other options. You can obtain forms by

- ✔ Visiting a local IRS office
- ✔ Lumbering over to your local library
- ✔ Going to other government offices
- ✔ Boogying to some banks
- ✔ Trying tax preparation software (see Chapter 2)
- ✔ Downloading the forms to your personal computer from an online service or the Internet (see Chapter 2)

Recorded Tax Information

Another free IRS service, paid for courtesy of your tax dollars, is TeleTax. TeleTax provides prerecorded answers to commonly asked tax questions. It's often quicker and more accurate than trying to find an IRS employee who knows the answer. Admittedly, a question like, "I am a U.S. citizen and have my primary residence in Lizard Lick, North Carolina; I own a business in Brazil; I bought a coffee farm there; I patented a new coffee bean and made gads of money off it; how much money can I deduct on my taxes?" will be difficult to answer through TeleTax. However, a question like, "I am a U.S. citizen and have my primary residence in Lizard Lick, North Carolina; I own a business in Brazil; I bought a coffee farm there in 1994; I patented a new coffee bean and made gads of money off it; I filled out my tax forms; where do I send them?" can be answered quickly. We have the answer to this question, too — later in this appendix.

TeleTax

800-829-4477
(TTY/TDD) 800-829-4059

TeleTax provides recorded tax information for about 150 topics. You can listen to up to three topics on each call you make. TeleTax is available 24 hours a day, 7 days a week, 365 days a year. Call at midnight on New Year's Eve just to test it!

When you call, you're asked if you want to listen to a TeleTax topic or if you're inquiring about a refund. You have to use a touch-tone phone after the main recording gives the basic instructions. TeleTax also explains the neat function of the (R)EPEAT and (C)ANCEL buttons on the touch-tone phone. The R button (#7) repeats your message as many times as you want — maybe until you understand! If you have a rotary phone, you're out of luck.

Your Form 1040 booklet has a complete listing of topics, or you can access the directory over the phone when you call TeleTax.

Automated refund information

800-829-4477 (same number as TeleTax)
(TTY/TDD) 800-829-4059

You haven't received your refund check, and you're getting antsy? Have you already spent your anticipated refund? Before you pick up the phone to call the IRS to check on the status of your refund, make sure that you have a copy of your tax return handy. For the IRS to check on the status of your refund, you will need to know the first Social Security number shown on your return, your filing status, and the exact whole-dollar amount of your refund.

Simply place your call to 800-829-4477 and follow the cheerful recorded instructions. The IRS updates refund information every seven days. If you call to find out about the status of your refund and do not receive a refund mailing date, wait a few days before calling back. Also, it's important to note that this touch-tone service is available Monday through Friday from 7:00 a.m. to 11:30 p.m. (Eastern time).

Toll-free tax help

800-829-1040

The IRS prefers that you contact a local IRS office to rap about your tax questions. But a toll-free 800 number is also available. Remember to have the necessary information at your fingertips to help you get to the root of your question or problem.

If the IRS provides an incorrect answer to your question, you are still responsible for the payment of the correct tax. But if this situation occurs, you won't be charged any penalty. (Gee, thanks, IRS!)

Be sure that you obtain the name of the person to whom you spoke and record the date (as well as the time of the call) in order to abate for reasonable cause any penalty that may be imposed (see Chapter 19 for the lowdown on abating penalties). For example, when you call, you should always have in front of you the tax form, schedule, or notice to which your question relates. Don't be embarrassed if you don't understand the answer. If you don't, just say so, and ask the IRS representative to explain it again. Even better, call the IRS again and get a "second opinion" from another representative.

IRS Problem Resolution Program

Any problems you have that cannot be resolved through normal channels, as we discuss in Chapter 19, may qualify for the IRS Problem Resolution Program. (Don't worry; this has nothing to do with the Witness Relocation Program!)

Begin this journey by calling 800-829-1040. Explain your problem to a specially trained representative who will try to fix it. If the representative can't fix it, he or she will evaluate your case to see whether it meets the necessary criteria for the Problem Resolution Program. The IRS representative will then assign you to a caseworker at your local district service center.

This may take some time on the phone, but it's generally better than corresponding by mail. The process could take months if you send your letter to the wrong address (or sometimes even if you send it to the correct address).

2003 Tax Forms

On the following pages, you can find many of the IRS tax forms that you may need to complete your tax return. We include the forms for your convenience and use. Feel free to tear them out, cut them out, or photocopy them (yes, you can use photocopied forms to complete your tax return). We suggest the following uses for the forms, but you're welcome to come up with your own:

- They are final, IRS-approved forms. You can file them with your tax return.
- Use the forms for your first draft tax return when you sit down with *Taxes For Dummies* and lay the foundation for preparing your return.
- Refer to the forms and follow along, line by line, as you read our tips and warnings in the rest of this book.

Form
1040EZ

Department of the Treasury—Internal Revenue Service

Income Tax Return for Single and Joint Filers With No Dependents (99) **2003**

OMB No. 1545-0675

Label

(See page 12.)

Use the IRS label. Otherwise, please print or type.

L A B E L   H E R E

Your first name and initial	Last name	Your social security number
If a joint return, spouse's first name and initial	Last name	Spouse's social security number
Home address (number and street). If you have a P.O. box, see page 12.	Apt. no.	
City, town or post office, state, and ZIP code. If you have a foreign address, see page 12.		

▲ **Important!** ▲

You **must** enter your SSN(s) above.

Presidential Election Campaign (page 12) ▶

Note. Checking "Yes" will not change your tax or reduce your refund.
Do you, or your spouse if a joint return, want $3 to go to this fund? . . . . . ▶

	You	Spouse
	☐ Yes ☐ No	☐ Yes ☐ No

Income

Attach Form(s) W-2 here.
Enclose, but do not attach, any payment.

Note. You **must** check Yes or No.

1	Wages, salaries, and tips. This should be shown in box 1 of your Form(s) W-2. Attach your Form(s) W-2.	**1**
2	Taxable interest. If the total is over $1,500, you cannot use Form 1040EZ.	**2**
3	Unemployment compensation and Alaska Permanent Fund dividends (see page 14).	**3**
4	Add lines 1, 2, and 3. This is your **adjusted gross income.**	**4**
5	Can your parents (or someone else) claim you on their return? **Yes.** ☐ Enter amount from worksheet on back. **No.** ☐ If **single,** enter $7,800. If **married filing jointly,** enter $15,600. See back for explanation.	**5**
6	Subtract line 5 from line 4. If line 5 is larger than line 4, enter -0-. This is your **taxable income.** ▶	**6**

Payments and tax

7	Federal income tax withheld from box 2 of your Form(s) W-2.	**7**
8	**Earned income credit (EIC).**	**8**
9	Add lines 7 and 8. These are your **total payments.** ▶	**9**
10	**Tax.** Use the amount on **line 6 above** to find your tax in the tax table on pages 24–28 of the booklet. Then, enter the tax from the table on this line.	**10**

Refund

Have it directly deposited! See page 19 and fill in 11b, 11c, and 11d.

11a	If line 9 is larger than line 10, subtract line 10 from line 9. This is your **refund.** ▶	**11a**
▶ **b**	Routing number ⬚⬚⬚⬚⬚⬚⬚⬚⬚ ▶ **c** Type: ☐ Checking ☐ Savings	
▶ **d**	Account number ⬚⬚⬚⬚⬚⬚⬚⬚⬚⬚⬚⬚⬚⬚⬚⬚⬚	

Amount you owe

12	If line 10 is larger than line 9, subtract line 9 from line 10. This is the **amount you owe.** For details on how to pay, see page 20. ▶	**12**

Third party designee

Do you want to allow another person to discuss this return with the IRS (see page 20)? ☐ **Yes.** Complete the following. ☐ **No**

Designee's name ▶	Phone no. ▶ ( )	Personal identification number (PIN) ▶ ⬚⬚⬚⬚⬚

Sign here

Joint return? See page 11.

Keep a copy for your records.

Under penalties of perjury, I declare that I have examined this return, and to the best of my knowledge and belief, it is true, correct, and accurately lists all amounts and sources of income I received during the tax year. Declaration of preparer (other than the taxpayer) is based on all information of which the preparer has any knowledge.

Your signature	Date	Your occupation	Daytime phone number ( )
Spouse's signature. If a joint return, **both** must sign.	Date	Spouse's occupation	

Paid preparer's use only

Preparer's signature ▶	Date	Check if self-employed ☐	Preparer's SSN or PTIN
Firm's name (or yours if self-employed), address, and ZIP code ▶		EIN	
		Phone no. ( )	

For Disclosure, Privacy Act, and Paperwork Reduction Act Notice, see page 23.
Cat. No. 11329W
Form **1040EZ** (2003)

Use this form if

- Your filing status is single or married filing jointly.
- You (and your spouse if married filing jointly) were under age 65 and not blind at the end of 2003. If you were born on January 1, 1939, you are considered to be age 65 at the end of 2003.
- You do not claim any dependents.
- Your taxable income (line 6) is less than $50,000.
- You do not claim a deduction for educator expenses, the student loan interest deduction, or the tuition and fees deduction.
- You do not claim an education credit, the retirement savings contributions credit, or the health coverage tax credit.
- You had **only** wages, salaries, tips, taxable scholarship or fellowship grants, unemployment compensation, or Alaska Permanent Fund dividends, and your taxable interest was not over $1,500. **But** if you earned tips, including allocated tips, that are not included in box 5 and box 7 of your W-2, you may not be able to use Form 1040EZ (see page 13). If you are planning to use Form 1040EZ for a child who received Alaska Permanent Fund dividends, see page 14.
- You did not receive any advance earned income credit payments.

If you are not sure about your filing status, see page 11. If you have questions about dependents, use TeleTax topic 354 (see page 6). If you **cannot use this form,** use TeleTax topic 352 (see page 6).

Filling in your return

For tips on how to avoid common mistakes, see page 21.

If you received a scholarship or fellowship grant or tax-exempt interest income, such as on municipal bonds, see the booklet before filling in the form. Also, see the booklet if you received a Form 1099-INT showing Federal income tax withheld or if Federal income tax was withheld from your unemployment compensation or Alaska Permanent Fund dividends.

Remember, you must report all wages, salaries, and tips even if you do not get a Form W-2 from your employer. You must also report all your taxable interest, including interest from banks, savings and loans, credit unions, etc., even if you do not get a Form 1099-INT.

Worksheet for dependents who checked "Yes" on line 5

(keep a copy for your records)

Use this worksheet to figure the amount to enter on line 5 if someone can claim you (or your spouse if married filing jointly) as a dependent, even if that person chooses not to do so. To find out if someone can claim you as a dependent, use TeleTax topic 354 (see page 6).

A. Amount, if any, from line 1 on front _____

+ 250.00 Enter total ▶ A. _____

B. Minimum standard deduction . . . . B. _____ 750.00

C. Enter the **larger** of line A or line B here . . . . C. _____

D. Maximum standard deduction. If **single,** enter $4,750; if **married filing jointly,** enter $9,500 . . . . D. _____

E. Enter the **smaller** of line C or line D here. This is your standard deduction . . . . E. _____

F. Exemption amount.
- If single, enter -0-.
- If married filing jointly and—
  —both you and your spouse can be claimed as dependents, enter -0-.
  —only one of you can be claimed as a dependent, enter $3,050.

F. _____

G. Add lines E and F. Enter the total here and on line 5 on the front . G. _____

If you checked "No" on line 5 because no one can claim you (or your spouse if married filing jointly) as a dependent, enter on line 5 the amount shown below that applies to you.

- Single, enter $7,800. This is the total of your standard deduction ($4,750) and your exemption ($3,050).
- Married filing jointly, enter $15,600. This is the total of your standard deduction ($9,500), your exemption ($3,050), and your spouse's exemption ($3,050).

Mailing return

Mail your return by **April 15, 2004.** Use the envelope that came with your booklet. If you do not have that envelope or if you moved during the year, see the back cover for the address to use.

Form

1040A

Department of the Treasury—Internal Revenue Service

U.S. Individual Income Tax Return (99) 2003

IRS Use Only—Do not write or staple in this space.

Label

(See page 19.)

Use the IRS label.

Otherwise, please print or type.

L A B E L   H E R E

Your first name and initial	Last name

OMB No. 1545-0085

Your social security number

If a joint return, spouse's first name and initial	Last name

Spouse's social security number

Home address (number and street). If you have a P.O. box, see page 20.	Apt. no.

City, town or post office, state, and ZIP code. If you have a foreign address, see page 20.

▲ **Important!** ▲

You **must** enter your SSN(s) above.

Presidential Election Campaign

(See page 20.)

▶ **Note.** Checking "Yes" will not change your tax or reduce your refund.
Do you, or your spouse if filing a joint return, want $3 to go to this fund? . . . ▶

You		Spouse	
☐ Yes	☐ No	☐ Yes	☐ No

Filing status

Check only one box.

1 ☐ Single
2 ☐ Married filing jointly (even if only one had income)
3 ☐ Married filing separately. Enter spouse's SSN above and full name here. ▶
4 ☐ Head of household (with qualifying person). (See page 20.) If the qualifying person is a child but not your dependent, enter this child's name here. ▶
5 ☐ Qualifying widow(er) with dependent child (See page 21.)

Exemptions

If more than six dependents, see page 21.

6a ☐ **Yourself.** If your parent (or someone else) can claim you as a dependent on his or her tax return, **do not** check box 6a.

b ☐ **Spouse**

c **Dependents:**

(1) First name Last name	(2) Dependent's social security number	(3) Dependent's relationship to you	(4) ✓ if qualifying child for child tax credit (see page 23)
			☐
			☐
			☐
			☐
			☐
			☐

No. of boxes checked on 6a and 6b _____

No. of children on 6c who:
lived with you _____
did not live with you due to divorce or separation (see page 23) _____
Dependents on 6c not entered above _____

Add numbers on lines above ☐

d Total number of exemptions claimed.

Income

Attach Form(s) W-2 here. Also attach Form(s) 1099-R if tax was withheld.

If you did not get a W-2, see page 24.

Enclose, but do not attach, any payment.

7 Wages, salaries, tips, etc. Attach Form(s) W-2. · 7

8a **Taxable** interest. Attach Schedule 1 if required. · 8a

b **Tax-exempt** interest. **Do not** include on line 8a. 8b

9a Ordinary dividends. Attach Schedule 1 if required. · 9a

b Qualified dividends (see page 25). 9b

10a Capital gain distributions (see page 25). · 10a

b Post-May 5 capital gain distributions (see page 25). 10b

11a IRA distributions. 11a | 11b Taxable amount (see page 25). 11b

12a Pensions and annuities. 12a | 12b Taxable amount (see page 26). 12b

13 Unemployment compensation and Alaska Permanent Fund dividends. 13

14a Social security benefits. 14a | 14b Taxable amount (see page 28). 14b

15 Add lines 7 through 14b (far right column). This is your **total income.** ▶ 15

Adjusted gross income

16 Educator expenses (see page 28). 16
17 IRA deduction (see page 28). 17
18 Student loan interest deduction (see page 31). 18
19 Tuition and fees deduction (see page 31). 19
20 Add lines 16 through 19. These are your **total adjustments.** 20

21 Subtract line 20 from line 15. This is your **adjusted gross income.** ▶ 21

Tax, credits, and payments	**22**	Enter the amount from line 21 (adjusted gross income).	22	

23a Check if: ☐ **You** were born before January 2, 1939, ☐ Blind **Total boxes**
☐ **Spouse** was born before January 2, 1939, ☐ Blind **checked ►** 23a ☐

b If you are married filing separately and your spouse itemizes deductions, see page 32 and check here ► 23b ☐

Standard Deduction for—

• People who checked any box on line 23a or 23b **or** who can be claimed as a dependent, see page 32.

• All others:

Single or Married filing separately, $4,750

Married filing jointly or Qualifying widow(er), $9,500

Head of household, $7,000

24	Enter your **standard deduction** (see left margin).	24	
25	Subtract line 24 from line 22. If line 24 is more than line 22, enter -0-.	25	
26	Multiply $3,050 by the total number of exemptions claimed on line 6d.	26	
27	Subtract line 26 from line 25. If line 26 is more than line 25, enter -0-. This is your **taxable income.** ►	27	
28	**Tax,** including any alternative minimum tax (see page 33).	28	
29	Credit for child and dependent care expenses. Attach Schedule 2.	29	
30	Credit for the elderly or the disabled. Attach Schedule 3.	30	
31	Education credits. Attach Form 8863.	31	
32	Retirement savings contributions credit. Attach Form 8880.	32	
33	Child tax credit (see page 37).	33	
34	Adoption credit. Attach Form 8839.	34	
35	Add lines 29 through 34. These are your **total credits.**	35	
36	Subtract line 35 from line 28. If line 35 is more than line 28, enter -0-.	36	
37	Advance earned income credit payments from Form(s) W-2.	37	
38	Add lines 36 and 37. This is your **total tax.** ►	38	
39	Federal income tax withheld from Forms W-2 and 1099.	39	
40	2003 estimated tax payments and amount applied from 2002 return.	40	

If you have a qualifying child, attach Schedule EIC.

41	**Earned income credit (EIC).**	41	
42	Additional child tax credit. Attach Form 8812.	42	
43	Add lines 39 through 42. These are your **total payments.** ►	43	

Refund	**44**	If line 43 is more than line 38, subtract line 38 from line 43. This is the amount you **overpaid.**	44	

Direct deposit? See page 50 and fill in 45b, 45c, and 45d.

45a	Amount of line 44 you want **refunded to you.** ►	45a	
► **b**	Routing number ☐☐☐☐☐☐☐☐☐ ► **c** Type: ☐ Checking ☐ Savings		
► **d**	Account number ☐☐☐☐☐☐☐☐☐☐☐☐☐☐☐☐☐		
46	Amount of line 44 you want **applied to your 2004 estimated tax.**	46	

Amount you owe	**47**	**Amount you owe.** Subtract line 43 from line 38. For details on how to pay, see page 51. ►	47	
	48	Estimated tax penalty (see page 52).	48	

Third party designee

Do you want to allow another person to discuss this return with the IRS (see page 52)? ☐ **Yes.** Complete the following. ☐ **No**

Designee's name ► ___ Phone no. ► ( ) ___ Personal identification number (PIN) ☐☐☐☐☐

Sign here

Joint return? See page 20.

Keep a copy for your records.

Under penalties of perjury, I declare that I have examined this return and accompanying schedules and statements, and to the best of my knowledge and belief, they are true, correct, and accurately list all amounts and sources of income I received during the tax year. Declaration of preparer (other than the taxpayer) is based on all information of which the preparer has any knowledge.

Your signature	Date	Your occupation	Daytime phone number ( )
Spouse's signature. If a joint return, **both** must sign.	Date	Spouse's occupation	

Paid preparer's use only

Preparer's signature ►	Date	Check if self-employed ☐	Preparer's SSN or PTIN
Firm's name (or yours if self-employed), address, and ZIP code ►		EIN	
		Phone no. ( )	

Schedule 1
(Form 1040A)

Department of the Treasury—Internal Revenue Service

**Interest and Ordinary Dividends
for Form 1040A Filers** (99)

2003

OMB No. 1545-0085

Name(s) shown on Form 1040A | Your social security number

Part I

Interest

(See back
of schedule
and the
instructions
for Form
1040A,
line 8a.)

Note. If you received a Form 1099-INT, Form 1099-OID, or substitute statement from a brokerage firm, enter the firm's name and the total interest shown on that form.

1 List name of payer. If any interest is from a seller-financed mortgage and the buyer used the property as a personal residence, see back of schedule and list this interest first. Also, show that buyer's social security number and address.

	Amount
1	

2 Add the amounts on line 1. | 2 |

3 Excludable interest on series EE and I U.S. savings bonds issued after 1989. Attach Form 8815. | 3 |

4 Subtract line 3 from line 2. Enter the result here and on Form 1040A, line 8a. | 4 |

Part II

**Ordinary
dividends**

(See back
of schedule
and the
instructions
for Form
1040A,
line 9a.)

Note. If you received a Form 1099-DIV or substitute statement from a brokerage firm, enter the firm's name and the ordinary dividends shown on that form.

5 List name of payer.	Amount
5	

6 Add the amounts on line 5. Enter the total here and on Form 1040A, line 9a. | 6 |

Schedule 2
(Form 1040A)

Department of the Treasury—Internal Revenue Service

Child and Dependent Care Expenses for Form 1040A Filers (99) **2003**

OMB No. 1545-0085

Name(s) shown on Form 1040A

Your social security number

Before you begin: You need to understand the following terms. See **Definitions** on page 1 of the separate instructions.
 ● Dependent Care Benefits   ● Qualifying Person(s)   ● Qualified Expenses   ● Earned Income

Part I

Persons or organizations who provided the care

You **must** complete this part.

1

	(a) Care provider's name	(b) Address (number, street, apt. no., city, state, and ZIP code)	(c) Identifying number (SSN or EIN)	(d) Amount paid (see instructions)

(If you need more space, use the bottom of page 2.)

Did you receive **dependent care benefits?**	No ———→	Complete only Part II below.
	Yes ———→	Complete Part III on the back next.

Caution. If the care was provided in your home, you may owe employment taxes. If you do, you must use Form 1040. See **Schedule H** and its instructions for details.

Part II

Credit for child and dependent care expenses

2 Information about your **qualifying person(s).** If you have more than two qualifying persons, see the instructions.

(a) Qualifying person's name		(b) Qualifying person's social security number	(c) Qualified expenses you incurred and paid in 2003 for the person listed in column (a)
First	Last		

3 Add the amounts in column (c) of line 2. **Do not** enter more than $3,000 for one qualifying person or $6,000 for two or more persons. If you completed Part III, enter the amount from line 26. **3**

4 Enter your **earned income.** **4**

5 If married filing jointly, enter your spouse's earned income (if your spouse was a student or was disabled, see the instructions); **all others,** enter the amount from line 4. **5**

6 Enter the **smallest** of line 3, 4, or 5. **6**

7 Enter the amount from Form 1040A, line 22. **7**

8 Enter on line 8 the decimal amount shown below that applies to the amount on line 7.

If line 7 is:			If line 7 is:		
Over	But not over	Decimal amount is	Over	But not over	Decimal amount is
$0—15,000		.35	$29,000—31,000		.27
15,000—17,000		.34	31,000—33,000		.26
17,000—19,000		.33	33,000—35,000		.25
19,000—21,000		.32	35,000—37,000		.24
21,000—23,000		.31	37,000—39,000		.23
23,000—25,000		.30	39,000—41,000		.22
25,000—27,000		.29	41,000—43,000		.21
27,000—29,000		.28	43,000—No limit		.20

8

9 Multiply **line 6** by the decimal amount on line 8. If you paid 2002 expenses in 2003, see the instructions. **9**

10 Enter the amount from Form 1040A, line 28. **10**

11 **Credit for child and dependent care expenses.** Enter the **smaller** of line 9 or line 10 here and on Form 1040A, line 29. **11**

Part III **Dependent care benefits**	**12** Enter the total amount of **dependent care benefits** you received for 2003. This amount should be shown in box 10 of your W-2 form(s). **Do not** include amounts that were reported to you as wages in box 1 of Form(s) W-2.	12
	13 Enter the amount forfeited, if any. See the instructions.	13
	14 Subtract line 13 from line 12.	14
	15 Enter the total amount of **qualified expenses** incurred in 2003 for the care of the qualifying person(s). 15	
	16 Enter the **smaller** of line 14 or 15. 16	
	17 Enter your **earned income.** 17	

	18 Enter the amount shown below that applies to you.
	  • If married filing jointly, enter your spouse's earned income (if your spouse was a student or was disabled, see the instructions for line 5).
	  • If married filing separately, see the instructions for the amount to enter.
	  • All others, enter the amount from line 17. 18	

	19 Enter the **smallest** of line 16, 17, or 18. 19	

	20 Excluded benefits. Enter here the **smaller** of the following:
	  • The amount from line 19 or
	  • $5,000 ($2,500 if married filing separately **and** you were required to enter your spouse's earned income on line 18).
		20

	21 Taxable benefits. Subtract line 20 from line 14. Also, include this amount on Form 1040A, line 7. In the space to the left of line 7, enter "DCB."	21

To claim the child and dependent care credit, complete lines 22–26 below.

22 Enter $3,000 ($6,000 if two or more qualifying persons).	22
23 Enter the amount from line 20.	23
24 Subtract line 23 from line 22. If zero or less, **stop.** You cannot take the credit. **Exception.** If you paid 2002 expenses in 2003, see the instructions for line 9.	24
25 Complete line 2 on the front of this schedule. **Do not** include in column (c) any benefits shown on line 20 above. Then, add the amounts in column (c) and enter the total here.	25
26 Enter the **smaller** of line 24 or 25. Also, enter this amount on line 3 on the front of this schedule and complete lines 4–11.	26

Schedule 3
(Form 1040A)

Department of the Treasury—Internal Revenue Service

Credit for the Elderly or the Disabled
for Form 1040A Filers   (99)   **2003**

OMB No. 1545-0085

Name(s) shown on Form 1040A

Your social security number

You may be able to take this credit and reduce your tax if by the end of 2003:
- You were age 65 or older   **or**   • You were under age 65, you retired on **permanent and total** disability, and you received taxable disability income.

But you must also meet other tests. See the separate instructions for Schedule 3.

TIP In most cases, the IRS can figure the credit for you. See the instructions.

Part I

Check the box for your filing status and age

If your filing status is:	And by the end of 2003:	Check only one box:

Single, Head of household, or Qualifying widow(er)

1 You were 65 or older . . . . 1 ☐

2 You were under 65 and you retired on permanent and total disability . . . . 2 ☐

Married filing jointly

3 Both spouses were 65 or older . . . . 3 ☐

4 Both spouses were under 65, but only one spouse retired on permanent and total disability . . . . . 4 ☐

5 Both spouses were under 65, and both retired on permanent and total disability . . . . 5 ☐

6 One spouse was 65 or older, and the other spouse was under 65 and retired on permanent and total disability . . . . 6 ☐

7 One spouse was 65 or older, and the other spouse was under 65 and **not** retired on permanent and total disability . . . . 7 ☐

Married filing separately

8 You were 65 or older and you lived apart from your spouse for all of 2003 . . . . 8 ☐

9 You were under 65, you retired on permanent and total disability, and you lived apart from your spouse for all of 2003 . . . . 9 ☐

┌─────────────────┐
│ **Did you check** │ ── **Yes** ──→ Skip Part II and complete Part III on the back.
│ **box 1, 3, 7, or** │
│ **8?**   │ ── **No** ──→ Complete Parts II and III.
└─────────────────┘

Part II

Statement of permanent and total disability

Complete this part **only** if you checked box 2, 4, 5, 6, or 9 above.

If: **1** You filed a physician's statement for this disability for 1983 or an earlier year, or you filed or got a statement for tax years after 1983 and your physician signed line B on the statement, **and**

2 Due to your continued disabled condition, you were unable to engage in any substantial gainful activity in 2003, check this box . . . . ▶ ☐

- If you checked this box, you do not have to get another statement for 2003.
- If you **did not** check this box, have your physician complete the statement on page 4 of the instructions. You **must** keep the statement for your records.

Part III **Figure your credit**	**10**	If you checked (in Part I): **Enter:** Box 1, 2, 4, or 7 . . . . $5,000 Box 3, 5, or 6 . . . . $7,500 Box 8 or 9 . . . . $3,750	**10**

> **Did you check box 2, 4, 5, 6, or 9 in Part I?** — Yes ➔ You **must** complete line 11.
>
> — No ➔ Enter the amount from line 10 on line 12 and go to line 13.

11	If you checked (in Part I):	
	• Box 6, add $5,000 to the taxable disability income of the spouse who was under age 65. Enter the total.	
	• Box 2, 4, or 9, enter your taxable disability income.	
	• Box 5, add your taxable disability income to your spouse's taxable disability income. Enter the total.	
	TIP For more details on what to include on line 11, see the instructions.	**11**
12	If you completed line 11, enter the **smaller** of line 10 or line 11; **all others,** enter the amount from line 10.	**12**
13	Enter the following pensions, annuities, or disability income that you (and your spouse if filing a joint return) received in 2003.	
a	Nontaxable part of social security benefits and Nontaxable part of railroad retirement benefits treated as social security (see instructions). **13a**	
b	Nontaxable veterans' pensions and Any other pension, annuity, or disability benefit that is excluded from income under any other provision of law (see instructions). **13b**	
c	Add lines 13a and 13b. (Even though these income items are not taxable, they **must** be included here to figure your credit.) If you did not receive any of the types of nontaxable income listed on line 13a or 13b, enter -0- on line 13c. **13c**	
14	Enter the amount from Form 1040A, line 22. **14**	
15	If you checked (in Part I): **Enter:** Box 1 or 2 . . . . $7,500 Box 3, 4, 5, 6, or 7 . . . . . . $10,000 Box 8 or 9 . . . . $5,000 **15**	
16	Subtract line 15 from line 14. If zero or less, enter -0-. **16**	
17	Enter one-half of line 16. **17**	
18	Add lines 13c and 17.	**18**
19	Subtract line 18 from line 12. If zero or less, **stop;** you **cannot** take the credit. Otherwise, go to line 20.	**19**
20	Multiply line 19 by 15% (.15).	**20**
21	Enter the amount from Form 1040A, line 28, minus any amount on Form 1040A, line 29.	**21**
22	**Credit for the elderly or the disabled.** Enter the **smaller** of line 20 or line 21 here and on Form 1040A, line 30.	**22**

Form **1040**

Department of the Treasury—Internal Revenue Service
U.S. Individual Income Tax Return **2003** (99) IRS Use Only—Do not write or staple in this space.

For the year Jan. 1–Dec. 31, 2003, or other tax year beginning , 2003, ending , 20

OMB No. 1545-0074

Label

(See instructions on page 19.)

Use the IRS label. Otherwise, please print or type.

L A B E L H E R E

Your first name and initial	Last name		Your social security number
If a joint return, spouse's first name and initial	Last name		Spouse's social security number
Home address (number and street). If you have a P.O. box, see page 19.		Apt. no.	
City, town or post office, state, and ZIP code. If you have a foreign address, see page 19.			

▲ **Important!** ▲
You **must** enter your SSN(s) above.

Presidential Election Campaign
(See page 19.) ▶

Note. Checking "Yes" will not change your tax or reduce your refund.
Do you, or your spouse if filing a joint return, want $3 to go to this fund? . . . ▶

	You		Spouse
	☐ Yes ☐ No		☐ Yes ☐ No

Filing Status

Check only one box.

1 ☐ Single
2 ☐ Married filing jointly (even if only one had income)
3 ☐ Married filing separately. Enter spouse's SSN above and full name here. ▶
4 ☐ Head of household (with qualifying person). (See page 20.) If the qualifying person is a child but not your dependent, enter this child's name here. ▶
5 ☐ Qualifying widow(er) with dependent child. (See page 20.)

Exemptions

6a ☐ **Yourself.** If your parent (or someone else) can claim you as a dependent on his or her tax return, **do not** check box 6a . . . .

b ☐ **Spouse** . . . .

c **Dependents:**

(1) First name Last name	(2) Dependent's social security number	(3) Dependent's relationship to you	(4) ✓ if qualifying child for child tax credit (see page 21)
			☐
			☐
			☐
			☐
			☐

If more than five dependents, see page 21.

No. of boxes checked on 6a and 6b	
No. of children on 6c who:	
lived with you	
did not live with you due to divorce or separation (see page 21)	
Dependents on 6c not entered above	
Add numbers on lines above ▶	

d Total number of exemptions claimed . . . .

Income

Attach Forms W-2 and W-2G here. Also attach Form(s) 1099-R if tax was withheld.

If you did not get a W-2, see page 22.

Enclose, but do not attach, any payment. Also, please use Form 1040-V.

7	Wages, salaries, tips, etc. Attach Form(s) W-2	**7**	
8a	**Taxable** interest. Attach Schedule B if required	**8a**	
b	**Tax-exempt** interest. **Do not** include on line 8a . . .	**8b**	
9a	Ordinary dividends. Attach Schedule B if required	**9a**	
b	Qualified dividends (see page 23)	**9b**	
10	Taxable refunds, credits, or offsets of state and local income taxes (see page 23) . .	**10**	
11	Alimony received	**11**	
12	Business income or (loss). Attach Schedule C or C-EZ	**12**	
13a	Capital gain or (loss). Attach Schedule D if required. If not required, check here ▶ ☐	**13a**	
b	If box on 13a is checked, enter post-May 5 capital gain distributions	**13b**	
14	Other gains or (losses). Attach Form 4797	**14**	
15a	IRA distributions . .	**15a**	b Taxable amount (see page 25)	**15b**	
16a	Pensions and annuities	**16a**	b Taxable amount (see page 25)	**16b**	
17	Rental real estate, royalties, partnerships, S corporations, trusts, etc. Attach Schedule E	**17**	
18	Farm income or (loss). Attach Schedule F	**18**	
19	Unemployment compensation	**19**	
20a	Social security benefits	**20a**	b Taxable amount (see page 27)	**20b**	
21	Other income. List type and amount (see page 27)	**21**	
22	Add the amounts in the far right column for lines 7 through 21. This is your **total income** ▶	**22**	

Adjusted Gross Income

23	Educator expenses (see page 29)	**23**	
24	IRA deduction (see page 29)	**24**	
25	Student loan interest deduction (see page 31) . . .	**25**	
26	Tuition and fees deduction (see page 32)	**26**	
27	Moving expenses. Attach Form 3903	**27**	
28	One-half of self-employment tax. Attach Schedule SE	**28**	
29	Self-employed health insurance deduction (see page 33)	**29**	
30	Self-employed SEP, SIMPLE, and qualified plans .	**30**	
31	Penalty on early withdrawal of savings	**31**	
32a	Alimony paid b Recipient's SSN ▶	**32a**	
33	Add lines 23 through 32a	**33**	
34	Subtract line 33 from line 22. This is your **adjusted gross income** . . . . . ▶	**34**	

Tax and Credits	35	Amount from line 34 (adjusted gross income) . . .			35	
	36a	Check if:	☐ **You** were born before January 2, 1939, ☐ Blind. ☐ **Spouse** was born before January 2, 1939, ☐ Blind.	**Total boxes** checked ▶ 36a		
Standard Deduction for—	b	If you are married filing separately and your spouse itemizes deductions, or you were a dual-status alien, see page 34 and check here . . . ▶ 36b ☐				
People who checked any box on line 36a or 36b **or** who can be claimed as a dependent, see page 34.	37	**Itemized deductions** (from Schedule A) **or** your **standard deduction** (see left margin) . .			37	
	38	Subtract line 37 from line 35			38	
	39	If line 35 is $104,625 or less, multiply $3,050 by the total number of exemptions claimed on line 6d. If line 35 is over $104,625, see the worksheet on page 35			39	
All others:	40	**Taxable income.** Subtract line 39 from line 38. If line 39 is more than line 38, enter -0-			40	
Single or Married filing separately, $4,750	41	**Tax** (see page 36). Check if any tax is from: **a** ☐ Form(s) 8814 **b** ☐ Form 4972 . . .			41	
	42	**Alternative minimum tax** (see page 38). Attach Form 6251			42	
Married filing jointly or Qualifying widow(er), $9,500	43	Add lines 41 and 42 . . . . ▶			43	
	44	Foreign tax credit. Attach Form 1116 if required . . .	44			
	45	Credit for child and dependent care expenses. Attach Form 2441	45			
Head of household, $7,000	46	Credit for the elderly or the disabled. Attach Schedule R . .	46			
	47	Education credits. Attach Form 8863	47			
	48	Retirement savings contributions credit. Attach Form 8880 .	48			
	49	Child tax credit (see page 40)	49			
	50	Adoption credit. Attach Form 8839	50			
	51	Credits from: **a** ☐ Form 8396 **b** ☐ Form 8859 . .	51			
	52	Other credits. Check applicable box(es): **a** ☐ Form 3800 **b** ☐ Form 8801 **c** ☐ Specify _____	52			
	53	Add lines 44 through 52. These are your **total credits** . .			53	
	54	Subtract line 53 from line 43. If line 53 is more than line 43, enter -0- . . . . . ▶			54	
Other Taxes	55	Self-employment tax. Attach Schedule SE			55	
	56	Social security and Medicare tax on tip income not reported to employer. Attach Form 4137 .			56	
	57	Tax on qualified plans, including IRAs, and other tax-favored accounts. Attach Form 5329 if required .			57	
	58	Advance earned income credit payments from Form(s) W-2			58	
	59	Household employment taxes. Attach Schedule H			59	
	60	Add lines 54 through 59. This is your **total tax** . . . . ▶			60	
Payments	61	Federal income tax withheld from Forms W-2 and 1099 . .	61			
	62	2003 estimated tax payments and amount applied from 2002 return	62			
If you have a qualifying child, attach Schedule EIC.	63	**Earned income credit (EIC)**	63			
	64	Excess social security and tier 1 RRTA tax withheld (see page 56)	64			
	65	Additional child tax credit. Attach Form 8812	65			
	66	Amount paid with request for extension to file (see page 56)	66			
	67	Other payments from: **a** ☐ Form 2439 **b** ☐ Form 4136 **c** ☐ Form 8885	67			
	68	Add lines 61 through 67. These are your **total payments** . . . . . . ▶			68	
Refund	69	If line 68 is more than line 60, subtract line 60 from line 68. This is the amount you **overpaid**			69	
Direct deposit? See page 56 and fill in 70b, 70c, and 70d.	70a	Amount of line 69 you want **refunded to you** . . . . ▶			70a	
	▶ b	Routing number ☐☐☐☐☐☐☐☐☐ ▶ **c** Type: ☐ Checking ☐ Savings				
	▶ d	Account number ☐☐☐☐☐☐☐☐☐☐☐☐☐☐☐☐☐				
	71	Amount of line 69 you want **applied to your 2004 estimated tax** ▶	71			
Amount You Owe	72	**Amount you owe.** Subtract line 68 from line 60. For details on how to pay, see page 57 ▶			72	
	73	Estimated tax penalty (see page 58)	73			

Third Party Designee	Do you want to allow another person to discuss this return with the IRS (see page 58)? ☐ **Yes.** Complete the following. ☐ **No**
	Designee's name ▶ _____ Phone no. ▶ ( ) Personal identification number (PIN) ▶ ☐☐☐☐☐

Sign Here	Under penalties of perjury, I declare that I have examined this return and accompanying schedules and statements, and to the best of my knowledge and belief, they are true, correct, and complete. Declaration of preparer (other than taxpayer) is based on all information of which preparer has any knowledge.			
Joint return? See page 20.	Your signature	Date	Your occupation	Daytime phone number ( )
Keep a copy for your records.	Spouse's signature. If a joint return, **both** must sign.	Date	Spouse's occupation	

Paid Preparer's Use Only	Preparer's signature ▶	Date	Check if self-employed ☐	Preparer's SSN or PTIN
	Firm's name (or yours if self-employed), address, and ZIP code ▶		EIN	
			Phone no. ( )	

SCHEDULES A&B
(Form 1040)

Department of the Treasury
Internal Revenue Service (99)

Schedule A—Itemized Deductions

(Schedule B is on back)

► **Attach to Form 1040.** ► **See Instructions for Schedules A and B (Form 1040).**

OMB No. 1545-0074

2003

Attachment
Sequence No. **07**

Name(s) shown on Form 1040

Your social security number

Medical and Dental Expenses		**Caution.** Do not include expenses reimbursed or paid by others.	
	1	Medical and dental expenses (see page A-2) . . .	1
	2	Enter amount from Form 1040, line 35 └ 2 ┘	
	3	Multiply line 2 by 7.5% (.075) .	3
	4	Subtract line 3 from line 1. If line 3 is more than line 1, enter -0-	4
Taxes You Paid (See page A-2.)	5	State and local income taxes	5
	6	Real estate taxes (see page A-2)	6
	7	Personal property taxes	7
	8	Other taxes. List type and amount ► -----------------	8
	9	Add lines 5 through 8	9
Interest You Paid (See page A-3.) **Note.** Personal interest is not deductible.	10	Home mortgage interest and points reported to you on Form 1098	10
	11	Home mortgage interest not reported to you on Form 1098. If paid to the person from whom you bought the home, see page A-3 and show that person's name, identifying no., and address ► -----------------	11
	12	Points not reported to you on Form 1098. See page A-3 for special rules	12
	13	Investment interest. Attach Form 4952 if required. (See page A-4.)	13
	14	Add lines 10 through 13	14
Gifts to Charity If you made a gift and got a benefit for it, see page A-4.	15	Gifts by cash or check. If you made any gift of $250 or more, see page A-4	15
	16	Other than by cash or check. If any gift of $250 or more, see page A-4. You **must** attach Form 8283 if over $500	16
	17	Carryover from prior year	17
	18	Add lines 15 through 17	18
Casualty and Theft Losses	19	Casualty or theft loss(es). Attach Form 4684. (See page A-5.)	19
Job Expenses and Most Other Miscellaneous Deductions (See page A-5.)	20	Unreimbursed employee expenses—job travel, union dues, job education, etc. Attach Form 2106 or 2106-EZ if required. (See page A-5.) ► -----------------	20
	21	Tax preparation fees	21
	22	Other expenses—investment, safe deposit box, etc. List type and amount ► -----------------	22
	23	Add lines 20 through 22	23
	24	Enter amount from Form 1040, line 35 └ 24 ┘	
	25	Multiply line 24 by 2% (.02)	25
	26	Subtract line 25 from line 23. If line 25 is more than line 23, enter -0-	26
Other Miscellaneous Deductions	27	Other—from list on page A-6. List type and amount ► -----------------	27
Total Itemized Deductions	28	Is Form 1040, line 35, over $139,500 (over $69,750 if married filing separately)?	
		☐ **No.** Your deduction is not limited. Add the amounts in the far right column for lines 4 through 27. Also, enter this amount on Form 1040, line 37. } ►	28
		☐ **Yes.** Your deduction may be limited. See page A-6 for the amount to enter. }	

For Paperwork Reduction Act Notice, see Form 1040 instructions.   Cat. No. 11330X   Schedule A (Form 1040) 2003

OMB No. 1545-0074   Page **2**

Name(s) shown on Form 1040. Do not enter name and social security number if shown on other side. | **Your social security number**

Schedule B—Interest and Ordinary Dividends

Attachment Sequence No. **08**

Part I
Interest

(See page B-1 and the instructions for Form 1040, line 8a.)

Note. If you received a Form 1099-INT, Form 1099-OID, or substitute statement from a brokerage firm, list the firm's name as the payer and enter the total interest shown on that form.

	Amount
1 List name of payer. If any interest is from a seller-financed mortgage and the buyer used the property as a personal residence, see page B-1 and list this interest first. Also, show that buyer's social security number and address ▶	
2 Add the amounts on line 1 . . . . **2**	
3 Excludable interest on series EE and I U.S. savings bonds issued after 1989. Attach Form 8815 . . . . **3**	
4 Subtract line 3 from line 2. Enter the result here and on Form 1040, line 8a ▶ **4**	

Note. If line 4 is over $1,500, you must complete Part III.

Part II
Ordinary Dividends

(See page B-1 and the instructions for Form 1040, line 9a.)

Note. If you received a Form 1099-DIV or substitute statement from a brokerage firm, list the firm's name as the payer and enter the ordinary dividends shown on that form.

	Amount
5 List name of payer ▶	
6 Add the amounts on line 5. Enter the total here and on Form 1040, line 9a . ▶ **6**	

Note. If line 6 is over $1,500, you must complete Part III.

Part III
Foreign Accounts and Trusts

(See page B-2.)

You must complete this part if you **(a)** had over $1,500 of taxable interest or ordinary dividends; or **(b)** had a foreign account; or **(c)** received a distribution from, or were a grantor of, or a transferor to, a foreign trust.

	Yes	No
7a At any time during 2003, did you have an interest in or a signature or other authority over a financial account in a foreign country, such as a bank account, securities account, or other financial account? See page B-2 for exceptions and filing requirements for Form TD F 90-22.1		
b If "Yes," enter the name of the foreign country ▶		
8 During 2003, did you receive a distribution from, or were you the grantor of, or transferor to, a foreign trust? If "Yes," you may have to file Form 3520. See page B-2		

For Paperwork Reduction Act Notice, see Form 1040 instructions.

Schedule B (Form 1040) 2003

SCHEDULE C
(Form 1040)

Department of the Treasury
Internal Revenue Service   (99)

Profit or Loss From Business
(Sole Proprietorship)
Partnerships, joint ventures, etc., must file Form 1065 or 1065-B.
▶ **Attach to Form 1040 or 1041.**   ▶ **See Instructions for Schedule C (Form 1040).**

OMB No. 1545-0074

2003

Attachment
Sequence No. **09**

Name of proprietor

Social security number (SSN)

A	Principal business or profession, including product or service (see page C-2 of the instructions)	**B** Enter code from pages C-7, 8, & 9 ▶
C	Business name. If no separate business name, leave blank.	**D** Employer ID number (EIN), if any

E   Business address (including suite or room no.) ▶
City, town or post office, state, and ZIP code

F   Accounting method: **(1)** ☐ Cash   **(2)** ☐ Accrual   **(3)** ☐ Other (specify) ▶

G   Did you "materially participate" in the operation of this business during 2003? If "No," see page C-3 for limit on losses   . ☐ Yes ☐ No

H   If you started or acquired this business during 2003, check here   .   .   .   .   ▶ ☐

Part I   Income

1	Gross receipts or sales. **Caution.** If this income was reported to you on Form W-2 and the "Statutory employee" box on that form was checked, see page C-3 and check here . . . . . . ▶ ☐	**1**	
2	Returns and allowances	**2**	
3	Subtract line 2 from line 1	**3**	
4	Cost of goods sold (from line 42 on page 2)	**4**	
5	**Gross profit.** Subtract line 4 from line 3	**5**	
6	Other income, including Federal and state gasoline or fuel tax credit or refund (see page C-3) . . .	**6**	
7	**Gross income.** Add lines 5 and 6 . . . . ▶	**7**	

Part II   Expenses. Enter expenses for business use of your home **only** on line 30.

8	Advertising	**8**		**19** Pension and profit-sharing plans	**19**	
9	Car and truck expenses (see page C-3) . . .	**9**		**20** Rent or lease (see page C-5):		
				a Vehicles, machinery, and equipment .	**20a**	
10	Commissions and fees . .	**10**		**b** Other business property . .	**20b**	
11	Contract labor (see page C-4)	**11**		**21** Repairs and maintenance . .	**21**	
12	Depletion	**12**		**22** Supplies (not included in Part III) .	**22**	
13	Depreciation and section 179 expense deduction (not included in Part III) (see page C-4) . .	**13**		**23** Taxes and licenses	**23**	
				24 Travel, meals, and entertainment:		
				a Travel	**24a**	
14	Employee benefit programs (other than on line 19) . . .	**14**		**b** Meals and entertainment		
15	Insurance (other than health) .	**15**		**c** Enter nondeduct-ible amount in-cluded on line 24b (see page C-5) .		
16	Interest:					
a	Mortgage (paid to banks, etc.) .	**16a**		**d** Subtract line 24c from line 24b .	**24d**	
b	Other	**16b**		**25** Utilities	**25**	
17	Legal and professional services	**17**		**26** Wages (less employment credits) .	**26**	
18	Office expense	**18**		**27** Other expenses (from line 48 on page 2)	**27**	

28	**Total expenses** before expenses for business use of home. Add lines 8 through 27 in columns . . . ▶	**28**	
29	Tentative profit (loss). Subtract line 28 from line 7	**29**	
30	Expenses for business use of your home. Attach **Form 8829**	**30**	
31	**Net profit or (loss).** Subtract line 30 from line 29. • If a profit, enter on **Form 1040, line 12,** and **also** on **Schedule SE, line 2** (statutory employees, see page C-6). Estates and trusts, enter on Form 1041, line 3. • If a loss, you **must** go to line 32.	**31**	

32   If you have a loss, check the box that describes your investment in this activity (see page C-6).
   • If you checked 32a, enter the loss on **Form 1040, line 12,** and **also** on **Schedule SE, line 2** (statutory employees, see page C-6). Estates and trusts, enter on Form 1041, line 3.
   • If you checked 32b, you **must** attach **Form 6198.**

32a ☐ All investment is at risk.
32b ☐ Some investment is not at risk.

For Paperwork Reduction Act Notice, see Form 1040 instructions.   Cat. No. 11334P   Schedule C (Form 1040) 2003

Part III Cost of Goods Sold (see page C-6)

33 Method(s) used to value closing inventory: **a** ☐ Cost **b** ☐ Lower of cost or market **c** ☐ Other (attach explanation)

34 Was there any change in determining quantities, costs, or valuations between opening and closing inventory? If "Yes," attach explanation ☐ Yes ☐ No

35 Inventory at beginning of year. If different from last year's closing inventory, attach explanation	35	
36 Purchases less cost of items withdrawn for personal use	36	
37 Cost of labor. Do not include any amounts paid to yourself	37	
38 Materials and supplies	38	
39 Other costs	39	
40 Add lines 35 through 39	40	
41 Inventory at end of year	41	
42 **Cost of goods sold.** Subtract line 41 from line 40. Enter the result here and on page 1, line 4	42	

Part IV Information on Your Vehicle. Complete this part **only** if you are claiming car or truck expenses on line 9 and are not required to file Form 4562 for this business. See the instructions for line 13 on page C-4 to find out if you must file Form 4562.

43 When did you place your vehicle in service for business purposes? (month, day, year) ▶ ____ / ____ / ____ .

44 Of the total number of miles you drove your vehicle during 2003, enter the number of miles you used your vehicle for:

a Business _____ **b** Commuting _____ **c** Other _____

45 Do you (or your spouse) have another vehicle available for personal use? ☐ Yes ☐ No

46 Was your vehicle available for personal use during off-duty hours? ☐ Yes ☐ No

47a Do you have evidence to support your deduction? ☐ Yes ☐ No

  b If "Yes," is the evidence written? ☐ Yes ☐ No

Part V Other Expenses. List below business expenses not included on lines 8–26 or line 30.

48 **Total other expenses.** Enter here and on page 1, line 27	48	

SCHEDULE C-EZ
(Form 1040)

Department of the Treasury
Internal Revenue Service   (99)

Net Profit From Business

(Sole Proprietorship)

▶ **Partnerships, joint ventures, etc., must file Form 1065 or 1065-B.**

▶ **Attach to Form 1040 or 1041.** ▶ **See instructions on back.**

OMB No. 1545-0074

2003

Attachment
Sequence No. **09A**

Name of proprietor

Social security number (SSN)

Part I   General Information

**You May Use
Schedule C-EZ
Instead of
Schedule C
Only If You:**

- Had business expenses of $2,500 or less.

  Use the cash method of accounting.
- Did not have an inventory at any time during the year.
- Did not have a net loss from your business.
- Had only one business as a sole proprietor.

And You:

- Had no employees during the year.
- Are not required to file **Form 4562,** Depreciation and Amortization, for this business. See the instructions for Schedule C, line 13, on page C-4 to find out if you must file.
- Do not deduct expenses for business use of your home.
- Do not have prior year unallowed passive activity losses from this business.

A Principal business or profession, including product or service

B Enter code from pages C-7, 8, & 9
▶

C Business name. If no separate business name, leave blank.

D Employer ID number (EIN), if any

E Business address (including suite or room no.). Address not required if same as on Form 1040, page 1.

City, town or post office, state, and ZIP code

Part II   Figure Your Net Profit

1 Gross receipts. Caution. If this income was reported to you on Form W-2 and the "Statutory employee" box on that form was checked, see **Statutory Employees** in the instructions for Schedule C, line 1, on page C-3 and check here . . . . ▶ ☐	**1**	
2 Total expenses (see instructions). If more than $2,500, you **must** use Schedule C	**2**	
3 Net profit. Subtract line 2 from line 1. If less than zero, you **must** use Schedule C. Enter on **Form 1040, line 12,** and also on **Schedule SE, line 2.** (Statutory employees **do not** report this amount on Schedule SE, line 2. Estates and trusts, enter on Form 1041, line 3.)	**3**	

Part III   Information on Your Vehicle. Complete this part **only** if you are claiming car or truck expenses on line 2.

4 When did you place your vehicle in service for business purposes? (month, day, year) ▶ ..../......../........ .

5 Of the total number of miles you drove your vehicle during 2003, enter the number of miles you used your vehicle for:

a Business .... **b** Commuting .... **c** Other ....

6 Do you (or your spouse) have another vehicle available for personal use? . . . . ☐ **Yes** ☐ **No**

7 Was your vehicle available for personal use during off-duty hours? . . . . ☐ **Yes** ☐ **No**

8a Do you have evidence to support your deduction? . . . . ☐ **Yes** ☐ **No**

b If "Yes," is the evidence written? . . . . ☐ **Yes** ☐ **No**

Instructions

You may use Schedule C-EZ instead of Schedule C if you operated a business or practiced a profession as a sole proprietorship and you have met all the requirements listed in Part I of Schedule C-EZ.

Line A

Describe the business or professional activity that provided your principal source of income reported on line 1. Give the general field or activity and the type of product or service.

Line B

Enter the six-digit code that identifies your principal business or professional activity. See pages C-7 through C-9 of the Instructions for Schedule C for the list of codes.

Line D

You need an employer identification number (EIN) only if you had a qualified retirement plan or were required to file an employment, excise, estate, trust, or alcohol, tobacco, and firearms tax return. If you need an EIN, file **Form SS-4,** Application for Employer Identification Number. If you do not have an EIN, leave line D blank. **Do not** enter your SSN.

Line E

Enter your business address. Show a street address instead of a box number. Include the suite or room number, if any.

Line 1

Enter gross receipts from your trade or business. Include amounts you received in your trade or business that were properly shown on **Forms 1099-MISC.** If the total amounts that were reported in box 7 of Forms 1099-MISC are more than the total you are reporting on line 1, attach a statement explaining the difference. You must show all items of taxable income actually or constructively received during the year (in cash, property, or services). Income is constructively received when it is credited to your account or set aside for you to use. Do not offset this amount by any losses.

Line 2

Enter the total amount of all deductible business expenses you actually paid during the year. Examples of these expenses include advertising, car and truck expenses, commissions and fees, insurance, interest, legal and professional services, office expense, rent or lease expenses, repairs and maintenance, supplies, taxes, travel, the allowable percentage of business meals and entertainment, and utilities (including telephone). For details, see the instructions for Schedule C, Parts II and V, on pages C-3 through C-7. If you wish, you may use the optional worksheet below to record your expenses.

If you claim car or truck expenses, be sure to complete Part III of Schedule C-EZ.

Optional Worksheet for Line 2 (keep a copy for your records)

a Business meals and entertainment	a	
b Enter nondeductible amount included on line **a** (see the instructions for lines 24b and 24c on page C-5)	b	
c Deductible business meals and entertainment. Subtract line **b** from line **a**	c	
d _____	d	
e _____	e	
f _____	f	
g _____	g	
h _____	h	
i _____	i	
j **Total.** Add lines **c** through **i.** Enter here and on line 2	j	

Schedule C-EZ (Form 1040) 2003

SCHEDULE D
(Form 1040)

Department of the Treasury
Internal Revenue Service   (99)

Capital Gains and Losses

► Attach to Form 1040.   ► See Instructions for Schedule D (Form 1040).

► Use Schedule D-1 to list additional transactions for lines 1 and 8.

OMB No. 1545-0074

20**03**

Attachment
Sequence No. **12**

Name(s) shown on Form 1040

Your social security number

Part I   Short-Term Capital Gains and Losses—Assets Held One Year or Less

(a) Description of property (Example: 100 sh. XYZ Co.)	(b) Date acquired (Mo., day, yr.)	(c) Date sold (Mo., day, yr.)	(d) Sales price (see page D-6 of the instructions)	(e) Cost or other basis (see page D-6 of the instructions)	(f) Gain or (loss) for the entire year Subtract (e) from (d)	(g) Post-May 5 gain or (loss)* (see below)
1						

2 Enter your short-term totals, if any, from Schedule D-1, line 2 . . . .   **2**

3 **Total short-term sales price amounts.** Add lines 1 and 2 in column (d) **3**

4 Short-term gain from Form 6252 and short-term gain or (loss) from Forms 4684, 6781, and 8824 . . . .   **4**

5 Net short-term gain or (loss) from partnerships, S corporations, estates, and trusts from Schedule(s) K-1 . . . .   **5**

6 Short-term capital loss carryover. Enter the amount, if any, from line 8 of your 2002 Capital Loss Carryover Worksheet . . . .   **6** (   )

7a Combine lines 1 through 5 in column (g). If the result is a loss, enter the result. Otherwise, enter -0-. **Do not** enter more than zero . . . .   **7a**   (   )

b **Net short-term capital gain or (loss).** Combine lines 1 through 6 in column (f) .   **7b**

Part II   Long-Term Capital Gains and Losses—Assets Held More Than One Year

(a) Description of property (Example: 100 sh. XYZ Co.)	(b) Date acquired (Mo., day, yr.)	(c) Date sold (Mo., day, yr.)	(d) Sales price (see page D-6 of the instructions)	(e) Cost or other basis (see page D-6 of the instructions)	(f) Gain or (loss) for the entire year Subtract (e) from (d)	(g) Post-May 5 gain or (loss)* (see below)
8						

9 Enter your long-term totals, if any, from Schedule D-1, line 9 . . . .   **9**

10 **Total long-term sales price amounts.** Add lines 8 and 9 in column (d) **10**

11 Gain from Form 4797, Part I; long-term gain from Forms 2439 and 6252; and long-term gain or (loss) from Forms 4684, 6781, and 8824 . . . . . .   **11**

12 Net long-term gain or (loss) from partnerships, S corporations, estates, and trusts from Schedule(s) K-1 . . . .   **12**

13 Capital gain distributions. See page D-2 of the instructions **13**

14 Long-term capital loss carryover. Enter the amount, if any, from line 13 of your 2002 Capital Loss Carryover Worksheet . . . .   **14** (   )

15 Combine lines 8 through 13 in column (g). If zero or less, enter -0- **15**

16 **Net long-term capital gain or (loss).** Combine lines 8 through 14 in column (f)   **16**
Next: Go to Part III on the back.

*Include in column (g) all gains and losses from column (f) from sales, exchanges, or conversions (including installment payments received) **after** May 5, 2003. However, **do not** include gain attributable to unrecaptured section 1250 gain, "collectibles gains and losses" (as defined on page D-8 of the instructions) or eligible gain on qualified small business stock (see page D-4 of the instructions).

Part III	Taxable Gain or Deductible Loss

17a Combine lines 7b and 16 and enter the result. If a loss, enter -0- on line 17b and go to line 18.
If a gain, enter the gain on Form 1040, line 13a, and go to line 17b below **17a**

b Combine lines 7a and 15. If zero or less, enter -0-. Then complete Form 1040 through line 40 . **17b**

Next: If line 16 of Schedule D is a gain **or** you have qualified dividends on Form 1040, line 9b, complete **Part IV** below.

Otherwise, skip the rest of Schedule D and complete the rest of Form 1040.

18 If line 17a is a loss, enter here and on Form 1040, line 13a, the **smaller** of **(a)** that loss or **(b)** ($3,000) (or, if married filing separately, ($1,500)) (see page D-7 of the instructions) . . . **18** (　　　　　)

Next: If you have qualified dividends on Form 1040, line 9b, complete Form 1040 through line 40, and then complete **Part IV** below (but skip lines 19 and 20).

Otherwise, skip **Part IV** below and complete the rest of Form 1040.

Part IV	Tax Computation Using Maximum Capital Gains Rates

If line 16 or line 17a is zero or less, skip lines 19 and 20 and go to line 21. Otherwise, go to line 19.

19 Enter your unrecaptured section 1250 gain, if any, from line 18 of the worksheet on page D-7 . . **19**

20 Enter your 28% rate gain, if any, from line 7 of the worksheet on page D-8 of the instructions . . **20**

If lines 19 and 20 are zero, go to line 21. Otherwise, complete the worksheet on page D-11 of the instructions to figure the amount to enter on lines 35 and 53 below, and skip all other lines below.

21 Enter your taxable income from Form 1040, line 40 . . . . **21**

22 Enter the **smaller** of line 16 or line 17a, but not less than zero . . **22**

23 Enter your qualified dividends from Form 1040, line 9b **23**

24 Add lines 22 and 23 . . . . **24**

25 Amount from line 4g of Form 4952 (investment interest expense) . **25**

26 Subtract line 25 from line 24. If zero or less, enter -0- **26**

27 Subtract line 26 from line 21. If zero or less, enter -0- **27**

28 Enter the **smaller** of line 21 **or:**
  • $56,800 if married filing jointly or qualifying widow(er);
  • $28,400 if single or married filing separately; or ⎬ **28**
  • $38,050 if head of household

If line 27 is more than line 28, skip lines 29–39 and go to line 40.

29 Enter the amount from line 27 . . . . **29**

30 Subtract line 29 from line 28. If zero or less, enter -0- and go to line 40 **30**

31 Add lines 17b and 23* **31**

32 Enter the **smaller** of line 30 or line 31 . . . . . **32**

33 Multiply line 32 by 5% (.05) **33**

If lines 30 and 32 are the same, skip lines 34–39 and go to line 40.

34 Subtract line 32 from line 30 . . . . **34**

35 Enter your qualified 5-year gain, if any, from line 8 of the worksheet on page D-10 . . **35**

36 Enter the **smaller** of line 34 or line 35 . . . . . . **36**

37 Multiply line 36 by 8% (.08) **37**

38 Subtract line 36 from line 34 . . . . **38**

39 Multiply line 38 by 10% (.10) **39**

If lines 26 and 30 are the same, skip lines 40–49 and go to line 50.

40 Enter the **smaller** of line 21 or line 26 . . . . . . **40**

41 Enter the amount from line 30 (if line 30 is blank, enter -0-) . . . **41**

42 Subtract line 41 from line 40 . . . . **42**

43 Add lines 17b and 23* **43**

44 Enter the amount from line 32 (if line 32 is blank, enter -0-) **44**

45 Subtract line 44 from line 43 . . . . . . **45**

46 Enter the **smaller** of line 42 or line 45 . . . . **46**

47 Multiply line 46 by 15% (.15) **47**

48 Subtract line 46 from line 42 . . . . **48**

49 Multiply line 48 by 20% (.20) **49**

50 Figure the tax on the amount on **line 27**. Use the Tax Table or Tax Rate Schedules, whichever applies **50**

51 Add lines 33, 37, 39, 47, 49, and 50 . . . . **51**

52 Figure the tax on the amount on **line 21**. Use the Tax Table or Tax Rate Schedules, whichever applies **52**

53 **Tax on all taxable income.** Enter the **smaller** of line 51 or line 52 here and on Form 1040, line 41 **53**

*If lines 23 and 25 are more than zero, see **Lines 31 and 43** on page D-9 for the amount to enter. ✪　　　　　　　　**Schedule D (Form 1040) 2003**

SCHEDULE D-1
(Form 1040)

Department of the Treasury
Internal Revenue Service   (99)

Continuation Sheet for Schedule D
(Form 1040)

▶ See instructions for Schedule D (Form 1040).
▶ Attach to Schedule D to list additional transactions for lines 1 and 8.

OMB No. 1545-0074

2003

Attachment
Sequence No. **12A**

Name(s) shown on Form 1040

Your social security number

Part I   Short-Term Capital Gains and Losses—Assets Held One Year or Less

(a) Description of property (Example: 100 sh. XYZ Co.)	(b) Date acquired (Mo., day, yr.)	(c) Date sold (Mo., day, yr.)	(d) Sales price (see page D-6 of the instructions)	(e) Cost or other basis (see page D-6 of the instructions)	(f) Gain or (loss) for the entire year Subtract (e) from (d)	(g) Post-May 5 gain or (loss)* (see page 2)
1						
2 **Totals.** Combine columns (d), (f) and (g). Enter here and on Schedule D, line 2 . . . . . ▶ **2**						

For Paperwork Reduction Act Notice, see Form 1040 instructions.

Cat. No. 10424K

Schedule D-1 (Form 1040) 2003

Name(s) shown on Form 1040. Do not enter name and social security number if shown on other side. | **Your social security number**

| **Part II** | **Long-Term Capital Gains and Losses—Assets Held More Than One Year** |

(a) Description of property (Example: 100 sh. XYZ Co.)	(b) Date acquired (Mo., day, yr.)	(c) Date sold (Mo., day, yr.)	(d) Sales price (see page D-6 of the instructions)	(e) Cost or other basis (see page D-6 of the instructions)	(f) Gain or (loss) for the entire year Subtract (e) from (d)	(g) Post-May 5 gain or (loss)* (see below)
8						
9 Totals. Combine columns (d), (f), and (g). Enter here and on Schedule D, line 9 . . . . . ▶ **9**						

*Include in column (g) all gains and losses from column (f) from sales, exchanges, or conversions (including installment payments received) **after** May 5, 2003. However, **do not** include gain attributable to unrecaptured section 1250 gain, "collectibles gains and losses" (as defined on page D-8 of the instructions) or eligible gain on qualified small business stock (see page D-4 of the instructions).

SCHEDULE E
(Form 1040)

Department of the Treasury
Internal Revenue Service (99)

Supplemental Income and Loss

**(From rental real estate, royalties, partnerships,
S corporations, estates, trusts, REMICs, etc.)**

▶ Attach to Form 1040 or Form 1041.   ▶ See Instructions for Schedule E (Form 1040).

OMB No. 1545-0074

2003

Attachment
Sequence No. **13**

Name(s) shown on return

Your social security number

Part I	**Income or Loss From Rental Real Estate and Royalties** Note. If you are in the business of renting personal property, use Schedule **C** or **C-EZ** (see page E-2). Report farm rental income or loss from **Form 4835** on page 2, line 40.

1 Show the kind and location of each **rental real estate property:**

A ....

B ....

C ....

2 For each rental real estate property listed on line 1, did you or your family use it during the tax year for personal purposes for more than the greater of:
- 14 days **or**
- 10% of the total days rented at fair rental value?
(See page E-3.)

	Yes	No
A		
B		
C		

Income:

			Properties			Totals
		A	B	C		(Add columns A, B, and C.)
3 Rents received	3		3			
4 Royalties received	4					4

Expenses:

5 Advertising	5					
6 Auto and travel (see page E-4) .	6					
7 Cleaning and maintenance . . .	7					
8 Commissions	8					
9 Insurance	9					
10 Legal and other professional fees	10					
11 Management fees	11					
12 Mortgage interest paid to banks, etc. (see page E-4)	12					12
13 Other interest	13					
14 Repairs	14					
15 Supplies	15					
16 Taxes	16					
17 Utilities	17					
18 Other (list) ▶	18					
19 Add lines 5 through 18	19					19
20 Depreciation expense or depletion (see page E-4)	20					20
21 Total expenses. Add lines 19 and 20	21					
22 Income or (loss) from rental real estate or royalty properties. Subtract line 21 from line 3 (rents) or line 4 (royalties). If the result is a (loss), see page E-4 to find out if you must file **Form 6198**. . .	22					
23 Deductible rental real estate loss. **Caution.** Your rental real estate loss on line 22 may be limited. See page E-4 to find out if you must file **Form 8582**. Real estate professionals must complete line 43 on page 2	23	(	) (	) (	)	

24 **Income.** Add positive amounts shown on line 22. **Do not** include any losses . . . . | 24 | |

25 **Losses.** Add royalty losses from line 22 and rental real estate losses from line 23. Enter total losses here | 25 | ( ) |

26 **Total rental real estate and royalty income or (loss).** Combine lines 24 and 25. Enter the result here. If Parts II, III, IV, and line 40 on page 2 do not apply to you, also enter this amount on Form 1040, line 17. Otherwise, include this amount in the total on line 41 on page 2 . . . . | 26 | |

For Paperwork Reduction Act Notice, see Form 1040 instructions.   Cat. No. 11344L   Schedule E (Form 1040) 2003

Name(s) shown on return. Do not enter name and social security number if shown on other side.	Your social security number

Part II　Income or Loss From Partnerships and S Corporations

Note. If you report a loss from an at-risk activity for which **any** amount is **not** at risk, you **must** check column **(e)** on line 28 and attach **Form 6198**. See page E-1.

27 Are you reporting losses not allowed in prior years due to the at-risk or basis limitations, passive losses not reported on Form 8582, or unreimbursed partnership expenses? . . . . ☐ **Yes**　☐ **No**

If you answered "Yes," see page E-5 before completing this section.

Caution: The IRS compares amounts reported on your tax return with amounts shown on Schedule(s) K-1.

28	**(a)** Name	**(b)** Enter **P** for partnership; **S** for S corporation	**(c)** Check if foreign partnership	**(d)** Employer identification number	**(e)** Check if any amount is not at risk
A					
B					
C					
D					

	Passive Income and Loss		Nonpassive Income and Loss		
	(f) Passive loss allowed (attach **Form 8582** if required)	**(g)** Passive income from **Schedule K-1**	**(h)** Nonpassive loss from **Schedule K-1**	**(i)** Section 179 expense deduction from **Form 4562**	**(j)** Nonpassive income from **Schedule K-1**
A					
B					
C					
D					
29a Totals					
b Totals					

30 Add columns (g) and (j) of line 29a **30**

31 Add columns (f), (h), and (i) of line 29b . . . . **31** ( )

32 **Total partnership and S corporation income or (loss).** Combine lines 30 and 31. Enter the result here and include in the total on line 41 below **32**

Part III　Income or Loss From Estates and Trusts

33	**(a)** Name	**(b)** Employer identification number
A		
B		

	Passive Income and Loss		Nonpassive Income and Loss	
	(c) Passive deduction or loss allowed (attach **Form 8582** if required)	**(d)** Passive income from **Schedule K-1**	**(e)** Deduction or loss from **Schedule K-1**	**(f)** Other income from **Schedule K-1**
A				
B				
34a Totals				
b Totals				

35 Add columns (d) and (f) of line 34a **35**

36 Add columns (c) and (e) of line 34b . . . . **36** ( )

37 **Total estate and trust income or (loss).** Combine lines 35 and 36. Enter the result here and include in the total on line 41 below **37**

Part IV　Income or Loss From Real Estate Mortgage Investment Conduits (REMICs)—Residual Holder

38	**(a)** Name	**(b)** Employer identification number	**(c)** Excess inclusion from **Schedules Q**, line 2c (see page E-6)	**(d)** Taxable income (net loss) from **Schedules Q**, line 1b	**(e)** Income from **Schedules Q**, line 3b

39 Combine columns (d) and (e) only. Enter the result here and include in the total on line 41 below . . **39**

Part V　Summary

40 Net farm rental income or (loss) from **Form 4835**. Also, complete line 42 below **40**

41 **Total income or (loss).** Combine lines 26, 32, 37, 39, and 40. Enter the result here and on Form 1040, line 17 ▶ **41**

42 **Reconciliation of Farming and Fishing Income.** Enter your **gross** farming and fishing income reported on Form 4835, line 7; Schedule K-1 (Form 1065), line 15b; Schedule K-1 (Form 1120S), line 23; and Schedule K-1 (Form 1041), line 14 (see page E-6) **42**

43 **Reconciliation for Real Estate Professionals.** If you were a real estate professional (see page E-1), enter the net income or (loss) you reported anywhere on Form 1040 from all rental real estate activities in which you materially participated under the passive activity loss rules . . . **43**

SCHEDULE EIC
(Form 1040A or 1040)

Department of the Treasury
Internal Revenue Service   (99)

Earned Income Credit

Qualifying Child Information

Complete and attach to Form 1040A or 1040
only if you have a qualifying child.

1040A
1040
EIC

OMB No. 1545-0074

20**03**

Attachment
Sequence No. **43**

Name(s) shown on return

Your social security number

Before you begin: See the instructions for Form 1040A, line 41, or Form 1040, line 63, to make sure that (**a**) you can take the EIC and (**b**) you have a qualifying child.

- If you take the EIC even though you are not eligible, you may not be allowed to take the credit for up to 10 years. See back of schedule for details.
- It will take us longer to process your return and issue your refund if you do not fill in all lines that apply for each qualifying child.
- Be sure the child's name on line 1 and social security number (SSN) on line 2a agree with the child's social security card. Otherwise, at the time we process your return, we may reduce or disallow your EIC. If the name or SSN on the child's social security card is not correct, call the Social Security Administration at 1-800-772-1213.

Qualifying Child Information

	Child 1	Child 2
1 Child's name If you have more than two qualifying children, you only have to list two to get the maximum credit.	First name Last name	First name Last name
2a Child's SSN The child must have an SSN as defined on page 43 of the Form 1040A instructions or page 47 of the Form 1040 instructions unless the child was born and died in 2003. If your child was born and died in 2003 and did not have an SSN, enter "Died" on this line and attach a copy of the child's birth certificate.		
b Child's year of birth	Year ___ ___ ___ ___ *If born after 1984, skip lines 3a and 3b; go to line 4.*	Year ___ ___ ___ ___ *If born after 1984, skip lines 3a and 3b; go to line 4.*
3 If the child was born before 1985— **a** Was the child under age 24 at the end of 2003 and a student?	☐ **Yes.** *Go to line 4.* ☐ **No.** *Continue*	☐ **Yes.** *Go to line 4.* ☐ **No.** *Continue*
b Was the child permanently and totally disabled during any part of 2003?	☐ **Yes.** *Continue* ☐ **No.** The child is not a qualifying child.	☐ **Yes.** *Continue* ☐ **No.** The child is not a qualifying child.
4 Child's relationship to you (for example, son, daughter, grandchild, niece, nephew, foster child, etc.)		
5 Number of months child lived with you in the United States during 2003 • If the child lived with you for more than half of 2003 but less than 7 months, enter "7". • If the child was born or died in 2003 and your home was the child's home for the entire time he or she was alive during 2003, enter "12".	_____ months *Do not enter more than 12 months.*	_____ months *Do not enter more than 12 months.*

    You may also be able to take the additional child tax credit if your child (**a**) was under age 17 at the end of 2003, (**b**) is claimed as your dependent on line 6c of Form 1040A or Form 1040, **and** (**c**) is a U.S. citizen or resident alien. For more details, see the instructions for line 42 of Form 1040A or line 65 of Form 1040.

For Paperwork Reduction Act Notice, see Form 1040A or 1040 instructions.   Cat. No. 13339M   **Schedule EIC (Form 1040A or 1040) 2003**

Purpose of Schedule

The purpose of this schedule is to give the IRS information about your qualifying child after you have figured your earned income credit (EIC).

To figure the amount of your credit or to have the IRS figure it for you, see the instructions for Form 1040A, line 41, or Form 1040, line 63.

Taking the EIC When Not Eligible. If you take the EIC even though you are not eligible and it is determined that your error is due to reckless or intentional disregard of the EIC rules, you will not be allowed to take the credit for 2 years even if you are otherwise eligible to do so. If you fraudulently take the EIC, you will not be allowed to take the credit for 10 years. You may also have to pay penalties.

Qualifying Child

A qualifying child is a child who is your . . .

Son, daughter, adopted child, stepchild, or a descendant of any of them (for example, your grandchild)

or

Brother, sister, stepbrother, stepsister, or a descendant of any of them (for example, your niece or nephew) whom you cared for as you would your own child

or

Foster child (any child placed with you by an authorized placement agency whom you cared for as you would your own child)

 AND

was at the end of 2003 . . .

Under age 19

or

Under age 24 and a student

or

Any age and permanently and totally disabled

 AND

who . . .

Lived with you in the United States for more than half of 2003. If the child did not live with you for the required time, see Exception to ì Time Lived With Youî Condition on page 42 of the Form 1040A instructions or page 46 of the Form 1040 instructions.

Note. If the child was married or meets the conditions to be a qualifying child of another person (other than your spouse if filing a joint return), special rules apply. For details, see page 43 of the Form 1040A instructions or page 47 of the Form 1040 instructions.

 Do you want part of the EIC added to your take-home pay in 2004? To see if you qualify, get Form W-5 from your employer, call the IRS at 1-800-TAX-FORM (1-800-829-3676), or go to www.irs.gov.

SCHEDULE F
(Form 1040)

Department of the Treasury
Internal Revenue Service   (99)

Profit or Loss From Farming

▶ Attach to Form 1040, Form 1041, Form 1065, or Form 1065-B.

▶ See Instructions for Schedule F (Form 1040).

OMB No. 1545-0074

2003

Attachment
Sequence No. **14**

Name of proprietor

Social security number (SSN)

A Principal product. Describe in one or two words your principal crop or activity for the current tax year.

B Enter code from Part IV
▶

D Employer ID number (EIN), if any

C Accounting method: (1) ☐ Cash (2) ☐ Accrual

E Did you "materially participate" in the operation of this business during 2003? If "No," see page F-2 for limit on passive losses. ☐ Yes ☐ No

Part I   Farm Income—Cash Method. Complete Parts I and II (Accrual method taxpayers complete Parts II and III, and line 11 of Part I.)
Do not include sales of livestock held for draft, breeding, sport, or dairy purposes; report these sales on Form 4797.

1	Sales of livestock and other items you bought for resale	1	
2	Cost or other basis of livestock and other items reported on line 1	2	
3	Subtract line 2 from line 1		3
4	Sales of livestock, produce, grains, and other products you raised		4
5a	Total cooperative distributions (Form(s) 1099-PATR)	5a 5b Taxable amount	5b
6a	Agricultural program payments (see page F-2)	6a 6b Taxable amount	6b
7	Commodity Credit Corporation (CCC) loans (see page F-3):		
a	CCC loans reported under election		7a
b	CCC loans forfeited	7b 7c Taxable amount	7c
8	Crop insurance proceeds and certain disaster payments (see page F-3):		
a	Amount received in 2003	8a 8b Taxable amount	8b
c	If election to defer to 2004 is attached, check here ▶ ☐ 8d Amount deferred from 2002		8d
9	Custom hire (machine work) income		9
10	Other income, including Federal and state gasoline or fuel tax credit or refund (see page F-3)		10
11	**Gross income.** Add amounts in the right column for lines 3 through 10. If accrual method taxpayer, enter the amount from page 2, line 51 ▶		11

Part II   Farm Expenses—Cash and Accrual Method. Do not include personal or living expenses such as taxes, insurance, repairs, etc., on your home.

12	Car and truck expenses (see page F-4—also attach **Form 4562**)	12	25	Pension and profit-sharing plans	25
13	Chemicals	13	26	Rent or lease (see page F-5):	
14	Conservation expenses (see page F-4)	14	a	Vehicles, machinery, and equipment	26a
15	Custom hire (machine work)	15	b	Other (land, animals, etc.)	26b
16	Depreciation and section 179 expense deduction not claimed elsewhere (see page F-4)	16	27	Repairs and maintenance	27
			28	Seeds and plants purchased	28
			29	Storage and warehousing	29
17	Employee benefit programs other than on line 25	17	30	Supplies purchased	30
18	Feed purchased	18	31	Taxes	31
19	Fertilizers and lime	19	32	Utilities	32
20	Freight and trucking	20	33	Veterinary, breeding, and medicine	33
21	Gasoline, fuel, and oil	21	34	Other expenses (specify):	
22	Insurance (other than health)	22	a	....	34a
23	Interest:		b	....	34b
a	Mortgage (paid to banks, etc.)	23a	c	....	34c
b	Other	23b	d	....	34d
24	Labor hired (less employment credits)	24	e	....	34e
			f		34f

35	**Total expenses.** Add lines 12 through 34f ▶	35
36	**Net farm profit or (loss).** Subtract line 35 from line 11. If a profit, enter on **Form 1040, line 18,** and also on **Schedule SE, line 1.** If a loss, you **must** go on to line 37 (estates, trusts, and partnerships, see page F-6)	36

37   If you have a loss, you **must** check the box that describes your investment in this activity (see page F-6).
 • If you checked 37a, enter the loss on **Form 1040, line 18,** and **also** on **Schedule SE, line 1.**
 • If you checked 37b, you **must** attach **Form 6198.**

37a ☐ All investment is at risk.
37b ☐ Some investment is not at risk.

For Paperwork Reduction Act Notice, see Form 1040 instructions.   Cat. No. 11346H   Schedule F (Form 1040) 2003

Part III **Farm Income—Accrual Method** (see page F-6)

Do not include sales of livestock held for draft, breeding, sport, or dairy purposes; report these sales on Form 4797 and do not include this livestock on line 46 below.

38	Sales of livestock, produce, grains, and other products during the year	38	
39a	Total cooperative distributions (Form(s) 1099-PATR) **39a**	**39b** Taxable amount	39b
40a	Agricultural program payments **40a**	**40b** Taxable amount	40b
41	Commodity Credit Corporation (CCC) loans:		
a	CCC loans reported under election	41a	
b	CCC loans forfeited **41b**	**41c** Taxable amount	41c
42	Crop insurance proceeds	42	
43	Custom hire (machine work) income	43	
44	Other income, including Federal and state gasoline or fuel tax credit or refund	44	
45	Add amounts in the right column for lines 38 through 44	45	

46	Inventory of livestock, produce, grains, and other products at beginning of the year.	**46**	
47	Cost of livestock, produce, grains, and other products purchased during the year.	**47**	
48	Add lines 46 and 47	**48**	
49	Inventory of livestock, produce, grains, and other products at end of year	**49**	
50	Cost of livestock, produce, grains, and other products sold. Subtract line 49 from line 48*	50	
51	**Gross income.** Subtract line 50 from line 45. Enter the result here and on page 1, line 11 . . . . . ▶	51	

*If you use the unit-livestock-price method or the farm-price method of valuing inventory and the amount on line 49 is larger than the amount on line 48, subtract line 48 from line 49. Enter the result on line 50. Add lines 45 and 50. Enter the total on line 51.

Part IV **Principal Agricultural Activity Codes**

File **Schedule C** (Form 1040), Profit or Loss From Business, or **Schedule C-EZ** (Form 1040), Net Profit From Business, instead of Schedule F if:

● Your principal source of income is from providing agricultural services such as soil preparation, veterinary, farm labor, horticultural, or management for a fee or on a contract basis or

● You are engaged in the business of breeding, raising, and caring for dogs, cats, or other pet animals.

These codes for the Principal Agricultural Activity classify farms by the type of activity they are engaged in to facilitate the administration of the Internal Revenue Code. These six-digit codes are based on the North American Industry Classification System (NAICS).

Select one of the following codes and enter the six-digit number on page 1, line B.

Crop Production

111100	Oilseed and grain farming
111210	Vegetable and melon farming
111300	Fruit and tree nut farming
111400	Greenhouse, nursery, and floriculture production
111900	Other crop farming

Animal Production

112111	Beef cattle ranching and farming
112112	Cattle feedlots
112120	Dairy cattle and milk production
112210	Hog and pig farming
112300	Poultry and egg production
112400	Sheep and goat farming
112510	Animal aquaculture
112900	Other animal production

Forestry and Logging

113000	Forestry and logging (including forest nurseries and timber tracts)

SCHEDULE H (Form 1040) Department of the Treasury Internal Revenue Service (99)	**Household Employment Taxes** (For Social Security, Medicare, Withheld Income, and Federal Unemployment (FUTA) Taxes) ▶ **Attach to Form 1040, 1040NR, 1040-SS, or 1041.** ▶ **See separate instructions.**	OMB No. 1545-0074 2003 Attachment Sequence No. **44**

Name of employer	Social security number
	Employer identification number

A Did you pay **any one** household employee cash wages of $1,400 or more in 2003? (If any household employee was your spouse, your child under age 21, your parent, or anyone under age 18, see the line A instructions on page 3 before you answer this question.)

    ☐ **Yes.** Skip lines B and C and go to line 1.
    ☐ **No.** Go to line B.

B Did you withhold Federal income tax during 2003 for any household employee?

    ☐ **Yes.** Skip line C and go to line 5.
    ☐ **No.** Go to line C.

C Did you pay **total** cash wages of $1,000 or more in **any** calendar **quarter** of 2002 or 2003 to **all** household employees? (**Do not** count cash wages paid in 2002 or 2003 to your spouse, your child under age 21, or your parent.)

    ☐ **No.** **Stop.** Do not file this schedule.
    ☐ **Yes.** Skip lines 1-9 and go to line 10 on the back. (Calendar year taxpayers having no household employees in 2003 **do not** have to complete this form for 2003.)

Part I   **Social Security, Medicare, and Income Taxes**

1	Total cash wages subject to social security taxes (see page 3)	**1**	
2	Social security taxes. Multiply line 1 by 12.4% (.124)	**2**	
3	Total cash wages subject to Medicare taxes (see page 3)	**3**	
4	Medicare taxes. Multiply line 3 by 2.9% (.029)	**4**	
5	Federal income tax withheld, if any	**5**	
6	**Total social security, Medicare, and income taxes** (add lines 2, 4, and 5)	**6**	
7	Advance earned income credit (EIC) payments, if any	**7**	
8	**Net taxes** (subtract line 7 from line 6)	**8**	

9 Did you pay **total** cash wages of $1,000 or more in **any** calendar **quarter** of 2002 or 2003 to household employees? (**Do not** count cash wages paid in 2002 or 2003 to your spouse, your child under age 21, or your parent.)

    ☐ **No.** **Stop.** Enter the amount from line 8 above on Form 1040, line 60. If you are not required to file Form 1040, see the line 9 instructions on page 4.

    ☐ **Yes.** Go to line 10 on the back.

For Paperwork Reduction Act Notice, see Form 1040 instructions.   Cat. No. 12187K   **Schedule H (Form 1040) 2003**

Part II   Federal Unemployment (FUTA) Tax

			Yes	No
10	Did you pay unemployment contributions to only one state?	**10**		
11	Did you pay all state unemployment contributions for 2003 by April 15, 2004? Fiscal year filers, see page 4	**11**		
12	Were all wages that are taxable for FUTA tax also taxable for your state's unemployment tax? . . .	**12**		

Next: If you checked the **"Yes"** box on **all** the lines above, complete Section A.

       If you checked the **"No"** box on **any** of the lines above, skip Section A and complete Section B.

Section A

13	Name of the state where you paid unemployment contributions ▶ - - - - - - - - - - - - - - -		
14	State reporting number as shown on state unemployment tax return ▶ - - - - - - - - - - - - - - -		
15	Contributions paid to your state unemployment fund (see page 4) .	**15**	
16	Total cash wages subject to FUTA tax (see page 4)		**16**
17	**FUTA tax.** Multiply line 16 by .008. Enter the result here, skip Section B, and go to line 26 . .		**17**

Section B

18   Complete all columns below that apply (if you need more space, see page 4):

(a) Name of state	(b) State reporting number as shown on state unemployment tax return	(c) Taxable wages (as defined in state act)	(d) State experience rate period From	(d) To	(e) State experience rate	(f) Multiply col. (c) by .054	(g) Multiply col. (c) by col. (e)	(h) Subtract col. (g) from col. (f). If zero or less, enter -0-.	(i) Contributions paid to state unemployment fund

19	Totals		**19**	
20	Add columns (h) and (i) of line 19	**20**		
21	Total cash wages subject to FUTA tax (see the line 16 instructions on page 4)		**21**	
22	Multiply line 21 by 6.2% (.062)		**22**	
23	Multiply line 21 by 5.4% (.054)	**23**		
24	Enter the **smaller** of line 20 or line 23		**24**	
25	**FUTA tax.** Subtract line 24 from line 22. Enter the result here and go to line 26		**25**	

Part III   Total Household Employment Taxes

26	Enter the amount from line 8	**26**	
27	Add line 17 (or line 25) and line 26	**27**	

28   Are you required to file Form 1040?

     ☐   **Yes.**   **Stop.** Enter the amount from line 27 above on Form 1040, line 60. **Do not** complete Part IV below.

     ☐   **No.**   You may have to complete Part IV. See page 4 for details.

Part IV   Address and Signature—Complete this part **only** if required. See the line 28 instructions on page 4.

Address (number and street) or P.O. box if mail is not delivered to street address	Apt., room, or suite no.

City, town or post office, state, and ZIP code

Under penalties of perjury, I declare that I have examined this schedule, including accompanying statements, and to the best of my knowledge and belief, it is true, correct, and complete. No part of any payment made to a state unemployment fund claimed as a credit was, or is to be, deducted from the payments to employees.

▶ _____   ▶ _____
    Employer's signature   Date

SCHEDULE J
(Form 1040)

Department of the Treasury
Internal Revenue Service   (99)

Farm Income Averaging

► Attach to Form 1040.

► See Instructions for Schedule J (Form 1040).

OMB No. 1545-0074

2003

Attachment
Sequence No. **20**

Name(s) shown on Form 1040

Social security number (SSN)

1	Enter the taxable income from your 2003 Form 1040, line 40	**1**
2	Enter your **elected farm income** (see page J-1). **Do not** enter more than the amount on line 1	**2**
3	Subtract line 2 from line 1	**3**
4	Figure the tax on the amount on line 3. Use the **2003** Tax Table, Tax Rate Schedules, Qualified Dividends and Capital Gain Tax Worksheet, or Schedule D, whichever applies	**4**
5	If you used Schedule J to figure your tax for 2002, enter the amount from line 11 of your 2002 Schedule J. If you used Schedule J for 2001 but not 2002, enter the amount from line 15 of your 2001 Schedule J. If you used Schedule J for 2000 but not 2001 nor 2002, enter the amount from line 3 of your 2000 Schedule J. Otherwise, enter the taxable income from your **2000** Form 1040, line 39; Form 1040A, line 25; or Form 1040EZ, line 6. If zero or less, see page J-2	**5**
6	Divide the amount on **line 2** by 3.0	**6**
7	Combine lines 5 and 6. If zero or less, enter -0-	**7**
8	Figure the tax on the amount on line 7 using **2000** tax rates (see page J-3)	**8**
9	If you used Schedule J to figure your tax for 2002, enter the amount from line 15 of your 2002 Schedule J. If you used Schedule J for 2001 but not 2002, enter the amount from line 3 of your 2001 Schedule J. Otherwise, enter the taxable income from your **2001** Form 1040, line 39; Form 1040A, line 25; or Form 1040EZ, line 6. If zero or less, see page J-4	**9**
10	Enter the amount from line 6	**10**
11	Combine lines 9 and 10. If less than zero, enter as a negative amount	**11**
12	Figure the tax on the amount on line 11 using **2001** tax rates (see page J-5)	**12**
13	If you used Schedule J to figure your tax for 2002, enter the amount from line 3 of your 2002 Schedule J. Otherwise, enter the taxable income from your **2002** Form 1040, line 41; Form 1040A, line 27; or Form 1040EZ, line 6. If zero or less, see page J-7	**13**
14	Enter the amount from line 6	**14**
15	Combine lines 13 and 14. If less than zero, enter as a negative amount	**15**
16	Figure the tax on the amount on line 15 using **2002** tax rates (see page J-8)	**16**
17	Add lines 4, 8, 12, and 16	**17**
18	If you used Schedule J to figure your tax for 2002, enter the amount from line 12 of your 2002 Schedule J. If you used Schedule J for 2001 but not 2002, enter the amount from line 16 of your 2001 Schedule J. If you used Schedule J for 2000 but not 2001 nor 2002, enter the amount from line 4 of your 2000 Schedule J. Otherwise, enter the tax from your **2000** Form 1040, line 40*; Form 1040A, line 26*; or Form 1040EZ, line 10 . . .	**18**
19	If you used Schedule J to figure your tax for 2002, enter the amount from line 16 of your 2002 Schedule J. If you used Schedule J for 2001 but not 2002, enter the amount from line 4 of your 2001 Schedule J. Otherwise, enter the tax from your **2001** Form 1040, line 40*; Form 1040A, line 26*; or Form 1040EZ, line 11 . . .	**19**
20	If you used Schedule J to figure your tax for 2002, enter the amount from line 4 of your 2002 Schedule J. Otherwise, enter the tax from your **2002** Form 1040, line 42*; Form 1040A, line 28*; or Form 1040EZ, line 10	**20**

*Do not include tax from Form 4972 or 8814 or from recapture of an education credit. Also, do not include alternative minimum tax from Form 1040A.

21	Add lines 18 through 20	**21**
22	Subtract line 21 from line 17. Also include this amount on Form 1040, line 41	**22**

Caution. Your tax may be less if you figure it using the 2003 Tax Table, Tax Rate Schedules, Qualified Dividends and Capital Gain Tax Worksheet, or Schedule D. Attach Schedule J only if you are using it to figure your tax.

For Paperwork Reduction Act Notice, see Form 1040 instructions.   Cat. No. 25513Y   **Schedule J (Form 1040) 2003**

Schedule R
(Form 1040)

Department of the Treasury
Internal Revenue Service   (99)

Credit for the Elderly or the Disabled

► **Attach to Form 1040.**   ► **See Instructions for Schedule R (Form 1040).**

OMB No. 1545-0074

20**03**

Attachment
Sequence No. **16**

Name(s) shown on Form 1040

Your social security number

You may be able to take this credit and reduce your tax if by the end of 2003:

● You were age 65 or older **or** ● You were under age 65, you retired on **permanent and total** disability, and you received taxable disability income.

But you must also meet other tests. See page R-1.

TIP In most cases, the IRS can figure the credit for you. See page R-1.

Part I   Check the Box for Your Filing Status and Age

If your filing status is:	And by the end of 2003:	Check only one box:
Single, Head of household, or Qualifying widow(er)	**1** You were 65 or older **1**	☐
	2 You were under 65 and you retired on permanent and total disability **2**	☐
Married filing jointly	**3** Both spouses were 65 or older. **3**	☐
	4 Both spouses were under 65, but only one spouse retired on permanent and total disability **4**	☐
	5 Both spouses were under 65, and both retired on permanent and total disability **5**	☐
	6 One spouse was 65 or older, and the other spouse was under 65 and retired on permanent and total disability **6**	☐
	7 One spouse was 65 or older, and the other spouse was under 65 and **not** retired on permanent and total disability **7**	☐
Married filing separately	**8** You were 65 or older and you lived apart from your spouse for all of 2003 . . . . **8**	☐
	9 You were under 65, you retired on permanent and total disability, and you lived apart from your spouse for all of 2003 . . . . **9**	☐

Did you check box 1, 3, 7, or 8?	Yes ──►	Skip Part II and complete Part III on back.
	No ──►	Complete Parts II and III.

Part II   Statement of Permanent and Total Disability (Complete **only** if you checked box 2, 4, 5, 6, or 9 above.)

If: 1 You filed a physician's statement for this disability for 1983 or an earlier year, or you filed or got a statement for tax years after 1983 and your physician signed line B on the statement, **and**

2 Due to your continued disabled condition, you were unable to engage in any substantial gainful activity in 2003, check this box . . . . ► ☐

● If you checked this box, you do not have to get another statement for 2003.

● If you **did not** check this box, have your physician complete the statement on page R-4. You **must** keep the statement for your records.

For Paperwork Reduction Act Notice, see Form 1040 instructions.   Cat. No. 11359K   **Schedule R (Form 1040) 2003**

Part III   **Figure Your Credit**

10   If you checked (in Part I):   Enter:
     Box 1, 2, 4, or 7 . . . . $5,000 ⎫
     Box 3, 5, or 6 . . . . $7,500 ⎬ **10**
     Box 8 or 9 . . . . $3,750 ⎭

     ┌─────────────┐
     │ Did you check │──── Yes ───▶ You **must** complete line 11.
     │ box 2, 4, 5, 6, │
     │ or 9 in Part I? │──── No ───▶ Enter the amount from line 10
     └─────────────┘   on line 12 and go to line 13.

11   If you checked (in Part I):
     ● Box 6, add $5,000 to the taxable disability income of the   ⎫
       spouse who was under age 65. Enter the total.   ⎪
     ● Box 2, 4, or 9, enter your taxable disability income.   ⎬ **11**
     ● Box 5, add your taxable disability income to your spouse's   ⎪
       taxable disability income. Enter the total.   ⎭

     (TIP) For more details on what to include on line 11, see page R-3.

12   If you completed line 11, enter the **smaller** of line 10 or line 11; **all others,** enter the
     amount from line 10 . . . .   **12**

13   Enter the following pensions, annuities, or disability income
     that you (and your spouse if filing a joint return) received in
     2003.
   a Nontaxable part of social security benefits and   ⎫
     Nontaxable part of railroad retirement benefits   ⎬ . . .   **13a**
     treated as social security (see page R-3).   ⎭

   b Nontaxable veterans' pensions and   ⎫
     Any other pension, annuity, or disability benefit that   ⎬ . . .   **13b**
     is excluded from income under any other provision   ⎪
     of law (see page R-3).   ⎭

   c Add lines 13a and 13b. (Even though these income items are
     not taxable, they **must** be included here to figure your credit.)
     If you did not receive any of the types of nontaxable income
     listed on line 13a or 13b, enter -0- on line 13c **13c**

14   Enter the amount from Form 1040,
     line 35 . . . .   **14**

15   If you checked (in Part I):   Enter:
     Box 1 or 2 . . . . $7,500 ⎫
     Box 3, 4, 5, 6, or 7 . . . $10,000 ⎬   **15**
     Box 8 or 9 . . . . . . $5,000 ⎭
16   Subtract line 15 from line 14. If zero or
     less, enter -0- **16**
17   Enter one-half of line 16 . . . .   **17**

18   Add lines 13c and 17 . . . .   **18**
19   Subtract line 18 from line 12. If zero or less, **stop;** you **cannot** take the credit. Otherwise,
     go to line 20 . . . .   **19**
20   Multiply line 19 by 15% (.15) **20**
21   Enter the amount from Form 1040, line 43 . . . .   **21**
22   Add the amounts from Form 1040, lines 44 and 45, and enter
     the total **22**
23   Subtract line 22 from line 21 . . . .   **23**

24   **Credit for the elderly or the disabled.** Enter the **smaller** of line 20 or line 23 here and
     on Form 1040, line 46 . . . .   **24**

SCHEDULE SE
(Form 1040)

Department of the Treasury
Internal Revenue Service (99)

Self-Employment Tax

▶ Attach to Form 1040. ▶ See Instructions for Schedule SE (Form 1040).

OMB No. 1545-0074

2003

Attachment
Sequence No. **17**

Name of person with **self-employment** income (as shown on Form 1040)	Social security number of person with **self-employment** income

Who Must File Schedule SE

You must file Schedule SE if:

● You had net earnings from self-employment from **other than** church employee income (line 4 of Short Schedule SE or line 4c of Long Schedule SE) of $400 or more **or**

● You had church employee income of $108.28 or more. Income from services you performed as a minister or a member of a religious order **is not** church employee income (see page SE-1).

Note. Even if you had a loss or a small amount of income from self-employment, it may be to your benefit to file Schedule SE and use either "optional method" in Part II of Long Schedule SE (see page SE-3).

Exception. If your only self-employment income was from earnings as a minister, member of a religious order, or Christian Science practitioner **and** you filed Form 4361 and received IRS approval not to be taxed on those earnings, **do not** file Schedule SE. Instead, write "Exempt–Form 4361" on Form 1040, line 55.

May I Use Short Schedule SE or Must I Use Long Schedule SE?

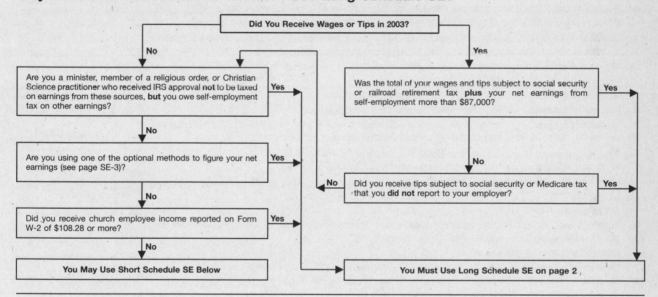

Section A—Short Schedule SE. Caution. Read above to see if you can use Short Schedule SE.

1	Net farm profit or (loss) from Schedule F, line 36, and farm partnerships, Schedule K-1 (Form 1065), line 15a	1	
2	Net profit or (loss) from Schedule C, line 31; Schedule C-EZ, line 3; Schedule K-1 (Form 1065), line 15a (other than farming); and Schedule K-1 (Form 1065-B), box 9. Ministers and members of religious orders, see page SE-1 for amounts to report on this line. See page SE-2 for other income to report	2	
3	Combine lines 1 and 2	3	
4	**Net earnings from self-employment.** Multiply line 3 by 92.35% (.9235). If less than $400, **do not** file this schedule; you do not owe self-employment tax . . . . ▶	4	
5	**Self-employment tax.** If the amount on line 4 is: ● $87,000 or less, multiply line 4 by 15.3% (.153). Enter the result here and on **Form 1040, line 55.** ● More than $87,000, multiply line 4 by 2.9% (.029). Then, add $10,788.00 to the result. Enter the total here and on **Form 1040, line 55.**	5	
6	**Deduction for one-half of self-employment tax.** Multiply line 5 by 50% (.5). Enter the result here and on **Form 1040, line 28**	6		

Name of person with **self-employment** income (as shown on Form 1040)	Social security number of person with **self-employment** income ▶		

Section B—Long Schedule SE

Part I Self-Employment Tax

Note. If your only income subject to self-employment tax is **church employee income**, skip lines 1 through 4b. Enter -0- on line 4c and go to line 5a. Income from services you performed as a minister or a member of a religious order **is not** church employee income. See page SE-1.

A If you are a minister, member of a religious order, or Christian Science practitioner **and** you filed Form 4361, but you had $400 or more of **other** net earnings from self-employment, check here and continue with Part I . . . . . . ▶ ☐

1	Net farm profit or (loss) from Schedule F, line 36, and farm partnerships, Schedule K-1 (Form 1065), line 15a. **Note.** Skip this line if you use the farm optional method (see page SE-4) . .	**1**	
2	Net profit or (loss) from Schedule C, line 31; Schedule C-EZ, line 3; Schedule K-1 (Form 1065), line 15a (other than farming); and Schedule K-1 (Form 1065-B), box 9. Ministers and members of religious orders, see page SE-1 for amounts to report on this line. See page SE-2 for other income to report. **Note.** Skip this line if you use the nonfarm optional method (see page SE-4)	**2**	
3	Combine lines 1 and 2	**3**	
4a	If line 3 is more than zero, multiply line 3 by 92.35% (.9235). Otherwise, enter amount from line 3	**4a**	
b	If you elect one or both of the optional methods, enter the total of lines 15 and 17 here . .	**4b**	
c	Combine lines 4a and 4b. If less than $400, **do not** file this schedule; you do not owe self-employment tax. **Exception.** If less than $400 and you had **church employee income,** enter -0- and continue ▶	**4c**	
5a	Enter your **church employee income** from Form W-2. See page SE-1 for definition of church employee income. **5a**		
b	Multiply line 5a by 92.35% (.9235). If less than $100, enter -0-	**5b**	
6	**Net earnings from self-employment.** Add lines 4c and 5b	**6**	
7	Maximum amount of combined wages and self-employment earnings subject to social security tax or the 6.2% portion of the 7.65% railroad retirement (tier 1) tax for 2003	**7**	87,000 00
8a	Total social security wages and tips (total of boxes 3 and 7 on Form(s) W-2) and railroad retirement (tier 1) compensation. If $87,000 or more, skip lines 8b through 10, and go to line 11 . . . . **8a**		
b	Unreported tips subject to social security tax (from Form 4137, line 9) **8b**		
c	Add lines 8a and 8b	**8c**	
9	Subtract line 8c from line 7. If zero or less, enter -0- here and on line 10 and go to line 11 . ▶	**9**	
10	Multiply the **smaller** of line 6 or line 9 by 12.4% (.124)	**10**	
11	Multiply line 6 by 2.9% (.029)	**11**	
12	**Self-employment tax.** Add lines 10 and 11. Enter here and on **Form 1040, line 55** . .	**12**	
13	**Deduction for one-half of self-employment tax.** Multiply line 12 by 50% (.5). Enter the result here and on **Form 1040, line 28** **13**		

Part II Optional Methods To Figure Net Earnings (see page SE-3)

Farm Optional Method. You may use this method **only** if:

● Your gross farm income[1] was not more than $2,400 **or**

● Your net farm profits[2] were less than $1,733.

14	Maximum income for optional methods	**14**	1,600 00
15	Enter the **smaller** of: two-thirds (⅔) of gross farm income[1] (not less than zero) or $1,600. Also include this amount on line 4b above	**15**	

Nonfarm Optional Method. You may use this method **only** if:

● Your net nonfarm profits[3] were less than $1,733 and also less than 72.189% of your gross nonfarm income[4] **and**

● You had net earnings from self-employment of at least $400 in 2 of the prior 3 years.

Caution. You may use this method no more than five times.

16	Subtract line 15 from line 14	**16**	
17	Enter the **smaller** of: two-thirds (⅔) of gross nonfarm income[4] (not less than zero) **or** the amount on line 16. Also include this amount on line 4b above	**17**	

[1]From Sch. F, line 11, and Sch. K-1 (Form 1065), line 15b.
[2]From Sch. F, line 36, and Sch. K-1 (Form 1065), line 15a.
[3]From Sch. C, line 31; Sch. C-EZ, line 3; Sch. K-1 (Form 1065), line 15a; and Sch. K-1 (Form 1065-B), box 9.
[4]From Sch. C, line 7; Sch. C-EZ, line 1; Sch. K-1 (Form 1065), line 15c; and Sch. K-1 (Form 1065-B), box 9.

Form **1040X** (Rev. November 2003)	Department of the Treasury—Internal Revenue Service **Amended U.S. Individual Income Tax Return** ► See separate instructions.	OMB No. 1545-0091

This return is for calendar year ►   **, or fiscal year ended ►**   ,   .

Please print or type

Your first name and initial	Last name	Your social security number
If a joint return, spouse's first name and initial	Last name	Spouse's social security number
Home address (no. and street) or P.O. box if mail is not delivered to your home	Apt. no.	Phone number ( )
City, town or post office, state, and ZIP code. If you have a foreign address, see page 2 of the instructions.		**For Paperwork Reduction Act Notice, see page 6.**

A If the name or address shown above is different from that shown on the original return, check here . . . . ► ☐

B Has the original return been changed or audited by the IRS or have you been notified that it will be? . . ☐ **Yes** ☐ **No**

C Filing status. Be sure to complete this line. **Note.** You cannot change from joint to separate returns after the due date.

On original return ► ☐ Single   ☐ Married filing jointly   ☐ Married filing separately   ☐ Head of household   ☐ Qualifying widow(er)

On this return ► ☐ Single   ☐ Married filing jointly   ☐ Married filing separately   ☐ Head of household*   ☐ Qualifying widow(er)

* If the qualifying person is a child but not your dependent, see page 2.

Use Part II on the back to explain any changes

		A. Original amount or as previously adjusted (see page 2)	**B. Net change**—amount of increase or (decrease)—explain in Part II	**C. Correct amount**
Income and Deductions (see pages 2–6)				
1 Adjusted gross income (see page 3)	**1**			
2 Itemized deductions or standard deduction (see page 3) . .	**2**			
3 Subtract line 2 from line 1	**3**			
4 Exemptions. If changing, fill in Parts I and II on the back	**4**			
5 Taxable income. Subtract line 4 from line 3	**5**			

Tax Liability

		A	B	C
6 Tax (see page 4). Method used in col. C_____	**6**			
7 Credits (see page 4)	**7**			
8 Subtract line 7 from line 6. Enter the result but not less than zero	**8**			
9 Other taxes (see page 4)	**9**			
10 Total tax. Add lines 8 and 9	**10**			

Payments

		A	B	C
11 Federal income tax withheld and excess social security and tier 1 RRTA tax withheld. If changing, see page 4 . . .	**11**			
12 Estimated tax payments, including amount applied from prior year's return	**12**			
13 Earned income credit (EIC)	**13**			
14 Additional child tax credit from Form 8812	**14**			
15 Credits from Form 2439, Form 4136, or Form 8885 . . .	**15**			
16 Amount paid with request for extension of time to file (see page 4)				**16**
17 Amount of tax paid with original return plus additional tax paid after it was filed				**17**
18 Total payments. Add lines 11 through 17 in column C				**18**

Refund or Amount You Owe

19 Overpayment, if any, as shown on original return or as previously adjusted by the IRS . . .	**19**
20 Subtract line 19 from line 18 (see page 5)	**20**
21 **Amount you owe.** If line 10, column C, is more than line 20, enter the difference and see page 5	**21**
22 If line 10, column C, is less than line 20, enter the difference	**22**
23 Amount of line 22 you want **refunded to you**	**23**
24 Amount of line 22 you want **applied to your** **estimated tax**	**24**

Sign Here

Joint return? See page 2. Keep a copy for your records.

Under penalties of perjury, I declare that I have filed an original return and that I have examined this amended return, including accompanying schedules and statements, and to the best of my knowledge and belief, this amended return is true, correct, and complete. Declaration of preparer (other than taxpayer) is based on all information of which the preparer has any knowledge.

Your signature	Date	Spouse's signature. If a joint return, **both** must sign.	Date

Paid Preparer's Use Only

Preparer's signature	Date	Check if self-employed ☐	Preparer's SSN or PTIN
Firm's name (or yours if self-employed), address, and ZIP code		EIN	
		Phone no. ( )	

Cat. No. 11360L   Form **1040X** (Rev. 11-2003)

Part I Exemptions. See Form 1040 or 1040A instructions.

If you are **not changing your exemptions,** do not complete this part.
If claiming **more exemptions,** complete lines 25–31.
If claiming **fewer exemptions,** complete lines 25–30.

		A. Original number of exemptions reported or as previously adjusted	B. Net change	C. Correct number of exemptions
25	Yourself and spouse			
	Caution. If your parents (or someone else) can claim you as a dependent (even if they chose not to), you cannot claim an exemption for yourself.			
26	Your dependent children who lived with you			
27	Your dependent children who did not live with you due to divorce or separation			
28	Other dependents			
29	Total number of exemptions. Add lines 25 through 28			
30	Multiply the number of exemptions claimed on line 29 by the amount listed below for the tax year you are amending. Enter the result here and on line 4.			

Tax year	Exemption amount	But see the instructions for line 4 on page 3 if the amount on line 1 is over:
2003	$3,050	$104,625
2002	3,000	103,000
2001	2,900	99,725
2000	2,800	96,700

31 Dependents (children and other) not claimed on original (or adjusted) return:

No. of your children on line 31 who:

(a) First name	Last name	(b) Dependent's social security number	(c) Dependent's relationship to you	(d) ✓ if qualifying child for child tax credit (see page 5)
				☐
				☐
				☐
				☐
				☐
				☐

- ● lived with you . . . ▶ ☐
- ● **did not** live with you due to divorce or separation (see page 5). . ▶ ☐
- Dependents on line 31 not entered above ▶ ☐

Part II Explanation of Changes to Income, Deductions, and Credits

Enter the line number from the front of the form for each item you are changing and give the reason for each change. Attach only the supporting forms and schedules for the items changed. If you do not attach the required information, your Form 1040X may be returned. Be sure to include your name and social security number on any attachments.

If the change relates to a net operating loss carryback or a general business credit carryback, attach the schedule or form that shows the year in which the loss or credit occurred. See page 2 of the instructions. Also, check here . . . . . ▶ ☐

Part III Presidential Election Campaign Fund. Checking below will not increase your tax or reduce your refund.

If you did not previously want $3 to go to the fund but now want to, check here . . . . ▶ ☐

If a joint return and your spouse did not previously want $3 to go to the fund but now wants to, check here . . . . ▶ ☐

Form **2106**	**Employee Business Expenses**	OMB No. 1545-0139

Form **2106**

Department of the Treasury
Internal Revenue Service (99)

Employee Business Expenses

▶ See separate instructions.

▶ Attach to Form 1040.

OMB No. 1545-0139

2003

Attachment
Sequence No. **54**

Your name	Occupation in which you incurred expenses	Social security number

Part I Employee Business Expenses and Reimbursements

Step 1 Enter Your Expenses

			Column A Other Than Meals and Entertainment	Column B Meals and Entertainment
1	Vehicle expense from line 22 or line 29. (Rural mail carriers: See instructions.)	**1**		
2	Parking fees, tolls, and transportation, including train, bus, etc., that **did not** involve overnight travel or commuting to and from work . .	**2**		
3	Travel expense while away from home overnight, including lodging, airplane, car rental, etc. **Do not** include meals and entertainment	**3**		
4	Business expenses not included on lines 1 through 3. **Do not** include meals and entertainment	**4**		
5	Meals and entertainment expenses (see instructions)	**5**		
6	**Total expenses.** In Column A, add lines 1 through 4 and enter the result. In Column B, enter the amount from line 5	**6**		

Note: *If you were not reimbursed for any expenses in Step 1, skip line 7 and enter the amount from line 6 on line 8.*

Step 2 Enter Reimbursements Received From Your Employer for Expenses Listed in Step 1

7	Enter reimbursements received from your employer that were **not** reported to you in box 1 of Form W-2. Include any reimbursements reported under code "L" in box 12 of your Form W-2 (see instructions)	**7**		

Step 3 Figure Expenses To Deduct on Schedule A (Form 1040)

8	Subtract line 7 from line 6. If zero or less, enter -0-. However, if line 7 is greater than line 6 in Column A, report the excess as income on Form 1040, line 7	**8**		
	Note: *If both columns of line 8 are zero, you cannot deduct employee business expenses. Stop here and attach Form 2106 to your return.*			
9	In Column A, enter the amount from line 8. In Column B, multiply line 8 by 50% (.50). (Employees subject to Department of Transportation (DOT) hours of service limits: Multiply meal expenses by 65% (.65) instead of 50%. For details, see instructions.)	**9**		
10	Add the amounts on line 9 of both columns and enter the total here. **Also, enter the total on Schedule A (Form 1040), line 20.** (Fee-basis state or local government officials, qualified performing artists, and individuals with disabilities: See the instructions for special rules on where to enter the total.) . . . . ▶	**10**		

Part II	Vehicle Expenses

Section A—General Information (You must complete this section if you are claiming vehicle expenses.)

			(a) Vehicle 1	(b) Vehicle 2
11	Enter the date the vehicle was placed in service	11	/ /	/ /
12	Total miles the vehicle was driven during 2003	12	miles	miles
13	Business miles included on line 12	13	miles	miles
14	Percent of business use. Divide line 13 by line 12	14	%	%
15	Average daily roundtrip commuting distance	15	miles	miles
16	Commuting miles included on line 12	16	miles	miles
17	Other miles. Add lines 13 and 16 and subtract the total from line 12 . . .	17	miles	miles

18	Do you (or your spouse) have another vehicle available for personal use?	☐ Yes	☐ No
19	Was your vehicle available for personal use during off-duty hours?	☐ Yes	☐ No
20	Do you have evidence to support your deduction?	☐ Yes	☐ No
21	If "Yes," is the evidence written?	☐ Yes	☐ No

Section B—Standard Mileage Rate (See the instructions for Part II to find out whether to complete this section or Section C.)

22	Multiply line 13 by 36¢ (.36)	22		

Section C—Actual Expenses		(a) Vehicle 1		(b) Vehicle 2	
23	Gasoline, oil, repairs, vehicle insurance, etc.	23				
24a	Vehicle rentals	24a				
b	Inclusion amount (see instructions)	24b				
c	Subtract line 24b from line 24a	24c				
25	Value of employer-provided vehicle (applies only if 100% of annual lease value was included on Form W-2—see instructions)	25				
26	Add lines 23, 24c, and 25 . .	26				
27	Multiply line 26 by the percentage on line 14 . . .	27				
28	Depreciation. Enter amount from line 38 below	28				
29	Add lines 27 and 28. Enter total here and on line 1	29				

Section D—Depreciation of Vehicles (Use this section only if you owned the vehicle and are completing Section C for the vehicle.)

			(a) Vehicle 1		(b) Vehicle 2	
30	Enter cost or other basis (see instructions)	30				
31	Enter section 179 deduction and special allowance (see instructions)	31				
32	Multiply line 30 by line 14 (see instructions if you claimed the section 179 deduction or special allowance)	32				
33	Enter depreciation method and percentage (see instructions) .	33				
34	Multiply line 32 by the percentage on line 33 (see instructions) . .	34				
35	Add lines 31 and 34	35				
36	Enter the applicable limit explained in the line 36 instructions. . . .	36				
37	Multiply line 36 by the percentage on line 14 . . .	37				
38	Enter the **smaller** of line 35 or line 37. Also enter this amount on line 28 above	38				

Form **2106-EZ**	**Unreimbursed Employee Business Expenses**	OMB No. 1545-1441

Form **2106-EZ**

Department of the Treasury
Internal Revenue Service   (99)

Unreimbursed Employee Business Expenses

▶ **Attach to Form 1040.**

OMB No. 1545-1441

20**03**

Attachment
Sequence No. **54A**

Your name	Occupation in which you incurred expenses	Social security number

You May Use This Form Only if All of the Following Apply.

- You are an employee deducting ordinary and necessary expenses attributable to your job. An ordinary expense is one that is common and accepted in your field of trade, business, or profession. A necessary expense is one that is helpful and appropriate for your business. An expense does not have to be required to be considered necessary.
- You **do not** get reimbursed by your employer for any expenses (amounts your employer included in box 1 of your Form W-2 are not considered reimbursements).
- If you are claiming vehicle expense, you are using the standard mileage rate for 2003.

Caution: *You can use the standard mileage rate for 2003 only if:* (a) *you owned the vehicle and used the standard mileage rate for the first year you placed the vehicle in service* or (b) *you leased the vehicle and used the standard mileage rate for the portion of the lease period after 1997.*

Part I	**Figure Your Expenses**	
1	Vehicle expense using the standard mileage rate. Complete Part II and multiply line 8a by 36¢ (.36)	**1**
2	Parking fees, tolls, and transportation, including train, bus, etc., that **did not** involve overnight travel or commuting to and from work	**2**
3	Travel expense while away from home overnight, including lodging, airplane, car rental, etc. **Do not** include meals and entertainment	**3**
4	Business expenses not included on lines 1 through 3. **Do not** include meals and entertainment	**4**
5	Meals and entertainment expenses: $ _____ x 50% (.50) (Employees subject to Department of Transportation (DOT) hours of service limits: Multiply meal expenses by 65% (.65) instead of 50%. For details, see instructions.)	**5**
6	**Total expenses.** Add lines 1 through 5. Enter here and **on line 20 of Schedule A (Form 1040).** (Fee-basis state or local government officials, qualified performing artists, and individuals with disabilities: See the instructions for special rules on where to enter this amount.)	**6**

Part II	**Information on Your Vehicle. Complete this part only if you are claiming vehicle expense on line 1.**

7 When did you place your vehicle in service for business use? (month, day, year) ▶ _____ / _____ / _____

8 Of the total number of miles you drove your vehicle during 2003, enter the number of miles you used your vehicle for:

a Business _____   **b** Commuting _____   **c** Other _____

9	Do you (or your spouse) have another vehicle available for personal use?	☐ Yes ☐ No
10	Was your vehicle available for personal use during off-duty hours?	☐ Yes ☐ No
11a	Do you have evidence to support your deduction?	☐ Yes ☐ No
b	If "Yes," is the evidence written?	☐ Yes ☐ No

General Instructions

Section references are to the Internal Revenue Code.

A Change To Note

Standard mileage rate. The standard mileage rate is 36 cents for each mile of business use in 2003.

Purpose of Form

You may use Form 2106-EZ instead of Form 2106 to claim your unreimbursed employee business expenses if you meet all the requirements listed above Part I.

Recordkeeping

You cannot deduct expenses for travel (including meals, unless you used the standard meal allowance), entertainment, gifts, or use of a car or other listed property, unless you keep records to prove the time, place, business purpose, business relationship (for entertainment and gifts), and amounts of these expenses. Generally, you must also have receipts for all lodging expenses (regardless of the amount) and any other expense of $75 or more.

Additional Information

For more details about employee business expenses, see:

Pub. 463, Travel, Entertainment, Gift, and Car Expenses

Pub. 529, Miscellaneous Deductions

Pub. 587, Business Use of Your Home (Including Use by Daycare Providers)

Pub. 946, How To Depreciate Property

Specific Instructions

Part I—Figure Your Expenses

Line 2. See the line 8b instructions for the definition of commuting.

Line 3. Enter lodging and transportation expenses connected with overnight travel away from your tax home (defined on this page). You cannot deduct expenses for travel away from your tax home for any period of temporary employment of more than 1 year. **Do not** include expenses for meals and entertainment. For more details, including limits, see Pub. 463.

Instead of keeping records of your actual incidental expenses, you can use an **optional method for deducting incidental expenses only** if you did **not** pay or incur meal expenses on a day you were traveling away

from your tax home. The amount of the deduction is $2 a day for the period from January 1 through October 31, 2003, and $3 a day for the period from November 1 through December 31, 2003. Incidental expenses include fees and tips given to porters, baggage carriers, bellhops, hotel maids, stewards or stewardesses and others on ships, and hotel servants in foreign countries. They do **not** include expenses for laundry, cleaning and pressing of clothing, lodging taxes, or the costs of telegrams or telephone calls. You cannot use this method on any day that you use the standard meal allowance (as explained in the instructions for line 5).

Generally, your **tax home** is your main place of business or post of duty regardless of where you maintain your family home. If you do not have a regular or main place of business because of the nature of your work, then your tax home is the place where you regularly live. If you do not fit in either of these categories, you are considered an itinerant and your tax home is wherever you work. As an itinerant, you are never away from home and cannot claim a travel expense deduction. For more details on your tax home, see Pub. 463.

Line 4. Enter other job-related expenses not listed on any other line of this form. Include expenses for business gifts, education (tuition and books), home office, trade publications, etc. For details, including limits, see Pub. 463 and Pub. 529. **Do not** include on line 4 any tuition and fees you deducted on Form 1040, line 26, or any educator expenses you deducted on Form 1040, line 23. If you are deducting home office expenses, see Pub. 587 for special instructions on how to report these expenses. If you are deducting depreciation or claiming a section 179 deduction on a cellular telephone or other similar telecommunications equipment, a home computer, etc., see **Form 4562,** Depreciation and Amortization, to figure the depreciation and section 179 deduction to enter on line 4.

 You may be able to take a credit for your educational expenses instead of a deduction. See **Form 8863,** Education Credits (Hope and Lifetime Learning Credits), for details.

Do not include expenses for meals and entertainment, taxes, or interest on line 4. Deductible taxes are entered on lines 5 through 9 of Schedule A (Form 1040). Employees **cannot** deduct car loan interest.

Note: *If line 4 is your only entry, do not complete Form 2106-EZ unless you are claiming:*

- *Expenses for performing your job as a fee-basis state or local government official,*
- *Performing-arts-related business expenses as a qualified performing artist, or*
- *Impairment-related work expenses as an individual with a disability.*

See the line 6 instructions for definitions. If you are not required to file Form 2106-EZ, enter your expenses directly on Schedule A (Form 1040), line 20.

Line 5. Generally, you may deduct only 50% of your business meal and entertainment expenses, including meals incurred while away from home on business. If you were an employee subject to the Department of Transportation (DOT) hours of service limits, that percentage is increased to 65% for business meals consumed during, or incident to, any period of duty for which those limits are in effect.

Employees subject to the DOT hours of service limits include certain air transportation employees, such as pilots, crew, dispatchers, mechanics, and control tower operators; interstate truck operators and interstate bus drivers; certain railroad employees, such as engineers, conductors, train crews, dispatchers, and control operations personnel; and certain merchant mariners.

Instead of actual cost, you may be able to claim the **standard meal allowance** for your daily meals and incidental expenses while away from your tax home overnight. Under this method, you deduct a specified amount, depending on where you travel, instead of keeping records of your actual meal expenses. However, you must still keep records to prove the time, place, and business purpose of your travel.

The standard meal allowance is the Federal M&IE rate. For most small localities in the United States, this rate is $30 a day for the period from January 1 through September 30, 2003, and $31 a day for the period from October 1 through December 31, 2003. localities in the United States are designated as high-cost areas and qualify for higher rates. You can find these rates on the Internet at **www.policyworks.gov/perdiem.** Click on "2003 Domestic Per Diem Rates" for the

period January 1, 2003 – September 30, 2003 and on "2004 Domestic Per Diem Rates" for the period October 1, 2003 – December 31, 2003. However, you may apply the rates in effect before October 1, 2003, for expenses of all travel within the United States for 2003 instead of the updated rates. You must consistently use either the rates for the first 9 months of 2003 or the updated rates for the period of October 1, 2003, through December 31, 2003. For locations outside the continental United States, the applicable rates are published monthly. You can find these rates on the Internet at **www.state.gov/m/a/als/prdm/2003.**

See Pub. 463 for details on how to figure your deduction using the standard meal allowance, including special rules for partial days of travel, transportation workers, and taxpayers related to their employer.

Line 6. If you were a **fee-basis state or local government official** (defined below), include the expenses you incurred for services performed in that job in the total on Form 1040, line 33. Write "FBO" and the amount in the space to the left of line 33. Your employee business expenses are deductible whether or not you itemize deductions. A fee-basis state or local government official is an official who is an employee of a state or political subdivision of a state and is compensated, in whole or in part, on a fee basis.

If you were a **qualified performing artist** (defined below), include your performing-arts-related expenses in the total on Form 1040, line 33. Write "QPA" and the amount in the space to the left of line 33. Your performing-arts-related business expenses are deductible whether or not you itemize deductions. The expenses are not subject to the 2% limit that applies to most other employee business expenses.

A qualified performing artist is an individual who:

1. Performed services in the performing arts as an employee for at least two employers during the tax year,

2. Received from at least two of those employers wages of $200 or more per employer,

3. Had allowable business expenses attributable to the performing arts of more than 10% of gross income from the performing arts, and

4. Had adjusted gross income of $16,000 or less before deducting expenses as a performing artist.

To be treated as a qualified performing artist, a married individual must also file a joint return, unless the individual and his or her spouse lived apart for all of 2003. On a joint return, requirements **1, 2,** and **3** must be figured separately for each spouse. However, requirement **4** applies to the combined adjusted gross income of both spouses.

If you were an **individual with a disability** and are claiming impairment-related work expenses (defined below), enter the part of the line 6 amount attributable to those expenses on Schedule A (Form 1040), line 27, instead of on Schedule A (Form 1040), line 20. Your impairment-related work expenses are not subject to the 2% limit that applies to most other employee business expenses. Impairment-related work expenses are the allowable expenses of an individual with physical or mental disabilities for attendant care at his or her place of employment. They also include other expenses in connection

with the place of employment that enable the employee to work. See Pub. 463 for details.

Part II—Information on Your Vehicle

If you claim vehicle expense, you must provide certain information on the use of your vehicle by completing Part II. Include an attachment listing the information requested in Part II for any additional vehicles you used for business during the year.

Line 7. Date placed in service is generally the date you first start using your vehicle. However, if you first start using your vehicle for personal use and later convert it to business use, the vehicle is treated as placed in service on the date you started using it for business.

Line 8a. Do not include commuting miles on this line; commuting miles are not considered business miles. See below for the definition of commuting.

Line 8b. If you do not know the total actual miles you used your vehicle for commuting during the year, figure the amount to enter on line 8b by multiplying the number of days during the year that you used your vehicle for commuting by the average daily roundtrip commuting distance in miles.

Generally, **commuting** is travel between your home and a work location. However, travel that meets **any** of the following conditions is not commuting.

1. You have at least one regular work location away from your home and the travel is to a temporary work location in the same trade or business, regardless of the distance. Generally, a temporary work location is one where your employment is expected to last 1 year or less. See Pub. 463 for details.

2. The travel is to a temporary work location outside the metropolitan area where you live and normally work.

3. Your home is your principal place of business under section 280A(c)(1)(A) (for purposes of deducting expenses for business use of your home) and the travel is to another work location in the same trade or business, regardless of whether that location is regular or temporary and regardless of distance.

Paperwork Reduction Act Notice. We ask for the information on this form to carry out the Internal Revenue laws of the United States. You are required to give us the information. We need it to ensure that you are complying with these laws and to allow us to figure and collect the right amount of tax.

You are not required to provide the information requested on a form that is subject to the Paperwork Reduction Act unless the form displays a valid OMB control number. Books or records relating to a form or its instructions must be retained as long as their contents may become material in the administration of any Internal Revenue law. Generally, tax returns and return information are confidential, as required by section 6103.

The time needed to complete and file this form will vary depending on individual circumstances. The estimated average time is: **Recordkeeping,** 39 min.; **Learning about the law or the form,** 12 min.; **Preparing the form,** 24 min.; **Copying, assembling, and sending the form to the IRS,** 20 min.

If you have comments concerning the accuracy of these time estimates or suggestions for making this form simpler, we would be happy to hear from you. See the Instructions for Form 1040.

Form **2688**	**Application for Additional Extension of Time To File U.S. Individual Income Tax Return** ► See instructions on back. ► You must complete all items that apply to you.	OMB No. 1545-0066 20**03**

Department of the Treasury
Internal Revenue Service

Please type or print.	Your first name and initial	Last name	**Your social security number**
	If a joint return, spouse's first name and initial	Last name	**Spouse's social security number**
File by the due date for filing your return.	Home address (number and street)		
	City, town or post office, state, and ZIP code		

Please fill in the Return Label at the bottom of this page.

1 I request an extension of time until .... , to file Form 1040EZ, Form 1040A, Form 1040, Form 1040NR-EZ, or Form 1040NR for the calendar year 2003, or other tax year ending ....

2 Explain why you need an extension. You must give an adequate explanation ► ....

....

....

....

3 Have you filed Form 4868 to request an automatic extension of time to file for this tax year? . . . . ☐ **Yes** ☐ **No**
If you checked "No," we will grant your extension only for undue hardship. Fully explain the hardship in item 2. Attach any information you have that helps explain the hardship.

If you expect to file a gift or generation-skipping transfer (GST) tax return, complete line 4.

4 If you or your spouse plan to file a gift or GST tax return (Form 709 or 709-A) for 2003, generally due by April 15, 2004, see the instructions and check here . . . . } **Yourself** . . ► ☐
Spouse . . ► ☐

Signature and Verification

Under penalties of perjury, I declare that I have examined this form, including accompanying schedules and statements, and to the best of my knowledge and belief, it is true, correct, and complete; and, if prepared by someone other than the taxpayer, that I am authorized to prepare this form.

Signature of taxpayer ► _____ Date ► _____

Signature of spouse ► _____ Date ► _____
(If filing jointly, **both** must sign even if only one had income.)

Signature of preparer other than taxpayer ► _____ Date ► _____

Please fill in the **Return Label** below with your name, address, and social security number. The IRS will complete the **Notice to Applicant** and return it to you. If you want it sent to another address or to an agent acting for you, enter the other address and add the agent's name.

(Do not detach)

Notice to Applicant **To Be Completed by the IRS**	☐ We **have** approved your application. ☐ We **have not** approved your application. However, we have granted a 10-day grace period to .... This grace period is considered a valid extension of time for elections otherwise required to be made on a timely return. ☐ We **have not** approved your application. After considering the information you provided in item 2 above, we cannot grant your request for an extension of time to file. We are not granting a 10-day grace period. ☐ We cannot consider your application because it was filed after the due date of your return. ☐ Other........................

_____ _____
Director Date

Return Label (Please type or print)	**Taxpayer's name** (and agent's name, if applicable). If a joint return, also give spouse's name.		**Taxpayer's social security number**
	Number and street (include suite, room, or apt. no.) or P.O. box number		**Spouse's social security number**
	City, town or post office, state, and ZIP code		**Agents:** Always include taxpayer's name on Return Label.

For Privacy Act and Paperwork Reduction Act Notice, see back of form.   Cat. No. 11958F   Form **2688** (2003)

General Instructions

 It's Convenient, Safe, and Secure

IRS *e-file* is the IRS's electronic filing program. Now you can get an additional extension of time to file your tax return by filing Form 2688 electronically. You will receive an electronic acknowledgment once you complete the transaction. Keep it with your records. **Do not** send in Form 2688 if you file electronically.

E-file Using Your Personal Computer or Through a Tax Professional. Refer to your software package or tax preparer for ways to file electronically. Be sure to have a copy of last year's tax return—you will be asked to provide information from the return for taxpayer verification.

Purpose of Form

Use Form 2688 to ask for more time to file **Form 1040EZ, Form 1040A, Form 1040, Form 1040NR-EZ,** or **Form 1040NR.** Generally, use it only if you already asked for more time on **Form 4868** (the "automatic" extension form) and that time was not enough. We will make an exception **only** for undue hardship. The maximum extension of time allowed by law is 6 months.

To get the extra time, you **must (a)** complete and file Form 2688 on time **and (b)** have a good reason why the first 4 months were not enough. Explain this on line 2.

Generally, we will not give you more time to file just for the convenience of your tax return preparer. But if the reasons for being late are beyond his or her control or, despite a good effort, you cannot get professional help in time to file, we will usually give you the extra time.

Caution: *If we give you more time to file and later find that the statements made on this form are false or misleading, the extension is null and void. You will owe the late filing penalty explained on this page.*

You cannot have the IRS figure your tax if you file after the regular due date of your return.

Form 709 or 709-A. An extension of time to file your 2003 **calendar year** income tax return also extends the time to file a gift or GST tax return for 2003. See Line 4 on this page.

If you live abroad. U.S. citizens or resident aliens living abroad may qualify for special tax treatment if they meet the foreign residence or presence tests. If you do not expect to meet either of those tests by the due date of your return, request an extension to a date after you expect to qualify, using **Form 2350,** Application for Extension of Time To File U.S. Income Tax Return. See **Pub. 54,** Tax Guide for U.S. Citizens and Resident Aliens Abroad.

Total Time Allowed

Generally, we cannot extend the due date of your return for more than 6 months. This includes the 4 extra months allowed by Form 4868. There may be an exception if you live abroad. See the previous discussion.

When To File

If you filed Form 4868, file Form 2688 by the extended due date of your return. For most people, this is August 16, 2004. If you did not file Form 4868 first because you need more than a 4-month extension due to an undue hardship, file Form 2688 as early as possible, but no later than the due date of your return. The due date is April 15, 2004, for a calendar year return. Be sure to fully explain on line 2 why you are filing Form 2688 first. Also, file Form 2688 early so that if your request is not approved, you can still file your return on time.

If you are a U.S. citizen or resident out of the country (defined on this page) on the regular due date of your return, you are allowed 2 extra months to file your return. For a calendar year return, this is June 15, 2004. To get an additional extension, first file Form 4868 (to get 2

extra months), and then, if necessary, file Form 2688 by the extended due date.

Out of the country means either **(a)** you live outside the United States and Puerto Rico **and** your main place of work is outside the United States and Puerto Rico or **(b)** you are in military or naval service outside the United States and Puerto Rico. If you qualify as being "out of the country," you will still be eligible for the extension, even if you are physically present in the United States or Puerto Rico on the regular due date of the return.

Where To File

Mail **Form 2688** to the Internal Revenue Service Center where you will file your return.

Filing Your Tax Return

You may file your tax return any time before the extension expires. Do **not** attach Form 2688 to your tax return.

Form 2688 does not extend the time to pay taxes. If you do not pay the amount due by the regular due date, you will owe interest and may also be charged penalties.

Interest. You will owe interest on any tax not paid by the regular due date of your return even if you had a good reason for not paying on time. The interest runs until you pay the tax.

Penalties. The **late payment penalty** is usually ½ of 1% of any tax (other than estimated tax) not paid by the regular due date. It is charged for each month or part of a month the tax is unpaid. The maximum penalty is 25%.

The **late filing penalty** is usually charged if your return is filed after the due date (including extensions). The penalty is usually 5% of the amount due for each month or part of a month your return is late. Generally, the maximum penalty is 25%. If your return is more than 60 days late, the minimum penalty is $100 or the balance of tax due on your return, whichever is smaller.

You might not owe these penalties if you have a good reason for paying and/or filing late. Attach a statement to your return, not Form 2688, explaining the reason.

How to claim credit for payment made with this form. The instructions for the following line of your tax return will tell you how to report any payment you sent with Form 2688.

Form 1040, line 66.

Form 1040A, line 43.

Form 1040EZ, line 9.

Form 1040NR, line 61.

Form 1040NR-EZ, line 21.

If you and your spouse each filed a separate Form 2688 but later file a joint return for 2003, enter the total paid with both Forms 2688 on the appropriate line of your joint return.

If you and your spouse jointly filed Form 2688 but later file separate returns for 2003, you may enter the total amount paid with Form 2688 on either of your separate returns. Or you and your spouse may divide the payment in any agreed amounts. Be sure each separate return has the social security numbers of both spouses.

Specific Instructions

Name, Address, and Social Security Number (SSN). If you plan to file a joint return, include your spouse's name and SSN in the same order they will appear on your return.

If you are filing Form 1040NR-EZ or Form 1040NR, and do not have (and are not eligible to obtain) an SSN, enter your IRS-issued individual taxpayer identification number (ITIN). For information on obtaining an ITIN, get **Form W-7,** Application for IRS Individual Taxpayer Identification Number.

Line 2. Clearly describe the reasons that will delay your return. We cannot accept incomplete reasons, such as "illness" or "practitioner too busy," without adequate explanations. If it is

clear that you have no important reason but only want more time, we will deny your request. The 10-day grace period will also be denied.

Line 4. If you or your spouse plan to file Form 709 or 709-A for 2003, check whichever box applies. Also, write "Gift Tax" at the top of the form. But if your spouse files a separate Form 2688, do not check the box for your spouse.

Signature and Verification. This form must be signed. If you plan to file a joint return, both of you should sign. If there is a good reason why one of you cannot, the other spouse may sign for both. Attach a statement explaining why the other spouse cannot sign.

Others who can sign for you. Anyone with a power of attorney can sign. Attorneys, CPAs, and enrolled agents can sign for you without a power of attorney. Also, a person in a close personal or business relationship to you can sign without a power of attorney if you cannot sign. There must be a good reason why you cannot sign, such as illness or absence. Attach an explanation.

Notice to Applicant and Return Label. You must complete the **Return Label** to receive the **Notice to Applicant.** We will use it to tell you if your application has been approved. Do not attach it to your return—keep it for your records.

If the post office does not deliver mail to your street address, enter the P.O. box number instead.

Note: *If you changed your mailing address after you filed your last return, use* **Form 8822,** *Change of Address, to notify the IRS of the change. Showing a new address on Form 2688 will not update your record. You can get Form 8822 by calling 1-800-829-3676.*

Privacy Act and Paperwork Reduction Act Notice. We ask for the information on this form to carry out the Internal Revenue laws of the United States. We need this information to determine your eligibility for an additional extension of time to file your individual income tax return. If you choose to apply for an additional extension of time to file, you are required by Internal Revenue Code sections 6001, 6011(a), and 6081 to provide the information requested on this form. Under section 6109 you must disclose your social security number (SSN) or individual taxpayer identification number (ITIN). Routine uses of this information include giving it to the Department of Justice for civil and criminal litigation, and to cities, states, and the District of Columbia for use in administering their tax laws. We may also disclose this information to other countries under a tax treaty, or to Federal and state agencies to enforce Federal nontax criminal laws and to combat terrorism. If you fail to provide this information in a timely manner, or provide incomplete or false information, you may be liable for interest and penalties.

You are not required to provide the information requested on a form that is subject to the Paperwork Reduction Act unless the form displays a valid OMB control number. Books or records relating to a form or its instructions must be retained as long as their contents may become material in the administration of any Internal Revenue law. Generally, tax returns and return information are confidential, as required by section 6103.

The time needed to complete and file this form will vary depending on individual circumstances. The estimated average time is: **Learning about the law or the form,** 12 min.; **Preparing the form,** 15 min.; and **Copying, assembling, and sending the form to the IRS,** 16 min.

If you have comments concerning the accuracy of these time estimates or suggestions for making this form simpler, we would be happy to hear from you. You can write to the Tax Products Coordinating Committee, Western Area Distribution Center, Rancho Cordova, CA 95743-0001. **Do not** send the form to this address. Instead, see **Where To File** on this page.

Form **6251**	**Alternative Minimum Tax—Individuals**	OMB No. 1545-0227
Department of the Treasury Internal Revenue Service (99)	▶ See separate instructions. ▶ Attach to Form 1040 or Form 1040NR.	**2003** Attachment Sequence No. **32**

Name(s) shown on Form 1040   Your social security number

Part I   Alternative Minimum Taxable Income (See instructions for how to complete each line.)

1	If filing Schedule A (Form 1040), enter the amount from Form 1040, line 38, and go to line 2. Otherwise, enter the amount from Form 1040, line 35, and go to line 7. (If zero or less, enter as a negative amount.)	**1**	
2	Medical and dental. Enter the **smaller** of Schedule A (Form 1040), line 4, **or** 2½% of Form 1040, line 35	**2**	
3	Taxes from Schedule A (Form 1040), line 9	**3**	
4	Certain interest on a home mortgage **not** used to buy, build, or improve your home	**4**	
5	Miscellaneous deductions from Schedule A (Form 1040), line 26	**5**	
6	If Form 1040, line 35, is over $139,500 (over $69,750 if married filing separately), enter the amount from line 9 of the worksheet for Schedule A (Form 1040), line 28	**6**	( )
7	Tax refund from Form 1040, line 10 or line 21	**7**	( )
8	Investment interest expense (difference between regular tax and AMT)	**8**	
9	Depletion (difference between regular tax and AMT)	**9**	
10	Net operating loss deduction from Form 1040, line 21. Enter as a positive amount	**10**	
11	Interest from specified private activity bonds exempt from the regular tax	**11**	
12	Qualified small business stock (see instructions)	**12**	
13	Exercise of incentive stock options (excess of AMT income over regular tax income)	**13**	
14	Estates and trusts (amount from Schedule K-1 (Form 1041), line 9)	**14**	
15	Electing large partnerships (amount from Schedule K-1 (Form 1065-B), box 6)	**15**	
16	Disposition of property (difference between AMT and regular tax gain or loss)	**16**	
17	Depreciation on assets placed in service after 1986 (difference between regular tax and AMT)	**17**	
18	Passive activities (difference between AMT and regular tax income or loss)	**18**	
19	Loss limitations (difference between AMT and regular tax income or loss)	**19**	
20	Circulation costs (difference between regular tax and AMT)	**20**	
21	Long-term contracts (difference between AMT and regular tax income)	**21**	
22	Mining costs (difference between regular tax and AMT)	**22**	
23	Research and experimental costs (difference between regular tax and AMT)	**23**	
24	Income from certain installment sales before January 1, 1987	**24**	( )
25	Intangible drilling costs preference	**25**	
26	Other adjustments, including income-based related adjustments	**26**	
27	Alternative tax net operating loss deduction	**27**	( )
28	**Alternative minimum taxable income.** Combine lines 1 through 27. (If married filing separately and line 28 is more than $191,000, see page 7 of the instructions.)	**28**	

Part II   Alternative Minimum Tax

29   Exemption. (If this form is for a child under age 14, see page 7 of the instructions.)

IF your filing status is . . .	AND line 28 is not over . . .	THEN enter on line 29 . . .	
Single or head of household	$112,500	$40,250	
Married filing jointly or qualifying widow(er)	150,000	58,000	**29**
Married filing separately	75,000	29,000	

     If line 28 is **over** the amount shown above for your filing status, see page 7 of the instructions.

30	Subtract line 29 from line 28. If zero or less, enter -0- here and on lines 33 and 35 and stop here	**30**	
31	• If you reported capital gain distributions directly on Form 1040, line 13a; you reported qualified dividends on Form 1040, line 9b; **or** you had a gain on both lines 16 and 17a of Schedule D (Form 1040) (as refigured for the AMT, if necessary), complete Part III on the back and enter the amount from line 65 here.	**31**	
	• All others: If line 30 is $175,000 or less ($87,500 or less if married filing separately), multiply line 30 by 26% (.26). Otherwise, multiply line 30 by 28% (.28) and subtract $3,500 ($1,750 if married filing separately) from the result.		
32	Alternative minimum tax foreign tax credit (see page 7 of the instructions)	**32**	
33	Tentative minimum tax. Subtract line 32 from line 31	**33**	
34	Tax from Form 1040, line 41 (minus any tax from Form 4972 and any foreign tax credit from Form 1040, line 44)	**34**	
35	**Alternative minimum tax.** Subtract line 34 from line 33. If zero or less, enter -0-. Enter here and on Form 1040, line 42	**35**	

For Paperwork Reduction Act Notice, see page 8 of the instructions.   Cat. No. 13600G   Form **6251** (2003)

Part III **Tax Computation Using Maximum Capital Gains Rates**

Caution: *If you did not complete Part IV of Schedule D (Form 1040), see page 8 of the instructions before you complete this part.*

36 Enter the amount from Form 6251, line 30 . . . . **36**

37 Enter the amount from Schedule D (Form 1040), line 26, or line 13 of the Schedule D Tax Worksheet on page D-11 of the instructions for Schedule D (Form 1040), whichever applies (as refigured for the AMT, if necessary) (see page 8 of the instructions) **37**

38 Enter the amount from Schedule D (Form 1040), line 19 (as refigured for the AMT, if necessary) (see page 8 of the instructions) **38**

39 If you did not complete a Schedule D Tax Worksheet for the regular tax or the AMT, enter the amount from line 37. Otherwise, add lines 37 and 38, and enter the **smaller** of that result or the amount from line 10 of the Schedule D Tax Worksheet (as refigured for the AMT, if necessary). **39**

40 Enter the **smaller** of line 36 or line 39 . . . . **40**

41 Subtract line 40 from line 36 . . . . **41**

42 If line 41 is $175,000 or less ($87,500 or less if married filing separately), multiply line 41 by 26% (.26). Otherwise, multiply line 41 by 28% (.28) and subtract $3,500 ($1,750 if married filing separately) from the result . . . . ▶ **42**

43 Enter the amount from Schedule D (Form 1040), line 30, or line 19 of the Schedule D Tax Worksheet on page D-11 of the instructions for Schedule D (Form 1040), whichever applies (as figured for the regular tax) (see page 8 of the instructions) **43**

44 Enter the **smaller** of line 36 or line 37 . . . . **44**

45 Enter the **smaller** of line 43 or line 44 . . . . **45**

46 Enter the amount from Schedule D (Form 1040), line 31 or line 20 of the Schedule D Tax Worksheet on page D-11 of the instructions for Schedule D (Form 1040), whichever applies (as refigured for the AMT, if necessary) (see page 8 of the instructions) **46**

47 Enter the **smaller** of line 45 or line 46. If line 45 is zero, go to line 55 . . **47**

48 Multiply line 47 by 5% (.05) . . . . ▶ **48**

49 Subtract line 47 from line 45. If zero or less, enter -0- and go to line 55 . . **49**

50 Enter your qualified 5-year gain, if any, from Schedule D (Form 1040), line 35 (as refigured for the AMT, if necessary) (see page 8 of the instructions) **50**

51 Enter the **smaller** of line 49 or line 50 . . . . **51**

52 Multiply line 51 by 8% (.08) . . . . ▶ **52**

53 Subtract line 51 from line 49 . . . . **53**

54 Multiply line 53 by 10% (.10) . . . . ▶ **54**

55 Subtract line 47 from line 46 . . . . **55**

56 Subtract line 45 from line 44 . . . . **56**

57 Enter the **smaller** of line 55 or line 56 . . . . **57**

58 Multiply line 57 by 15% (.15) . . . . ▶ **58**

59 Subtract line 57 from line 56 . . . . **59**

60 Multiply line 59 by 20% (.20) . . . . ▶ **60**

If line 38 is zero or blank, skip lines 61 and 62 and go to line 63. Otherwise, go to line 61.

61 Subtract line 44 from line 40 . . . . **61**

62 Multiply line 61 by 25% (.25) . . . . ▶ **62**

63 Add lines 42, 48, 52, 54, 58, 60, and 62 . . . . **63**

64 If line 36 is $175,000 or less ($87,500 or less if married filing separately), multiply line 36 by 26% (.26). Otherwise, multiply line 36 by 28% (.28) and subtract $3,500 ($1,750 if married filing separately) from the result **64**

65 Enter the **smaller** of line 63 or line 64 here and on line 31 . . . . . . **65**

Form **8615**

Department of the Treasury
Internal Revenue Service (99)

Tax for Children Under Age 14 With Investment Income of More Than $1,500
▶ Attach only to the child's Form 1040, Form 1040A, or Form 1040NR.
▶ See separate instructions.

OMB No. 1545-0998

2003

Attachment
Sequence No. **33**

Child's name shown on return

Child's social security number

Before you begin: If the child, the parent, or any of the parent's other children under age 14 received capital gains (including capital gain distributions), or qualified dividends, or farm income, see **Pub. 929,** Tax Rules for Children and Dependents. It explains how to figure the child's tax using the **Qualified Dividends and Capital Gain Tax Worksheet** in the Form 1040 or Form 1040A instructions, or **Schedule D** or **J** (Form 1040).

A Parent's name (first, initial, and last). **Caution:** See instructions before completing.

B Parent's social security number

C Parent's filing status (check one):

☐ Single   ☐ Married filing jointly   ☐ Married filing separately   ☐ Head of household   ☐ Qualifying widow(er)

Part I   Child's Net Investment Income

1	Enter the child's investment income (see instructions)	**1**
2	If the child **did not** itemize deductions on **Schedule A** (Form 1040 or Form 1040NR), enter $1,500. Otherwise, see instructions	**2**
3	Subtract line 2 from line 1. If zero or less, **stop;** do not complete the rest of this form but **do** attach it to the child's return	**3**
4	Enter the child's **taxable income** from Form 1040, line 40; Form 1040A, line 27; or Form 1040NR, line 38	**4**
5	Enter the **smaller** of line 3 or line 4. If zero, **stop;** do not complete the rest of this form but **do** attach it to the child's return	**5**

Part II   Tentative Tax Based on the Tax Rate of the Parent

6	Enter the parent's **taxable income** from Form 1040, line 40; Form 1040A, line 27; Form 1040EZ, line 6; TeleFile Tax Record, line K(1); Form 1040NR, line 38; or Form 1040NR-EZ, line 14. If zero or less, enter -0-	**6**
7	Enter the total, if any, from Forms 8615, line 5, of **all other** children of the parent named above. **Do not** include the amount from line 5 above	**7**
8	Add lines 5, 6, and 7.	**8**
9	Enter the tax on the amount on line 8 based on the **parent's** filing status above (see instructions). If the Qualified Dividends and Capital Gain Tax Worksheet or Schedule D or J (Form 1040) is used, check here ▶ ☐	**9**
10	Enter the parent's tax from Form 1040, line 41; Form 1040A, line 28, minus any alternative minimum tax; Form 1040EZ, line 10; TeleFile Tax Record, line K(2); Form 1040NR, line 39; or Form 1040NR-EZ, line 15. **Do not** include any tax from **Form 4972** or **8814.** If the Qualified Dividends and Capital Gain Tax Worksheet or Schedule D or J (Form 1040) was used to figure the tax, check here ▶ ☐	**10**
11	Subtract line 10 from line 9 and enter the result. If line 7 is blank, also enter this amount on line 13 and go to **Part III**	**11**
12a	Add lines 5 and 7 **12a**	
b	Divide line 5 by line 12a. Enter the result as a decimal (rounded to at least three places)	**12b** × .
13	Multiply line 11 by line 12b	**13**

Part III   Child's Tax—If lines 4 and 5 above are the same, enter -0- on line 15 and go to line 16.

14	Subtract line 5 from line 4 **14**	
15	Enter the tax on the amount on line 14 based on the **child's** filing status (see instructions). If the Qualified Dividends and Capital Gain Tax Worksheet or Schedule D or J (Form 1040) is used to figure the tax, check here ▶ ☐	**15**
16	Add lines 13 and 15	**16**
17	Enter the tax on the amount on line 4 based on the **child's** filing status (see instructions). If the Qualified Dividends and Capital Gain Tax Worksheet or Schedule D or J (Form 1040) is used to figure the tax, check here ▶ ☐	**17**
18	Enter the **larger** of line 16 or line 17 here and on the **child's** Form 1040, line 41; Form 1040A, line 28; or Form 1040NR, line 39	**18**

For Paperwork Reduction Act Notice, see the instructions.   Cat. No. 64113U   Form **8615** (2003)

Form **8814**

Department of the Treasury
Internal Revenue Service

Parents' Election To Report
Child's Interest and Dividends

▶ See instructions below and on back.
▶ Attach to parents' Form 1040 or Form 1040NR.

OMB No. 1545-1128

20**03**

Attachment
Sequence No. **40**

Name(s) shown on your return

Your social security number

Caution: *The Federal income tax on your child's income, including qualified dividends and capital gain distributions, may be less if you file a separate tax return for the child instead of making this election. This is because you cannot take certain tax benefits that your child could take on his or her own return. For details, see* **Tax Benefits You May Not Take** *on the back.*

A	Child's name (first, initial, and last)	B	Child's social security number

C If more than one Form 8814 is attached, check here . . . . ▶ ☐

Part I   Child's Interest and Dividends To Report on Your Return

1a Enter your child's **taxable** interest. If this amount is different from the amounts shown on the child's Forms 1099-INT and 1099-OID, see the instructions . . . . | **1a** |

b Enter your child's **tax-exempt** interest. **Do not** include this amount on line 1a . . . . | **1b** |

2 Enter your child's ordinary dividends, including any Alaska Permanent Fund dividends. If your child received any ordinary dividends as a nominee, see the instructions . . . . | **2** |

3 Enter your child's capital gain distributions. If your child received any capital gain distributions as a nominee, see the instructions . . . . | **3** |

4 Add lines 1a, 2, and 3. If the total is $1,500 or less, skip lines 5 and 6 and go to line 7. If the total is $7,500 or more, **do not** file this form. Your child **must** file his or her own return to report the income . . . . | **4** |

5 Base amount . . . . | **5** | 1,500 | 00 |

6 Subtract line 5 from line 4. See the instructions for where to report this amount. Go to line 7 below . . . . ▶ | **6** |

Part II   Tax on the First $1,500 of Child's Interest and Dividends

7 Amount not taxed . . . . | **7** | 750 | 00 |

8 Subtract line 7 from line 4. If the result is zero or less, enter -0- . . . . | **8** |

9 **Tax.** Is the amount on line 8 less than $750?
☐ **No.** Enter $75 here and see the **Note** below.
☐ **Yes.** Multiply line 8 by 10% (.10). Enter the result here and see the **Note** below.   } . . | **9** |

Note: *If you checked the box on line C above, see the instructions. Otherwise, include the amount from line 9 in the tax you enter on Form 1040, line 41, or Form 1040NR, line 39. Be sure to check box **a** on Form 1040, line 41, or Form 1040NR, line 39.*

General Instructions

Purpose of Form. Use this form if you elect to report your child's income on your return. If you do, your child will not have to file a return. You can make this election if your child meets **all** of the following conditions.

• The child was under age 14 at the end of 2003. A child born on January 1, 1990, is considered to be age 14 at the end of 2003.

• The child's only income was from interest and dividends, including capital gain distributions and Alaska Permanent Fund dividends.

• The child's gross income for 2003 was less than $7,500.

• The child is required to file a 2003 return.

• There were no estimated tax payments for the child for 2003 (including any overpayment of tax from his or her 2002 return applied to 2003 estimated tax).

• There was no Federal income tax withheld from the child's income.

You must also qualify. See **Parents Who Qualify To Make the Election** below.

How To Make the Election. To make the election, complete and attach Form(s) 8814 to your tax return and file your return by the due date (including extensions). A separate Form 8814 must be filed for **each** child whose income you choose to report.

Parents Who Qualify To Make the Election. You qualify to make this election if you file Form 1040 or Form 1040NR and **any** of the following apply.

• You are filing a joint return for 2003 with the child's other parent.

• You and the child's other parent were married to each other but file separate returns for 2003 **and** you had the **higher** taxable income.

• You were unmarried, treated as unmarried for Federal income tax purposes, or separated from the child's other parent by a divorce or separate maintenance decree. You must have had custody of your child for most of the year (you were the custodial parent). If you were the custodial parent and you remarried, you may make the election on a joint return with your new spouse. But if you and your new spouse do not file a joint return, you qualify to make the election only if you had **higher** taxable income than your new spouse.

(continued)

For Paperwork Reduction Act Notice, see back of form.   Cat. No. 10750J   Form **8814** (2003)

Note: *If you and the child's other parent were not married but lived together during the year with the child, you qualify to make the election only if you are the parent with the **higher** taxable income.*

Tax Benefits You May Not Take. If you elect to report your child's income on your return, you may not take any of the following deductions that your child could take on his or her own return.

• Standard deduction of $1,900 for a blind child.

• Penalty on early withdrawal of child's savings.

• Itemized deductions such as child's investment expenses or charitable contributions.

If your child received qualified dividends or capital gain distributions, you may pay up to $37.50 more tax if you make this election instead of filing a separate tax return for the child. This is because the tax rate on the child's income between $750 and $1,500 is 10% if you make this election. However, if you file a separate return for the child, the tax rate may be as low as 5% because of the preferential tax rates for qualified dividends and post-May 5 capital gain distributions (8% on qualified 5-year gain).

If any of the above apply to your child, first figure the tax on your child's income as if he or she is filing a return. Next, figure the tax as if you are electing to report your child's income on **your** return. Then, compare the methods to determine which results in the lower tax.

Alternative Minimum Tax. If your child received tax-exempt interest (or exempt-interest dividends paid by a regulated investment company) from certain private activity bonds, you must take this into account in determining if you owe the alternative minimum tax. See **Form 6251,** Alternative Minimum Tax— Individuals, and its instructions for details.

Investment Interest Expense. Your child's income (other than qualified dividends, Alaska Permanent Fund dividends, and capital gain distributions) that you report on your return is considered to be **your** investment income for purposes of figuring your investment interest expense deduction. If your child received qualified dividends, Alaska Permanent Fund dividends, or capital gain distributions, see **Pub. 550,** Investment Income and Expenses, to figure the amount you may treat as your investment income.

Foreign Accounts and Trusts. Complete Part III of **Schedule B** (Form 1040) for your child if he or she **(a)** had a foreign financial account or **(b)** received a distribution from, or was the grantor of, or transferor to, a foreign trust. If you answer "Yes" to either question, you must file this Schedule B with **your** return. Enter "Form 8814" next to line 7a or line 8, whichever applies. Also, complete line 7b if applicable.

Change of Address. If your child filed a return for a previous year and the address shown on the last return filed is not your child's current address, be sure to notify the IRS, in writing, of the new address. To do this, you may use **Form 8822,** Change of Address.

Additional Information. See **Pub. 929,** Tax Rules for Children and Dependents, for more details.

Line Instructions

Name and Social Security Number. If filing a joint return, include your spouse's name but enter the social security number of the person whose name is shown first on the return.

Line 1a. Enter **all** taxable interest income received by your child in 2003. If your child received a **Form 1099-INT** for tax-exempt interest, such as from municipal bonds, enter the amount and "Tax-exempt interest" on the dotted line next to line 1a. **Do not** include this interest in the total for line 1a but be sure to include it on line 1b.

If your child received, as a **nominee,** interest that actually belongs to another person, enter the amount and "ND" (for nominee distribution) on the dotted line next to line 1a. **Do not** include amounts received as a nominee in the total for line 1a.

If your child had accrued interest that was paid to the seller of a bond, amortizable bond premium (ABP) allowed as a reduction to interest income, or if any original issue discount (OID) is less than the amount shown on your child's **Form 1099-OID,** enter the nontaxable amount on the dotted line next to line 1a and "Accrued interest," "ABP adjustment," or "OID adjustment," whichever applies. **Do not** include any nontaxable amounts in the total for line 1a.

Line 1b. If your child received any tax-exempt interest income, such as from certain state and municipal bonds, report it on line 1b. Also, include any exempt-interest dividends your child received as a shareholder in a mutual fund or other regulated investment company.

Note: *If line 1b includes tax-exempt interest or exempt-interest dividends paid by a regulated investment company from private activity bonds, see **Alternative Minimum Tax** on this page.*

Line 2. Enter the ordinary dividends received by your child in 2003. Ordinary dividends should be shown in box 1a of **Form 1099-DIV.** Also, include ordinary dividends your child received through a partnership, an S corporation, or an estate or trust.

If your child received, as a **nominee,** ordinary dividends that actually belong to another person, enter the amount and "ND" on the dotted line next to line 2. **Do not** include amounts received as a nominee in the total for line 2.

Line 3. Enter the capital gain distributions received by your child in 2003. Capital gain distributions should be shown in box 2a of Form 1099-DIV. Also, see the instructions for line 6.

If your child received, as a **nominee,** capital gain distributions that actually belong to another person, enter the amount and "ND" on the dotted line next to line 3. **Do not** include amounts received as a nominee in the total for line 3.

Line 6. If you checked the box on line C, add the amounts from line 6 of **all** your Forms 8814. Unless the exception below applies, include this amount in the total on line 21 of Form 1040 or Form 1040NR, whichever applies. Be sure to enter "Form 8814" and the total of the line 6 amounts in the space next to line 21.

Exception. If your child received qualified dividends or capital gain distributions, part or all of that income must be reported on your Form 1040 or Form 1040NR instead of on Form 8814, line 6. See Pub. 929 for details.

Line 9. If you checked the box on line C, add the amounts from line 9 of **all** your Forms 8814. Include the total on Form 1040, line 41, or Form 1040NR, line 39. Be sure to check box **a** on that line.

Form **8829**

Department of the Treasury
Internal Revenue Service   (99)

Expenses for Business Use of Your Home

▶ File only with Schedule C (Form 1040). Use a separate Form 8829 for each home you used for business during the year.

▶ See separate instructions.

OMB No. 1545-1266

2003

Attachment
Sequence No. **66**

Name(s) of proprietor(s)

Your social security number

Part I   Part of Your Home Used for Business

1	Area used regularly and exclusively for business, regularly for day care, or for storage of inventory or product samples (see instructions)	1	
2	Total area of home	2	
3	Divide line 1 by line 2. Enter the result as a percentage	3	%

● **For day-care facilities not used exclusively for business, also complete lines 4–6.**

● **All others, skip lines 4–6 and enter the amount from line 3 on line 7.**

4	Multiply days used for day care during year by hours used per day	4	hr.
5	Total hours available for use during the year (365 days × 24 hours) (see instructions)	5	8,760 hr.
6	Divide line 4 by line 5. Enter the result as a decimal amount	6	.
7	Business percentage. For day-care facilities not used exclusively for business, multiply line 6 by line 3 (enter the result as a percentage). All others, enter the amount from line 3 ▶	7	%

Part II   Figure Your Allowable Deduction

8   Enter the amount from Schedule C, line 29, **plus** any net gain or (loss) derived from the business use of your home and shown on Schedule D or Form 4797. If more than one place of business, see instructions ... **8**

See instructions for columns (a) and (b) before completing lines 9–20.

		(a) Direct expenses	(b) Indirect expenses	
9	Casualty losses (see instructions)			
10	Deductible mortgage interest (see instructions)			
11	Real estate taxes (see instructions)			
12	Add lines 9, 10, and 11			
13	Multiply line 12, column (b) by line 7		13	
14	Add line 12, column (a) and line 13			14
15	Subtract line 14 from line 8. If zero or less, enter -0-			15
16	Excess mortgage interest (see instructions)			
17	Insurance			
18	Repairs and maintenance			
19	Utilities			
20	Other expenses (see instructions)			
21	Add lines 16 through 20			
22	Multiply line 21, column (b) by line 7	22		
23	Carryover of operating expenses from 2002 Form 8829, line 41	23		
24	Add line 21 in column (a), line 22, and line 23			24
25	Allowable operating expenses. Enter the **smaller** of line 15 or line 24			25
26	Limit on excess casualty losses and depreciation. Subtract line 25 from line 15			26
27	Excess casualty losses (see instructions)	27		
28	Depreciation of your home from Part III below	28		
29	Carryover of excess casualty losses and depreciation from 2002 Form 8829, line 42	29		
30	Add lines 27 through 29			30
31	Allowable excess casualty losses and depreciation. Enter the **smaller** of line 26 or line 30			31
32	Add lines 14, 25, and 31			32
33	Casualty loss portion, if any, from lines 14 and 31. Carry amount to **Form 4684**, Section B			33
34	Allowable expenses for business use of your home. Subtract line 33 from line 32. Enter here and on Schedule C, line 30. If your home was used for more than one business, see instructions ▶			34

Part III   Depreciation of Your Home

35	Enter the **smaller** of your home's adjusted basis or its fair market value (see instructions)	35	
36	Value of land included on line 35	36	
37	Basis of building. Subtract line 36 from line 35	37	
38	Business basis of building. Multiply line 37 by line 7	38	
39	Depreciation percentage (see instructions)	39	%
40	Depreciation allowable (see instructions). Multiply line 38 by line 39. Enter here and on line 28 above	40	

Part IV   Carryover of Unallowed Expenses to 2004

41	Operating expenses. Subtract line 25 from line 24. If less than zero, enter -0-	41	
42	Excess casualty losses and depreciation. Subtract line 31 from line 30. If less than zero, enter -0-	42	

For Paperwork Reduction Act Notice, see page 4 of separate instructions.   Cat. No. 13232M   Form **8829** (2003)

Form **8857**
(Rev. May 2002)
Department of the Treasury
Internal Revenue Service

Request for Innocent Spouse Relief
(And Separation of Liability and Equitable Relief)

▶ Do not file with your tax return.　▶ See instructions.

OMB No. 1545-1596

Do not file this form if:

- You did not file a joint return for the year(s) for which you are requesting relief. However, if you lived in a community property state, see instructions.

- All or part of your overpayment was (or is expected to be) applied against your spouse's past-due debt (such as child support). Instead, file **Form 8379,** Injured Spouse Claim and Allocation, to apply to have your share of the overpayment refunded to you.

(TIP) *To see if you may qualify for **Innocent Spouse Relief,** go to www.irs.gov, click on "Individuals," "Innocent Spouses," and "Explore if you are an Eligible Innocent Spouse"; or see **Pub. 971,** Innocent Spouse Relief.*

Part I See **Spousal Notification** in the instructions.	Your current name (see instructions)	Your social security number
	Your current home address (number and street). If a P.O. box, see instructions.	Apt. no.
	City, town or post office, state, and ZIP code. If a foreign address, see instructions.	Daytime phone number ( )

If you have been a victim of domestic abuse and fear that filing a claim for innocent spouse relief will result in retaliation, check here . . . . ▶ ☐

Part II

1 Enter the year(s) for which you are requesting relief from liability of tax ▶ ....

2 Information about the person to whom you were married as of the end of the year(s) on line 1.

Name	Social security number
Current home address (number and street). If a P.O. box, see instructions.	Apt. no.
City, town or post office, state, and ZIP code. If a foreign address, see instructions.	Daytime phone number ( )

3 Do you have an **Understatement of Tax** (that is, the IRS has determined there is a difference between the tax shown on your return and the tax that should have been shown)?

☐ **Yes.** Go to Part III. ☐ **No.** Go to Part V.

Part III

4 Are you divorced from the person listed on line 2 or has that person died?

☐ **Yes.** Go to line 7. ☐ **No.** Go to line 5.

5 Are you legally separated from the person listed on line 2?

☐ **Yes.** Go to line 7. ☐ **No.** Go to line 6.

6 Have you lived apart from the person listed on line 2 at all times during the 12-month period prior to filing this form?

☐ **Yes.** Go to line 7. ☐ **No.** Go to Part IV.

7 If line **4, 5,** or **6** is **Yes,** you may request **Separation of Liability** by **attaching a statement** (see instructions). Check here ▶ ☐ and go to Part IV.

Part IV

8 Is the understatement of tax due to the **Erroneous Items** of your spouse (see instructions)?

☐ **Yes.** You may request **Innocent Spouse Relief** by **attaching a statement** (see instructions). Go to Part V. ☐ **No.** You may request **Equitable Relief** for the understatement of tax. Check **Yes** in Part V.

Part V

9 Do you have an **Underpayment of Tax** (that is, tax that is properly shown on your return but not paid) or another tax liability that qualifies for **Equitable Relief** (see instructions)?

☐ **Yes.** You may request **Equitable Relief** by **attaching a statement** (see instructions). ☐ **No.** You cannot file this form unless line 3 is **Yes.**

Under penalties of perjury, I declare that I have examined this form and any accompanying schedules and statements, and to the best of my knowledge and belief, they are true, correct, and complete. Declaration of preparer (other than taxpayer) is based on all information of which preparer has any knowledge.

| **Sign Here**
Keep a copy for your records. ▶ | Your signature | Date |

Paid Preparer's Use Only	Preparer's signature ▶	Date	Check if self-employed ☐	Preparer's SSN or PTIN
	Firm's name (or yours if self-employed), address, and ZIP code ▶		EIN	
			Phone no. ( )	

For Privacy Act and Paperwork Reduction Act Notice, see instructions.　Cat. No. 24647V　Form **8857** (Rev. 5-2002)

General Instructions

Purpose of Form

Use Form 8857 to request relief from liability for tax, plus related penalties and interest, for which you believe only your spouse or former spouse should be held liable. Generally, you must have filed a joint return for the year(s) for which you are requesting relief (but see **Community Property Laws).** The IRS will evaluate your request and tell you if you qualify.

You may be allowed one or more of these three types of relief:

- Separation of liability,
- Innocent spouse relief, or
- Equitable relief.

Statement To Attach

You must attach a statement to Form 8857 explaining why you qualify for relief. Complete the statement using the best information you have available. Include your name and social security number (SSN) on the statement.

If you are requesting relief for more than 1 tax year, you only need to file one Form 8857. However, you must include a separate statement for each year. Clearly indicate in the statement(s) the type(s) of relief you are requesting for each year. You must provide certain information for each type of relief you are requesting. See the specific instructions for Parts III, IV, and V for details on the information to include with your statement(s).

Generally, the IRS will request additional information from you. You can help the processing of your request for relief by completing and attaching **Form 12510,** Questionnaire for Requesting Spouse. To get Form 12510, go to **www.irs.gov** or call 1-800-TAX-FORM (1-800-829-3676).

Additional Information

See **Pub. 971,** Innocent Spouse Relief. To get Pub. 971, go to **www.irs.gov** or call 1-800-TAX-FORM (1-800-829-3676).

The IRS can help you with your request. If you are working with an IRS employee, you can ask that employee, or you can call 1-800-829-1040.

When To File

You should file Form 8857 as soon as you become aware of a tax liability for which you believe only your spouse or former spouse should be held liable. The following are some of the ways you may become aware of such a liability.

- The IRS is examining your tax return and proposing a deficiency.
- The IRS sends you a notice.

You generally must file Form 8857 no later than 2 years after the first IRS attempt to collect the tax from you that occurs after July 22, 1998. Examples of attempts to collect the tax from you are garnishment of your wages or applying your income tax refund to the tax due.

Note: *The time that the IRS will be allowed to collect taxes, interest, and penalties does not include the time that your request for relief is being considered.*

Where To File

Do not file Form 8857 with your tax return or fax it to the IRS. Instead, see below.

IF . . .	THEN file Form 8857 with . . .
You are meeting with an IRS employee for an examination, examination appeal, or collection	That IRS employee.
You received an IRS notice of deficiency, and the 90-day period specified in the notice has not expired*	The IRS employee named in the notice. Attach a copy of the notice. **Do not** file Form 8857 with the Tax Court.
Neither situation above applies to you	**Internal Revenue Service Stop 840M, 201 W. Rivercenter Blvd., Covington, KY 41019**

*Before the end of the 90-day period, you should file a petition with the Tax Court, as explained in the notice. By doing so, you preserve your rights if the IRS is unable to properly consider your request before the end of the 90-day period. Include the information that supports your position, including when and why you filed Form 8857 with the IRS, in your petition to the Tax Court. The time for filing with the Tax Court is **not** extended while the IRS is considering your request.

Definitions

Understatement of Tax

An understatement of tax, or deficiency, is generally the difference between the total amount of tax that the IRS determines should have been shown on the return, and the amount that actually was shown on the return.

Example. You and your former spouse filed a joint return showing $5,000 of tax, which was fully paid. The IRS later examines the return and finds $10,000 of income that your former spouse earned but did not report. With the additional income, the total tax becomes $6,500. The understatement of tax is $1,500, for which you and your former spouse are both liable.

Underpayment of Tax

An underpayment is tax that is properly shown on your return but has not been paid.

Example. You and your former spouse filed a joint return that properly reflects your income and deductions but showed an unpaid balance due of $5,000. The underpayment of tax is $5,000. You gave your former spouse $2,500 and he or she promised to pay the full $5,000, but did not. There is still an underpayment of tax of $5,000, for which you and your former spouse are both liable.

Note: *If you have both an underpayment and understatement of tax, you may have to request different types of relief. If you have an underpayment of tax, you may only request equitable relief. Complete Parts III and IV to see which type(s) of relief you can request for the understatement of tax.*

Joint and Several Liability

Generally, joint and several liability applies to all joint returns. This means that both you and your spouse or former spouse are jointly and individually responsible for any underpayment of tax plus any understatement of tax that may become due later. This is true even if a divorce decree states that your former spouse will be responsible for any amounts due on previously filed joint returns.

Community Property Laws

Generally, you must follow community property laws when filing a tax return if you are married and live in a community property state. Community property states are: Arizona, California, Idaho, Louisiana, Nevada, New Mexico, Texas, Washington, and Wisconsin. Generally, community property laws provide that you and your spouse are both entitled to one-half of your total community income and expenses. If you and your spouse filed a joint return in a community property state, you are both jointly and severally liable for the total liability on the return. If you request relief from joint and several liability, state community property laws are not taken into account in determining whether an item belongs to you or your spouse or former spouse.

If you and your spouse filed separate returns, each of you must report one-half of your total community income and expenses on your separate returns. See **Pub. 555,** Community Property, for details.

If you were married and filed a separate return in a community property state and are now liable for an underpayment or understatement of tax, you have two ways to get relief.

1. Relief from separate return liability for community income. You are not responsible for the tax related to an item of community income if **all** the following conditions exist.

● You filed a separate return for the tax year.

● You did not include the item in gross income on your separate return.

● You establish that you did not know of, and had no reason to know of, that item.

● Under all facts and circumstances, it would not be fair to include the item in your gross income.

If you meet the above conditions, write "Innocent Spouse Relief Under IRC 66(c)" across the top of Form 8857. Complete Parts I, II, and V. Attach a statement to the form explaining why you believe you qualify for relief.

2. Equitable relief. If you do not qualify for the relief described above and are now liable for an underpayment or understatement of tax you believe should be paid only by your spouse or former spouse, you may request equitable relief (see the instructions for Part V).

Tax Court Review of Request

You may petition (ask) the Tax Court to review your request for relief if:

● The IRS sends you a final determination notice regarding your request for relief or

● You do not receive a final determination notice from the IRS within 6 months from the date you filed Form 8857.

The petition must be made no later than the 90th day after the date the IRS mails you a final determination notice. If you do not file a petition, or if you file it late, the Tax Court cannot review your request for relief. See Pub. 971 for details on petitioning the Tax Court.

Specific Instructions

Foreign address. Enter the information in the following order: City, province or state, and country. Follow the country's practice for entering the postal code. **Do not** abbreviate the country name.

Part I

Name. Enter your current name. If your current name is different from your name as shown on your tax return for any year for which you are requesting relief, enter it in parentheses after your current name. For example, enter "Jane Maple (formerly Jane Oak)."

P.O. box. Enter your box number **only** if your post office does not deliver mail to your home.

Spousal Notification

The law requires the IRS to inform your spouse or former spouse of the request for relief from liability. The IRS is also required to allow your spouse or former spouse to provide information that may assist in determining the amount of relief from liability. The IRS will **not** provide information to your spouse or former spouse that could infringe on your privacy. The IRS will not provide your new name, address, information about your employer, phone number, or any other information that does not relate to making a determination about your request for relief from liability.

Victim of Domestic Abuse

If you have been a victim of domestic abuse and fear that filing a request for relief of liability will result in retaliation, check the box in Part I. Checking this box will alert us to the sensitivity of your situation. It does not grant you special consideration when we make our decision. However, evidence of abuse is one factor that the IRS may consider for certain types of relief. You should fully explain to us your concerns in the statement attached to your request.

Part II
Line 1

Enter the tax year(s) for which you have an understatement or underpayment. **Do not** enter any year(s) that the IRS used your refund to offset the understatement or underpayment.

Example: You were due a refund for tax year 2001 on your single return but the IRS applied the refund to unpaid joint taxes for tax year 1999. You enter "1999" on line 1.

Line 2

Enter the current name and SSN of the person to whom you were married at the end of the year(s) listed on line 1. If the name of the person shown on that year's tax return(s) is different from the current name, enter it in parentheses after the current name. For example, enter "Jane Maple (formerly Jane Oak)." Also enter the current address and phone number if you know it.

P.O. box. Enter the box number **only** if:

● You do not know the street address or

● The post office does not deliver mail to the street address.

Part III—Separation of Liability

You may request separation of liability for any understatement of tax shown on the joint return(s) you filed with the person listed on line 2 if that person died or you and that person:

● Are divorced, or

● Are legally separated, or

● Have lived apart at all times during the 12-month period prior to the date you file Form 8857.

See **Pub. 504,** Divorced or Separated Individuals, for details on divorce and separation.

Separation of liability applies only to amounts owed that are not paid. The IRS cannot give you a refund of amounts already paid.

Requesting Separation of Liability

You must attach a statement to Form 8857. Show the total amount of the understatement of tax. For each item that resulted in an understatement of tax, explain whether the item is attributable to you, the person listed on line 2, or both of you. For example, unreported income earned by the person listed on line 2, plus any related self-employment tax, would be allocated to that person. See Pub. 971 for more details.

Exception. If, at the time you signed the joint return, you knew about any item that resulted in part or all of the understatement, then your request will not apply to that part of the understatement.

Part IV—Innocent Spouse Relief

You may be allowed innocent spouse relief only if **all** of the following apply.

● You filed a joint return for the year(s) entered on line 1.

● There is an understatement of tax on the return(s) that is due to erroneous items (defined below) of the person listed on line 2.

● You can show that when you signed the return(s) you did not know and had no reason to know that the understatement of tax existed (or the extent to which the understatement existed).

● Taking into account all the facts and circumstances, it would be unfair to hold you liable for the understatement of tax.

Erroneous Items

Any income, deduction, credit, or basis is an erroneous item if it is omitted from or incorrectly reported on the joint return.

Partial Innocent Spouse Relief

If you knew about any of the erroneous items, but not the full extent of the item(s), you may be allowed relief for the part of the understatement you did not know about. Explain in the statement you attach to Form 8857 how much you knew and why you did not know, and had no reason to know, the full extent of the item(s).

Requesting Innocent Spouse Relief

You must attach a statement to Form 8857 explaining why you believe you qualify. The statement will vary depending on your circumstances, but should include **all** of the following.

● The amount of the understatement of tax for which you are liable and are seeking relief.

● The amount and a detailed description of each erroneous item, including why you had no reason to know about the item or the extent to which you knew about the item.

● Why you believe it would be unfair to hold you liable for the understatement of tax.

For additional information on innocent spouse relief, see Pub. 971.

Part V—Equitable Relief

You may be allowed equitable relief if, taking into account all the facts and circumstances, the IRS determines you should not be held liable for any understatement or underpayment of tax.

Equitable relief generally applies only to:

● An underpayment of tax or

● Part or all of any understatement of tax that does not qualify for both separation of liability and innocent spouse relief.

You should request separation of liability or innocent spouse relief for any understatement of tax if you are eligible. The IRS will consider equitable relief for any understatement of tax if it determines that innocent spouse relief and separation of liability do not apply.

Equitable relief is generally available only for amounts owed that are not paid. However, you may be able to receive a refund of certain installment payments made after you file Form 8857.

For additional information on equitable relief, see Pub. 971 and Rev. Proc. 2000-15, 2000-1 C.B. 447. You can find Rev. Proc. 2000-15 on page 447 of Internal Revenue Bulletin 2000-05 at **www.irs.gov/bus_info/bullet.html.**

Requesting Equitable Relief

You must attach an explanation of why you believe it would be unfair to hold you liable for the tax instead of the person listed on line 2. If you are attaching a statement for separation of liability or innocent spouse relief, only include any additional information you believe supports your request for equitable relief.

Privacy Act and Paperwork Reduction Act Notice. We ask for the information on this form to carry out the Internal Revenue laws of the United States. We need it to determine the amount of liability, if any, of which you may be relieved. Internal Revenue Code section 6015 allows relief from liability. If you request relief of liability, you must give us the information requested on this form. Code section 6109 requires you to provide your social security number. Routine uses of this information include giving it to the Department of Justice for civil and criminal litigation, and to cities, states, and the District of Columbia for use in administering their tax laws. We may also disclose this information to Federal, state, or local agencies that investigate or respond to acts or threats of terrorism or participate in intelligence or counterintelligence activities concerning terrorism. If you do not provide all the information in a timely manner, we may not be able to process your request.

You are not required to provide the information requested on a form that is subject to the Paperwork Reduction Act unless the form displays a valid OMB control number. Books or records relating to a form or its instructions must be retained as long as their contents may become material in the administration of any Internal Revenue law. Generally, tax returns and return information are confidential, as required by Code section 6103.

The time needed to complete and file this form will vary depending on individual circumstances. The estimated average time is: **Learning about the law or the form,** 16 min.; **Preparing the form,** 22 min.; and **Copying, assembling, and sending the form to the IRS,** 20 min.

If you have comments concerning the accuracy of this time estimate or suggestions for making this form simpler, we would be happy to hear from you. You can write to the Tax Forms Committee, Western Area Distribution Center, Rancho Cordova, CA 95743-0001. **Do not** send the form to this address. Instead, see **Where To File** on page 2.

2003 Tax Table

Use if your taxable income is less than $100,000.
If $100,000 or more, use the Tax Rate Schedules.

Example. Mr. and Mrs. Brown are filing a joint return. Their taxable income on line 40 of Form 1040 is $25,300. First, they find the $25,300–25,350 income line. Next, they find the column for married filing jointly and read down the column. The amount shown where the income line and filing status column meet is $3,099. This is the tax amount they should enter on line 41 of their Form 1040.

Sample Table

At least	But less than	Single	Married filing jointly *	Married filing sepa-rately	Head of a house-hold
			Your tax is—		
25,200	25,250	3,434	3,084	3,434	3,284
25,250	25,300	3,441	(3,091)	3,441	3,291
25,300	25,350	3,449	(3,099)	3,449	3,299
25,350	25,400	3,456	3,106	3,456	3,306

If line 40 (taxable income) is— At least	But less than	Single	Married filing jointly *	Married filing sepa-rately	Head of a house-hold
			Your tax is—		
0	5	0	0	0	0
5	15	1	1	1	1
15	25	2	2	2	2
25	50	4	4	4	4
50	75	6	6	6	6
75	100	9	9	9	9
100	125	11	11	11	11
125	150	14	14	14	14
150	175	16	16	16	16
175	200	19	19	19	19
200	225	21	21	21	21
225	250	24	24	24	24
250	275	26	26	26	26
275	300	29	29	29	29
300	325	31	31	31	31
325	350	34	34	34	34
350	375	36	36	36	36
375	400	39	39	39	39
400	425	41	41	41	41
425	450	44	44	44	44
450	475	46	46	46	46
475	500	49	49	49	49
500	525	51	51	51	51
525	550	54	54	54	54
550	575	56	56	56	56
575	600	59	59	59	59
600	625	61	61	61	61
625	650	64	64	64	64
650	675	66	66	66	66
675	700	69	69	69	69
700	725	71	71	71	71
725	750	74	74	74	74
750	775	76	76	76	76
775	800	79	79	79	79
800	825	81	81	81	81
825	850	84	84	84	84
850	875	86	86	86	86
875	900	89	89	89	89
900	925	91	91	91	91
925	950	94	94	94	94
950	975	96	96	96	96
975	1,000	99	99	99	99

1,000

At least	But less than	Single	Married filing jointly *	Married filing sepa-rately	Head of a house-hold
1,000	1,025	101	101	101	101
1,025	1,050	104	104	104	104
1,050	1,075	106	106	106	106
1,075	1,100	109	109	109	109
1,100	1,125	111	111	111	111
1,125	1,150	114	114	114	114
1,150	1,175	116	116	116	116
1,175	1,200	119	119	119	119
1,200	1,225	121	121	121	121
1,225	1,250	124	124	124	124
1,250	1,275	126	126	126	126
1,275	1,300	129	129	129	129

If line 40 (taxable income) is— At least	But less than	Single	Married filing jointly *	Married filing sepa-rately	Head of a house-hold
			Your tax is—		
1,300	1,325	131	131	131	131
1,325	1,350	134	134	134	134
1,350	1,375	136	136	136	136
1,375	1,400	139	139	139	139
1,400	1,425	141	141	141	141
1,425	1,450	144	144	144	144
1,450	1,475	146	146	146	146
1,475	1,500	149	149	149	149
1,500	1,525	151	151	151	151
1,525	1,550	154	154	154	154
1,550	1,575	156	156	156	156
1,575	1,600	159	159	159	159
1,600	1,625	161	161	161	161
1,625	1,650	164	164	164	164
1,650	1,675	166	166	166	166
1,675	1,700	169	169	169	169
1,700	1,725	171	171	171	171
1,725	1,750	174	174	174	174
1,750	1,775	176	176	176	176
1,775	1,800	179	179	179	179
1,800	1,825	181	181	181	181
1,825	1,850	184	184	184	184
1,850	1,875	186	186	186	186
1,875	1,900	189	189	189	189
1,900	1,925	191	191	191	191
1,925	1,950	194	194	194	194
1,950	1,975	196	196	196	196
1,975	2,000	199	199	199	199

2,000

At least	But less than	Single	Married filing jointly *	Married filing sepa-rately	Head of a house-hold
2,000	2,025	201	201	201	201
2,025	2,050	204	204	204	204
2,050	2,075	206	206	206	206
2,075	2,100	209	209	209	209
2,100	2,125	211	211	211	211
2,125	2,150	214	214	214	214
2,150	2,175	216	216	216	216
2,175	2,200	219	219	219	219
2,200	2,225	221	221	221	221
2,225	2,250	224	224	224	224
2,250	2,275	226	226	226	226
2,275	2,300	229	229	229	229
2,300	2,325	231	231	231	231
2,325	2,350	234	234	234	234
2,350	2,375	236	236	236	236
2,375	2,400	239	239	239	239
2,400	2,425	241	241	241	241
2,425	2,450	244	244	244	244
2,450	2,475	246	246	246	246
2,475	2,500	249	249	249	249
2,500	2,525	251	251	251	251
2,525	2,550	254	254	254	254
2,550	2,575	256	256	256	256
2,575	2,600	259	259	259	259
2,600	2,625	261	261	261	261
2,625	2,650	264	264	264	264
2,650	2,675	266	266	266	266
2,675	2,700	269	269	269	269

If line 40 (taxable income) is— At least	But less than	Single	Married filing jointly *	Married filing sepa-rately	Head of a house-hold
			Your tax is—		
2,700	2,725	271	271	271	271
2,725	2,750	274	274	274	274
2,750	2,775	276	276	276	276
2,775	2,800	279	279	279	279
2,800	2,825	281	281	281	281
2,825	2,850	284	284	284	284
2,850	2,875	286	286	286	286
2,875	2,900	289	289	289	289
2,900	2,925	291	291	291	291
2,925	2,950	294	294	294	294
2,950	2,975	296	296	296	296
2,975	3,000	299	299	299	299

3,000

At least	But less than	Single	Married filing jointly *	Married filing sepa-rately	Head of a house-hold
3,000	3,050	303	303	303	303
3,050	3,100	308	308	308	308
3,100	3,150	313	313	313	313
3,150	3,200	318	318	318	318
3,200	3,250	323	323	323	323
3,250	3,300	328	328	328	328
3,300	3,350	333	333	333	333
3,350	3,400	338	338	338	338
3,400	3,450	343	343	343	343
3,450	3,500	348	348	348	348
3,500	3,550	353	353	353	353
3,550	3,600	358	358	358	358
3,600	3,650	363	363	363	363
3,650	3,700	368	368	368	368
3,700	3,750	373	373	373	373
3,750	3,800	378	378	378	378
3,800	3,850	383	383	383	383
3,850	3,900	388	388	388	388
3,900	3,950	393	393	393	393
3,950	4,000	398	398	398	398

4,000

At least	But less than	Single	Married filing jointly *	Married filing sepa-rately	Head of a house-hold
4,000	4,050	403	403	403	403
4,050	4,100	408	408	408	408
4,100	4,150	413	413	413	413
4,150	4,200	418	418	418	418
4,200	4,250	423	423	423	423
4,250	4,300	428	428	428	428
4,300	4,350	433	433	433	433
4,350	4,400	438	438	438	438
4,400	4,450	443	443	443	443
4,450	4,500	448	448	448	448
4,500	4,550	453	453	453	453
4,550	4,600	458	458	458	458
4,600	4,650	463	463	463	463
4,650	4,700	468	468	468	468
4,700	4,750	473	473	473	473
4,750	4,800	478	478	478	478
4,800	4,850	483	483	483	483
4,850	4,900	488	488	488	488
4,900	4,950	493	493	493	493
4,950	5,000	498	498	498	498

(Continued on page 63)

* This column must also be used by a qualifying widow(er).

5,000

If line 40 (taxable income) is—		And you are—			
At least	But less than	Single	Married filing jointly *	Married filing separately	Head of a household
		Your tax is—			
5,000	5,050	503	503	503	503
5,050	5,100	508	508	508	508
5,100	5,150	513	513	513	513
5,150	5,200	518	518	518	518
5,200	5,250	523	523	523	523
5,250	5,300	528	528	528	528
5,300	5,350	533	533	533	533
5,350	5,400	538	538	538	538
5,400	5,450	543	543	543	543
5,450	5,500	548	548	548	548
5,500	5,550	553	553	553	553
5,550	5,600	558	558	558	558
5,600	5,650	563	563	563	563
5,650	5,700	568	568	568	568
5,700	5,750	573	573	573	573
5,750	5,800	578	578	578	578
5,800	5,850	583	583	583	583
5,850	5,900	588	588	588	588
5,900	5,950	593	593	593	593
5,950	6,000	598	598	598	598

6,000

At least	But less than	Single	Married filing jointly *	Married filing separately	Head of a household
6,000	6,050	603	603	603	603
6,050	6,100	608	608	608	608
6,100	6,150	613	613	613	613
6,150	6,200	618	618	618	618
6,200	6,250	623	623	623	623
6,250	6,300	628	628	628	628
6,300	6,350	633	633	633	633
6,350	6,400	638	638	638	638
6,400	6,450	643	643	643	643
6,450	6,500	648	648	648	648
6,500	6,550	653	653	653	653
6,550	6,600	658	658	658	658
6,600	6,650	663	663	663	663
6,650	6,700	668	668	668	668
6,700	6,750	673	673	673	673
6,750	6,800	678	678	678	678
6,800	6,850	683	683	683	683
6,850	6,900	688	688	688	688
6,900	6,950	693	693	693	693
6,950	7,000	698	698	698	698

7,000

At least	But less than	Single	Married filing jointly *	Married filing separately	Head of a household
7,000	7,050	704	703	704	703
7,050	7,100	711	708	711	708
7,100	7,150	719	713	719	713
7,150	7,200	726	718	726	718
7,200	7,250	734	723	734	723
7,250	7,300	741	728	741	728
7,300	7,350	749	733	749	733
7,350	7,400	756	738	756	738
7,400	7,450	764	743	764	743
7,450	7,500	771	748	771	748
7,500	7,550	779	753	779	753
7,550	7,600	786	758	786	758
7,600	7,650	794	763	794	763
7,650	7,700	801	768	801	768
7,700	7,750	809	773	809	773
7,750	7,800	816	778	816	778
7,800	7,850	824	783	824	783
7,850	7,900	831	788	831	788
7,900	7,960	839	793	839	793
7,950	8,000	846	798	846	798

8,000

At least	But less than	Single	Married filing jointly *	Married filing separately	Head of a household
8,000	8,050	854	803	854	803
8,050	8,100	861	808	861	808
8,100	8,150	869	813	869	813
8,150	8,200	876	818	876	818
8,200	8,250	884	823	884	823
8,250	8,300	891	828	891	828
8,300	8,350	899	833	899	833
8,350	8,400	906	838	906	838
8,400	8,450	914	843	914	843
8,450	8,500	921	848	921	848
8,500	8,550	929	853	929	853
8,550	8,600	936	858	936	858
8,600	8,650	944	863	944	863
8,650	8,700	951	868	951	868
8,700	8,750	959	873	959	873
8,750	8,800	966	878	966	878
8,800	8,850	974	883	974	883
8,850	8,900	981	888	981	888
8,900	8,950	989	893	989	893
8,950	9,000	996	898	996	898

9,000

At least	But less than	Single	Married filing jointly *	Married filing separately	Head of a household
9,000	9,050	1,004	903	1,004	903
9,050	9,100	1,011	908	1,011	908
9,100	9,150	1,019	913	1,019	913
9,150	9,200	1,026	918	1,026	918
9,200	9,250	1,034	923	1,034	923
9,250	9,300	1,041	928	1,041	928
9,300	9,350	1,049	933	1,049	933
9,350	9,400	1,056	938	1,056	938
9,400	9,450	1,064	943	1,064	943
9,450	9,500	1,071	948	1,071	948
9,500	9,550	1,079	953	1,079	953
9,550	9,600	1,086	958	1,086	958
9,600	9,650	1,094	963	1,094	963
9,650	9,700	1,101	968	1,101	968
9,700	9,750	1,109	973	1,109	973
9,750	9,800	1,116	978	1,116	978
9,800	9,850	1,124	983	1,124	983
9,850	9,900	1,131	988	1,131	988
9,900	9,950	1,139	993	1,139	993
9,950	10,000	1,146	998	1,146	998

10,000

At least	But less than	Single	Married filing jointly *	Married filing separately	Head of a household
10,000	10,050	1,154	1,003	1,154	1,004
10,050	10,100	1,161	1,008	1,161	1,011
10,100	10,150	1,169	1,013	1,169	1,019
10,150	10,200	1,176	1,018	1,176	1,026
10,200	10,250	1,184	1,023	1,184	1,034
10,250	10,300	1,191	1,028	1,191	1,041
10,300	10,350	1,199	1,033	1,199	1,049
10,350	10,400	1,206	1,038	1,206	1,056
10,400	10,450	1,214	1,043	1,214	1,064
10,450	10,500	1,221	1,048	1,221	1,071
10,500	10,550	1,229	1,053	1,229	1,079
10,550	10,600	1,236	1,058	1,236	1,086
10,600	10,650	1,244	1,063	1,244	1,094
10,650	10,700	1,251	1,068	1,251	1,101
10,700	10,750	1,259	1,073	1,259	1,109
10,750	10,800	1,266	1,078	1,266	1,116
10,800	10,850	1,274	1,083	1,274	1,124
10,850	10,900	1,281	1,088	1,281	1,131
10,900	10,950	1,289	1,093	1,289	1,139
10,950	11,000	1,296	1,098	1,296	1,146

11,000

At least	But less than	Single	Married filing jointly *	Married filing separately	Head of a household
11,000	11,050	1,304	1,103	1,304	1,154
11,050	11,100	1,311	1,108	1,311	1,161
11,100	11,150	1,319	1,113	1,319	1,169
11,150	11,200	1,326	1,118	1,326	1,176
11,200	11,250	1,334	1,123	1,334	1,184
11,250	11,300	1,341	1,128	1,341	1,191
11,300	11,350	1,349	1,133	1,349	1,199
11,350	11,400	1,356	1,138	1,356	1,206
11,400	11,450	1,364	1,143	1,364	1,214
11,450	11,500	1,371	1,148	1,371	1,221
11,500	11,550	1,379	1,153	1,379	1,229
11,550	11,600	1,386	1,158	1,386	1,236
11,600	11,650	1,394	1,163	1,394	1,244
11,650	11,700	1,401	1,168	1,401	1,251
11,700	11,750	1,409	1,173	1,409	1,259
11,750	11,800	1,416	1,178	1,416	1,266
11,800	11,850	1,424	1,183	1,424	1,274
11,850	11,900	1,431	1,188	1,431	1,281
11,900	11,950	1,439	1,193	1,439	1,289
11,950	12,000	1,446	1,198	1,446	1,296

12,000

At least	But less than	Single	Married filing jointly *	Married filing separately	Head of a household
12,000	12,050	1,454	1,203	1,454	1,304
12,050	12,100	1,461	1,208	1,461	1,311
12,100	12,150	1,469	1,213	1,469	1,319
12,150	12,200	1,476	1,218	1,476	1,326
12,200	12,250	1,484	1,223	1,484	1,334
12,250	12,300	1,491	1,228	1,491	1,341
12,300	12,350	1,499	1,233	1,499	1,349
12,350	12,400	1,506	1,238	1,506	1,356
12,400	12,450	1,514	1,243	1,514	1,364
12,450	12,500	1,521	1,248	1,521	1,371
12,500	12,550	1,529	1,253	1,529	1,379
12,550	12,600	1,536	1,258	1,536	1,386
12,600	12,650	1,544	1,263	1,544	1,394
12,650	12,700	1,551	1,268	1,551	1,401
12,700	12,750	1,559	1,273	1,559	1,409
12,750	12,800	1,566	1,278	1,566	1,416
12,800	12,850	1,574	1,283	1,574	1,424
12,850	12,900	1,581	1,288	1,581	1,431
12,900	12,950	1,589	1,293	1,589	1,439
12,950	13,000	1,596	1,298	1,596	1,446

13,000

At least	But less than	Single	Married filing jointly *	Married filing separately	Head of a household
13,000	13,050	1,604	1,303	1,604	1,454
13,050	13,100	1,611	1,308	1,611	1,461
13,100	13,150	1,619	1,313	1,619	1,469
13,150	13,200	1,626	1,318	1,626	1,476
13,200	13,250	1,634	1,323	1,634	1,484
13,250	13,300	1,641	1,328	1,641	1,491
13,300	13,350	1,649	1,333	1,649	1,499
13,350	13,400	1,656	1,338	1,656	1,506
13,400	13,450	1,664	1,343	1,664	1,514
13,450	13,500	1,671	1,348	1,671	1,521
13,500	13,550	1,679	1,353	1,679	1,529
13,550	13,600	1,686	1,358	1,686	1,536
13,600	13,650	1,694	1,363	1,694	1,544
13,650	13,700	1,701	1,368	1,701	1,551
13,700	13,750	1,709	1,373	1,709	1,559
13,750	13,800	1,716	1,378	1,716	1,566
13,800	13,850	1,724	1,383	1,724	1,574
13,850	13,900	1,731	1,388	1,731	1,581
13,900	13,950	1,739	1,393	1,739	1,589
13,950	14,000	1,746	1,398	1,746	1,596

* This column must also be used by a qualifying widow(er).

(Continued on page 64)

14,000

At least	But less than	Single	Married filing jointly*	Married filing separately	Head of a household
14,000	14,050	1,754	1,404	1,754	1,604
14,050	14,100	1,761	1,411	1,761	1,611
14,100	14,150	1,769	1,419	1,769	1,619
14,150	14,200	1,776	1,426	1,776	1,626
14,200	14,250	1,784	1,434	1,784	1,634
14,250	14,300	1,791	1,441	1,791	1,641
14,300	14,350	1,799	1,449	1,799	1,649
14,350	14,400	1,806	1,456	1,806	1,656
14,400	14,450	1,814	1,464	1,814	1,664
14,450	14,500	1,821	1,471	1,821	1,671
14,500	14,550	1,829	1,479	1,829	1,679
14,550	14,600	1,836	1,486	1,836	1,686
14,600	14,650	1,844	1,494	1,844	1,694
14,650	14,700	1,851	1,501	1,851	1,701
14,700	14,750	1,859	1,509	1,859	1,709
14,750	14,800	1,866	1,516	1,866	1,716
14,800	14,850	1,874	1,524	1,874	1,724
14,850	14,900	1,881	1,531	1,881	1,731
14,900	14,950	1,889	1,539	1,889	1,739
14,950	15,000	1,896	1,546	1,896	1,746

15,000

At least	But less than	Single	Married filing jointly*	Married filing separately	Head of a household
15,000	15,050	1,904	1,554	1,904	1,754
15,050	15,100	1,911	1,561	1,911	1,761
15,100	15,150	1,919	1,569	1,919	1,769
15,150	15,200	1,926	1,576	1,926	1,776
15,200	15,250	1,934	1,584	1,934	1,784
15,250	15,300	1,941	1,591	1,941	1,791
15,300	15,350	1,949	1,599	1,949	1,799
15,350	15,400	1,956	1,606	1,956	1,806
15,400	15,450	1,964	1,614	1,964	1,814
15,450	15,500	1,971	1,621	1,971	1,821
15,500	15,550	1,979	1,629	1,979	1,829
15,550	15,600	1,986	1,636	1,986	1,836
15,600	15,650	1,994	1,644	1,994	1,844
15,650	15,700	2,001	1,651	2,001	1,851
15,700	15,750	2,009	1,659	2,009	1,859
15,750	15,800	2,016	1,666	2,016	1,866
15,800	15,850	2,024	1,674	2,024	1,874
15,850	15,900	2,031	1,681	2,031	1,881
15,900	15,950	2,039	1,689	2,039	1,889
15,950	16,000	2,046	1,696	2,046	1,896

16,000

At least	But less than	Single	Married filing jointly*	Married filing separately	Head of a household
16,000	16,050	2,054	1,704	2,054	1,904
16,050	16,100	2,061	1,711	2,061	1,911
16,100	16,150	2,069	1,719	2,069	1,919
16,150	16,200	2,076	1,726	2,076	1,926
16,200	16,250	2,084	1,734	2,084	1,934
16,250	16,300	2,091	1,741	2,091	1,941
16,300	16,350	2,099	1,749	2,099	1,949
16,350	16,400	2,106	1,756	2,106	1,956
16,400	16,450	2,114	1,764	2,114	1,964
16,450	16,500	2,121	1,771	2,121	1,971
16,500	16,550	2,129	1,779	2,129	1,979
16,550	16,600	2,136	1,786	2,136	1,986
16,600	16,650	2,144	1,794	2,144	1,994
16,650	16,700	2,151	1,801	2,151	2,001
16,700	16,750	2,159	1,809	2,159	2,009
16,750	16,800	2,166	1,816	2,166	2,016
16,800	16,850	2,174	1,824	2,174	2,024
16,850	16,900	2,181	1,831	2,181	2,031
16,900	16,950	2,189	1,839	2,189	2,039
16,950	17,000	2,196	1,846	2,196	2,046

17,000

At least	But less than	Single	Married filing jointly*	Married filing separately	Head of a household
17,000	17,050	2,204	1,854	2,204	2,054
17,050	17,100	2,211	1,861	2,211	2,061
17,100	17,150	2,219	1,869	2,219	2,069
17,150	17,200	2,226	1,876	2,226	2,076
17,200	17,250	2,234	1,884	2,234	2,084
17,250	17,300	2,241	1,891	2,241	2,091
17,300	17,350	2,249	1,899	2,249	2,099
17,350	17,400	2,256	1,906	2,256	2,106
17,400	17,450	2,264	1,914	2,264	2,114
17,450	17,500	2,271	1,921	2,271	2,121
17,500	17,550	2,279	1,929	2,279	2,129
17,550	17,600	2,286	1,936	2,286	2,136
17,600	17,650	2,294	1,944	2,294	2,144
17,650	17,700	2,301	1,951	2,301	2,151
17,700	17,750	2,309	1,959	2,309	2,159
17,750	17,800	2,316	1,966	2,316	2,166
17,800	17,850	2,324	1,974	2,324	2,174
17,850	17,900	2,331	1,981	2,331	2,181
17,900	17,950	2,339	1,989	2,339	2,189
17,950	18,000	2,346	1,996	2,346	2,196

18,000

At least	But less than	Single	Married filing jointly*	Married filing separately	Head of a household
18,000	18,050	2,354	2,004	2,354	2,204
18,050	18,100	2,361	2,011	2,361	2,211
18,100	18,150	2,369	2,019	2,369	2,219
18,150	18,200	2,376	2,026	2,376	2,226
18,200	18,250	2,384	2,034	2,384	2,234
18,250	18,300	2,391	2,041	2,391	2,241
18,300	18,350	2,399	2,049	2,399	2,249
18,350	18,400	2,406	2,056	2,406	2,256
18,400	18,450	2,414	2,064	2,414	2,264
18,450	18,500	2,421	2,071	2,421	2,271
18,500	18,550	2,429	2,079	2,429	2,279
18,550	18,600	2,436	2,086	2,436	2,286
18,600	18,650	2,444	2,094	2,444	2,294
18,650	18,700	2,451	2,101	2,451	2,301
18,700	18,750	2,459	2,109	2,459	2,309
18,750	18,800	2,466	2,116	2,466	2,316
18,800	18,850	2,474	2,124	2,474	2,324
18,850	18,900	2,481	2,131	2,481	2,331
18,900	18,950	2,489	2,139	2,489	2,339
18,950	19,000	2,496	2,146	2,496	2,346

19,000

At least	But less than	Single	Married filing jointly*	Married filing separately	Head of a household
19,000	19,050	2,504	2,154	2,504	2,354
19,050	19,100	2,511	2,161	2,511	2,361
19,100	19,150	2,519	2,169	2,519	2,369
19,150	19,200	2,526	2,176	2,526	2,376
19,200	19,250	2,534	2,184	2,534	2,384
19,250	19,300	2,541	2,191	2,541	2,391
19,300	19,350	2,549	2,199	2,549	2,399
19,350	19,400	2,556	2,206	2,556	2,406
19,400	19,450	2,564	2,214	2,564	2,414
19,450	19,500	2,571	2,221	2,571	2,421
19,500	19,550	2,579	2,229	2,579	2,429
19,550	19,600	2,586	2,236	2,586	2,436
19,600	19,650	2,594	2,244	2,594	2,444
19,650	19,700	2,601	2,251	2,601	2,451
19,700	19,750	2,609	2,259	2,609	2,459
19,750	19,800	2,616	2,266	2,616	2,466
19,800	19,850	2,624	2,274	2,624	2,474
19,850	19,900	2,631	2,281	2,631	2,481
19,900	19,950	2,639	2,289	2,639	2,489
19,950	20,000	2,646	2,296	2,646	2,496

20,000

At least	But less than	Single	Married filing jointly*	Married filing separately	Head of a household
20,000	20,050	2,654	2,304	2,654	2,504
20,050	20,100	2,661	2,311	2,661	2,511
20,100	20,150	2,669	2,319	2,669	2,519
20,150	20,200	2,676	2,326	2,676	2,526
20,200	20,250	2,684	2,334	2,684	2,534
20,250	20,300	2,691	2,341	2,691	2,541
20,300	20,350	2,699	2,349	2,699	2,549
20,350	20,400	2,706	2,356	2,706	2,556
20,400	20,450	2,714	2,364	2,714	2,564
20,450	20,500	2,721	2,371	2,721	2,571
20,500	20,550	2,729	2,379	2,729	2,579
20,550	20,600	2,736	2,386	2,736	2,586
20,600	20,650	2,744	2,394	2,744	2,594
20,650	20,700	2,751	2,401	2,751	2,601
20,700	20,750	2,759	2,409	2,759	2,609
20,750	20,800	2,766	2,416	2,766	2,616
20,800	20,850	2,774	2,424	2,774	2,624
20,850	20,900	2,781	2,431	2,781	2,631
20,900	20,950	2,789	2,439	2,789	2,639
20,950	21,000	2,796	2,446	2,796	2,646

21,000

At least	But less than	Single	Married filing jointly*	Married filing separately	Head of a household
21,000	21,050	2,804	2,454	2,804	2,654
21,050	21,100	2,811	2,461	2,811	2,661
21,100	21,150	2,819	2,469	2,819	2,669
21,150	21,200	2,826	2,476	2,826	2,676
21,200	21,250	2,834	2,484	2,834	2,684
21,250	21,300	2,841	2,491	2,841	2,691
21,300	21,350	2,849	2,499	2,849	2,699
21,350	21,400	2,856	2,506	2,856	2,706
21,400	21,450	2,864	2,514	2,864	2,714
21,450	21,500	2,871	2,521	2,871	2,721
21,500	21,550	2,879	2,529	2,879	2,729
21,550	21,600	2,886	2,536	2,886	2,736
21,600	21,650	2,894	2,544	2,894	2,744
21,650	21,700	2,901	2,551	2,901	2,751
21,700	21,750	2,909	2,559	2,909	2,759
21,750	21,800	2,916	2,566	2,916	2,766
21,800	21,850	2,924	2,574	2,924	2,774
21,850	21,900	2,931	2,581	2,931	2,781
21,900	21,950	2,939	2,589	2,939	2,789
21,950	22,000	2,946	2,596	2,946	2,796

22,000

At least	But less than	Single	Married filing jointly*	Married filing separately	Head of a household
22,000	22,050	2,954	2,604	2,954	2,804
22,050	22,100	2,961	2,611	2,961	2,811
22,100	22,150	2,969	2,619	2,969	2,819
22,150	22,200	2,976	2,626	2,976	2,826
22,200	22,250	2,984	2,634	2,984	2,834
22,250	22,300	2,991	2,641	2,991	2,841
22,300	22,350	2,999	2,649	2,999	2,849
22,350	22,400	3,006	2,656	3,006	2,856
22,400	22,450	3,014	2,664	3,014	2,864
22,450	22,500	3,021	2,671	3,021	2,871
22,500	22,550	3,029	2,679	3,029	2,879
22,550	22,600	3,036	2,686	3,036	2,886
22,600	22,650	3,044	2,694	3,044	2,894
22,650	22,700	3,051	2,701	3,051	2,901
22,700	22,750	3,059	2,709	3,059	2,909
22,750	22,800	3,066	2,716	3,066	2,916
22,800	22,850	3,074	2,724	3,074	2,924
22,850	22,900	3,081	2,731	3,081	2,931
22,900	22,950	3,089	2,739	3,089	2,939
22,950	23,000	3,096	2,746	3,096	2,946

* This column must also be used by a qualifying widow(er).

(Continued on page 65)

23,000

At least	But less than	Single	Married filing jointly *	Married filing separately	Head of a household
23,000	23,050	3,104	2,754	3,104	2,954
23,050	23,100	3,111	2,761	3,111	2,961
23,100	23,150	3,119	2,769	3,119	2,969
23,150	23,200	3,126	2,776	3,126	2,976
23,200	23,250	3,134	2,784	3,134	2,984
23,250	23,300	3,141	2,791	3,141	2,991
23,300	23,350	3,149	2,799	3,149	2,999
23,350	23,400	3,156	2,806	3,156	3,006
23,400	23,450	3,164	2,814	3,164	3,014
23,450	23,500	3,171	2,821	3,171	3,021
23,500	23,550	3,179	2,829	3,179	3,029
23,550	23,600	3,186	2,836	3,186	3,036
23,600	23,650	3,194	2,844	3,194	3,044
23,650	23,700	3,201	2,851	3,201	3,051
23,700	23,750	3,209	2,859	3,209	3,059
23,750	23,800	3,216	2,866	3,216	3,066
23,800	23,850	3,224	2,874	3,224	3,074
23,850	23,900	3,231	2,881	3,231	3,081
23,900	23,950	3,239	2,889	3,239	3,089
23,950	24,000	3,246	2,896	3,246	3,096

24,000

At least	But less than	Single	Married filing jointly *	Married filing separately	Head of a household
24,000	24,050	3,254	2,904	3,254	3,104
24,050	24,100	3,261	2,911	3,261	3,111
24,100	24,150	3,269	2,919	3,269	3,119
24,150	24,200	3,276	2,926	3,276	3,126
24,200	24,250	3,284	2,934	3,284	3,134
24,250	24,300	3,291	2,941	3,291	3,141
24,300	24,350	3,299	2,949	3,299	3,149
24,350	24,400	3,306	2,956	3,306	3,156
24,400	24,450	3,314	2,964	3,314	3,164
24,450	24,500	3,321	2,971	3,321	3,171
24,500	24,550	3,329	2,979	3,329	3,179
24,550	24,600	3,336	2,986	3,336	3,186
24,600	24,650	3,344	2,994	3,344	3,194
24,650	24,700	3,351	3,001	3,351	3,201
24,700	24,750	3,359	3,009	3,359	3,209
24,750	24,800	3,366	3,016	3,366	3,216
24,800	24,850	3,374	3,024	3,374	3,224
24,850	24,900	3,381	3,031	3,381	3,231
24,900	24,950	3,389	3,039	3,389	3,239
24,950	25,000	3,396	3,046	3,396	3,246

25,000

At least	But less than	Single	Married filing jointly *	Married filing separately	Head of a household
25,000	25,050	3,404	3,054	3,404	3,254
25,050	25,100	3,411	3,061	3,411	3,261
25,100	25,150	3,419	3,069	3,419	3,269
25,150	25,200	3,426	3,076	3,426	3,276
25,200	25,250	3,434	3,084	3,434	3,284
25,250	25,300	3,441	3,091	3,441	3,291
25,300	25,350	3,449	3,099	3,449	3,299
25,350	25,400	3,456	3,106	3,456	3,306
25,400	25,450	3,464	3,114	3,464	3,314
25,450	25,500	3,471	3,121	3,471	3,321
25,500	25,550	3,479	3,129	3,479	3,329
25,550	25,600	3,486	3,136	3,486	3,336
25,600	25,650	3,494	3,144	3,494	3,344
25,650	25,700	3,501	3,151	3,501	3,351
25,700	25,750	3,509	3,159	3,509	3,359
25,750	25,800	3,516	3,166	3,516	3,366
25,800	25,850	3,524	3,174	3,524	3,374
25,850	25,900	3,531	3,181	3,531	3,381
25,900	25,950	3,539	3,189	3,539	3,389
25,950	26,000	3,546	3,196	3,546	3,396

26,000

At least	But less than	Single	Married filing jointly *	Married filing separately	Head of a household
26,000	26,050	3,554	3,204	3,554	3,404
26,050	26,100	3,561	3,211	3,561	3,411
26,100	26,150	3,569	3,219	3,569	3,419
26,150	26,200	3,576	3,226	3,576	3,426
26,200	26,250	3,584	3,234	3,584	3,434
26,250	26,300	3,591	3,241	3,591	3,441
26,300	26,350	3,599	3,249	3,599	3,449
26,350	26,400	3,606	3,256	3,606	3,456
26,400	26,450	3,614	3,264	3,614	3,464
26,450	26,500	3,621	3,271	3,621	3,471
26,500	26,550	3,629	3,279	3,629	3,479
26,550	26,600	3,636	3,286	3,636	3,486
26,600	26,650	3,644	3,294	3,644	3,494
26,650	26,700	3,651	3,301	3,651	3,501
26,700	26,750	3,659	3,309	3,659	3,509
26,750	26,800	3,666	3,316	3,666	3,516
26,800	26,850	3,674	3,324	3,674	3,524
26,850	26,900	3,681	3,331	3,681	3,531
26,900	26,950	3,689	3,339	3,689	3,539
26,950	27,000	3,696	3,346	3,696	3,546

27,000

At least	But less than	Single	Married filing jointly *	Married filing separately	Head of a household
27,000	27,050	3,704	3,354	3,704	3,554
27,050	27,100	3,711	3,361	3,711	3,561
27,100	27,150	3,719	3,369	3,719	3,569
27,150	27,200	3,726	3,376	3,726	3,576
27,200	27,250	3,734	3,384	3,734	3,584
27,250	27,300	3,741	3,391	3,741	3,591
27,300	27,350	3,749	3,399	3,749	3,599
27,350	27,400	3,756	3,406	3,756	3,606
27,400	27,450	3,764	3,414	3,764	3,614
27,450	27,500	3,771	3,421	3,771	3,621
27,500	27,550	3,779	3,429	3,779	3,629
27,550	27,600	3,786	3,436	3,786	3,636
27,600	27,650	3,794	3,444	3,794	3,644
27,650	27,700	3,801	3,451	3,801	3,651
27,700	27,750	3,809	3,459	3,809	3,659
27,750	27,800	3,816	3,466	3,816	3,666
27,800	27,850	3,824	3,474	3,824	3,674
27,850	27,900	3,831	3,481	3,831	3,681
27,900	27,950	3,839	3,489	3,839	3,689
27,950	28,000	3,846	3,496	3,846	3,696

28,000

At least	But less than	Single	Married filing jointly *	Married filing separately	Head of a household
28,000	28,050	3,854	3,504	3,854	3,704
28,050	28,100	3,861	3,511	3,861	3,711
28,100	28,150	3,869	3,519	3,869	3,719
28,150	28,200	3,876	3,526	3,876	3,726
28,200	28,250	3,884	3,534	3,884	3,734
28,250	28,300	3,891	3,541	3,891	3,741
28,300	28,350	3,899	3,549	3,899	3,749
28,350	28,400	3,906	3,556	3,906	3,756
28,400	28,450	3,916	3,564	3,916	3,764
28,450	28,500	3,929	3,571	3,929	3,771
28,500	28,550	3,941	3,579	3,941	3,779
28,550	28,600	3,954	3,586	3,954	3,786
28,600	28,650	3,966	3,594	3,966	3,794
28,650	28,700	3,979	3,601	3,979	3,801
28,700	28,750	3,991	3,609	3,991	3,809
28,750	28,800	4,004	3,616	4,004	3,816
28,800	28,850	4,016	3,624	4,016	3,824
28,850	28,900	4,029	3,631	4,029	3,831
28,900	28,950	4,041	3,639	4,041	3,839
28,950	29,000	4,054	3,646	4,054	3,846

29,000

At least	But less than	Single	Married filing jointly *	Married filing separately	Head of a household
29,000	29,050	4,066	3,654	4,066	3,854
29,050	29,100	4,079	3,661	4,079	3,861
29,100	29,150	4,091	3,669	4,091	3,869
29,150	29,200	4,104	3,676	4,104	3,876
29,200	29,250	4,116	3,684	4,116	3,884
29,250	29,300	4,129	3,691	4,129	3,891
29,300	29,350	4,141	3,699	4,141	3,899
29,350	29,400	4,154	3,706	4,154	3,906
29,400	29,450	4,166	3,714	4,166	3,914
29,450	29,500	4,179	3,721	4,179	3,921
29,500	29,550	4,191	3,729	4,191	3,929
29,550	29,600	4,204	3,736	4,204	3,936
29,600	29,650	4,216	3,744	4,216	3,944
29,650	29,700	4,229	3,751	4,229	3,951
29,700	29,750	4,241	3,759	4,241	3,959
29,750	29,800	4,254	3,766	4,254	3,966
29,800	29,850	4,266	3,774	4,266	3,974
29,850	29,900	4,279	3,781	4,279	3,981
29,900	29,950	4,291	3,789	4,291	3,989
29,950	30,000	4,304	3,796	4,304	3,996

30,000

At least	But less than	Single	Married filing jointly *	Married filing separately	Head of a household
30,000	30,050	4,316	3,804	4,316	4,004
30,050	30,100	4,329	3,811	4,329	4,011
30,100	30,150	4,341	3,819	4,341	4,019
30,150	30,200	4,354	3,826	4,354	4,026
30,200	30,250	4,366	3,834	4,366	4,034
30,250	30,300	4,379	3,841	4,379	4,041
30,300	30,350	4,391	3,849	4,391	4,049
30,350	30,400	4,404	3,856	4,404	4,056
30,400	30,450	4,416	3,864	4,416	4,064
30,450	30,500	4,429	3,871	4,429	4,071
30,500	30,550	4,441	3,879	4,441	4,079
30,550	30,600	4,454	3,886	4,454	4,086
30,600	30,650	4,466	3,894	4,466	4,094
30,650	30,700	4,479	3,901	4,479	4,101
30,700	30,750	4,491	3,909	4,491	4,109
30,750	30,800	4,504	3,916	4,504	4,116
30,800	30,850	4,516	3,924	4,516	4,124
30,850	30,900	4,529	3,931	4,529	4,131
30,900	30,950	4,541	3,939	4,541	4,139
30,950	31,000	4,554	3,946	4,554	4,146

31,000

At least	But less than	Single	Married filing jointly *	Married filing separately	Head of a household
31,000	31,050	4,566	3,954	4,566	4,154
31,050	31,100	4,579	3,961	4,579	4,161
31,100	31,150	4,591	3,969	4,591	4,169
31,150	31,200	4,604	3,976	4,604	4,176
31,200	31,250	4,616	3,984	4,616	4,184
31,250	31,300	4,629	3,991	4,629	4,191
31,300	31,350	4,641	3,999	4,641	4,199
31,350	31,400	4,654	4,006	4,654	4,206
31,400	31,450	4,666	4,014	4,666	4,214
31,450	31,500	4,679	4,021	4,679	4,221
31,500	31,550	4,691	4,029	4,691	4,229
31,550	31,600	4,704	4,036	4,704	4,236
31,600	31,650	4,716	4,044	4,716	4,244
31,650	31,700	4,729	4,051	4,729	4,251
31,700	31,750	4,741	4,059	4,741	4,259
31,750	31,800	4,754	4,066	4,754	4,266
31,800	31,850	4,766	4,074	4,766	4,274
31,850	31,900	4,779	4,081	4,779	4,281
31,900	31,950	4,791	4,089	4,791	4,289
31,950	32,000	4,804	4,096	4,804	4,296

* This column must also be used by a qualifying widow(er).

(Continued on page 66)

If line 40 (taxable income) is—		And you are—				If line 40 (taxable income) is—		And you are—				If line 40 (taxable income) is—		And you are—			
At least	But less than	Single	Married filing jointly *	Married filing separately	Head of a household	At least	But less than	Single	Married filing jointly *	Married filing separately	Head of a household	At least	But less than	Single	Married filing jointly *	Married filing separately	Head of a household
		Your tax is—						Your tax is—						Your tax is—			
32,000						**35,000**						**38,000**					
32,000	32,050	4,816	4,104	4,816	4,304	35,000	35,050	5,566	4,554	5,566	4,754	38,000	38,050	6,316	5,004	6,316	5,204
32,050	32,100	4,829	4,111	4,829	4,311	35,050	35,100	5,579	4,561	5,579	4,761	38,050	38,100	6,329	5,011	6,329	5,214
32,100	32,150	4,841	4,119	4,841	4,319	35,100	35,150	5,591	4,569	5,591	4,769	38,100	38,150	6,341	5,019	6,341	5,226
32,150	32,200	4,854	4,126	4,854	4,326	35,150	35,200	5,604	4,576	5,604	4,776	38,150	38,200	6,354	5,026	6,354	5,239
32,200	32,250	4,866	4,134	4,866	4,334	35,200	35,250	5,616	4,584	5,616	4,784	38,200	38,250	6,366	5,034	6,366	5,251
32,250	32,300	4,879	4,141	4,879	4,341	35,250	35,300	5,629	4,591	5,629	4,791	38,250	38,300	6,379	5,041	6,379	5,264
32,300	32,350	4,891	4,149	4,891	4,349	35,300	35,350	5,641	4,599	5,641	4,799	38,300	38,350	6,391	5,049	6,391	5,276
32,350	32,400	4,904	4,156	4,904	4,356	35,350	35,400	5,654	4,606	5,654	4,806	38,350	38,400	6,404	5,056	6,404	5,289
32,400	32,450	4,916	4,164	4,916	4,364	35,400	35,450	5,666	4,614	5,666	4,814	38,400	38,450	6,416	5,064	6,416	5,301
32,450	32,500	4,929	4,171	4,929	4,371	35,450	35,500	5,679	4,621	5,679	4,821	38,450	38,500	6,429	5,071	6,429	5,314
32,500	32,550	4,941	4,179	4,941	4,379	35,500	35,550	5,691	4,629	5,691	4,829	38,500	38,550	6,441	5,079	6,441	5,326
32,550	32,600	4,954	4,186	4,954	4,386	35,550	35,600	5,704	4,636	5,704	4,836	38,550	38,600	6,454	5,086	6,454	5,339
32,600	32,650	4,966	4,194	4,966	4,394	35,600	35,650	5,716	4,644	5,716	4,844	38,600	38,650	6,466	5,094	6,466	5,351
32,650	32,700	4,979	4,201	4,979	4,401	35,650	35,700	5,729	4,651	5,729	4,851	38,650	38,700	6,479	5,101	6,479	5,364
32,700	32,750	4,991	4,209	4,991	4,409	35,700	35,750	5,741	4,659	5,741	4,859	38,700	38,750	6,491	5,109	6,491	5,376
32,750	32,800	5,004	4,216	5,004	4,416	35,750	35,800	5,754	4,666	5,754	4,866	38,750	38,800	6,504	5,116	6,504	5,389
32,800	32,850	5,016	4,224	5,016	4,424	35,800	35,850	5,766	4,674	5,766	4,874	38,800	38,850	6,516	5,124	6,516	5,401
32,850	32,900	5,029	4,231	5,029	4,431	35,850	35,900	5,779	4,681	5,779	4,881	38,850	38,900	6,529	5,131	6,529	5,414
32,900	32,950	5,041	4,239	5,041	4,439	35,900	35,950	5,791	4,689	5,791	4,889	38,900	30,950	6,541	5,139	6,541	5,426
32,950	33,000	5,054	4,246	5,054	4,446	35,950	36,000	5,804	4,696	5,804	4,896	38,950	39,000	6,554	5,146	6,554	5,439
33,000						**36,000**						**39,000**					
33,000	33,050	5,066	4,254	5,066	4,454	36,000	36,050	5,816	4,704	5,816	4,904	39,000	39,050	6,566	5,154	6,566	5,451
33,050	33,100	5,079	4,261	5,079	4,461	36,050	36,100	5,829	4,711	5,829	4,911	39,050	39,100	6,579	5,161	6,579	5,464
33,100	33,150	5,091	4,269	5,091	4,469	36,100	36,150	5,841	4,719	5,841	4,919	39,100	39,150	6,591	5,169	6,591	5,476
33,150	33,200	5,104	4,276	5,104	4,476	36,150	36,200	5,854	4,726	5,854	4,926	39,150	39,200	6,604	5,176	6,604	5,489
33,200	33,250	5,116	4,284	5,116	4,484	36,200	36,250	5,866	4,734	5,866	4,934	39,200	39,250	6,616	5,184	6,616	5,501
33,250	33,300	5,129	4,291	5,129	4,491	36,250	36,300	5,879	4,741	5,879	4,941	39,250	39,300	6,629	5,191	6,629	5,514
33,300	33,350	5,141	4,299	5,141	4,499	36,300	36,350	5,891	4,749	5,891	4,949	39,300	39,350	6,641	5,199	6,641	5,526
33,350	33,400	5,154	4,306	5,154	4,506	36,350	36,400	5,904	4,756	5,904	4,956	39,350	39,400	6,654	5,206	6,654	5,539
33,400	33,450	5,166	4,314	5,166	4,514	36,400	36,450	5,916	4,764	5,916	4,964	39,400	39,450	6,666	5,214	6,666	5,551
33,450	33,500	5,179	4,321	5,179	4,521	36,450	36,500	5,929	4,771	5,929	4,971	39,450	39,500	6,679	5,221	6,679	5,564
33,500	33,550	5,191	4,329	5,191	4,529	36,500	36,550	5,941	4,779	5,941	4,979	39,500	39,550	6,691	5,229	6,691	5,576
33,550	33,600	5,204	4,336	5,204	4,536	36,550	36,600	5,954	4,786	5,954	4,986	39,550	39,600	6,704	5,236	6,704	5,589
33,600	33,650	5,216	4,344	5,216	4,544	36,600	36,650	5,966	4,794	5,966	4,994	39,600	39,650	6,716	5,244	6,716	5,601
33,650	33,700	5,229	4,351	5,229	4,551	36,650	36,700	5,979	4,801	5,979	5,001	39,650	39,700	6,729	5,251	6,729	5,614
33,700	33,750	5,241	4,359	5,241	4,559	36,700	36,750	5,991	4,809	5,991	5,009	39,700	39,750	6,741	5,259	6,741	5,626
33,750	33,800	5,254	4,366	5,254	4,566	36,750	36,800	6,004	4,816	6,004	5,016	39,750	39,800	6,754	5,266	6,754	5,639
33,800	33,850	5,266	4,374	5,266	4,574	36,800	36,850	6,016	4,824	6,016	5,024	39,800	39,850	6,766	5,274	6,766	5,651
33,850	33,900	5,279	4,381	5,279	4,581	36,850	36,900	6,029	4,831	6,029	5,031	39,850	39,900	6,779	5,281	6,779	5,664
33,900	33,950	5,291	4,389	5,291	4,589	36,900	36,950	6,041	4,839	6,041	5,039	39,900	39,950	6,791	5,289	6,791	5,676
33,950	34,000	5,304	4,396	5,304	4,596	36,950	37,000	6,054	4,846	6,054	5,046	39,950	40,000	6,804	5,296	6,804	5,689
34,000						**37,000**						**40,000**					
34,000	34,050	5,316	4,404	5,316	4,604	37,000	37,050	6,066	4,854	6,066	5,054	40,000	40,050	6,816	5,304	6,816	5,701
34,050	34,100	5,329	4,411	5,329	4,611	37,050	37,100	6,079	4,861	6,079	5,061	40,050	40,100	6,829	5,311	6,829	5,714
34,100	34,150	5,341	4,419	5,341	4,619	37,100	37,150	6,091	4,869	6,091	5,069	40,100	40,150	6,841	5,319	6,841	5,726
34,150	34,200	5,354	4,426	5,354	4,626	37,150	37,200	6,104	4,876	6,104	5,076	40,150	40,200	6,854	5,326	6,854	5,739
34,200	34,250	5,366	4,434	5,366	4,634	37,200	37,250	6,116	4,884	6,116	5,084	40,200	40,250	6,866	5,334	6,866	5,751
34,250	34,300	5,379	4,441	5,379	4,641	37,250	37,300	6,129	4,891	6,129	5,091	40,250	40,300	6,879	5,341	6,879	5,764
34,300	34,350	5,391	4,449	5,391	4,649	37,300	37,350	6,141	4,899	6,141	5,099	40,300	40,350	6,891	5,349	6,891	5,776
34,350	34,400	5,404	4,456	5,404	4,656	37,350	37,400	6,154	4,906	6,154	5,106	40,350	40,400	6,904	5,356	6,904	5,789
34,400	34,450	5,416	4,464	5,416	4,664	37,400	37,450	6,166	4,914	6,166	5,114	40,400	40,450	6,916	5,364	6,916	5,801
34,450	34,500	5,429	4,471	5,429	4,671	37,450	37,500	6,179	4,921	6,179	5,121	40,450	40,500	6,929	5,371	6,929	5,814
34,500	34,550	5,441	4,479	5,441	4,679	37,500	37,550	6,191	4,929	6,191	5,129	40,500	40,550	6,941	5,379	6,941	5,826
34,550	34,600	5,454	4,486	5,454	4,686	37,550	37,600	6,204	4,936	6,204	5,136	40,550	40,600	6,954	5,386	6,954	5,839
34,600	34,650	5,466	4,494	5,466	4,694	37,600	37,650	6,216	4,944	6,216	5,144	40,600	40,650	6,966	5,394	6,966	5,851
34,650	34,700	5,479	4,501	5,479	4,701	37,650	37,700	6,229	4,951	6,229	5,151	40,650	40,700	6,979	5,401	6,979	5,864
34,700	34,750	5,491	4,509	5,491	4,709	37,700	37,750	6,241	4,959	6,241	5,159	40,700	40,750	6,991	5,409	6,991	5,876
34,750	34,800	5,504	4,516	5,504	4,716	37,750	37,800	6,254	4,966	6,254	5,166	40,750	40,800	7,004	5,416	7,004	5,889
34,800	34,850	5,516	4,524	5,516	4,724	37,800	37,850	6,266	4,974	6,266	5,174	40,800	40,850	7,016	5,424	7,016	5,901
34,850	34,900	5,529	4,531	5,529	4,731	37,850	37,900	6,279	4,981	6,279	5,181	40,850	40,900	7,029	5,431	7,029	5,914
34,900	34,950	5,541	4,539	5,541	4,739	37,900	37,950	6,291	4,989	6,291	5,189	40,900	40,950	7,041	5,439	7,041	5,926
34,950	35,000	5,554	4,546	5,554	4,746	37,950	38,000	6,304	4,996	6,304	5,196	40,950	41,000	7,054	5,446	7,054	5,939

* This column must also be used by a qualifying widow(er).

(Continued on page 67)

If line 40 (taxable income) is—		And you are—			
At least	But less than	Single	Married filing jointly *	Married filing separately	Head of a house-hold
		Your tax is—			

41,000

At least	But less than	Single	Married filing jointly	Married filing separately	Head of a household
41,000	41,050	7,066	5,454	7,066	5,951
41,050	41,100	7,079	5,461	7,079	5,964
41,100	41,150	7,091	5,469	7,091	5,976
41,150	41,200	7,104	5,476	7,104	5,989
41,200	41,250	7,116	5,484	7,116	6,001
41,250	41,300	7,129	5,491	7,129	6,014
41,300	41,350	7,141	5,499	7,141	6,026
41,350	41,400	7,154	5,506	7,154	6,039
41,400	41,450	7,166	5,514	7,166	6,051
41,450	41,500	7,179	5,521	7,179	6,064
41,500	41,550	7,191	5,529	7,191	6,076
41,550	41,600	7,204	5,536	7,204	6,089
41,600	41,650	7,216	5,544	7,216	6,101
41,650	41,700	7,229	5,551	7,229	6,114
41,700	41,750	7,241	5,559	7,241	6,126
41,750	41,800	7,254	5,566	7,254	6,139
41,800	41,850	7,266	5,574	7,266	6,151
41,850	41,900	7,279	5,581	7,279	6,164
41,900	41,950	7,291	5,589	7,291	6,176
41,950	42,000	7,304	5,596	7,304	6,189

42,000

At least	But less than	Single	Married filing jointly	Married filing separately	Head of a household
42,000	42,050	7,316	5,604	7,316	6,201
42,050	42,100	7,329	5,611	7,329	6,214
42,100	42,150	7,341	5,619	7,341	6,226
42,150	42,200	7,354	5,626	7,354	6,239
42,200	42,250	7,366	5,634	7,366	6,251
42,250	42,300	7,379	5,641	7,379	6,264
42,300	42,350	7,391	5,649	7,391	6,276
42,350	42,400	7,404	5,656	7,404	6,289
42,400	42,450	7,416	5,664	7,416	6,301
42,450	42,500	7,429	5,671	7,429	6,314
42,500	42,550	7,441	5,679	7,441	6,326
42,550	42,600	7,454	5,686	7,454	6,339
42,600	42,650	7,466	5,694	7,466	6,351
42,650	42,700	7,479	5,701	7,479	6,364
42,700	42,750	7,491	5,709	7,491	6,376
42,750	42,800	7,504	5,716	7,504	6,389
42,800	42,850	7,516	5,724	7,516	6,401
42,850	42,900	7,529	5,731	7,529	6,414
42,900	42,950	7,541	5,739	7,541	6,426
42,950	43,000	7,554	5,746	7,554	6,439

43,000

At least	But less than	Single	Married filing jointly	Married filing separately	Head of a household
43,000	43,050	7,566	5,754	7,566	6,451
43,050	43,100	7,579	5,761	7,579	6,464
43,100	43,150	7,591	5,769	7,591	6,476
43,150	43,200	7,604	5,776	7,604	6,489
43,200	43,250	7,616	5,784	7,616	6,501
43,250	43,300	7,629	5,791	7,629	6,514
43,300	43,350	7,641	5,799	7,641	6,526
43,350	43,400	7,654	5,806	7,654	6,539
43,400	43,450	7,666	5,814	7,666	6,551
43,450	43,500	7,679	5,821	7,679	6,564
43,500	43,550	7,691	5,829	7,691	6,576
43,550	43,600	7,704	5,836	7,704	6,589
43,600	43,650	7,716	5,844	7,716	6,601
43,650	43,700	7,729	5,851	7,729	6,614
43,700	43,750	7,741	5,859	7,741	6,626
43,750	43,800	7,754	5,866	7,754	6,639
43,800	43,850	7,766	5,874	7,766	6,651
43,850	43,900	7,779	5,881	7,779	6,664
43,900	43,950	7,791	5,889	7,791	6,676
43,950	44,000	7,804	5,896	7,804	6,689

44,000

At least	But less than	Single	Married filing jointly	Married filing separately	Head of a household
44,000	44,050	7,816	5,904	7,816	6,701
44,050	44,100	7,829	5,911	7,829	6,714
44,100	44,150	7,841	5,919	7,841	6,726
44,150	44,200	7,854	5,926	7,854	6,739
44,200	44,250	7,866	5,934	7,866	6,751
44,250	44,300	7,879	5,941	7,879	6,764
44,300	44,350	7,891	5,949	7,891	6,776
44,350	44,400	7,904	5,956	7,904	6,789
44,400	44,450	7,916	5,964	7,916	6,801
44,450	44,500	7,929	5,971	7,929	6,814
44,500	44,550	7,941	5,979	7,941	6,826
44,550	44,600	7,954	5,986	7,954	6,839
44,600	44,650	7,966	5,994	7,966	6,851
44,650	44,700	7,979	6,001	7,979	6,864
44,700	44,750	7,991	6,009	7,991	6,876
44,750	44,800	8,004	6,016	8,004	6,889
44,800	44,850	8,016	6,024	8,016	6,901
44,850	44,900	8,029	6,031	8,029	6,914
44,900	44,950	8,041	6,039	8,041	6,926
44,950	45,000	8,054	6,046	8,054	6,939

45,000

At least	But less than	Single	Married filing jointly	Married filing separately	Head of a household
45,000	45,050	8,066	6,054	8,066	6,951
45,050	45,100	8,079	6,061	8,079	6,964
45,100	45,150	8,091	6,069	8,091	6,976
45,150	45,200	8,104	6,076	8,104	6,989
45,200	45,250	8,116	6,084	8,116	7,001
45,250	45,300	8,129	6,091	8,129	7,014
45,300	45,350	8,141	6,099	8,141	7,026
45,350	45,400	8,154	6,106	8,154	7,039
45,400	45,450	8,166	6,114	8,166	7,051
45,450	45,500	8,179	6,121	8,179	7,064
45,500	45,550	8,191	6,129	8,191	7,076
45,550	45,600	8,204	6,136	8,204	7,089
45,600	45,650	8,216	6,144	8,216	7,101
45,650	45,700	8,229	6,151	8,229	7,114
45,700	45,750	8,241	6,159	8,241	7,126
45,750	45,800	8,254	6,166	8,254	7,139
45,800	45,850	8,266	6,174	8,266	7,151
45,850	45,900	8,279	6,181	8,279	7,164
45,900	45,950	8,291	6,189	8,291	7,176
45,950	46,000	8,304	6,196	8,304	7,189

46,000

At least	But less than	Single	Married filing jointly	Married filing separately	Head of a household
46,000	46,050	8,316	6,204	8,316	7,201
46,050	46,100	8,329	6,211	8,329	7,214
46,100	46,150	8,341	6,219	8,341	7,226
46,150	46,200	8,354	6,226	8,354	7,239
46,200	46,250	8,366	6,234	8,366	7,251
46,250	46,300	8,379	6,241	8,379	7,264
46,300	46,350	8,391	6,249	8,391	7,276
46,350	46,400	8,404	6,256	8,404	7,289
46,400	46,450	8,416	6,264	8,416	7,301
46,450	46,500	8,429	6,271	8,429	7,314
46,500	46,550	8,441	6,279	8,441	7,326
46,550	46,600	8,454	6,286	8,454	7,339
46,600	46,650	8,466	6,294	8,466	7,351
46,650	46,700	8,479	6,301	8,479	7,364
46,700	46,750	8,491	6,309	8,491	7,376
46,750	46,800	8,504	6,316	8,504	7,389
46,800	46,850	8,516	6,324	8,516	7,401
46,850	46,900	8,529	6,331	8,529	7,414
46,900	46,950	8,541	6,339	8,541	7,426
46,950	47,000	8,554	6,346	8,554	7,439

47,000

At least	But less than	Single	Married filing jointly	Married filing separately	Head of a household
47,000	47,050	8,566	6,354	8,566	7,451
47,050	47,100	8,579	6,361	8,579	7,464
47,100	47,150	8,591	6,369	8,591	7,476
47,150	47,200	8,604	6,376	8,604	7,489
47,200	47,250	8,616	6,384	8,616	7,501
47,250	47,300	8,629	6,391	8,629	7,514
47,300	47,350	8,641	6,399	8,641	7,526
47,350	47,400	8,654	6,406	8,654	7,539
47,400	47,450	8,666	6,414	8,666	7,551
47,450	47,500	8,679	6,421	8,679	7,564
47,500	47,550	8,691	6,429	8,691	7,576
47,550	47,600	8,704	6,436	8,704	7,589
47,600	47,650	8,716	6,444	8,716	7,601
47,650	47,700	8,729	6,451	8,729	7,614
47,700	47,750	8,741	6,459	8,741	7,626
47,750	47,800	8,754	6,466	8,754	7,639
47,800	47,850	8,766	6,474	8,766	7,651
47,850	47,900	8,779	6,481	8,779	7,664
47,900	47,950	8,791	6,489	8,791	7,676
47,950	48,000	8,804	6,496	8,804	7,689

48,000

At least	But less than	Single	Married filing jointly	Married filing separately	Head of a household
48,000	48,050	8,816	6,504	8,816	7,701
48,050	48,100	8,829	6,511	8,829	7,714
48,100	48,150	8,841	6,519	8,841	7,726
48,150	48,200	8,854	6,526	8,854	7,739
48,200	48,250	8,866	6,534	8,866	7,751
48,250	48,300	8,879	6,541	8,879	7,764
48,300	48,350	8,891	6,549	8,891	7,776
48,350	48,400	8,904	6,556	8,904	7,789
48,400	48,450	8,916	6,564	8,916	7,801
48,450	48,500	8,929	6,571	8,929	7,814
48,500	48,550	8,941	6,579	8,941	7,826
48,550	48,600	8,954	6,586	8,954	7,839
48,600	48,650	8,966	6,594	8,966	7,851
48,650	48,700	8,979	6,601	8,979	7,864
48,700	48,750	8,991	6,609	8,991	7,876
48,750	48,800	9,004	6,616	9,004	7,889
48,800	48,850	9,016	6,624	9,016	7,901
48,850	48,900	9,029	6,631	9,029	7,914
48,900	48,950	9,041	6,639	9,041	7,926
48,950	49,000	9,054	6,646	9,054	7,939

49,000

At least	But less than	Single	Married filing jointly	Married filing separately	Head of a household
49,000	49,050	9,066	6,654	9,066	7,951
49,050	49,100	9,079	6,661	9,079	7,964
49,100	49,150	9,091	6,669	9,091	7,976
49,150	49,200	9,104	6,676	9,104	7,989
49,200	49,250	9,116	6,684	9,116	8,001
49,250	49,300	9,129	6,691	9,129	8,014
49,300	49,350	9,141	6,699	9,141	8,026
49,350	49,400	9,154	6,706	9,154	8,039
49,400	49,450	9,166	6,714	9,166	8,051
49,450	49,500	9,179	6,721	9,179	8,064
49,500	49,550	9,191	6,729	9,191	8,076
49,550	49,600	9,204	6,736	9,204	8,089
49,600	49,650	9,216	6,744	9,216	8,101
49,650	49,700	9,229	6,751	9,229	8,114
49,700	49,750	9,241	6,759	9,241	8,126
49,750	49,800	9,254	6,766	9,254	8,139
49,800	49,850	9,266	6,774	9,266	8,151
49,850	49,900	9,279	6,781	9,279	8,164
49,900	49,950	9,291	6,789	9,291	8,176
49,950	50,000	9,304	6,796	9,304	8,189

* This column must also be used by a qualifying widow(er).

(Continued on page 68)

50,000

At least	But less than	Single	Married filing jointly *	Married filing separately	Head of a household
50,000	50,050	9,316	6,804	9,316	8,201
50,050	50,100	9,329	6,811	9,329	8,214
50,100	50,150	9,341	6,819	9,341	8,226
50,150	50,200	9,354	6,826	9,354	8,239
50,200	50,250	9,366	6,834	9,366	8,251
50,250	50,300	9,379	6,841	9,379	8,264
50,300	50,350	9,391	6,849	9,391	8,276
50,350	50,400	9,404	6,856	9,404	8,289
50,400	50,450	9,416	6,864	9,416	8,301
50,450	50,500	9,429	6,871	9,429	8,314
50,500	50,550	9,441	6,879	9,441	8,326
50,550	50,600	9,454	6,886	9,454	8,339
50,600	50,650	9,466	6,894	9,466	8,351
50,650	50,700	9,479	6,901	9,479	8,364
50,700	50,750	9,491	6,909	9,491	8,376
50,750	50,800	9,504	6,916	9,504	8,389
50,800	50,850	9,516	6,924	9,516	8,401
50,850	50,900	9,529	6,931	9,529	8,414
50,900	50,950	9,541	6,939	9,541	8,426
50,950	51,000	9,554	6,946	9,554	8,439

51,000

At least	But less than	Single	Married filing jointly *	Married filing separately	Head of a household
51,000	51,050	9,566	6,954	9,566	8,451
51,050	51,100	9,579	6,961	9,579	8,464
51,100	51,150	9,591	6,969	9,591	8,476
51,150	51,200	9,604	6,976	9,604	8,489
51,200	51,250	9,616	6,984	9,616	8,501
51,250	51,300	9,629	6,991	9,629	8,514
51,300	51,350	9,641	6,999	9,641	8,526
51,350	51,400	9,654	7,006	9,654	8,539
51,400	51,450	9,666	7,014	9,666	8,551
51,450	51,500	9,679	7,021	9,679	8,564
51,500	51,550	9,691	7,029	9,691	8,576
51,550	51,600	9,704	7,036	9,704	8,589
51,600	51,650	9,716	7,044	9,716	8,601
51,650	51,700	9,729	7,051	9,729	8,614
51,700	51,750	9,741	7,059	9,741	8,626
51,750	51,800	9,754	7,066	9,754	8,639
51,800	51,850	9,766	7,074	9,766	8,651
51,850	51,900	9,779	7,081	9,779	8,664
51,900	51,950	9,791	7,089	9,791	8,676
51,950	52,000	9,804	7,096	9,804	8,689

52,000

At least	But less than	Single	Married filing jointly *	Married filing separately	Head of a household
52,000	52,050	9,816	7,104	9,816	8,701
52,050	52,100	9,829	7,111	9,829	8,714
52,100	52,150	9,841	7,119	9,841	8,726
52,150	52,200	9,854	7,126	9,854	8,739
52,200	52,250	9,866	7,134	9,866	8,751
52,250	52,300	9,879	7,141	9,879	8,764
52,300	52,350	9,891	7,149	9,891	8,776
52,350	52,400	9,904	7,156	9,904	8,789
52,400	52,450	9,916	7,164	9,916	8,801
52,450	52,500	9,929	7,171	9,929	8,814
52,500	52,550	9,941	7,179	9,941	8,826
52,550	52,600	9,954	7,186	9,954	8,839
52,600	52,650	9,966	7,194	9,966	8,851
52,650	52,700	9,979	7,201	9,979	8,864
52,700	52,750	9,991	7,209	9,991	8,876
52,750	52,800	10,004	7,216	10,004	8,889
52,800	52,850	10,016	7,224	10,016	8,901
52,850	52,900	10,029	7,231	10,029	8,914
52,900	52,950	10,041	7,239	10,041	8,926
52,950	53,000	10,054	7,246	10,054	8,939

53,000

At least	But less than	Single	Married filing jointly *	Married filing separately	Head of a household
53,000	53,050	10,066	7,254	10,066	8,951
53,050	53,100	10,079	7,261	10,079	8,964
53,100	53,150	10,091	7,269	10,091	8,976
53,150	53,200	10,104	7,276	10,104	8,989
53,200	53,250	10,116	7,284	10,116	9,001
53,250	53,300	10,129	7,291	10,129	9,014
53,300	53,350	10,141	7,299	10,141	9,026
53,350	53,400	10,154	7,306	10,154	9,039
53,400	53,450	10,166	7,314	10,166	9,051
53,450	53,500	10,179	7,321	10,179	9,064
53,500	53,550	10,191	7,329	10,191	9,076
53,550	53,600	10,204	7,336	10,204	9,089
53,600	53,650	10,216	7,344	10,216	9,101
53,650	53,700	10,229	7,351	10,229	9,114
53,700	53,750	10,241	7,359	10,241	9,126
53,750	53,800	10,254	7,366	10,254	9,139
53,800	53,850	10,266	7,374	10,266	9,151
53,850	53,900	10,279	7,381	10,279	9,164
53,900	53,950	10,291	7,389	10,291	9,176
53,950	54,000	10,304	7,396	10,304	9,189

54,000

At least	But less than	Single	Married filing jointly *	Married filing separately	Head of a household
54,000	54,050	10,316	7,404	10,316	9,201
54,050	54,100	10,329	7,411	10,329	9,214
54,100	54,150	10,341	7,419	10,341	9,226
54,150	54,200	10,354	7,426	10,354	9,239
54,200	54,250	10,366	7,434	10,366	9,251
54,250	54,300	10,379	7,441	10,379	9,264
54,300	54,350	10,391	7,449	10,391	9,276
54,350	54,400	10,404	7,456	10,404	9,289
54,400	54,450	10,416	7,464	10,416	9,301
54,450	54,500	10,429	7,471	10,429	9,314
54,500	54,550	10,441	7,479	10,441	9,326
54,550	54,600	10,454	7,486	10,454	9,339
54,600	54,650	10,466	7,494	10,466	9,351
54,650	54,700	10,479	7,501	10,479	9,364
54,700	54,750	10,491	7,509	10,491	9,376
54,750	54,800	10,504	7,516	10,504	9,389
54,800	54,850	10,516	7,524	10,516	9,401
54,850	54,900	10,529	7,531	10,529	9,414
54,900	54,950	10,541	7,539	10,541	9,426
54,950	55,000	10,554	7,546	10,554	9,439

55,000

At least	But less than	Single	Married filing jointly *	Married filing separately	Head of a household
55,000	55,050	10,566	7,554	10,566	9,451
55,050	55,100	10,579	7,561	10,579	9,464
55,100	55,150	10,591	7,569	10,591	9,476
55,150	55,200	10,604	7,576	10,604	9,489
55,200	55,250	10,616	7,584	10,616	9,501
55,250	55,300	10,629	7,591	10,629	9,514
55,300	55,350	10,641	7,599	10,641	9,526
55,350	55,400	10,654	7,606	10,654	9,539
55,400	55,450	10,666	7,614	10,666	9,551
55,450	55,500	10,679	7,621	10,679	9,564
55,500	55,550	10,691	7,629	10,691	9,576
55,550	55,600	10,704	7,636	10,704	9,589
55,600	55,650	10,716	7,644	10,716	9,601
55,650	55,700	10,729	7,651	10,729	9,614
55,700	55,750	10,741	7,659	10,741	9,626
55,750	55,800	10,754	7,666	10,754	9,639
55,800	55,850	10,766	7,674	10,766	9,651
55,850	55,900	10,779	7,681	10,779	9,664
55,900	55,950	10,791	7,689	10,791	9,676
55,950	56,000	10,804	7,696	10,804	9,689

56,000

At least	But less than	Single	Married filing jointly *	Married filing separately	Head of a household
56,000	56,050	10,816	7,704	10,816	9,701
56,050	56,100	10,829	7,711	10,829	9,714
56,100	56,150	10,841	7,719	10,841	9,726
56,150	56,200	10,854	7,726	10,854	9,739
56,200	56,250	10,866	7,734	10,866	9,751
56,250	56,300	10,879	7,741	10,879	9,764
56,300	56,350	10,891	7,749	10,891	9,776
56,350	56,400	10,904	7,756	10,904	9,789
56,400	56,450	10,916	7,764	10,916	9,801
56,450	56,500	10,929	7,771	10,929	9,814
56,500	56,550	10,941	7,779	10,941	9,826
56,550	56,600	10,954	7,786	10,954	9,839
56,600	56,650	10,966	7,794	10,966	9,851
56,650	56,700	10,979	7,801	10,979	9,864
56,700	56,750	10,991	7,809	10,991	9,876
56,750	56,800	11,004	7,816	11,004	9,889
56,800	56,850	11,016	7,826	11,016	9,901
56,850	56,900	11,029	7,839	11,029	9,914
56,900	56,950	11,041	7,851	11,041	9,926
56,950	57,000	11,054	7,864	11,054	9,939

57,000

At least	But less than	Single	Married filing jointly *	Married filing separately	Head of a household
57,000	57,050	11,066	7,876	11,066	9,951
57,050	57,100	11,079	7,889	11,079	9,964
57,100	57,150	11,091	7,901	11,091	9,976
57,150	57,200	11,104	7,914	11,104	9,989
57,200	57,250	11,116	7,926	11,116	10,001
57,250	57,300	11,129	7,939	11,129	10,014
57,300	57,350	11,141	7,951	11,141	10,026
57,350	57,400	11,154	7,964	11,155	10,039
57,400	57,450	11,166	7,976	11,169	10,051
57,450	57,500	11,179	7,989	11,183	10,064
57,500	57,550	11,191	8,001	11,197	10,076
57,550	57,600	11,204	8,014	11,211	10,089
57,600	57,650	11,216	8,026	11,225	10,101
57,650	57,700	11,229	8,039	11,239	10,114
57,700	57,750	11,241	8,051	11,253	10,126
57,750	57,800	11,254	8,064	11,267	10,139
57,800	57,850	11,266	8,076	11,281	10,151
57,850	57,900	11,279	8,089	11,295	10,164
57,900	57,950	11,291	8,101	11,309	10,176
57,950	58,000	11,304	8,114	11,323	10,189

58,000

At least	But less than	Single	Married filing jointly *	Married filing separately	Head of a household
58,000	58,050	11,316	8,126	11,337	10,201
58,050	58,100	11,329	8,139	11,351	10,214
58,100	58,150	11,341	8,151	11,365	10,226
58,150	58,200	11,354	8,164	11,379	10,239
58,200	58,250	11,366	8,176	11,393	10,251
58,250	58,300	11,379	8,189	11,407	10,264
58,300	58,350	11,391	8,201	11,421	10,276
58,350	58,400	11,404	8,214	11,435	10,289
58,400	58,450	11,416	8,226	11,449	10,301
58,450	58,500	11,429	8,239	11,463	10,314
58,500	58,550	11,441	8,251	11,477	10,326
58,550	58,600	11,454	8,264	11,491	10,339
58,600	58,650	11,466	8,276	11,505	10,351
58,650	58,700	11,479	8,289	11,519	10,364
58,700	58,750	11,491	8,301	11,533	10,376
58,750	58,800	11,504	8,314	11,547	10,389
58,800	58,850	11,516	8,326	11,561	10,401
58,850	58,900	11,529	8,339	11,575	10,414
58,900	58,950	11,541	8,351	11,589	10,426
58,950	59,000	11,554	8,364	11,603	10,439

* This column must also be used by a qualifying widow(er).

(Continued on page 69)

59,000

If line 40 (taxable income) is— At least	But less than	Single	Married filing jointly *	Married filing separately	Head of a household
59,000	59,050	11,566	8,376	11,617	10,451
59,050	59,100	11,579	8,389	11,631	10,464
59,100	59,150	11,591	8,401	11,645	10,476
59,150	59,200	11,604	8,414	11,659	10,489
59,200	59,250	11,616	8,426	11,673	10,501
59,250	59,300	11,629	8,439	11,687	10,514
59,300	59,350	11,641	8,451	11,701	10,526
59,350	59,400	11,654	8,464	11,715	10,539
59,400	59,450	11,666	8,476	11,729	10,551
59,450	59,500	11,679	8,489	11,743	10,564
59,500	59,550	11,691	8,501	11,757	10,576
59,550	59,600	11,704	8,514	11,771	10,589
59,600	59,650	11,716	8,526	11,785	10,601
59,650	59,700	11,729	8,539	11,799	10,614
59,700	59,750	11,741	8,551	11,813	10,626
59,750	59,800	11,754	8,564	11,827	10,639
59,800	59,850	11,766	8,576	11,841	10,651
59,850	59,900	11,779	8,589	11,855	10,664
59,900	59,950	11,791	8,601	11,869	10,676
59,950	60,000	11,804	8,614	11,883	10,689

60,000

At least	But less than	Single	Married filing jointly *	Married filing separately	Head of a household
60,000	60,050	11,816	8,626	11,897	10,701
60,050	60,100	11,829	8,639	11,911	10,714
60,100	60,150	11,841	8,651	11,925	10,726
60,150	60,200	11,854	8,664	11,939	10,739
60,200	60,250	11,866	8,676	11,953	10,751
60,250	60,300	11,879	8,689	11,967	10,764
60,300	60,350	11,891	8,701	11,981	10,776
60,350	60,400	11,904	8,714	11,995	10,789
60,400	60,450	11,916	8,726	12,009	10,801
60,450	60,500	11,929	8,739	12,023	10,814
60,500	60,550	11,941	8,751	12,037	10,826
60,550	60,600	11,954	8,764	12,051	10,839
60,600	60,650	11,966	8,776	12,065	10,851
60,650	60,700	11,979	8,789	12,079	10,864
60,700	60,750	11,991	8,801	12,093	10,876
60,750	60,800	12,004	8,814	12,107	10,889
60,800	60,850	12,016	8,826	12,121	10,901
60,850	60,900	12,029	8,839	12,135	10,914
60,900	60,950	12,041	8,851	12,149	10,926
60,950	61,000	12,054	8,864	12,163	10,939

61,000

At least	But less than	Single	Married filing jointly *	Married filing separately	Head of a household
61,000	61,050	12,066	8,876	12,177	10,951
61,050	61,100	12,079	8,889	12,191	10,964
61,100	61,150	12,091	8,901	12,205	10,976
61,150	61,200	12,104	8,914	12,219	10,989
61,200	61,250	12,116	8,926	12,233	11,001
61,250	61,300	12,129	8,939	12,247	11,014
61,300	61,350	12,141	8,951	12,261	11,026
61,350	61,400	12,154	8,964	12,275	11,039
61,400	61,450	12,166	8,976	12,289	11,051
61,450	61,500	12,179	8,989	12,303	11,064
61,500	61,550	12,191	9,001	12,317	11,076
61,550	61,600	12,204	9,014	12,331	11,089
61,600	61,650	12,216	9,026	12,345	11,101
61,650	61,700	12,229	9,039	12,359	11,114
61,700	61,750	12,241	9,051	12,373	11,126
61,750	61,800	12,254	9,064	12,387	11,139
61,800	61,850	12,266	9,076	12,401	11,151
61,850	61,900	12,279	9,089	12,415	11,164
61,900	61,950	12,291	9,101	12,429	11,176
61,950	62,000	12,304	9,114	12,443	11,189

62,000

At least	But less than	Single	Married filing jointly *	Married filing separately	Head of a household
62,000	62,050	12,316	9,126	12,457	11,201
62,050	62,100	12,329	9,139	12,471	11,214
62,100	62,150	12,341	9,151	12,485	11,226
62,150	62,200	12,354	9,164	12,499	11,239
62,200	62,250	12,366	9,176	12,513	11,251
62,250	62,300	12,379	9,189	12,527	11,264
62,300	62,350	12,391	9,201	12,541	11,276
62,350	62,400	12,404	9,214	12,555	11,289
62,400	62,450	12,416	9,226	12,569	11,301
62,450	62,500	12,429	9,239	12,583	11,314
62,500	62,550	12,441	9,251	12,597	11,326
62,550	62,600	12,454	9,264	12,611	11,339
62,600	62,650	12,466	9,276	12,625	11,351
62,650	62,700	12,479	9,289	12,639	11,364
62,700	62,750	12,491	9,301	12,653	11,376
62,750	62,800	12,504	9,314	12,667	11,389
62,800	62,850	12,516	9,326	12,681	11,401
62,850	62,900	12,529	9,339	12,695	11,414
62,900	62,950	12,541	9,351	12,709	11,426
62,950	63,000	12,554	9,364	12,723	11,439

63,000

At least	But less than	Single	Married filing jointly *	Married filing separately	Head of a household
63,000	63,050	12,566	9,376	12,737	11,451
63,050	63,100	12,579	9,389	12,751	11,464
63,100	63,150	12,591	9,401	12,765	11,476
63,150	63,200	12,604	9,414	12,779	11,489
63,200	63,250	12,616	9,426	12,793	11,501
63,250	63,300	12,629	9,439	12,807	11,514
63,300	63,350	12,641	9,451	12,821	11,526
63,350	63,400	12,654	9,464	12,835	11,539
63,400	63,450	12,666	9,476	12,849	11,551
63,450	63,500	12,679	9,489	12,863	11,564
63,500	63,550	12,691	9,501	12,877	11,576
63,550	63,600	12,704	9,514	12,891	11,589
63,600	63,650	12,716	9,526	12,905	11,601
63,650	63,700	12,729	9,539	12,919	11,614
63,700	63,750	12,741	9,551	12,933	11,626
63,750	63,800	12,754	9,564	12,947	11,639
63,800	63,850	12,766	9,576	12,961	11,651
63,850	63,900	12,779	9,589	12,975	11,664
63,900	63,950	12,791	9,601	12,989	11,676
63,950	64,000	12,804	9,614	13,003	11,689

64,000

At least	But less than	Single	Married filing jointly *	Married filing separately	Head of a household
64,000	64,050	12,816	9,626	13,017	11,701
64,050	64,100	12,829	9,639	13,031	11,714
64,100	64,150	12,841	9,651	13,045	11,726
64,150	64,200	12,854	9,664	13,059	11,739
64,200	64,250	12,866	9,676	13,073	11,751
64,250	64,300	12,879	9,689	13,087	11,764
64,300	64,350	12,891	9,701	13,101	11,776
64,350	64,400	12,904	9,714	13,115	11,789
64,400	64,450	12,916	9,726	13,129	11,801
64,450	64,500	12,929	9,739	13,143	11,814
64,500	64,550	12,941	9,751	13,157	11,826
64,550	64,600	12,954	9,764	13,171	11,839
64,600	64,650	12,966	9,776	13,185	11,851
64,650	64,700	12,979	9,789	13,199	11,864
64,700	64,750	12,991	9,801	13,213	11,876
64,750	64,800	13,004	9,814	13,227	11,889
64,800	64,850	13,016	9,826	13,241	11,901
64,850	64,900	13,029	9,839	13,255	11,914
64,900	64,950	13,041	9,851	13,269	11,926
64,950	65,000	13,054	9,864	13,283	11,939

65,000

At least	But less than	Single	Married filing jointly *	Married filing separately	Head of a household
65,000	65,050	13,066	9,876	13,297	11,951
65,050	65,100	13,079	9,889	13,311	11,964
65,100	65,150	13,091	9,901	13,325	11,976
65,150	65,200	13,104	9,914	13,339	11,989
65,200	65,250	13,116	9,926	13,353	12,001
65,250	65,300	13,129	9,939	13,367	12,014
65,300	65,350	13,141	9,951	13,381	12,026
65,350	65,400	13,154	9,964	13,395	12,039
65,400	65,450	13,166	9,976	13,409	12,051
65,450	65,500	13,179	9,989	13,423	12,064
65,500	65,550	13,191	10,001	13,437	12,076
65,550	65,600	13,204	10,014	13,451	12,089
65,600	65,650	13,216	10,026	13,465	12,101
65,650	65,700	13,229	10,039	13,479	12,114
65,700	65,750	13,241	10,051	13,493	12,126
65,750	65,800	13,254	10,064	13,507	12,139
65,800	65,850	13,266	10,076	13,521	12,151
65,850	65,900	13,279	10,089	13,535	12,164
65,900	65,950	13,291	10,101	13,549	12,176
65,950	66,000	13,304	10,114	13,563	12,189

66,000

At least	But less than	Single	Married filing jointly *	Married filing separately	Head of a household
66,000	66,050	13,316	10,126	13,577	12,201
66,050	66,100	13,329	10,139	13,591	12,214
66,100	66,150	13,341	10,151	13,605	12,226
66,150	66,200	13,354	10,164	13,619	12,239
66,200	66,250	13,366	10,176	13,633	12,251
66,250	66,300	13,379	10,189	13,647	12,264
66,300	66,350	13,391	10,201	13,661	12,276
66,350	66,400	13,404	10,214	13,675	12,289
66,400	66,450	13,416	10,226	13,689	12,301
66,450	66,500	13,429	10,239	13,703	12,314
66,500	66,550	13,441	10,251	13,717	12,326
66,550	66,600	13,454	10,264	13,731	12,339
66,600	66,650	13,466	10,276	13,745	12,351
66,650	66,700	13,479	10,289	13,759	12,364
66,700	66,750	13,491	10,301	13,773	12,376
66,750	66,800	13,504	10,314	13,787	12,389
66,800	66,850	13,516	10,326	13,801	12,401
66,850	66,900	13,529	10,339	13,815	12,414
66,900	66,950	13,541	10,351	13,829	12,426
66,950	67,000	13,554	10,364	13,843	12,439

67,000

At least	But less than	Single	Married filing jointly *	Married filing separately	Head of a household
67,000	67,050	13,566	10,376	13,857	12,451
67,050	67,100	13,579	10,389	13,871	12,464
67,100	67,150	13,591	10,401	13,885	12,476
67,150	67,200	13,604	10,414	13,899	12,489
67,200	67,250	13,616	10,426	13,913	12,501
67,250	67,300	13,629	10,439	13,927	12,514
67,300	67,350	13,641	10,451	13,941	12,526
67,350	67,400	13,654	10,464	13,955	12,539
67,400	67,450	13,666	10,476	13,969	12,551
67,450	67,500	13,679	10,489	13,983	12,564
67,500	67,550	13,691	10,501	13,997	12,576
67,550	67,600	13,704	10,514	14,011	12,589
67,600	67,650	13,716	10,526	14,025	12,601
67,650	67,700	13,729	10,539	14,039	12,614
67,700	67,750	13,741	10,551	14,053	12,626
67,750	67,800	13,754	10,564	14,067	12,639
67,800	67,850	13,766	10,576	14,081	12,651
67,850	67,900	13,779	10,589	14,095	12,664
67,900	67,950	13,791	10,601	14,109	12,676
67,950	68,000	13,804	10,614	14,123	12,689

* This column must also be used by a qualifying widow(er).

(Continued on page 70)

2003 Tax Table—Continued

If line 40 (taxable income) is— At least	But less than	Single	Married filing jointly *	Married filing separately	Head of a household
		Your tax is—			
68,000					
68,000	68,050	13,816	10,626	14,137	12,701
68,050	68,100	13,829	10,639	14,151	12,714
68,100	68,150	13,841	10,651	14,165	12,726
68,150	68,200	13,854	10,664	14,179	12,739
68,200	68,250	13,866	10,676	14,193	12,751
68,250	68,300	13,879	10,689	14,207	12,764
68,300	68,350	13,891	10,701	14,221	12,776
68,350	68,400	13,904	10,714	14,235	12,789
68,400	68,450	13,916	10,726	14,249	12,801
68,450	68,500	13,929	10,739	14,263	12,814
68,500	68,550	13,941	10,751	14,277	12,826
68,550	68,600	13,954	10,764	14,291	12,839
68,600	68,650	13,966	10,776	14,305	12,851
68,650	68,700	13,979	10,789	14,319	12,864
68,700	68,750	13,991	10,801	14,333	12,876
68,750	68,800	14,004	10,814	14,347	12,889
68,800	68,850	14,017	10,826	14,361	12,901
68,850	68,900	14,031	10,839	14,375	12,914
68,900	68,950	14,045	10,851	14,389	12,926
68,950	69,000	14,059	10,864	14,403	12,939
69,000					
69,000	69,050	14,073	10,876	14,417	12,951
69,050	69,100	14,087	10,889	14,431	12,964
69,100	69,150	14,101	10,901	14,445	12,976
69,150	69,200	14,115	10,914	14,459	12,989
69,200	69,250	14,129	10,926	14,473	13,001
69,250	69,300	14,143	10,939	14,487	13,014
69,300	69,350	14,157	10,951	14,501	13,026
69,350	69,400	14,171	10,964	14,515	13,039
69,400	69,450	14,185	10,976	14,529	13,051
69,450	69,500	14,199	10,989	14,543	13,064
69,500	69,550	14,213	11,001	14,557	13,076
69,550	69,600	14,227	11,014	14,571	13,089
69,600	69,650	14,241	11,026	14,585	13,101
69,650	69,700	14,255	11,039	14,599	13,114
69,700	69,750	14,269	11,051	14,613	13,126
69,750	69,800	14,283	11,064	14,627	13,139
69,800	69,850	14,297	11,076	14,641	13,151
69,850	69,900	14,311	11,089	14,655	13,164
69,900	69,950	14,325	11,101	14,669	13,176
69,950	70,000	14,339	11,114	14,683	13,189
70,000					
70,000	70,050	14,353	11,126	14,697	13,201
70,050	70,100	14,367	11,139	14,711	13,214
70,100	70,150	14,381	11,151	14,725	13,226
70,150	70,200	14,395	11,164	14,739	13,239
70,200	70,250	14,409	11,176	14,753	13,251
70,250	70,300	14,423	11,189	14,767	13,264
70,300	70,350	14,437	11,201	14,781	13,276
70,350	70,400	14,451	11,214	14,795	13,289
70,400	70,450	14,465	11,226	14,809	13,301
70,450	70,500	14,479	11,239	14,823	13,314
70,500	70,550	14,493	11,251	14,837	13,326
70,550	70,600	14,507	11,264	14,851	13,339
70,600	70,650	14,521	11,276	14,865	13,351
70,650	70,700	14,535	11,289	14,879	13,364
70,700	70,750	14,549	11,301	14,893	13,376
70,750	70,800	14,563	11,314	14,907	13,389
70,800	70,850	14,577	11,326	14,921	13,401
70,850	70,900	14,591	11,339	14,935	13,414
70,900	70,950	14,605	11,351	14,949	13,426
70,950	71,000	14,619	11,364	14,963	13,439
71,000					
71,000	71,050	14,633	11,376	14,977	13,451
71,050	71,100	14,647	11,389	14,991	13,464
71,100	71,150	14,661	11,401	15,005	13,476
71,150	71,200	14,675	11,414	15,019	13,489
71,200	71,250	14,689	11,426	15,033	13,501
71,250	71,300	14,703	11,439	15,047	13,514
71,300	71,350	14,717	11,451	15,061	13,526
71,350	71,400	14,731	11,464	15,075	13,539
71,400	71,450	14,745	11,476	15,089	13,551
71,450	71,500	14,759	11,489	15,103	13,564
71,500	71,550	14,773	11,501	15,117	13,576
71,550	71,600	14,787	11,514	15,131	13,589
71,600	71,650	14,801	11,526	15,145	13,601
71,650	71,700	14,815	11,539	15,159	13,614
71,700	71,750	14,829	11,551	15,173	13,626
71,750	71,800	14,843	11,564	15,187	13,639
71,800	71,850	14,857	11,576	15,201	13,651
71,850	71,900	14,871	11,589	15,215	13,664
71,900	71,950	14,885	11,601	15,229	13,676
71,950	72,000	14,899	11,614	15,243	13,689
72,000					
72,000	72,050	14,913	11,626	15,257	13,701
72,050	72,100	14,927	11,639	15,271	13,714
72,100	72,150	14,941	11,651	15,285	13,726
72,150	72,200	14,955	11,664	15,299	13,739
72,200	72,250	14,969	11,676	15,313	13,751
72,250	72,300	14,983	11,689	15,327	13,764
72,300	72,350	14,997	11,701	15,341	13,776
72,350	72,400	15,011	11,714	15,355	13,789
72,400	72,450	15,025	11,726	15,369	13,801
72,450	72,500	15,039	11,739	15,383	13,814
72,500	72,550	15,053	11,751	15,397	13,826
72,550	72,600	15,067	11,764	15,411	13,839
72,600	72,650	15,081	11,776	15,425	13,851
72,650	72,700	15,095	11,789	15,439	13,864
72,700	72,750	15,109	11,801	15,453	13,876
72,750	72,800	15,123	11,814	15,467	13,889
72,800	72,850	15,137	11,826	15,481	13,901
72,850	72,900	15,151	11,839	15,495	13,914
72,900	72,950	15,165	11,851	15,509	13,926
72,950	73,000	15,179	11,864	15,523	13,939
73,000					
73,000	73,050	15,193	11,876	15,537	13,951
73,050	73,100	15,207	11,889	15,551	13,964
73,100	73,150	15,221	11,901	15,565	13,976
73,150	73,200	15,235	11,914	15,579	13,989
73,200	73,250	15,249	11,926	15,593	14,001
73,250	73,300	15,263	11,939	15,607	14,014
73,300	73,350	15,277	11,951	15,621	14,026
73,350	73,400	15,291	11,964	15,635	14,039
73,400	73,450	15,305	11,976	15,649	14,051
73,450	73,500	15,319	11,989	15,663	14,064
73,500	73,550	15,333	12,001	15,677	14,076
73,550	73,600	15,347	12,014	15,691	14,089
73,600	73,650	15,361	12,026	15,705	14,101
73,650	73,700	15,375	12,039	15,719	14,114
73,700	73,750	15,389	12,051	15,733	14,126
73,750	73,800	15,403	12,064	15,747	14,139
73,800	73,850	15,417	12,076	15,761	14,151
73,850	73,900	15,431	12,089	15,775	14,164
73,900	73,950	15,445	12,101	15,789	14,176
73,950	74,000	15,459	12,114	15,803	14,189
74,000					
74,000	74,050	15,473	12,126	15,817	14,201
74,050	74,100	15,487	12,139	15,831	14,214
74,100	74,150	15,501	12,151	15,845	14,226
74,150	74,200	15,515	12,164	15,859	14,239
74,200	74,250	15,529	12,176	15,873	14,251
74,250	74,300	15,543	12,189	15,887	14,264
74,300	74,350	15,557	12,201	15,901	14,276
74,350	74,400	15,571	12,214	15,915	14,289
74,400	74,450	15,585	12,226	15,929	14,301
74,450	74,500	15,599	12,239	15,943	14,314
74,500	74,550	15,613	12,251	15,957	14,326
74,550	74,600	15,627	12,264	15,971	14,339
74,600	74,650	15,641	12,276	15,985	14,351
74,650	74,700	15,655	12,289	15,999	14,364
74,700	74,750	15,669	12,301	16,013	14,376
74,750	74,800	15,683	12,314	16,027	14,389
74,800	74,850	15,697	12,326	16,041	14,401
74,850	74,900	15,711	12,339	16,055	14,414
74,900	74,950	15,725	12,351	16,069	14,426
74,950	75,000	15,739	12,364	16,083	14,439
75,000					
75,000	75,050	15,753	12,376	16,097	14,451
75,050	75,100	15,767	12,389	16,111	14,464
75,100	75,150	15,781	12,401	16,125	14,476
75,150	75,200	15,795	12,414	16,139	14,489
75,200	75,250	15,809	12,426	16,153	14,501
75,250	75,300	15,823	12,439	16,167	14,514
75,300	75,350	15,837	12,451	16,181	14,526
75,350	75,400	15,851	12,464	16,195	14,539
75,400	75,450	15,865	12,476	16,209	14,551
75,450	75,500	15,879	12,489	16,223	14,564
75,500	75,550	15,893	12,501	16,237	14,576
75,550	75,600	15,907	12,514	16,251	14,589
75,600	75,650	15,921	12,526	16,265	14,601
75,650	75,700	15,935	12,539	16,279	14,614
75,700	75,750	15,949	12,551	16,293	14,626
75,750	75,800	15,963	12,564	16,307	14,639
75,800	75,850	15,977	12,576	16,321	14,651
75,850	75,900	15,991	12,589	16,335	14,664
75,900	75,950	16,005	12,601	16,349	14,676
75,950	76,000	16,019	12,614	16,363	14,689
76,000					
76,000	76,050	16,033	12,626	16,377	14,701
76,050	76,100	16,047	12,639	16,391	14,714
76,100	76,150	16,061	12,651	16,405	14,726
76,150	76,200	16,075	12,664	16,419	14,739
76,200	76,250	16,089	12,676	16,433	14,751
76,250	76,300	16,103	12,689	16,447	14,764
76,300	76,350	16,117	12,701	16,461	14,776
76,350	76,400	16,131	12,714	16,475	14,789
76,400	76,450	16,145	12,726	16,489	14,801
76,450	76,500	16,159	12,739	16,503	14,814
76,500	76,550	16,173	12,751	16,517	14,826
76,550	76,600	16,187	12,764	16,531	14,839
76,600	76,650	16,201	12,776	16,545	14,851
76,650	76,700	16,215	12,789	16,559	14,864
76,700	76,750	16,229	12,801	16,573	14,876
76,750	76,800	16,243	12,814	16,587	14,889
76,800	76,850	16,257	12,826	16,601	14,901
76,850	76,900	16,271	12,839	16,615	14,914
76,900	76,950	16,285	12,851	16,629	14,926
76,950	77,000	16,299	12,864	16,643	14,939

* This column must also be used by a qualifying widow(er).

(Continued on page 71)

If line 40 (taxable income) is—		And you are—			
At least	But less than	Single	Married filing jointly *	Married filing separately	Head of a household
		Your tax is—			

77,000

At least	But less than	Single	Married filing jointly *	Married filing separately	Head of a household
77,000	77,050	16,313	12,876	16,657	14,951
77,050	77,100	16,327	12,889	16,671	14,964
77,100	77,150	16,341	12,901	16,685	14,976
77,150	77,200	16,355	12,914	16,699	14,989
77,200	77,250	16,369	12,926	16,713	15,001
77,250	77,300	16,383	12,939	16,727	15,014
77,300	77,350	16,397	12,951	16,741	15,026
77,350	77,400	16,411	12,964	16,755	15,039
77,400	77,450	16,425	12,976	16,769	15,051
77,450	77,500	16,439	12,989	16,783	15,064
77,500	77,550	16,453	13,001	16,797	15,076
77,550	77,600	16,467	13,014	16,811	15,089
77,600	77,650	16,481	13,026	16,825	15,101
77,650	77,700	16,495	13,039	16,839	15,114
77,700	77,750	16,509	13,051	16,853	15,126
77,750	77,800	16,523	13,064	16,867	15,139
77,800	77,850	16,537	13,076	16,881	15,151
77,850	77,900	16,551	13,089	16,895	15,164
77,900	77,950	16,565	13,101	16,909	15,176
77,950	78,000	16,579	13,114	16,923	15,189

78,000

At least	But less than	Single	Married filing jointly *	Married filing separately	Head of a household
78,000	78,050	16,593	13,126	16,937	15,201
78,050	78,100	16,607	13,139	16,951	15,214
78,100	78,150	16,621	13,151	16,965	15,226
78,150	78,200	16,635	13,164	16,979	15,239
78,200	78,250	16,649	13,176	16,993	15,251
78,250	78,300	16,663	13,189	17,007	15,264
78,300	78,350	16,677	13,201	17,021	15,276
78,350	78,400	16,691	13,214	17,035	15,289
78,400	78,450	16,705	13,226	17,049	15,301
78,450	78,500	16,719	13,239	17,063	15,314
78,500	78,550	16,733	13,251	17,077	15,326
78,550	78,600	16,747	13,264	17,091	15,339
78,600	78,650	16,761	13,276	17,105	15,351
78,650	78,700	16,775	13,289	17,119	15,364
78,700	78,750	16,789	13,301	17,133	15,376
78,750	78,800	16,803	13,314	17,147	15,389
78,800	78,850	16,817	13,326	17,161	15,401
78,850	78,900	16,831	13,339	17,175	15,414
78,900	78,950	16,845	13,351	17,189	15,426
78,950	79,000	16,859	13,364	17,203	15,439

79,000

At least	But less than	Single	Married filing jointly *	Married filing separately	Head of a household
79,000	79,050	16,873	13,376	17,217	15,451
79,050	79,100	16,887	13,389	17,231	15,464
79,100	79,150	16,901	13,401	17,245	15,476
79,150	79,200	16,915	13,414	17,259	15,489
79,200	79,250	16,929	13,426	17,273	15,501
79,250	79,300	16,943	13,439	17,287	15,514
79,300	79,350	16,957	13,451	17,301	15,526
79,350	79,400	16,971	13,464	17,315	15,539
79,400	79,450	16,985	13,476	17,329	15,551
79,450	79,500	16,999	13,489	17,343	15,564
79,500	79,550	17,013	13,501	17,357	15,576
79,550	79,600	17,027	13,514	17,371	15,589
79,600	79,650	17,041	13,526	17,385	15,601
79,650	79,700	17,055	13,539	17,399	15,614
79,700	79,750	17,069	13,551	17,413	15,626
79,750	79,800	17,083	13,564	17,427	15,639
79,800	79,850	17,097	13,576	17,441	15,651
79,850	79,900	17,111	13,589	17,455	15,664
79,900	79,950	17,125	13,601	17,469	15,676
79,950	80,000	17,139	13,614	17,483	15,689

80,000

At least	But less than	Single	Married filing jointly *	Married filing separately	Head of a household
80,000	80,050	17,153	13,626	17,497	15,701
80,050	80,100	17,167	13,639	17,511	15,714
80,100	80,150	17,181	13,651	17,525	15,726
80,150	80,200	17,195	13,664	17,539	15,739
80,200	80,250	17,209	13,676	17,553	15,751
80,250	80,300	17,223	13,689	17,567	15,764
80,300	80,350	17,237	13,701	17,581	15,776
80,350	80,400	17,251	13,714	17,595	15,789
80,400	80,450	17,265	13,726	17,609	15,801
80,450	80,500	17,279	13,739	17,623	15,814
80,500	80,550	17,293	13,751	17,637	15,826
80,550	80,600	17,307	13,764	17,651	15,839
80,600	80,650	17,321	13,776	17,665	15,851
80,650	80,700	17,335	13,789	17,679	15,864
80,700	80,750	17,349	13,801	17,693	15,876
80,750	80,800	17,363	13,814	17,707	15,889
80,800	80,850	17,377	13,826	17,721	15,901
80,850	80,900	17,391	13,839	17,735	15,914
80,900	80,950	17,405	13,851	17,749	15,926
80,950	81,000	17,419	13,864	17,763	15,939

81,000

At least	But less than	Single	Married filing jointly *	Married filing separately	Head of a household
81,000	81,050	17,433	13,876	17,777	15,951
81,050	81,100	17,447	13,889	17,791	15,964
81,100	81,150	17,461	13,901	17,805	15,976
81,150	81,200	17,475	13,914	17,819	15,989
81,200	81,250	17,489	13,926	17,833	16,001
81,250	81,300	17,503	13,939	17,847	16,014
81,300	81,350	17,517	13,951	17,861	16,026
81,350	81,400	17,531	13,964	17,875	16,039
81,400	81,450	17,545	13,976	17,889	16,051
81,450	81,500	17,559	13,989	17,903	16,064
81,500	81,550	17,573	14,001	17,917	16,076
81,550	81,600	17,587	14,014	17,931	16,089
81,600	81,650	17,601	14,026	17,945	16,101
81,650	81,700	17,615	14,039	17,959	16,114
81,700	81,750	17,629	14,051	17,973	16,126
81,750	81,800	17,643	14,064	17,987	16,139
81,800	81,850	17,657	14,076	18,001	16,151
81,850	81,900	17,671	14,089	18,015	16,164
81,900	81,950	17,685	14,101	18,029	16,176
81,950	82,000	17,699	14,114	18,043	16,189

82,000

At least	But less than	Single	Married filing jointly *	Married filing separately	Head of a household
82,000	82,050	17,713	14,126	18,057	16,201
82,050	82,100	17,727	14,139	18,071	16,214
82,100	82,150	17,741	14,151	18,085	16,226
82,150	82,200	17,755	14,164	18,099	16,239
82,200	82,250	17,769	14,176	18,113	16,251
82,250	82,300	17,783	14,189	18,127	16,264
82,300	82,350	17,797	14,201	18,141	16,276
82,350	82,400	17,811	14,214	18,155	16,289
82,400	82,450	17,825	14,226	18,169	16,301
82,450	82,500	17,839	14,239	18,183	16,314
82,500	82,550	17,853	14,251	18,197	16,326
82,550	82,600	17,867	14,264	18,211	16,339
82,600	82,650	17,881	14,276	18,225	16,351
82,650	82,700	17,895	14,289	18,239	16,364
82,700	82,750	17,909	14,301	18,253	16,376
82,750	82,800	17,923	14,314	18,267	16,389
82,800	82,850	17,937	14,326	18,281	16,401
82,850	82,900	17,951	14,339	18,295	16,414
82,900	82,950	17,965	14,351	18,309	16,426
82,950	83,000	17,979	14,364	18,323	16,439

83,000

At least	But less than	Single	Married filing jointly *	Married filing separately	Head of a household
83,000	83,050	17,993	14,376	18,337	16,451
83,050	83,100	18,007	14,389	18,351	16,464
83,100	83,150	18,021	14,401	18,365	16,476
83,150	83,200	18,035	14,414	18,379	16,489
83,200	83,250	18,049	14,426	18,393	16,501
83,250	83,300	18,063	14,439	18,407	16,514
83,300	83,350	18,077	14,451	18,421	16,526
83,350	83,400	18,091	14,464	18,435	16,539
83,400	83,450	18,105	14,476	18,449	16,551
83,450	83,500	18,119	14,489	18,463	16,564
83,500	83,550	18,133	14,501	18,477	16,576
83,550	83,600	18,147	14,514	18,491	16,589
83,600	83,650	18,161	14,526	18,505	16,601
83,650	83,700	18,175	14,539	18,519	16,614
83,700	83,750	18,189	14,551	18,533	16,626
83,750	83,800	18,203	14,564	18,547	16,639
83,800	83,850	18,217	14,576	18,561	16,651
83,850	83,900	18,231	14,589	18,575	16,664
83,900	83,950	18,245	14,601	18,589	16,676
83,950	84,000	18,259	14,614	18,603	16,689

84,000

At least	But less than	Single	Married filing jointly *	Married filing separately	Head of a household
84,000	84,050	18,273	14,626	18,617	16,701
84,050	84,100	18,287	14,639	18,631	16,714
84,100	84,150	18,301	14,651	18,645	16,726
84,150	84,200	18,315	14,664	18,659	16,739
84,200	84,250	18,329	14,676	18,673	16,751
84,250	84,300	18,343	14,689	18,687	16,764
84,300	84,350	18,357	14,701	18,701	16,776
84,350	84,400	18,371	14,714	18,715	16,789
84,400	84,450	18,385	14,726	18,729	16,801
84,450	84,500	18,399	14,739	18,743	16,814
84,500	84,550	18,413	14,751	18,757	16,826
84,550	84,600	18,427	14,764	18,771	16,839
84,600	84,650	18,441	14,776	18,785	16,851
84,650	84,700	18,455	14,789	18,799	16,864
84,700	84,750	18,469	14,801	18,813	16,876
84,750	84,800	18,483	14,814	18,827	16,889
84,800	84,850	18,497	14,826	18,841	16,901
84,850	84,900	18,511	14,839	18,855	16,914
84,900	84,950	18,525	14,851	18,869	16,926
84,950	85,000	18,539	14,864	18,883	16,939

85,000

At least	But less than	Single	Married filing jointly *	Married filing separately	Head of a household
85,000	85,050	18,553	14,876	18,897	16,951
85,050	85,100	18,567	14,889	18,911	16,964
85,100	85,150	18,581	14,901	18,925	16,976
85,150	85,200	18,595	14,914	18,939	16,989
85,200	85,250	18,609	14,926	18,953	17,001
85,250	85,300	18,623	14,939	18,967	17,014
85,300	85,350	18,637	14,951	18,981	17,026
85,350	85,400	18,651	14,964	18,995	17,039
85,400	85,450	18,665	14,976	19,009	17,051
85,450	85,500	18,679	14,989	19,023	17,064
85,500	85,550	18,693	15,001	19,037	17,076
85,550	85,600	18,707	15,014	19,051	17,089
85,600	85,650	18,721	15,026	19,065	17,101
85,650	85,700	18,735	15,039	19,079	17,114
85,700	85,750	18,749	15,051	19,093	17,126
85,750	85,800	18,763	15,064	19,107	17,139
85,800	85,850	18,777	15,076	19,121	17,151
85,850	85,900	18,791	15,089	19,135	17,164
85,900	85,950	18,805	15,101	19,149	17,176
85,950	86,000	18,819	15,114	19,163	17,189

* This column must also be used by a qualifying widow(er).

(Continued on page 72)

If line 40 (taxable income) is—		And you are—			
At least	But less than	Single	Married filing jointly *	Married filing separately	Head of a house-hold
		Your tax is—			

86,000

At least	But less than	Single	Married filing jointly	Married filing separately	Head of household
86,000	86,050	18,833	15,126	19,177	17,201
86,050	86,100	18,847	15,139	19,191	17,214
86,100	86,150	18,861	15,151	19,205	17,226
86,150	86,200	18,875	15,164	19,219	17,239
86,200	86,250	18,889	15,176	19,233	17,251
86,250	86,300	18,903	15,189	19,247	17,264
86,300	86,350	18,917	15,201	19,261	17,276
86,350	86,400	18,931	15,214	19,275	17,289
86,400	86,450	18,945	15,226	19,289	17,301
86,450	86,500	18,959	15,239	19,303	17,314
86,500	86,550	18,973	15,251	19,317	17,326
86,550	86,600	18,987	15,264	19,331	17,339
86,600	86,650	19,001	15,276	19,345	17,351
86,650	86,700	19,015	15,289	19,359	17,364
86,700	86,750	19,029	15,301	19,373	17,376
86,750	86,800	19,043	15,314	19,387	17,389
86,800	86,850	19,057	15,326	19,401	17,401
86,850	86,900	19,071	15,339	19,415	17,414
86,900	86,950	19,085	15,351	19,429	17,426
86,950	87,000	19,099	15,364	19,443	17,439

87,000

At least	But less than	Single	Married filing jointly	Married filing separately	Head of household
87,000	87,050	19,113	15,376	19,457	17,451
87,050	87,100	19,127	15,389	19,471	17,464
87,100	87,150	19,141	15,401	19,485	17,476
87,150	87,200	19,155	15,414	19,499	17,489
87,200	87,250	19,169	15,426	19,513	17,501
87,250	87,300	19,183	15,439	19,527	17,514
87,300	87,350	19,197	15,451	19,541	17,526
87,350	87,400	19,211	15,464	19,557	17,539
87,400	87,450	19,225	15,476	19,573	17,551
87,450	87,500	19,239	15,489	19,590	17,564
87,500	87,550	19,253	15,501	19,606	17,576
87,550	87,600	19,267	15,514	19,623	17,589
87,600	87,650	19,281	15,526	19,639	17,601
87,650	87,700	19,295	15,539	19,656	17,614
87,700	87,750	19,309	15,551	19,672	17,626
87,750	87,800	19,323	15,564	19,689	17,639
87,800	87,850	19,337	15,576	19,705	17,651
87,850	87,900	19,351	15,589	19,722	17,664
87,900	87,950	19,365	15,601	19,738	17,676
87,950	88,000	19,379	15,614	19,755	17,689

88,000

At least	But less than	Single	Married filing jointly	Married filing separately	Head of household
88,000	88,050	19,393	15,626	19,771	17,701
88,050	88,100	19,407	15,639	19,788	17,714
88,100	88,150	19,421	15,651	19,804	17,726
88,150	88,200	19,435	15,664	19,821	17,739
88,200	88,250	19,449	15,676	19,837	17,751
88,250	88,300	19,463	15,689	19,854	17,764
88,300	88,350	19,477	15,701	19,870	17,776
88,350	88,400	19,491	15,714	19,887	17,789
88,400	88,450	19,505	15,726	19,903	17,801
88,450	88,500	19,519	15,739	19,920	17,814
88,500	88,550	19,533	15,751	19,936	17,826
88,550	88,600	19,547	15,764	19,953	17,839
88,600	88,650	19,561	15,776	19,969	17,851
88,650	88,700	19,575	15,789	19,986	17,864
88,700	88,750	19,589	15,801	20,002	17,876
88,750	88,800	19,603	15,814	20,019	17,889
88,800	88,850	19,617	15,826	20,035	17,901
88,850	88,900	19,631	15,839	20,052	17,914
88,900	88,950	19,645	15,851	20,068	17,926
88,950	89,000	19,659	15,864	20,085	17,939

89,000

At least	But less than	Single	Married filing jointly	Married filing separately	Head of household
89,000	89,050	19,673	15,876	20,101	17,951
89,050	89,100	19,687	15,889	20,118	17,964
89,100	89,150	19,701	15,901	20,134	17,976
89,150	89,200	19,715	15,914	20,151	17,989
89,200	89,250	19,729	15,926	20,167	18,001
89,250	89,300	19,743	15,939	20,184	18,014
89,300	89,350	19,757	15,951	20,200	18,026
89,350	89,400	19,771	15,964	20,217	18,039
89,400	89,450	19,785	15,976	20,233	18,051
89,450	89,500	19,799	15,989	20,250	18,064
89,500	89,550	19,813	16,001	20,266	18,076
89,550	89,600	19,827	16,014	20,283	18,089
89,600	89,650	19,841	16,026	20,299	18,101
89,650	89,700	19,855	16,039	20,316	18,114
89,700	89,750	19,869	16,051	20,332	18,126
89,750	89,800	19,883	16,064	20,349	18,139
89,800	89,850	19,897	16,076	20,365	18,151
89,850	89,900	19,911	16,089	20,382	18,164
89,900	89,950	19,925	16,101	20,398	18,176
89,950	90,000	19,939	16,114	20,415	18,189

90,000

At least	But less than	Single	Married filing jointly	Married filing separately	Head of household
90,000	90,050	19,953	16,126	20,431	18,201
90,050	90,100	19,967	16,139	20,448	18,214
90,100	90,150	19,981	16,151	20,464	18,226
90,150	90,200	19,995	16,164	20,481	18,239
90,200	90,250	20,009	16,176	20,497	18,251
90,250	90,300	20,023	16,189	20,514	18,264
90,300	90,350	20,037	16,201	20,530	18,276
90,350	90,400	20,051	16,214	20,547	18,289
90,400	90,450	20,065	16,226	20,563	18,301
90,450	90,500	20,079	16,239	20,580	18,314
90,500	90,550	20,093	16,251	20,596	18,326
90,550	90,600	20,107	16,264	20,613	18,339
90,600	90,650	20,121	16,276	20,629	18,351
90,650	90,700	20,135	16,289	20,646	18,364
90,700	90,750	20,149	16,301	20,662	18,376
90,750	90,800	20,163	16,314	20,679	18,389
90,800	90,850	20,177	16,326	20,695	18,401
90,850	90,900	20,191	16,339	20,712	18,414
90,900	90,950	20,205	16,351	20,728	18,426
90,950	91,000	20,219	16,364	20,745	18,439

91,000

At least	But less than	Single	Married filing jointly	Married filing separately	Head of household
91,000	91,050	20,233	16,376	20,761	18,451
91,050	91,100	20,247	16,389	20,778	18,464
91,100	91,150	20,261	16,401	20,794	18,476
91,150	91,200	20,275	16,414	20,811	18,489
91,200	91,250	20,289	16,426	20,827	18,501
91,250	91,300	20,303	16,439	20,844	18,514
91,300	91,350	20,317	16,451	20,860	18,526
91,350	91,400	20,331	16,464	20,877	18,539
91,400	91,450	20,345	16,476	20,893	18,551
91,450	91,500	20,359	16,489	20,910	18,564
91,500	91,550	20,373	16,501	20,926	18,576
91,550	91,600	20,387	16,514	20,943	18,589
91,600	91,650	20,401	16,526	20,959	18,601
91,650	91,700	20,415	16,539	20,976	18,614
91,700	91,750	20,429	16,551	20,992	18,626
91,750	91,800	20,443	16,564	21,009	18,639
91,800	91,850	20,457	16,576	21,025	18,651
91,850	91,900	20,471	16,589	21,042	18,664
91,900	91,950	20,485	16,601	21,058	18,676
91,950	92,000	20,499	16,614	21,075	18,689

92,000

At least	But less than	Single	Married filing jointly	Married filing separately	Head of household
92,000	92,050	20,513	16,626	21,091	18,701
92,050	92,100	20,527	16,639	21,108	18,714
92,100	92,150	20,541	16,651	21,124	18,726
92,150	92,200	20,555	16,664	21,141	18,739
92,200	92,250	20,569	16,676	21,157	18,751
92,250	92,300	20,583	16,689	21,174	18,764
92,300	92,350	20,597	16,701	21,190	18,776
92,350	92,400	20,611	16,714	21,207	18,789
92,400	92,450	20,625	16,726	21,223	18,801
92,450	92,500	20,639	16,739	21,240	18,814
92,500	92,550	20,653	16,751	21,256	18,826
92,550	92,600	20,667	16,764	21,273	18,839
92,600	92,650	20,681	16,776	21,289	18,851
92,650	92,700	20,695	16,789	21,306	18,864
92,700	92,750	20,709	16,801	21,322	18,876
92,750	92,800	20,723	16,814	21,339	18,889
92,800	92,850	20,737	16,826	21,355	18,901
92,850	92,900	20,751	16,839	21,372	18,914
92,900	92,950	20,765	16,851	21,388	18,926
92,950	93,000	20,779	16,864	21,405	18,939

93,000

At least	But less than	Single	Married filing jointly	Married filing separately	Head of household
93,000	93,050	20,793	16,876	21,421	18,951
93,050	93,100	20,807	16,889	21,438	18,964
93,100	93,150	20,821	16,901	21,454	18,976
93,150	93,200	20,835	16,914	21,471	18,989
93,200	93,250	20,849	16,926	21,487	19,001
93,250	93,300	20,863	16,939	21,504	19,014
93,300	93,350	20,877	16,951	21,520	19,026
93,350	93,400	20,891	16,964	21,537	19,039
93,400	93,450	20,905	16,976	21,553	19,051
93,450	93,500	20,919	16,989	21,570	19,064
93,500	93,550	20,933	17,001	21,586	19,076
93,550	93,600	20,947	17,014	21,603	19,089
93,600	93,650	20,961	17,026	21,619	19,101
93,650	93,700	20,975	17,039	21,636	19,114
93,700	93,750	20,989	17,051	21,652	19,126
93,750	93,800	21,003	17,064	21,669	19,139
93,800	93,850	21,017	17,076	21,685	19,151
93,850	93,900	21,031	17,089	21,702	19,164
93,900	93,950	21,045	17,101	21,718	19,176
93,950	94,000	21,059	17,114	21,735	19,189

94,000

At least	But less than	Single	Married filing jointly	Married filing separately	Head of household
94,000	94,050	21,073	17,126	21,751	19,201
94,050	94,100	21,087	17,139	21,768	19,214
94,100	94,150	21,101	17,151	21,784	19,226
94,150	94,200	21,115	17,164	21,801	19,239
94,200	94,250	21,129	17,176	21,817	19,251
94,250	94,300	21,143	17,189	21,834	19,264
94,300	94,350	21,157	17,201	21,850	19,276
94,350	94,400	21,171	17,214	21,867	19,289
94,400	94,450	21,185	17,226	21,883	19,301
94,450	94,500	21,199	17,239	21,900	19,314
94,500	94,550	21,213	17,251	21,916	19,326
94,550	94,600	21,227	17,264	21,933	19,339
94,600	94,650	21,241	17,276	21,949	19,351
94,650	94,700	21,255	17,289	21,966	19,364
94,700	94,750	21,269	17,301	21,982	19,376
94,750	94,800	21,283	17,314	21,999	19,389
94,800	94,850	21,297	17,326	22,015	19,401
94,850	94,900	21,311	17,339	22,032	19,414
94,900	94,950	21,325	17,351	22,048	19,426
94,950	95,000	21,339	17,364	22,065	19,439

* This column must also be used by a qualifying widow(er).

(Continued on page 73)

If line 40 (taxable income) is—		And you are—			
At least	But less than	Single	Married filing jointly *	Married filing separately	Head of a house-hold
		Your tax is—			

95,000

At least	But less than	Single	Married filing jointly *	Married filing separately	Head of a household
95,000	95,050	21,353	17,376	22,081	19,451
95,050	95,100	21,367	17,389	22,098	19,464
95,100	95,150	21,381	17,401	22,114	19,476
95,150	95,200	21,395	17,414	22,131	19,489
95,200	95,250	21,409	17,426	22,147	19,501
95,250	95,300	21,423	17,439	22,164	19,514
95,300	95,350	21,437	17,451	22,180	19,526
95,350	95,400	21,451	17,464	22,197	19,539
95,400	95,450	21,465	17,476	22,213	19,551
95,450	95,500	21,479	17,489	22,230	19,564
95,500	95,550	21,493	17,501	22,246	19,576
95,550	95,600	21,507	17,514	22,263	19,589
95,600	95,650	21,521	17,526	22,279	19,601
95,650	95,700	21,535	17,539	22,296	19,614
95,700	95,750	21,549	17,551	22,312	19,626
95,750	95,800	21,563	17,564	22,329	19,639
95,800	95,850	21,577	17,576	22,345	19,651
95,850	95,900	21,591	17,589	22,362	19,664
95,900	95,950	21,605	17,601	22,378	19,676
95,950	96,000	21,619	17,614	22,395	19,689

96,000

At least	But less than	Single	Married filing jointly *	Married filing separately	Head of a household
96,000	96,050	21,633	17,626	22,411	19,701
96,050	96,100	21,647	17,639	22,428	19,714
96,100	96,150	21,661	17,651	22,444	19,726
96,150	96,200	21,675	17,664	22,461	19,739
96,200	96,250	21,689	17,676	22,477	19,751
96,250	96,300	21,703	17,689	22,494	19,764
96,300	96,350	21,717	17,701	22,510	19,776
96,350	96,400	21,731	17,714	22,527	19,789
96,400	96,450	21,745	17,726	22,543	19,801
96,450	96,500	21,759	17,739	22,560	19,814
96,500	96,550	21,773	17,751	22,576	19,826
96,550	96,600	21,787	17,764	22,593	19,839
96,600	96,650	21,801	17,776	22,609	19,851
96,650	96,700	21,815	17,789	22,626	19,864
96,700	96,750	21,829	17,801	22,642	19,876
96,750	96,800	21,843	17,814	22,659	19,889
96,800	96,850	21,857	17,826	22,675	19,901
96,850	96,900	21,871	17,839	22,692	19,914
96,900	96,950	21,885	17,851	22,708	19,926
96,950	97,000	21,899	17,864	22,725	19,939

97,000

At least	But less than	Single	Married filing jointly *	Married filing separately	Head of a household
97,000	97,050	21,913	17,876	22,741	19,951
97,050	97,100	21,927	17,889	22,758	19,964
97,100	97,150	21,941	17,901	22,774	19,976
97,150	97,200	21,955	17,914	22,791	19,989
97,200	97,250	21,969	17,926	22,807	20,001
97,250	97,300	21,983	17,939	22,824	20,014
97,300	97,350	21,997	17,951	22,840	20,026
97,350	97,400	22,011	17,964	22,857	20,039
97,400	97,450	22,025	17,976	22,873	20,051
97,450	97,500	22,039	17,989	22,890	20,064
97,500	97,550	22,053	18,001	22,906	20,076
97,550	97,600	22,067	18,014	22,923	20,089
97,600	97,650	22,081	18,026	22,939	20,101
97,650	97,700	22,095	18,039	22,956	20,114
97,700	97,750	22,109	18,051	22,972	20,126
97,750	97,800	22,123	18,064	22,989	20,139
97,800	97,850	22,137	18,076	23,005	20,151
97,850	97,900	22,151	18,089	23,022	20,164
97,900	97,950	22,165	18,101	23,038	20,176
97,950	98,000	22,179	18,114	23,055	20,189

98,000

At least	But less than	Single	Married filing jointly *	Married filing separately	Head of a household
98,000	98,050	22,193	18,126	23,071	20,201
98,050	98,100	22,207	18,139	23,088	20,214
98,100	98,150	22,221	18,151	23,104	20,226
98,150	98,200	22,235	18,164	23,121	20,239
98,200	98,250	22,249	18,176	23,137	20,251
98,250	98,300	22,263	18,189	23,154	20,265
98,300	98,350	22,277	18,201	23,170	20,279
98,350	98,400	22,291	18,214	23,187	20,293
98,400	98,450	22,305	18,226	23,203	20,307
98,450	98,500	22,319	18,239	23,220	20,321
98,500	98,550	22,333	18,251	23,236	20,335
98,550	98,600	22,347	18,264	23,253	20,349
98,600	98,650	22,361	18,276	23,269	20,363
98,650	98,700	22,375	18,289	23,286	20,377
98,700	98,750	22,389	18,301	23,302	20,391
98,750	98,800	22,403	18,314	23,319	20,405
98,800	98,850	22,417	18,326	23,335	20,419
98,850	98,900	22,431	18,339	23,352	20,433
98,900	98,950	22,445	18,351	23,368	20,447
98,950	99,000	22,459	18,364	23,385	20,461

99,000

At least	But less than	Single	Married filing jointly *	Married filing separately	Head of a household
99,000	99,050	22,473	18,376	23,401	20,475
99,050	99,100	22,487	18,389	23,418	20,489
99,100	99,150	22,501	18,401	23,434	20,503
99,150	99,200	22,515	18,414	23,451	20,517
99,200	99,250	22,529	18,426	23,467	20,531
99,250	99,300	22,543	18,439	23,484	20,545
99,300	99,350	22,557	18,451	23,500	20,559
99,350	99,400	22,571	18,464	23,517	20,573
99,400	99,450	22,585	18,476	23,533	20,587
99,450	99,500	22,599	18,489	23,550	20,601
99,500	99,550	22,613	18,501	23,566	20,615
99,550	99,600	22,627	18,514	23,583	20,629
99,600	99,650	22,641	18,526	23,599	20,643
99,650	99,700	22,655	18,539	23,616	20,657
99,700	99,750	22,669	18,551	23,632	20,671
99,750	99,800	22,683	18,564	23,649	20,685
99,800	99,850	22,697	18,576	23,665	20,699
99,850	99,900	22,711	18,589	23,682	20,713
99,900	99,950	22,725	18,601	23,698	20,727
99,950	100,000	22,739	18,614	23,715	20,741

$100,000 or over — use the Tax Rate Schedules on page 74

* This column must also be used by a qualifying widow(er).

2003 Tax Rate Schedules

Use **only** if your taxable income (Form 1040, line 40) is $100,000 or more. If less, use the **Tax Table.** Even though you cannot use the Tax Rate Schedules below if your taxable income is less than $100,000, all levels of taxable income are shown so taxpayers can see the tax rate that applies to each level.

Schedule X—Use if your filing status is **Single**

If the amount on Form 1040, line 40, is: Over—	But not over—	Enter on Form 1040, line 41	of the amount over—
$0	$7,000	.... 10%	$0
7,000	28,400	$700.00 + 15%	7,000
28,400	68,800	3,910.00 + 25%	28,400
68,800	143,500	14,010.00 + 28%	68,800
143,500	311,950	34,926.00 + 33%	143,500
311,950	....	90,514.50 + 35%	311,950

Schedule Y-1—Use if your filing status is **Married filing jointly** or **Qualifying widow(er)**

If the amount on Form 1040, line 40, is: Over—	But not over—	Enter on Form 1040, line 41	of the amount over—
$0	$14,000	.... 10%	$0
14,000	56,800	$1,400.00 + 15%	14,000
56,800	114,650	7,820.00 + 25%	56,800
114,650	174,700	22,282.50 + 28%	114,650
174,700	311,950	39,096.50 + 33%	174,700
311,950	....	84,389.00 + 35%	311,950

Schedule Y-2—Use if your filing status is **Married filing separately**

If the amount on Form 1040, line 40, is: Over—	But not over—	Enter on Form 1040, line 41	of the amount over—
$0	$7,000	.... 10%	$0
7,000	28,400	$700.00 + 15%	7,000
28,400	57,325	3,910.00 + 25%	28,400
57,325	87,350	11,141.25 + 28%	57,325
87,350	155,975	19,548.25 + 33%	87,350
155,975	....	42,194.50 + 35%	155,975

Schedule Z—Use if your filing status is **Head of household**

If the amount on Form 1040, line 40, is: Over—	But not over—	Enter on Form 1040, line 41	of the amount over—
$0	$10,000	.... 10%	$0
10,000	38,050	$1,000.00 + 15%	10,000
38,050	98,250	5,207.50 + 25%	38,050
98,250	159,100	20,257.50 + 28%	98,250
159,100	311,950	37,295.50 + 33%	159,100
311,950	....	87,736.00 + 35%	311,950

Form **4868**
Department of the Treasury
Internal Revenue Service (99)

Application for Automatic Extension of Time To File U.S. Individual Income Tax Return

OMB No. 1545-0188

2003

 **It's Convenient, Safe, and Secure**

IRS e-file is the IRS's electronic filing program. Now you can get an automatic extension of time to file your tax return by filing Form 4868 electronically. You will receive an electronic acknowledgment or confirmation number once you complete the transaction. Keep it with your records. **Do not** send in Form 4868 if you file electronically.

Complete Form 4868 to use as a worksheet. If you think you may owe tax when you file your return, you will need to estimate your total tax liability and subtract how much you have already paid (lines 4, 5, and 6 below).

If you think you may owe tax and wish to make a payment, you may pay by electronic funds withdrawal using option 1 or 2 below or you may pay by credit card using option 3.

1 **E-file by Phone—February 2–April 15**
Call toll free **1-888-796-1074**

Anyone who filed a tax return for 2002 can file Form 4868 by phone. The telephone system will accept extensions any time from February 2 through April 15, 2004, and your extension will be good through August 16, 2004. Filing by telephone is advantageous because it is free and you get a confirmation number.

If you wish to make a payment by electronic funds withdrawal you will be asked for the adjusted gross income (AGI) from your 2002 tax return. Your AGI for that year is located on line 35 of your Form 1040, line 21 of your 1040A, line 4 of your 1040EZ, or line I of your TeleFile Tax Record. If you choose, you may also file your extension by phone and mail a payment to the address shown in the middle column on page 4.

2 **E-file Using Your Personal Computer or Through a Tax Professional**

Refer to your tax software package or tax preparer for ways to file electronically. Be sure to have a copy of last year's tax return

— you will be asked to provide information from the return for taxpayer verification. If you wish to make a payment, you can pay by electronic funds withdrawal (see page 4) or send your payment to the address shown in the middle column on page 4.

3 **E-file and Pay by Credit Card**

You can get an extension if you pay part or all of your estimate of income tax due by using a credit card (American Express® Card, Discover® Card, MasterCard® card, or Visa® card). Your payment must be at least $1. You may pay by phone or over the Internet through one of the service providers listed below.

Each service provider will charge a convenience fee based on the amount of the tax payment you are making. Fees may vary between service providers. You will be told what the fee is during the transaction and will have the option to continue or cancel the transaction. You may also obtain the convenience fee by calling the service providers' automated customer service numbers or visiting their websites. All calls are toll free. Do not add the convenience fee to your tax payment.

Link2Gov Corporation
1-888-PAY-1040 ˢᵐ
(1-888-729-1040)
1-888-658-5465 (Customer Service)
www.PAY1040.com

Official Payments Corporation
1-800-2PAY-TAX ˢᵐ
(1-800-272-9829)
1-877-754-4413 (Customer Service)
www.officialpayments.com

Form 709 or 709-A. Although an extension of time to file your income tax return also extends the time to file Form 709 or 709-A, you cannot make payments of the gift or GST tax with a credit card. To make a payment of the gift or GST tax, send a check or money order to the Internal Revenue Service Center where the donor's gift tax return will be filed. Enter "2003 Form 709" and the donor's name and social security number on the payment.

File a Paper Form 4868

If you wish to file on paper instead of electronically, fill in the Form 4868 below and mail it to the address shown on page 4.

▼ DETACH HERE ▼

Form **4868**
Department of the Treasury
Internal Revenue Service

Application for Automatic Extension of Time To File U.S. Individual Income Tax Return

For calendar year 2003, or other tax year beginning , 2003, ending , .

OMB No. 1545-0188

2003

Part I	Identification

1 Your name(s) (see instructions)

Address (see instructions)

City, town or post office, state, and ZIP code

2 Your social security number **3** Spouse's social security number

Part II	Complete ONLY If Filing Gift/GST Tax Return

Caution: *Only for gift/GST tax extension! Checking box(es) may result in correspondence if Form 709 or 709-A is not filed.*

This form also extends the time for filing a gift or generation-skipping transfer (GST) tax return if you file a calendar (not fiscal) year income tax return. Enter your gift or GST tax payment(s) in Part IV and:

If **you** are requesting a **Gift or GST tax** return extension, check this box . . . . ▶ ☐

If **your spouse** is requesting a **Gift or GST tax** return extension, check this box . . . . ▶ ☐

Part III	Individual Income Tax

4 Estimate of total tax liability for 2003 $ _____
5 Total 2003 payments . . . . . . _____
6 **Balance due.** Subtract 5 from 4 _____

Part IV	Gift/GST Tax—If you are **not filing** a gift or GST tax return, go to Part V now. See the instructions.

7 Your gift or GST tax payment . . $ _____
8 **Your spouse's** gift/GST tax payment _____

Part V	Total

9 **Total liability.** Add lines 6, 7, and 8 $ _____
10 Amount you are paying . . . . . ▶ _____

Confirmation Number

If you file electronically, you will receive a confirmation number telling you that your Form 4868 has been accepted. Enter the confirmation number here and keep it for your records . . . . ▶

For Privacy Act and Paperwork Reduction Act Notice, see page 4.

Cat. No. 13141W

Form **4868** (2003)

Index